AF801640

ANOTHER MUST READ FROM DANIEL STORM

Surviving the Alphabet Soup

FIFTH EDITION

By:

daniel storm

William J Pulkinen and Associates

705 Sunny Slope Road

Elm Grove, Wisconsin 53122

Pulkinen@wi.rr.com

PREFACE

This book is crafted for the layman, without the Latin terms generally associated with the law, statutes and interpretations. There have been a lot of changes since I first published this book in 2009. As a study guide, this text paints the general landscape of the federal criminal justice system and is not meant to supplant seasoned legal counsel or enable oneself to authoritatively represent themselves.

In combination with counsel, this treatise will help you more fully understand the procedural measures that may confront you if you are a target of an investigation by a federal agency or have been arrested.

The complexities of a federal prosecution encompass a variety of topics, which I discuss thoughtfully and slanted towards protecting your rights. Being more fully informed, you will now be succinct in your questions of counsel and the judge, if called upon.

"Surviving the Alphabet Soup" is the product of over thirty years of formal and practical experience. However, as the law is in a constant state of flux and decisions are being made frequently by the Courts of Appeals and the Supreme Court, your counsel will be able to research any changes or amendments for you.

Remember that this book does not constitute legal advice. Or do I as an author in any way suggest that after reading the contents, one is qualified to represent themselves. I am sure you will find the content accurate, informative and thorough. It represents the culmination of my passion for legal theory and a need to enlighten the general public.

daniel

The Alphabet Soup

The citizen will be better able to survive encounters with various government agencies by becoming familiar with those agencies, their duties, and powers:

ATF	Alcohol, Tobacco and
DHS	Department of Homeland Security
FBI	Federal Bureau
IRS	Internal Revenue Service
BOP	Bureau of Prisons
DOJ	Department of Justice
USMS	United States Marshals Service

User's Guide

As you read, there will be what are called "citations" given from which the legal authority for that particular statement derives. It will be a legal case reference where a court has issued a ruling which includes a decision on a particular statement or issue.

A case citation consists of:

1.) The name of the case or parties involved;

2.) The volume number, which appears on the book's spine;

3.) An abbreviation indicating the reporter wherein the case is published;

4.) The page number where the case begins;

5.) The page number where the referenced authority or material is located; and,

6.) In parenthesis, the court which decided the case and the year in which decided.

Example: ***United States –v- Ginglen***, 467 F.3d 1071, 1075 (7th Cir. 2006)

The United States Supreme Court cases, such as ***Ginglen,*** above, are reported in the United States Reports, (U.S) or Supreme Court Reporter, (S. Ct).

Courts of Appeals are found in the Federal Reporters, Second (2d) or Third (3d) series. The Third series are newer cases, but these Reporters are generally found in every law library or easily located on the internet websites such as findlaw.com or research services such as West's Publishing, for a small fee.

Chapter I

Investigations

The Fourth Amendment to the United States Constitution states:

"The right of the people to be secure in their persons, houses, papers, and effects, against unreasonable searches and seizure, shall not be violated and no Warrants shall be issued, but upon probable cause, supported by Oath or affirmation and particularly describing the place to be searched and the person or things to be seized."

The Fifth Amendment, in pertinent part, states; **"...no person... shall be compelled in any criminal case to be a witness against himself."**

These two Amendments are crucial to the American way of life and the judicial system that sets this nation distinctively apart from every other.

The Framers or craftsmen who wrote the Constitution deeply embraced these two fundamental rights or liberties. With these Amendments in mind we will discuss the various types of government agency investigations into which you may find yourself cast.

Informal Investigations

These investigations may range from a spouse rummaging through your clothes searching for signs of infidelity or cheating to surveys of your emails and online activities.. They may also encompass questioning you about your habits, likes, dislikes, travels or any number of innocent questions while dating for example, while someone gets to know you. Make no mistake, however, these are investigations and you always retain the right to refuse to answer. When asked in a context of employment, such as on a job application or by security personnel after being hired, you then transition into the next type of investigation and heightened standards or rules apply.

Formal Investigations

For the purposes of this book, we differentiate this type of investigation from a law enforcement context, for the sake of clarity.

Formal investigations, being non-criminal at that time, may include financial audits or verifications, background checks or numerous others that people simply encounter in daily life.

If you work for a company, for example, that is undergoing an internal audit, any profit-loss statement submitted by you or co-workers will be investigated for accuracy. When you apply for credit, when the lender obtains credit history, references and employment verification, this is a formal investigation.

Because in most instances, you sign or execute documents under an oath or affirmation that your statements are true and factual to the best of your knowledge or beliefs, if the investigation reveals fraud or deceit, intentionally and knowingly, then these formal investigations may result in the next more serious type of investigation.

Official Investigations

For functional purposes, this is where law enforcement becomes involved and the umbrella of examples for this type range from traffic accidents to sophisticated white collar crime. Once an agent becomes involved, the Amendments we previously mentioned become far more important.

When investigations include questioning, the intent of the agent is of primary concern. If you are a suspect in a crime, the agent is required to advise you of your rights.[1] These rights are focused on the Fifth Amendment above, but include the use of your statements in court against you and your right to have an attorney present, which falls into the Sixth Amendment of the Constitution[2]

If an agent questions you as a suspect, the complexion of the encounter dictates Miranda warnings. An agent is not required to Mirandize you during "investigatory detentions." These typically arise during vehicular stops or what are called "Police-citizen

---

[1] ***Miranda v. Arizona*, 384 U.S. 436 (1966), was a landmark 5–4 decision of the United States Supreme Court. The Court held that both inculpatory and exculpatory statements made in response to interrogation by a defendant in police custody will be admissible at trial only if the prosecution can show that the defendant was informed of the right to consult with an attorney before and during questioning and of the right against self-incrimination prior to questioning by police, and that the defendant not only understood these rights, but voluntarily waived them.**

[2] ***Miranda***, Ibid.

encounters." This term stems from the U. S. Supreme Court ruling in ***Terry***.[3] In that decision, the Court addressed the probable cause officers have when approaching citizens that are suspicious, but not yet suspects in an actual crime. In permitting officers to pat search a citizen for weapons and request identification, the Court articulated a median degree assigned to these investigations, based upon reasonable suspicion. The citizens in ***Terry***, were in a high crime rate area, acting suspiciously and the officers believed that they may be about to commit a crime or had just committed the crime of burglary. Agents are permitted this heightened authority, but only to the point where their intent changes and you as a citizen become a crime suspect.[4] If the intent of the officer changes from that of checking a suspect to interrogating and/or taking in a suspect of a crime, at that point, Miranda rights implications come into focus.

When a criminal change argues that the legality of statements obtained as a result of a transition from a Terry stop to a custodial interrogation requiring Miranda warnings, counsel will set forth these contentions in a pre-trial motion,[5] which generally results in the court holding an evidentiary hearing to ascertain the law enforcement agent's intent at the time the statements were made and the totality of circumstances. There are a number of circumstances under which a reasonable person may believe they are in custody and not free to leave, such as law enforcement agent's use of force or threatened use of force, weapons drawn by agents, the officer blocking an exit, or even the sheer number of agents surrounding someone. These subtleties of the law are addressed by the courts and seasoned legal counsel. If you bring it to the attention of your counsel immediately, an effective legal representative will look into the matter for substance and viability in a *pre-trial motion*. It is by such motions <u>before a trial</u> that damaging statements made to police or agents and even evidence is ruled not admissible or what is known in legal terms as "suppressed" because the government obtained those statements and evidence in violation of civil rights guaranteed under the Fourth and/or Fifth Amendments to the U.S. Constitution, noted above.

<u>Grand Jury Investigations</u>

---

[3] ***Terry v. Ohio***, 392 U.S. 1, June 1968.

[4] ***Yarborbough v Alvardo*** , 541 U.S. 652, 663-665 (2004).

[5] See Chapter VI.

Everyone who is entertained by television series like the "Sopranos," "Law and Order" and "CSI," all have heard the term "grand jury" and people being compelled to appear and serve as a member of the grand jury.

The make-up of a grand jury ranges from 18 to 23 people who are selected from administrative rolls maintained by voter registration or drivers license divisions of state agencies. These people receive notices in the main that they have been selected for service and to report to a particular Clerk's Office on a specific date and time, where they are sworn in as jurors and are taken to a courtroom or other suitable space where the prosecutors present witnesses and evidence in order to obtain an Indictment.

As an investigatory tool, the grand jury is a potent weapon in its considerable arsenal against crime. If a witness decides to lie or commit perjury, they are subject to criminal prosecution and face stiff punishments ranging from financial sanctions to prison terms. It is that threat or inducement that has witnesses being more forthright, after being placed under oath and sitting before the jurors. **(See Chapter III)**

If you are summoned before a grand jury, you possess a series of rights which are critical. If you are a "target" of the grand jury investigation, you have a right to be advised of that status, *if you make that inquiry.*[6] If you are a target, of an investigation, you have the right to invoke the Fifth Amendment right against self-incrimination.

There are exceptions to this distinction, however, if you are summoned to appear for the purpose of providing handwriting examples, hair follicles, blood, voice examples or records. [7] The bases for these exceptions are derived from the legal concept that obtaining hair or blood for example, is not compelling you to incriminate yourself. It has been argued that obtaining blood or hair for DNA testing is the essence of the body testifying against the person. These arguments have failed in the Courts.[8]

The production of documents presents a much different analysis than those above. Business records of a public entity like a corporation are subject to grand jury probes to

---

[6] ***United States v. Luxenberg***, 374 F.2d 241 (6th Cir. 1967).

[7] ***U.S. –v- Dionisio***, 410 U.S. 1, 5-13 (1973).

[8] ***In re: Solomon***; 465 F. 3 d 114, 112 (3rd Cir. 2006); 135 and ***Federal Rules of Criminal Procedure***, **Rule 17** (c) (1***); US –v- Mars***, 410 U.S. 19, 21-22 (1973).

protect the public investors, thus the exception is carved out of the concern that stock holders would have, that their investments are not fraudulently mishandled or converted. [9]

Subpoena Power

The Subpoena is a document that is issued by the Clerk of Courts where the grand jury is sitting. Once a date and time are ascertained, the subpoena must advise you of the exact location and room where you are to appear. It will bear the Court seal and have the Clerk's signature or that of an appropriate designee.

In the event records are sought, a slightly different form is used and given a Latin name, "deuces tecum" which simply means, "to produce". There is a specific section which must succinctly describe what documents or records you are required to bring with you and surrender to prosecutors.

If you are served with this form of subpoena, it would be prudent to consult with counsel, so they may determine your involvement in the investigation, your rights and any legal maneuvers they may deem appropriate, including negotiations with prosecutors or filing formal motions before the courts to quash or limit the disclosures of your documents and records.

Contempt

In the event that you ignore the subpoena and refuse to appear when directed, you may be arrested and held in civil contempt. This means you will likely remain in physical custody until such time as you agree and appear before the grand jury. This is called "purging," where you absolve yourself of refusing to appear and testify.

A person may be held in civil contempt for the life of the grand jury, which is up to 18 to 24 months, if the grand jury is extended by the Chief Judge of the district court, upon filing of an official motion by the prosecutors. A "contemnor" as they are called at that juncture, will be held without bail until one of the three instances occur.

a. they purge the contempt and appear;[10] or

---

[9] ***Braswell –v- U.S.,*** 487 U.S. 99.104 (1988).

[10] ***Title 18 U.S.C.*§ 401** and ***Title 28 U.S.C.* §1826** (a) (purging).

b. The grand jury expires and they are released; or

c. They are charged by the prosecutors with the companion to civil contempt, criminal contempt.

d. If the prosecutors can prove beyond a reasonable doubt that you possess material evidence or information and are intentionally impeding justice or the grand jury, you are subject to being charged with criminal contempt and face stiff penalties which include prison terms and fines.

There is a timing concern with the transformation from civil to criminal contempt of which you should be aware. When the prosecutors believe that civil contempt will not induce you to cooperate and appear before the grand jury, it is then their responsibility to either charge you criminally or move for your release from custody."

If you are serving a sentence and are found to be in contempt by a court of competent jurisdiction, service of your sentence will cease at that moment and you will not receive credit towards that sentence for any time spent in contempt status.[11]

A sentence for criminal contempt will be most similar to the conduct which provoked the contempt determination. Under the Federal Sentencing Guidelines, this is discussed at Section 2 x 5.1 and you should consult counsel or the Guidelines Manual in this instance.

NOTES

[11] ***Title 18 U.S.C. § 3583***

Chapter II

Arrest

As we discussed earlier in Chapter I, there is a distinction between a detention and arrest, or formal custody. Detentions can include being placed in restraints or in the rear seat of a patrol car, under the reasoning that doing so is for the mutual protection of you and the other agents. This is a temporary moment and when it extends into unreasonable time frames, it's tantamount to an arrest. The circumstances and intent of officers or agents is critical to when a detention transposed into an arrest and will likely result in an evidentiary hearing before a court in order to ferret out the legalities.

Warrantless Arres

The Supreme Court announced the exception to the warrant requirement contemplated by the Constitution in 1975 when it held; "although a warrant requirement for all arrests may assure maximum protection of individual rights... such a requirement would constitute an intolerable handicap for legitimate law enforcement."[12] The offense was committed in the presence of the agent, which is defined as when the agent, with the aid of his or her senses, determines that an offense is being committed. [13]

The Pringle case demonstrates how occupants of vehicles become entrenched in crime, as well as the driver. The illusion that because one is not driving the vehicle where narcotics or weapons are found and therefore not subject to arrest, is not etched in granite. Recently, the Supreme Court addressed vehicular searches, in the case of ***Arizona –v- Gant.***[14] One must always remember that individual cases present circumstances unique to every situation and your particular circumstances may constitute a reasonable basis to challenge the lawfulness of your arrest. You should consult counsel immediately to determine if there was cause to arrest you without a warrant.

---

[12] ***VonSt. -v- Brigmoni-Ponce***, 422 U.S. 873, 880-81 (1975) see also; ***Gerstein -v-Pugh***, 420 U.S. 103,113 (1975).

[13] ***Maryland –v-Pringle*** 540 U.S. 366, 373-374 (2003).

[14] ***Arizona –v- Gant***, 556 U.S. (2009)

It must be noted that an unlawful arrest or seizure under the auspices of the Fourth, Fifth or Sixth Amendments, does not automatically entitle you to dismissal of charges and your release from custody. It does entitle you to the sweeping benefits of what is called the **"exclusionary rule."**

In order to deter law enforcement personnel from violating the enumerated rights of citizens by searching whatever and whenever they pleased, the Supreme Court created a remedy. The Constitution does not speak to remedies for violations, only what the Framers held as inalienable citizen rights. As a result, the Supreme Court conceived the "exclusionary rule." [15] When agents offend the rights of citizens, the evidence uncovered and brought before the court, it is excluded and the prosecution is denied the ability to introduce that evidence against the defendant at trial. This exclusion can range from murder, weapons, drugs, forensics traces or even a body itself. This rule of law has come under tremendous fire by prosecutors, law makers and victim's rights advocates, as being the most serious "loophole" in law that can be twisted so as to permit murderers to walk out of a courtroom free.

Over the years, due to the sustained outpouring of public concern for murders walking out of the court instead of into prison, the Supreme Court responded and carefully crafted exceptions to this drastic rule. Today, the complexities of this rule involve intricate instances where exclusion will not result.

Probably the most popular exception is "good faith," where the law enforcement agent believed he was acting within the scope of his duties and was not intentionally violating the rights of citizens.[16]

Then, you enter the realm of the theoretical exceptions and will require your counsel's assistance in explaining how these may or may not apply to your situation. "Attenuation" is the first of these technical exceptions and without question the most problematic for the layman to understand.

The confusing word "attenuated" is better defined by giving an example. In 1963, the Supreme Court was faced with a case involving the illegal arrest, without warrant or probable cause, of a defendant named Wong Sun. After being released on bail, Wong Sun returned to

---

[15] ***US –v- Leon,*** 468 U.S. 897, 906 (1989).

[16] ***Leon*** @ pp. 918-919

the agent's offices and gave a voluntary, but unsigned, confession. Wong Sun's counsel filed pre-trial motions to exclude the confession from the upcoming trial, based upon the illegal arrest or seizure, in the first instance. The Supreme Court then concluded that, indeed, the arrest was illegal and that issue was not in real dispute. However, the confession would not be excluded because the confession was sufficiently attenuated so as to remove the taint of the unlawful arrest. [17]

This holding has become deeply entrenched in American jurisprudence as the Wong Sun doctrine and you will encounter the term "fruits of the poisonous tree." In other words, had the confession been given immediately upon the illegal arrest, after being Mirandized, it would in all likelihood, have been excluded from trial.

In conjunction with how courts should determine the sufficiency of the attenuation, the Supreme Court has developed a three part test for lower courts to consider when factoring in the causal chain for the attenuation.[18] While the additional term of "causation" may seem confusing, the three factors listed should erase the confusion and clarify when a confession or statement may still be used. The three factors are:

1) The time which elapsed between the illegality and the acquisition of the evidence sought to be excluded; and

2) The presence of intervening circumstances; and

3) The purpose and flagrancy of the official misconduct. [19]

Briefly, even the layman not trained in the law can accept the first factor, which deals with the timing of the violation to obtaining the evidence. In Wong Sun's case, his confession or change of mind returned days subsequent to arrest and volunteered a confession. Remember, however, that the law is fluidic and the product of humans, which will vary from court to court, circuit to circuit and will change with the seasons of the Supreme Court. There is no hardline rule that will enable a victory or defeat, simply based upon timing.

Intervening circumstances is a little more problematic to grasp for even seasoned legal veterans, as every case has its own twists and turns. In Wong Sun, the intervening

---

[17] ***Wong Sun –v- U.S.,*** 371 U.S. 471, 488 (1963).

[18] ***Brown –v – Ill.***, 422 U.S. 590, 603 (1975).

[19] ***Brown –v – Ill.*** @ pp. 603-04.

circumstances include the fact Wong Sun was on bail and no longer in custody, and he returned to the offices voluntarily and gave a confession, which was unsigned as some perceived legal maneuver or deficiency.

The third factor calls into question the subjective intent of the agents and how egregious the violation was. In other words, did the offending agents possess some ill-intent in violating the citizen's rights? If they simply disregarded the Constitutional rights of the suspect, the courts will then look at how badly they offended those rights.

Every law enforcement officer attends classes and is schooled in the technicalities associated with their official capacity in an effort to ensure that arrests are lawful and within Constitutional boundaries. The courts, mindful of this education and the wisdom which comes from experience and oversight by the superior officers, holds agents and officers to a higher standard than those of us not trained in such technical fields.

There is a delicate balance that courts must weigh when deciding motions under the exclusionary rule. There is no steadfast equation which will decide the success or failure of any motion filed in such cases, but will remain in a constant state of flux from court to court.

The first exception is more easily understood, but without question, not agreeable to defendants seeking relief. "**Inevitable discovery**" is simply defined as a means where a court may admit illegally obtained evidence if the evidence would inevitably or eventually have been discovered through independent, lawful means.[20] That is not to say that prosecutors will be able to avoid exclusion of tainted evidence by simply arguing that the evidence would be discovered at some point, anyhow.

For example, in 1984, the Supreme Court. addressed this argument where a victim's body was located in violation of the defendant's right to counsel. [21]

In affirming the introduction of the discovery of the victim's remains, the Court ruled that the body, which was located in close proximity to where a massive sweep by the officers was

---

[20] ***Murray –v - US***, 487 U.S. 533, 537 (1988).

[21] ***Nix –v- Williams***, 467 U.S. 431 (1984)

already underway, would have eventually been found anyway and in essence the illegally obtained location merely shortened the time required by the officers to locate the body. [22]

The last exception to the exclusionary rule is more understandable and is called "collateral uses." This is where prosecutors may still use illegally obtained evidence outside its "case-in-chief" against a criminal defendant.

As a defendant you should be aware that illegally obtained statements may be used to impeach your testimony at trial. [23]

Before making decisions regarding applications of the exclusion- any rule, it is a prudent measure to consult with counsel and plan accordingly. Every case is different in some respect and outcomes will vary, but diligent counsel will file viable motions, not only to seek justice, but preserve those issues for an appeal that may result.

Arrest by Warrant

Arrests are also made pursuant to a judicial warrant, which is the term given the specific document which is directed to all sworn law enforcement officers, commanding them to take the person identified therein, into physical custody.

Arrests are also made upon Complaints and indictments, where neutral judges or grand juries have made a determination of probable cause that a person or persons, has or have engaged in certain specified criminal activity.

It must be remembered, as discussed at the beginning of this text, probable cause is all that is Constitutionally mandated in the order to arrest or seize a citizen.

"...when police have, at the moment of arrest, knowledge of facts and circumstances grounded in reasonably trustworthy information and sufficient in and of itself to warrant a belief by a prudent person that an offense has been or is being committed." [24]

---

[22] ***Nix –v- Williams***, @ pp 448 -50 (1984).

[23] ***Michigan – Harvey***, 494 U.S. 334,336 (1990).

[24] ***Beck – v – Ohio***, 379 US 89,91 (1964).

An arresting officer need not have physical possession in hand at the time of arrest, as long as knowledge of its existence is known. For example, during a traffic stop, if the patrolman is informed by a dispatcher that a driver or occupant is wanted by a jurisdiction, that officer is within police power to take physical custody of that individual, relying on the information given by the dispatcher.

The dispatcher, routinely enters an inquiry to the National Crime Information Center, or NCIC, and receives a printout with verification of the warrant's existence, the agency responsible for the execution of the warrant, the charged offense or offenses and in most cases, the amount of bail the court set at the time of issuance.

Warrants are sometimes called a "capias" or "body attachment", the latter term referring more to civil matters, like contempt. In that instance, the customary practice is to hold that person without admitting them to bail until they are brought before the court which issued the warrant.

Miranda –v – Arizona

As discussed before when briefly touching on the subject of when a police-citizen encounter becomes custodial in nature, or a seizure, which triggers the Miranda warnings, whenever a person is arrested pursuant to a Warrant or capias, ***Miranda*** implications are more automatic when interrogation is about to occur.[25]

"Interrogation" is defined as "express questioning or its functional equivalent."[26] This does not extend to normal booking procedures, such as Fingerprinting, photography or requesting your name, address and date of birth. [27] These types of questions and record keeping are not intended to elicit incriminating evidence, but as a means to accurately identify you.

The linchpin consideration when addressing Miranda allegations and challenges, is whether or not the person was in custody and therefore becoming a suspect. In other words, if you are in custody as a suspect, you have the right to be informed of that and to be alert to

---

[25] ***Illinois - v- Perkins***, 496 U.S. 292, 297.

[26] ***Rhode Island – v- Innis***, 446, U.S. 291, 300.01 (1980).

[27] ***Pennsylvania –v Muniz***, 496 U.S. 582, 600-602 (1990).

protect your own interests. The custodial status (are you in custody when you make a statement) is the epicenter of judicial hearings and inquiries. Without that element being satisfied, the courts have no need to move to the question of whether or not the person was subjected to interrogation without being Mirandized beforehand.

Be forewarned, that there is a devilish term called "spontaneous utterances", where a suspect simply blurts out a statement which incriminates them. For example, agents appear at your door and ask to talk to you before they read you your rights, and you say the them, "I told John Doe not to shoot the guy. We only wanted the money." That spontaneous account of your complicity in the crime will haunt you at trial. [28]

Jailhouse Snitches

The use of informants by prosecutors has evolved into more of a necessity, than an option. Historically, criminals associated with other criminals and hang out in the most likely place where criminals and criminal activity were likely to abound. If you have read my companion textbook, "***Drug Dealing for Dummies*** "you will already be familiar with techniques used by agents when working with snitches, or formally referred to "confidential informants" or CI's.

Assuming, however, that you find yourself in custody and no CI was employed by agents in the community, ***take heed of what I am about to impart to you***.

Jailhouse snitches are like sharks in a tank full of gold fish. Veterans of the criminal justice system are almost experts in the laws or provisions which earn them reduced sentences or their freedom, depending on the quality or quantity of others they cooperate against. Prosecutors routinely interview these informers and enter into "Cooperation Agreements", wherein they assure the informant that if they testify against a defendant or a group of defendants, truthfully and completely, they will file a motion with the court to reduce their sentence exposure or drop various charges completely. These bargains are Constitutional and those swarming around you while you await bail or trial are well aware of the benefits that come from knowing your business.

[28] ***U.S. - v.- Younger***, 398 F. 3d. 1179, 1186, (CA9 2005).

WARNING

Do not discuss your offence with anyone, other than your attorney and only in-person. Telephones in jails and detention centers are recorded and monitored, which means anything you say on them will be given to prosecutors for use against you in court. Do not let others read any materials given you by your counsel. In doing so, it gives the snitch credibility when he or she testifies that you confided in them and made incriminating admissions. Also, do not leave materials lying about where a snitch can read them when you are not around.

Constitutionally speaking, prosecutors cannot approach a jail-house informant and request that they gain your confidence and trust, so as to elicit incriminating statements. The reason for this is founded in the Sixth Amendment right to counsel. The informant, if agreeing to gain your confidence and trust, is acting as an agent at that point and once counsel appears on your behalf, no agent or prosecutor may approach you or question you, without the prior consent of your attorney. While instances have occurred where prosecutors have disregarded this tenet of law, as a general rule, prosecutors will avoid such implications to avoid the risk of charges being dismissed by an angry court or facing formal disciplinary measures before the American Bar Association.

This will not inhibit them from employing *an informant who approaches them* with information about you, either through their counsel or by contacting agents directly. As long as they did not initiate the contact, they are within Constitutional Parameters.

The safest measure you can employ is by staying to yourself and never discussing your offense. I cannot emphasize that Rule enough. It has brought down some of the biggest defendants ever to face a federal court.

Right to Remain Silent

Hopefully, you have exercised both your right to remain silent and your right to counsel, as contemplated by Miranda. Unless advised by counsel to do otherwise, it would be foolish and reckless on your part to circumvent counsel and approach the agents or prosecutors in your case or someone else's. To do so would constitute a waiver of those rights.

The right to counsel automatically attaches upon initiation of any adversarial, criminal proceedings against you.[29] You do not have to make a formal demand at this juncture. However, under Miranda, since the formal proceedings have not yet been undertaken, you must assert that you want counsel prior to any questioning. The bright line distinction is evident. Once you are brought before a judge, your right to counsel is self-proclaiming.

Unlike the right to counsel under the Sixth Amendment above you also possess the Fifth Amendment right to remain silent and not incriminate yourself.

Waivers

There are two types of waivers; 1) express, there you execute a form acknowledging your rights and waive them in order for an agent to question you. 2) The second type is "implied" and this is far more complex than express waivers and will be discussed separately.

The burden rests with prosecutors to prove that you waived your rights, and must show by a "preponderance of evidence" that you did so. Also, it must be shown that you waived your rights voluntarily and without threat or coercion.[30] Also, it must be shown that the waiver was a "knowingly and intelligently" made.[31]

Courts will look to a variety of factors in analyzing whether or not you waived your rights. These factors will include how the questioning occurred, your education or intelligence level, your age, your familiarity with the justice system, whether or not you were under the influence of drugs or alcohol at the time and your mental fitness. In combination, the courts will generally address the totality of the circumstances and render a decision.

An important consideration also extends to language barriers, as in Spanish suspects being questioned by non-Spanish speaking agents. One who does not understand the language cannot "knowingly and intelligently" waive his rights.[32]

---

[29] ***Brever –v –Williams***, 430 U.S. 387, 404 (1977).

[30] ***Colorado – v- Connelly***, 479 U.S. 157, 169-70 (1986).

[31] ***N. Carolina – v- Butler***, 441 U.S. 369, 373, 375-76 (1979).

[32] ***U.S. – v – Broussard***, 80 F.3d 1025, 1034 (5th Cir 1996).

Federal agents are customarily provided wavier forms, in English and Spanish. It would be difficult to overcome such a waiver at a hearing, if you have signed one and then incriminated yourself during a police interrogation.

Implied Waivers

"Implied Waivers" waivers are not formal and become perplexing to the average defendant.

To use an example, a suspect, after being Mirandized, could acknowledge that he understands those rights, never invoked them by asserting them and subsequently answering questions.[33] As a suspect, one must always be cognizant of these pitfalls and rely on counsel for guidance before initiating any official contact or comments to the police.

Inasmuch as the rule prohibits agents from questioning after a suspect has asserted their rights, the remedy has exclusively been limited to the exclusion of the testimonial evidence obtained in violation of Miranda.[34] Thus, a suspect_will not necessarily gain freedom because they were not Mirandized or if they made incriminating statements under circumstances above which offend or negate those rights.

There is a "public safety" exception, which permits evidence to be introduced at trial, which was obtained contrary to Miranda.[35] A couple examples are self-explanatory.

An agent, who has prior knowledge that a suspect has a prior conviction for violence, asks if there are any guns present in the house immediately prior to giving the Miranda warning. The public safety interest associated with this line of questioning is acceptable.[36]

Anyone who has watched episodes of "Cops" has seen officers ask people if they "had any needles" in their pockets that could injure them during a pat-down search. These questions meet the public safety exception and the admission that such needles do exist and the needles will be admissible in court.[37] If you question the validity of statements or evidence which you

---

[33] ***Flamer –v- Delaware*** 68 F. 3d 710, 719-20 (3rd Cir. 1995).

[34] ***Michigan – v – Tucker***, 417 U.S. 433, 451-52 (1974).

[35] ***N.Y. – v – Quareles***, 467 U.S. 649, 655-56 (1984).

[36] ***U.S. –v – Estrada***, 430 F. 3d 606, 613 (2nd Cir. 2005).

[37] ***U.S. –v- Webster***, 162 F.3d 308, 332 (5th Cir. 1998).

believe contrary to Miranda or other Supreme Court holdings, you should immediately consult with counsel, privately.

Booking

After being arrested, the suspect will be transported to a contract jail or a federal detention center, where they will be processed.

Processing will include fingerprinting, where the physical cards are maintained by the F.B.I. in Washington, D.C. and the arresting authority as well. This will explain the numerous cards you are requested to sign after your prints are taken.

Currently, the FBI is employing an electronic method for taking fingerprints, retention and identification. This system is called AFIS, or Automated Fingerprint Identification System.

Not only will AFIS obtain smuggles prints by rolling the subjects fingers across a clear glass square for scanning, but once entered into the data bank, it will retain those virtual points forever or until recalled for physical use. Another AFIS advantage is that by using sophisticated computer technology and programming, AFIS will electronically search, match and identify unknown suspect prints from crime scenes and produce the owner of those prints.

While it may seem to be, photographing, both profile and frontal images, is not an invasion of privacy or a violation of a suspect's rights. It is a reasonable means to identify the suspect without the rigors of constant fingerprint analysis. These photos, or "mug shots" are maintained by AFIS and the arresting/detaining authorities. In the event that charges are dismissed against you or you are found not guilty, you can petition the court for an expungement order upon the FBI/USMS and anyone having custody of fingerprints and photos, to surrender them to you and purge their files of any such arrest.

Any clothing or personal property you possessed at the time of arrest are generally held by the detaining authority, unless such items constitute evidence and are seized by agents. A suspect is searched and issued institutional clothing before being housed in the jail or detention center, into general population. Refusing to cooperate with standard booking procedures as noted above, will result in delay in appearing before a judge for bail consideration, or in more extreme cases, prints and photos will be forcefully obtained.

Standard booking procedures do not include "line – ups" where you are placed in a line with several others, for identification purposes by witnesses or victims.

Identifications

The Sixth Amendment assures the right to counsel during any post-indictment, pretrial line-ups or identifications.[38] This is deemed necessary to avoid any impermissible or suggestive identifications which would taint later identifications. Notice, however that I use the terminology, "post-indictment, partial identifications", as the Supreme Court has held that the same constrictions do not apply until the beginning of adversarial proceedings. This means that a suspect does not have a right to counsel during a photo array, where booking photos are laid out with others who have similar characteristics, for victims or witnesses to identify. [39]

Likewise a suspect is not entitled to counsel being present when scientific comparisons are performed on fingerprints, hair blood, or other forensic trace elements, including DNA testing. [40]

Identification issues are as complex as those under the exclusionary rule and will require research and the learned hand of counsel.

In the event a suspect is asked to appear physically in a line-up, it is prudent for them to request counsel prior to their freely participating.

Any challenges to the identification will necessitate the filing of a formal motion to suppress and require an evidentiary hearing in most cases.

NOTES

____

____

____

____

[38] ***U.S. – v- Wade***, 388 U.S. 218, 224 (1967).

[39] ***US – v- Ash***, 413 US 300, 321 (1973).

[40] ***US –v – Lewis***, 483 F 3d871, 874 (8th Cir. 207.

Chapter III

Initial Appearance

There are three basic types of "initial appearance";

1. ***Gerstein*** hearing
2. Initial appearance hearing
3. Preliminary hearing

The Supreme Court., as well as the Constitution, has consistently held that a judge must make a determination of probable cause.[41] Having been arrested, a suspect is entitled to a prompt hearing and determination, so as to limit the restraint on his or her liberty. The brevity of this period before such hearing shall not exceed 48 hours.[42] However, courts are reluctant to grant relief, unless a defendant can clearly demonstrate prejudice that has resulted from the delay.

A ***Gerstein*** hearing does not apply, if a suspect was arrested pursuant to a valid Warrant or Indictment, as both methods have probable cause determinations built into the process. (There must be sufficient cause to issue a warrant.)

If a suspect is arrested without a Warrant or Indictment, and is not promptly brought before a judge, then they should consult their attorney immediately. If they cannot afford counsel and a judge has not appointed the Federal Defender to represent them as yet, then the suspect or family member should contact the Federal Defender's office immediately and explain the circumstances. Someone from that agency will initiate contact or investigate the situation and cause some remedial measure.

Gerstein hearings are informal, allowing hearsay and the formal rules of evidence are relaxed or do not apply. In fact, this hearing may not even require the suspect's appearance or counsel, as it is considered non-adversarial. This means that the judge is only going to rule on

---

[41] ***Gerstein –v- Pugh***, 420 U.S. 103, 123-24 (1975).

[42] ***Riverside County –v- McLaughlin***, 500 U.S. 44,56 (1991) Fourth Amendment.

whether probable cause exits to hold the defendant as to not guilt or innocence. As discussed earlier, the definition of probable cause does not require much evidence.

While a weekend or holiday will justify the delay in bringing a suspect before the bench, a five day delay has been held as unreasonable, as police are still investigating during that time and should have had sufficient evidence to arrest in the first place. [43]

Initial Appearance

Unlike a ***Gerstein*** hearing, with or without the arrest being pursuant to a Warrant, the suspect is to be brought before a magistrate judge without unnecessary delay.[44] While a magistrate judge is not a district court judge, they are empowered to handle pre-trial matters such as the initial appearance, bail hearings, and conduct evidentiary hearings for their "Report and Recommendation" which will be reviewed by the district judge.

At the initial appearance, the Magistrate Judge will advise the accused of the charges against them and of their rights to remain silent and counsel. As a standard practice, counsel from the Federal Defender's Office will be on stand by and file their limited appearance for the sake of the initial appearance.

If the accused meets the financial criteria for indigence status, or a pauper, the court will appoint the Federal Defender to represent them.

Another function of this hearing is release on bail. [45] This is required under the **F. R. Cr. P., Rule 5 (d) (3).**

The accused has a right to consult with counsel before the appearance and unless retained counsel appears, it will most likely be counsel from the Federal Defender's Office who conducts this interview.

Some district courts are equipped with video monitors, where the accused will appear from a remote location, like the jail or detention center. This practice is sanctioned by the **F.R.**

---

[43] ***Lopez –v- Chicago***, 464 F3d 711, 721-22 (7th Cir. 2006).

[44] **Federal Rules Ct. Procedure, Rule 5 (d)**

[45] **Federal Rules Ct. Procedure, Rule 5 (d)**

Cr. P. Rule 5 (f), but only with the consent of the accused.

If an accused is held beyond a reasonable period of time before being brought for an initial appearance, such unwarranted delay offends the Due Process rights under the Constitution and could result in dismissal of the charges and release. [46] The factual basis for the delay will determine whether or not it was justified, but the burden rests with prosecutors to substantiate the reasonableness.

If an accused believes that they were held for an unreasonable period before an initial appearance, say, more than five days, they should consult with their counsel immediately.

Preliminary Hearings

At this juncture, the suspect or accused now becomes a defendant and is named in an official case file opened by the Clerk of the District Court.

The purpose of this hearing before a Magistrate Judge is the determination of a probable cause to hold the defendant for further proceedings and potentially on to trial. [47] This hearing must be conducted within 10 days of the initial appearance if the defendant is in custody [48] and twenty days if the defendant is admitted to bail.[49]

If an Indictment has been returned by a grand jury and filed, this obviates the need to determine probable cause. However, if no such Indictment has been filed and the defendant does not waive the preliminary hearing, the adversarial process begins and the defendant is entitled to counsel, to cross-examine witnesses and if the defendant chooses, introduce evidence.

As a tactical maneuver, defense attorneys enjoy the testimonial benefits of preliminary hearings and insight into the strengths or weaknesses in the prosecution's case. Although the depth of the cross-examination can be restricted by the magistrate judge, a certain degree of knowledge is gained and a transcript generally may become invaluable for impeachment use, if the matter proceeds to trial.

---

[46] ***Baker –v- McColum***, 443 U.S. 137, 145 (1979).

[47] **F.R.Cr.P. Rule 5.1 (a).**

[48] **F.R. Cr.P. Rule 5.1 (c).**

[49] **F.R.Cr..P. Rule 5.1 (a)** and ***Title 18 U.S.C. §* 3060 (e).**

Aside from the logistical advantages above, there will be occasions where defense counsel may advise the defendant to waive the hearing, as there may be an agreement on bail reduction or continuation and even a forthcoming plea agreement which may be favorable.

There are reasons for and against holding prosecutors to task regarding preliminary hearings.

Once the determination is made that probable cause does exist to continue the prosecution, the magistrate judge will "bind" the defendant over for trial and whatever offense or offenses the determination of probable cause has been found.

If probable cause is not found, the magistrate judge will dismiss the matter and discharge the defendant. This does not preclude or prevent the prosecution from presenting the case to a grand jury and obtaining an Indictment to sustain the prosecution. That option still resides within prosecutorial discretion.[50] _50_/

One other point that is worth mentioning here, is that someone may be taken into custody as a "material witness" and held until they are brought before a mag. jud. to determine whether or not the witness should be held without bail or released. In such cases, the agents fear that the witness will flee and not appear at a trial and that their knowledge of a crime is critical to the prosecution. Although such instances are rare, a material witness who presents a flight risk and undercutting of the prosecution's case, could be held in custody to assure their appearance.

NOTES

[50] ***U.S. Kendrick***, 853 F. 2d 492, 496 (6th Cir. 1988).

Chapter IV

Bail

The Constitution, pursuant to the Eighth Amendment, provides that no citizen shall be held in lieu of excessive bail, in other than a capital offense. A "capital" offense is where the defendant can receive the death penalty, which comes from cases such as murder, treason or convictions of that ilk.

The "***Bail Reform Act of 1984,***" which accompanied the Sentence Reform Act, or the "new law" and the federal sentencing guidelines, make substantial changes to how federal courts would approach how a defendant was reviewed for bail hearings. (see below)

The federal statute which most applies to the defendant's situation in bail considerations, is Title 18 United States Code, § 3142, which states:

§ 3142. RELEASE OR DETENTION OF A DEFENDANT PENDING TRIAL

(a) In General.— Upon the appearance before a judicial officer of a person charged with an offense, the judicial officer shall issue an order that, pending trial, the person be—

(1) released on personal recognizance or upon execution of an unsecured appearance bond, under subsection (b) of this section;

(2) released on a condition or combination of conditions under subsection (c) of this section;

(3) temporarily detained to permit revocation of conditional release, deportation, or exclusion under subsection (d) of this section; or

(4) detained under subsection (e) of this section.

(b) Release on Personal Recognizance or Unsecured Appearance Bond.— The judicial officer shall order the pretrial release of the person on personal recognizance, or upon execution of an unsecured appearance bond in an amount specified by the court, subject to the condition that the person not commit a Federal, State, or local crime during the period of release and subject to the condition that the person cooperate in the collection of a DNA sample from the person if the collection of such a sample is authorized pursuant to section 3 of the DNA Analysis Backlog Elimination Act of 2000 (42 U.S.C. 14135a), unless the judicial officer determines that such release will not reasonably assure the appearance of the person as required or will endanger the safety of any other person or the community.

(c) Release on Conditions.—

(1) If the judicial officer determines that the release described in subsection (b) of this section will not reasonably assure the appearance of the person as required or will endanger the safety of any other person or the community, such judicial officer shall order the pretrial release of the person—

(A) subject to the condition that the person not commit a Federal, State, or local crime during the period of release and subject to the condition that the person cooperate in the collection of a DNA sample from the person if the collection of such a sample is authorized pursuant to section 3 of the DNA Analysis Backlog Elimination Act of 2000 (42 U.S.C. 14135a); and

(B) subject to the least restrictive further condition, or combination of conditions, that such judicial officer determines will reasonably assure the appearance of the person as required and the safety of any other person and the community, which may include the condition that the person—

(i) remain in the custody of a designated person, who agrees to assume supervision and to report any violation of a release condition to the court, if the designated person is able reasonably to assure the judicial officer that the person will appear as required and will not pose a danger to the safety of any other person or the community;

(ii) maintain employment, or, if unemployed, actively seek employment;

(iii) maintain or commence an educational program;

(iv) abide by specified restrictions on personal associations, place of abode, or travel;

(v) avoid all contact with an alleged victim of the crime and with a potential witness who may testify concerning the offense;

(vi) report on a regular basis to a designated law enforcement agency, pretrial services agency, or other agency;

(vii) comply with a specified curfew;

(viii) refrain from possessing a firearm, destructive device, or other dangerous weapon;

(ix) refrain from excessive use of alcohol, or any use of a narcotic drug or other controlled substance, as defined in section 102 of the Controlled Substances Act (21 U.S.C. 802), without a prescription by a licensed medical practitioner;

(x) undergo available medical, psychological, or psychiatric treatment, including treatment for drug or alcohol dependency, and remain in a specified institution if required for that purpose;

(xi) execute an agreement to forfeit upon failing to appear as required, property of a sufficient unencumbered value, including money, as is reasonably necessary to assure the appearance of the person as required, and shall provide the court with proof of ownership and the value of the property along with information regarding existing encumbrances as the judicial office may require;

(xii) execute a bail bond with solvent sureties; who will execute an agreement to forfeit in such amount as is reasonably necessary to assure appearance of the person as required and shall provide the court with information regarding the value of the assets and liabilities of the surety if other than an approved surety and the nature and extent of encumbrances against the surety's property; such surety shall have a net worth which shall have sufficient unencumbered value to pay the amount of the bail bond;

(xiii) return to custody for specified hours following release for employment, schooling, or other limited purposes; and

(xiv) satisfy any other condition that is reasonably necessary to assure the appearance of the person as required and to assure the safety of any other person and the community. In any case, that involves a minor victim under
Section 1201, 1591, 2241,2242, 2244 (a)(1), 2245, 2251, 2251A, 2252 (a)(1), 2252 (a)(2), 2252 (a)(3),2252A (a)(1), 2252A (a)(2), 2252A (a)(3), 2252A (a)(4), 2260, 2421, 2422,2423, or 2425 of this title, or a failure to register offense under section 2250of this title, any release order shall contain, at a minimum, a condition of electronic monitoring and each of the conditions specified at subparagraphs (iv), (v), (vi), (vii), and (viii).

(2) The judicial officer may not impose a financial condition that results in the pretrial detention of the person.

(3) The judicial officer may at any time amend the order to impose additional or different conditions of release.

(d) Temporary Detention To Permit Revocation of Conditional Release, Deportation, or Exclusion.— If the judicial officer determines that—

(1) such person—

(A) is, and was at the time the offense was committed, on—

(i) release pending trial for a felony under Federal, State, or local law;

(ii) release pending imposition or execution of sentence, appeal of sentence or conviction, or completion of sentence, for any offense under Federal, State, or local law; or

(iii) probation or parole for any offense under Federal, State, or local law; or

(B) is not a citizen of the United States or lawfully admitted for permanent residence, as defined in section 101(a)(20) of the Immigration and Nationality Act (8 U.S.C. 1101 (a)(20)); and

(2) such person may flee or pose a danger to any other person or the community;

such judicial officer shall order the detention of such person, for a period of not more than ten days, excluding Saturdays, Sundays, and holidays, and direct the attorney for the Government to notify the appropriate court, probation or parole official, or State or local law enforcement official, or the appropriate official of the Immigration and Naturalization Service. If the official fails or declines to take such person into custody during that period, such person shall be treated in accordance with the other provisions of this section, notwithstanding the applicability of other provisions of law governing release pending trial or deportation or exclusion proceedings. If temporary detention is sought under paragraph (1)(B) of this subsection, such person has the burden of proving to the court such person's United States citizenship or lawful admission for permanent residence.

(e) Detention.—

(1) If, after a hearing pursuant to the provisions of subsection (f) of this section, the judicial officer finds that no condition or combination of conditions will reasonably assure the appearance of the person as required and the safety of any other person and the community, such judicial officer shall order the detention of the person before trial.

(2) In a case described in subsection (f)(1) of this section, a rebuttable presumption arises that no condition or combination of conditions will reasonably assure the safety of any other person and the community if such judicial officer finds that—

(A) the person has been convicted of a Federal offense that is described in subsection (f)(1) of this section, or of a State or local offense that would have been an offense described in subsection (f)(1) of this section if a circumstance giving rise to Federal jurisdiction had existed;
(B) the offense described in subparagraph (A) was committed while the person was on release pending trial for a Federal, State, or local offense; and
(C) a period of not more than five years has elapsed since the date of conviction, or the release of the person from imprisonment, for the offense described in subparagraph (A), whichever is later.
(3) Subject to rebuttal by the person, it shall be presumed that no condition or combination of conditions will reasonably assure the appearance of the person as required and the safety of the community if the judicial officer finds that there is probable cause to believe that the person committed—
(A) an offense for which a maximum term of imprisonment of ten years or more is prescribed in the Controlled Substances Act (21 U.S.C. 801 et seq.), the Controlled Substances Import and Export Act (21 U.S.C. 951 et seq.), or chapter 705 of title 46;
(B) an offense under section 924 (c), 956 (a), or 2332b of this title;
(C) an offense listed in section 2332b (g)(5)(B) of title 18, United States Code, for which a maximum term of imprisonment of 10 years or more is prescribed;
(D) an offense under chapter 77 of this title for which a maximum term of imprisonment of 20 years or more is prescribed; or
(E) an offense involving a minor victim under section 1201, 1591, 2241,2242, 2244 (a)(1), 2245, 2251, 2251A, 2252 (a)(1), 2252 (a)(2), 2252 (a)(3),2252A (a)(1), 2252A (a)(2), 2252A (a)(3), 2252A (a)(4), 2260, 2421, 2422,2423, or 2425 of this title.
(f) Detention Hearing.— The judicial officer shall hold a hearing to determine whether any condition or combination of conditions set forth in subsection (c) of this section will reasonably assure the appearance of such person as required and the safety of any other person and the community—
(1) upon motion of the attorney for the Government, in a case that involves—
(A) a crime of violence, a violation of section 1591, or an offense listed in section 2332b (g)(5)(B) for which a maximum term of imprisonment of 10 years or more is prescribed;
(B) an offense for which the maximum sentence is life imprisonment or death;
(C) an offense for which a maximum term of imprisonment of ten years or more is prescribed in the Controlled Substances Act (21 U.S.C. 801 et seq.), the Controlled Substances Import and Export Act (21 U.S.C. 951 et seq.), or chapter 705 of title 46;
(D) any felony if such person has been convicted of two or more offenses described in subparagraphs (A) through (C) of this paragraph, or two or more State or local offenses that would have been offenses described in subparagraphs (A) through (C) of this paragraph if a circumstance giving rise to Federal jurisdiction had existed, or a combination of such offenses; or

(E) any felony that is not otherwise a crime of violence that involves a minor victim or that involves the possession or use of a firearm or destructive device (as those terms are defined in section 921), or any other dangerous weapon, or involves a failure to register under section 2250 of title 18, United States Code; or

(2) upon motion of the attorney for the Government or upon the judicial officer's own motion in a case, that involves—

(A) a serious risk that such person will flee; or

(B) a serious risk that such person will obstruct or attempt to obstruct justice, or threaten, injure, or intimidate, or attempt to threaten, injure, or intimidate, a prospective witness or juror.

The hearing shall be held immediately upon the person's first appearance before the judicial officer unless that person, or the attorney for the Government, seeks a continuance. Except for good cause, a continuance on motion of such person may not exceed five days (not including any intermediate Saturday, Sunday, or legal holiday), and a continuance on motion of the attorney for the Government may not exceed three days (not including any intermediate Saturday, Sunday, or legal holiday). During a continuance, such person shall be detained, and the judicial officer, on motion of the attorney for the Government or sua sponte, may order that, while in custody, a person who appears to be a narcotics addict receive a medical examination to determine whether such person is an addict. At the hearing, such person has the right to be represented by counsel, and, if financially unable to obtain adequate representation, to have counsel appointed. The person shall be afforded an opportunity to testify, to present witnesses, to cross-examine witnesses who appear at the hearing, and to present information by proffer or otherwise. The rules concerning admissibility of evidence in criminal trials do not apply to the presentation and consideration of information at the hearing. The facts the judicial officer uses to support a finding pursuant to subsection (e) that no condition or combination of conditions will reasonably assure the safety of any other person and the community shall be supported by clear and convincing evidence. The person may be detained pending completion of the hearing. The hearing may be reopened, before or after a determination by the judicial officer, at any time before trial if the judicial officer finds that information exists that was not known to the movant at the time of the hearing and that has a material bearing on the issue whether there are conditions of release that will reasonably assure the appearance of such person as required and the safety of any other person and the community.

(g) Factors To Be Considered.— The judicial officer shall, in determining whether there are conditions of release that will reasonably assure the appearance of the person as required and the safety of any other person and the community, take into account the available information concerning—

(1) the nature and circumstances of the offense charged, including whether the offense is a crime of violence, a violation of section 1591, a Federal crime of terrorism, or involves a minor victim or a controlled substance, firearm, explosive, or destructive device;

(2) the weight of the evidence against the person;

(3) the history and characteristics of the person, including—

(A) the person's character, physical and mental condition, family ties, employment, financial resources, length of residence in the community, community ties, past conduct, history relating to drug or alcohol abuse, criminal history, and record concerning appearance at court proceedings; and
(B) whether, at the time of the current offense or arrest, the person was on probation, on parole, or on other release pending trial, sentencing, appeal, or completion of sentence for an offense under Federal, State, or local law; and
(4) the nature and seriousness of the danger to any person or the community that would be posed by the person's release. In considering the conditions of release described in subsection (c)(1)(B)(xi) or (c)(1)(B)(xii) of this section, the judicial officer may upon his own motion, or shall upon the motion of the Government, conduct an inquiry into the source of the property to be designated for potential forfeiture or offered as collateral to secure a bond, and shall decline to accept the designation, or the use as collateral, of property that, because of its source, will not reasonably assure the appearance of the person as required.
(h) Contents of Release Order.— In a release order issued under subsection (b) or (c) of this section, the judicial officer shall—
(1) include a written statement that sets forth all the conditions to which the release is subject, in a manner sufficiently clear and specific to serve as a guide for the person's conduct; and
(2) advise the person of—
(A) the penalties for violating a condition of release, including the penalties for committing an offense while on pretrial release;
(B) the consequences of violating a condition of release, including the immediate issuance of a warrant for the person's arrest; and
(C) sections 1503 of this title (relating to intimidation of witnesses, jurors, and officers of the court), 1510 (relating to obstruction of criminal investigations), 1512 (tampering with a witness, victim, or an informant), and 1513 (retaliating against a witness, victim, or an informant).
(i) Contents of Detention Order.— In a detention order issued under subsection (e) of this section, the judicial officer shall—
(1) include written findings of fact and a written statement of the reasons for the detention;
(2) direct that the person be committed to the custody of the Attorney General for confinement in a corrections facility separate, to the extent practicable, from persons awaiting or serving sentences or being held in custody pending appeal;
(3) direct that the person be afforded reasonable opportunity for private consultation with counsel; and
(4) direct that, on order of a court of the United States or on request of an attorney for the Government, the person in charge of the corrections facility in which the person is confined deliver the person to a United States marshal for the purpose of an appearance in connection with a court proceeding.
The judicial officer may, by subsequent order, permit the temporary release of the person, in the custody of a United States marshal or another appropriate person, to the extent that the judicial

officer determines such release to be necessary for preparation of the person's defense or for another compelling reason.

(j) Presumption of Innocence.— Nothing in this section shall be construed as modifying or limiting the presumption of innocence.

Since most federal defendants face narcotics offenses, we will use the offense for example purposes. Each situation will vary, but the primary factors will remain fairly consistent.

A defendant arrested in the mid to upper level drug deliveries, are more culpable to prosecutors than the street corner hustler with a pocket full of gray rocks. Prosecutors want the big fish, not the minnows. [51] There are two realities which compete in a prosecutor's mind, whether they will admit to the existence of both or not. The emotional adjective, "ambitious" is one of the considerations at play, while the criminal justice goal of crime deterrence competes for the judicial spotlight. We will address the conventional wisdom which poses the more thoughtful issue, first.

From a criminal justice standpoint, deterrence is of paramount concern. There are complementary approaches to this goal. If you incarcerate the defendant for decades, obviously that person is deterred from selling drugs on America's streets. The actual term that this approach conjures up is, "warehousing". The 100:1 ratio used to sentence crack dealers is a prime example. In its purest from, this practice was tantamount to warehousing.

When you introduce an economical sense to criminal justice, you approach the drug dealing more sensibly. In Economics 101, you learn that in any free market, there are two fundamental factors, namely, a supply and demand. In contemporary history, prosecutors and agents have sought to win their quest for attacking the supply side of the equation. You interdict drug shipments using sophisticated Navy resources, chase the multi-million dollar money laundering and transports for seizure and forfeiture, along with a sharp focus on upper crust and mid-level vendors of the narcotics. If an addict cannot find a source, presumably, the addict surrenders the habit. Unfortunately, history has proven this approach to be ineffective and like the moonshine and imported whiskey from Ireland, federal agents like Elliot Ness chased the misguided policy. During the "Prohibition Era," gangsters reaped millions from running shipments and distilleries.

All of these government resources proved so ineffective, that Congress eventually repealed and Amendment prohibiting alcohol.

Today's approach is not too far displaced from the "Prohibition" times, except Congress has not accepted the conventional wisdom that if people wish to self-medicate using drugs to reduce anxiety or depression, there is no method, short of placing addicts inside of some sort of Impenetrable bubble, to prevent them from fulfilling their goals. The inescapable failure that dooms this approach, does little to dampen prosecutorial spirits. Thus, the likely targets are the upper echelon purveyors of the narcotics industry. That equates to targeting those who present the larger target.

---

[51] US –v- Webster, 162 F.3d 308, 332 (5th Cir. 1998).

With that said, the emotional side of prosecutorial discretion interacts. Prosecutors do not see themselves locked into such salaried positions forever and the means to the higher rewards financially, come from private practice. To reach the six-figure incomes from being a partner of a major law firm, a large number of prosecutors use their record of successful trials and prosecutions as a testament to the skills and knowledge they possess. Getting "tough on crime" became the 1980's mantra, coined by Nancy Reagan and has sense become a politically popular foundation. The most newsworthy the defendant is, the more media exposure the prosecutor captures and attention from major firms grows in leaps and bounds. You may fall into a category where you become a media darling and the prosecutor seeks to harvest exposure and to make you an "event." An "event" in his/her career, that is.

Title 18 U.S.C.§3142 provides for a presumption in certain cases, where admitting a defendant to bail is imprudent or contra-indicated. In crimes of violence and narcotics cases, there is what is referred to as a "rebuttable presumption" of; a) risk of flight; or b) a danger to the community. [52]

Bail is first addressed at a defendant's initial appearance, unless the defendant or prosecution sought a continuance.[53] Be mindful, that deviation of the customary practices involving bail, does not entitle one to release.

If prosecutors demonstrate, during a "detention hearing" that a defendant poses a danger to the community or risk of flight, the Eight Amendment is not offered and that defendant can be held without bail until trial and sentencing.[54]

The standard of proof in assessing bail, is the civil standard of "by the preponderance of evidence," which basically means whoever manages to tip the scales in their favor. In cases where a defendant faces extradition or removal from one

In theory, "rebuttable" means that the allegation is not in-defensible or is mechanical. For example, a prosecutor may allege your role as a primary supplier of cocaine and by reason of that position; you have international ties and likely fee in order to avoid a conviction and lengthy prison sentence. As your defense counsel, it would be logical to argue that you are presumed innocent until proven guilty, which will carry a greater weight prior to a preliminary hearing or indictment being returned. Other defense arguments would include the family ties in the community, especially adolescent children; homeownership and other holdings; the length of time in the community; the employment history of the defendant; the defendants health; even citizenship and education are tentative factors. Surrendering a passport to the judge, could serve the interests in determining whether or not the defendant would be a risk of flight.

Obviously, if a defendant has a history of "failure to appear" or a fugitive on other charges, the likelihood of pretrial release is severely diminished.

---

[52] 18 U.S.C.§ 3142(f) release on bail. (See ***Wright –v – Henkel***, 190 U.S. 40.63 (1903).

[53] ***U.S. – v – Salerno***, 481 U.S. 739, 754-55 (1987) (appendix).

[54] ***Ingram –v- Wright***, 430 U.S. 651, 671 note 40 (1977).

In sum, the drug charge itself should not stand in the way of release on bail. The presumption is rebuttable, but be cognizant of the statutory wording of 18U.S.C. § 3142 (e):

Considerations Regarding Temporary Detention Orders: Title 18, United States Code, Section 3142(d) requires a judicial officer to enter an order of temporary detention in cases where a factual determination is made that:

the defendant: is, and was at the time the offense was committed, on release pending trial for a felony under Federal, State, or local law; release pending imposition or execution of sentence, appeal of sentence or conviction, or completion of sentence, for any offense under Federal, State, or local law; or probation or parole for any offense under Federal, State, or local law; OR

is not a citizen of the United States or lawfully admitted for permanent residence, as defined in section 101(a)(20) of the Immigration and Nationality Act (8 U.S.C. 1101(a)(2); *AND* the defendant may flee or pose a danger to any other person or the community.

Once indicted, the defendant bears the burden of proof to overcome the presumption, by producing credible evidence.

If a defendant is detained with bail, the judge is required to state the reason for that action on the record, enabling the defendant to appeal that decision.[55] There are two methods for appealing an unfavorable bail decision. If a magistrate judge denied bail, a defendant has the right to appeal that decision to the district court judge, who can affirm the magistrate's Order or modify it in any fashion it decides.

If a district judge denies bail, a defendant has the ability to appeal to the Court of Appeals on an expedited schedule and obtain a decision within weeks. [56] A defendant is not required to wait until a final resolution has been reached, as is usually the case, in order to seek release on bail pending trial or final resolution.

The standards for review in the various Courts of Appeal, are varied. Some circuits employ the more difficult "clearly erroneous" standard for a defendant to succeed on appeal, where one must demonstrate that the district judge clearly erred. Asking counsel will answer the question of which standard is used in the appellate circuit where you are located.

---

[55] **F. R. A. P., Rule 9 (a) (1)**

[56] **18 U.S.C. § 3142**

Bail Pending Appeal

This topic deserves its own section, as a number of defendants have often compared to federal system to state systems regarding rights to remain on bail pending and appeal after being convicted and sentenced. The federal statute which related to this particular topic is rather certain in its wording. [57]

18 U.S.C. § 3143 reads as follows:

§ 3143. RELEASE OR DETENTION OF A DEFENDANT PENDING SENTENCE OR APPEAL

(a) Release or Detention Pending Sentence.—

(1) Except as provided in paragraph (2), the judicial officer shall order that a person who has been found guilty of an offense and who is awaiting imposition or execution of sentence, other than a person for whom the applicable guideline promulgated pursuant to 28 U.S.C. 994 does not recommend a term of imprisonment, be detained, unless the judicial officer finds by clear and convincing evidence that the person is not likely to flee or pose a danger to the safety of any other person or the community if released under section 3142 (b) or (c). If the judicial officer makes such a finding, such judicial officer shall order the release of the person in accordance with section 3142 (b) or (c).

(2) The judicial officer shall order that a person who has been found guilty of an offense in a case described in subparagraph (A), (B), or (C) of subsection (f)(1) of section 3142 and is awaiting imposition or execution of sentence be detained unless—

(A)

(i) the judicial officer finds there is a substantial likelihood that a motion for acquittal or new trial will be granted; or

(ii) an attorney for the Government has recommended that no sentence of imprisonment be imposed on the person; and

(B) the judicial officer finds by clear and convincing evidence that the person is not likely to flee or pose a danger to any other person or the community.

(b) Release or Detention Pending Appeal by the Defendant.—

---

[57] **18 U.S.C. § 3143 as follows:**

(1) Except as provided in paragraph (2), the judicial officer shall order that a person who has been found guilty of an offense and sentenced to a term of imprisonment, and who has filed an appeal or a petition for a writ of certiorari, be detained, unless the judicial officer finds—

(A) by clear and convincing evidence that the person is not likely to flee or pose a danger to the safety of any other person or the community if released under section 3142 (b) or (c) of this title; and

(B) that the appeal is not for the purpose of delay and raises a substantial question of law or fact likely to result in—

(i) reversal,

(ii) an order for a new trial,

(iii) a sentence that does not include a term of imprisonment, or

(iv) a reduced sentence to a term of imprisonment less than the total of the time already served plus the expected duration of the appeal process.

If the judicial officer makes such findings, such judicial officer shall order the release of the person in accordance with section 3142 (b) or (c) of this title, except that in the circumstance described in subparagraph (B)(iv) of this paragraph, the judicial officer shall order the detention terminated at the expiration of the likely reduced sentence.

(2) The judicial officer shall order that a person who has been found guilty of an offense in a case described in subparagraph (A), (B), or (C) of subsection (f)(1) of section 3142 and sentenced to a term of imprisonment, and who has filed an appeal or a petition for a writ of certiorari, be detained.

(c) Release or Detention Pending Appeal by the Government.— The judicial officer shall treat a defendant in a case in which an appeal has been taken by the United States under section 3731 of this title, in accordance with section 3142 of this title, unless the defendant is otherwise subject to a release or detention order. Except as provided in subsection (b) of this section, the judicial officer, in a case in which an appeal has been taken by the United States under section 3742, shall—

(1) if the person has been sentenced to a term of imprisonment, order that person detained; and

(2) in any other circumstance, release or detain the person under section 3142.

Simply stated, the ***Bail Reform Act*** requires a district judge to detain the defendant, unless the defendant demonstrates that:

1) The defendant, by clear and convincing evidence, is not likely to flee or pose a danger to the community; and,

2) The appeal raises a substantial question of law or fact which is likely to result in a reversal or a new trial or the equivalent of a "time served" sentence. [58]

Most of the federal circuits have defined the term "substantial question of law or fact," to equate to a judicial determination that the appeal could go either way, not that it would likely result in a new trial.[59]

Bail Revocation

It is worth mentioning that if someone violates the conditions of bail, that the prosecution will file a formal motion before the judge to seek a hearing. The motion must set out a factual basis for the proposed revocation, sufficient enough to enable the defendant to prepare a meaningful defense. The defendant will also enjoy the right to counsel at the hearings.

In addition, the prosecutors can initiate a civil action against the defendant who violates the condition of bail, for the full amount of the bail.[60] For example, if a defendant is released on a recognizance bond in the amount of $100,000.00 and violates the conditions of bond, the prosecutors may initiate an action seeking a civil judgment in that amount. Once that judgment is obtained, the prosecutors could begin attaching property, both real and personal, in which to satisfy that amount.

A civil action will not preclude the prosecution from also seeking a forfeiture petition in the criminal action, as well. [61]

NOTES

---

[58] 18:U.S.C. § 3143 (b) (1)(B) and ***U.S. –v- Giraldi***, 86 F.3d 1368, 1379 (CA5 1996).

[59] ***U.S. –v-Bayko*** 774 F.2d 516, 521-23, (CA 1 1985)

[60] **F.R.C.P. Rule 46 (f) (1)**

[61] **F.R.C.P. Rule 46 (f) (1)**

Chapter V

Indictments

The Fifth Amendment to the Constitution requires the government to initiate prosecutions for capital and felony cases by indictment.

"No person shall be held to answer for a capital or otherwise infamous crime, unless on a presentment or indictment of a Grand Jury." [62]

An Indictment, or True Bill, is a document which sets forth the statutory offenses with which a defendant is charged and a determination of probable cause has been found. For example, narcotics offenses are set forth in Title 21 of the United States Code, which most other offenses that are generally encountered are found in Title 18.

In remaining within the previous examples we will look at typical narcotics offenses. Sample Indictments alleging drug offenses are found within the Appendix. [63]

Since 2001, the courts have held prosecutors to tighter standards on pleading drug offenses and the statutory enhancements associated. There are certain "elements" that must be stated within the body of the Indictment. For example, if a defendant is charged with possessing five or more grams of "crack," or cocaine base, that creates a statutory mandatory minimum of five years imprisonment and must be set forth in the Indictment. [64] It is this statutory shift requiring a minimum of five years imprisonment that mandates the prosecution to include this element. Likewise, if a defendant had five hundred grams of powder cocaine. The next statutory shift in mandatory minimum sentences comes into play if a defendant possessed fifty or more grams of crack or five or more Kilograms of powder cocaine. In the instances, the statutory mandatory minimum is ten years, not five. [65] Prosecutors must be careful in statutory pleadings or risk waiving the enhanced sentences.

The Indictment must be sufficient to give every defendant enough information upon which to prepare a defense. In legal terminology, this is called "notice" and does not require the inclusion of every aspect of the prosecution's case, but only enough information to include the proximate time or date, the location, offense conduct or statute violated and statutory provisions allegedly violated.

---

[62] see also Chapter 1 for discussion on grand juries.

[63] see Appendix

[64] **Title 21, U.S.C. § 841 (a) (1) and (b)**

[65] **Title 21 U.S.C. § 841(b)**

If a defendant believes that they lack sufficient notice upon which to prepare a defense, such as date for example, where they may have an alibi defense, they may file a "Motion for Bill of Particulars." If the judge grants this Motion, the prosecutors will be required to be more definitive and expose more facts from their case to the defendant. Such motions are rarely granted, but there are instances where a defendant may prevail. A defendant must remember that a grand jury only needs probable cause and courts will not dismiss facially valid indictments. [66]

The Supreme Court, in 2001, issued a blockbuster decision which altered the landscape of criminal prosecutions across the country. [67] Essentially, when prosecutors seek statutory enhancements, which includes shifts in mandatory minimums, they must "Plead" the particular statute and "prove that element to a jury beyond a reasonable doubt." [68]

Be cautious when interpreting ***Apprendi***_and subsequent decisions, by confusing statutory shifts, versus guidelines enhancements. [69]

When a judge is sentencing a defendant, there are sentencing factors, not elements of the crime itself, which can be taken into consideration. [70] For purposes of this Chapter, however the importance attached to Indictments and elements of offenses is critical.

In obtaining the Indictment, prosecutors present evidence to a grand jury. The finding of a grand jury to indict does not have to be unanimous and is based only on probable cause, which the prosecutors need to prove by a preponderance of evidence. Once the decision is made by the jurors to indict, prosecutors provide a "True Bill of Indictment" for the person to sign. The Indictment will contain "counts", in sequential order. Since each offense constitutes a crime, these offenses are set forth in Counts. For example, a defendant delivers crack cocaine to an undercover officer or informant, ten times over a period of time. Each delivery will be reflected as a Count in the Indictment. In addition to the ten Counts for the deliveries, the indictment will likely contain a Count for "conspiracy", pursuant to Subsection 846 and/ or a more broad allegation of "possession with intent to deliver"' under Subsection 841. These would be separate Counts.

The theory behind this practice is a bit complicated. The prosecution must prove you committed a crime beyond a reasonable doubt. If constrained to the broader offense of "Possession with intent to deliver" under Subsection 841, a jury could be confused in determining a defendant's guilt or innocence. For example, the jury may or may not believe you made all ten of the alleged deliveries used as an example above. By reducing these deliveries to Counts, the jury can reject the allegations, systematically and with a rationale. If these

---

[66] ***Costello – v – US***, 350 U.S. 359, 363-64 (1956).

[67] ***Appendi –v- N.J.***, 530 U.S. 466, (2001).

[68] **Id**. 475.76, see also ***Ring v – Arizona***, 536 US. 584 (2002.

[69] ***Costello – v – US***, 350 U.S. 359, 363-64 (1956).

[70] _70_/ see **Chapter IX.**

individual offences were not divided up the jury simply had one charge to decide upon, like "possession with intent to deliver'" a defendant would be convicted of the offense, if the jury believed the prosecutors had proved one or more of the alleged deliveries. By separating the drug transactions, they jury definitely decides which, if any, of the drug transactions the defendant was guilty.

By requiring prosecutors to identify the offenses and their respective elements in the Indictment, prosecutors are then prohibited from changing offenses during trial. In legal terminology, there are two basic types of changes:

a) variance and b) amendment.

A "variance" occurs when the wording, terms and elements of the offense/offenses remain unchanged, but the evidence adduced at the trial varies. For example, a defendant may be indicted for a conspiring with John Doe, but at trial the prosecutors argue and present evidence the defendant conspired with Dennis Hermann. Variances are unlikely to resort in a mistrial, unless the defendant can demonstrate prejudice. [71] An "amendment", on the other hand, is considered a more serious infringement on a defendant's rights. An amendment occurs when the prosecutors and/or judge literally change the wording, terms or elements of the offense or "constructively" make those changes.

A literal amendment would occur if prosecutors or judge, after a grand jury returned a True Bill, simply re-wrote the changes before or during the trial, without returning to the Grand Jury beforehand. This would infringe upon the defendants rights under the Fifth Amendment. [72] A "constructive" amendment occurs when the evidence at trial is different from the charged offenses or when the jury is given instructions which broaden the charged conduct.[73]

The following, is from the ***U.S. Attorneys Manual***, so that you know how the prosecutor will approach your case.

The general rule is that indictments cannot be amended in substance. "An amendment to an indictment occurs when the charging terms of an indictment are altered." *United States v. Cancelliere*, 69 F.3d 1116, 1121 (11th Cir. 1995). This follows from the fundamental distinction between the information and the indictment , which must be returned by a grand jury. If the indictment could be changed by the court or by the prosecutor, then it would no longer be the indictment returned by the grand jury. Indeed, in *Russell v. United States*, 369 U.S. 749, 769 (1962), the Court pointed out that a consequence of amending the indictment is that the defendant "could then be convicted on the basis of facts not found by, and perhaps not even presented to, the grand jury which indicted him." "Thus, the Fifth Amendment forbids amendment of an indictment by the Court, whether actual or constructive." *United States v.*

[71] **F.R.Cr. P. Rule 52 (a).**

[72] **F.R.Cr.P. Rules 6 & 7**; see also, ***Stirone –v- U.S.,*** 361 U.S. 212, 217-219 (1960).

[73] ***Stirone*** @ 217.

Wacker, 72 F.3d 1453, 1474 (10th Cir. 1995), *petition for cert. filed*, (Jun. 10, 1996)(No. 95-9284).

The Supreme Court, reviewing the history of the grand jury, quotes Lord Mansfield on the subject: There is a great difference between amending indictments and amending informations. Indictments are found upon the oaths of a jury, and ought only to be amended by themselves; but informations are as declarations in the king's suit. An officer of the Crown has the right of framing them originally; he may, with leave, amend in like manner, as any plaintiff may do. .*Ex parte Bain*, 121 U.S. 1, 6 (1887). *Cf. United States v. Miller*, 105 S.Ct. 1811 (1985)(it does not constitute an unconstitutional amendment to an indictment to drop those allegations which are unnecessary to an offense that is clearly contained within it). In one case, *Stirone v. United States*, 361 U.S. 212 (1960), the defendant was convicted of unlawful interference with interstate commerce in violation of the Hobbs Act, 18 U.S.C. § 1951. The indictment charged that the victim's contract was to supply ready-mix concrete from his Pennsylvania plant to be used in the erection of a steel mill in Allenport, Pennsylvania. Performance of the contract involved, according to the indictment, shipment of sand from various points in the United States to the victim's ready-mix concrete plant. The trial court permitted the government to offer evidence of the effect upon interstate commerce not only of the sand thus brought into Pennsylvania but also the interstate shipment of steel from the steel mill to be constructed from the ready-mix concrete.

The Supreme Court reversed the defendant's conviction on the ground that he was convicted of a different crime from that charged, in violation of his Fifth Amendment right to be indicted by a grand jury:

The grand jury which found this indictment was satisfied to charge that Stirone's conduct interfered with interstate importation of sand. But neither this nor any other court can know that the grand jury would have been willing to charge that Stirone's conduct would interfere with interstate exportation of steel from a mill later to be built with Rider's concrete. . . Although the trial court did not permit a formal amendment of the indictment, the effect of what it did was the same. *Stirone*, at 217.

An amendment for the excising of surplusage that has the effect of narrowing a defendant's liability without changing the meaning of the charge as it was presented to the grand jury is permissible. In *United States v. Whitman*, 665 F.2d 313 (10th Cir. 1981), the court held it was proper for the government to strike the references to overvaluation of property in an 18 U.S.C. § 1014 count alleging false statements to a federally insured bank. A similar deletion was approved in *United States v. Ramirez*, 670 F.2d 27 (5th Cir. 1982), even though the defendant's theory of defense was thereby altered.

The Supreme Court, reviewing the history of the grand jury, quotes Lord Mansfield on the subject: There is a great difference between amending indictments and amending informations. Indictments are found upon the oaths of a jury, and ought only to be amended by themselves; but informations are as declarations in the king's suit. An officer of the Crown has the right of framing them originally; he may, with leave, amend in like manner, as any plaintiff may do. .*Ex parte Bain*, 121 U.S. 1, 6 (1887). *Cf. United States v. Miller*, 105 S.Ct. 1811 (1985)(it does not constitute an unconstitutional amendment to an indictment to drop those allegations which are unnecessary to an offense that is clearly contained within it). In one case, *Stirone v. United States*, 361 U.S. 212 (1960), the defendant was convicted of unlawful interference with interstate commerce in violation of the Hobbs Act, 18 U.S.C. § 1951. The indictment charged that the victim's contract was to supply ready-mix concrete from his Pennsylvania plant to be used in the erection of a steel mill in Allenport, Pennsylvania. Performance of the contract

An issue, as yet unresolved, exists concerning amendment of an indictment for an offense that could have been initiated by an information. In *United States v. Goldstein*, 502 F.2d 526 (3d Cir. 1974), the Third Circuit considered the issue in the case of an indictment for failure to file an income tax return by April 15, which was a misdemeanor. The evidence showed that the defendant had obtained an extension until May 7. The government argued that had the offense been prosecuted by information, it could have been amended and therefore similar liberality should apply to the indictment. The court relied in part upon the fact that Fed. R. Crim. P. 7(e), which permits the amendment of informations, is silent about the amendment of indictments and, therefore, by implication must prohibit their amendment. The court also cited *United States v. Fischetti*, 450 F.2d 34, 39 (5th Cir. 1971),*cert. denied*, 405 U.S. 1016 (1922), where the Fifth Circuit indicated that having chosen to proceed by indictment, the government is bound by the principles applicable to indictments.

In *United States v. Pandilidis*, 524 F.2d 644 (6th Cir. 1975), *cert. denied*, 424 U.S. 933 (1976), the Sixth Circuit, confronting the issue in virtually an identical case, upheld amendment of the indictment. The indictment alleged a failure to file by April 15 and the government corrected this with a bill of particulars setting out the extensions to file. The Sixth Circuit identified the rights involved as: (1) fair notice under the Sixth Amendment, (2) protection from double jeopardy under the Fifth Amendment, and (3) the right not to be held for an infamous crime except upon an indictment by a grand jury. The court held that the defendant's right to fair notice was not infringed because he was apprised be protected from double jeopardy, since the record of the case provided full protection. As for the right of the defendant to be indicted by a grand jury, the court noted that although the defendant had a constitutional right to be indicted for an infamous crime, the offense with which he was charged was not such an offense. "[S]ince the error permitting amendment to the indictment in this case did not reach constitutional dimensions, the appropriateness of reversal must be determined under Rule 52(a) [harmless error]. . . ." *SeePandilidis*, at 649.

The correction of an error in an indictment by substitution of a superseding information, where the offense could have been initiated by information, was upheld in *United States v. Brewer*, 681 F.2d 973 (5th Cir. 1982). *See also United States v. Talbot* 51 F.3d 183, 186 (9th Cir. 1995); *United States v. Saussy*, 802 F.2d 849, 852 (6th Cir. 1986), *cert. denied*, 480 U.S. 907 (1987).

Requirement of Specificity

The second part of the sufficiency test, apprising the defendant of what he or she must be prepared to meet incorporates the specificity requirement of the Sixth Amendment. The specificity requirement serves to insure that a defendant only has to answer to charges actually brought by the grand jury and not a prosecutor's interpretation of the charges, that the defendant is apprised of the charges against him in order to permit preparation of his defense, and that the defendant is protected against double jeopardy. *See United States v. Haas*, 583 F.2d 216 (5th Cir.),*reh'g denied*, 588 F.2d 829, *cert. denied*, 440 U.S. 981 (1978).

An example of an indictment which failed this test is provided by *United States v. Nance*, 533 F.2d 699 (D.C. Cir. 1976). The indictment in Nance charged a false pretense violation pursuant to the D.C. Code. It listed the name of each victim, the date of the false representation, the amount each victim lost, and the date the sum was paid to the defendants, but was fatally defective as a consequence of its failure to specify the false representation which induced the victims to pay the money to the defendants. *See also United States v. Brown*, 995 F.2d 1493, 1504-05 (10th Cir.)(indictment charging controlling premises and making them available for storing and distributing cocaine base insufficient because failed to state how control was exercised), *cert. denied*, 114 S.Ct. 353 (1993).

The indictment, though, need only satisfy a defendant's constitutional right to know what he or she is charged with and not the evidentiary details which will be used to establish his commission of the offense. *See United States v. Blinder*, 10 F.3d 1468, 1476 (9th Cir. 1993)(indictment charging RICO violation in omitting material facts sufficient despite lack of detailed explanations of omissions); *United States v. Chappell*, 6 F.3d 1095, 1099-100 (5th Cir. 1993)(indictment met requirements of alerting defendants to charges and was sufficient despite possibility of being more carefully drafted), *cert. denied*, 114 S.Ct. 1235 (1994); *United States v. Diecidue*, 603 F.2d 535, 547 (5th Cir.), *cert. denied*, *Gispert v. United States*, 445 U.S. 946 (1980).

In determining whether an indictment sufficiently informs the defendant of the offense, courts give the indictment a common sense construction. *United States v. Drew*, 722 F.2d 551, 552-53 (9th Cir. 1983)(indictments charging defendants with acting knowingly and willfully sufficient although failing to track statutory language alleging "unlawful or fraudulent intent" because, under common sense reading, defendants informed of charge), *cert. denied*, 467 U.S. 1216 (1984); *United States v. Reed*, 721 F.2d 1059, 1061-62 (6th Cir. 1983)(indictment charging defendants with conspiring with others sufficient because, under common sense reading, it also charged defendants with conspiring with one another). [74]

NOTES

____

____

____

____

____

[74] Criminal Resource Manual 206

Chapter VI

Offenses

While the entire ***Crimes and Offenses*** provisions of ***Titles 18 & 21, United States Code*** fills thousands of pages, the greatest per centum of offenders facing federal prosecution fall into narcotics, firearms, a combination of both or conspiracy to commit one or more of those offenses. Therefore, we will focus on the actual statutes for these offenses.

Title 18 U.S.C.

§2. PRINCIPALS

(a) Whoever commits an offense against the United States or aids, abets, counsels, commands, induces or procures its commission, is punishable as a principal.

(b) Whoever willfully causes an act to be done which if directly performed by him or another would be an offense against the United States, is punishable as a principal.

§ 3. ACCESSORY AFTER THE FACT

Whoever, knowing that an offense against the United States has been committed, receives, relieves, comforts or assists the offender in order to hinder or prevent his apprehension, trial or punishment, is an accessory after the fact.

Except as otherwise expressly provided by any Act of Congress, an accessory after the fact shall be imprisoned not more than one-half the maximum term of imprisonment or (notwithstanding section 3571) fined not more than one-half the maximum fine prescribed for the punishment of the principal, or both; or if the principal is punishable by life imprisonment or death, the accessory shall be imprisoned not more than 15 years.

§ 371. CONSPIRACY TO COMMIT OFFENSE OR TO DEFRAUD UNITED STATES

If two or more persons conspire either to commit any offense against the United States, or to defraud the United States, or any agency thereof in any manner or for any purpose, and one or more of such persons do any act to effect the object of the conspiracy, each shall be fined under this title or imprisoned not more than five years, or both.

If, however, the offense, the commission of which is the object of the conspiracy, is a misdemeanor only, the punishment for such conspiracy shall not exceed the maximum punishment provided for such misdemeanor.

§ 922. UNLAWFUL ACTS

(a) It shall be unlawful—

(1) for any person—

(A) except a licensed importer, licensed manufacturer, or licensed dealer, to engage in the business of importing, manufacturing, or dealing in firearms, or in the course of such business to ship, transport, or receive any firearm in interstate or foreign commerce; or

(B) except a licensed importer or licensed manufacturer, to engage in the business of importing or manufacturing ammunition, or in the course of such business, to ship, transport, or receive any ammunition in interstate or foreign commerce;

(2) for any importer, manufacturer, dealer, or collector licensed under the provisions of this chapter to ship or transport in interstate or foreign commerce any firearm to any person other than a licensed importer, licensed manufacturer, licensed dealer, or licensed collector, except that—

(A) this paragraph and subsection (b)(3) shall not be held to preclude a licensed importer, licensed manufacturer, licensed dealer, or licensed collector from returning a firearm or replacement firearm of the same kind and type to a person from whom it was received; and this paragraph shall not be held to preclude an individual from mailing a firearm owned in compliance with Federal, State, and local law to a licensed importer, licensed manufacturer, licensed dealer, or licensed collector;

(B) this paragraph shall not be held to preclude a licensed importer, licensed manufacturer, or licensed dealer from depositing a firearm for conveyance in the mails to any officer, employee, agent, or watchman who, pursuant to the provisions of section 1715 of this title, is eligible to receive through the mails pistols, revolvers, and other firearms capable of being concealed on the person, for use in connection with his official duty; and

(C) nothing in this paragraph shall be construed as applying in any manner in the District of Columbia, the Commonwealth of Puerto Rico, or any possession of the United States differently than it would apply if the District of Columbia, the Commonwealth of Puerto Rico, or the possession were in fact a State of the United States;

(3) for any person, other than a licensed importer, licensed manufacturer, licensed dealer, or licensed collector to transport into or receive in the State where he resides (or if the person is a corporation or other business entity, the State where it maintains a place of business) any firearm purchased or otherwise obtained by such person outside that State, except that this paragraph (A) shall not preclude any person who lawfully acquires a firearm by bequest or intestate succession in a State other than his State of residence from transporting the firearm into or receiving it in that State, if it is lawful for such person to purchase or possess such firearm in that State, (B) shall not apply to the transportation or receipt of a firearm obtained in conformity with subsection (b)(3) of this section, and (C) shall not apply to the transportation of any firearm acquired in any State prior to the effective date of this chapter;

(4) for any person, other than a licensed importer, licensed manufacturer, licensed dealer, or licensed collector, to transport in interstate or foreign commerce any destructive device, machinegun (as defined in section 5845 of the Internal Revenue Code of 1986), short-barreled shotgun, or short-barreled rifle, except as specifically authorized by the Attorney General consistent with public safety and necessity;

(5) for any person (other than a licensed importer, licensed manufacturer, licensed dealer, or licensed collector) to transfer, sell, trade, give, transport, or deliver any firearm to any person (other than a licensed importer, licensed manufacturer, licensed dealer, or licensed collector) who the transferor knows or has reasonable cause to believe does not reside in (or if the person is a corporation or other business entity, does not maintain a place of business in) the State in which the transferor resides; except that this paragraph shall not apply to

(A) the transfer, transportation, or delivery of a firearm made to carry out a bequest of a firearm to, or an acquisition by intestate succession of a firearm by, a person who is permitted to acquire or possess a firearm under the laws of the State of his residence, and

(B) the loan or rental of a firearm to any person for temporary use for lawful sporting purposes;

(6) for any person in connection with the acquisition or attempted acquisition of any firearm or ammunition from a licensed importer, licensed manufacturer, licensed dealer, or licensed collector, knowingly to make any false or fictitious oral or written statement or to furnish or exhibit any false, fictitious, or misrepresented identification, intended or likely to deceive such importer, manufacturer, dealer, or collector with respect to any fact material to the lawfulness of the sale or other disposition of such firearm or ammunition under the provisions of this chapter;

(7) for any person to manufacture or import armor piercing ammunition, unless—

(A) the manufacture of such ammunition is for the use of the United States, any department or agency of the United States, any State, or any department, agency, or political subdivision of a State;

(B) the manufacture of such ammunition is for the purpose of exportation; or

(C) the manufacture or importation of such ammunition is for the purpose of testing or experimentation and has been authorized by the Attorney General;

(8) for any manufacturer or importer to sell or deliver armor piercing ammunition, unless such sale or delivery—

(A) is for the use of the United States, any department or agency of the United States, any State, or any department, agency, or political subdivision of a State;

(B) is for the purpose of exportation; or

(C) is for the purpose of testing or experimentation and has been authorized by the Attorney General; [1]

(9) for any person, other than a licensed importer, licensed manufacturer, licensed dealer, or licensed collector, who does not reside in any State to receive any firearms unless such receipt is for lawful sporting purposes.

(b) It shall be unlawful for any licensed importer, licensed manufacturer, licensed dealer, or licensed collector to sell or deliver—

(1) any firearm or ammunition to any individual who the licensee knows or has reasonable cause to believe is less than eighteen years of age, and, if the firearm, or ammunition is other than a shotgun or rifle, or ammunition for a shotgun or rifle, to any individual who the licensee knows or has reasonable cause to believe is less than twenty-one years of age;

(2) any firearm to any person in any State where the purchase or possession by such person of such firearm would be in violation of any State law or any published ordinance applicable at the place of sale, delivery or other disposition, unless the licensee knows or has reasonable cause to believe that the purchase or possession would not be in violation of such State law or such published ordinance;

(3) any firearm to any person who the licensee knows or has reasonable cause to believe does not reside in (or if the person is a corporation or other business entity, does not maintain a place of business in) the State in which the licensee's place of business is located, except that this paragraph (A) shall not apply to the sale or delivery of any rifle or shotgun to a resident of a State other than a State in which the licensee's place of business is located if the transferee meets in person with the transferor to accomplish the transfer, and the sale, delivery, and receipt fully comply with the legal conditions of sale in both such States (and any licensed manufacturer, importer or dealer shall be presumed, for purposes of this subparagraph, in the absence of evidence to the contrary, to have had actual knowledge of the State laws and published ordinances of both States), and (B) shall not apply to the loan or rental of a firearm to any person for temporary use for lawful sporting purposes;

(4) to any person any destructive device, machinegun (as defined in section 5845 of the Internal Revenue Code of 1986), short-barreled shotgun, or short-barreled rifle, except as specifically authorized by the Attorney General consistent with public safety and necessity; and

(5) any firearm or armor-piercing ammunition to any person unless the licensee notes in his records, required to be kept pursuant to section 923 of this chapter, the name, age, and place of residence of such person if the person is an individual, or the identity and principal and local places of business of such person if the person is a corporation or other business entity.

Paragraphs (1), (2), (3), and (4) of this subsection shall not apply to transactions between licensed importers, licensed manufacturers, licensed dealers, and licensed collectors. Paragraph (4) of this subsection shall not apply to a sale or delivery to any research organization designated by the Attorney General.

(c) In any case not otherwise prohibited by this chapter, a licensed importer, licensed manufacturer, or licensed dealer may sell a firearm to a person who does not appear in person at the licensee's business premises (other than another licensed importer, manufacturer, or dealer) only if—

(1) the transferee submits to the transferor a sworn statement in the following form:

"Subject to penalties provided by law, I swear that, in the case of any firearm other than a shotgun or a rifle, I am twenty-one years or more of age, or that, in the case of a shotgun or a rifle, I am eighteen years or more of age; that I am not prohibited by the provisions of chapter 44 of title 18, United States Code, from receiving a firearm in interstate or foreign commerce; and that my receipt of this firearm will not be in violation of any statute of the State and published ordinance applicable to the locality in which I reside. Further, the true title, name, and address of the principal law enforcement officer of the locality to which the firearm will be delivered are XXXXXXXXXXXXXXXXXXXXXXXXXXXXXXXXXX

Signature XXXXXXXXX Date XXXX."

and containing blank spaces for the attachment of a true copy of any permit or other information required pursuant to such statute or published ordinance;

(2) the transferor has, prior to the shipment or delivery of the firearm, forwarded by registered or certified mail (return receipt requested) a copy of the sworn statement, together with a description of the firearm, in a form prescribed by the Attorney General, to the chief law enforcement officer of the transferee's place of residence, and has received a return receipt evidencing delivery of the statement or has had the statement returned due to the refusal of the named addressee to accept such letter in accordance with United States Post Office Department regulations; and

(3) the transferor has delayed shipment or delivery for a period of at least seven days following receipt of the notification of the acceptance or refusal of delivery of the statement.

A copy of the sworn statement and a copy of the notification to the local law enforcement officer, together with evidence of receipt or rejection of that notification shall be retained by the licensee as a part of the records required to be kept under section 923 (g).

(d) It shall be unlawful for any person to sell or otherwise dispose of any firearm or ammunition to any person knowing or having reasonable cause to believe that such person—

(1) is under indictment for, or has been convicted in any court of, a crime punishable by imprisonment for a term exceeding one year;

(2) is a fugitive from justice;

(3) is an unlawful user of or addicted to any controlled substance (as defined in section 102 of the Controlled Substances Act (21 U.S.C. 802));

(4) has been adjudicated as a mental defective or has been committed to any mental institution;

(5) who, being an alien—

(A) is illegally or unlawfully in the United States; or

(B) except as provided in subsection (y)(2), has been admitted to the United States under a nonimmigrant visa (as that term is defined in section 101(a)(26) of the Immigration and Nationality Act (8 U.S.C. 1101 (a)(26)));

(6) who [2] has been discharged from the Armed Forces under dishonorable conditions;

(7) who, having been a citizen of the United States, has renounced his citizenship;

(8) is subject to a court order that restrains such person from harassing, stalking, or threatening an intimate partner of such person or child of such intimate partner or person, or engaging in other conduct that would place an intimate partner in reasonable fear of bodily injury to the partner or child, except that this paragraph shall only apply to a court order that—

(A) was issued after a hearing of which such person received actual notice, and at which such person had the opportunity to participate; and

(B)

(i) includes a finding that such person represents a credible threat to the physical safety of such intimate partner or child; or

(ii) by its terms explicitly prohibits the use, attempted use, or threatened use of physical force against such intimate partner or child that would reasonably be expected to cause bodily injury; or

(9) has been convicted in any court of a misdemeanor crime of domestic violence.

This subsection shall not apply with respect to the sale or disposition of a firearm or ammunition to a licensed importer, licensed manufacturer, licensed dealer, or licensed collector who pursuant to subsection (b) of section 925 of this chapter is not precluded from dealing in firearms or ammunition, or to a person who has been granted relief from disabilities pursuant to subsection (c) of section 925 of this chapter.

(e) It shall be unlawful for any person knowingly to deliver or cause to be delivered to any common or contract carrier for transportation or shipment in interstate or foreign commerce, to persons other than licensed importers, licensed manufacturers, licensed dealers, or licensed collectors, any package or other container in which there is any firearm or ammunition without written notice to the carrier that such firearm or ammunition is being transported or shipped; except that any passenger who owns or legally possesses a firearm or ammunition being transported aboard any common or contract carrier for movement with the passenger in interstate or foreign commerce may deliver said firearm or ammunition into the custody of the pilot, captain, conductor or operator of such common or contract carrier for the duration of the trip without violating any of the provisions of this chapter. No common or contract carrier shall require or cause any label, tag, or other written notice to be placed on the outside of any package, luggage, or other container that such package, luggage, or other container contains a firearm.

(f)

(1) It shall be unlawful for any common or contract carrier to transport or deliver in interstate or foreign commerce any firearm or ammunition with knowledge or reasonable cause to believe that the shipment, transportation, or receipt thereof would be in violation of the provisions of this chapter.

(2) It shall be unlawful for any common or contract carrier to deliver in interstate or foreign commerce any firearm without obtaining written acknowledgement of receipt from the recipient of the package or other container in which there is a firearm.

(g) It shall be unlawful for any person—

(1) who has been convicted in any court of, a crime punishable by imprisonment for a term exceeding one year;

(2) who is a fugitive from justice;

(3) who is an unlawful user of or addicted to any controlled substance (as defined in section 102 of the Controlled Substances Act (21 U.S.C. 802));

(4) who has been adjudicated as a mental defective or who has been committed to a mental institution;

(5) who, being an alien—

(A) is illegally or unlawfully in the United States; or

(B) except as provided in subsection (y)(2), has been admitted to the United States under a nonimmigrant visa (as that term is defined in section 101(a)(26) of the Immigration and Nationality Act (8 U.S.C. 1101 (a)(26)));

(6) who has been discharged from the Armed Forces under dishonorable conditions;

(7) who, having been a citizen of the United States, has renounced his citizenship;
(8) who is subject to a court order that—
(A) was issued after a hearing of which such person received actual notice, and at which such person had an opportunity to participate;
(B) restrains such person from harassing, stalking, or threatening an intimate partner of such person or child of such intimate partner or person, or engaging in other conduct that would place an intimate partner in reasonable fear of bodily injury to the partner or child; and
(C)
(i) includes a finding that such person represents a credible threat to the physical safety of such intimate partner or child; or
(ii) by its terms explicitly prohibits the use, attempted use, or threatened use of physical force against such intimate partner or child that would reasonably be expected to cause bodily injury; or
(9) who has been convicted in any court of a misdemeanor crime of domestic violence,
to ship or transport in interstate or foreign commerce, or possess in or affecting commerce, any firearm or ammunition; or to receive any firearm or ammunition which has been shipped or transported in interstate or foreign commerce.
(h) It shall be unlawful for any individual, who to that individual's knowledge and while being employed for any person described in any paragraph of subsection (g) of this section, in the course of such employment—
(1) to receive, possess, or transport any firearm or ammunition in or affecting interstate or foreign commerce; or
(2) to receive any firearm or ammunition which has been shipped or transported in interstate or foreign commerce.
(i) It shall be unlawful for any person to transport or ship in interstate or foreign commerce, any stolen firearm or stolen ammunition, knowing or having reasonable cause to believe that the firearm or ammunition was stolen.
(j) It shall be unlawful for any person to receive, possess, conceal, store, barter, sell, or dispose of any stolen firearm or stolen ammunition, or pledge or accept as security for a loan any stolen firearm or stolen ammunition, which is moving as, which is a part of, which constitutes, or which has been shipped or transported in, interstate or foreign commerce, either before or after it was stolen, knowing or having reasonable cause to believe that the firearm or ammunition was stolen.
(k) It shall be unlawful for any person knowingly to transport, ship, or receive, in interstate or foreign commerce, any firearm which has had the importer's or manufacturer's serial number removed, obliterated, or altered or to possess or receive any firearm which has had the importer's or manufacturer's serial number removed, obliterated, or altered and has, at any time, been shipped or transported in interstate or foreign commerce.
(l) Except as provided in section 925 (d) of this chapter, it shall be unlawful for any person knowingly to import or bring into the United States or any possession thereof any firearm or ammunition; and it shall be unlawful for any person knowingly to receive any firearm or

ammunition which has been imported or brought into the United States or any possession thereof in violation of the provisions of this chapter.

(m) It shall be unlawful for any licensed importer, licensed manufacturer, licensed dealer, or licensed collector knowingly to make any false entry in, to fail to make appropriate entry in, or to fail to properly maintain, any record which he is required to keep pursuant to section 923 of this chapter or regulations promulgated thereunder.

(n) It shall be unlawful for any person who is under indictment for a crime punishable by imprisonment for a term exceeding one year to ship or transport in interstate or foreign commerce any firearm or ammunition or receive any firearm or ammunition which has been shipped or transported in interstate or foreign commerce.

(o)

(1) Except as provided in paragraph (2), it shall be unlawful for any person to transfer or possess a machinegun.

(2) This subsection does not apply with respect to—

(A) a transfer to or by, or possession by or under the authority of, the United States or any department or agency thereof or a State, or a department, agency, or political subdivision thereof; or

(B) any lawful transfer or lawful possession of a machinegun that was lawfully possessed before the date this subsection takes effect.

(p)

(1) It shall be unlawful for any person to manufacture, import, sell, ship, deliver, possess, transfer, or receive any firearm—

(A) that, after removal of grips, stocks, and magazines, is not as detectable as the Security Exemplar, by walk-through metal detectors calibrated and operated to detect the Security Exemplar; or

(B) any major component of which, when subjected to inspection by the types of x-ray machines commonly used at airports, does not generate an image that accurately depicts the shape of the component. Barium sulfate or other compounds may be used in the fabrication of the component.

(2) For purposes of this subsection—

(A) the term "firearm" does not include the frame or receiver of any such weapon;

(B) the term "major component" means, with respect to a firearm, the barrel, the slide or cylinder, or the frame or receiver of the firearm; and

(C) the term "Security Exemplar" means an object, to be fabricated at the direction of the Attorney General, that is—

(i) constructed of, during the 12-month period beginning on the date of the enactment of this subsection, 3.7 ounces of material type 17–4 PH stainless steel in a shape resembling a handgun; and

(ii) suitable for testing and calibrating metal detectors:

Provided, however, That at the close of such 12-month period, and at appropriate times thereafter the Attorney General shall promulgate regulations to permit the manufacture, importation, sale, shipment, delivery, possession, transfer, or receipt of firearms previously prohibited under this subparagraph that are as detectable as a "Security Exemplar" which contains 3.7 ounces of material type 17–4 PH stainless steel, in a shape resembling a handgun, or such lesser amount as is detectable in view of advances in state-of-the-art developments in weapons detection technology.

(3) Under such rules and regulations as the Attorney General shall prescribe, this subsection shall not apply to the manufacture, possession, transfer, receipt, shipment, or delivery of a firearm by a licensed manufacturer or any person acting pursuant to a contract with a licensed manufacturer, for the purpose of examining and testing such firearm to determine whether paragraph (1) applies to such firearm. The Attorney General shall ensure that rules and regulations adopted pursuant to this paragraph do not impair the manufacture of prototype firearms or the development of new technology.

(4) The Attorney General shall permit the conditional importation of a firearm by a licensed importer or licensed manufacturer, for examination and testing to determine whether or not the unconditional importation of such firearm would violate this subsection.

(5) This subsection shall not apply to any firearm which—

(A) has been certified by the Secretary of Defense or the Director of Central Intelligence, after consultation with the Attorney General and the Administrator of the Federal Aviation Administration, as necessary for military or intelligence applications; and

(B) is manufactured for and sold exclusively to military or intelligence agencies of the United States.

(6) This subsection shall not apply with respect to any firearm manufactured in, imported into, or possessed in the United States before the date of the enactment of the Undetectable Firearms Act of 1988.

(q)

(1) The Congress finds and declares that—

(A) crime, particularly crime involving drugs and guns, is a pervasive, nationwide problem;

(B) crime at the local level is exacerbated by the interstate movement of drugs, guns, and criminal gangs;

(C) firearms and ammunition move easily in interstate commerce and have been found in increasing numbers in and around schools, as documented in numerous hearings in both the Committee on the Judiciary [3] the House of Representatives and the Committee on the Judiciary of the Senate;

(D) in fact, even before the sale of a firearm, the gun, its component parts, ammunition, and the raw materials from which they are made have considerably moved in interstate commerce;

(E) while criminals freely move from State to State, ordinary citizens and foreign visitors may fear to travel to or through certain parts of the country due to concern about violent crime and gun violence, and parents may decline to send their children to school for the same reason;

(F) the occurrence of violent crime in school zones has resulted in a decline in the quality of education in our country;

(G) this decline in the quality of education has an adverse impact on interstate commerce and the foreign commerce of the United States;

(H) States, localities, and school systems find it almost impossible to handle gun-related crime by themselves—even States, localities, and school systems that have made strong efforts to prevent, detect, and punish gun-related crime find their efforts unavailing due in part to the failure or inability of other States or localities to take strong measures; and

(I) the Congress has the power, under the interstate commerce clause and other provisions of the Constitution, to enact measures to ensure the integrity and safety of the Nation's schools by enactment of this subsection.

(2)

(A) It shall be unlawful for any individual knowingly to possess a firearm that has moved in or that otherwise affects interstate or foreign commerce at a place that the individual knows, or has reasonable cause to believe, is a school zone.

(B) Subparagraph (A) does not apply to the possession of a firearm—

(i) on private property not part of school grounds;

(ii) if the individual possessing the firearm is licensed to do so by the State in which the school zone is located or a political subdivision of the State, and the law of the State or political subdivision requires that, before an individual obtains such a license, the law enforcement authorities of the State or political subdivision verify that the individual is qualified under law to receive the license;

(iii) that is—

(I) not loaded; and

(II) in a locked container, or a locked firearms rack that is on a motor vehicle;

(iv) by an individual for use in a program approved by a school in the school zone;

(v) by an individual in accordance with a contract entered into between a school in the school zone and the individual or an employer of the individual;

(vi) by a law enforcement officer acting in his or her official capacity; or

(vii) that is unloaded and is possessed by an individual while traversing school premises for the purpose of gaining access to public or private lands open to hunting, if the entry on school premises is authorized by school authorities.

(3)

(A) Except as provided in subparagraph (B), it shall be unlawful for any person, knowingly or with reckless disregard for the safety of another, to discharge or attempt to discharge a firearm that has moved in or that otherwise affects interstate or foreign commerce at a place that the person knows is a school zone.

(B) Subparagraph (A) does not apply to the discharge of a firearm—

(i) on private property not part of school grounds;

(ii) as part of a program approved by a school in the school zone, by an individual who is participating in the program;

(iii) by an individual in accordance with a contract entered into between a school in a school zone and the individual or an employer of the individual; or

(iv) by a law enforcement officer acting in his or her official capacity.
(4) Nothing in this subsection shall be construed as preempting or preventing a State or local government from enacting a statute establishing gun free school zones as provided in this subsection.
(r) It shall be unlawful for any person to assemble from imported parts any semiautomatic rifle or any shotgun which is identical to any rifle or shotgun prohibited from importation under section 925 (d)(3) of this chapter as not being particularly suitable for or readily adaptable to sporting purposes except that this subsection shall not apply to—
(1) the assembly of any such rifle or shotgun for sale or distribution by a licensed manufacturer to the United States or any department or agency thereof or to any State or any department, agency, or political subdivision thereof; or
(2) the assembly of any such rifle or shotgun for the purposes of testing or experimentation authorized by the Attorney General.
(s)
(1) Beginning on the date that is 90 days after the date of enactment of this subsection and ending on the day before the date that is 60 months after such date of enactment, it shall be unlawful for any licensed importer, licensed manufacturer, or licensed dealer to sell, deliver, or transfer a handgun (other than the return of a handgun to the person from whom it was received) to an individual who is not licensed under section 923, unless—
(A) after the most recent proposal of such transfer by the transferee—
(i) the transferor has—
(I) received from the transferee a statement of the transferee containing the information described in paragraph (3);
(II) verified the identity of the transferee by examining the identification document presented;
(III) within 1 day after the transferee furnishes the statement, provided notice of the contents of the statement to the chief law enforcement officer of the place of residence of the transferee; and
(IV) within 1 day after the transferee furnishes the statement, transmitted a copy of the statement to the chief law enforcement officer of the place of residence of the transferee; and
(ii)
(I) 5 business days (meaning days on which State offices are open) have elapsed from the date the transferor furnished notice of the contents of the statement to the chief law enforcement officer, during which period the transferor has not received information from the chief law enforcement officer that receipt or possession of the handgun by the transferee would be in violation of Federal, State, or local law; or
(II) the transferor has received notice from the chief law enforcement officer that the officer has no information indicating that receipt or possession of the handgun by the transferee would violate Federal, State, or local law;
(B) the transferee has presented to the transferor a written statement, issued by the chief law enforcement officer of the place of residence of the transferee during the 10-day period ending on the date of the most recent proposal of such transfer by the transferee, stating that the

transferee requires access to a handgun because of a threat to the life of the transferee or of any member of the household of the transferee;

(C)

(i) the transferee has presented to the transferor a permit that—

(I) allows the transferee to possess or acquire a handgun; and

(II) was issued not more than 5 years earlier by the State in which the transfer is to take place; and

(ii) the law of the State provides that such a permit is to be issued only after an authorized government official has verified that the information available to such official does not indicate that possession of a handgun by the transferee would be in violation of the law;

(D) the law of the State requires that, before any licensed importer, licensed manufacturer, or licensed dealer completes the transfer of a handgun to an individual who is not licensed under section 923, an authorized government official verify that the information available to such official does not indicate that possession of a handgun by the transferee would be in violation of law;

(E) the Attorney General has approved the transfer under section 5812 of the Internal Revenue Code of 1986; or

(F) on application of the transferor, the Attorney General has certified that compliance with subparagraph (A)(i)(III) is impracticable because—

(i) the ratio of the number of law enforcement officers of the State in which the transfer is to occur to the number of square miles of land area of the State does not exceed 0.0025;

(ii) the business premises of the transferor at which the transfer is to occur are extremely remote in relation to the chief law enforcement officer; and

(iii) there is an absence of telecommunications facilities in the geographical area in which the business premises are located.

(2) A chief law enforcement officer to whom a transferor has provided notice pursuant to paragraph (1)(A)(i)(III) shall make a reasonable effort to ascertain within 5 business days whether receipt or possession would be in violation of the law, including research in whatever State and local recordkeeping systems are available and in a national system designated by the Attorney General.

(3) The statement referred to in paragraph (1)(A)(i)(I) shall contain only—

(A) the name, address, and date of birth appearing on a valid identification document (as defined in section 1028 (d)(1) [4]) of the transferee containing a photograph of the transferee and a description of the identification used;

(B) a statement that the transferee—

(i) is not under indictment for, and has not been convicted in any court of, a crime punishable by imprisonment for a term exceeding 1 year, and has not been convicted in any court of a misdemeanor crime of domestic violence;

(ii) is not a fugitive from justice;

(iii) is not an unlawful user of or addicted to any controlled substance (as defined in section 102 of the Controlled Substances Act);

(iv) has not been adjudicated as a mental defective or been committed to a mental institution;
(v) is not an alien who—
(I) is illegally or unlawfully in the United States; or
(II) subject to subsection (y)(2), has been admitted to the United States under a nonimmigrant visa (as that term is defined in section 101(a)(26) of the Immigration and Nationality Act (8 U.S.C. 1101 (a)(26)));
(vi) has not been discharged from the Armed Forces under dishonorable conditions; and
(vii) is not a person who, having been a citizen of the United States, has renounced such citizenship;
(C) the date the statement is made; and
(D) notice that the transferee intends to obtain a handgun from the transferor.
(4) Any transferor of a handgun who, after such transfer, receives a report from a chief law enforcement officer containing information that receipt or possession of the handgun by the transferee violates Federal, State, or local law shall, within 1 business day after receipt of such request, communicate any information related to the transfer that the transferor has about the transfer and the transferee to—
(A) the chief law enforcement officer of the place of business of the transferor; and
(B) the chief law enforcement officer of the place of residence of the transferee.
(5) Any transferor who receives information, not otherwise available to the public, in a report under this subsection shall not disclose such information except to the transferee, to law enforcement authorities, or pursuant to the direction of a court of law.
(6)
(A) Any transferor who sells, delivers, or otherwise transfers a handgun to a transferee shall retain the copy of the statement of the transferee with respect to the handgun transaction, and shall retain evidence that the transferor has complied with subclauses (III) and (IV) of paragraph (1)(A)(i) with respect to the statement.
(B) Unless the chief law enforcement officer to whom a statement is transmitted under paragraph (1)(A)(i)(IV) determines that a transaction would violate Federal, State, or local law—
(i) the officer shall, within 20 business days after the date the transferee made the statement on the basis of which the notice was provided, destroy the statement, any record containing information derived from the statement, and any record created as a result of the notice required by paragraph (1)(A)(i)(III);
(ii) the information contained in the statement shall not be conveyed to any person except a person who has a need to know in order to carry out this subsection; and
(iii) the information contained in the statement shall not be used for any purpose other than to carry out this subsection.
(C) If a chief law enforcement officer determines that an individual is ineligible to receive a handgun and the individual requests the officer to provide the reason for such determination, the officer shall provide such reasons to the individual in writing within 20 business days after receipt of the request.

(7) A chief law enforcement officer or other person responsible for providing criminal history background information pursuant to this subsection shall not be liable in an action at law for damages—

(A) for failure to prevent the sale or transfer of a handgun to a person whose receipt or possession of the handgun is unlawful under this section; or

(B) for preventing such a sale or transfer to a person who may lawfully receive or possess a handgun.

(8) For purposes of this subsection, the term "chief law enforcement officer" means the chief of police, the sheriff, or an equivalent officer or the designee of any such individual.

(9) The Attorney General shall take necessary actions to ensure that the provisions of this subsection are published and disseminated to licensed dealers, law enforcement officials, and the public.

(t)

(1) Beginning on the date that is 30 days after the Attorney General notifies licensees under section 103(d) of the Brady Handgun Violence Prevention Act that the national instant criminal background check system is established, a licensed importer, licensed manufacturer, or licensed dealer shall not transfer a firearm to any other person who is not licensed under this chapter, unless—

(A) before the completion of the transfer, the licensee contacts the national instant criminal background check system established under section 103 of that Act;

(B)

(i) the system provides the licensee with a unique identification number; or

(ii) 3 business days (meaning a day on which State offices are open) have elapsed since the licensee contacted the system, and the system has not notified the licensee that the receipt of a firearm by such other person would violate subsection (g) or (n) of this section; and

(C) the transferor has verified the identity of the transferee by examining a valid identification document (as defined in section 1028 (d) of this title) of the transferee containing a photograph of the transferee.

(2) If receipt of a firearm would not violate subsection (g) or (n) or State law, the system shall—

(A) assign a unique identification number to the transfer;

(B) provide the licensee with the number; and

(C) destroy all records of the system with respect to the call (other than the identifying number and the date the number was assigned) and all records of the system relating to the person or the transfer.

(3) Paragraph (1) shall not apply to a firearm transfer between a licensee and another person if—

(A)

(i) such other person has presented to the licensee a permit that—

(I) allows such other person to possess or acquire a firearm; and

(II) was issued not more than 5 years earlier by the State in which the transfer is to take place; and

(ii) the law of the State provides that such a permit is to be issued only after an authorized government official has verified that the information available to such official does not indicate that possession of a firearm by such other person would be in violation of law;
(B) the Attorney General has approved the transfer under section 5812 of the Internal Revenue Code of 1986; or
(C) on application of the transferor, the Attorney General has certified that compliance with paragraph (1)(A) is impracticable because—
(i) the ratio of the number of law enforcement officers of the State in which the transfer is to occur to the number of square miles of land area of the State does not exceed 0.0025;
(ii) the business premises of the licensee at which the transfer is to occur are extremely remote in relation to the chief law enforcement officer (as defined in subsection (s)(8)); and
(iii) there is an absence of telecommunications facilities in the geographical area in which the business premises are located.
(4) If the national instant criminal background check system notifies the licensee that the information available to the system does not demonstrate that the receipt of a firearm by such other person would violate subsection (g) or (n) or State law, and the licensee transfers a firearm to such other person, the licensee shall include in the record of the transfer the unique identification number provided by the system with respect to the transfer.
(5) If the licensee knowingly transfers a firearm to such other person and knowingly fails to comply with paragraph (1) of this subsection with respect to the transfer and, at the time such other person most recently proposed the transfer, the national instant criminal background check system was operating and information was available to the system demonstrating that receipt of a firearm by such other person would violate subsection (g) or (n) of this section or State law, the Attorney General may, after notice and opportunity for a hearing, suspend for not more than 6 months or revoke any license issued to the licensee under section923, and may impose on the licensee a civil fine of not more than $5,000.
(6) Neither a local government nor an employee of the Federal Government or of any State or local government, responsible for providing information to the national instant criminal background check system shall be liable in an action at law for damages—
(A) for failure to prevent the sale or transfer of a firearm to a person whose receipt or possession of the firearm is unlawful under this section; or
(B) for preventing such a sale or transfer to a person who may lawfully receive or possess a firearm.
(u) It shall be unlawful for a person to steal or unlawfully take or carry away from the person or the premises of a person who is licensed to engage in the business of importing, manufacturing, or dealing in firearms, any firearm in the licensee's business inventory that has been shipped or transported in interstate or foreign commerce.
[(v) , (w) Repealed. Pub. L. 103–322, title XI, § 110105(2), Sept. 13, 1994, 108 Stat. 2000.]
(x)
(1) It shall be unlawful for a person to sell, deliver, or otherwise transfer to a person who the transferor knows or has reasonable cause to believe is a juvenile—

(A) a handgun; or

(B) ammunition that is suitable for use only in a handgun.

(2) It shall be unlawful for any person who is a juvenile to knowingly possess—

(A) a handgun; or

(B) ammunition that is suitable for use only in a handgun.

(3) This subsection does not apply to—

(A) a temporary transfer of a handgun or ammunition to a juvenile or to the possession or use of a handgun or ammunition by a juvenile if the handgun and ammunition are possessed and used by the juvenile—

(i) in the course of employment, in the course of ranching or farming related to activities at the residence of the juvenile (or on property used for ranching or farming at which the juvenile, with the permission of the property owner or lessee, is performing activities related to the operation of the farm or ranch), target practice, hunting, or a course of instruction in the safe and lawful use of a handgun;

(ii) with the prior written consent of the juvenile's parent or guardian who is not prohibited by Federal, State, or local law from possessing a firearm, except—

(I) during transportation by the juvenile of an unloaded handgun in a locked container directly from the place of transfer to a place at which an activity described in clause (i) is to take place and transportation by the juvenile of that handgun, unloaded and in a locked container, directly from the place at which such an activity took place to the transferor; or

(II) with respect to ranching or farming activities as described in clause (i), a juvenile may possess and use a handgun or ammunition with the prior written approval of the juvenile's parent or legal guardian and at the direction of an adult who is not prohibited by Federal, State or local law from possessing a firearm;

(iii) the juvenile has the prior written consent in the juvenile's possession at all times when a handgun is in the possession of the juvenile; and

(iv) in accordance with State and local law;

(B) a juvenile who is a member of the Armed Forces of the United States or the National Guard who possesses or is armed with a handgun in the line of duty;

(C) a transfer by inheritance of title (but not possession) of a handgun or ammunition to a juvenile; or

(D) the possession of a handgun or ammunition by a juvenile taken in defense of the juvenile or other persons against an intruder into the residence of the juvenile or a residence in which the juvenile is an invited guest.

(4) A handgun or ammunition, the possession of which is transferred to a juvenile in circumstances in which the transferor is not in violation of this subsection shall not be subject to permanent confiscation by the Government if its possession by the juvenile subsequently becomes unlawful because of the conduct of the juvenile, but shall be returned to the lawful owner when such handgun or ammunition is no longer required by the Government for the purposes of investigation or prosecution.

(5) For purposes of this subsection, the term "juvenile" means a person who is less than 18 years of age.

(6)

(A) In a prosecution of a violation of this subsection, the court shall require the presence of a juvenile defendant's parent or legal guardian at all proceedings.

(B) The court may use the contempt power to enforce subparagraph (A).

(C) The court may excuse attendance of a parent or legal guardian of a juvenile defendant at a proceeding in a prosecution of a violation of this subsection for good cause shown.

(y) Provisions Relating to Aliens Admitted Under Nonimmigrant Visas.—

(1) Definitions.— In this subsection—

(A) the term "alien" has the same meaning as in section 101(a)(3) of the Immigration and Nationality Act (8 U.S.C. 1101 (a)(3)); and

(B) the term "nonimmigrant visa" has the same meaning as in section 101(a)(26) of the Immigration and Nationality Act (8 U.S.C. 1101 (a)(26)).

(2) Exceptions.— Subsections (d)(5)(B), (g)(5)(B), and (s)(3)(B)(v)(II) do not apply to any alien who has been lawfully admitted to the United States under a nonimmigrant visa, if that alien is—

(A) admitted to the United States for lawful hunting or sporting purposes or is in possession of a hunting license or permit lawfully issued in the United States;

(B) an official representative of a foreign government who is—

(i) accredited to the United States Government or the Government's mission to an international organization having its headquarters in the United States; or

(ii) en route to or from another country to which that alien is accredited;

(C) an official of a foreign government or a distinguished foreign visitor who has been so designated by the Department of State; or

(D) a foreign law enforcement officer of a friendly foreign government entering the United States on official law enforcement business.

(3) Waiver.—

(A) Conditions for waiver.— Any individual who has been admitted to the United States under a nonimmigrant visa may receive a waiver from the requirements of subsection (g)(5), if—

(i) the individual submits to the Attorney General a petition that meets the requirements of subparagraph (C); and

(ii) the Attorney General approves the petition.

(B) Petition.— Each petition under subparagraph (B) shall—

(i) demonstrate that the petitioner has resided in the United States for a continuous period of not less than 180 days before the date on which the petition is submitted under this paragraph; and

(ii) include a written statement from the embassy or consulate of the petitioner, authorizing the petitioner to acquire a firearm or ammunition and certifying that the alien would not, absent the application of subsection (g)(5)(B), otherwise be prohibited from such acquisition under subsection (g).

(C) Approval of petition.— The Attorney General shall approve a petition submitted in accordance with this paragraph, if the Attorney General determines that waiving the requirements of subsection (g)(5)(B) with respect to the petitioner—

(i) would be in the interests of justice; and

(ii) would not jeopardize the public safety.

(z) Secure Gun Storage or Safety Device.—

(1) In general.— Except as provided under paragraph (2), it shall be unlawful for any licensed importer, licensed manufacturer, or licensed dealer to sell, deliver, or transfer any handgun to any person other than any person licensed under this chapter, unless the transferee is provided with a secure gun storage or safety device (as defined in section 921 (a)(34)) for that handgun.

(2) Exceptions.— Paragraph (1) shall not apply to—

(A)

(i) the manufacture for, transfer to, or possession by, the United States, a department or agency of the United States, a State, or a department, agency, or political subdivision of a State, of a handgun; or

(ii) the transfer to, or possession by, a law enforcement officer employed by an entity referred to in clause (i) of a handgun for law enforcement purposes (whether on or off duty); or

(B) the transfer to, or possession by, a rail police officer employed by a rail carrier and certified or commissioned as a police officer under the laws of a State of a handgun for purposes of law enforcement (whether on or off duty);

(C) the transfer to any person of a handgun listed as a curio or relic by the Secretary pursuant to section 921 (a)(13); or

(D) the transfer to any person of a handgun for which a secure gun storage or safety device is temporarily unavailable for the reasons described in the exceptions stated in section 923 (e), if the licensed manufacturer, licensed importer, or licensed dealer delivers to the transferee within 10 calendar days from the date of the delivery of the handgun to the transferee a secure gun storage or safety device for the handgun.

(3) Liability for use.—

(A) In general.— Notwithstanding any other provision of law, a person who has lawful possession and control of a handgun, and who uses a secure gun storage or safety device with the handgun, shall be entitled to immunity from a qualified civil liability action.

(B) Prospective actions.— A qualified civil liability action may not be brought in any Federal or State court.

(C) Defined term.— As used in this paragraph, the term "qualified civil liability action"—

(i) means a civil action brought by any person against a person described in subparagraph (A) for damages resulting from the criminal or unlawful misuse of the handgun by a third party, if—

(I) the handgun was accessed by another person who did not have the permission or authorization of the person having lawful possession and control of the handgun to have access to it; and

(II) at the time access was gained by the person not so authorized, the handgun had been made inoperable by use of a secure gun storage or safety device; and

(ii) shall not include an action brought against the person having lawful possession and control of the handgun for negligent entrustment or negligence per se. [APPENDIX A Repealed. Pub. L. 103–322, title XI, § 110105(2), Sept. 13, 1994, 108 Stat. 2000]

Title 21 U.S.C.

§ 841. PROHIBITED ACTS A

(a) Unlawful acts

Except as authorized by this subchapter, it shall be unlawful for any person knowingly or intentionally—

(1) to manufacture, distribute, or dispense, or possess with intent to manufacture, distribute, or dispense, a controlled substance; or

(2) to create, distribute, or dispense, or possess with intent to distribute or dispense, a counterfeit substance.

(b) Penalties

Except as otherwise provided in section 849, 859, 860, or 861 of this title, any person who violates subsection (a) of this section shall be sentenced as follows:

(1)

(A) In the case of a violation of subsection (a) of this section involving—

(i) 1 kilogram or more of a mixture or substance containing a detectable amount of heroin;

(ii) 5 kilograms or more of a mixture or substance containing a detectable amount of—

(I) coca leaves, except coca leaves and extracts of coca leaves from which cocaine, ecgonine, and derivatives of ecgonine or their salts have been removed;

(II) cocaine, its salts, optical and geometric isomers, and salts of isomers;

(III) ecgonine, its derivatives, their salts, isomers, and salts of isomers; or

(IV) any compound, mixture, or preparation which contains any quantity of any of the substances referred to in subclauses (I) through (III);

(iii) 50 grams or more of a mixture or substance described in clause (ii) which contains cocaine base;

(iv) 100 grams or more of phencyclidine (PCP) or 1 kilogram or more of a mixture or substance containing a detectable amount of phencyclidine (PCP);

(v) 10 grams or more of a mixture or substance containing a detectable amount of lysergic acid diethylamide (LSD);

(vi) 400 grams or more of a mixture or substance containing a detectable amount of N-phenyl-N-[1-(2-phenylethyl) -4-piperidinyl] propanamide or 100 grams or more of a mixture or substance containing a detectable amount of any analogue of N-phenyl-N-[1-(2-phenylethyl)-4-piperidinyl] propanamide;

(vii) 1000 kilograms or more of a mixture or substance containing a detectable amount of marihuana, or 1,000 or more marihuana plants regardless of weight; or

(viii) 50 grams or more of methamphetamine, its salts, isomers, and salts of its isomers or 500 grams or more of a mixture or substance containing a detectable amount of methamphetamine, its salts, isomers, or salts of its isomers;

such person shall be sentenced to a term of imprisonment which may not be less than 10 years or more than life and if death or serious bodily injury results from the use of such substance shall be not less than 20 years or more than life, a fine not to exceed the greater of that authorized in accordance with the provisions of title 18 or $4,000,000 if the defendant is an individual or $10,000,000 if the defendant is other than an individual, or both. If any person commits such a violation after a prior conviction for a felony drug offense has become final, such person shall be sentenced to a term of imprisonment which may not be less than 20 years and not more than life imprisonment and if death or serious bodily injury results from the use of such substance shall be sentenced to life imprisonment, a fine not to exceed the greater of twice that authorized in accordance with the provisions of title 18 or $8,000,000 if the defendant is an individual or $20,000,000 if the defendant is other than an individual, or both. If any person commits a violation of this subparagraph or of section 849, 859, 860, or 861 of this title after two or more prior convictions for a felony drug offense have become final, such person shall be sentenced to a mandatory term of life imprisonment without release and fined in accordance with the preceding sentence. Notwithstanding section 3583 of title 18, any sentence under this subparagraph shall, in the absence of such a prior conviction, impose a term of supervised release of at least 5 years in addition to such term of imprisonment and shall, if there was such a prior conviction, impose a term of supervised release of at least 10 years in addition to such term of imprisonment. Notwithstanding any other provision of law, the court shall not place on probation or suspend the sentence of any person sentenced under this subparagraph. No person sentenced under this subparagraph shall be eligible for parole during the term of imprisonment imposed therein.

(B) In the case of a violation of subsection (a) of this section involving—

(i) 100 grams or more of a mixture or substance containing a detectable amount of heroin;

(ii) 500 grams or more of a mixture or substance containing a detectable amount of—

(I) coca leaves, except coca leaves and extracts of coca leaves from which cocaine, ecgonine, and derivatives of ecgonine or their salts have been removed;

(II) cocaine, its salts, optical and geometric isomers, and salts of isomers;

(III) ecgonine, its derivatives, their salts, isomers, and salts of isomers; or

(IV) any compound, mixture, or preparation which contains any quantity of any of the substances referred to in subclauses (I) through (III);

(iii) 5 grams or more of a mixture or substance described in clause (ii) which contains cocaine base;

(iv) 10 grams or more of phencyclidine (PCP) or 100 grams or more of a mixture or substance containing a detectable amount of phencyclidine (PCP);

(v) 1 gram or more of a mixture or substance containing a detectable amount of lysergic acid diethylamide (LSD);

(vi) 40 grams or more of a mixture or substance containing a detectable amount of N-phenyl-N-[1- (2-phenylethyl) -4-piperidinyl] propanamide or 10 grams or more of a mixture or substance containing a detectable amount of any analogue of N-phenyl-N-[1-(2-phenylethyl)-4-piperidinyl] propanamide;

(vii) 100 kilograms or more of a mixture or substance containing a detectable amount of marihuana, or 100 or more marihuana plants regardless of weight; or

(viii) 5 grams or more of methamphetamine, its salts, isomers, and salts of its isomers or 50 grams or more of a mixture or substance containing a detectable amount of methamphetamine, its salts, isomers, or salts of its isomers;

such person shall be sentenced to a term of imprisonment which may not be less than 5 years and not more than 40 years and if death or serious bodily injury results from the use of such substance shall be not less than 20 years or more than life, a fine not to exceed the greater of that authorized in accordance with the provisions of title 18 or $2,000,000 if the defendant is an individual or $5,000,000 if the defendant is other than an individual, or both. If any person commits such a violation after a prior conviction for a felony drug offense has become final, such person shall be sentenced to a term of imprisonment which may not be less than 10 years and not more than life imprisonment and if death or serious bodily injury results from the use of such substance shall be sentenced to life imprisonment, a fine not to exceed the greater of twice that authorized in accordance with the provisions of title 18 or $4,000,000 if the defendant is an individual or $10,000,000 if the defendant is other than an individual, or both. Notwithstanding section 3583of title 18, any sentence imposed under this subparagraph shall, in the absence of such a prior conviction, include a term of supervised release of at least 4 years in addition to such term of imprisonment and shall, if there was such a prior conviction, include a term of supervised release of at least 8 years in addition to such term of imprisonment. Notwithstanding any other provision of law, the court shall not place on probation or suspend the sentence of any person sentenced under this subparagraph. No person sentenced under this subparagraph shall be eligible for parole during the term of imprisonment imposed therein.

(C) In the case of a controlled substance in schedule I or II, gamma hydroxybutyric acid (including when scheduled as an approved drug product for purposes of section 3(a)(1)(B) of the Hillory J. Farias and Samantha Reid Date-Rape Drug Prohibition Act of 2000), or 1 gram of flunitrazepam, except as provided in subparagraphs (A), (B), and (D), such person shall be sentenced to a term of imprisonment of not more than 20 years and if death or serious bodily injury results from the use of such substance shall be sentenced to a term of imprisonment of not less than twenty years or more than life, a fine not to exceed the greater of that authorized in accordance with the provisions of title 18 or $1,000,000 if the defendant is an individual or $5,000,000 if the defendant is other than an individual, or both. If any person commits such a violation after a prior conviction for a felony drug offense has become final, such person shall be sentenced to a term of imprisonment of not more than 30 years and if death or serious bodily injury results from the use of such substance shall be sentenced to life imprisonment, a fine not to exceed the greater of twice that authorized in accordance with the provisions of title 18 or $2,000,000 if the defendant is an individual or $10,000,000 if the defendant is other than an individual, or both. Notwithstanding section 3583of title 18, any sentence imposing a term of imprisonment under this paragraph shall, in the absence of such a prior conviction, impose a term of supervised release of at least 3 years in addition to such term of imprisonment and shall, if there was such a prior conviction, impose a term of supervised release of at least 6 years in addition to such term of imprisonment. Notwithstanding any other provision of law, the court shall not place on probation or suspend the sentence of any person sentenced under the provisions of this subparagraph which provide for a mandatory term of imprisonment if death or serious bodily injury results, nor shall a person so sentenced be eligible for parole during the term of such a sentence.

(D) In the case of less than 50 kilograms of marihuana, except in the case of 50 or more marihuana plants regardless of weight, 10 kilograms of hashish, or one kilogram of hashish oil, such person shall, except as provided in paragraphs (4) and (5) of this subsection, be sentenced to a term of imprisonment of not more than 5 years, a fine not to exceed the greater of that authorized in accordance with the provisions of title 18 or $250,000 if the defendant is an individual or $1,000,000 if the defendant is other than an individual, or both. If any person commits such a violation after a prior conviction for a felony drug offense has become final, such person shall be sentenced to a term of imprisonment of not more than 10 years, a fine not to exceed the greater of twice that authorized in accordance with the provisions of title 18 or $500,000 if the defendant is an individual or $2,000,000 if the defendant is other than an individual, or both. Notwithstanding section 3583of title 18, any sentence imposing a term of imprisonment under this paragraph shall, in the absence of such a prior conviction, impose a term of supervised release of at least 2 years in addition to such term of imprisonment and shall, if there was such a prior conviction, impose a term of supervised release of at least 4 years in addition to such term of imprisonment.

(E)

(i) Except as provided in subparagraphs (C) and (D), in the case of any controlled substance in schedule III, such person shall be sentenced to a term of imprisonment of not more than 10 years and if death or serious bodily injury results from the use of such substance shall be sentenced to a term of imprisonment of not more than 15 years, a fine not to exceed the greater of that authorized in accordance with the provisions of title 18 or $500,000 if the defendant is an individual or $2,500,000 if the defendant is other than an individual, or both.

(ii) If any person commits such a violation after a prior conviction for a felony drug offense has become final, such person shall be sentenced to a term of imprisonment of not more than 20 years and if death or serious bodily injury results from the use of such substance shall be sentenced to a term of imprisonment of not more than 30 years, a fine not to exceed the greater of twice that authorized in accordance with the provisions of title 18 or $1,000,000 if the defendant is an individual or $5,000,000 if the defendant is other than an individual, or both.

(iii) Any sentence imposing a term of imprisonment under this subparagraph shall, in the absence of such a prior conviction, impose a term of supervised release of at least 2 years in addition to such term of imprisonment and shall, if there was such a prior conviction, impose a term of supervised release of at least 4 years in addition to such term of imprisonment.

(2) In the case of a controlled substance in schedule IV, such person shall be sentenced to a term of imprisonment of not more than 5 years, a fine not to exceed the greater of that authorized in accordance with the provisions of title 18 or $250,000 if the defendant is an individual or $1,000,000 if the defendant is other than an individual, or both. If any person commits such a violation after a prior conviction for a felony drug offense has become final, such person shall be sentenced to a term of imprisonment of not more than 10 years, a fine not to exceed the greater of twice that authorized in accordance with the provisions of title 18 or $500,000 if the defendant is an individual or $2,000,000 if the defendant is other than an individual, or both. Any sentence imposing a term of imprisonment under this paragraph shall, in the absence of such a prior conviction, impose a term of supervised release of at least one year in addition to such term of imprisonment and shall, if there was such a prior conviction, impose a term of supervised release of at least 2 years in addition to such term of imprisonment.
(3) In the case of a controlled substance in schedule V, such person shall be sentenced to a term of imprisonment of not more than one year, a fine not to exceed the greater of that authorized in accordance with the provisions of title 18 or $100,000 if the defendant is an individual or $250,000 if the defendant is other than an individual, or both. If any person commits such a violation after a prior conviction for a felony drug offense has become final, such person shall be sentenced to a term of imprisonment of not more than 4 years, a fine not to exceed the greater of twice that authorized in accordance with the provisions of title 18 or $200,000 if the defendant is an individual or $500,000 if the defendant is other than an individual, or both. Any sentence imposing a term of imprisonment under this paragraph may, if there was a prior conviction, impose a term of supervised release of not more than 1 year, in addition to such term of imprisonment.
(4) Notwithstanding paragraph (1)(D) of this subsection, any person who violates subsection (a) of this section by distributing a small amount of marihuana for no remuneration shall be treated as provided in section 844 of this title and section3607 of title 18.
(5) Any person who violates subsection (a) of this section by cultivating or manufacturing a controlled substance on Federal property shall be imprisoned as provided in this subsection and shall be fined any amount not to exceed—
(A) the amount authorized in accordance with this section;
(B) the amount authorized in accordance with the provisions of title 18;
(C) $500,000 if the defendant is an individual; or
(D) $1,000,000 if the defendant is other than an individual;
or both.
(6) Any person who violates subsection (a) of this section, or attempts to do so, and knowingly or intentionally uses a poison, chemical, or other hazardous substance on Federal land, and, by such use—
(A) creates a serious hazard to humans, wildlife, or domestic animals,
(B) degrades or harms the environment or natural resources, or
(C) pollutes an aquifer, spring, stream, river, or body of water,
shall be fined in accordance with title 18 or imprisoned not more than five years, or both.

(7) Penalties for distribution.—

(A) In general.— Whoever, with intent to commit a crime of violence, as defined in section 16 of title 18 (including rape), against an individual, violates subsection (a) of this section by distributing a controlled substance or controlled substance analogue to that individual without that individual's knowledge, shall be imprisoned not more than 20 years and fined in accordance with title 18.

(B) Definition.— For purposes of this paragraph, the term "without that individual's knowledge" means that the individual is unaware that a substance with the ability to alter that individual's ability to appraise conduct or to decline participation in or communicate unwillingness to participate in conduct is administered to the individual.

(c) Offenses involving listed chemicals

Any person who knowingly or intentionally—

(1) possesses a listed chemical with intent to manufacture a controlled substance except as authorized by this subchapter;

(2) possesses or distributes a listed chemical knowing, or having reasonable cause to believe, that the listed chemical will be used to manufacture a controlled substance except as authorized by this subchapter; or

(3) with the intent of causing the evasion of the recordkeeping or reporting requirements of section 830 of this title, or the regulations issued under that section, receives or distributes a reportable amount of any listed chemical in units small enough so that the making of records or filing of reports under that section is not required;

shall be fined in accordance with title 18 or imprisoned not more than 20 years in the case of a violation of paragraph (1) or (2) involving a list I chemical or not more than 10 years in the case of a violation of this subsection other than a violation of paragraph (1) or (2) involving a list I chemical, or both.

(d) Boobytraps on Federal property; penalties; "boobytrap" defined

(1) Any person who assembles, maintains, places, or causes to be placed a boobytrap on Federal property where a controlled substance is being manufactured, distributed, or dispensed shall be sentenced to a term of imprisonment for not more than 10 years or fined under title 18, or both.

(2) If any person commits such a violation after 1 or more prior convictions for an offense punishable under this subsection, such person shall be sentenced to a term of imprisonment of not more than 20 years or fined under title 18, or both.

(3) For the purposes of this subsection, the term "boobytrap" means any concealed or camouflaged device designed to cause bodily injury when triggered by any action of any unsuspecting person making contact with the device. Such term includes guns, ammunition, or explosive devices attached to trip wires or other triggering mechanisms, sharpened stakes, and lines or wires with hooks attached.

(e) Ten-year injunction as additional penalty

In addition to any other applicable penalty, any person convicted of a felony violation of this section relating to the receipt, distribution, manufacture, exportation, or importation of a listed chemical may be enjoined from engaging in any transaction involving a listed chemical for not more than ten years.

(f) Wrongful distribution or possession of listed chemicals

(1) Whoever knowingly distributes a listed chemical in violation of this subchapter (other than in violation of a recordkeeping or reporting requirement of section830 of this title) shall, except to the extent that paragraph (12), (13), or (14) of section 842 (a) of this title applies, be fined under title 18 or imprisoned not more than 5 years, or both.

(2) Whoever possesses any listed chemical, with knowledge that the recordkeeping or reporting requirements of section 830 of this title have not been adhered to, if, after such knowledge is acquired, such person does not take immediate steps to remedy the violation shall be fined under title 18 or imprisoned not more than one year, or both.

(g) Internet sales of date rape drugs

(1) Whoever knowingly uses the Internet to distribute a date rape drug to any person, knowing or with reasonable cause to believe that—

(A) the drug would be used in the commission of criminal sexual conduct; or

(B) the person is not an authorized purchaser;

shall be fined under this subchapter or imprisoned not more than 20 years, or both.

(2) As used in this subsection:

(A) The term "date rape drug" means—

(i) gamma hydroxybutyric acid (GHB) or any controlled substance analogue of GHB, including gamma butyrolactone (GBL) or 1,4–butanediol;

(ii) ketamine;

(iii) flunitrazepam; or

(iv) any substance which the Attorney General designates, pursuant to the rulemaking procedures prescribed by section 553 of title 5, to be used in committing rape or sexual assault. The Attorney General is authorized to remove any substance from the list of date rape drugs pursuant to the same rulemaking authority.

(B) The term "authorized purchaser" means any of the following persons, provided such person has acquired the controlled substance in accordance with this chapter:

(i) A person with a valid prescription that is issued for a legitimate medical purpose in the usual course of professional practice that is based upon a qualifying medical relationship by a practitioner registered by the Attorney General. A "qualifying medical relationship" means a medical relationship that exists when the practitioner has conducted at least 1 medical evaluation with the authorized purchaser in the physical presence of the practitioner, without regard to whether portions of the evaluation are conducted by other heath [1] professionals. The preceding sentence shall not be construed to imply that 1 medical evaluation demonstrates that a prescription has been issued for a legitimate medical purpose within the usual course of professional practice.

(ii) Any practitioner or other registrant who is otherwise authorized by their registration to dispense, procure, purchase, manufacture, transfer, distribute, import, or export the substance under this chapter.

(iii) A person or entity providing documentation that establishes the name, address, and business of the person or entity and which provides a legitimate purpose for using any "date rape drug" for which a prescription is not required.

(3) The Attorney General is authorized to promulgate regulations for record-keeping and reporting by persons handling 1,4–butanediol in order to implement and enforce the provisions of this section. Any record or report required by such regulations shall be considered a record or report required under this chapter.

(h) Offenses involving dispensing of controlled substances by means of the Internet

(1) In general

It shall be unlawful for any person to knowingly or intentionally—

(A) deliver, distribute, or dispense a controlled substance by means of the Internet, except as authorized by this subchapter; or

(B) aid or abet (as such terms are used in section 2 of title 18) any activity described in subparagraph (A) that is not authorized by this subchapter.

(2) Examples

Examples of activities that violate paragraph (1) include, but are not limited to, knowingly or intentionally—

(A) delivering, distributing, or dispensing a controlled substance by means of the Internet by an online pharmacy that is not validly registered with a modification authorizing such activity as required by section 823 (f) of this title (unless exempt from such registration);

(B) writing a prescription for a controlled substance for the purpose of delivery, distribution, or dispensation by means of the Internet in violation of section 829(e) of the title;

(C) serving as an agent, intermediary, or other entity that causes the Internet to be used to bring together a buyer and seller to engage in the dispensing of a controlled substance in a manner not authorized by sections [2] 823(f) or 829(e) of this title;

(D) offering to fill a prescription for a controlled substance based solely on a consumer's completion of an online medical questionnaire; and

(E) making a material false, fictitious, or fraudulent statement or representation in a notification or declaration under subsection (d) or (e), respectively, of section 831 of this title.

(3) Inapplicability

(A) This subsection does not apply to—

(i) the delivery, distribution, or dispensation of controlled substances by nonpractitioners to the extent authorized by their registration under this subchapter;

(ii) the placement on the Internet of material that merely advocates the use of a controlled substance or includes pricing information without attempting to propose or facilitate an actual transaction involving a controlled substance; or

(iii) except as provided in subparagraph (B), any activity that is limited to—

(I) the provision of a telecommunications service, or of an Internet access service or Internet information location tool (as those terms are defined in section 231 of title 47); or

(II) the transmission, storage, retrieval, hosting, formatting, or translation (or any combination thereof) of a communication, without selection or alteration of the content of the communication, except that deletion of a particular communication or material made by another person in a manner consistent with section 230 (c) of title 47shall not constitute such selection or alteration of the content of the communication.

(B) The exceptions under subclauses (I) and (II) of subparagraph (A)(iii) shall not apply to a person acting in concert with a person who violates paragraph (1).

(4) Knowing or intentional violation

Any person who knowingly or intentionally violates this subsection shall be sentenced in accordance with subsection (b).

§ 844. PENALTIES FOR SIMPLE POSSESSION

(a) Unlawful acts; penalties

It shall be unlawful for any person knowingly or intentionally to possess a controlled substance unless such substance was obtained directly, or pursuant to a valid prescription or order, from a practitioner, while acting in the course of his professional practice, or except as otherwise authorized by this subchapter or subchapter II of this chapter. It shall be unlawful for any person knowingly or intentionally to possess any list I chemical obtained pursuant to or under authority of a registration issued to that person under section 823 of this title or section 958 of this title if that registration has been revoked or suspended, if that registration has expired, or if the registrant has ceased to do business in the manner contemplated by his registration. It shall be unlawful for any person to knowingly or intentionally purchase at retail during a 30 day period more than 9 grams of ephedrine base, pseudoephedrine base, or phenylpropanolamine base in a scheduled listed chemical product, except that, of such 9 grams, not more than 7.5 grams may be imported by means of shipping through any private or commercial carrier or the Postal Service. Any person who violates this subsection may be sentenced to a term of imprisonment of not more than 1 year, and shall be fined a minimum of $1,000, or both, except that if he commits such offense after a prior conviction under this subchapter or subchapter II of this chapter, or a prior conviction for any drug, narcotic, or chemical offense chargeable under the law of any State, has become final, he shall be sentenced to a term of imprisonment for not less than 15 days but not more than 2 years, and shall be fined a minimum of $2,500, except, further, that if he commits such offense after two or more prior convictions under this subchapter or subchapter II of this chapter, or two or more prior convictions for any drug, narcotic, or chemical offense chargeable under the law of any State, or a combination of two or more such offenses have become final, he shall be sentenced to a term of imprisonment for not less than 90 days but not more than 3 years, and shall be fined a minimum of $5,000. Notwithstanding the preceding sentence, a person convicted under this subsection for the possession of a mixture or substance which contains cocaine base shall be imprisoned not less than 5 years and not more than 20 years, and fined a minimum of $1,000, if the conviction is a first conviction under this subsection and the amount of the mixture or substance exceeds 5 grams, if the conviction is after a prior conviction for the possession of such a mixture or substance under this subsection becomes final and the amount of the mixture or substance exceeds 3 grams, or if the conviction is after 2 or more prior convictions for the possession of such a mixture or substance under this subsection become final and the amount of the mixture or substance exceeds 1 gram. Notwithstanding any penalty provided in this subsection, any person convicted under this subsection for the possession of flunitrazepam shall be imprisoned for not more than 3 years, shall be fined as otherwise provided in this section, or both. The imposition or execution of a minimum sentence required to be imposed under this subsection shall not be suspended or deferred. Further, upon conviction, a person who violates this subsection shall be fined the reasonable costs of the investigation and prosecution of the offense, including the costs of prosecution of an offense as defined in sections 1918 and 1920 of title 28, except that this sentence shall not apply and a fine under this section need not be imposed if the court determines under the provision of title 18 that the defendant lacks the ability to pay.

(b) Repealed. Pub. L. 98–473, title II, § 219(a), Oct. 12, 1984, 98 Stat. 2027

(c) "Drug, narcotic, or chemical offense" defined

As used in this section, the term "drug, narcotic, or chemical offense" means any offense which proscribes the possession, distribution, manufacture, cultivation, sale, transfer, or the attempt or conspiracy to possess, distribute, manufacture, cultivate, sell or transfer any substance the possession of which is prohibited under this subchapter.

§ 846. ATTEMPT AND CONSPIRACY

Any person who attempts or conspires to commit any offense defined in this subchapter shall be subject to the same penalties as those prescribed for the offense, the commission of which was the object of the attempt or conspiracy.

NOTICE

When the prosecution charges "conspiracy" in narcotics violations, **Title 21 U.S.C. § 846** is always used, not the "generic" conspiracy found in **Title 18 U.S.C. § 371**, which is constrained to non-narcotic offenses, such as weapons, fraud, etc.

NOTES

Chapter VII

Pretrial Issues and Concerns

The initial concern of defense counsel in a federal criminal case should be pretrial matters such as discovery, pretrial motions, and investigations. This Chapter will deal with discovery under Federal Rule of Criminal Procedure 16, as well as other procedural rules and case law that must be considered in the early preparation of a federal criminal matter.

A. DISCOVERY IN CRIMINAL CASES IN FEDERAL COURT

One of the most startling, disorienting, and disturbing differences between the practice of criminal law in the New Jersey District Court and the New Jersey Superior Court is the discovery process. While the practice in New Jersey Superior Court is generally characterized by disclosure and candor, which promote fairness and ensure the integrity of the process, the discovery practice in New Jersey District Court is byzantine, archaic, and designed to impede candor and disclosure.

The result often is an aura of distrust, a culture of concealment, and a disturbing level of gamesmanship. Although this result is in part an unavoidable by-product of the Federal Rules of Criminal Procedure and the ancillary discovery procedures, it is both unfortunate and unnecessary.

It is unfortunate for a number of reasons, not the least of which are the perceptions of unfairness and the doubts regarding the integrity of the process that it creates. An ancillary problem is the perception among many defense lawyers that prosecutors do not diligently investigate for information that is subject to Rule 16 disclosure, much less for Brady and Giglio material. Likewise, there is a perception that definitions are narrowed to the point that disclosure is strictly limited to the bare minimum required by the most rigid reading of the rules. This problem is compounded by the perception that government discovery violations are often subject to no discernible sanction. The problems this creates for the criminal justice system are profound and troubling. Court time is wasted on last minute discovery motions and related hearings concerning whether a particular item is indeed subject to disclosure and what, if any, remedy is appropriate. These hearings are, frankly, one of defense counsel's best opportunities to change the focus of a trial, and it is truly unfathomable why government attorneys consistently put themselves in this position.

Despite this opportunity, the down sides to dilatory discovery practice far outweigh any advantages. Clients, particularly those who have been through the state system are, at a minimum, astounded when they are advised of how little discovery they will receive. More often, they doubt their attorney's commitment, and their suspicions about the resolve of appointed counsel are heightened. Even worse is the wholly inexcusable effect created when discovery is provided incrementally. Not only is the client's initial optimism shattered, but the resultant anger he/she feels is then directed at counsel for the failure to obtain the discovery at an earlier date. any confidence that had developed is eviscerated and the integrity of the process consequently suffers.

The final tangible effect of current government policy is that AUSAs appear to resist compliance with even the minimal obligations imposed by law. From a defense lawyer's perspective, it often appears that federal prosecutors feel little institutional incentive to provide discovery. Indeed, the perception is that there is some fear that by providing discovery, defense counsel will gain some advantage as a result of access to information about the case. It is difficult to imagine a concept that could be more contrary to any reasonable person's expectations about how a criminal justice system should operate. The idea that a trial should be characterized by surprise, deception, and mystery is medieval, if not malevolent. The theory seems to be that if defense counsel is prepared, the government's evidence may not hold up and a conviction may not result. To put it another way, the restrictive discovery practice is not designed to promote justice, but is instead intended to give the government an unfair advantage.

The justification for the practice, of course, is something more benign. Usually, the argument is that early disclosure of witness statements, agent reports, grand jury testimony documents, and other materials will lead to witness tampering, obstruction of justice, and other instances of misconduct designed to undermine the trial process. Whatever legitimacy these concerns may hold in a particular case, they nonetheless cannot justify the blanket approach that exists within this district. Years of far more open discovery practice in state court demonstrate that the government's concerns are more illusory than real. Moreover, with the erosion of any real distinction between the types of cases brought in federal court and state court, any legitimacy that might have attached to those concerns is further undermined. The fact is that cases where concerns about witness tampering and obstruction of justice are real are few and far between, and can be handled on a case-by-case basis.

Further evidence of the lack of foundation for the government's unduly strict adherence to Rule 16 and other discovery rules is found through comparing the practice in this district to the approach taken by other U.S. Attorney Offices and by other District Courts. It is not uncommon for federal prosecutors in other districts to institute open discovery policies within their offices. This practice greatly diminishes the need for last minute discovery motions as well as the likelihood that discovery violations will occur. Additionally, open discovery policies help eliminate problems for counsel, and, ultimately, the court, that are occasioned by late or piecemeal discovery.

Similarly, a sampling of standing discovery orders from around the country discloses that other courts have recognized the problem and attempted to address it by institutionalizing a more progressive approach. Among the many examples of more enlightened discovery practices are the following:

1. Witness lists. Witness lists are exchanged at a designated time before trial. Southern District of Mississippi, District of New Hampshire, District of Vermont.
2. Preservation of tapes, notes, and other memoranda. This provision orders the government not to purposefully destroy any tapes, notes, reports, or communications generated in connection with a case until it is resolved. District of New Mexico, Middle District of Tennessee.
3. Jencks disclosure. This provision is phrased as an agreement by the government to disclose Jencks material at a specific time before trial. The provision permits the government to withdraw from the agreement in a particular case at its discretion. District of New Hampshire, Eastern District of Kentucky, District of Connecticut, Eastern District of Virginia.

4. Additional Jencks disclosure. Disclosure of Jencks material for other proceedings. This provision incorporates the Rule 26.2 requirements in the standing order. District of Connecticut, Eastern District of Oklahoma.
5. Search warrants. An explicit direction to provide all warrants, applications, supporting affidavits, testimony, returns and inventories. District of Connecticut, District of Vermont.
6. Brady disclosure. The Brady provision includes a reminder to the government to disclose information relevant to guilt or to punishment. District of Connecticut, District of Vermont.
7. Identification procedures. A number of orders contain a reference to identification procedures. The disclosure requirement includes a specific request that the government produce photographs used in a line-up, show-up, photo spread, or, if no photograph exists, a requirement that the government notify the defendant whether an identification procedure took place and the results of the procedure. District of Connecticut, District of Hawaii, Middle District of Tennessee, Western District of Washington.
8. Giglio disclosure. Giglio material is subject to disclosure at least twenty days before trial. District of New Hampshire.
9. Inspection of property. The government is required to permit the defendant, counsel, and any experts to inspect any automobile, vessel, or aircraft, and further requires the government counsel to assist defense efforts to gain access to such property by advising the agency in possession of the items that inspection was permitted by court order. Middle District of Tennessee.
10. Entrapment as a defense. If a defendant advises the government of an intention to rely upon an entrapment defense and provides a written summary of the evidence of that defense, the government is required to disclose a synopsis of any other crimes, wrongs, or acts upon which the government would rely to rebut the defense. Western District of Washington.

These are only a few of the provisions contained in standing orders for discovery in other United States District Courts. Their existence and use demonstrate that a more progressive approach to discovery can be used without posing any threat to the government's ability to prosecute its cases.

B. DISCOVERY REQUESTS AND FED. R. CRIM. P. 16

Discovery requests should be made early, to allow as much time as possible before deciding whether the defendant should accept a plea offer from the government or proceed to trial and to review the materials before trial strategy decisions are made. Also, discovery material often proves invaluable in predicting the potential guideline sentencing range in the event of conviction. Most United States District Judges in New Jersey enter a formal, pre-printed standard order for discovery and inspection, referencing certain provisions of Fed. R. Crim. P.16.56 This order is generally entered on the date of arraignment on the indictment, and sets certain time limits for compliance.[75]

The first four paragraphs of Fed. R. Crim. P. 16(a)(1) begin **"Upon request by the defendant** the government **shall . . . ."** (emphasis added). This language makes clear that Rule

---

[75] (failure to disclose evidence after specific request more likely to be held "material" since defense counsel may have detrimentally relied on evidence not being in existence).[75]

16 becomes applicable upon the specific request of defense counsel. In certain cases, in addition to sending the prosecutor a letter requesting discovery, consider filing a discovery motion in order to preserve the record adequately.

1. Fed. R. Crim. P. 16(a)(1)(A) – Statements Of The Defendant

Rule 16 includes all written or recorded statements by the defendant in the possession of the government including statements that will be used only for impeachment purposes by thegovernment. This material includes the substance of any relevant oral statement made to a known government agent. Those statements should be produced pretrial. The rough notes of agents who may have spoken to the defendant during the course of their investigation should also be requested.58

2. Fed. R. Crim. P. 16(a)(1)(B) – Criminal Records

Upon request, the prosecution must provide a defendant with his/her prior criminal record. Be very familiar with the defendant's record and anticipate Fed. R. Evid. 404(b) problems well in advance of trial in order to file a motion in limine opposing the government's use of such evidence. Review the criminal history thoroughly, particularly the out-of-state annotations of the extract, which may be unfamiliar. Traffic matters, such as D.U.I., should be explored as well because of possible guideline impact.

The defendant's prior criminal record is of paramount importance given the impact it has on sentencing considerations. Always check the record and the charges to see if the defendant is in mandatory minimum, career offender, or armed career criminal territory. The most immediate source of information concerning the defendant's criminal history is Pretrial Services, which will have run a check of the defendant's history prior to the bail/detention hearing.

3. Fed. R. Crim. P. 16(a)(1)(C) – Documents And Tangible Objects

This rule allows for the inspection of all physical evidence that the government intends to use in its case-in-chief at trial, that is material to the defense, or that was obtained from the defendant. This rule allows the material in possession of the government to be inspected, tested, weighed, analyzed, etc. For example, the government must allow the defense to weigh the drugs because of the impact the weight has on sentencing under the guidelines.

4. Fed. R. Crim. P. 16(a)(1)(D) – Scientific Reports And Examinations

Rule 16(a)(1)(D) allows access to all such reports that are in possession of the government or may become known by exercise of due diligence and that are material to preparation of the defense or are intended for use by the government as evidence at the trial.

5. Fed. R. Crim. P. 16(a)(1)(E) – Expert Witnesses

Upon request, counsel is entitled to a written summary of the testimony of any expert witness that the government intends to use in its case-in-chief. The witness' qualifications, opinion, and bases for the opinion should be provided. Be aware that the government takes a rather narrow view of this rule and that it may therefore become necessary to file a pretrial motion in order to obtain full compliance.

6. Fed. R. Crim. P. 16(b) – Reciprocal Discovery

Rule 16(b) applies to the same type of documents requested by the defense that were covered in paragraphs three, four, and five above. The rule requires that **"upon compliance with such request by the government[,]"** the defense shall provide reciprocal discovery. The reciprocal provisions regarding experts can be triggered by the defense filing notice pursuant to Fed. R. Crim. P. 12.2. Special concern arises under § (b)(1)(C) with respect to expert witnesses. The defense may be required to reveal important aspects of the defense and subject its expert to pretrial interviews by the government.

C. OTHER DISCLOSURE BURDENS PLACED ON THE DEFENSE

Several of the Federal Rules of Criminal Procedure place the burden on the defense to give the government notice of its intent to present affirmative defenses or produce defense witness statements. The government will usually request this information when it provides discovery in a case.

1. Fed. R. Crim. P. 26.2 - Production Of Statements Of Witnesses

This rule governs which statements the defense must produce should the government request statements of defense witnesses. This rule is, in essence, reverse Jencks, and it applies only upon request by the government. Review the definition of "statement" in the rule, because it may protect investigators' reports. In any case, the need to have the investigator make contemporaneous notes when interviewing a potential witness should be considered. 59 Fed. R. Crim. P. 12.2(a).-

2. Fed. R. Crim. P. 12.1 - Notice Of Alibi

Be sure to read and to abide by this rule when an alibi defense is anticipated, or the defense or may be precluded pursuant to Fed. R. Crim. P. 12.1(d). Disclosure must be made within ten days of a written demand by the prosecutor. Be aware that § (f) prohibits the use of any such information provided by the defendant if the alibi defense is later withdrawn.

3. Fed. R. Crim. P. 12.2 - The Insanity and Other Defenses

Rule 12.2 governs the insanity defense as well as other mental health based offenses and discovery obligations incumbent upon the defendant in such cases. Be aware that the rule directs that "[i]f there is a failure to comply with the requirements of this subdivision, insanity may not be raised as a defense." The notice must be given within the time for filing of pretrial motions, although the court may allow late filing for good cause. Note also that § (c) may allow for a government expert to examine the defendant.

4. Fed. R. Crim. P. 12.3 - Notice Of Defense Based Upon Public Authority

The defendant must provide the government with the names, agencies, and witnesses that he/she will rely upon to establish this defense. The government should respond with an admission or denial of such public authority.

D. DEPOSITIONS AND 18 U.S.C. § 3503 – FED. R. CRIM. P. 15

Depositions may be taken in criminal cases and the testimony introduced at trial, if the proponent of such testimony can show that the witness is unavailable pursuant to Fed. R. Evid. 804(a)(5) and that exceptional circumstances exist. Should the government attempt to introduce, the defendant can challenge the deposition if they were not present for the deposition or the witness is available for cross-examination at trial.

The rule governing the introduction of deposition testimony in the Third Circuit was set forth in United States v. Wilson, 601 F.2d 95 (3d Cir. 1979). For deposition evidence, a Sixth Amendment confrontation clause objection should be made. The deposition will, however, probably be admissible at trial under Fed. R. Evid. 804(2) if the witness is unavailable.

E. SUBPOENAS – FED. R. CRIM. P. 17

Rule 17(e)(1) allows the defense to subpoena potential witnesses in any part of the United States, while Fed. R. Crim. P. 17(e)(2) provides a mechanism to subpoena witnesses abroad. Pursuant to Fed. R. Crim. P. 17(b), the court can order that defense witnesses be brought to court at the government's expense. Rule 17(c) allows the court to order pretrial production of documents in order to determine whether they should be turned over to the defendant.[76]

However, because a subpoena duces tecum is not intended as a discovery tool, counsel should be prepared to show that the documents sought are needed to prepare for trial.

F. PRETRIAL CONFERENCES – FED. R. CRIM. P. 17.1

Once the indictment or information has been filed, a pre-trial conference is available at the request of the court, the defense, or the government. If counsel believes that the government is not providing all appropriate discovery, resolution of that issue may be addressed by means of a pretrial conference.

G. TRANSCRIPTS

The court must provide an indigent defendant with transcripts of prior proceedings if the transcripts are needed to prepare and to present an effective defense or appeal.[77] See United States v. Passodelis, 615 F.2d 975, 977 (3d Cir. 1980).

---

[76] See United States v. Nixon, 418 U.S. 683, 698 (1974).

[77] 62 See Britt v. North Carolina, 404 U.S. 226, 227 (1971).

H. RULES GOVERNING THE TRANSFER OF CASES FROM ONE FEDERAL JURISDICTION TO ANOTHER

1. Fed. R. Crim. P. 20 – Transfer Where Defendant Pleads Guilty

Rule 20 applies to cases where the defendant has been arrested in a district other than the one in which the offense was indicted. In these cases, the defendant may be given the opportunity to plead guilty in the arresting jurisdiction, as opposed to being returned to the charging jurisdiction **subject to the approval of the United States Attorney for each district**. These proceedings are best coordinated prior to the court appearance by speaking to the local AUSA and, if need be, to an AUSA in the demanding jurisdiction. Keep in mind, however, that this rule only applies to cases that will be disposed of through a guilty plea.

2. Fed. R. Crim. P. 21 - Transfer Of Trial

Rule 21 applies to the transfer of a trial from one jurisdiction to another upon motion by the defendant alleging prejudice in the district where the case has been brought.

3. Fed. R. Crim. P. 22 - Timing Of Transfer Motions

Rule 22 provides a time frame for transfer motions brought pursuant to Rules 20 and 21.

4. Fed. R. Crim. P. 5 - Commitment To Another District

These hearings are also known as "removal hearings." They occur when the defendant has been arrested in a district other than the one in which the indictment or complaint and warrant originated and the prosecuting (demanding) jurisdiction wants him/her back for prosecution. Be sure to consider the possibility of the previously discussed Rule 20 transfer of the case to this district for a plea when that would be in the defendant's best interest. Explain the choice to the defendant, and then explore the option with the prosecutor if the defendant wishes to transfer the case.

Removal hearings take place before the duty magistrate judge. When an indictment has been filed, the government need only establish the defendant's identity. With a complaint and warrant, the government must establish identity and probable cause. Be aware that hearsay is admissible at these hearings and that anything the defendant says can and will be used against him/her in the demanding jurisdiction.

The identification hearing determines whether the defendant is the same individual named in the indictment by the demanding jurisdiction. Identification is proven by photographs, fingerprints, and/or by the testimony of agents from the demanding jurisdiction. Assuming identification is **not** an issue, stipulating to identification may avoid the probable extended detention of the defendant in New Jersey to await an evidentiary hearing, but limit the stipulation for purposes of the removal hearing **only**.

Bail issues will also be decided at these hearings. On occasion, the magistrate judge will release the defendant on bail and allow him/her to surrender to the demanding jurisdiction. Factors that affect the bail decision include the nature of the pending charges, prior record, family considerations, Pretrial Services' recommendation, and/or the consent of the demanding jurisdiction.

Procedures for individuals arrested due to violations of probation or supervised release also are outlined in Fed. R. Crim. P. 5(d). Note that there is no language in this section of the rule mandating detention of the defendant pending his/her removal to the demanding jurisdiction. In reality, however, convincing a magistrate judge to afford bail to such individuals is difficult. It is a good practice to call the AUSA in the demanding jurisdiction to try to negotiate bail, reasonable release conditions, and a surrender date on the violation.

On the other hand, individuals arrested for failing to appear in the demanding jurisdiction shall be held by the magistrate:

(e) Arrest for Failure to Appear: Upon production of the warrant or a certified copy thereof and upon a finding that the person before the magistrate is the person named in the warrant, the federal magistrate shall hold the person to answer in the district in which the warrant was issued. (Emphasis added). Magistrate Judges are afforded more latitude in situations where an individual was previously detained or conditionally released in the demanding jurisdiction:

(f) Release or Detention: . . . [T]he federal magistrate shall take into account the decision previously made and the reasons set forth therefor, if any, **but will not be bound by that decision**. If the federal magistrate amends the release or detention decision or alters the conditions of release, the magistrate shall set forth the reasons in writing. (Emphasis added).

I. THE JENCKS ACT– 18 U.S.C. § 3500

The Jencks Act was passed by Congress in response to Jencks v. United States, 353 U.S. 657 (1957), which held that a defendant is entitled to **pretrial** discovery of government witnesses statements. The act, in relevant part, changed the time frame regarding disclosure of prior testimony so that production is not required **until after the witness has testified** on direct examination at trial. 18 U.S.C. § 3500 provides in pertinent part:

(b) After a witness called by the United States has testified on direct examination, the court shall, on motion of the defendant, order the United States to produce any statement (as hereinafter defined) of the witness in the possession of the United States which relates to the subject matter as to which the witness has testified.

Generally, the practice in this district is that the government will provide Jencks material at 64 See Fed. R. Crim. P. 26.2(g). 65 See 18 U.S.C. §§ 3500(e)(2) & (3). 66 See 18 U.S.C. § 3500(e)(1); see also Goldberg v. United States, 425 U.S. 94, 98 (1976) (notes taken during witness interview qualified as Jencks material where information was read back to witness for corrections); United States v. Ogbuehi, 18 F.3d 807, 810-11 (9th Cir. 1994) (in camera review of interview notes taken by prosecutor proper when prosecutor read back notes to witness for accuracy, although notes were not verbatim or ever shown to witness). At least one day in advance of the witness' appearance at trial, but at times a prosecutor will not deviate from the letter of the rule. In those situations, counsel should consider filing a motion for the early production of Jencks material. A pretrial conference could also be requested to explain the defense position to the judge, who may be able to persuade the prosecutor to reach some agreement with respect to the production of Jencks material. If nothing else, the conference will put the judge on notice that if the prosecutor does not provide Jencks prior to trial, a substantial recess will be needed in order to review the material and to conduct follow-up investigation. However, remember that Fed. R. Crim. P. 26.2 allows for disclosure when a witness testifies at other hearings as well.64 The other critical Jencks issue is whether a "statement" by a witness qualifies as Jencks material, as defined in 18 U.S.C. § 3500(e). All grand jury testimony qualifies, as well as other recorded, verbatim statements made by the witness.65 The troublesome area involves government reports relating to the substance of witness interviews. When a government agent interviews a prospective government witness, there are usually rough notes taken and almost always the interviewing agent prepares a report. The rough notes taken by a government agent are not discoverable as the witness' "statement" unless the witness reviewed or approved the notes,66 or the notes were "a substantially verbatim recital of an oral statement made by said witness and 67 See 18 U.S.C. § 3500(e)(2); see also United States v. Smith, 984 F.2d 1084 (10th Cir. 1993) (agent's interview notes of government witness are Jencks "statements" if substantially verbatim), cert. denied, 510 U.S. 873 (1993); United States v. Rewald, 889 F.2d 836 (9th Cir. 1989) (court's failure to review FBI reports of witness interviews for Jencks material required remand.) See United States v. Griffin, 659 F.2d 932, 937-38 (9th Cir. 1981), cert. denied, 456 U.S. 949 (1982). See United States v. Harris, 543 F.2d 1247, 1251 (9th Cir. 1976). See 18 U.S.C. §§ 3500(b) & (d). See United States v. Well, 572 F.2d 1383, 1384 (9th Cir. 1978). recorded contemporaneously . . . ."

Rough notes taken by the interviewing agent are probably not discoverable as Jencks statements of the agent. However, if the notes contain material that is arguably exculpatory, they should be preserved for a determination by the court of whether they must be disclosed as

Brady material. For this reason, counsel should ask the court to order the preservation of rough notes at an early stage. If a defendant can show that Jencks material has been destroyed, the witness' testimony should be stricken. No showing of prejudice is required. notwithstanding this provision, the agent's destruction of those notes is generally held to be harmless error.[78] Nonetheless, the agent's reports, which incorporates these notes, are discoverable.

J. BRADY MATERIAL

The prosecutor must disclose all evidence favorable to the defendant which is "material either to guilt or punishment."[79] United States v. Bagley, 473 U.S. 667 (1985) explained that evidence was material if there was a reasonable probability that had the evidence been disclosed to the defense, the result would have been different. Impeachment evidence may come within the Brady rule if the reliability of the witness may be determinative of the defendant's guilt or innocence. Also, there appears to be no denial of due process if the Brady material is disclosed in time for its effective use of trial.[80]

Be aware that Brady suggests that the defense must request the information. While Brady must be interpreted expansively by defense counsel, all Brady requests must be **SPECIFIC** in order to protect the record and to force the government to comply with the requests. Absence of specificity may affect the perception of the Court on appeal and the ultimate likelihood of success.

In ***Kyles v. Whitley***, 514 U.S. 419 (1995), the government was found to have a duty to disclose exculpatory evidence, even in the absence of a request, if the withheld evidence, considered as a whole, results in a "reasonable probability" that a different outcome would have obtained. The

---

[78] See ***United States v. Ammar***, 714 F.2d 238 (3d Cir.), cert. denied, 464 U.S. 936 (1983); see also ***United States v, McKoy***, 78 F.3d 446, 451 (9th Cir. 1996) (Jencks Act violation should have resulted in mistrial, not suppression), cert. denied, 519 U.S. 817 (1996).

[79] See ***Brady v. Maryland***, 373 U.S. 83, 87 (1963).

[80] See ***United States v. Starusko***, 729 F.2d 256, 260 (3d Cir. 1984). ***United States v. Higgs***, 713 F.2d 39, 44 (3d Cir. 1983). ***United States v. Strifler***, 851 F.2d 1197, 1202 (9th Cir. 1988), cert. denied, 489 U.S. 1032 (1989). ***Jackson v. Wainwright***, 390 F.2d 288, 298 (5th Cir. 1968). United States v. Wilkins, 326 F.2d 135, 136 (2d Cir. 1964). ***Ashley v. Texas***, 319 F.2d 80, 85 (5th Cir.), cert. denied, 375 U.S. 931 (1963).

defendant should show that the suppression of the evidence "undermined confidence in the outcome of the trial." The question of good faith is irrelevant, and the obligation exists even if the police have failed to disclose the evidence to the prosecutor. Categories of evidence generally considered to be Brady material are a witness' prior record, witness statements that are favorable to the defendant, the existence of witnesses favorable to the defense,78 and psychiatric reports showing the defendant's legal insanity. Other examples of Brady material which must be produced include promises of immunity to a government witness[81] and prior contrary statements of a prosecution witness.81 "Out of the ordinary" Brady requests, that is, information other than informant records and open cases pending against the informant should be made well in advance of trial for two reasons.[82] One, the prosecutor may rethink his/her position regarding the indictment after reviewing all the material available against its informant, and two, the information may take some time to get from other agencies, particularly the I.N.S. and the I.R.S. Cases such as Kyles v. Whitley, 514 U.S. 419 (1995), and United States v. Perdomo, 929 F.2d 967 (3d Cir. 1991), make clear that it does not matter whether the requested information is in the immediate possession of the United States Attorney's Office. If any agency of the United States government or local law enforcement has the information, it is available to the prosecutor and the defense is entitled to it if it qualifies as Brady or Giglio material. Giglio v. United States, 405 U.S. 150 (1972), clarified that any evidence which would affect the credibility of a government witness could be construed as Brady material. This category would include any information that shows bias of the witness, motive for the witness to lie or to exaggerate testimony, credibility issues of a government witness (such as prior bad acts of dishonesty or felony convictions), and a lack of memory by the witness. The defense should also request that the personnel files of government witnesses be produced so that those files can be reviewed for possible Brady material.

---

[81] See ***Giglio v. United States***, 405 U.S. 150, 154 (1972).

[82] See ***Giles v. Maryland***, 386 U.S. 66, 81 (1967); see also ***United States v. Hanna***, 55 F.3d 1456, 1459-61 (9th Cir. 1995) (failure to produce grand jury testimony and pretrial statements of arresting officer which might have been inconsistent with trial testimony was reversible error).

If the exculpatory nature of the evidence is doubtful, the prosecutor should turn over the evidence.[83]

PRETRIAL MOTIONS

This Chapter contains a discussion of selected pretrial motions and motions in limine frequently filed. Rule 12, 3d Cir. R. 12.1, and 3d Cir. R. 7.1(a), (b)(1), (d)(1) & (g), made specifically applicable to criminal cases via Local R. 1.1, define the parameters of pre-trial motion practice.85 Although Fed. R. Crim. P. 12(b) allows oral motions to be filed at the judge's discretion and does not specify when the motions must be filed, Local R. 12.1 sets a time frame for filing motions: Defenses or objections permitted pursuant to Fed. R. Crim. P. 12 shall be made before pleading or within 30 days thereafter unless the Court at the time of arraignment on application of counsel otherwise specifies, or unless good cause is shown.[84]

A. MOTIONS REQUESTING ENLARGEMENT OF TIME TO FILE PRETRIAL MOTIONS

Motions requesting enlargements of time in which to file pretrial motions may be filed in this district. Typically, extensions are granted for a thirty to sixty day period. Rule 45 governs the computation of time, the procedure, and the criteria for such requests: (b) Enlargement. When an act is required or allowed to be done at or within a specified time, the court for cause shown may at any time in its discretion (1) with or without motion or notice, order the period enlarged if a request is made before the expiration of the period originally prescribed by a previous order or

---

[83] See ***United States v. Lloyd***, 992 F.2d 348, 352 (D.C. Cir. 1993) (case remanded for government to make redetermination as to materiality of documents that its investigation produced, and any documents not turned over to the defendant should be reviewed in camera); accord ***United States v. Cadet***, 727 F.2d 1453, 1467 (9th Cir. 1984); ***United States v. Griggs***, 713 F.2d 672, 674 (11th Cir. 1983); ***Hamric v. Bailey***, 386 F.2d 390, 393 (4th Cir. 1967). 83 But see ***United States v. Gardner***, 611 F.2d 770, 775 (9th Cir. 1980) (with trial court permission, prosecutor may submit for in camera inspection only materials it deems discoverable under Brady).

[84] See ***United States v. Gaston***, 608 F.2d 607, 612-14 (5th Cir. 1979).

(2) upon motion made after the expiration of the specified period permit the act to be done if the failure to act was the result of excusable neglect; .[85] .

Motions to enlarge are typically filed because defense counsel has not received complete discovery from the AUSA or has not had ample opportunity to review the discovery within the time frame allocated in 3d Cir. R. 12.1. In cases involving complex legal and/or factual issues or situations in which the AUSA informs counsel that discovery will not be available within the thirty day time frame, a request to extend the pretrial filing date to ten days after the AUSA anticipates the completion of discovery should be made. If discovery is not completed by the anticipated date, the AUSA should be contacted for consent for a further continuance order. If, in the alternative, the AUSA is not being diligent in the production of discovery, counsel should consider filing a motion to compel discovery or to dismiss the indictment, whichever is more appropriate.

B. MOTIONS TO CONTINUE TRIAL AND THE RIGHT TO A SPEEDY TRIAL

Once motions have been filed and argued and a trial date has been set, motions to continue trial are frowned upon by the District Court Judges in the District of New Jersey. Most judges, and more importantly, their deputy clerks, make reasonable efforts to accommodate the attorneys' schedules. Scheduling problems should be brought to the attention of the judge at the return date for pretrial motions, because that is typically the juncture when a "real" trial date is set. District Court Judges in this district run individual calendars and are solely responsible for compliance with the Speedy Trial Act for cases on their dockets.88 Once an actual trial date is set, most judges are reluctant to grant a trial continuance, and will do so only in exceptional See 18 U.S.C. § 3161(b) (thirty days from arrest to indictment); § 3161(c)(1) (trial is seventy days after indictment is filed).

See 18 U.S.C. § 3161(c)(2) (absent written consent of defendant, matter shall not be tried less than thirty days from date on which defendant first appears through counsel or expressly waives counsel and elects to proceed pro se). 9118 U.S.C. § 3164(b). 9218 U.S.C. § 3161(h)(8)(B)(ii). circumstances. Nonetheless, some judges are more accommodating than others; it is therefore advisable to learn the practice of the particular judge prior to requesting a continuance.

1. The Speedy Trial Act

---

[85] **Fed. R. Crim. P. 45**. See ***United States v. Rivera Constr. Co***., 863 F.2d 293, 296-97 (3d Cir. 1988).

a. Generally

Under the Speedy Trial Act, the critical time periods are thirty days from the arrest to the indictment and seventy days from the date the indictment is filed to trial. The Act also provides for a mandatory thirty day defense preparatory period. In setting trial schedules, the Speedy Trial Act gives priority to defendants who have been detained: The trial of any person described in subsection (a)(1) or (a)(2) of this section shall commence not later than ninety days following the beginning of such continuous detention or designation of high risk by the attorney for the Government. The periods of delay enumerated in Section 3161(h) are excluded in computing the time limitation specified in this section. Cases involving unusually complex fact patterns and/or legal issues may be considered for a continuance:

(ii) Whether the case is so unusual or so complex, due to the number of defendants, the nature of the prosecution, or the existence of novel questions of fact or law, that it is unreasonable to expect adequate preparation for pre-trial proceedings or for trial itself within the time limits established by this section.

Sanctions for failure to comply with the Speedy Trial Act are covered in 18 U.S.C. §3162 (a)(2). The criteria a court is to consider when deciding to dismiss the case with or without prejudice to the government are: among others, each of the following factors: the seriousness of the offense; the facts and circumstances of the case which led to the dismissal; and the impact of a reprosecution on the administration of justice. Failure of the defendant to move for dismissal prior to trial or entry of a plea of guilty or nolo contendere shall constitute a waiver of the right to dismissal under this section.[86]

Failure to comply with the Act permits reconsideration by the court of the conditions of confinement: No detainee, as defined in subsection (a), shall be held in custody pending trial after the expiration of such ninety-day period required for the commencement of his trial.

b. Tolling The Statute

---

[86] 18 U.S.C. § 3162; see also ***United States v. Taylor***, 487 U.S. 326, 337 (1988) (applying test for determining whether dismissal should be with or without prejudice). 9418 U.S.C. § 3164(c). 18 U.S.C. § 3161(h)(1)(F) (delay resulting from any pretrial motion or its disposition is excludable); see also ***United States v. Felton***, 811 F.2d 190, 196 (3d Cir. 1987) (indicating that subsection (h)(1)(F) does not exclude time where court does not establish set, specific time frame for consideration of motions, as intended by Congress in Speedy Trial Act), cert. denied, 483 U.S. 1008 (1987).

Section 3161(h) of Title 18 governs the computation of excludable time. In effect, the filing of a pretrial motion will toll the Speedy Trial Act until the timely disposition of the motion by the trial court.95 The Speedy Trial Act should be reviewed carefully prior to challenging an indictment based on post-indictment, pretrial delay. Post-arrest pre-indictment requests for a continuance are often initiated jointly by the government and defendant on the grounds that the defendant is cooperating, may decide cooperate, or may agree to waive indictment and to proceed by an information. Post-indictment requests for a continuance based on incomplete or untimely discovery are initiated by the defendant. Both types of continuance motions are usually granted, particularly when they are presented as a joint request.[87]

2. The Sixth Amendment Guarantee To A Speedy Trial

The Sixth Amendment provides in pertinent part that "[i]n all criminal prosecutions, the accused shall enjoy the right to a speedy and public trial." The right to speedy trial does not attach until the defendant is indicted, arrested, or otherwise officially accused.97

The Sixth Amendment right to a speedy trial is not primarily intended to prevent prejudice to the defense caused by passage of time. The Due Process Clause and statutes of limitations serve that function.98 The Sixth Amendment speedy trial guarantee is instead designed to minimize the possibility of lengthy incarceration prior to trial, to reduce the lesser, but nevertheless substantial, impairment of liberty imposed on an accused while released on bail, and to shorten the disruption of life caused by arrest and the presence of unresolved criminal charges.99 In Barker v. Wingo,100 the Supreme Court set forth a four-part test for evaluating a Sixth Amendment challenge. The Court announced the factors to be considered in evaluating a speedy trial challenge: the length of the delay, the reason for the delay, the prejudice suffered by the 101 See id. at 530; see also, e.g.***, Doggett v. United States***, 505 U.S. 647, 651 (1992) (8 ½ year delay; ***United States v. Dent***, 149 F.3d 180, 184 (3d Cir. 1998) (applying Barker v. Wingo test to five year delay); ***United States v. Shell***, 974 F.2d 1035, 1036 (9th Cir. 1992) (five year delay between indictment and arrest, attributable to government's negligence, is presumptively prejudicial; indictment dismissed despite defendant's concession

---

[87] See 18 U.S.C. § 3161(c)(1***); United States v. McKinley***, 23 F.3d 181, 184 (7th Cir. 1994).

United States v. MacDonald, 456 U.S. 1, 8 (1982). id. at 8; see also ***United States v. Loud*** Hawk, 474 U.S. 302, 310-11 (1986) (expanded MacDonald to cover situations where government appealed pretrial order dismissing indictment ; 407 U.S. 514 (1972).

that most essential witnesses and documentary evidence were still available because government failed to rebut presumption).

The Court also stated that the length of the delay operates as a triggering mechanism, and that until a presumptively prejudicial delay has occurred, there is no need to engage in the remainder of the analysis.[88]

3. Statute Of Limitations

There is no statute of limitations for capital offenses.[89] Most other offenses have a five year statute of limitations, although bank frauds and other types of frauds have a ten year statute of limitations.[90]

C. MOTIONS TO SUPPRESS EVIDENCE BASED ON VIOLATIONS OF THE FOURTH, FIFTH, AND SIXTH AMENDMENTS

Pursuant to Fed. R. Crim. P.12(b), motions to suppress may be presented to the court orally or in writing, at the discretion of the particular judge. At times, the court may decide the motion based upon the papers filed in the case without an evidentiary hearing. A discussion of the broad array of suppression motions available under the Fourth, Fifth, and Sixth Amendments is well beyond the scope of this manual. There are a myriad of excellent hornbooks and treatises available on the subject, and they should be consulted whenever counsel is faced with the advantages of joinder in terms of judicial economy. . . it is well established that judicial economy favors a joint trial where defendants are jointly indicted[91] . . . . Consequently, the burden is on the defendant to establish a reason for a severance"), cert. denied, 494 U.S. 1089 (1990); ***United States v. Gorecki***, 813 F.2d 40, 42 (3d Cir. 1987) (defendant claiming improper joinder under Fed. R. Crim. P. 8(a) must prove actual prejudice from misjoinder); see also Quintero, 38 F.3d at 1339 (no mandatory requirement for severance, and mutually antagonistic defenses are

---

[88] See 407 U.S. at 530-31.

[89] See 18 U.S.C. § 3281.

[90] See 18 U.S.C. § 3282.

[91] See U.S.S.G. § 1B1.3. ***United States v. Quintero***, 38 F.3d 1317, 1339 (3d Cir. 1994) (defendant bears burden of establishing that separate trials are necessary to prevent prejudice), cert. denied, 513 U.S. 1195 (1995); ***United States v. Sandini***, 888 F.2d 300, 305 (3d Cir. 1989)

not prejudicial per se; there must be serious risk that joint trial will compromise specific trial right of one defendant or prevent the jury from making reliable judgment about guilt or innocence). See ***Sandini***, 888 F.2d at 305 (decision to sever is reviewed for abuse of discretion). Always remain cognizant of the possibility of a suppression issue. Careful research coupled with creative thinking and advice from seasoned colleagues will significantly expand the possibilities. A sampling of some of the materials available regarding suppression motions includes: ***Wayne R. LaFave, Search and Seizure: A Treatise on the Fourth Amendment*** (2004-2011) Joseph G. Cook, ***Constitutional Rights of the Accused (3d ed. 1996)*** William A. Grimes, ***Criminal Law Outline (1997)***

D. JOINDER AND SEVERANCE MOTIONS – FED. R. CRIM. P. 8, 12, 13 & 14

Rule 8 permits joinder of offenses and of defendants. Joinder can and often will be detrimental to individual defendants at trial. It will likely also be detrimental at sentencing, given the language of the relevant conduct section of the sentencing guidelines. The defendant can move to sever if he/she can show that the joinder was improper and that he/she was prejudiced by the joinder. The decision to sever, however, rests within the discretion of the trial court. Fed. R. Crim. P. 13.

111 See United States v. Ingio, 925 F.2d 641, 655 (3d Cir. 1991) (defendant entitled to severance when evidence against one defendant cannot be compartmentalized by jury; jury must be unable to make individualized determination of guilt)[92].

Rule 13 is implicated when there are multiple but related indictments.109 Under Rule 13, the court can try two or more indictments together if the court determines that the defendants could have been charged in a single indictment.[93]

---

[92] See ***United States v. Tootick***, 952 F.2d 1078, 1081 (9th Cir. 1991). But see ***United States v. Zafiro***, 506 U.S. 534, 537-38 (1993) (Rule 14 does not require severance as matter of law when co-defenses are mutually exclusive; severance required only if there exists serious risk that joint trial would compromise specific trial right or prevent jury from making reliable judgment of guilt or innocence); ***United States v. Voight***, 89 F.3d 1050, 1095 (3d Cir. 1996) (asserted defenses, while in conflict with one another, were not so irreconcilable that jury could not have been able to assess guilt or innocence of defendant on an individual, independent basis; mutually antagonistic defenses exist rarely in practice), cert. denied, 519 U.S. 104 (1996).

[93] See ***United States v. Gonzalez***, 918 F.2d 1129, 1137 (3d Cir. 1990), cert. denied, 499 U.S. 982 (1991) (citing ***United States v. Bosica***, 573 F.2d 827, cert. denied, 436 U.S. 911 (1979));

Severance of defendants and/or charges is governed by Fed. R. Crim. P. 14, which provides for severance (or any other relief justice requires) should either party establish that joinder will prejudice his/her case. Mutually exclusive defenses may sometimes require severance, such as when acquittal of one co-defendant necessarily calls for the conviction of the other. A motion to sever will be reviewed on appeal only for abuse of discretion. The procedure for motions to sever is governed by Fed. R. Crim. P. 12. Rule 12 requires that a motion to sever must be brought prior to trial.114

115 See generally Marshall v. Jerrico, 446 U.S. 238 (1980) (Due Process Clause entitles person to impartial and disinterested tribunal in both civil and criminal cases).

116 Actual Prejudice:

See Irvin v. Dowd, 366 U.S. 717, 723 (1961) (test for prejudice is whether nature and strength of opinion formed necessarily raises presumption of partiality; impartiality is not technical conception but rather state of mind).

Inherent Prejudice: See Murphy v. Florida, 421 U.S. 794, 799 (1975) (juror exposure to information concerning defendant's priors and/or news accounts of crime charged does not presumptively deprive defendant of due process; exposure is to be reviewed by "totality of the circumstances" analysis, and once juror has given court assurances that he/she can be fair, it remains open to defendant to demonstrate "the actual existence of such an opinion in the mind of the juror as will rise the presumption of partiality."); see also Chapter Six, supra, for a discussion of Mu'Min v. Virginia, 500 U.S. 415 (1991).

Reasonable Likelihood Standard:

See Sheppard v. Maxwell, 384 U.S. 333, 362 (1966) (due process requires that accused receive trial by impartial jury, free from outside influences; given modern communications and difficulty of effacing prejudicial

E. MOTIONS FOR RECUSAL AND FOR A CHANGE OF VENUE – FED. R. CRIM.P. 21(A)

1. Recusal Of Trial Judge

---

see also id. (four factors court should consider when determining whether to sever are likelihood that co-defendant will testify, degree to which such testimony would be exculpatory, degree to which testifying co-defendants could be impeached, and effect on judicial economy). While other circuits have held that the motion must also be made at the close of trial in order to preserve the issue for appeal, see, e.g.*, **United States v. Allen***, 160 F.3d 1096, 1106-07 (6th Cir. 1998), the Third Circuit has not yet spoken on this requirement.

Section 455(a) of Title 28 directs that: "Any justice or judge of the United States shall disqualify himself in any proceeding in which his impartiality might reasonably be questioned."115

2. Transfer Of Cases To Other Jurisdictions

The transfer of a case due to pretrial publicity that may prejudice the defendant is governed by Fed. R. Crim. P. 21(a):

For Prejudice in the District. The court upon motion of the defendant shall transfer the proceeding as to that defendant to another district whether or not such district is specified in the defendant's motion if the court is satisfied that there exists in the district where the prosecution is pending so great a prejudice against the defendant that the defendant cannot obtain a fair and impartial trial at any place fixed by law for holding court in that district.116 publicity from minds of the jurors, trial court must take strong measures to ensure that balance is never weighed against accused); see also United States v. Inigo, 925 F.2d 641, 655 (3d Cir. 1991) (trial was not partial despite corporate victim's unique prominence in economic and social communities where case was litigated and attention drawn to case by media); Martin v. Warden, 653 F.2d 799, 804 (3d Cir. 1981) (pre-trial publicity will not automatically taint juror; person may serve if he/she can set aside prior impression and render fair verdict based on evidence presented at trial); cert. denied, 454 U.S. 1151 (1982). See generally Government of the Virgin Islands v. Riley, 973 F.2d 224, 226 (3d Cir. 1992) (question is not whether community remembers case, but whether jurors had such fixed opinions that they could not judge guilt of defendant impartially; pretrial publicity will not automatically taint juror). 117 See United States v. Dyal, 868 F.2d 424, 428-429 (11th Cir. 1989) (in dismissing indictment, information, or complaint under Rule 48(a), government is entitled to presumption of good faith); see also id. (prosecutor abides by standards of fair play and decency if s/he refuses to seek indictments until completely satisfied that s/he should prosecute and that s/he will be able promptly to establish guilt beyond reasonable doubt); United States v. Welborn, 849 F.2d 980, 983 (5th Cir. 1988) (prosecutor's request for dismissal is improper if made in bad faith, which arises when prosecution is motivated "by considerations `clearly contrary to the public interest[;]'" "the public interest is not served by harassing a defendant. When a court considers a prosecutor's motion to dismiss it must begin with the presumption that the prosecutor acted in good faith. . . . . Whether deliberate or not, unjustified failure to contest a motion to dismiss waives any right to later complain that the prosecutor requested dismissal in bad faith.").Rule 21(b) for the transfer of cases to another district upon motion by the defendant for the convenience of parties and witnesses and in the interests of justice.

F. MOTIONS TO DISMISS INDICTMENTS

1. Government Motion To Withdraw An Indictment

Government motions to dismiss indictments are governed by Fed. R. Crim. P. 48(a). The government is entitled to a presumption of good faith in dismissing the charging document.117 Be wary if the government moves to withdraw the indictment for "no apparent reason." The indictment will more than likely resurface in a new and improved version, adding charges that will invariably expose the defendant to more severe penalties. Make a record and preserve the right to question whether the government acted in good faith in dismissing the original indictment.

2. Indictments Dismissed By The Court

Rule 48(b) provides a mechanism by which the court may dismiss an indictment due to pretrial delay:

If there is unnecessary delay in presenting the charge to a grand jury or in filing an Information against a defendant who has been held to answer to the district court, or if there has been unnecessary delay in bringing a defendant to trial, the court may dismiss the Indictment, Information or Complaint. Rule 48(b) does not be apply in lieu of the Sixth Amendment guarantee to a speedy trial or the Speedy Trial Act but, rather, reinforces the court's inherent power to dismiss a case. Needless to say, such dismissals are rarely granted.

3. Miscellaneous Defense Motions Requesting A Dismissal Of The Indictment

a. Double Jeopardy

Motions to dismiss on grounds of double jeopardy merit special mention given the number of state court cases that are assumed by the federal government. The federal authorities in the District of New Jersey are assuming a significant number of cases that begin as state court prosecutions because defendants can be detained under the Bail Reform Act and because they are subject to lengthier sentences under the sentencing guidelines. However, when a defendant is convicted in state court, the United States Attorney's Office, will, in most cases, adhere to the Justice Department's Petite policy prior to bringing a case in federal court.

120 See Blockburger v. United States, 284 U.S. 299, 303-04 (1932); see also United States v. Dixon, 509 U.S. 688, 704 (1993) (successive prosecution need not satisfy "same conduct" test to avoid double jeopardy bar) (overruling Grady v. Corbin, 495 U.S. 508 (1990)).

121 For a general discussion on the theory of double jeopardy and dual sovereignty, see generally Rinaldi v. United States, 434 U.S. 22 (1977), and Heath v. Alabama, 474 U.S. 82 (1985). See also United States v. Pungitore, 910 F.2d 1084, 1105 (3d Cir. 1990) ("'dual sovereignty' doctrine rests on premise that where both sovereigns legitimately claim strong interest in penalizing same behavior, they have concurrent jurisdiction to vindicate those

interests, and need not yield to each other"; acquittal in state court does not preclude federal prosecution, especially for RICO violations), cert. denied, 500 U.S. 915 (1991).

122 See United States v. Conley, 37 F.3d 970, 977 (3d Cir. 1994) (applying Blockburger test to money laundering and illegal gambling conspiracies); see also United States v. Calderone, 982 F.2d 42, 48 (2d Cir. 1992) (conspiracy wholly contained within longer conspiracy that was already prosecuted is barred by double jeopardy).

123 See United States v. Felix, 503 U.S. 378, 388 (1992).

124 See Hudson v. United States, 522 U.S. 93, 99 (1997) (remanded for determination whether monetary sanctions were merely remedial and did not constitute "punishment" that would preclude subsequent criminal prosecution); United States v. $184,505.01 in U.S. Currency, 72 F.3d 1160, 1167 (3d Cir. 1995) (forfeiture does not constitute punishment within meaning of double jeopardy clause); United States v. Cullen, 979 F.2d 992, 994 (4th Cir. 1992) (forfeiture is not primarily an act of punishment but protects community from threat of continued

The Double Jeopardy Clause protects only against the imposition of multiple criminal punishments for the same offense. The Supreme Court has held that the proper analysis in reviewing double jeopardy claims evaluates whether each offense contains an element not contained in the other.120 When a case has already been tried in state court, double jeopardy is not a bar to a subsequent federal prosecution.121 Only if the same sovereign is involved and if the elements are the same, will the double jeopardy clause bar a subsequent prosecution and punishment.

The Double Jeopardy Clause also does not bar prosecution where some of the alleged overt acts are proven with conduct that was prosecuted as a substantive crime in an earlier prosecution. Conspiracy and the underlying crime itself are separate offenses. The clause will likewise not bar a later criminal prosecution for conduct that was punished in an earlier civil proceeding.

Double Jeopardy Clause does not apply to civil forfeitures where property itself has been instrument of criminal activity).

125 See Oregon v. Kennedy, 456 U.S. 667, 675-76 (1982).

126 See United States v. Wallach, 979 F.2d 912, 916 (2d Cir.), cert. denied, 508 U.S. 939 (1993); United States v. Coleman, 862 F.2d 455, 460 (3d Cir. 1988).

127 See Government of the Virgin Islands v. Paniagua, 922 F.2d 178, 182 (3d Cir. 1990).

128 18 U.S.C. § 3006A(e)(1);

Double jeopardy might, however, bar retrial if a prosecutor engages in misconduct to thwart an imminent acquittal. Double jeopardy bars a second trial where a defendant successfully moved for a mistrial, but only if the conduct giving rise to the mistrial was prosecutorial or judicial conduct intended to provoke the defendant into moving for a mistrial.125 Extensions of this principle should be limited to situations in which prosecutors act with the intent to avoid an acquittal that they believe is likely.126 Note that the Double Jeopardy Clause is not offended when a defendant is retried after the magistrate judge has declared a mistrial, upon the defendant's request because the jury could not reach a unanimous verdict.

G. MOTIONS CONCERNING EXPERTS

1. Motions For Appointment of Experts

The Criminal Justice Act allows counsel to obtain "investigative, expert, or other services necessary for adequate representation."128 Section 3006A(e)(2) of Title 18 permits appointed counsel to retain experts without court approval provided the cost does not exceed $300.00. Costs in excess of $300.00 require pre-approval. Pursuant to Fed. R. Crim. P. 17(b), these requests can and should be made on an ex parte basis:

129 See also 18 U.S.C. § 3006A(e)(1).

130 See 509 U.S. 579 (1993) (superseding Frye v. United States, 293 F.2d 1013 (D.C. Cir. 1923)).

131 See id. at 593.

132 See id. at 596.

133 See id.

Defendant Unable to Pay. Upon a defendant's ex parte application, the court must order that a subpoena be issued for a named witness if the defendant shows an inability to pay the witness's fees and the necessity of the witness's presence for an adequate defense. If the court orders a subpoena to be issued, the process costs and witness fees will be paid in the same manner as those paid for witnesses the government subpoenas.

2. Motions to Challenge The Basis of Expert Testimony

In Daubert v. Merrell Dow Pharmaceuticals, Inc., the Supreme Court held that Fed. R. Evid. 702 provides a more liberal basis for admitting relevant scientific evidence than that of general acceptance in the relevant scientific community.130 Among the factors a court should consider are whether the scientific knowledge being offered has been tested, whether the underlying theory could be falsified, whether it has been subject to peer review and publication, and whether the evidence has a particular degree of acceptance in the relevant community.131 Additionally, the Court held that trial courts have broad discretion under the "gatekeeping" function to consider the Daubert factors, to the extent relevant, in determining the reliability of all types of expert testimony.

132 The Court emphasized that the role of the Daubert factors as reasonable measures of reliability will vary from case to case and that the trial court has broad discretion in considering the specific factors.

133 The "gatekeeping" obligation announced in Daubert was extended by the Supreme Court

134 see 526 U.S. 137, 147 (1999)

135 See id.

136 See id. at 152.

137 See 753 F.2d 1224, 1237 (3d Cir. 1985).

138 Id.

Kumho Tire Co., Ltd. v. Carmichael to encompass not only "scientific" expert testimony, but testimony based on technical or other specialized knowledge as well.134 In Kumho Tire, the Supreme Court opined that although Daubert limited its "gatekeeping" requirement to scientific testimony, which was the testimony at issue in Daubert, Fed. R. Evid. 702 makes no relevant distinctions between scientific knowledge and technical or other specialized knowledge.135 Consequently, the gatekeeping function properly applies to all specialized knowledge.136 The Third Circuit had previously developed its own reliability criteria in United States v. Downing.137 While Daubert now controls the analysis, the factors identified in Downing remain useful. Those factors include:

(1) the soundness and reliability of the process or technique used in generating the evidence, (2) the possibility that admitting the evidence would overwhelm, confuse, or mislead the jury, and (3) the proffered connection between the scientific research or test result to be presented, and particular disputed factual issues in the case.138

On a final note, remember that Fed. R. Crim. P. 16(b)(1)(C) imposes reciprocal discovery obligations on defense counsel with respect to expert testimony when the expert will testify.

H. MOTIONS IN LIMINE

A formal notice of motion and accompanying legal memoranda can be filed with the court. Motions in limine are not among the motions that must be filed pretrial pursuant to Fed. R. Crim. P. 12(b)(1)-(5).

141 See United States v. Console, 13 F.3d 641, 659 (3d Cir. 1993) (citing United States v. Sampson, 980 F.2d 883, 886 (3d Cir. 1992)), cert. denied, 511 U.S. 1076 , and 513 U.S. 812 (1994); see also Huddleston v. United States, 485 U.S. 681, 687 (1988) (threshold inquiry court must make before admitting similar acts evidence is whether that evidence is probative of material issue other than character; court is not required to make preliminary finding that government has proved "other act" by preponderance of evidence before it submits similar

evidence to jury, but, rather, evidence should be admitted if there is sufficient evidence to support finding by jury that defendant committed similar acts); cf. United States v. Murray, 103 F.3d 310, 317 (3d Cir. 1997) (evidence that defendant committed uncharged murder was not admissible in prosecution for intentional killing in furtherance of continuing criminal enterprise); United States v. Himelwright, 42 F.3d 777, 782 (3d Cir. 1994) (when evidence of prior bad acts is offered, proponent must clearly articulate how that evidence fits into chain of logical inferences, no link of which may be inference that defendant has propensity to commit crime charged).

142 See Console, 13 F.3d at 659.

or submitted informally as letter applications. If the issue is novel or involves extensive research, it may be helpful to file the motion several days in advance of trial. If the issue is fairly rudimentary, filing on the eve of trial may be acceptable. Following is a non-exhaustive list of motions routinely filed.

1. Fed. R. Evid. 404(b) Motions

Among the most common motions in limine are 404(b) motions, which attempt to limit the prior bad act evidence that a prosecutor will be permitted to introduce against the defendant. In order to admit prior bad act evidence, a court must be satisfied that the following criteria are met:

(1) the evidence must have a proper purpose under Rule 404(b);

(2) it must be relevant under Rule 402; and (3) its probative value must outweigh its prejudicial effect under Rule 403. If the evidence is admitted, the court must charge the jury to consider the evidence only for the limited purpose for which it is admitted.

Rule 404(b) in limine motions should be used to limit or preclude the introduction of the Be advised that Fed. R. Evid. 404(b) issues may arise should the defendant opt to introduce character evidence on his/her behalf. See United States v. Curtis, 644 F.2d 263, 268 (3d Cir. 1981), for a good discussion of the differences between opinion and reputation evidence when introduced to establish good character pursuant to Fed. R. Evid. 405. See United States v. Vue, 13 F.3d 1206, 1211 (8th Cir. 1994) (reversing conviction of two brothers of Hmong descent because government called agent to testify that 95% of cases involving heroin involve individuals of Hmong descent; court relied on Fed. R. Evid. 401 & 403 and found due process and equal protection violations); United States v. Rodriguez Cortes 949 F.2d 532, 541 (1st Cir. 1991) (admission at cocaine conspiracy trial of Columbian identity card bearing photo of defendant who was U.S. resident was sufficiently prejudicial to spoil conviction); see also United States v. Doe, 903 F.2d 16, 20 (D.C. Ct. App. 1990) (expert testimony that local retail drug market had been taken over by Jamaicans was irrelevant and unfairly prejudicial where defendants were Jamaican). But see United States v. Alzanti, 54 F.3d 994, 1007-08 (1st Cir. 1995) (permitting evidence of repressive Kuwaiti customs and practices toward domestic workers in trial of defendant on charge of holding household employee in involuntary servitude).

145 See United States v. Karas, 950 F.2d 31, 37 (1st Cir. 1991).

146 519 U.S. 172, 174 (1997) regarding defendant's prior arrests, convictions, use of aliases, probation/parole status, etc. Additionally, given the negative stereotype many jurors have toward non-American nationals, several appellate courts have also held that introducing information concerning the nationality of a defendant may be unduly prejudicial. Admission of 404(b) evidence may also be contingent upon the defense presented. Notably, the First Circuit has held that if no defense is presented, defense counsel's opening statement cannot open the door to other crimes evidence.145 Additionally, the Supreme Court, in Old Chief v. United States, held that: A district court abuses its discretion under Rule 403 if it spurns a defendant's offer to concede a prior judgment and admits the full judgment record over the defendant's objection, when the name or nature of the prior offense raises the risk of a verdict tainted by improper considerations, and when the purpose of the evidence is solely to prove the element of prior conviction.

There had been a split in the circuits on this issue when the stipulation concerned an element of the offense charged and the defense theory is that the offense charged never took 604 F.2d 748, 751 (2d Cir. 1979). 148 See, e.g.,United States v. Tokars, 95 F.3d 1520, 1537 (11th Cir. 1996) (admitting articles about money laundering where defendant, who was charged with that offense, never stipulated in writing that intent was not an issue for jury consideration yet asserted that he never denied knowing how to launder money); United States v. Colon, 880 F.2d 650, 660 (2d Cir. 1989); see also United States v. Williford, 764 F.2d 1493, 1498 (11th Cir. 1985) ("This circuit has refused to adopt a per se rule either for or against admission of evidence when that evidence is relevant to an issue to which the defendant offers to stipulate. Rather, we analyze the offer to stipulate as one factor in making the Rule 403 determination."). See United States v. Myers, 123 F.3d 350, 363 (6th Cir. 1997); United States v. Brown, 34 F.3d 569, 573 (7th Cir. 1994); United States v. Wallace, 32 F.3d 921, 927-28 (5th Cir. 1994); United States v. Mayans, 17 F.3d 1174, 1182 (9th Cir. 1994); United States v. Hernandez, 975 F.2d 1035, 1040 (4th Cir. 1992); United States v. Gano, 560 F.2d 990, 993 (10th Cir. 1977).

150 United States v. Garcia, 983 F.2d 1160, 1175 (1st Cir. 1993).

151 United States v. Jemal, 26 F.3d 1267, 1274 (3d Cir. 1994).

place. In United States v. Mohel, the Second Circuit held that "under Rule 404(b) bad acts evidence must be relevant to an 'actual' issue and that an offer to stipulate to an issue removes it from the case."147 This remains the general rule in both the Second and the Eleventh Circuits, although the Eleventh Circuit has never reversed a conviction on this basis and appears to have embraced a contrary position in earlier cases.148 The Fourth, Fifth, Sixth, Seventh, Ninth, and Tenth Circuits have rejected the position of the Second Circuit, concluding that bad acts evidence may be admissible to prove an element of a crime regardless whether that element is "in dispute."149

Other circuits have been somewhat equivocal. The First Circuit, while suggesting that a defendant's offer to stipulate to an element renders evidence of other bad acts inadmissible to prove that element, has also stated that "[i]n the final analysis, . . . whether such an offer is accepted remains in the sound discretion of the district judge."150 The Third Circuit has noted that "district courts should generally deem prior bad acts evidence inadmissible to prove an issue that the defendant makes clear he is not contesting,"151 but has refused to adopt a per se rule of 152 See id.; United States v. Provenzano, 620 F.2d 985, 1003-04 (3d Cir. 1980).

Compare United States v. Sumner, 119 F.3d 658, 660-61 (8th Cir. 1997) (supporting per se rule of exclusion) with United States v. Barry, 133 F.3d 580, 582 (8th Cir. 1998) (acknowledging general rule of circuit that "the government is not bound by a defendant's offer to stipulate") (internal quotation and citation marks omitted).

154See United States v. Spence, 125 F.3d 1192, 1194 n. 2 (8th Cir. 1997).

155United States v. Crowder, 141 F.3d 1202, 1209 (D.C. Cir. 1998) (citations omitted).

exclusion.152

The Eighth Circuit seems to have taken inconsistent positions on the issue.153 In a decision handed down after Old Chief, however, the Eighth Circuit acknowledged that the Supreme Court's decision may have resolved the Rule 404 (b) question concerning stipulated conduct once and for all.154 Finally, in a case on remand for reconsideration in light of Old Chief, the D.C. Circuit held that [A] defendant's offer to stipulate to an element of an offense does not render the government's other crimes evidence inadmissible under Rule 404(b) to prove that element, even if the defendant's proposed stipulation is unequivocal, and even if the defendant agrees to a jury instruction . . . Other rules of evidence may bear on the admissibility of evidence satisfying Rule 404(b) . . . For now it is enough to repeat the words of the advisory committee on Rule 404(b): if evidence is offered for a purpose Rule 404(b) permits, such as proving knowledge or intent, Rule 404(b) "does not require that the evidence be excluded."155

2. Fed. R. Evid. 609 Motions

Rule 609 motions restrict impeachment by evidence of prior criminal convictions. This rule must be reviewed carefully prior to deciding who will testify on the defendant's behalf, whether the defendant will testify, and how to impeach prosecution witnesses. Take particular note of the following language of Rule 609(b): However, evidence of a conviction more than ten years old as 156 463 F.2d 721 (3d Cir. 1972). 157 Id. at 721.

158 Id. at 724-25.

Whether a prior conviction is calculated herein, is not admissible unless the proponent gives the adverse party sufficient written notice of intent to use such evidence to provide the adverse party with a fair opportunity to contest the use of such evidence.

3. Motions To Strike Aliases From Indictment

While this issue can often be disposed of by a 404(b) motion, a separate motion premised on United States v. Beedle156, may also be appropriate. In Beedle, the alias was included in the indictment because the prosecutor did not have the correct spelling of the defendant's name when the indictment was filed.157 The government and the defense agreed to have the alias removed from the indictment. The judge, however, made reference to the alias and failed to explain the reason for the appearance of the alias on the indictment to the jury. The trial court's reference to the defendant's alias was among the reasons the Third Circuit cited in remanding this case and ordering a new trial.158

4. Government Motions In Limine

In limine motions by the government have become increasingly common and should be anticipated. This is particularly so when the government expects that the defendant will raise an affirmative defense or pursue a line of cross-examination with respect to the background of a government witness. The object of the motions is to prevent the jury from hearing anything about the issue at trial.

I. BILL OF PARTICULARS – FED. R. CRIM. P. 7(f)

A request for a bill of particulars should be filed in cases involving complicated fact 159 See generally United States v. Rosa, 891 F.2d 1074 (3d Cir. 1989), for a detailed discussion of the use of bills of particulars in the Third Circuit. See also Appendix - Sample Motion for Bill of Particulars. patterns. A bill of particulars is also advisable where the indictment is written in vague terms and provides little information as to the exact conduct that the government is alleging is criminal in nature or that constitutes the overt acts underlying a conspiracy indictment. The bill of particulars may not, however, be used to circumvent the discovery scheme of Fed. R. Crim. P. 16.159 If ordered, the government's theory and evidence at trial will be limited by the bill of particulars.

J. MOTIONS TO CONTINUE SENTENCING

Although there are no Speedy Trial Act, statutory, or case law considerations governing the expedient imposition of sentence, there is a standing order in this district regarding guideline sentencing. This order was revised to expand the time allotted for the preparation of the Presentence report and to adjust the time frame for the dissemination of the report, comments, and submission of memoranda to the court.160 Section (f)(1) requires that: [n]ot less than fifteen calendar days prior to the date for sentencing, the government shall submit its sentencing memorandum and any motions for departure to the Court, to the probation officer and to defense counsel. The motions for departure shall include motions based upon U.S.S.G. § 5K1.1 and/or 18 U.S.C. § 3553(e).

The standing order has also been revised to require that the defendant submit his/her sentencing memorandum and motions for departure to the Court, to the probation officer and to the government, not less than ten calendar days before the date of sentencing and any response by the government is to be submitted five calendar days prior to sentencing. For cooperating defendants, the government will often seek a continuance of the Should the defendant opt to cooperate after sentencing, Fed. R. Crim. P. 35(b) allows modification of his/her sentencing within one year of the date of sentencing.

A cooperating defendant's sentencing should be delayed until after the government has fully taken advantage of his/her assistance. This request may be either informal or in writing, depending on the preferred practice of the court. Generally, a defendant will not be sentenced until he/she has been fully debriefed, has testified at any and all grand jury appearances, trials, sentencing hearings, and/or any other collateral proceedings in which his/her testimony may be desired. It is presumed that the cooperator's testimony is more credible at trial if sentence has yet to be imposed. Although the defendant may wish to be sentenced as soon as possible, it is often in his/her best interest to agree to the continuance until his/her cooperation has been fully exhausted so that he/she can get the maximum benefit at sentencing.

NOTES

Chapter VIII

Trial Strategies

THE TRIAL AND SPECIFIC DEFENSES

This Chapter addresses the procedural and practical aspects of trying a case in the District of New Jersey, and includes a substantive discussion of some specific defenses available in federal court.197 Refer also to the manual published by the Federal Defenders of San Diego, Inc., which contains an excellent discussion of several defenses, in particular, duress/necessity, entrapment, outrageous government conduct, and insanity.

A. THE TRIAL

1. Scheduling The Trial

At the arraignment, the court usually sets a trial date. While in most cases, this date is flexible, in others, it is a firm date and adjournments will only be granted for compelling reasons. The judge's deputy clerk can inform counsel as to the practice of the court. If the trial needs to be rescheduled, contact the AUSA and the judge's deputy clerk immediately. Be aware that lengthy continuances are rarely granted.

2. Selecting The Jury Panel

Rule 24, 28 U.S.C. §§ 1861-1878, and the Jury Selection Plan for the District of New Jersey govern jury selection.199 Note, however, that jury selection varies according to the judge See Rosales-Lopez v. United States, 451 U.S. 182, 188 (1981) (federal judges accorded ample discretion in determining how to conduct voir dire); United States v. Greer, 968 F.2d 433, 435 (5th Cir. 1992), (same), cert. denied, 507 U.S. 962 (1993).

201 See Peretz v. United States, 501 U.S. 923, 931 (magistrate judges may, with parties' consent, supervise jury selection in felony trial); Government of the Virgin Islands v. Williams, 892 F.2d 305, 310 (3d Cir. 1989) (district court may delegate voir dire to magistrate judge as "additional duty" as long as defendant expresses no objection), cert. denied, 495 U.S. 949 (1990) .The film contains some useful information about jury duty in general. At some point, counsel should take the opportunity to view the orientation film.

Furthermore, jury selection may be conducted by either the district judge or the magistrate judge, depending on the defendant's consent. An orientation program for all potential jurors, which includes the viewing of a film on jury duty, is conducted by a deputy clerk.202 After the initial orientation and film, jury panels are directed to a courtroom where a trial is commencing.

Those jurors not selected during their first appearance will be required, depending upon the court, to return either the following day or week. (A few courts, however, select juries for multiple cases at one time and from one panel.) As a result, the panel in later cases often consists of jurors who have been stricken from other cases. If a juror serves on a jury and the trial ends before the next panel is due to report, the juror will often be required to return for additional service. Federal jurors generally serve for one month.

The size of the panel varies based on the number of jurors available and the type of case. Once the panel is assembled in the courtroom, the judge provides more specific instructions regarding the process and the case. Counsel will receive only a list of the jurors' names and addresses. The deputy clerk randomly selects twelve jurors and those jurors are seated in the order called. This procedure can be important if the judge designates juror number one as the foreperson. Some judges allow the jury to elect the foreperson. Counsel should ensure that the client is appropriately dressed during and in the courtroom (and, if in custody, is unshackled)

205 See generally Mu'Min v. Virginia, 500 U.S. 415 (1991).

206 See Rosales-Lopez v. United States, 451 U.S. 182, 191 (1981).

207 In multi-defendant cases, the judge may increase the number of defense peremptories and divide them among all defense counsel.

The jurors provide biographical information and answer questions posed by the judge. Attorney voir dire is generally not permitted in this district. It is therefore imperative that counsel submit proposed voir dire questions in writing before the start of the trial.204 Some judges will permit jury questionnaires to be used in complex or high publicity cases. Unfortunately, voir dire is often cursory at best.

The Supreme Court has traditionally afforded trial courts great latitude in conducting voir dire.205 In some cases, however, the judge must probe specific issues. For instance, where the defendant is accused of a violent crime against a victim of a different racial or ethnic group, the trial court is compelled to voir dire the panel on the issue of racial prejudice. Some judges will pre-qualify a panel before any peremptory challenges are exercised. Challenges for cause are discussed at side bar to avoid the potential of infecting an entire panel.

a. Peremptory Challenges

Rule 24(b) affords the defense ten peremptory challenges and the government six peremptory challenges.207 If the offense charged is punishable by death, each side is entitled to twenty peremptory challenges. As with every other facet of jury selection, the method for exercising peremptory challenges varies from court to court. Many judges require the attorney to stand and announce the strike: "Your Honor, please thank and excuse juror number five." Others provide a jury selection sheet to counsel during each round. If counsel wishes to exercise a peremptory, he/she does so by crossing a line through the juror's name. The deputy clerk will announce the strike and call another juror.

Alternatively, some courts require that attorneys exercise strikes in strict conformance with the federal rules. Under this system, counsel must use (or lose) any strikes in a given round. For example, if counsel has two strikes in a given round but only exercises one, the second is lost. Likewise, if counsel passes in a given round, those strikes are waived. Alternates are selected in a similar manner. After the twelve jurors are seated, each side has one peremptory challenge. Peremptory challenges not used when selecting the jury do not carry over to the alternate selection phase. The number of alternates selected will vary depending upon the length of the case. If more than two will be selected, generally in lengthy cases, judges will often permit additional peremptories. In some courts, the alternates will not know that they have been selected as alternates at the beginning of the case. Other courts are explicit about the distinction before the trial begins. Learn the procedure followed by the court prior to selection.

208 476 U.S. 79 (1986). Batson was decided under the Equal Protection Clause of the Fourteenth Amendment. For challenges based on the Sixth Amendment right to a jury that represents a fair cross-section of the community, see Holland v. Illinois, 493 U.S. 474 (1990).

209 499 U.S. 400 (1991).

210 505 U.S. 42 (1992).

211 See McCollum, 505 U.S. at 59 ("We hold that the Constitution prohibits a criminal defendant from engaging in purposeful discrimination on the grounds of race in the exercise of peremptory challenges. Accordingly, if the State demonstrates a prima facie case of racial discrimination by the defendants, the defendants must articulate a racially neutral explanation for peremptory challenges.")

212See id. at 57.

i. Peremptory Challenges - Race

Batson v. Kentucky,208 Powers v. Ohio,209 and Georgia v. McCollum,210 are the primary cases addressing jury selection. Batson established that race-based peremptory challenges are unconstitutional. Powers expanded Batson, declaring that white defendants likewise have standing to assert equal protection rights to keep the government from striking black venirepersons on the basis of race. Conversely, McCollum made the prohibitions of Batson applicable to the defense's use of peremptory challenges. Justice Blackmun's majority opinion in McCollum also served as notice of the precarious status of the peremptory challenge. He reconfirmed the Court's position that peremptory challenges are not a constitutionally protected fundamental right: As a preliminary matter, it is important to recall that peremptory challenges are not constitutionally protected fundamental rights; rather, they are but one state-created means to the constitutional end of an impartial jury and a fair trial. This Court has repeatedly stated that the right to a peremptory challenge may be withheld altogether without impairing the constitutional guarantee of an impartial jury and a fair trial. Defense attorneys can now expect that the government will ask for race-neutral

213 511 U.S. 127 (1994).

214 Id. at 131.

215 Id.

216 See also United States v. Omoruyi, 7 F.3d 880, 882 (9th Cir. 1993) (prosecutor's use of peremptory challenges to strike unmarried women violates Batson); United States v. DeGross, 960 F.2d 1433, 1440 (9th Cir. 1992) (en banc) (peremptory strikes based on gender are universally impermissible: "Whether the prosecutor or the defense exercises the strike, the excluded venire persons are harmed because discriminatory strikes are based on group membership whereas juror competence depends upon an individual's qualifications."). 217 500 U.S. 352 (1991). 218 Id. at 363.

Absent that explanation, the challenged juror will be impaneled. To use peremptory challenges effectively, defense attorneys must be familiar with the justifications for peremptory strikes that courts have accepted as race-neutral.

ii. Peremptory Challenges - Gender

The Supreme Court has expanded the teachings of Batson and McCollum to prohibit peremptory strikes based on gender.

216 In J.E.B. v. Alabama ex rel. T.B.,213 the Supreme Court held that a state actor's intentional discrimination on the basis of gender in the use of peremptory strikes violates the equal protection clause.214 This conclusion obtains because distinctions based on gender are afforded heightened equal protection scrutiny and gender-based peremptory challenges cannot survive such heightened scrutiny.215 The Court resolved a previous circuit split over this issue.

iii. Peremptory Challenges - Language Ability

In Hernandez v. New York, the Supreme Court permitted a prosecutor to strike Spanish-speaking Latinos because the prosecutor was uncertain whether Spanish-speaking jurors would be able to listen and to accept an interpreter's translation as the controlling testimony. See e.g. 28 U.S.C. §1865(b)(2), (3) (English-language ability required for federal jury service) 220 See 500 U.S. at 365.

221 See Pemberthy v. Beyer, 19 F.3d 857, 870 (3d Cir.), cert. denied, 513 U.S. 969 (1994).

222 See United States v. Clemons, 843 F.2d 741, 748 (3d Cir.), cert denied, 488 U.S. 835 (1988).

223 See United States v. Jimenez, 77 F.3d 95, 100 (5th Cir. 1996); see also Howard v. Moore, 131 F.3d 399, 408 (4th Cir. 1997) (both age and employment status are legitimate race-neutral factors), cert. denied, 525 U.S. 843 (1998).

Itis a harsh paradox that one may become proficient enough in English to participate in a trial, only to encounter disqualification because he/she knows a second language as well. Nonetheless, applying the analysis of Hernandez, the Third Circuit has held that Batson does not apply to peremptory challenges based on language ability because that classification, unlike gender or race, is not subject to heightened or strict scrutiny.

iv. Peremptory Challenges - Age, Employment & Education

Challenges based on age, unemployment, lack of education have been accepted as race neutral by the courts.

(1) Age

A prosecutor's explanation that he/she was striking all young, single panel members was held by the Third Circuit to be a race-neutral, non-pretextual reason sufficient to satisfy Batson The Fifth Circuit similarly ruled that the fact that a prospective African-American juror was too young, uneducated, and lacking a religious preference was a race-neutral reason for striking that juror.223

(2) Employment Status

A juror's unemployment status is, according to the Seventh Circuit, a race-neutral, valid reason for exclusion. See United States v. Lewis, 117 F.3d 980, 983 (7th Cir.), cert. denied, 522 U.S. 1035 (1997). 225See United States v. Pofahl, 990 F.2d 1456, 1465 (5th Cir.), cert. denied, 510 U.S. 898 (1993) and 510 U.S. 996 (1993); see also Garcia v. Excel Corp., 102 F.3d 758, 759-760 (5th Cir. 1997) (in work injury case, permissible to strike African-American and Hispanic jurors who were unemployed or had unemployed spouses)

226See Pofahl, 990 F.2d at 1466.

227See United States v. Uwaezhoke, 995 F.2d 388, 390-91, 393-95 (3d Cir. 1993), cert. denied, 510 U.S. 1091 (1994).

228See United States v. Moeller, 80 F.3d 1053, 1060 (5th Cir. 1996).

229See United States v. Gibson, 105 F.3d 1229, 1232 (8th Cir. 1997); United States v. Hunter, 86 F.3d 679, 683 (7th Cir.), cert. denied, 519 U.S. 985 (1996).

230See United States v. Casper, 956 F.2d 416, 419 (3d Cir. 1992).

224 The Fifth Circuit agreed, in United States v. Pofahl. In Pofahl, the government struck one Hispanic and two black jurors because of their occupations, school bus driver and auto mechanic, as well as their dress and demeanor.

225 The Fifth Circuit ruled that a tendency to strike jurors on economic grounds because the government wants a "middle class" jury is acceptable.

226 Finally, the Third Circuit has accepted as race-neutral the prosecutor's rationale that a black, single mother of modest means living in low-income housing was more likely to have been exposed to drug trafficking than someone who did not live in low income housing, and thus she could be stricken without violating Batson.

(3) Education

The Fifth Circuit has held that requiring jurors to have at least a high school education was appropriate in certain cases.

228 In the Eighth and Seventh Circuits, peremptory challenges based on jurors' lack of education and disinterest in or confusion about the proceedings have been upheld as race-neutral.

229 Finally, the Third Circuit has held that a challenge based on inarticulate and evasive responses to voir dire was race-neutral.230

231 959 F.2d 820 (9th Cir. 1992).

232 Id. at 825.

233 See id.; but see United States v. Uwaezhoke, 995 F.2d 388, 394 n. 15 (3d Cir. 1993) (nothing in Hernandez plurality opinion suggests that prosecutor must offer nexus between specific juror and particular case that tends to demonstrate that juror would be unable to fairly evaluate the evidence; disagreeing with Ninth Circuit's view that Hernandez "strongly suggests" that such nexus must exist for prosecutor's explanation to be facially valid), cert. denied, 510 U.S. 1091 (1994).

v. Peremptory Challenges - Challenges Using A Proxy For An Impermissible Reason

To use peremptory challenges effectively, to protect the record, and to guard against abuses by the government, defense counsel must ensure that peremptory challenges are not based on a race-neutral proxy for an unconstitutional justification. In United States v. Bishop,231 the Ninth Circuit held that a peremptory strike based on the fact that the juror lived in a poor, violent area was in fact not race-neutral.232 The Ninth Circuit found that the government's reasons for the strike constituted a proxy for a race-based peremptory strike:

To strike black jurors who reside in such communities (Compton) on the assumption they will sympathize with a black defendant rather than the police is akin to striking jurors who speak Spanish merely because the case involves Spanish-speaking witnesses. The Court in Hernandez strongly suggested that more was required – namely, the prosecutor's belief that the particular juror might not accept the proposed translation.233

3. Motions In Limine - F.Rule Evid.104

The defense will have an opportunity to argue and/or present motion(s) in limine before trial begins. Motions in limine based on Rule 404(b) and Rule 609 and motions to strike aliases, which are fairly typical in limine motions, are covered in some detail in Chapter Four § H, supra.

4. The Record

In this district, most judges use a stenographer. Some judges, however, utilize the tape

234 See Appendix - CJA Form 24.

235 See Fed. R. Crim. P. 29(a).

Recording system. There are two aspects to the tape recording system which must be recognized by counsel at the outset: **First, if the trial is tape recorded, all discussions will be on the record. More importantly, if the microphones at counsel table are activated, all conversations are heard, even when court is not in session.** Avoid having any discussions with the defendant recorded.

If daily transcripts of the trial are necessary, the judge's approval will be needed. The court reporter should be informed that daily transcripts have been ordered so that he/she will be able to accommodate the request. If the judge approves a request for transcripts, counsel should file a CJA Form 24 with the clerk.234 Counsel must confirm that the court has received and signed the completed CJA 24.

5. Pretrial Stipulations

The AUSA is likely to seek pretrial stipulations regarding chemical analysis results, the interstate commerce element of the offense, ballistics results, the defendant's prior conviction punishable by a term of imprisonment in excess of one year, chain of custody, and the authenticity of documents. Agreeing to a stipulation may be beneficial to the case. It may also precipitate the early disclosure of Jencks or facilitate a stipulation regarding another issue.

6. Motion For Judgment Of Acquittal - Fed. R. Crim. P. 29

A motion for judgment of acquittal pursuant to Fed. R. Crim. P. 29, which is the equivalent of a motion for directed verdict in state court, can be made by the defendant or the court.235 It can be made at the close of the government's case and/or after the defense rests, 236See Fed. R.

Crim. P. 43(b); see generally Crosby v. U.S., 506 U.S. 255, 262 (1993),outside the presence of the jury.

A motion for acquittal need not be directed at all charges. Under Rule 29(a), the court may order entry of judgment of acquittal as to one or more offenses charged in the indictment or information. Section 29(b) allows the judge to reserve decision on the motion, to consider the motion after the case has been submitted to the jury, and to decide the motion either before the jury returns a verdict or even after the jury returns a guilty verdict. Section 29(c) permits the court to consider a Rule 29 motion up to seven days after the discharge of the jury, regardless of whether a verdict was returned. The court may, during the seven days, extend that time-frame. Section 29(d) addresses conditional rulings on Rule 29 motions.

7. Presence Of Defendant – Fed. R. Crim. P. 43

Rule 43 outlines when the defendant must be present and when his/her presence is optional. Pursuant to Rule 43(a), a defendant must be present at arraignment, at the time of the plea, at every stage of the trial, and at the imposition of sentence, unless otherwise provided by the rule. Circumstances under which the continued presence of the defendant at trial is not required are listed in Rule 43(b). Those instances in which the defendant's presence is never required are identified in Rule 43(c).

Rule 43 directs that a defendant who is voluntarily absent before trial shall be treated differently from one who becomes absent after the trial has begun. If a defendant flees after trial has begun, he/she may be tried and sentenced in absentia.236

237 See www.ca3.uscourts.gov/modeljuryinstructions.htm.

238 Kevin O'Malley, Jay E. Grenig, Hon. William C. Lee, Federal Jury Practice and Instructions (6th ed. 2006).

239 See Mathews v. United States, 485 U.S. 58, 63 (1988) ("A defendant is entitled to an instruction as to any recognized defense for which there exists evidence sufficient for a reasonable jury to find in his favor"); United States v. Mercer, 853 F.2d 630, 633 (8th Cir. 1988) (defendant is entitled to have jury instructed on defense theory if defense timely submits instruction that correctly states applicable law and is supported by evidence), cert. denied, 488 U.S. 996 (1988) and cert. denied, 490 U.S. 1110 (1989).

8. Jury Charges

In September 2004, a committee appointed by the Third Circuit began drafting model jury instructions for use in the Circuit. The final set of model instructions includes preliminary and final instructions, instructions for use during trial and instructions covering the most frequently litigated federal crimes and defenses. In addition to model instructions, the committee also prepared Comments to accompany each instruction, summarizing relevant Third Circuit and Supreme Court precedent. The model instructions and accompanying comments are available on the Third Circuit's website in both WordPerfect and PDF formats.237

The government will submit proposed jury instructions in virtually all cases. The proposed instructions come from a number of sources, including the Third Circuit's model instructions, edited renditions of O'Malley, Grenig & Lee238 pattern instructions, or hybrid instructions developed by the government. Carefully review the submitted instructions – it is not uncommon for the proposed instructions to contain argument or overstatements of the holding in a particular case. Also, supplement or correct any inaccuracies the proposed instructions contain.

240 Defense counsel should also submit proposed instructions. A defendant generally is entitled to an instruction on his/her theory as long as evidence to support the instruction has been adduced at trial and the proposed instruction correctly states the applicable law.239 Note, See Edward J. Devitt, Charles B. Blackmar, Michael A. Wolff & Kevin F. O'Malley, Federal Jury Practice and Instructions § 19.01, at 723-24 (4th ed. 1992) ("A defendant is entitled to a theory of the defense instruction which is supported by the law and the evidence received in the case, and if it is not redundant with other instructions. The precise wording of the instruction is committed to the discretion of the trial court. If the theory of the defense instruction is a correct legal statement directed to an issue in the case, it should be given.").

241 362 U.S. 402 (1960).

242 See Godinez v. Moran, 509 U.S. 389, 397 (1993) (Dusky standard for competency to stand trial will also serve for determination of competency to plead guilty and to waive right to counsel). However, that the precise language of the point for charge is up to the court. Judges in this district generally give comprehensive instructions. Counsel should, therefore, consider submitting a select number of instructions and urge that these be given in addition to, or in lieu of, the judge's charge or the government's proposed instructions. Whether a printed version of the instructions will be provided to the jury is in the court's discretion.

B. COMPETENCY ISSUES AND INSANITY DEFENSES IN FEDERAL COURT

1. Competency To Stand Trial And/Or To Be Sentenced

Competency to stand trial differs from the defense of insanity. Competency issues address the accused's state of mind at the time of trial. Insanity issues concern the individual's state of mind at the time of the conduct that led to the charges.

The criteria to determine competency to stand trial in federal court were articulated by the Supreme Court in Dusky v. United States.241 A competency examination must evaluate whether the defendant has sufficient present ability to consult with his/her lawyer with a reasonable degree of rational understanding and whether he/she has a rational as well as factual understanding of the proceedings against him/her.242

Either the defendant or the government can file a motion to determine the competency of 243 See 18 U.S.C. § 4241(a); see also Appendix - Sample Notice of Motion for Competency Hearing and Psychiatric Study.

244 But see United States v. DiGilio, 538 F.2d 972, 988 n. 20 (3d Cir. 1976) ("The district court can, of course, allocate the burden of going forward with the evidence bearing on competence in any manner which will provide for the expeditious development of the facts relevant to its § 4244 determination."), cert. denied, 429 U.S. 1038 (1977).

245 See 18 U.S.C. § 4241(d)(1).

246 See 18 U.S.C. § 4241(d)(2)(A).

247 See 18 U.S.C. § 4241(f).

The individual to stand trial.243 The government, however, bears the burden of proof by a preponderance of the evidence at the hearing.244 The scope of the questions concerning competency should be limited, and the examiner should not discuss the facts of the instant case.

Upon a finding by a preponderance of the evidence that the individual is incompetent, the defendant will be committed to the custody of the Attorney General for treatment for a period not to exceed four months.245 Detention may be extended if the court makes an explicit finding that the defendant may become competent within a given period of time.246 If it appears that the defendant will not become competent within the specified time of detention, further detention can then be pursued under 18 U.S.C. § 4246. Finally, always object to the use of dual evaluations addressing competency and sanity in the same examination performed by the same doctor. A determination that the defendant is competent to stand trial does not preclude an insanity defense, and the competency conclusion is inadmissible at trial.247

2. Insanity Defense – 18 U.S.C. § 17

(a) Affirmative Defense - It is an affirmative defense to a

prosecution under any federal statute that, at the time of the commission of the acts constituting the offense, the defendant, as a 248 18 U.S.C. § 17.

249 See Appendix - Notice of Insanity Defense.

250 18 U.S.C. § 4242(a) (1998) (mandating the court, upon government motion, to order psychiatric or psychological examination of defendant once defense files notice under Fed. R. Crim. P. 12.2).

251 See Fed. R. Crim. P. 12.2(c). result of a severe mental disease or defect, was unable to appreciate the nature and quality or the wrongfulness of his acts. Mental disease or defect does not otherwise constitute a defense.

(b) Burden of proof - The defendant has the burden of proving the defense of insanity by clear and convincing evidence.248 Pursuant to Fed. R. Crim. P. 12.2(a), defense counsel must notify the government if it intends to argue insanity as a defense.249 Rule 12.2(b) requires that the defense must also notify the government if it intends to call an expert to testify. Rule 12.2(c) permits the court to order the defendant to submit to an examination upon the request of the government.250 Although Rule 12.2(c) so authorizes the court, nothing that the defendant says during such an examination can be used against the defendant, "except on an issue respecting mental condition on which the defendant has introduced testimony."251

Defense counsel should request that the client be evaluated locally, rather than at a distant Bureau of Prisons' mental health facility, in order to conserve time and resources. Counsel should also request to be present during the evaluation or, alternatively, request that a defense psychiatrist examine the defendant. Another alternative is to make a written request that the court order a videotaped evaluation under 18 U.S.C. § 4247(f). At a minimum, defense counsel should request that only the defendant and the court-appointed psychiatrist be present during the interview. Also, all information relied upon by the government's psychiatrist should be disclosed

252 See Shannon v. United States, 512 U.S. 573, 579 (1994); see also United States v. Fisher, 10 F.3d 115, 121 (3d Cir. 1993), cert. denied, 512 U.S. 1238 (1994).

253 Remember also that an imperfect insanity defense can constitute a ground for a downward departure at sentencing under U.S.S.G. §5K2.13 (Diminished Capacity). For a more detailed discussion of this issue, see Defending a Federal Criminal Case, supra Note 118, Volume II, Ch. 17, which includes an extensive bibliography of reference materials.

254 Refer to Defending a Federal Criminal Case, supra Note 118, Volume I, Ch. 8, for an extensive discussion of specific defenses (non-mental health).

To the defendant under Fed. R. Crim. P. 16(a)(1)(C)-(D).

The Insanity Defense Reform Act, 18 U.S.C. §§ 4241-47, does not require the trial court to instruct the jury regarding the consequences of a verdict of not guilty by reason of insanity.252 If a defendant is found not guilty by reason of insanity, § 4243(c) mandates that a hearing concerning a defendant's eligibility for discharge occur within forty days. Section 4243(d) places the burden of proof on the defendant, and the standard applicable is a function of the offense of conviction:

(d) Burden of proof - In a hearing under subsection (c) of this section, a person found not guilty by reason of insanity of an offense involving bodily injury to, or serious damage to the property of another person, or involving a substantial risk of such injury or damage, has the burden of proving by clear and convincing evidence that his release would not create a substantial risk of bodily injury to another person or serious damage of property of another due to a present mental disease or defect. With respect to any other offense, the person has the burden of such proof by a preponderance of the evidence.253

C. SPECIFIC DEFENSES

This section presents a brief overview of some of the more commonly employed legal defenses. It is not an exhaustive list of possible legal defenses, and it does not address factual defenses.254

255 See Appendix - Notice of Alibi Defense.

256 606 F.2d 47 (3d Cir. 1979).

257 Id. at 49.

The advisory sentencing guidelines must be considered before formulating any trial defense. Remember that an imperfect or unsuccessful trial defenses might, nevertheless, lead to a downward departure, including departures based on U.S.S.G. § 5K2.10, Victim's Conduct (self defense), U.S.S.G. § 5K2.11, Lesser Harms (justification), U.S.S.G. § 5K2.12, Coercion and Duress, and U.S.S.G. § 5K2.13, Diminished Capacity (competency/insanity). Be aware, however, that if the defendant testifies and the judge believes that he/she is less than truthful, that strategy could hurt the defendant at sentencing. It could also possibly be used to justify an upward departure and/or an adjustment under U.S.S.G. § 3C1.1.

1. Alibi

Rule 12.1, discussed in Chapter Three, § B(2), sets forth the procedural requirements for the use of an alibi defense.255 Be prepared, however, for the fact that the government will investigate the alibi and contact witnesses to interview them about the alibi. Witnesses should, therefore, be prepared accordingly.

2. Entrapment

The United States Attorney's office typically cites United States v. Levin256, to argue that defense counsel must give prompt notice of an entrapment defense. The relevant language in Levin does not go that far: Therefore, we hold that a defendant is not entitled to an instruction on entrapment unless he explicitly pleads, at a sufficiently early point in the trial, that he was entrapped.257

258 See generally Jacobson v. United States, 503 U.S. 540 (1992) (citations and internal quotation marks omitted).

259 United States v. Wright, 921 F.2d 42, 44 (3d Cir. 1990), cert. denied, 501 U.S. 1207 (1991).

260 See United States v. Bay, 852 F.2d 702, 705 (3d Cir. 1988) (evidence that defendant initiated conversations that led to indictment is enough to show predisposition); cf. United States v. Marino, 868 F.2d 549, 551 (3d Cir. 1989) (mere solicitation or request by law enforcement officials to engage in criminal activity is not by itself an inducement), cert. denied, 492 U.S. 918 (1989).

Although the entrapment defense is a viable defense, its requirements are exacting.258 The Third Circuit has articulated the proof needed for a successful entrapment defense: Entrapment is a relatively limited defense that may defeat a prosecution only when the government's deception actually implants the criminal design in the mind of the defendant. A valid entrapment defense has two related elements: (1) government inducement of the crime, and (2) a lack of predisposition on the part of the defendant to engage in the criminal conduct. The defendant has the burden of producing evidence of both inducement and non-predisposition to commit the crime. After the defendant has made this showing, . . . the government then has the burden of proving beyond a reasonable doubt that it did not entrap the defendant. We have held that the trial court should not instruct on entrapment unless the defendant has presented evidence on both prongs of the defense.259

Conversations with agents and co-defendants, prior convictions, arrests, and an assortment of other baggage that the typical defendant carries with him/her into a trial are likely admissible to rebut the defendant's asserted lack of predisposition element. This type of evidence thus often serves to defeat an entrapment defense.260

The government's evidence of predisposition must involve acts that occurred before the government initiated its plan to snare the defendant. Relevant factors in this analysis include the defendant's character, the identity of the individual who suggested the criminal activity, the nature of government's inducement, the defendant's purpose for engaging in the activity, and, most important, how the government entrapped the defendant.

261 See United States v. Skarie, 971 F.2d 317, 320 (9th Cir. 1992); see also United States v. Gambino, 788 F.2d 938, 945 (3d Cir.) (court looks to defendant's state of mind and inclinations before his initial exposure to government agents in determining predisposition), cert. denied, 479 U.S. 825 (1986).

262 See United States v. Allibhai, 939 F.2d 244, 249 (5th Cir. 1991), cert. denied, 502 U.S. 1072 (1992).

263 See Mathews v. United States, 485 U.S. 58, 62, 64-66 (1988).

264 See id.

265 See generally Hampton v. United States, 425 U.S. 484 (1976).

266 See United States v. Twigg, 588 F.2d 373, 377-81 (3d Cir. 1978); United States v. West, 511 F.2d 1083, 1086 (3d Cir. 1975).

267 See United States v. Voigt, 89 F.3d 1050, 1066 (3d Cir.) (claim of outrageous government conduct premised upon deliberate intrusion into attorney-client relationship was cognizable where defendant could point to actual and substantial prejudice), cert. denied, 519 U.S. 1047 (1996); United States v. Marshank, 777 F. Supp. 1507, 1522-25 (N. D. Cal. 1991) (deep involvement of defendant's attorney with government in making case against his

own client led district court to dismiss indictment) .Critically, the defendant's show of any reluctance.261 Note that the government needs no suspicion to target a person in an undercover sting operation.262 Importantly, a defendant need not admit to all elements of a given offense in order for the jury to be charged on entrapment.263 A defendant can deny one or more elements of the crime and still be entitled to an entrapment instruction as long as there exists sufficient evidence from which a jury could reasonably find that he/she was entrapped.264

3. Outrageous Government Conduct

Outrageous government conduct is similar to the entrapment defense, less the predisposition element that makes entrapment such a difficult proposition.265 This defense is available in theory when there has been severe overreaching by the government, and the overreaching was so overwhelming that it amounted to a denial of due process.266 Defense counsel should also be aware of cases in which outrageous conduct claims have arisen out of defense counsel's conduct.267

268 See United States v. Gonzales, 927 F.2d 139, 142-46 (3d Cir. 1991); see also United States v. Santana, 6 F.3d 1, 3, 7-8 (1st Cir. 1993) (federal authorities did not cross line by supplying 2,500 doses of heroin to member of distribution ring in order to gain credibility); see generally United States v. Cuervelo, 949 F.2d 559, 564-68 (2d Cir. 1991) (discussion of outrageous government conduct versus entrapment; case was remanded for an evidentiary hearing to determine whether DEA agent's sexual relationship with defendant amounted to outrageous government conduct).

269 444 U.S. 394 (1980).

270 See United States v. Bailey, 444 U.S. 394, 409-10 (1980); see also United States v. Santos, 932 F.2d 244, 253 (3d Cir.) (trial court's failure in narcotics prosecution to instruct jury

that defendant could establish duress as result of threats against her children was not plain error where it was unlikely that charge making specific reference to evidence of threats to children, in light of other evidence, would have affected verdict), cert. denied, 502 U.S. 985 (1991).

271 Refer to Defending a Federal Criminal Case, supra Note 118, Volume I, Ch. 8, for an extensive discussion of these two defenses.

Be aware that in this circuit, payment of informants does not generally constitute outrageous government conduct. In narcotics cases, the government may pay an informant literally hundreds of thousands of dollars. In many cases, the informant will receive a percentage of the proceeds. While many may find this practice outrageous, the Third Circuit does not. The court has held that the method of payment is an issue for the jury to consider in assessing credibility, and that it does not automatically constitute outrageous government conduct.268

4. Duress/Necessity

The Supreme Court distinguished between the defenses of duress and necessity in United States v. Bailey.269 The distinction turns on physical force. If the defendant acted under a threat of imminent death or serious bodily injury, duress is the appropriate defense. Where the defendant chose the lesser of two evils in response to threats, necessity should be argued.270 To establish either a duress or necessity defense, the defendant will likely have to testify as to the "forces" that compelled his/her actions.271 In either case, the defendant bears the burden of proof.

272 See Dixon v. United States, 548 U.S. 1, 4 (2006).

273 See United States v. Crittendon, 883 F.2d 326, 330 (4th Cir. 1989) (citation omitted); United States v. Romano, 849 F.2d 812, 816 n.7 (3d Cir. 1988); United States v. Lemon, 824 F.2d 763, 764 (9th Cir. 1987).

274 See Crittendon, 883 F.2d at 330 (citation omitted).

275 See United States v. Paolello 951 F.2d 537, 540 (3d. Cir. 1991) (citation omitted).

276 See United States v. Van Scoy, 654 F.2d 257, 266 (3d Cir.) ("Mere presence at the scene of a crime and knowledge that a crime is being committed are not sufficient to establish that the defendant aided and abetted the crime unless you find beyond a reasonable doubt that he was a participant and . . . not merely a knowing spectator."), cert. denied, 454 U.S. 1126 (1981).

Proving the defense by a preponderance of the evidence.272

5. Justification

The justification defense is similar to the duress/necessity defenses.273 Because justification is an affirmative defense, the judge will only instruct on justification if the defense establishes the elements of a justification defense.274 Note that in § 922(g) cases, the Third Circuit has taken a very restrictive approach toward a justification defense. In order to warrant an instruction on justification, the defense must establish that the defendant was subject to an immediate threat of death or serious bodily injury, that he/she had a well-grounded fear that the threat would be carried out, that he/she did not have a reasonably opportunity to escape the threatened harm without taking the gun, and that there was a direct causal link between the action and avoiding the threatened harm.275 To establish these elements, the defendant will have to testify. Therefore, consider Fed. R. Evid. 404(b), governing the use of prior bad act evidence, at the outset.

6. Mere Presence

The "mere presence" defense can be effective in those cases where the defendant was at the scene of the crime, but not as a participant. "Knowing spectators" are not criminally liable. See generally United States v. Wexler, 838 F.2d 88, 90-91 (3d Cir. 1988) ("One of the requisite elements the government must show in a conspiracy is that the alleged conspirators shared a 'unity of purpose,' the intent to achieve a common goal, and an agreement to work together toward the goal. . . . The inferences rising from 'keeping bad company' are not enough to convict a defendant for conspiracy.") (citations omitted) .

NOTES

Chapter IX

SENTENCING

The ***United States Sentencing Commission*** "Guideline Manual for 2011, is appended hereto as Appendix A.

The Bureau of Prisons

I. INTRODUCTION

The Bureau of Prisons (BOP) is charged with implementing the sentences imposed on federal offenders by the federal justice system and managing the facilities constructed for that purpose. Its 118 prisons, operated by both the federal government and private industry, address the range of possible security levels for the approximately 209,000 prisoners currently assigned to the BOP. The BOP also has responsibility for operating its administrative components, which include Federal Medical Centers conducting mental health evaluations for purposes of competency determinations and insanity defenses. Its role is therefore larger than post-judgment. The majority of attorneys will however encounter the BOP through its involvement in prisoner placement and calculation of release dates after a guilty plea enters. While the BOP has substantial authority in placing prisoners and utilizing its computations on good time credit, the sentence it is charged with implementing remains the judgment of a federal court or the U.S. Parole Commission in Prisoner Treaty Transfer cases, and only those organizations may change the underlying judgment itself.

II. BOP FACILITIES

The Bureau of Prisons operates institutions of five different security levels (i.e., minimum, low, medium, high, and administrative). Security levels are based on such features as the presence of external patrols, towers, security barriers, or detection devices; the type of housing within the institution; internal security features; and the staff-to-inmate ratio. The following is a brief description of BOP facilities, see U.S. Dep't of Justice, Bureau of Prisons, Prison Types & General Information (available at http://www.bop.gov/locations/institutions/index.jsp):

A. Minimum Security: Also known as Federal Prison Camps (FPCs), these facilities have dormitory housing, a relatively low staff-to-inmate ratio, and little to no perimeter fencing. They are work- and program-oriented; and many are located adjacent to larger institutions or on military bases, where inmates help serve the labor needs of the larger institution or base.

B. Low Security: Federal Correctional Institutions (FCIs) with double-fenced perimeters, typically dormitory or cubicle housing, and strong work and program components. The staff-to-inmate ratio in these institutions is higher than in minimum security facilities.

C. Medium Security: FCIs (and U.S. Penitentiaries (USPs) designated as medium 1Only applies to cases in which prisoner was not escorted to prison for service of sentence, surrender occurred post-sentencing and surrender was not to U.S. Marshals on security) with strengthened perimeters, such as double fences with electronic detection systems, largely cell-type housing, a wide variety of work and treatment programs, a higher staff-to-inmate ratio than low security FCIs, and even greater internal controls. Note there are no Medium security level institutions for female inmates.

D. High Security: USPs with highly-secured perimeters (featuring walls or reinforced fences), multiple- and single-occupant cell housing, the highest staff-to-inmate ratio, and close control of inmate movement.

E. Administrative: Administrative facilities have special missions, such as the detention of pretrial offenders; the treatment of inmates with serious or chronic medical problems; or the containment of extremely dangerous, violent, or escape-prone inmates. Administrative facilities include Metropolitan Correctional Centers (MCCs), Metropolitan Detention Centers (MDCs), Federal Detention Centers (FDCs), and Federal Medical Centers (FMCs), as well as the Federal Transfer Center (FTC), the Medical Center for Federal Prisoners (MCFP), and the Administrative-Maximum (ADX) U.S. Penitentiary. Administrative facilities are capable of holding inmates in all security categories.

III. INMATE CLASSIFICATION AND BOP DESIGNATION

Prisoners are classified by the BOP according to procedures set forth in Program Statement P5100.08. *See* U.S. Dep't of Justice, Bureau of Prisons, Program Statement P5100.08 (Sept. 2006). All biographical data for a particular prisoner is entered into the BOP database system, SENTRY, which produces a security score based on individual characteristics entered. This score determines the minimum security level permitted, at which point an appropriate facility is identified typically within 500 miles of the release residence designated by the prisoner. The placement authorized by the security score may be overridden, to the benefit or detriment of the individual prisoner, by variables known as Public Safety Factors or Management Variables. A custody level is also assigned to each inmate within any given security level institution.

A. SCORING

Prisoner scoring utilizes the following data: (1) sentencing, (2) programing recommendations, (3) background information from the Judgment, (4) the Statement of Reasons (SOR), and (5) the PSR. Individual components of that score are:

(1) Voluntary Surrender1? No (0 points) Yes (-3 points) sentencing date.

Assigned values according to definitions f 2 or individual offenses set forth in the Offense Severity Scale found in Policy Statement 5100.08. 3The BOP directs that the score is taken first from the judgment or SOR, then from the PSR. If no criminal history score is provided, the BOP independently applies the scoring system used by the *Guidelines* for its inmate scoring entry.

4This category assesses whether a finding entered by judgment, revocation or disciplinary hearing indicating an act of violence. The severity is assessed by the underlying conduct, not by the particular finding.

5 Escapes or attempted are graded as minor when involving minimal security and no violence or threat of violence and serious if from higher security and/or violence or a threat of violence.

6 This category assesses any pending charges and assigns points based on the severity of the pending offense using the table used to assign points to the current offense.

(2) Severity of Current Offense?2 Lowest (0 points) Low Moderate (1 point) Moderate (3 points) High (5 points) Greatest (7 points)

(3) Criminal History Score in PSR3? 0-1 (0 points) 2-3 (2 points) 4-6 (4 points) 7-9 (6 points) 10-12 (8 points) 13+ (10 points) (4) Documented History of Violence (minor/serious)4? None (0 points/0 points) >15 years (1 point/2 points) 10-15 years (1point/4 points) 5-10 years (3 points/6 points) <5 years (5 points/7 points)

(5) History of Escapes/Attempts?

(minor/serious)5? None (0 points/0 points) >15 years (1 point/3 points) 10-15 years (1 point/3 points) 5-10 years (2 points/3 points) < 5 years (3 points/3 points)

(6) Existing detainer6? None (0 points) Lowest/Low Moderate (1 point) Moderate (3 points) High (5 points) Greatest (7 points)

(7) Age? 0-1 (0 points) 55+ (0 points) 36-54 (2 points) 25-35 (4 points) <25 (6 points)

(8) Education Level? High School Graduate/GED (0 points) Progress on GED (1 point)

No Degree/Not Progressing (2 points)

(9) Drug/Alcohol Abuse? None/>5 years (0 points) <5 years (1 point)

The total of points assigned in these categories is the security score used for purposes of designation. Using the inmate's Security Score and Custody Level (discussed below), available designations are defined in P5100.08 according to the following table

Security

Level

Custody

Level

Male Female

MINIMUM COMMUNITY and OUT 0-11 points 0-15 points LOW OUT and IN 12-15 points 16-30 points MEDIUM OUT and IN 16-23 points * HIGH IN and MAXIMUM 24+ points 31+ points ADMINISTRATIVE All custody levels

PRACTICAL TIPS:

1. Under Severity of Current Offense, points are assessed reflecting the most severe documented instant offense behavior regardless of the conviction offense. Make sure you fight to remove any behavior that is not properly documented! Do your best to remove language regarding such behavior from the PSR.

2. Under History of Violence, the severity of the act of violence is assessed by the underlying conduct, not by the finding or conviction. Make sure you fight to remove any behavior that is not properly documented! Do your best to remove language regarding such behavior from the PSR.

3. If there is a pending charge, points are added under Detainer based on the documented behavior. No points are added for ICE detainers.

4. The Education Level requires that the inmate's education level be verified. Provide documentation to the probation officer if necessary.

B. PUBLIC SAFETY FACTORS

Separate from the above security score are Public Safety Factors (PSFs) that can individually effect designations. Up to three PSFs can be waived by the designation coordinator thereby giving an inmate the possibility of a lower security institution. The PSFs are as follows: (1) Sentence Length (males only). Unless waived, a male inmate with more than (1) ten years remaining to serve will be housed in at least a Low security level institution, (2) twenty years remaining will be housed in at least a Medium security level institution, and (3) thirty years remaining will be housed in at least a High security level institution.

(2) Disruptive Group (males only). If validated as a member of a disruptive group, prisoner will be assigned a "High" security level.

(3) Greatest Severity Offense (males only). If a current offense falls within the category of "Greatest Severity," prisoner may receive a minimum security level of "Low" unless waived.

(4) Sex Offender. If the PSR or other official documentation "clearly indicates" behavior that may be characterized as a sex offense, prisoner may receive a minimum security level of "Low" unless waived.

(5) Threat to Government Officials. If falling within this category, prisoner may receive a minimum security level of "Low" unless waived.

(6) Deportable Alien. Prisoner may receive a minimum security level of "Low."

(7) Violent Behavior (females only). A female inmate whose current term of confinement or history involves two convictions (or findings of commission of a prohibited act by the DHO) for serious incidents of violence within the last five years will be assigned to at least a Low security level institution unless waived.

(8) Serious Escape. A female inmate who has been involved in a serious escape within the last ten years will be assigned to the Carswell Administrative Unit, unless the PSF has been waived. A male inmate who has escaped from a secure facility (prior or instant offense) with or without the threat of violence or who escapes from an open institution or program with a threat of violence will be housed in at least a Medium security level institution, unless the PSF has been waived.

(9) Juvenile Violence. A male or female juvenile who has any documented instance of violent behavior, past or present, which resulted in a conviction, a delinquency adjudication, or finding of guilt.

(10) Serious Telephone Abuse. If the PSR or other official documentation clearly indicates that telephone communications were used to facilitate crimes (drug trafficking, threats, acts of violence, etc.), then the inmate must be housed in at least a Low security level institution, unless the PSF is waived.

(11) Prison Disturbance. A male inmate who was involved in a serious incident of violence within the institution will be housed in at least a High security level institution, unless the PSF is waived. A female inmate who was involved in a serious incident of violence within the institution will be housed in the Carswell Administrative Unit, unless the PSF has been waived.

PRACTICAL TIPS:

1. If an inmate is listed as being a member of a disruptive group, he can face an increased security level. Ask the court to remove any mention of a client's gang affiliation.

2. The Sex Offender PSF can be applied based on behavior listed in the PSR or other official documentation. Make sure you fight to remove any behavior that is not properly documented! Do your best to remove language regarding such behavior from the PSR

C. MANAGEMENT VARIABLES

Management Variables override the security level established by the security score. They may further override certain PSFs requiring higher security levels. Specific variables are as follows:

(1) Judicial Recommendation. "When consistent with policies or when such actions are consistent with sound correctional management, the [BOP] attempts to satisfy judicial recommendations."

(2) Release Residence. Directs placement within 500 miles of declared residence on release and may be used when prisoner is 36 months from scheduled release date.

(3) Population Management. Permits assignment to facility inconsistent with security level due to, for example, population pressures affecting available appropriate-level bed space within 500 miles of the inmate's anticipated release residence; gang/security concerns.

(4) Central Inmate Monitoring Assignment. Limitations on possible facilities based on special circumstances like the need to segregate from general population or special monitoring requirements.

(5) Medical or Psychiatric. Applicable to those whose current or historical medical and psychological conditions require evaluation or treatment.

(6) Program Participation. When an inmate's security level changes during participation in a special program not likely to be available in another appropriate facility, causing placement outside normal guidelines.

(7) Work Cadre. At secure facilities without satellite camps, the Regional Director may authorize a certain number of work cadre inmates to perform work outside the perimeter of the institution.

(8) PSF Waived. Up to 3 PSFs may be waived by designation coordinator.

(9) Long-term Detainee. Permits increase or reduction in security level of facility based on observed prisoner conduct.

(10) Greater Security. Catch-all provision for those prisoners whose characteristics result in a security score inadequately reflects security requirements.

(11) Lesser Security. Catch-all provision for those prisoners whose characteristics result in a security score that overstates security requirements.

PRACTICAL TIP: **Provide the probation officer with medical records so that the client can receive the appropriate medical treatment.**

D. CUSTODY LEVEL

Within any given security level institution, a custody level is assigned to each inmate. There are four custody levels in each institution:

1) COMMUNITY: The lowest custody level. An inmate may be eligible for the least secure housing, including any which is outside the institution's perimeter, may work on outside details with minimal supervision, and may participate in community based program activities if other eligibility requirements are satisfied.

2) IN: An inmate is assigned to regular quarters and is eligible for all regular work assignments and activities under a normal level of supervision. Inmates are not eligible for work details or programs outside the institution's secure perimeter.

3) OUT: An inmate may be assigned to less secure housing and may be eligible for work details outside the institution's secure perimeter with a minimum of two-hour intermittent staff supervision.

4) MAXIMUM: This classification us for individuals who, by their behavior, have been identified as assaultive, predacious, riotous, serious escape risks, or seriously disruptive to the orderly running of an institution. Accordingly, quarters and work assignments are assigned to ensure maximum control and supervision.

An inmate's custody level within any given security level institution is routinely reviewed and may change for various reasons during the period of incarceration.

IV. TRANSFER/RE-DESIGNATION

Transfers, also referred to as redesignations, are used to place inmates in different institutions.

Typical reasons for transfers include (1) institution classification, (2) nearer release, (3) disciplinary/close supervision, (4) adjustment, (5) medical/psychological treatment, (6) temporary transfers, (7) training purposes/program participation, (8) Institution Hearing Program, (9) pre-release and (10) transfers from CCC's.

Inmates may be considered for a nearer release transfer (moves the inmate closer to their legal residence or release destination) only after serving 18 consecutive months of clear conduct in a general population. Essentially these transfers are based on a change in circumstances from the inmate's original designation, and proceeds in the same manner as the original designation process.

V. EARLY RELEASE UNDER RESIDENTIAL DRUG ABUSE PROGRAM

According to statute, "[t]he period a prisoner convicted of a nonviolent offense remains in custody after successfully completing a treatment program may be reduced by the Bureau of Prisons, but such reduction may not be more than one year from the term the prisoner must otherwise serve." 18 U.S.C.A. § 3621(e)(2)(B).

The BOP has implemented early release procedures for successful completion in a Residential Drug Abuse Program (RDAP) in Program Statement P5331.02 (Mar. 16, 2009). This program applies to those inmates sentenced for a nonviolent offense with a diagnosed substance abuse disorder who successfully complete RDAP. The BOP interprets "successful completion" as (1) completion of the unit-based RDAP while in the institution, (2) if applicable, participation in follow-up treatment while in general population for 12 months or until release, whichever comes first, (3) completion of a community Transition Drug Abuse Treatment while residing in a Residential Reentry Center or on home confinement, and (4) comply with the Financial Responsibility Program.

The following inmates are considered by the BOP to be ineligible for RDAP:

(1) alien detainees,

(2) those in pretrial custody,

(3) State or military inmates,

(4) inmates with *prior* felony or misdemeanor conviction for homicide, forcible rape, robbery, aggravated assault, arson, kidnaping, or an offense that by its nature or conduct involves sexual abuse offenses committed upon minors,

(5) Inmates who have a current felony conviction for an offense that has as an element, the actual, attempted, or threatened use of physical force against the person or property of another, an offense that involved the carrying, possession, or use of a firearm or other dangerous weapon or explosives (including any explosive material or explosive device), an offense that, by its nature or conduct, presents a serious potential risk of physical force against the person or property of another; or an offense that, by its nature or conduct, involves sexual abuse offenses committed upon minors,

(6) inmates who have been convicted of an attempt, conspiracy, or other offense which involved an underlying offense listed in (4) or (5) of this section; or

(7) Inmates who previously received an early release under 18 U.S.C. § 3621(e). These prohibitions, in short, deny RDAP to inmates with prior enumerated crimes of violence and current convictions that meet the definition of crime of violence set forth in 18 U.S.C. § 16.

The eligibility for RDAP is a one-time deal if prior early release is granted.

VI. SEX OFFENDERS

While a discussion of this topic requires more than a cursory reference, given the BOP's role in registration, treatment and possible commitment, a brief summary of possible consequences is required.

The BOP has Program Statement 5141.02, Sex Offender Notification and Registration (Dec. 14, 1998), which provides for notification of local authorities for those with the "sex offender" PSF.

The law has evolved substantially since this Program Statement.

In 2006, Congress enacted the Sex Offender Registration and Notification Act (SORNA), 42 U.S.C. §§ 16901-16929. SORNA defines "sex offender" very broadly, creates a national sex offender database, requires that anyone who travels for more than a 3-day period update registration data with local authorities, and mandates in person verification of registry data, potentially for the rest of that individuals life. If one labeled a sex offender fails to update or register as required by SORNA, he or she faces a potential felony conviction under 18 U.S.C. § 2250. This process begins with the BOP's identification of an individual as a sex offender and notification and acknowledgment of the registration requirements of SORNA.

Likely a larger problem, as it may prohibit a prisoner from ever departing federal custody, is civil commitment under 18 U.S.C. § 4248. Under that statute, if the BOP certifies that an inmate scheduled for release meets the definition of a "sexually dangerous person," it may hold that inmate in custody, potentially indefinitely. This procedure was recently upheld by the Supreme Court in United States v. Comstock, 130 S. Ct. 1949 (2010). A "sexually dangerous person" is defined as a "person who has engaged or attempted to engage in sexually violent conduct or child molestation" and who "suffers from a serious mental illness, abnormality, or disorder as a result of which he would have serious difficulty in refraining from sexually violent conduct or child molestation if released. " 18 U.S.C. § 4247(a)(5) & (6). This definition is sufficiently broad to raise concerns as to how many may one day be swept in to indefinite civil commitment.

PRACTICAL TIP: Be careful with the information provided by your client to the probation officer and any evaluations done on your client prior to sentencing! Any of this information can be used to civilly commitment your client under the Adam Walsh Act.

VERY IMPORTANT

VII. THE BOP AND PRESENTENCE INVESTIGATION REPORTS

When attorneys review their client's Presentence Investigation Reports (PSRs), they may find themselves asking why the PSR provides what appears to be extraneous facts with little or no bearing on the sentence to be imposed. A minor entry in criminal history may be followed by paragraphs of details from arrest reports, while a major entry may be described in only a few lines. As United States Probation Offices are an arm of the court, by definition neutral in sentencing, it would seem PSRs should represent the complete and impartial facts intended for the court's consideration in sentencing. That is not always the case. As described by a former Probation Officer, the PSR is "like the Bible for the BOP. It extends way beyond the sentencing date." Nancy Glass, *The Social Workers of Sentencing? Probation Officers, Discretion, and the Accuracy of Presentence Reports Under the Federal Sentencing Guidelines*, 46 No. 1 Crim.

Law Bulletin Art. 2 (Jan.-Feb. 2010). Federal Rule of Criminal Procedure 32, governing sentencing, itself acknowledges that the PSR is submitted to the BOP (*See* FED. R. CRIM. P. 32(i)(3)(C)(providing "[a]t sentencing, the court . . . must append a copy of the court's determinations under this rule to any copy of the presentence report made available to the Bureau of Prisons"); see also id. Advisory Committee Notes to 1983 Amendment (providing "If the defendant is incarcerated, the presentence report accompanies him to the correctional institution and provides background information for the Bureau of Prisons' classification summary, which, in turn, determines the defendant's classification within the facility, his ability to obtain furloughs, and the choice of treatment programs" and "the Bureau of Prisons and the Parole Commission make substantial use of the presentence investigation report. Under current practice, this can result in reliance upon assertions of fact in the report in the making of critical determinations relating to custody or parole"). Given the substantial reliance on the facts contained in the PSR by the BOP, a critical role of the defense counsel in sentencing is insuring facts are both accurate and relevant to imposition of sentence. Alan Ellis, *Securing a Favorable Federal Prison Placement*, 30-APR Champion 22, 26 (2006). Failure to correct facts within the PSR, a record that remains with a prisoner long after a sentencing hearing is over, can have catastrophic long-term consequences. These consequences can include restrictions on facilities based on special offender characterizations, ineligibility for desired programs, and characterization as a "sex offender" — a label that may subject a defendant to civil commitment procedures after a criminal sentence has run its course. The prospects of correcting the factual record established by the PSR process after sentencing are grim, given the minimal obligation imposed on sentencing courts to correct the PSR. *See United States v. Saeteurn*, 504 F.3d 1175, 1179 (9th Cir. 2007)(concluding sentencing court need only resolve factual dispute involving "matters that will affect the determination and imposition of a correct sentence" and need not resolve "disputes that will affect only post-sentence decisions and the manner and location of service of the sentence").

PRACTICAL TIP: MAKE SURE THE FACTS IN THE PSR ARE ACCURATE AND RELEVANT TO IMPOSITION OF THE SENTENCE.

VIII. ROLE OF FEDERAL COURTS IN EXECUTION OF SENTENCE

As previously stated, federal courts dictate the length of a term of imprisonment required by a federal sentence. The BOP, in turn, determines when a sentence commences. *See, e.g., United States v. Wells*, 473 F.3d 640, 645 (6th Cir. 2007)(stating that the BOP, not the district judge, will determine when a sentence commences). A federal judge may make recommendations to the BOP regarding when a sentence is to start and designation of a prison at which an inmate will serve a sentence, *see, e.g.*, *United States v. Hayes*, 535 F.3d 907, 910 (8th Cir. 2008), but these are ultimately non-binding recommendations, not mandates to the BOP.

The BOP's determination of this date is established by statute: "A sentence to a term of imprisonment commences on the date the defendant is received in custody awaiting transportation to, or arrives voluntarily to commence service of sentence at, the official detention facility at which the sentence is to be served." 18 U.S.C. § 3585(a). Credit for time served is similarly determined by statute: "A defendant shall be given credit toward the service of a term of imprisonment for any time he has spent in official detention prior to the date the sentence commences-- (1) as a result of the offense for which the sentence was imposed; or (2) as a result of any other charge for which the defendant was arrested after the commission of the offense for which the sentence was imposed; that has not been credited against another sentence." *Id.* § 3585(b). The BOP, not sentencing courts, apply these statutory directives. *See, e.g.*, *Werber v. United States*, 149 F.3d 172, 179 (2d Cir. 1998) (holding "only the BOP is entitled to give credit for time served prior to the commencement of a sentence.").

The "time served" calculations turn on whether a prisoner was in "official detention" for the offense charged. It bears noting that federal courts have substantial authority over where a criminal defendant is held pending resolution of any criminal charges before it. If an offense involves immigration deportation or state custody, the act of permitting a defendant to remain in immigration detention or state custody can add additional time to the federal sentence ultimately served if there is a federal custody alternative. *See, e.g.*, BOP Program Statement 5880.28 at 14 ("Official detention does not include time spent in the custody of the U.S. Immigration & Naturalization Service (INS) . . . pending a final determination of deportability. An inmate being held by INS pending a civil deportation determination is not being held in "official detention" pending criminal charges.").

PRACTICAL TIP: IF YOUR CLIENT IS RELEASED OUT ON BOND FROM FEDERAL COURT BUT HE REMAINS IN IMMIGRATION DETENTION, THE TIME HE SERVES AT INS WILL NOT BE CREDITED TOWARDS HIS FEDERAL SENTENCE. AS HIS FEDERAL DEFENSE ATTORNEY, YOU SHOULD FILE A MOTION SURRENDERING THE BOND SO THAT HE CAN BE RETURNED TO FEDERAL CUSTODY AND EARN CREDIT FOR HIS FEDERAL SENTENCE.

IX. DESIGNATION OF STATE INSTITUTION FOR SERVICE OF FEDERAL SENTENCE

Governed by U.S. Dep't of Justice, Bureau of Prisons, Designation of State Institution for Service of Federal Sentence, Program Statement 5160.05 (Jan. 16, 2003). Consistent with its statutory authority to designate the place of imprisonment, 18 U.S.C. § 3621(b), the BOP may designate a state facility. By default, a sentence runs consecutively with any previously imposed sentence, whether state or federal. 18 U.S.C. § 3584. However, if a federal sentencing court orders that a sentence run concurrently with a state sentence already imposed, the BOP implements that order ordinarily by designating the state facility as the place to serve the federal sentence. Ordinarily, the reason for selecting the state institution is that primary non-federal custody (primary state custody) resided with the state jurisdiction and the federal sentencing court intended its sentence be served concurrently with the state sentence.

These designations are reviewed by the Regional Inmate Systems Administrator. As this issue is central to sentencing, no designation will be made unless consistent with the intent of the sentencing court reflected in the judgment, or unless subsequently approved by the sentencing court.

PRACTICAL TIPS:

1. I F YOUR CLIENT IS IN PRIMARY STATE CUSTODY (ON WRIT IN FEDERAL COURT), REQUEST THAT THE FEDERAL SENTENCING COURT ORDER THAT THE FEDERAL SENTENCE RUN CONCURRENTLY WITH THE STATE SENTENCE IN THE JUDGMENT BY STATING:

A) "SAID SENTENCE TO RUN CONCURRENTLY WITH THE STATE SENTENCE THE DEFENDANT IS PRESENTLY SERVING."

B) "S ENTENCE TO RUN CONCURRENTLY WITH SENTENCE IMPOSED UNDER DOCKET 168-88, SAN DIEGO COUNTY COURT, ON MAY 14, 1988."

C) " THAT THE DEFENDANT SERVE THIS SENTENCE AT THE STATE FACILITY, I.E., NEW MEXICO DEPARTMENT OF CORRECTIONS."

2. EVEN IF A FEDERAL JUDGE ORDERS THAT THE FEDERAL AND STATE SENTENCES RUN CONCURRENTLY, THEY WILL NOT RUN CONCURRENTLY IF THE STATE SENTENCE HAS ALREADY BEEN COMPLETED. IN THIS TYPE OF SITUATION, THE FEDERAL DEFENSE ATTORNEY SHOULD REQUEST A DEPARTURE OR VARIANCE FROM THE COURT REDUCING THE SENTENCE FOR THE AMOUNT OF TIME THE DEFENDANT WOULD HAVE BEEN CREDITED IF THE STATE AND FEDERAL SENTENCES WOULD HAVE RUN CONCURRENTLY.

3. I F A FEDERAL SENTENCE IS ORDERED TO RUN CONCURRENTLY WITH A STATE SENTENCE IN WHICH THE STATE HAS PRIMARY CUSTODY, THE FEDERAL SENTENCE WILL NOT BEGIN TO RUN UNTIL THE DATE THE FEDERAL SENTENCE IS IMPOSED.

THE FEDERAL SENTENCE WILL NOT BE CREDITED WITH ANY OF THE STATE TIME EARNED PRIOR TO THE DATE OF THE FEDERAL SENTENCING.

4. REGARDLESS OF WHICH AUTHORITIES HAVE PRIMARY CUSTODIAL JURISDICTION, IF THE DEFENDANT IS SENTENCED IN STATE COURT PRIOR TO BEING SENTENCED IN FEDERAL COURT, THERE WILL LIKELY BE AN INCREASE IN THE DEFENDANT'S CRIMINAL HISTORY IN FEDERAL COURT. THUS, IF POSSIBLE, A DEFENDANT SHOULD BE SENTENCED IN FEDERAL COURT FIRST.

5. REMEMBER THAT IF THE DEFENDANT IS RELEASED FROM THE CUSTODY OF THE AUTHORITY WITH PRIMARY CUSTODIAL JURISDICTION (FOR EXAMPLE, THE CHARGES ARE DISMISSED OR THE CLIENT IS RELEASED OUT ON BOND), PRIMARY CUSTODY MAY SHIFT TO THE OTHER AUTHORITY.

6. I F THE FEDERAL TERM EXPIRES PRIOR TO THE INMATE'S RELEASE FROM THE NON-FEDERAL JURISDICTION, A TERM OF SUPERVISED RELEASE THAT FOLLOWS

The Ninth Circuit invalidated this regulation based on a technical failure to articulate a rational basis for the BOP's interpretation of § 3624 as required by the Administrated Procedures Act. *Tablada v. Thomas*, 533 F.3d 800, 809 (9th Cir. 2008). It nonetheless deferred to the BOP's longstanding interpretation through its Program Statement.

A FEDERAL SENTENCE WILL NOT COMMENCE UNTIL THE INMATE IS RELEASED FROM ALL PERIODS OF CONFINEMENT. 7. KEEP IN MIND. THE COURT MAY, FROM TIME TO TIME, ORDER CONCURRENT SERVICE OF THE FEDERAL SENTENCE AT SOME TIME AFTER ITS IMPOSITION IF FOR INSTANCE, PRIMARY JURISDICTION RESIDED WITH THE STATE AND THE COURT MISTAKENLY BELIEVED THAT THE INMATE WAS IN FEDERAL CUSTODY FOR SERVICE OF THE FEDERAL SENTENCE ON THE DATE OF IMPOSITION. (SEE SECTION 9 OF PROGRAM STATEMENT 5160.05.)

X. GOOD CONDUCT TIME/GOOD TIME CREDIT

For sentences involving terms of imprisonment of more that 1 years, the BOP is authorized to award good conduct time, also referred to as good time credit, of up to 54 days if it finds the "prisoner has displayed exemplary compliance with institutional disciplinary regulations." 18 U.S.C.A. § 3624(b)(1). If the BOP finds a prisoners compliance is less than exemplary, it is authorized to award no credit or lesser credit.

The details of the BOP's implementation of the good time credit provision are found in both regulation, *see* 28 C.F.R. § 523.20,7 and BOP Program Statements, *see* Program Statement 5880.28 and Program Statement P5884.03 (Mar. 31, 2006). As the name suggests, any award of good time credit that has not vested may be reduced or eliminated for disciplinary issues.

While these proceedings are beyond the scope of this paper, details may be found in 28 C.F.R. § 541.13.

There are three different rules applied to determine good time credit based on the date of offense conduct for which a prisoner was sentenced. These rules are set forth as follows:

(1) For offenses committed on or after November 1, 1987, but before September 13, 1994, the BOP awards 54 days credit for each year served. This amount is prorated when the time served is less than a full year. Once good time credit vests, it cannot be disallowed.

(2) For offenses committed on or after September 13, 1994, but before April 26, 1996, inmates earn up to 54 days credit at the end of each full year if they have earned, or are making satisfactory progress toward earning, a GED.

(3) For inmates serving a sentence for an offense committed on or after April 26, 1996, the BOP awards 54 days credit for each year served (or a prorated amount when the time served is less than a full year) if the inmate has earned or is making satisfactory progress toward earning a GED credential or high school diploma. The BOP awards a maximum of 42 days credit for each year served (or a prorated amount for a period of less than a year) if the inmate has not earned or is not making satisfactory progress toward earning a GED credential or high school diploma.

(4) Under rules (2) and (3), an alien subject to a final order of removal is not required to participate in literacy/GED programs to receive the full award of good time credit. If an inmate disagrees with an assessment on good time credit, he or she must challenge the assessment using the Administrative Remedy Program, 28 CFR §§ 542.10-542.19.

PRACTICAL TIPS:

1. MAKE SURE THE PSR ACCURATELY REFLECTS YOUR CLIENT'S EDUCATIONAL HISTORY, INCLUDING IF HE HAS EARNED A GED CREDENTIAL OR A HIGH SCHOOL DIPLOMA.

2. YOU MIGHT WANT TO CONSIDER ASKING FOR A VARIANCE IN CASES INVOLVING LENGTHY SENTENCES BASED ON THE FACT THAT BOP CALCULATES GOOD TIME CREDIT BASED ON PRISON TIME SERVED RATHER THAN THE SENTENCE IMPOSED. IN *BARBER V. THOMAS,* IN WHICH THE UNITED STATES SUPREME COURT RECENTLY UPHELD THE BOP 'S METHOD OF CALCULATING GOOD-TIME CREDIT, JUSTICE BREYER WROTE" "[I]F IT TURNS OUT THAT THE CALCULATION OF GOOD TIME CREDIT BASED ON PRISON TIME SERVED RATHER THAN THE SENTENCE IMPOSED PRODUCES RESULTS THAT ARE MORE SEVERE THAT THE COMMISSION FINDS APPROPRIATE, THE COMMISSION REMAINS FREE TO ADJUST SENTENCE LEVELS ACCORDINGLY." NO. 09-5201, 2010 WL 2243706,AT *9 (U.S. JUNE 7, 2010).

XI. SECOND CHANCE ACT

On April 28, 2008, the President signed into law the Second Chance Act of 2007, 18 U.S.C. § 3624. was signed into law to improve the outcomes for people returning to communities from prisons and jails. This legislation authorizes federal grants to government agencies and nonprofit organizations to provide programs and services to help reduce recidivism.

A. APPROPRIATIONS

In fiscal year 2010, $144 million were appropriated for prisoner reentry programs, including reentry initiatives in the Federal Bureau of Prisons and Second Chance grant programs:

* Reentry demonstration projects under Sec. 101
* Mentoring grants to nonprofit organizations under Sec. 211
* Reentry Courts under Sec. 111
* Family-based, substance abuse treatment under Sec. 113
* Grants to evaluate and improve education in prisons, jails, and juvenile facilities under Sec. 114
* Technology career training demonstration grants under Sec. 115
* Reentry Substance Abuse and criminal justice collaboration under Sec. 201
* Reentry research under Sec. 245

B. PRERELEASE CUSTODY UNDER SEC. 251

This Act permits eligible inmates to spend some portion of the **final twelve months** of their sentence in a community correctional facility, also known as a half-way house or residential reentry center. "The Director of the Bureau of Prisons shall, to the extent practicable, ensure that a prisoner serving a term of imprisonment spends a portion of the final months of that term (not to exceed 12 months), under conditions that will afford that prisoner a reasonable opportunity to adjust to and prepare for the reentry of that prisoner into the community. Such conditions may include a community correctional facility." *Id.* § 3624(c)(1). This authority "may be used to place a prisoner in home confinement for the shorter of 10 percent of the term of imprisonment of that prisoner or 6 months." *Id.* § 3624(c)(2).

It should be noted that § 3624 expressly does not override the BOP's authority to designate an appropriate facility, thus a prisoner must meet general eligibility requirements discussed above for these placements.

The regulation implementing this mandate provides that "[i]nmates may be designated to community confinement as a condition of pre-release custody and programming during the final months of the inmate's term of imprisonment, not to exceed twelve months." 28 C.F.R. § 570.21(a). This regulation also provides for "home detention as a condition of pre-release custody and programming during the final months of the inmate's term of imprisonment, not to exceed the shorter of ten percent of the inmate's term of imprisonment or six months." Pursuant to the Second Chance Act, the BOP staff is required to review inmates for RRC placement 17-19 months before their projected release date, and inmates are to be individually considered using the five factors listed in §3621(b).

C. ELDERLY INMATE PILOT PROGRAM UNDER SEC. 231

Pursuant to the Second Chance Act, the Attorney General was directed to conduct a pilot program to determine the effectiveness of removing eligible elderly offenders from a Bureau of Prisons facility and placing such offenders on home detention until their term of confinement has expired. 42 U.S.C. §17451(g)(1)(A).

To be eligible for the Elderly Inmate Pilot Program, offenders must satisfy two sets requirements in addition to the requirement that the offender must be not less than 65 years of age: (1) the offender must be serving a term of imprisonment other than life imprisonment based on a conviction for an offense or offenses that do not include any crime of violence, sex offenses, or other offenses enumerated inn the statute;

(2) the offender must have served greater of 10 years or 75% of the term of imprisonment imposed at sentencing;

(3) the offender must not have been convicted in the past of any Federal or State crime of violence, sex offense, or other offense enumerated in the statute.

(4) the offender must not have been determined by the BOP to have a history of violence or of sex offenses or the other offenses described in the statute; (5) the offender must not have escaped or attempted to escape from a BOP institution;

(6) the BOP must determine that release of the offender to home detention will result in a substantial net reduction of costs to the federal government; and

(7) the BOP must determine that the offender poses no substantial risk of engaging in criminal conduct or of endangering any person if released to home detention. 42 U.S.C. §17541(g)(5)(A)(I-vii).

Chapter X

CONCLUSION

It is hoped these topics are informative and provide a basic understanding of the role of the BOP and considerations that may limit the time a client spends in custody. For specific issues, it is best to consult the individual Program Statements found on the BOP's Web site (http://www.bop.gov/). Typically, items of interest to attorneys would be found in the 5000 series Program Statements.

daniel storm

IMPORTANT:

For up to the minute changes in sentences, guidelines and Amendments, I have annexed the 2016-2017 Federal Sentencing Guidelines from the United States Sentencing Commission.

UNITED STATES SENTENCING COMMISSION

GUIDELINES MANUAL

[Incorporating guidelines amendments effective November 1, 2016, and earlier]

UNITED STATES
SENTENCING COMMISSION
GUIDELINES MANUAL

Chair

CHARLES R. BREYER

Vice Chair

DABNEY L. FRIEDRICH

Commissioner

RACHEL E. BARKOW

Commissioner

WILLIAM H. PRYOR, JR.

Commissioner

MICHELLE MORALES

Commissioner, *Ex-officio*

J. PATRICIA WILSON SMOOT

Commissioner, *Ex-officio*

This document contains the text of the *Guidelines Manual* incorporating amendments effective November 1, 2016, and earlier.

CITATION FORM

RECOMMENDED CITATION FORM

United States Sentencing Commission Guidelines, Policy Statements, and Commentary may be cited as follows:

I. Full citation form

United States Sentencing Commission, *Guidelines Manual*, §3E1.1 (Nov. 2016)

II. Abbreviated citation form

[using USSG as the designated short form for United States Sentencing Guidelines]

- a guideline —

USSG §2D1.1

- a policy statement —

USSG §6A1.1, p.s.

- commentary designated as an application note —

USSG §2B1.1, comment. (n.1)

- commentary designated as background —

USSG §2B1.1, comment. (backg'd.)

- commentary designated as an introduction —

USSG Ch.3, Pt.D, intro. comment.

- commentary designated as a conclusion —

USSG Ch.3, Pt.D, concl. comment.

- an appendix to the Guidelines Manual —

USSG App. C

TABLE OF CONTENTS

TABLE OF CONTENTS

SUPPLEMENTARY VOLUMES

Ch. 1 Pt. A

CHAPTER ONE
INTRODUCTION, AUTHORITY, AND GENERAL APPLICATION PRINCIPLES
PART A — INTRODUCTION AND AUTHORITY
Introductory Commentary
Subparts 1 and 2 of this Part provide an introduction to the Guidelines Manual describing the historical development and evolution of the federal sentencing guidelines. Subpart 1 sets forth the original introduction to the Guidelines Manual as it first appeared in 1987, with the inclusion of amendments made occasionally thereto between 1987 and 2000. The original introduction, as so amended, explained a number of policy decisions made by the United States Sentencing Commission ("Commission") when it promulgated the initial set of guidelines and therefore provides a useful reference for contextual and historical purposes. Subpart 2 further describes the evolution of the federal sentencing guidelines after the initial guidelines were promulgated.
Subpart 3 of this Part states the authority of the Commission to promulgate federal sentencing guidelines, policy statements, and commentary.
1. ORIGINAL INTRODUCTION TO THE GUIDELINES MANUAL
The following provisions of this Subpart set forth the original introduction to this manual, effective November 1, 1987, and as amended through November 1, 2000:
1. Authority
The United States Sentencing Commission ("Commission") is an independent agency in the judicial branch composed of seven voting and two non-voting, *ex officio* members. Its principal purpose is to establish sentencing policies and practices for the federal criminal justice system that will assure the ends of justice by promulgating detailed guidelines prescribing the appropriate sentences for offenders convicted of federal crimes.
The guidelines and policy statements promulgated by the Commission are issued pursuant to Section 994(a) of Title 28, United States Code.
2. The Statutory Mission
The Sentencing Reform Act of 1984 (Title II of the Comprehensive Crime Control Act of 1984) provides for the development of guidelines that will further

the basic purposes of criminal punishment: deterrence, incapacitation, just punishment, and rehabilitation. The Act delegates broad authority to the Commission to review and rationalize the federal sentencing process.
The Act contains detailed instructions as to how this determination should be made, the most important of which directs the Commission to create categories of offense behavior and offender characteristics. An offense behavior category might consist, for example, of "bank robbery/committed with a gun/$2500 taken." An offender characteristic category might be "offender with one prior conviction not resulting in imprisonment." The Commission is required to prescribe guideline ranges that specify an appropriate sentence for each class of convicted persons determined by coordinating the offense behavior categories with the offender characteristic categories. Where the guidelines call for imprisonment, the range must be narrow: the maximum of the range cannot exceed the minimum by more than the greater of 25 percent or six months. 28 U.S.C. § 994(b)(2).
Pursuant to the Act, the sentencing court must select a sentence from within the guideline range. If, however, a particular case presents atypical features, the Act allows the court to depart from the guidelines and sentence outside the prescribed range. In that case, the court must specify reasons for departure.
18 U.S.C. § 3553(b). If the court sentences within the guideline range, an appellate

court may review the sentence to determine whether the guidelines were correctly applied. If the court departs from the guideline range, an appellate court may review the reasonableness of the departure. 18 U.S.C. § 3742. The Act also abolishes parole, and substantially reduces and restructures good behavior adjustments.

The Commission's initial guidelines were submitted to Congress on April 13, 1987. After the prescribed period of Congressional review, the guidelines took effect on November 1, 1987, and apply to all offenses committed on or after that date. The Commission has the authority to submit guideline amendments each year to Congress between the beginning of a regular Congressional session and May 1. Such amendments automatically take effect 180 days after submission unless a law is enacted to the contrary. 28 U.S.C. § 994(p).

The initial sentencing guidelines and policy statements were developed after extensive hearings, deliberation, and consideration of substantial public comment. The Commission emphasizes, however, that it views the guideline-writing process as evolutionary. It expects, and the governing statute anticipates, that continuing research, experience, and analysis will result in modifications and revisions to the guidelines through submission of amendments to Congress. To this end, the Commission is established as a permanent agency to monitor sentencing practices in the federal courts.

3. The Basic Approach (Policy Statement)

To understand the guidelines and their underlying rationale, it is important to focus on the three objectives that Congress sought to achieve in enacting the Sentencing Reform Act of 1984. The Act's basic objective was to enhance the ability of the criminal justice system to combat crime through an effective, fair sentencing system. To achieve this end, Congress first sought honesty in sentencing.

It sought to avoid the confusion and implicit deception that arose out of the pre-guidelines sentencing system which required the court to impose an indeterminate sentence of imprisonment and empowered the parole commission to determine how much of the sentence an offender actually would serve in prison. This practice usually resulted in a substantial reduction in the effective length of the sentence imposed, with defendants often serving only about one-third of the sentence imposed by the court.

Second, Congress sought reasonable uniformity in sentencing by narrowing the wide disparity in sentences imposed for similar criminal offenses committed by similar offenders. Third, Congress sought proportionality in sentencing through a system that imposes appropriately different sentences for criminal conduct of differing severity.

Honesty is easy to achieve: the abolition of parole makes the sentence imposed by the court the sentence the offender will serve, less approximately fifteen percent for good behavior. There is a tension, however, between the mandate of uniformity and the mandate of proportionality. Simple uniformity — sentencing every offender to five years — destroys proportionality. Having only a few simple categories of crimes would make the guidelines uniform and easy to administer, but might lump together offenses that are different in important respects. For example, a single category for robbery that included armed and unarmed robberies, robberies with and without injuries, robberies of a few dollars and robberies of millions, would be far too broad.

A sentencing system tailored to fit every conceivable wrinkle of each case would quickly become unworkable and seriously compromise the certainty of punishment and its deterrent effect. For example: a bank robber with (or without) a gun, which the robber kept hidden (or brandished), might have frightened (or merely warned), injured seriously (or less seriously), tied up (or simply pushed) a guard, teller, or customer, at night (or at noon), in an effort to obtain money for other crimes (or for other purposes), in the company of a few (or many) other robbers, for the first (or fourth) time.

The list of potentially relevant features of criminal behavior is long; the fact that they can occur in multiple combinations means that the list of possible permutations of factors is virtually endless. The appropriate relationships among these different factors are exceedingly difficult to establish, for they are often context specific. Sentencing courts do not treat the occurrence of a simple bruise identically in all cases, irrespective of whether that bruise occurred in the context of a bank robbery or in the context of a breach of peace. This is so, in part, because

the risk that such a harm will occur differs depending on the underlying offense with which it is connected; and also because, in part, the relationship between punishment and multiple harms is not simply additive. The relation varies depending on how much other harm has occurred. Thus, it would not be proper to assign points for each kind of harm and simply add them up, irrespective of context and total amounts.

The larger the number of subcategories of offense and offender characteristics included in the guidelines, the greater the complexity and the less workable the system. Moreover, complex combinations of offense and offender characteristics would apply and interact in unforeseen ways to unforeseen situations, thus failing to cure the unfairness of a simple, broad category system. Finally, and perhaps most importantly, probation officers and courts, in applying a complex system having numerous subcategories, would be required to make a host of decisions regarding whether the underlying facts were sufficient to bring the case within a particular subcategory. The greater the number of decisions required and the greater their complexity, the greater the risk that different courts would apply the guidelines differently to situations that, in fact, are similar, thereby reintroducing the very disparity that the guidelines were designed to reduce.

In view of the arguments, it would have been tempting to retreat to the simple, broad category approach and to grant courts the discretion to select the proper point along a broad sentencing range. Granting such broad discretion, however, would have risked correspondingly broad disparity in sentencing, for different courts may exercise their discretionary powers in different ways. Such an approach would have risked a return to the wide disparity that Congress established the Commission to reduce and would have been contrary to the Commission's mandate set forth in the Sentencing Reform Act of 1984.

In the end, there was no completely satisfying solution to this problem. The Commission had to balance the comparative virtues and vices of broad, simple categorization and detailed, complex subcategorization, and within the constraints established by that balance, minimize the discretionary powers of the sentencing court. Any system will, to a degree, enjoy the benefits and suffer from the drawbacks of each approach.

A philosophical problem arose when the Commission attempted to reconcile the differing perceptions of the purposes of criminal punishment. Most observers of the criminal law agree that the ultimate aim of the law itself, and of punishment in particular, is the control of crime. Beyond this point, however, the consensus seems to break down. Some argue that appropriate punishment should be defined primarily on the basis of the principle of "just deserts." Under this principle, punishment should be scaled to the offender's culpability and the resulting harms. Others argue that punishment should be imposed primarily on the basis of practical "crime control" considerations. This theory calls for sentences that most effectively lessen the likelihood of future crime, either by deterring others or incapacitating the defendant.

Adherents of each of these points of view urged the Commission to choose between them and accord one primacy over the other. As a practical matter, however, this choice was unnecessary because in most sentencing decisions the application of either philosophy will produce the same or similar results.

In its initial set of guidelines, the Commission sought to solve both the practical and philosophical problems of developing a coherent sentencing system by taking an empirical approach that used as a starting point data estimating preguidelines sentencing practice. It analyzed data drawn from 10,000 presentence investigations, the differing elements of various crimes as distinguished in substantive criminal statutes, the United States Parole Commission's guidelines and statistics, and data from other relevant sources in order to determine which distinctions were important in pre-guidelines practice. After consideration, the Commission accepted, modified, or rationalized these distinctions.

This empirical approach helped the Commission resolve its practical problem by defining a list of relevant distinctions that, although of considerable length, was short enough to create a manageable set of guidelines. Existing categories are relatively broad and omit distinctions that some may believe important, yet they include most of the major distinctions that statutes and data suggest made a significant difference in sentencing decisions. Relevant distinctions not reflected in the guidelines probably will occur rarely and sentencing courts may take such unusual cases into account by departing from the guidelines.

The Commission's empirical approach also helped resolve its philosophical dilemma. Those who adhere to a just deserts philosophy may concede that the lack of consensus might make it difficult to say exactly what punishment is deserved for a particular crime. Likewise, those who subscribe to a philosophy of crime control may acknowledge that the lack of sufficient data might make it difficult to determine exactly the punishment that will best prevent that crime. Both groups might therefore recognize the wisdom of looking to those distinctions that judges and legislators have, in fact, made over the course of time. These established distinctions are ones that the community believes, or has found over time, to be important from either a just deserts or crime control perspective.

The Commission did not simply copy estimates of pre-guidelines practice as revealed by the data, even though establishing offense values on this basis would help eliminate disparity because the data represent averages. Rather, it departed from the data at different points for various important reasons. Congressional statutes, for example, suggested or required departure, as in the case of the Anti-Drug Abuse Act of 1986 that imposed increased and mandatory minimum sentences. In addition, the data revealed inconsistencies in treatment, such as punishing

economic crime less severely than other apparently equivalent behavior.
Despite these policy-oriented departures from pre-guidelines practice, the guidelines represent an approach that begins with, and builds upon, empirical data. The guidelines will not please those who wish the Commission to adopt a single philosophical theory and then work deductively to establish a simple and

perfect set of categorizations and distinctions. The guidelines may prove acceptable, however, to those who seek more modest, incremental improvements in the status quo, who believe the best is often the enemy of the good, and who recognize that these guidelines are, as the Act contemplates, but the first step in an evolutionary process. After spending considerable time and resources exploring alternative approaches, the Commission developed these guidelines as a practical effort toward the achievement of a more honest, uniform, equitable, proportional, and therefore effective sentencing system.

4. The Guidelines' Resolution of Major Issues (Policy Statement)

The guideline-drafting process required the Commission to resolve a host of important policy questions typically involving rather evenly balanced sets of competing considerations. As an aid to understanding the guidelines, this introduction briefly discusses several of those issues; commentary in the guidelines explains others.

(a) Real Offense vs. Charge Offense Sentencing.

One of the most important questions for the Commission to decide was whether to base sentences upon the actual conduct in which the defendant engaged regardless of the charges for which he was indicted or convicted ("real offense" sentencing), or upon the conduct that constitutes the elements of the offense for which the defendant was charged and of which he was convicted ("charge offense" sentencing). A bank robber, for example, might have used a gun, frightened bystanders, taken $50,000, injured a teller, refused to stop when ordered, and raced away damaging property during his escape. A pure real offense system would sentence on the basis of all identifiable conduct. A pure charge offense system would overlook some of the harms that did not constitute statutory elements of the offenses of which the defendant was convicted.

The Commission initially sought to develop a pure real offense system. After all, the pre-guidelines sentencing system was, in a sense, this type of system. The sentencing court and the parole commission took account of the conduct in which the defendant actually engaged, as determined in a presentence report, at the sentencing hearing, or before a parole commission hearing officer. The Commission's initial efforts in this direction, carried out in the spring and early summer of 1986, proved unproductive, mostly for practical reasons. To make such a system work, even to formalize and rationalize the status quo, would have required the Commission to decide precisely which harms to take into account, how to add them up, and what kinds of procedures the courts should use to determine the presence or absence of disputed factual elements. The Commission found no practical way to combine and account for the large number of diverse harms arising in different circumstances; nor did it find a practical way to reconcile the need for a fair adjudicatory procedure with the need for a speedy sentencing process given the potential existence of hosts of adjudicated "real harm" facts in many typical cases. The effort proposed as a solution to these problems required the use of, for example, quadratic roots and other mathematical operations that the Commission considered too complex to be workable. In the Commission's view, such a system risked return to wide disparity in sentencing practice.

In its initial set of guidelines submitted to Congress in April 1987, the Commission moved closer to a charge offense system. This system, however, does contain a significant number of real offense elements. For one thing, the hundreds of overlapping and duplicative statutory provisions that make up the federal criminal law forced the Commission to write guidelines that are descriptive of generic conduct rather than guidelines that track purely statutory language. For another, the guidelines take account of a number of important, commonly occurring real offense elements such as role in the offense, the presence of a gun, or the amount of money actually taken, through alternative base offense levels, specific offense characteristics, cross references, and adjustments.

The Commission recognized that a charge offense system has drawbacks of its own. One of the most important is the potential it affords prosecutors to influence sentences by increasing or decreasing the number of counts in an indictment. Of course, the defendant's actual conduct (that which the prosecutor can prove in court) imposes a natural limit upon the prosecutor's ability to increase a defendant's sentence. Moreover, the Commission has written its rules for the treatment of multicount convictions with an eye toward eliminating unfair treatment that might flow from count manipulation. For example, the guidelines treat a three-count indictment, each count of which charges sale of 100 grams of heroin or theft of $10,000, the same as a single-count indictment charging sale of 300 grams of heroin or theft of $30,000. Furthermore, a sentencing court may control any inappropriate manipulation of the indictment through use of its departure power. Finally, the Commission will closely monitor charging and plea agreement practices and will make appropriate adjustments should they become necessary.

(b) Departures.

The sentencing statute permits a court to depart from a guideline-specified sentence only when it finds "an aggravating or mitigating circumstance of a kind, or to a degree, not adequately taken into consideration by the Sentencing Commission in formulating the guidelines that should result in a sentence different from that described." 18 U.S.C. § 3553(b). The Commission intends the sentencing courts to treat each guideline as carving out a "heartland," a set of typical cases embodying the conduct that each guideline describes. When a court finds an atypical case, one to which a particular guideline linguistically applies but where conduct significantly differs from the norm, the court may consider whether a departure is warranted. Section 5H1.10 (Race, Sex, National Origin, Creed, Religion, and Socio-Economic Status), §5H1.12 (Lack of Guidance as a Youth and Similar Circumstances), the third sentence of §5H1.4 (Physical Condition, Including Drug or Alcohol Dependence or Abuse), the last sentence of §5K2.12 (Coercion and Duress), and §5K2.19 (Post-Sentencing Rehabilitative Efforts) list several factors that the court cannot take into account as grounds for

departure. With those specific exceptions, however, the Commission does not intend to limit the kinds of factors, whether or not mentioned anywhere else in the guidelines, that could constitute grounds for departure in an unusual case.

The Commission has adopted this departure policy for two reasons. First, it is difficult to prescribe a single set of guidelines that encompasses the vast range of human conduct potentially relevant to a sentencing decision. The Commission also recognizes that the initial set of guidelines need not do so. The Commission is a permanent body, empowered by law to write and rewrite guidelines, with progressive changes, over many years. By monitoring when courts depart from the guidelines and by analyzing their stated reasons for doing so and court decisions with references thereto, the Commission, over time, will be able to refine the guidelines to specify more precisely when departures should and should not be permitted.

Second, the Commission believes that despite the courts' legal freedom to depart from the guidelines, they will not do so very often. This is because the guidelines, offense by offense, seek to take account of those factors that the Commission's data indicate made a significant difference in pre-guidelines sentencing practice. Thus, for example, where the presence of physical injury made an important difference in pre-guidelines sentencing practice (as in the case of robbery or assault), the guidelines specifically include this factor to enhance the sentence. Where the guidelines do not specify an augmentation or diminution, this is generally because the sentencing data did not permit the Commission to conclude that the factor was empirically important in relation to the particular offense. Of course, an important factor (*e.g.*, physical injury) may infrequently occur in connection with a particular crime (*e.g.*, fraud). Such rare occurrences are precisely the type of events that the courts' departure powers were designed to cover — unusual cases outside the range of the more typical offenses for which the guidelines were designed.

It is important to note that the guidelines refer to two different kinds of departure. The first involves instances in which the guidelines provide specific guidance for departure by analogy or by other numerical or non-numerical suggestions. The Commission intends such suggestions as policy guidance for the courts. The Commission expects that most departures will reflect the suggestions and that the courts of appeals may prove more likely to find departures "unreasonable" where they fall outside suggested levels.

A second type of departure will remain unguided. It may rest upon grounds referred to in Chapter Five, Part K (Departures) or on grounds not mentioned in the guidelines. While Chapter Five, Part K lists factors that the Commission believes may constitute grounds for departure, the list is not exhaustive. The Commission recognizes that there may be other grounds for departure that are not mentioned; it also believes there may be cases in which a departure outside suggested levels is warranted. In its view, however, such cases will be highly infrequent.

(c) Plea Agreements.

Nearly ninety percent of all federal criminal cases involve guilty pleas and many of these cases involve some form of plea agreement. Some commentators on early Commission guideline drafts urged the Commission not to attempt any major reforms of the plea agreement process on the grounds that any set of guidelines that threatened to change pre-guidelines practice radically also threatened to make the federal system unmanageable. Others argued that guidelines that failed to control and limit plea agreements would leave untouched a "loophole" large enough to undo the good that sentencing guidelines would bring.

The Commission decided not to make major changes in plea agreement practices in the initial guidelines, but rather to provide guidance by issuing general policy statements concerning the acceptance of plea agreements in Chapter Six, Part B (Plea Agreements). The rules set forth in Fed. R. Crim. P. 11(e) govern the acceptance or rejection of such agreements. The Commission will collect data on the courts' plea practices and will analyze this information to determine when and why the courts accept or reject plea agreements and whether plea agreement practices are undermining the intent of the Sentencing Reform Act. In light of this information and analysis, the Commission will seek to further regulate the plea agreement process as appropriate. Importantly, if the policy statements relating to plea agreements are followed, circumvention of the Sentencing Reform Act and the guidelines should not occur.

The Commission expects the guidelines to have a positive, rationalizing impact upon plea agreements for two reasons. First, the guidelines create a clear, definite expectation in respect to the sentence that a court will impose if a trial takes place. In the event a prosecutor and defense attorney explore the possibility of a negotiated plea, they will no longer work in the dark. This fact alone should help to reduce irrationality in respect to actual sentencing outcomes. Second, the guidelines create a norm to which courts will likely refer when they decide whether, under Rule 11(e), to accept or to reject a plea agreement or recommendation.

(d) Probation and Split Sentences.

The statute provides that the guidelines are to "reflect the general appropriateness of imposing a sentence other than imprisonment in cases in which the defendant is a first offender who has not been convicted of a crime of violence or an otherwise serious offense . . . ." 28 U.S.C. § 994(j). Under pre-guidelines sentencing practice, courts sentenced to probation an inappropriately high percentage of offenders guilty of certain economic crimes, such as theft, tax evasion, antitrust offenses, insider trading, fraud, and embezzlement, that in the Commission's view are "serious."

The Commission's solution to this problem has been to write guidelines that classify as serious many offenses for which probation previously was frequently given and provide for at least a short period of imprisonment in such cases. The Commission concluded that the definite prospect of prison, even though the term

may be short, will serve as a significant deterrent, particularly when compared with pre-guidelines practice where probation, not prison, was the norm.

More specifically, the guidelines work as follows in respect to a first offender. For offense levels one through eight, the sentencing court may elect to sentence the offender to probation (with or without confinement conditions) or to a prison term. For offense levels nine and ten, the court may substitute probation for a prison term, but the probation must include confinement conditions (community confinement, intermittent confinement, or home detention). For offense levels eleven and twelve, the court must impose at least one-half the minimum confinement sentence in the form of prison confinement, the remainder to be served on supervised release with a condition of community confinement or home detention. The Commission, of course, has not dealt with the single acts of aberrant behavior that still may justify probation at higher offense levels through departures.*

*Note: Although the Commission had not addressed "single acts of aberrant behavior" at the time the Introduction to the Guidelines Manual originally was written, it subsequently addressed the issue in Amendment

603, effective November 1, 2000. (*See* Supplement to Appendix C, amendment 603.)

(e) Multi-Count Convictions.

The Commission, like several state sentencing commissions, has found it particularly difficult to develop guidelines for sentencing defendants convicted of multiple violations of law, each of which makes up a separate count in an indictment. The difficulty is that when a defendant engages in conduct that causes several harms, each additional harm, even if it increases the extent to which punishment is warranted, does not necessarily warrant a proportionate increase in punishment. A defendant who assaults others during a fight, for example, may warrant more punishment if he injures ten people than if he injures one, but his conduct does not necessarily warrant ten times the punishment. If it did, many of the simplest offenses, for reasons that are often fortuitous, would lead to sentences of life imprisonment — sentences that neither just deserts nor crime control theories of punishment would justify.

Several individual guidelines provide special instructions for increasing punishment when the conduct that is the subject of that count involves multiple occurrences or has caused several harms. The guidelines also provide general rules for aggravating punishment in light of multiple harms charged separately in separate counts. These rules may produce occasional anomalies, but normally they will permit an appropriate degree of aggravation of punishment for multiple offenses that are the subjects of separate counts.

These rules are set out in Chapter Three, Part D (Multiple Counts). They essentially provide: (1) when the conduct involves fungible items (*e.g.*, separate drug transactions or thefts of money), the amounts are added and the guidelines apply to the total amount; (2) when nonfungible harms are involved, the offense level for the most serious count is increased (according to a diminishing scale) to reflect the existence of other counts of conviction. The guidelines have been writ

ten in order to minimize the possibility that an arbitrary casting of a single transaction into several counts will produce a longer sentence. In addition, the sentencing court will have adequate power to prevent such a result through departures.

(f) Regulatory Offenses.

Regulatory statutes, though primarily civil in nature, sometimes contain criminal provisions in respect to particularly harmful activity. Such criminal provisions often describe not only substantive offenses, but also more technical, administratively-related offenses such as failure to keep accurate records or to provide requested information. These statutes pose two problems: first, which criminal regulatory provisions should the Commission initially consider, and second, how should it treat technical or administratively-related criminal violations?

In respect to the first problem, the Commission found that it could not comprehensively treat all regulatory violations in the initial set of guidelines. There are hundreds of such provisions scattered throughout the United States Code. To find all potential violations would involve examination of each individual federal regulation. Because of this practical difficulty, the Commission sought to determine, with the assistance of the Department of Justice and several regulatory agencies, which criminal regulatory offenses were particularly important in light of the need for enforcement of the general regulatory scheme. The Commission addressed these offenses in the initial guidelines.

In respect to the second problem, the Commission has developed a system for treating technical recordkeeping and reporting offenses that divides them into four categories. First, in the simplest of cases, the offender may have failed to fill out a form intentionally, but without knowledge or intent that substantive harm would likely follow. He might fail, for example, to keep an accurate record of toxic substance transport, but that failure may not lead, nor be likely to lead, to the release or improper handling of any toxic substance. Second, the same failure may be accompanied by a significant likelihood that substantive harm will occur; it may make a release of a toxic substance more likely. Third, the same failure may have led to substantive harm. Fourth, the failure may represent an effort to conceal a substantive harm that has occurred.

The structure of a typical guideline for a regulatory offense provides a low base offense level (*e.g.*, 6) aimed at the first type of recordkeeping or reporting offense. Specific offense characteristics designed to reflect substantive harms that do occur in respect to some regulatory offenses, or that are likely to occur, increase the offense level. A specific offense characteristic also provides that a recordkeeping or reporting offense that conceals a substantive offense will have the same offense level as the substantive offense.

(g) Sentencing Ranges.

In determining the appropriate sentencing ranges for each offense, the Commission estimated the average sentences served within each category under the

pre-guidelines sentencing system. It also examined the sentences specified in federal statutes, in the parole guidelines, and in other relevant, analogous sources. The Commission's Supplementary Report on the Initial Sentencing Guidelines (1987) contains a comparison between estimates of pre-guidelines sentencing practice and sentences under the guidelines.

While the Commission has not considered itself bound by pre-guidelines sentencing practice, it has not attempted to develop an entirely new system of sentencing on the basis of theory alone. Guideline sentences, in many instances, will approximate average pre-guidelines practice and adherence to the guidelines will help to eliminate wide disparity. For example, where a high percentage of persons received probation under pre-guidelines practice, a guideline may include one or more specific offense characteristics in an effort to distinguish those types of defendants who received probation from those who received more severe sentences. In some instances, short sentences of incarceration for all offenders in a category have been substituted for a pre-guidelines sentencing practice of very wide variability in which some defendants received probation while others received several years in prison for the same offense. Moreover, inasmuch as those who pleaded guilty under pre-guidelines practice often received lesser sentences, the guidelines permit the court to impose lesser sentences on those defendants who accept responsibility for their misconduct. For defendants who provide substantial assistance to the government in the investigation or prosecution of others, a downward departure may be warranted.

The Commission has also examined its sentencing ranges in light of their likely impact upon prison population. Specific legislation, such as the Anti-Drug Abuse Act of 1986 and the career offender provisions of the Sentencing Reform Act of 1984 (28 U.S.C. § 994(h)), required the Commission to promulgate guidelines that will lead to substantial prison population increases. These increases will occur irrespective of the guidelines. The guidelines themselves, insofar as they reflect policy decisions made by the Commission (rather than legislated mandatory minimum or career offender sentences), are projected to lead to an increase in prison population that computer models, produced by the Commission and the Bureau of Prisons in 1987, estimated at approximately 10 percent over a period of ten years.

(h) The Sentencing Table.

The Commission has established a sentencing table that for technical and practical reasons contains 43 levels. Each level in the table prescribes ranges that overlap with the ranges in the preceding and succeeding levels. By overlapping the ranges, the table should discourage unnecessary litigation. Both prosecution and defense will realize that the difference between one level and another will not necessarily make a difference in the sentence that the court imposes. Thus, little purpose will be served in protracted litigation trying to determine, for example, whether $10,000 or $11,000 was obtained as a result of a fraud. At the same time, the levels work to increase a sentence proportionately. A change of six levels roughly doubles the sentence irrespective of the level at which one

starts. The guidelines, in keeping with the statutory requirement that the maximum of any range cannot exceed the minimum by more than the greater of 25 percent or six months (28 U.S.C. § 994(b)(2)), permit courts to exercise the greatest permissible range of sentencing discretion. The table overlaps offense levels meaningfully, works proportionately, and at the same time preserves the maximum degree of allowable discretion for the court within each level.

Similarly, many of the individual guidelines refer to tables that correlate amounts of money with offense levels. These tables often have many rather than a few levels. Again, the reason is to minimize the likelihood of unnecessary litigation. If a money table were to make only a few distinctions, each distinction would become more important and litigation over which category an offender fell within would become more likely. Where a table has many small monetary distinctions, it minimizes the likelihood of litigation because the precise amount of money involved is of considerably less importance.

5. A Concluding Note

The Commission emphasizes that it drafted the initial guidelines with considerable caution. It examined the many hundreds of criminal statutes in the United States Code. It began with those that were the basis for a significant number of prosecutions and sought to place them in a rational order. It developed additional distinctions relevant to the application of these provisions and it applied sentencing ranges to each resulting category. In doing so, it relied upon preguidelines sentencing practice as revealed by its own statistical analyses based on summary reports of some 40,000 convictions, a sample of 10,000 augmented presentence reports, the parole guidelines, and policy judgments.

The Commission recognizes that some will criticize this approach as overly cautious, as representing too little a departure from pre-guidelines sentencing practice. Yet, it will cure wide disparity. The Commission is a permanent body that can amend the guidelines each year. Although the data available to it, like all data, are imperfect, experience with the guidelines will lead to additional information and provide a firm empirical basis for consideration of revisions.

Finally, the guidelines will apply to more than 90 percent of all felony and Class A misdemeanor cases in the federal courts. Because of time constraints and the nonexistence of statistical information, some offenses that occur infrequently are not considered in the guidelines. Their exclusion does not reflect any judgment regarding their seriousness and they will be addressed as the Commission refines the guidelines over time.

2. CONTINUING EVOLUTION AND ROLE OF THE GUIDELINES

The Sentencing Reform Act of 1984 changed the course of federal sentencing. Among other things, the Act created the United States Sentencing Commission as an

independent agency in the Judicial Branch, and directed it to develop guidelines and policy statements for sentencing courts to use when sentencing offenders convicted of federal crimes. Moreover, it empowered the Commission with ongoing responsibilities to monitor the guidelines, submit to Congress appropriate modifications of the guidelines and recommended changes in criminal statutes, and establish education and research programs. The mandate rested on congressional awareness that sentencing is a dynamic field that requires continuing review by an expert body to revise sentencing policies, in light of application experience, as new criminal statutes are enacted, and as more is learned about what motivates and controls criminal behavior.

This statement finds resonance in a line of Supreme Court cases that, taken together, echo two themes. The first theme is that the guidelines are the product of a deliberative process that seeks to embody the purposes of sentencing set forth in the Sentencing Reform Act, and as such they continue to play an important role in the sentencing court's determination of an appropriate sentence in a particular case. The Supreme Court alluded to this in *Mistretta v. United States*, 488 U.S. 361 (1989), which upheld the constitutionality of both the federal sentencing guidelines and the Commission against nondelegation and separation of powers challenges. Therein the Court stated:

Developing proportionate penalties for hundreds of different crimes by a virtually limitless array of offenders is precisely the sort of intricate, laborintensive task for which delegation to an expert body is especially appropriate.

Although Congress has delegated significant discretion to the Commission to draw judgments from its analysis of existing sentencing practice and alternative sentencing models, . . . [w]e have no doubt that in the hands of the Commission "the criteria which Congress has supplied are wholly adequate for carrying out the general policy and purpose" of the Act.

Id. at 379 (internal quotation marks and citations omitted).

The continuing importance of the guidelines in federal sentencing was further acknowledged by the Court in *United States v. Booker*, 543 U.S. 220 (2005), even as that case rendered the guidelines advisory in nature. In *Booker*, the Court held that the imposition of an enhanced sentence under the federal sentencing guidelines based on the sentencing judge's determination of a fact (other than a prior conviction) that was not found by the jury or admitted by the defendant violated the Sixth Amendment. The Court reasoned that an advisory guideline system, while lacking the mandatory features that Congress enacted, retains other features that help to further congressional objectives, including providing certainty and fairness in meeting the purposes of sentencing, avoiding unwarranted sentencing disparities, and maintaining sufficient flexibility to permit individualized sentences when warranted. The Court concluded that an advisory guideline system would "continue to move sentencing in Congress' preferred direction, helping to avoid excessive sentencing disparities while maintaining flexibility sufficient to individualize sentences where necessary." *Id.* at

264–65. An advisory guideline system continues to assure transparency by requiring that sentences be based on articulated reasons stated in open court that are subject to appellate review. An advisory guideline system also continues to promote certainty

and predictability in sentencing, thereby enabling the parties to better anticipate the likely sentence based on the individualized facts of the case.

The continuing importance of the guidelines in the sentencing determination is predicated in large part on the Sentencing Reform Act's intent that, in promulgating guidelines, the Commission must take into account the purposes of sentencing as set forth in 18 U.S.C. § 3553(a). *See* 28 U.S.C. §§ 994(f), 991(b)(1). The Supreme Court reinforced this view in *Rita v. United States*, 551 U.S. 338 (2007), which held that a court of appeals may apply a presumption of reasonableness to a sentence imposed by a district court within a properly calculated guideline range without violating the Sixth Amendment. In *Rita*, the Court relied heavily on the complementary roles of the Commission and the sentencing court in federal sentencing, stating:

[T]he presumption reflects the nature of the Guidelines-writing task that Congress set for the Commission and the manner in which the Commission carried out that task. In instructing both the *sentencing judge* and the *Commission* what to do, Congress referred to the basic sentencing objectives that the statute sets forth in 18 U.S.C. § 3553(a) . . . . The provision also tells the sentencing judge to "impose a sentence sufficient, but not greater than necessary, to comply with" the basic aims of sentencing as set out above. Congressional statutes then tell the *Commission* to write Guidelines that will carry out these same § 3553(a) objectives.

Id. at 347–48 (emphasis in original). The Court concluded that "[t]he upshot is that the sentencing statutes envision both the sentencing judge and the Commission as carrying out the same basic § 3553(a) objectives, the one, at retail, the other at wholesale[,]" *id.* at 348, and that the Commission's process for promulgating guidelines results in "a set of Guidelines that seek to embody the § 3553(a) considerations, both in principle and in practice." *Id.* at 350.

Consequently, district courts are required to properly calculate and consider the guidelines when sentencing, even in an advisory guideline system. *See* 18 U.S.C. § 3553(a)(4), (a)(5); *Booker*, 543 U.S. at 264 ("The district courts, while not bound to apply the Guidelines, must . . . take them into account when sentencing."); *Rita*, 551 U.S. at 351 (stating that a district court should begin all sentencing proceedings by correctly calculating the applicable Guidelines range); *Gall v. United States*, 552 U.S. 38, 49 (2007) ("As a matter of administration and to secure nationwide consistency, the Guidelines should be the starting point and the initial benchmark."). The district court, in determining the appropriate sentence in a particular case, therefore, must consider the properly calculated guideline range, the grounds for departure provided in the policy statements, and then the factors under 18 U.S.C. § 3553(a). *See Rita*, 551 U.S. at 351. The appellate court engages in a two-step process upon review. The appellate court "first ensure[s] that the district court committed no significant procedural error, such as failing to calculate (or improperly calculating) the Guidelines range . . . [and] then consider[s] the substantive reasonableness of the sentence imposed under an abuse-of-discretion standard[,] . . . tak[ing] into account the totality of the circumstances, including the extent of any variance from the Guidelines range." *Gall*, 552 U.S. at 51.

The second and related theme resonant in this line of Supreme Court cases is that, as contemplated by the Sentencing Reform Act, the guidelines are evolutionary in nature. They are the product of the Commission's fulfillment of its statutory duties to monitor federal sentencing law and practices, to seek public input on the operation of the guidelines, and to revise the guidelines accordingly. As the Court acknowledged in *Rita*:

The Commission's work is ongoing. The statutes and the Guidelines themselves foresee continuous evolution helped by the sentencing courts and courts of appeals in that process. The sentencing courts, applying the Guidelines in individual cases may depart (either pursuant to the Guidelines or, since *Booker*, by imposing a non-Guidelines sentence). The judges will set forth their reasons. The Courts of Appeals will determine the reasonableness of the resulting sentence. The Commission will collect and examine the results. In doing so, it may obtain advice from prosecutors, defenders, law enforcement groups, civil liberties associations, experts in penology, and others. And it can revise the Guidelines accordingly.

Rita, 551 U.S. at 350; *see also Booker*, 543 U.S. at 264 ("[T]he Sentencing Commission remains in place, writing Guidelines, collecting information about actual district court sentencing decisions, undertaking research, and revising the Guidelines accordingly."); *Gall*, 552 U.S. at 46 ("[E]ven though the Guidelines are advisory rather than mandatory, they are, as we pointed out in *Rita*, the product of careful study based on extensive empirical evidence derived from the review of thousands of individual sentencing decisions.").

Provisions of the Sentencing Reform Act promote and facilitate this evolutionary process. For example, pursuant to 28 U.S.C. § 994(x), the Commission publishes guideline amendment proposals in the *Federal Register* and conducts hearings to solicit input on those proposals from experts and other members of the public. Pursuant to 28 U.S.C. § 994(o), the Commission periodically reviews and revises the guidelines in consideration of comments it receives from members of the federal criminal justice system, including the courts, probation officers, the Department of Justice, the Bureau of Prisons, defense attorneys and the federal public defenders, and in consideration of data it receives from sentencing courts and other sources. Statutory mechanisms such as these bolster the Commission's ability to take into account fully the purposes of sentencing set forth in 18 U.S.C. § 3553(a)(2) in its promulgation of the guidelines.

Congress retains authority to require certain sentencing practices and may exercise its authority through specific directives to the Commission with respect to the guidelines. As the Supreme Court noted in *Kimbrough v. United States*, 552 U.S. 85 (2007), "Congress has shown that it knows how to direct sentencing practices in express terms. For example, Congress has specifically required the Sentencing Commission to set Guideline sentences for serious recidivist offenders 'at or near' the statutory maximum." *Id.* at 103; 28 U.S.C. § 994(h).

As envisioned by Congress, implemented by the Commission, and reaffirmed by the Supreme Court, the guidelines are the product of a deliberative and dynamic process that seeks to embody within federal sentencing policy the purposes of sentencing set forth in the Sentencing Reform Act. As such, the guidelines continue to be a key component of federal sentencing and to play an important role in the sentencing court's determination of an appropriate sentence in any particular case.

3. AUTHORITY

§1A3.1. Authority

The guidelines, policy statements, and commentary set forth in this Guidelines Manual, including amendments thereto, are promulgated by the United States Sentencing Commission pursuant to: (1) section 994(a) of title 28, United States Code; and (2) with respect to guidelines, policy statements, and commentary promulgated or amended pursuant to specific congressional directive, pursuant to the authority contained in that directive in addition to the authority under section 994(a) of title 28, United States Code.

Historical Note

Effective November 1, 1987. Amended effective November 1, 1989 (amendments 67 and 68); November 1, 1990 (amendment 307); November 1, 1992 (amendment 466); November 1, 1995 (amendment 534); November 1, 1996 (amendment 538); November 1, 2000 (amendments 602 and 603); October 27, 2003 (amendment 651); November 1, 2008 (amendments 717 and 725); November 1, 2014 (amendment 789).

PART B — GENERAL APPLICATION PRINCIPLES

§1B1.1. Application Instructions

(a) The court shall determine the kinds of sentence and the guideline range as set forth in the guidelines (*see* 18 U.S.C. § 3553(a)(4)) by applying the provisions of this manual in the following order, except as specifically directed:

(1) Determine, pursuant to §1B1.2 (Applicable Guidelines), the offense guideline section from Chapter Two (Offense Conduct) applicable to the offense of conviction. *See* §1B1.2.

(2) Determine the base offense level and apply any appropriate specific offense characteristics, cross references, and special instructions contained in the particular guideline in Chapter Two in the order listed.

(3) Apply the adjustments as appropriate related to victim, role, and obstruction of justice from Parts A, B, and C of Chapter Three.

(4) If there are multiple counts of conviction, repeat steps (1) through (3) for each count. Apply Part D of Chapter Three to group the various counts and adjust the offense level accordingly.

(5) Apply the adjustment as appropriate for the defendant's acceptance of responsibility from Part E of Chapter Three.

(6) Determine the defendant's criminal history category as specified in Part A of Chapter Four. Determine from Part B of Chapter Four any other applicable adjustments.

(7) Determine the guideline range in Part A of Chapter Five that corresponds to the offense level and criminal history category determined above.

(8) For the particular guideline range, determine from Parts B through G of Chapter Five the sentencing requirements and

options related to probation, imprisonment, supervision conditions, fines, and restitution.

(b) The court shall then consider Parts H and K of Chapter Five, Specific Offender Characteristics and Departures, and any other policy

statements or commentary in the guidelines that might warrant consideration in imposing sentence. *See* 18 U.S.C. § 3553(a)(5).

(c) The court shall then consider the applicable factors in 18 U.S.C. § 3553(a) taken as a whole. *See* 18 U.S.C. § 3553(a).

Commentary

Application Notes:

1. The following are definitions of terms that are used frequently in the guidelines and are of general applicability (except to the extent expressly modified in respect to a particular guideline or policy statement):

(A) "***Abducted***" means that a victim was forced to accompany an offender to a different location. For example, a bank robber's forcing a bank teller from the bank into a getaway car would constitute an abduction.

(B) "***Bodily injury***" means any significant injury; *e.g.*, an injury that is painful and obvious, or is of a type for which medical attention ordinarily would be sought.

(C) "***Brandished***" with reference to a dangerous weapon (including a firearm) means that all or part of the weapon was displayed, or the presence of the weapon was otherwise made known to another person, in order to intimidate that person, regardless of whether the weapon was directly visible to that person. Accordingly, although the dangerous weapon does not have to be directly visible, the weapon must be present.

(D) "***Dangerous weapon***" means (i) an instrument capable of inflicting death or serious bodily injury; or (ii) an object that is not an instrument capable of inflicting death or serious bodily injury but (I) closely resembles such an instrument; or (II) the defendant used the object in a manner that created the impression that the object was such an instrument (*e.g.* a defendant wrapped a hand in a towel during a bank robbery to create the appearance of a gun).

(E) "***Departure***" means (i) for purposes other than those specified in subdivision (ii), imposition of a sentence outside the applicable guideline range or of a sentence that is otherwise different from the guideline sentence; and (ii) for purposes of §4A1.3 (Departures Based on Inadequacy of Criminal History Category), assignment of a criminal history category other than the otherwise applicable criminal history category, in order to effect a sentence outside the applicable guideline range. "***Depart***" means grant a departure.

"***Downward departure***" means departure that effects a sentence less than a sentence that could be imposed under the applicable guideline range or a sentence that is otherwise less than the guideline sentence. "***Depart downward***" means grant a downward departure.

"***Upward departure***" means departure that effects a sentence greater than a sentence that could be imposed under the applicable guideline range or a sentence that is otherwise greater than the guideline sentence. "***Depart upward***" means grant an upward departure.

(F) "***Destructive device***" means any article described in 26 U.S.C. § 5845(f) (including an explosive, incendiary, or poison gas — (i) bomb, (ii) grenade, (iii) rocket having a propellant charge of more than four ounces, (iv) missile having an explosive or incendiary charge of more than one-quarter ounce, (v) mine, or (vi) device similar

to any of the devices described in the preceding clauses).
(G) "***Firearm***" means (i) any weapon (including a starter gun) which will or is designed to or may readily be converted to expel a projectile by the action of an explosive; (ii) the frame or receiver of any such weapon; (iii) any firearm muffler or silencer; or (iv) any destructive device. A weapon, commonly known as a "BB" or pellet gun, that uses air or carbon dioxide pressure to expel a projectile is a dangerous weapon but not a firearm.
(H) "***Offense***" means the offense of conviction and all relevant conduct under §1B1.3 (Relevant Conduct) unless a different meaning is specified or is otherwise clear from the context. The term "***instant***" is used in connection with "offense," "federal offense," or "offense of conviction," as the case may be, to distinguish the violation for which the defendant is being sentenced from a prior or subsequent offense, or from an offense before another court (*e.g.*, an offense before a state court involving the same underlying conduct).
(I) "***Otherwise used***" with reference to a dangerous weapon (including a firearm) means that the conduct did not amount to the discharge of a firearm but was more than brandishing, displaying, or possessing a firearm or other dangerous weapon.
(J) "***Permanent or life-threatening bodily injury***" means injury involving a substantial risk of death; loss or substantial impairment of the function of a bodily member, organ, or mental faculty that is likely to be permanent; or an obvious disfigurement that is likely to be permanent. In the case of a kidnapping, for example, maltreatment to a life-threatening degree (*e.g.*, by denial of food or medical care) would constitute life-threatening bodily injury.
(K) "***Physically restrained***" means the forcible restraint of the victim such as by being tied, bound, or locked up.
(L) "***Serious bodily injury***" means injury involving extreme physical pain or the protracted impairment of a function of a bodily member, organ, or mental faculty; or requiring medical intervention such as surgery, hospitalization, or physical rehabilitation. In addition, "serious bodily injury" is deemed to have occurred if the offense involved conduct constituting criminal sexual abuse under 18 U.S.C. § 2241 or § 2242 or any similar offense under state law.
2. Definitions of terms also may appear in other sections. Such definitions are not designed for general applicability; therefore, their applicability to sections other than those expressly referenced must be determined on a case by case basis.
The term "***includes***" is not exhaustive; the term "***e.g.***" is merely illustrative.
3. The list of "Statutory Provisions" in the Commentary to each offense guideline does not necessarily include every statute covered by that guideline. In addition, some statutes may be covered by more than one guideline.
4. (A) **Cumulative Application of Multiple Adjustments within One Guideline.—** The offense level adjustments from more than one specific offense characteristic

within an offense guideline are applied cumulatively (added together) unless the guideline specifies that only the greater (or greatest) is to be used. Within each specific offense characteristic subsection, however, the offense level adjustments are alternative; only the one that best describes the conduct is to be used. For example, in §2A2.2(b)(3), pertaining to degree of bodily injury, the subdivision that best describes the level of bodily injury is used; the adjustments for different degrees of bodily injury (subdivisions (A) – (E)) are not added together.
(B) **Cumulative Application of Multiple Adjustments from Multiple Guidelines.—** Absent an instruction to the contrary, enhancements under Chapter Two, adjustments under Chapter Three, and determinations under Chapter Four are to be applied cumulatively. In some cases, such enhancements, adjustments, and determinations may be triggered by the same conduct. For example, shooting a police officer during the commission of a robbery may warrant an injury enhancement

under §2B3.1(b)(3) and an official victim adjustment under §3A1.2, even though the enhancement and the adjustment both are triggered by the shooting of the officer.

5. Where two or more guideline provisions appear equally applicable, but the guidelines authorize the application of only one such provision, use the provision that results in the greater offense level. *E.g.*, in §2A2.2(b)(2), if a firearm is both discharged and brandished, the provision applicable to the discharge of the firearm would be used.

6. **Use of Abbreviated Guideline Titles.**—Whenever a guideline makes reference to another guideline, a parenthetical restatement of that other guideline's heading accompanies the initial reference to that other guideline. This parenthetical is provided only for the convenience of the reader and is not intended to have substantive effect. In the case of lengthy guideline headings, such a parenthetical restatement of the guideline heading may be abbreviated for ease of reference. For example, references to §2B1.1 (Larceny, Embezzlement, and Other Forms of Theft; Offenses Involving Stolen Property; Property Damage or Destruction; Fraud and Deceit; Forgery; Offenses Involving Altered or Counterfeit Instruments Other than Counterfeit Bearer Obligations of the United States) may be abbreviated as follows: §2B1.1 (Theft, Property Destruction, and Fraud).

Background: The court must impose a sentence "sufficient, but not greater than necessary," to comply with the purposes of sentencing set forth in 18 U.S.C. § 3553(a)(2). *See* 18 U.S.C. § 3553(a). Subsections (a), (b), and (c) are structured to reflect the three-step process used in determining the particular sentence to be imposed. If, after step (c), the court imposes a sentence that is outside the guidelines framework, such a sentence is considered a "***variance***". *See Irizarry v. United States*, 553 U.S. 708, 709–16 (2008) (describing within-range sentences and departures as "sentences imposed under the framework set out in the Guidelines").

Historical Note

Effective November 1, 1987. Amended effective January 15, 1988 (amendment 1); November 1, 1989 (amendments 69–72 and 303); November 1, 1990 (amendment 361); November 1, 1991 (amendment 388); November 1, 1993 (amendment 497); November 1, 1997 (amendments 545 and 546); November 1, 2000 (amendments 591 and 601); November 1, 2001 (amendment 617); October 27, 2003 (amendment 651); November 1, 2003 (amendment 661); November 1, 2006 (amendment 684); November 1, 2010 (amendment 741); November 1, 2014 (amendment 789).

§1B1.2. Applicable Guidelines

(a) Determine the offense guideline section in Chapter Two (Offense Conduct) applicable to the offense of conviction (*i.e.*, the offense conduct charged in the count of the indictment or information of which the defendant was convicted). However, in the case of a plea agreement (written or made orally on the record) containing a stipulation that specifically establishes a more serious offense than the offense of conviction, determine the offense guideline section in Chapter Two applicable to the stipulated offense.

Refer to the Statutory Index (Appendix A) to determine the Chapter Two offense guideline, referenced in the Statutory Index for the offense of conviction. If the offense involved a conspiracy, attempt, or solicitation, refer to §2X1.1 (Attempt, Solicitation, or Conspiracy) as well as the guideline referenced in the Statutory Index for the substantive offense. For statutory provisions not listed in the Statutory Index, use the most analogous guideline. *See* §2X5.1 (Other Offenses). The guidelines do not apply to any count of conviction that is a Class B or C misdemeanor or an infraction. *See* §1B1.9 (Class B or C Misdemeanors and Infractions).

(b) After determining the appropriate offense guideline section pursuant to subsection (a) of this section, determine the applicable guideline

range in accordance with §1B1.3 (Relevant Conduct).
(c) A plea agreement (written or made orally on the record) containing a stipulation that specifically establishes the commission of additional offense(s) shall be treated as if the defendant had been convicted of additional count(s) charging those offense(s).
(d) A conviction on a count charging a conspiracy to commit more than one offense shall be treated as if the defendant had been convicted on a separate count of conspiracy for each offense that the defendant conspired to commit.

Commentary

Application Notes:

1. This section provides the basic rules for determining the guidelines applicable to the offense conduct under Chapter Two (Offense Conduct). The court is to use the Chapter Two guideline section referenced in the Statutory Index (Appendix A) for the offense of conviction. However, (A) in the case of a plea agreement (written or made orally on the record) containing a stipulation that specifically establishes a more serious offense than the offense of conviction, the Chapter Two offense guideline section applicable to the stipulated offense is to be used; and (B) for statutory provisions not listed in the Statutory Index, the most analogous guideline, determined pursuant to §2X5.1 (Other Offenses), is to be used.

In the case of a particular statute that proscribes only a single type of criminal conduct, the offense of conviction and the conduct proscribed by the statute will coincide, and the Statutory Index will specify only one offense guideline for that offense of conviction. In the case of a particular statute that proscribes a variety of conduct that might constitute the subject of different offense guidelines, the Statutory Index may specify more than one offense guideline for that particular statute, and the court will determine which of the referenced guideline sections is most appropriate for the offense conduct charged in the count of which the defendant was convicted. If the offense involved a conspiracy, attempt, or solicitation, refer to §2X1.1 (Attempt, Solicitation, or Conspiracy) as well as the guideline referenced in the Statutory Index for the substantive offense. For statutory provisions not listed in the Statutory Index, the most analogous guideline is to be used. *See* §2X5.1 (Other Offenses).

As set forth in the first paragraph of this note, an exception to this general rule is that if a plea agreement (written or made orally on the record) contains a stipulation that establishes a more serious offense than the offense of conviction, the guideline section applicable to the stipulated offense is to be used. A factual statement or a stipulation contained in a plea agreement (written or made orally on the record) is a stipulation for purposes of subsection (a) only if both the defendant and the government explicitly agree that the factual statement or stipulation is a stipulation for such purposes. However, a factual statement or stipulation made after the plea agreement has been entered, or after any modification to the plea agreement has been made, is not a stipulation for purposes of subsection (a). The sentence that shall be imposed is limited, however, to the maximum authorized by the statute under which the defendant is convicted. *See* Chapter Five, Part G (Implementing the Total Sentence of Imprisonment). For example, if the defendant pleads guilty to theft, but admits the elements of robbery as part of the plea agreement, the robbery guideline is to be applied. The sentence, however, may not exceed the maximum sentence for theft. *See* H. Rep. 98-1017, 98th Cong., 2d Sess. 99 (1984).

The exception to the general rule has a practical basis. In a case in which the elements of an offense more serious than the offense of conviction are established by a plea agreement, it may unduly complicate the sentencing process if the applicable guideline does not reflect the seriousness of the defendant's actual conduct. Without this exception, the court would be forced to use an artificial guideline and then depart from it to the degree the court found necessary based upon the more serious conduct established by the plea agreement. The probation officer would first be required to calculate the guideline for the offense of conviction. However, this guideline might even contain characteristics that are difficult to establish or not very important in the context of the actual offense conduct. As a simple example, §2B1.1 (Theft, Property Destruction, and Fraud) contains monetary distinctions which are more significant and more detailed than the monetary distinctions in §2B3.1 (Robbery). Then, the probation officer might need to calculate the robbery guideline to assist the court in determining the appropriate degree of departure in a case in which the defendant pled guilty to theft but admitted committing robbery. This cumbersome, artificial procedure is avoided by using the exception rule in guilty or *nolo contendere* plea cases where it is applicable.

As with any plea agreement, the court must first determine that the agreement is acceptable, in accordance with the policies stated in Chapter Six, Part B (Plea Agreements). The limited exception provided here applies only after the court has determined that a plea, otherwise fitting the exception, is acceptable.

2. Section 1B1.2(b) directs the court, once it has determined the applicable guideline (*i.e.*, the applicable guideline section from Chapter Two) under §1B1.2(a) to determine

any applicable specific offense characteristics (under that guideline), and any other applicable sentencing factors pursuant to the relevant conduct definition in §1B1.3. Where there is more than one base offense level within a particular guideline, the determination of the applicable base offense level is treated in the same manner as a determination of a specific offense characteristic. Accordingly, the "relevant conduct" criteria of §1B1.3 are to be used, unless conviction under a specific statute is expressly required.

3. Subsections (c) and (d) address circumstances in which the provisions of Chapter Three, Part D (Multiple Counts) are to be applied although there may be only one count of conviction. Subsection (c) provides that in the case of a stipulation to the commission of additional offense(s), the guidelines are to be applied as if the defendant had been convicted of an additional count for each of the offenses stipulated. For example, if the defendant is convicted of one count of robbery but, as part of a plea agreement, admits to having committed two additional robberies, the guidelines are to be applied as if the defendant had been convicted of three counts of robbery. Subsection (d) provides that a conviction on a conspiracy count charging conspiracy to commit more than one offense is treated as if the defendant had been convicted of a separate conspiracy count for each offense that he conspired to commit. For example, where a conviction on a single count of conspiracy establishes that the defendant conspired to commit three robberies, the guidelines are to be applied as if the defendant had been convicted on one count of conspiracy to commit the first robbery, one count of conspiracy to commit the second robbery, and one count of conspiracy to commit the third robbery.

4. Particular care must be taken in applying subsection (d) because there are cases in which the verdict or plea does not establish which offense(s) was the object of the conspiracy. In such cases, subsection (d) should only be applied with respect to an object offense alleged in the conspiracy count if the court, were it sitting as a trier of fact, would convict the defendant of conspiring to commit that object offense. Note, however, if the object offenses specified in the conspiracy count would be grouped together under §3D1.2(d) (*e.g.*, a conspiracy to steal three government checks) it is not necessary to engage in the foregoing analysis, because §1B1.3(a)(2) governs consideration of the defendant's conduct.

Historical Note

Effective November 1, 1987. Amended effective January 15, 1988 (amendment 2); November 1, 1989 (amendments 73–75 and 303); November 1, 1991 (amendment 434); November 1, 1992 (amendment 438); November 1, 2000 (amendment 591); November 1, 2001 (amendments 613 and 617).

§1B1.3. Relevant Conduct (Factors that Determine the Guideline Range)

(a) CHAPTERS TWO (OFFENSE CONDUCT) AND THREE (ADJUSTMENTS). Unless otherwise specified, (i) the base offense level where the guideline specifies more than one base offense level, (ii) specific offense characteristics and (iii) cross references in Chapter Two, and (iv) adjustments in Chapter Three, shall be determined on the basis of the following:

(1) (A) all acts and omissions committed, aided, abetted, counseled, commanded, induced, procured, or willfully caused by the defendant; and

(B) in the case of a jointly undertaken criminal activity (a criminal plan, scheme, endeavor, or enterprise undertaken by the defendant in concert with others, whether or not charged as a conspiracy), all acts and omissions of others that were—

(i) within the scope of the jointly undertaken criminal activity,

(ii) in furtherance of that criminal activity, and

(iii) reasonably foreseeable in connection with that criminal activity;

that occurred during the commission of the offense of conviction, in preparation for that offense, or in the course of attempting to avoid detection or responsibility for that offense;

(2) solely with respect to offenses of a character for which §3D1.2(d) would require grouping of multiple counts, all acts and omissions described in subdivisions (1)(A) and (1)(B) above that were part of the same course of conduct or common scheme or plan as the offense of conviction;

(3) all harm that resulted from the acts and omissions specified in subsections (a)(1) and (a)(2) above, and all harm that was the object of such acts and omissions; and

(4) any other information specified in the applicable guideline.

(b) CHAPTERS FOUR (CRIMINAL HISTORY AND CRIMINAL LIVELIHOOD) AND FIVE (DETERMINING THE SENTENCE). Factors in Chapters Four and Five that establish the guideline range shall be determined on the basis of the conduct and information specified in the respective guidelines.

Commentary

Application Notes:

1. **Sentencing Accountability and Criminal Liability.**—The principles and limits of sentencing accountability under this guideline are not always the same as the principles and limits of criminal liability. Under subsections (a)(1) and (a)(2), the focus is on the specific acts and omissions for which the defendant is to be held accountable in determining the applicable guideline range, rather than on whether the defendant is criminally liable for an offense as a principal, accomplice, or conspirator.

2. **Accountability Under More Than One Provision.**—In certain cases, a defendant may be accountable for particular conduct under more than one subsection of this guide**§**

line. If a defendant's accountability for particular conduct is established under one provision of this guideline, it is not necessary to review alternative provisions under which such accountability might be established.

3. **Jointly Undertaken Criminal Activity (Subsection (a)(1)(B)).—**

(A) **In General.—**A "***jointly undertaken criminal activity***" is a criminal plan, scheme, endeavor, or enterprise undertaken by the defendant in concert with others, whether or not charged as a conspiracy.

In the case of a jointly undertaken criminal activity, subsection (a)(1)(B) provides that a defendant is accountable for the conduct (acts and omissions) of others that was:

(i) within the scope of the jointly undertaken criminal activity;

(ii) in furtherance of that criminal activity; and

(iii) reasonably foreseeable in connection with that criminal activity.

The conduct of others that meets all three criteria set forth in subdivisions (i) through (iii) (*i.e.*, "within the scope," "in furtherance," and "reasonably foreseeable") is relevant conduct under this provision. However, when the conduct of others does not meet any one of the criteria set forth in subdivisions (i) through (iii), the conduct is not relevant conduct under this provision.

(B) **Scope.—**Because a count may be worded broadly and include the conduct of many participants over a period of time, the scope of the "jointly undertaken criminal activity" is not necessarily the same as the scope of the entire conspiracy, and hence relevant conduct is not necessarily the same for every participant. In order to determine the defendant's accountability for the conduct of others under subsection (a)(1)(B), the court must first determine the scope of the criminal activity the particular defendant agreed to jointly undertake (*i.e.*, the scope of the specific conduct and objectives embraced by the defendant's agreement). In doing so, the court may consider any explicit agreement or implicit agreement fairly inferred from the conduct of the defendant and others. Accordingly, the accountability of the defendant for the acts of others is limited by the scope of his or her agreement to jointly undertake the particular criminal activity. Acts of others that were not within the scope of the defendant's agreement, even if those acts were known or reasonably foreseeable to the defendant, are not relevant conduct under subsection (a)(1)(B).

In cases involving contraband (including controlled substances), the scope of the jointly undertaken criminal activity (and thus the accountability of the defendant for the contraband that was the object of that jointly undertaken activity) may depend upon whether, in the particular circumstances, the nature of the offense is more appropriately viewed as one jointly undertaken criminal activity or as a number of separate criminal activities.

A defendant's relevant conduct does not include the conduct of members of a conspiracy prior to the defendant joining the conspiracy, even if the defendant knows of that conduct (*e.g.*, in the case of a defendant who joins an ongoing drug distribution conspiracy knowing that it had been selling two kilograms of cocaine per week, the cocaine sold prior to the defendant joining the conspiracy is not included as relevant conduct in determining the defendant's offense level). The Commission

does not foreclose the possibility that there may be some unusual set of circumstances in which the exclusion of such conduct may not adequately reflect the defendant's culpability; in such a case, an upward departure may be warranted.

(C) **In Furtherance.—**The court must determine if the conduct (acts and omissions) of others was in furtherance of the jointly undertaken criminal activity.

(D) **Reasonably Foreseeable.—**The court must then determine if the conduct (acts and omissions) of others that was within the scope of, and in furtherance of, the jointly undertaken criminal activity was reasonably foreseeable in connection with that criminal activity.

Note that the criminal activity that the defendant agreed to jointly undertake, and the reasonably foreseeable conduct of others in furtherance of that criminal activity, are not necessarily identical. For example, two defendants agree to commit a robbery and, during the course of that robbery, the first defendant assaults and injures a victim. The second defendant is accountable for the assault and injury to the victim (even if the second defendant had not agreed to the assault and had cautioned the first defendant to be careful not to hurt anyone) because the assaultive conduct was within the scope of the jointly undertaken criminal activity (the robbery), was in furtherance of that criminal activity (the robbery), and was reasonably foreseeable in connection with that criminal activity (given the nature of the offense).

With respect to offenses involving contraband (including controlled substances), the defendant is accountable under subsection (a)(1)(A) for all quantities of contraband with which he was directly involved and, in the case of a jointly undertaken criminal activity under subsection (a)(1)(B), all quantities of contraband that were involved in transactions carried out by other participants, if those transactions were within the scope of, and in furtherance of, the jointly undertaken criminal activity and were reasonably foreseeable in connection with that criminal activity.

The requirement of reasonable foreseeability applies only in respect to the conduct (*i.e.*, acts and omissions) of others under subsection (a)(1)(B). It does not apply to conduct that the defendant personally undertakes, aids, abets, counsels, commands, induces, procures, or willfully causes; such conduct is addressed under subsection (a)(1)(A).

4. **Illustrations of Conduct for Which the Defendant is Accountable under Subsections (a)(1)(A) and (B).—**

(A) **Acts and omissions aided or abetted by the defendant.—**

(i) Defendant A is one of ten persons hired by Defendant B to off-load a ship containing marihuana. The off-loading of the ship is interrupted by law enforcement officers and one ton of marihuana is seized (the amount on the ship as well as the amount off-loaded). Defendant A and the other off-loaders are arrested and convicted of importation of marihuana. Regardless of the number of bales he personally unloaded, Defendant A is accountable for the entire oneton quantity of marihuana. Defendant A aided and abetted the off-loading of the entire shipment of marihuana by directly participating in the off-loading of that shipment (*i.e.*, the specific objective of the criminal activity he joined was the off-loading of the entire shipment). Therefore, he is accountable for the entire shipment under subsection (a)(1)(A) without regard to the issue of

reasonable foreseeability. This is conceptually similar to the case of a defendant who transports a suitcase knowing that it contains a controlled substance and, therefore, is accountable for the controlled substance in the suitcase regardless of his knowledge or lack of knowledge of the actual type or amount of that controlled substance.

In certain cases, a defendant may be accountable for particular conduct under more than one subsection of this guideline. As noted in the preceding paragraph, Defendant A is accountable for the entire one-ton shipment of marihuana under subsection (a)(1)(A). Defendant A also is accountable for the entire one-ton shipment of marihuana on the basis of subsection (a)(1)(B) (applying to a jointly undertaken criminal activity). Defendant A engaged in a jointly undertaken criminal activity and all three criteria of subsection (a)(1)(B) are met. First, the conduct was within the scope of the criminal activity (the importation of the shipment of marihuana). Second, the off-loading of the shipment of marihuana was in furtherance of the criminal activity, as described above. And third, a finding that the one-ton quantity of marihuana was reasonably foreseeable is warranted from the nature of the undertaking itself (the importation of marihuana by ship typically involves very large quantities of marihuana). The specific circumstances of the case (the defendant was one of ten persons off-loading the marihuana in bales) also support this finding. In an actual case, of course, if a defendant's accountability for particular conduct is established under one provision of this guideline, it is not necessary to review alternative provisions under which such accountability might be established. *See* Application Note 2.

(B) **Acts and omissions aided or abetted by the defendant; acts and omissions in a jointly undertaken criminal activity.—**

(i) Defendant C is the getaway driver in an armed bank robbery in which $15,000 is taken and a teller is assaulted and injured. Defendant C is accountable for the money taken under subsection (a)(1)(A) because he aided and abetted the act of taking the money (the taking of money was the specific objective of the offense he joined). Defendant C is accountable for the injury to the teller under subsection (a)(1)(B) because the assault on the teller was within the scope and in furtherance of the jointly undertaken criminal activity (the robbery), and was reasonably foreseeable in connection with that criminal activity (given the nature of the offense).

As noted earlier, a defendant may be accountable for particular conduct under more than one subsection. In this example, Defendant C also is accountable for the money taken on the basis of subsection (a)(1)(B) because the taking of money was within the scope and in furtherance of the jointly undertaken criminal activity (the robbery), and was reasonably foreseeable (as noted, the taking of money was the specific objective of the jointly undertaken criminal activity).

(C) **Requirements that the conduct of others be within the scope of the jointly undertaken criminal activity, in furtherance of that criminal activity, and reasonably foreseeable.—**

(i) Defendant D pays Defendant E a small amount to forge an endorsement on an $800 stolen government check. Unknown to Defendant E, Defendant D then uses that check as a down payment in a scheme to fraudulently obtain

$15,000 worth of merchandise. Defendant E is convicted of forging the $800 check and is accountable for the forgery of this check under subsection (a)(1)(A). Defendant E is not accountable for the $15,000 because the fraudulent scheme to obtain $15,000 was not within the scope of the jointly undertaken criminal activity (*i.e.*, the forgery of the $800 check).

(ii) Defendants F and G, working together, design and execute a scheme to sell fraudulent stocks by telephone. Defendant F fraudulently obtains $20,000. Defendant G fraudulently obtains $35,000. Each is convicted of mail fraud. Defendants F and G each are accountable for the entire amount ($55,000). Each defendant is accountable for the amount he personally obtained under subsection (a)(1)(A). Each defendant is accountable for the amount obtained by his accomplice under subsection (a)(1)(B) because the conduct of each was within the scope of the jointly undertaken criminal activity (the scheme to sell fraudulent stocks), was in furtherance of that criminal activity, and was reasonably foreseeable in connection with that criminal activity.

(iii) Defendants H and I engaged in an ongoing marihuana importation conspiracy in which Defendant J was hired only to help off-load a single shipment. Defendants H, I, and J are included in a single count charging conspiracy to import marihuana. Defendant J is accountable for the entire single shipment of marihuana he helped import under subsection (a)(1)(A) and any acts and omissions of others related to the importation of that shipment on the basis of subsection (a)(1)(B) (*see* the discussion in example (A)(i) above). He is not accountable for prior or subsequent shipments of marihuana imported by Defendants H or I because those acts were not within the scope of his jointly undertaken criminal activity (the importation of the single shipment of marihuana).

(iv) Defendant K is a wholesale distributor of child pornography. Defendant L is a retail-level dealer who purchases child pornography from Defendant K and resells it, but otherwise operates independently of Defendant K. Similarly, Defendant M is a retail-level dealer who purchases child pornography from Defendant K and resells it, but otherwise operates independently of Defendant K. Defendants L and M are aware of each other's criminal activity but operate independently. Defendant N is Defendant K's assistant who recruits customers for Defendant K and frequently supervises the deliveries to Defendant K's customers. Each defendant is convicted of a count charging conspiracy to distribute child pornography. Defendant K is accountable under subsection (a)(1)(A) for the entire quantity of child pornography sold to Defendants L and M. Defendant N also is accountable for the entire quantity sold to those defendants under subsection (a)(1)(B) because the entire quantity was within the scope of his jointly undertaken criminal activity (to distribute child pornography with Defendant K), in furtherance of that criminal activity, and reasonably foreseeable. Defendant L is accountable under subsection (a)(1)(A) only for the quantity of child pornography that he purchased from Defendant K because he is not engaged in a jointly undertaken criminal activity with the other defendants. For the same reason, Defendant M is accountable under subsection (a)(1)(A) only for the quantity of child pornography that he purchased from Defendant K.

(v) Defendant O knows about her boyfriend's ongoing drug-trafficking activity, but agrees to participate on only one occasion by making a delivery for him at his request when he was ill. Defendant O is accountable under subsection

(a)(1)(A) for the drug quantity involved on that one occasion. Defendant O is not accountable for the other drug sales made by her boyfriend because those sales were not within the scope of her jointly undertaken criminal activity (*i.e.*, the one delivery).

(vi) Defendant P is a street-level drug dealer who knows of other street-level drug dealers in the same geographic area who sell the same type of drug as he sells. Defendant P and the other dealers share a common source of supply, but otherwise operate independently. Defendant P is not accountable for the quantities of drugs sold by the other street-level drug dealers because he is not engaged in a jointly undertaken criminal activity with them. In contrast, Defendant Q, another street-level drug dealer, pools his resources and profits with four other street-level drug dealers. Defendant Q is engaged in a jointly undertaken criminal activity and, therefore, he is accountable under subsection (a)(1)(B) for the quantities of drugs sold by the four other dealers during the course of his joint undertaking with them because those sales were within the scope of the jointly undertaken criminal activity, in furtherance of that criminal activity, and reasonably foreseeable in connection with that criminal activity.

(vii) Defendant R recruits Defendant S to distribute 500 grams of cocaine. Defendant S knows that Defendant R is the prime figure in a conspiracy involved in importing much larger quantities of cocaine. As long as Defendant S's agreement and conduct is limited to the distribution of the 500 grams, Defendant S is accountable only for that 500 gram amount (under subsection (a)(1)(A)), rather than the much larger quantity imported by Defendant R. Defendant S is not accountable under subsection (a)(1)(B) for the other quantities imported by Defendant R because those quantities were not within the scope of his jointly undertaken criminal activity (*i.e.*, the 500 grams).

(viii) Defendants T, U, V, and W are hired by a supplier to backpack a quantity of marihuana across the border from Mexico into the United States. Defendants T, U, V, and W receive their individual shipments from the supplier at the same time and coordinate their importation efforts by walking across the border together for mutual assistance and protection. Each defendant is accountable for the aggregate quantity of marihuana transported by the four defendants. The four defendants engaged in a jointly undertaken criminal activity, the object of which was the importation of the four backpacks containing marihuana (subsection (a)(1)(B)), and aided and abetted each other's actions (subsection (a)(1)(A)) in carrying out the jointly undertaken criminal activity (which under subsection (a)(1)(B) were also in furtherance of, and reasonably foreseeable in connection with, the criminal activity). In contrast, if Defendants T, U, V, and W were hired individually, transported their individual shipments at different times, and otherwise operated independently, each defendant would be accountable only for the quantity of marihuana he personally transported (subsection (a)(1)(A)). As this example illustrates, the scope of the jointly undertaken criminal activity may depend upon whether, in the particular circumstances, the nature of the offense is more appropriately viewed as one jointly undertaken criminal activity or as a number of separate criminal activities. *See* Application Note 3(B).

5. **Application of Subsection (a)(2).—**

(A) **Relationship to Grouping of Multiple Counts.**—"Offenses of a character for which §3D1.2(d) would require grouping of multiple counts," as used in subsection (a)(2), applies to offenses for which grouping of counts would be required under §3D1.2(d) had the defendant been convicted of multiple counts. Application of this provision does not require the defendant, in fact, to have been convicted of multiple counts. For example, where the defendant engaged in three drug sales of 10, 15, and 20 grams of cocaine, as part of the same course of conduct or common scheme or plan, subsection (a)(2) provides that the total quantity of cocaine involved (45 grams) is to be used to determine the offense level even if the defendant is convicted of a single count charging only one of the sales. If the defendant is convicted of multiple counts for the above noted sales, the grouping rules of Chapter Three, Part D (Multiple Counts) provide that the counts are grouped together. Although Chapter Three, Part D (Multiple Counts) applies to multiple counts of conviction, it does not limit the scope of subsection (a)(2). Subsection (a)(2) merely incorporates by reference the types of offenses set forth in §3D1.2(d); thus, as discussed above, multiple counts of conviction are not required for subsection (a)(2) to apply.

As noted above, subsection (a)(2) applies to offenses of a character for which §3D1.2(d) would require grouping of multiple counts, had the defendant been convicted of multiple counts. For example, the defendant sells 30 grams of cocaine (a violation of 21 U.S.C. § 841) on one occasion and, as part of the same course of conduct or common scheme or plan, attempts to sell an additional 15 grams of cocaine (a violation of 21 U.S.C. § 846) on another occasion. The defendant is convicted of one count charging the completed sale of 30 grams of cocaine. The two offenses (sale of cocaine and attempted sale of cocaine), although covered by different statutory provisions, are of a character for which §3D1.2(d) would require the grouping of counts, had the defendant been convicted of both counts. Therefore, subsection (a)(2) applies and the total amount of cocaine (45 grams) involved is used to determine the offense level.

(B) **"Same Course of Conduct or Common Scheme or Plan".**—"Common scheme or plan" and "same course of conduct" are two closely related concepts.

(i) **Common scheme or plan.** For two or more offenses to constitute part of a common scheme or plan, they must be substantially connected to each other by at least one common factor, such as common victims, common accomplices, common purpose, or similar *modus operandi*. For example, the conduct of five defendants who together defrauded a group of investors by computer manipulations that unlawfully transferred funds over an eighteen-month period would qualify as a common scheme or plan on the basis of any of the above listed factors; *i.e.*, the commonality of victims (the same investors were defrauded on an ongoing basis), commonality of offenders (the conduct constituted an ongoing conspiracy), commonality of purpose (to defraud the group of investors), or similarity of *modus operandi* (the same or similar computer manipulations were used to execute the scheme).

(ii) **Same course of conduct**. Offenses that do not qualify as part of a common scheme or plan may nonetheless qualify as part of the same course of conduct if they are sufficiently connected or related to each other as to warrant the conclusion that they are part of a single episode, spree, or ongoing series of offenses. Factors that are appropriate to the determination of whether offenses are sufficiently connected or related to each other to be considered as

part of the same course of conduct include the degree of similarity of the offenses, the regularity (repetitions) of the offenses, and the time interval between the offenses. When one of the above factors is absent, a stronger presence of at least one of the other factors is required. For example, where the conduct alleged to be relevant is relatively remote to the offense of conviction, a stronger showing of similarity or regularity is necessary to compensate for the absence of temporal proximity. The nature of the offenses may also be a relevant consideration (*e.g.*, a defendant's failure to file tax returns in three consecutive years appropriately would be considered as part of the same course of conduct because such returns are only required at yearly intervals).

(C) **Conduct Associated with a Prior Sentence.**—For the purposes of subsection (a)(2), offense conduct associated with a sentence that was imposed prior to the acts or omissions constituting the instant federal offense (the offense of conviction) is not considered as part of the same course of conduct or common scheme or plan as the offense of conviction.

Examples: (1) The defendant was convicted for the sale of cocaine and sentenced to state prison. Immediately upon release from prison, he again sold cocaine to the same person, using the same accomplices and *modus operandi*. The instant federal offense (the offense of conviction) charges this latter sale. In this example, the offense conduct relevant to the state prison sentence is considered as prior criminal history, not as part of the same course of conduct or common scheme or plan as the offense of conviction. The prior state prison sentence is counted under Chapter Four (Criminal History and Criminal Livelihood). (2) The defendant engaged in two cocaine sales constituting part of the same course of conduct or common scheme or plan. Subsequently, he is arrested by state authorities for the first sale and by federal authorities for the second sale. He is convicted in state court for the first sale and sentenced to imprisonment; he is then convicted in federal court for the second sale. In this case, the cocaine sales are not separated by an intervening sentence. Therefore, under subsection (a)(2), the cocaine sale associated with the state conviction is considered as relevant conduct to the instant federal offense. The state prison sentence for that sale is not counted as a prior sentence; *see* §4A1.2(a)(1).

Note, however, in certain cases, offense conduct associated with a previously imposed sentence may be expressly charged in the offense of conviction. Unless otherwise provided, such conduct will be considered relevant conduct under subsection (a)(1), not (a)(2).

6. **Application of Subsection (a)(3).**—

(A) **Definition of "Harm".**—"***Harm***" includes bodily injury, monetary loss, property damage and any resulting harm.

(B) **Risk or Danger of Harm.**—If the offense guideline includes creating a risk or danger of harm as a specific offense characteristic, whether that risk or danger was created is to be considered in determining the offense level. *See, e.g.*, §2K1.4 (Arson; Property Damage by Use of Explosives); §2Q1.2 (Mishandling of Hazardous or Toxic Substances or Pesticides). If, however, the guideline refers only to harm sustained (*e.g.*, §2A2.2 (Aggravated Assault); §2B3.1 (Robbery)) or to actual, attempted or intended harm (*e.g.*, §2B1.1 (Theft, Property Destruction, and Fraud); §2X1.1 (Attempt, Solicitation, or Conspiracy)), the risk created enters into the determination of the offense level only insofar as it is incorporated into the base offense level. Unless clearly indicated by the guidelines, harm that is merely risked is not to be

treated as the equivalent of harm that occurred. In a case in which creation of risk is not adequately taken into account by the applicable offense guideline, an upward departure may be warranted. *See generally* §1B1.4 (Information to be Used in Imposing Sentence); §5K2.0 (Grounds for Departure). The extent to which harm that was attempted or intended enters into the determination of the offense level should be determined in accordance with §2X1.1 (Attempt, Solicitation, or Conspiracy) and the applicable offense guideline.

7. **Factors Requiring Conviction under a Specific Statute.**—A particular guideline (in the base offense level or in a specific offense characteristic) may expressly direct that a particular factor be applied only if the defendant was convicted of a particular statute. For example, in §2S1.1 (Laundering of Monetary Instruments; Engaging in Monetary Transactions in Property Derived from Unlawful Activity), subsection (b)(2)(B) applies if the defendant "was convicted under 18 U.S.C. § 1956". Unless such an express direction is included, conviction under the statute is not required. Thus, use of a statutory reference to describe a particular set of circumstances does not require a conviction under the referenced statute. An example of this usage is found in §2A3.4(a)(2) ("if the offense involved conduct described in 18 U.S.C. § 2242").

Unless otherwise specified, an express direction to apply a particular factor only if the defendant was convicted of a particular statute includes the determination of the offense level where the defendant was convicted of conspiracy, attempt, solicitation, aiding or abetting, accessory after the fact, or misprision of felony in respect to that particular statute. For example, §2S1.1(b)(2)(B) (which is applicable only if the defendant is convicted under 18 U.S.C. § 1956) would be applied in determining the offense level under §2X3.1 (Accessory After the Fact) in a case in which the defendant was convicted of accessory after the fact to a violation of 18 U.S.C. § 1956 but would not be applied in a case in which the defendant is convicted of a conspiracy under 18 U.S.C. § 1956(h) and the sole object of that conspiracy was to commit an offense set forth in 18 U.S.C. § 1957. *See* Application Note 3(C) of §2S1.1.

8. **Partially Completed Offense.**—In the case of a partially completed offense (*e.g.*, an offense involving an attempted theft of $800,000 and a completed theft of $30,000), the offense level is to be determined in accordance with §2X1.1 (Attempt, Solicitation, or Conspiracy) whether the conviction is for the substantive offense, the inchoate offense (attempt, solicitation, or conspiracy), or both. *See* Application Note 4 in the Commentary to §2X1.1. Note, however, that Application Note 4 is not applicable where the offense level is determined under §2X1.1(c)(1).

9. **Solicitation, Misprision, or Accessory After the Fact.**—In the case of solicitation, misprision, or accessory after the fact, the conduct for which the defendant is accountable includes all conduct relevant to determining the offense level for the underlying offense that was known, or reasonably should have been known, by the defendant.

Background: This section prescribes rules for determining the applicable guideline sentencing range, whereas §1B1.4 (Information to be Used in Imposing Sentence) governs the range of information that the court may consider in adjudging sentence once the guideline sentencing range has been determined. Conduct that is not formally charged or is not an element of the

offense of conviction may enter into the determination of the applicable guideline sentencing range. The range of information that may be considered at sentencing is broader than the range of information upon which the applicable sentencing range is determined.
Subsection (a) establishes a rule of construction by specifying, in the absence of more explicit instructions in the context of a specific guideline, the range of conduct that is relevant

to determining the applicable offense level (except for the determination of the applicable offense guideline, which is governed by §1B1.2(a)). No such rule of construction is necessary with respect to Chapters Four and Five because the guidelines in those Chapters are explicit as to the specific factors to be considered.

Subsection (a)(2) provides for consideration of a broader range of conduct with respect to one class of offenses, primarily certain property, tax, fraud and drug offenses for which the guidelines depend substantially on quantity, than with respect to other offenses such as assault, robbery and burglary. The distinction is made on the basis of §3D1.2(d), which provides for grouping together (*i.e.*, treating as a single count) all counts charging offenses of a type covered by this subsection. However, the applicability of subsection (a)(2) does not depend upon whether multiple counts are alleged. Thus, in an embezzlement case, for example, embezzled funds that may not be specified in any count of conviction are nonetheless included in determining the offense level if they were part of the same course of conduct or part of the same scheme or plan as the count of conviction. Similarly, in a drug distribution case, quantities and types of drugs not specified in the count of conviction are to be included in determining the offense level if they were part of the same course of conduct or part of a common scheme or plan as the count of conviction. On the other hand, in a robbery case in which the defendant robbed two banks, the amount of money taken in one robbery would *not* be taken into account in determining the guideline range for the other robbery, even if both robberies were part of a single course of conduct or the same scheme or plan. (This is true whether the defendant is convicted of one or both robberies.)

Subsections (a)(1) and (a)(2) adopt different rules because offenses of the character dealt with in subsection (a)(2) (*i.e.*, to which §3D1.2(d) applies) often involve a pattern of misconduct that cannot readily be broken into discrete, identifiable units that are meaningful for purposes of sentencing. For example, a pattern of embezzlement may consist of several acts of taking that cannot separately be identified, even though the overall conduct is clear. In addition, the distinctions that the law makes as to what constitutes separate counts or offenses often turn on technical elements that are not especially meaningful for purposes of sentencing. Thus, in a mail fraud case, the scheme is an element of the offense and each mailing may be the basis for a separate count; in an embezzlement case, each taking may provide a basis for a separate count. Another consideration is that in a pattern of small thefts, for example, it is important to take into account the full range of related conduct. Relying on the entire range of conduct, regardless of the number of counts that are alleged or on which a conviction is obtained, appears to be the most reasonable approach to writing workable guidelines for these offenses.

Conversely, when §3D1.2(d) does not apply, so that convictions on multiple counts are considered separately in determining the guideline sentencing range, the guidelines prohibit aggregation of quantities from other counts in order to prevent "double counting" of the conduct and harm from each count of conviction. Continuing offenses present similar practical problems. The reference to §3D1.2(d), which provides for grouping of multiple counts arising out of a continuing offense when the offense guideline takes the continuing nature into account, also prevents double counting.

Subsection (a)(4) requires consideration of any other information specified in the applicable guideline. For example, §2A1.4 (Involuntary Manslaughter) specifies consideration of the defendant's state of mind; §2K1.4 (Arson; Property Damage By Use of Explosives) specifies consideration of the risk of harm created.

Historical
Note

Effective November 1, 1987. Amended effective January 15, 1988 (amendment 3); November 1, 1989 (amendments 76–78 and 303); November 1, 1990 (amendment 309); November 1, 1991 (amendment 389); November

1, 1992 (amendment 439); November 1, 1994 (amendment 503); November 1, 2001 (amendments 617 and 634); November 1, 2004 (amendment 674); November 1, 2010 (amendment 746); November 1, 2015 (amendments 790 and 797).

§1B1.4. Information to be Used in Imposing Sentence (Selecting a Point Within the Guideline Range or Departing from the Guidelines)

In determining the sentence to impose within the guideline range, or whether a departure from the guidelines is warranted, the court may consider, without limitation, any information concerning the background, character and conduct of the defendant, unless otherwise prohibited by law. *See* 18 U.S.C. § 3661.

Commentary

Background: This section distinguishes between factors that determine the applicable guideline sentencing range (§1B1.3) and information that a court may consider in imposing sentence within that range. The section is based on 18 U.S.C. § 3661, which recodifies 18 U.S.C. § 3577. The recodification of this 1970 statute in 1984 with an effective date of 1987 (99 Stat. 1728), makes it clear that Congress intended that no limitation would be placed on the information that a court may consider in imposing an appropriate sentence under the future guideline sentencing system. A court is not precluded from considering information that the guidelines do not take into account in determining a sentence within the guideline range or from considering that information in determining whether and to what extent to depart from the guidelines. For example, if the defendant committed two robberies, but as part of a plea negotiation entered a guilty plea to only one, the robbery that was not taken into account by the guidelines would provide a reason for sentencing at the top of the guideline range and may provide a reason for an upward departure. Some policy statements do, however, express a Commission policy that certain factors should not be considered for any purpose, or should be considered only for limited purposes. *See, e.g.*, Chapter Five, Part H (Specific Offender Characteristics).

Historical Note

Effective November 1, 1987. Amended effective January 15, 1988 (amendment 4); November 1, 1989 (amendment 303); November 1, 2000 (amendment 604); November 1, 2004 (amendment 674).

§1B1.5. Interpretation of References to Other Offense Guidelines

(a) A cross reference (an instruction to apply another offense guideline) refers to the entire offense guideline (*i.e.*, the base offense level, specific offense characteristics, cross references, and special instructions).

(b) (1) An instruction to use the offense level from another offense guideline refers to the offense level from the entire offense guideline (*i.e.*, the base offense level, specific offense characteristics, cross references, and special instructions), except as provided in subdivision (2) below.

(2) An instruction to use a particular subsection or table from another offense guideline refers only to the particular subsection or table referenced, and not to the entire offense guideline.

(c) If the offense level is determined by a reference to another guideline under subsection (a) or (b)(1) above, the adjustments in Chapter Three (Adjustments) also are determined in respect to the referenced offense guideline, except as otherwise expressly provided.

(d) A reference to another guideline under subsection (a) or (b)(1) above may direct that it be applied only if it results in the greater offense level. In such case, the greater offense level means the greater Chapter Two offense level, except as otherwise expressly provided.

Commentary

Application Notes:

1. References to other offense guidelines are most frequently designated "Cross References," but may also appear in the portion of the guideline entitled "Base Offense Level" (*e.g.*, §2D1.2(a)(1) and (2)), or "Specific Offense Characteristics" (*e.g.*, §2A4.1(b)(7)). These references may be to a specific guideline, or may be more general (*e.g.*, to the guideline for the "underlying offense"). Such references incorporate the specific offense characteristics, cross references, and special instructions as well as the base offense level. For example, if the guideline reads "2 plus the offense level from §2A2.2 (Aggravated Assault)," the user would determine the offense level from §2A2.2, including any applicable adjustments for planning, weapon use, degree of injury and motive, and then increase by 2 levels. A reference may also be to a specific subsection of another guideline; *e.g.*, the reference in §2D1.10(a)(1) to "3 plus the offense level from the Drug Quantity Table in §2D1.1". In such case, only the specific subsection of that other guideline is used.
2. A reference to another guideline may direct that such reference is to be used only if it results in a greater offense level. In such cases, the greater offense level means the offense level taking into account only the Chapter Two offense level, unless the offense guideline expressly provides for consideration of both the Chapter Two offense level and applicable Chapter Three adjustments. For situations in which a comparison involving both Chapters Two and Three is necessary, *see* the Commentary to §§2C1.1 (Offering, Giving, Soliciting, or Receiving a Bribe; Extortion Under Color of Official Right; Fraud Involving the Deprivation of the Intangible Right to Honest Services of Public Officials; Conspiracy to Defraud by Interference with Governmental Functions); 2E1.1 (Unlawful Conduct Relating to Racketeer Influenced and Corrupt Organizations); and 2E1.2 (Interstate or Foreign Travel or Transportation in Aid of a Racketeering Enterprise).
3. A reference may direct that, if the conduct involved another offense, the offense guideline for such other offense is to be applied. Consistent with the provisions of §1B1.3 (Relevant Conduct), such other offense includes conduct that may be a state or local offense and conduct that occurred under circumstances that would constitute a federal offense had the conduct taken place within the territorial or maritime jurisdiction of the United States. Where there is more than one such other offense, the most serious such offense (or group of closely related offenses in the case of offenses that would be grouped together under §3D1.2(d)) is to be used. For example, if a defendant convicted of possession of a firearm by a felon, to which §2K2.1 (Unlawful Receipt, Possession, or Transportation of Firearms or Ammunition; Prohibited Transactions Involving Firearms or Ammunition) applies, is found to have possessed that firearm during commission of a series of offenses,

the cross reference at §2K2.1(c) is applied to the offense resulting in the greatest offense level.

Historical Note

Effective November 1, 1987. Amended effective November 1, 1989 (amendments 79, 80, and 302); November 1, 1991 (amendment 429); November 1, 1992 (amendment 440); November 1, 1995 (amendment 534); November 1, 1997 (amendment 547); November 1, 2001 (amendment 616); November 1, 2004 (amendment 666).

§1B1.6. Structure of the Guidelines

The guidelines are presented in numbered chapters divided into alphabetical parts. The parts are divided into subparts and individual guidelines. Each guideline is identified by three numbers and a letter corresponding to the chapter, part, subpart and individual guideline. The first number is the chapter, the letter represents the part of the chapter, the second number is the subpart, and the final number is the guideline. Section 2B1.1, for example, is the first guideline in the first subpart in Part B of Chapter Two. Or, §3A1.2 is the second guideline in the first subpart in Part A of Chapter Three. Policy statements are similarly identified.

To illustrate:

Historical Note

Effective November 1, 1987.

§1B1.7. Significance of Commentary

The Commentary that accompanies the guideline sections may serve a number of purposes. First, it may interpret the guideline or explain how it is to be applied. Failure to follow such commentary could constitute an incorrect application of the guidelines, subjecting the sentence to possible reversal on appeal. *See* 18 U.S.C. § 3742. Second, the commentary may suggest circumstances which, in the view of the Commission, may warrant departure from the guidelines. Such commentary is to be

treated as the legal equivalent of a policy statement. Finally, the commentary may provide background information, including factors considered in promulgating the guideline or reasons underlying promulgation of the guideline. As with a policy statement, such commentary may provide guidance in assessing the reasonableness of any departure from the guidelines.

Commentary

Portions of this document not labeled as guidelines or commentary also express the policy of the Commission or provide guidance as to the interpretation and application of the guidelines. These are to be construed as commentary and thus have the force of policy statements.

"[C]ommentary in the *Guidelines Manual* that interprets or explains a guideline is authoritative unless it violates the Constitution or a federal statute, or is inconsistent with, or a plainly erroneous reading of, that guideline." *Stinson v. United States*, 508 U.S. 36, 38 (1993).

Historical Note

Effective November 1, 1987. Amended effective November 1, 1993 (amendment 498).

§1B1.8. Use of Certain Information

(a) Where a defendant agrees to cooperate with the government by providing information concerning unlawful activities of others, and as part of that cooperation agreement the government agrees that self-incriminating information provided pursuant to the agreement will not be used against the defendant, then such information shall not be used in determining the applicable guideline range, except to the extent provided in the agreement.

(b) The provisions of subsection (a) shall not be applied to restrict the use of information:

(1) known to the government prior to entering into the cooperation agreement;

(2) concerning the existence of prior convictions and sentences in determining §4A1.1 (Criminal History Category) and §4B1.1 (Career Offender);

(3) in a prosecution for perjury or giving a false statement;

(4) in the event there is a breach of the cooperation agreement by

the defendant; or

§1B1.8

(5) in determining whether, or to what extent, a downward departure from the guidelines is warranted pursuant to a government motion under §5K1.1 (Substantial Assistance to Authorities).

Commentary

Application Notes:

1. This provision does not authorize the government to withhold information from the court but provides that self-incriminating information obtained under a cooperation agreement is not to be used to determine the defendant's guideline range. Under this provision, for example, if a defendant is arrested in possession of a kilogram of cocaine and, pursuant to an agreement to provide information concerning the unlawful activities of co-conspirators, admits that he assisted in the importation of an additional three kilograms of cocaine, a fact not previously known to the government, this admission would not be used to increase his applicable guideline range, except to the extent provided in the agreement. Although the guideline itself affects only the determination of the guideline range, the policy of the Commission, as a corollary, is that information prohibited from being used to determine the applicable guideline range shall not be used to depart upward. In contrast, subsection (b)(5) provides that consideration of such information is appropriate in determining whether, and to what extent, a downward departure is warranted pursuant to a government motion under §5K1.1 (Substantial Assistance to Authorities); *e.g.*, a court may refuse to depart downward on the basis of such information.
2. Subsection (b)(2) prohibits any cooperation agreement from restricting the use of information as to the existence of prior convictions and sentences in determining adjustments under §4A1.1 (Criminal History Category) and §4B1.1 (Career Offender). The probation office generally will secure information relevant to the defendant's criminal history independent of information the defendant provides as part of his cooperation agreement.
3. On occasion the defendant will provide incriminating information to the government during plea negotiation sessions before a cooperation agreement has been reached. In the event no agreement is reached, use of such information in a sentencing proceeding is restricted by Rule 11(f) (Admissibility or Inadmissibility of a Plea, Plea Discussions, and Related Statements) of the Federal Rules of Criminal Procedure and Rule 410 (Pleas, Plea Discussions, and Related Statements) of the Rules of Evidence.
4. As with the statutory provisions governing use immunity, 18 U.S.C. § 6002, this guideline does not apply to information used against the defendant in a prosecution for perjury, giving a false statement, or in the event the defendant otherwise fails to comply with the cooperation agreement.
5. This guideline limits the use of certain incriminating information furnished by a defendant in the context of a defendant-government agreement for the defendant to provide information concerning the unlawful activities of other persons. The guideline operates as a limitation on the use of such incriminating information in determining the applicable guideline range, and not merely as a restriction of the government's presentation of such information (*e.g.*, where the defendant, subsequent to having entered into a cooperation agreement, provides such information to the probation officer preparing the presentence report, the use of such information remains protected by this section).

§1B1.9

6. Unless the cooperation agreement relates to the provision of information concerning the unlawful activities of others, this guideline does not apply (*i.e.*, an agreement by the defendant simply to detail the extent of his own unlawful activities, not involving an agreement to provide information concerning the unlawful activity of another person, is not covered by this guideline).

Historical

Note
Effective June 15, 1988 (amendment 5). Amended effective November 1, 1990 (amendment 308); November 1, 1991 (amendment 390); November 1, 1992 (amendment 441); November 1, 2004 (amendment 674); November 1, 2009 (amendment 736); November 1, 2010 (amendment 746); November 1, 2013 (amendment 778).

§1B1.9. Class B or C Misdemeanors and Infractions

The sentencing guidelines do not apply to any count of conviction that is a Class B or C misdemeanor or an infraction.

Commentary

Application Notes:

1. Notwithstanding any other provision of the guidelines, the court may impose any sentence authorized by statute for each count that is a Class B or C misdemeanor or an infraction. A Class B misdemeanor is any offense for which the maximum authorized term of imprisonment is more than thirty days but not more than six months; a Class C misdemeanor is any offense for which the maximum authorized term of imprisonment is more than five days but not more than thirty days; an infraction is any offense for which the maximum authorized term of imprisonment is not more than five days or for which no imprisonment is authorized. *See* 18 U.S.C. § 3559.

2. The guidelines for sentencing on multiple counts do not apply to counts that are Class B or C misdemeanors or infractions. Sentences for such offenses may be consecutive to or concurrent with sentences imposed on other counts. In imposing sentence, the court should, however, consider the relationship between the Class B or C misdemeanor or infraction and any other offenses of which the defendant is convicted.

Background: For the sake of judicial economy, the Commission has exempted all Class B and C misdemeanors and infractions from the coverage of the guidelines.

Historical
Note
Effective June 15, 1988 (amendment 6). Amended effective November 1, 1989 (amendment 81); November 1, 2010 (amendment 746).

§1B1.10. Reduction in Term of Imprisonment as a Result of Amended Guideline Range (Policy Statement)

(a) AUTHORITY.—

(1) IN GENERAL.—In a case in which a defendant is serving a term of imprisonment, and the guideline range applicable to that defendant has subsequently been lowered as a result of an amendment to the Guidelines Manual listed in subsection (d) below, the court may reduce the defendant's term of imprisonment as provided by 18 U.S.C. § 3582(c)(2). As required by 18 U.S.C. § 3582(c)(2), any such reduction in the defendant's term of imprisonment shall be consistent with this policy statement.

(2) EXCLUSIONS.—A reduction in the defendant's term of imprisonment is not consistent with this policy statement and therefore is not authorized under 18 U.S.C. § 3582(c)(2) if—

(A) none of the amendments listed in subsection (d) is applicable to the defendant; or

(B) an amendment listed in subsection (d) does not have the effect of lowering the defendant's applicable guideline range.

(3) LIMITATION.—Consistent with subsection (b), proceedings under 18 U.S.C. § 3582(c)(2) and this policy statement do not constitute a full resentencing of the defendant.

(b) DETERMINATION OF REDUCTION IN TERM OF IMPRISONMENT.—

(1) IN GENERAL.—In determining whether, and to what extent, a reduction in the defendant's term of imprisonment under 18 U.S.C. § 3582(c)(2) and this policy statement is warranted, the court shall determine the amended guideline range that would have been applicable to the defendant if the amendment(s) to the guidelines listed in subsection (d) had been in effect at the time the defendant was sentenced. In making such determination, the court shall substitute only the amendments listed in subsection (d) for the corresponding guideline provisions that were applied when the defendant was sentenced and shall leave all other guideline application decisions unaffected.

(2) LIMITATION AND PROHIBITION ON EXTENT OF REDUCTION.—

(A) LIMITATION.—Except as provided in subdivision (B), the court shall not reduce the defendant's term of imprisonment under 18 U.S.C. § 3582(c)(2) and this policy statement to a term that is less than the minimum of the amended guideline range determined under subdivision (1) of this subsection.

(B) EXCEPTION FOR SUBSTANTIAL ASSISTANCE.—If the term of imprisonment imposed was less than the term of imprisonment provided by the guideline range applicable to the defendant at the time of sentencing pursuant to a government motion to reflect the defendant's substantial assistance to authorities, a reduction comparably less than the amended guideline range determined under subdivision (1) of this subsection may be appropriate.

(C) PROHIBITION.—In no event may the reduced term of imprisonment be less than the term of imprisonment the defendant has already served.

(c) CASES INVOLVING MANDATORY MINIMUM SENTENCES AND SUBSTANTIAL ASSISTANCE.—If the case involves a statutorily required minimum sentence and the court had the authority to impose a sentence below the statutorily required minimum sentence pursuant to a government motion to reflect the defendant's substantial assistance to authorities, then for purposes of this policy statement the amended guideline range shall be determined without regard to the operation of §5G1.1 (Sentencing on a Single Count of Conviction) and §5G1.2 (Sentencing on Multiple Counts of Conviction).

(d) COVERED AMENDMENTS.—Amendments covered by this policy statement are listed in Appendix C as follows: 126, 130, 156, 176, 269, 329, 341, 371, 379, 380, 433, 454, 461, 484, 488, 490, 499, 505, 506, 516, 591, 599, 606, 657, 702, 706 as amended by 711, 715, 750 (parts A and C only), and 782 (subject to subsection (e)(1)).

(e) SPECIAL INSTRUCTION.—

(1) The court shall not order a reduced term of imprisonment based on Amendment 782 unless the effective date of the

court's order is November 1, 2015, or later.

Commentary

Application Notes:

1. **Application of Subsection (a).—**

(A) **Eligibility.**—Eligibility for consideration under 18 U.S.C. § 3582(c)(2) is triggered only by an amendment listed in subsection (d) that lowers the applicable guideline range (*i.e.*, the guideline range that corresponds to the offense level and criminal history category determined pursuant to §1B1.1(a), which is determined before consideration of any departure provision in the Guidelines Manual or any variance).

Accordingly, a reduction in the defendant's term of imprisonment is not authorized under 18 U.S.C. § 3582(c)(2) and is not consistent with this policy statement if: (i) none of the amendments listed in subsection (d) is applicable to the defendant; or (ii) an amendment listed in subsection (d) is applicable to the defendant but the amendment does not have the effect of lowering the defendant's applicable guideline range because of the operation of another guideline or statutory provision (*e.g.*, a statutory mandatory minimum term of imprisonment).

(B) **Factors for Consideration.—**

(i) **In General.**—Consistent with 18 U.S.C. § 3582(c)(2), the court shall consider the factors set forth in 18 U.S.C. § 3553(a) in determining: (I) whether a reduction in the defendant's term of imprisonment is warranted; and (II) the extent of such reduction, but only within the limits described in subsection (b).

(ii) **Public Safety Consideration.**—The court shall consider the nature and seriousness of the danger to any person or the community that may be posed by a reduction in the defendant's term of imprisonment in determining: (I) whether such a reduction is warranted; and (II) the extent of such reduction, but only within the limits described in subsection (b).

(iii) **Post-Sentencing Conduct.**—The court may consider post-sentencing conduct of the defendant that occurred after imposition of the term of imprisonment in determining: (I) whether a reduction in the defendant's term of imprisonment is warranted; and (II) the extent of such reduction, but only within the limits described in subsection (b).

2. **Application of Subsection (b)(1).**—In determining the amended guideline range under subsection (b)(1), the court shall substitute only the amendments listed in subsection (d) for the corresponding guideline provisions that were applied when the defendant was sentenced. All other guideline application decisions remain unaffected.

3. **Application of Subsection (b)(2).**—Under subsection (b)(2), the amended guideline range determined under subsection (b)(1) and the term of imprisonment already served by the defendant limit the extent to which the court may reduce the defendant's term of imprisonment under 18 U.S.C. § 3582(c)(2) and this policy statement. Specifically, as provided in subsection (b)(2)(A), if the term of imprisonment imposed was within the guideline range applicable to the defendant at the time of sentencing, the court may reduce the defendant's term of imprisonment to a term that is no less than the minimum term of imprisonment provided by the amended guideline range determined under subsection (b)(1). For example, in a case in which: (A) the guideline range applicable to the defendant at the time of sentencing was 70 to 87 months; (B) the term of imprisonment

imposed was 70 months; and (C) the amended guideline range determined under subsection (b)(1) is 51 to 63 months, the court may reduce the defendant's term of imprisonment, but shall not reduce it to a term less than 51 months.

If the term of imprisonment imposed was outside the guideline range applicable to the defendant at the time of sentencing, the limitation in subsection (b)(2)(A) also applies.

Thus, if the term of imprisonment imposed in the example provided above was not a sentence of 70 months (within the guidelines range) but instead was a sentence of 56 months (constituting a downward departure or variance), the court likewise may reduce the defendant's term of imprisonment, but shall not reduce it to a term less than 51 months.

Subsection (b)(2)(B) provides an exception to this limitation, which applies if the term of imprisonment imposed was less than the term of imprisonment provided by the guideline range applicable to the defendant at the time of sentencing pursuant to a government motion to reflect the defendant's substantial assistance to authorities. In such a case, the court may reduce the defendant's term, but the reduction is not limited by subsection (b)(2)(A) to the minimum of the amended guideline range. Instead, as provided in subsection (b)(2)(B), the court may, if appropriate, provide a reduction comparably less than the amended guideline range. Thus, if the term of imprisonment imposed in the example provided above was 56 months pursuant to a government motion to reflect the defendant's substantial assistance to authorities (representing a downward departure of 20 percent below the minimum term of imprisonment provided by the guideline range applicable to the defendant at the time of sentencing), a reduction to a term of imprisonment of 41 months (representing a reduction of approximately 20 percent below the minimum term of imprisonment provided by the amended guideline range) would amount to a comparable reduction and may be appropriate.

The provisions authorizing such a government motion are §5K1.1 (Substantial Assistance to Authorities) (authorizing, upon government motion, a downward departure based on the defendant's substantial assistance); 18 U.S.C. § 3553(e) (authorizing the court, upon government motion, to impose a sentence below a statutory minimum to reflect the defendant's substantial assistance); and Fed. R. Crim. P. 35(b) (authorizing the court, upon government motion, to reduce a sentence to reflect the defendant's substantial assistance).

In no case, however, shall the term of imprisonment be reduced below time served. *See* subsection (b)(2)(C). Subject to these limitations, the sentencing court has the discretion to determine whether, and to what extent, to reduce a term of imprisonment under this section.

4. **Application of Subsection (c).**—As stated in subsection (c), if the case involves a statutorily required minimum sentence and the court had the authority to impose a sentence below the statutorily required minimum sentence pursuant to a government motion to reflect the defendant's substantial assistance to authorities, then for purposes of this policy statement the amended guideline range shall be determined without regard to the operation of §5G1.1 (Sentencing on a Single Count of Conviction) and §5G1.2 (Sentencing on Multiple Counts of Conviction). For example:

(A) Defendant A is subject to a mandatory minimum term of imprisonment of 120 months. The original guideline range at the time of sentencing was 135 to 168 months, which is entirely above the mandatory minimum, and the court imposed a sentence of 101 months pursuant to a government motion to reflect the defendant's substantial assistance to authorities. The court determines that the

amended guideline range as calculated on the Sentencing Table is 108 to 135 months. Ordinarily, §5G1.1 would operate to restrict the amended guideline range to 120 to 135 months, to reflect the mandatory minimum term of imprisonment. For purposes of this policy statement, however, the amended guideline range remains 108 to 135 months.

To the extent the court considers it appropriate to provide a reduction comparably less than the amended guideline range pursuant to subsection (b)(2)(B), Defendant A's original sentence of 101 months amounted to a reduction of approximately 25 percent below the minimum of the original guideline range of 135 months. Therefore, an amended sentence of 81 months (representing a reduction of approximately

25 percent below the minimum of the amended guideline range of 108 months) would amount to a comparable reduction and may be appropriate.

(B) Defendant B is subject to a mandatory minimum term of imprisonment of 120 months. The original guideline range at the time of sentencing (as calculated on the Sentencing Table) was 108 to 135 months, which was restricted by operation of §5G1.1 to a range of 120 to 135 months. *See* §5G1.1(c)(2). The court imposed a sentence of 90 months pursuant to a government motion to reflect the defendant's substantial assistance to authorities. The court determines that the amended guideline range as calculated on the Sentencing Table is 87 to 108 months. Ordinarily, §5G1.1 would operate to restrict the amended guideline range to precisely 120 months, to reflect the mandatory minimum term of imprisonment. *See* §5G1.1(b). For purposes of this policy statement, however, the amended guideline range is considered to be 87 to 108 months (*i.e.*, unrestricted by operation of §5G1.1 and the statutory minimum of 120 months).

To the extent the court considers it appropriate to provide a reduction comparably less than the amended guideline range pursuant to subsection (b)(2)(B), Defendant B's original sentence of 90 months amounted to a reduction of approximately 25 percent below the original guideline range of 120 months. Therefore, an amended sentence of 65 months (representing a reduction of approximately 25 percent below the minimum of the amended guideline range of 87 months) would amount to a comparable reduction and may be appropriate.

5. **Application to Amendment 750 (Parts A and C Only).**—As specified in subsection (d), the parts of Amendment 750 that are covered by this policy statement are Parts A and C only. Part A amended the Drug Quantity Table in §2D1.1 for crack cocaine and made related revisions to the Drug Equivalency Tables in the Commentary to §2D1.1 (*see* §2D1.1, comment. (n.8)). Part C deleted the cross reference in §2D2.1(b) under which an offender who possessed more than 5 grams of crack cocaine was sentenced under §2D1.1.

6. **Application to Amendment 782.**—As specified in subsection (d) and (e)(1), Amendment 782 (generally revising the Drug Quantity Table and chemical quantity tables across drug and chemical types) is covered by this policy statement only in cases in which the order reducing the defendant's term of imprisonment has an effective date of November 1, 2015, or later.

A reduction based on retroactive application of Amendment 782 that does not comply with the requirement that the order take effect on November 1, 2015, or later is not consistent with this policy statement and therefore is not authorized under 18 U.S.C. § 3582(c)(2).

Subsection (e)(1) does not preclude the court from conducting sentence reduction proceedings and entering orders under 18 U.S.C. § 3582(c)(2) and this policy statement before November 1, 2015, provided that any order reducing the defendant's term of imprisonment has an effective date of November 1, 2015, or later.

7. **Supervised Release.**—

(A) **Exclusion Relating to Revocation.**—Only a term of imprisonment imposed as part of the original sentence is authorized to be reduced under this section. This section does not authorize a reduction in the term of imprisonment imposed upon revocation of supervised release.

(B) **Modification Relating to Early Termination.**—If the prohibition in subsection (b)(2)(C) relating to time already served precludes a reduction in the term of imprisonment to the extent the court determines otherwise would have been appropriate as a result of the amended guideline range determined under subsection (b)(1), the court may consider any such reduction that it was unable to grant in connection with any motion for early termination of a term of supervised release under 18 U.S.C. § 3583(e)(1). However, the fact that a defendant may have served a longer term of imprisonment than the court determines would have been appropriate in view of the amended guideline range determined under subsection (b)(1) shall not, without more, provide a basis for early termination of supervised release. Rather, the court should take into account the totality of circumstances relevant to a decision to terminate supervised release, including the term of supervised release that would have been appropriate in connection with a sentence under the amended guideline range determined under subsection (b)(1).

8. **Use of Policy Statement in Effect on Date of Reduction.**—Consistent with subsection (a) of §1B1.11 (Use of Guidelines Manual in Effect on Date of Sentencing), the court shall use the version of this policy statement that is in effect on the date on which the court reduces the defendant's term of imprisonment as provided by 18 U.S.C. § 3582(c)(2).

Background: Section 3582(c)(2) of Title 18, United States Code, provides: "[I]n the case of a defendant who has been sentenced to a term of imprisonment based on a sentencing range that has subsequently been lowered by the Sentencing Commission pursuant to 28 U.S.C. § 994(o), upon motion of the defendant or the Director of the Bureau of Prisons, or on its own motion, the court may reduce the term of imprisonment, after considering the factors set forth in section 3553(a) to the extent that they are applicable, if such a reduction is consistent with applicable policy statements issued by the Sentencing Commission."

This policy statement provides guidance and limitations for a court when considering a motion under 18 U.S.C. § 3582(c)(2) and implements 28 U.S.C. § 994(u), which provides: "If the Commission reduces the term of imprisonment recommended in the guidelines applicable to a particular offense or category of offenses, it shall specify in what circumstances and by what amount the sentences of prisoners serving terms of imprisonment for the offense may be reduced." The Supreme Court has concluded that proceedings under section 3582(c)(2) are not governed by *United States v. Booker*, 543 U.S. 220 (2005), and this policy statement remains binding on courts in such proceedings. *See Dillon v. United States*, 560 U.S. 817 (2010).

Among the factors considered by the Commission in selecting the amendments included in subsection (d) were the purpose of the amendment, the magnitude of the change in the guideline range made by the amendment, and the difficulty of applying the amendment retroactively to determine an amended guideline range under subsection (b)(1).

The listing of an amendment in subsection (d) reflects policy determinations by the Commission that a reduced guideline range is sufficient to achieve the purposes of sentencing and that, in the sound discretion of the court, a reduction in the term of imprisonment may be appropriate for previously sentenced, qualified defendants. The authorization of such a discretionary reduction does not otherwise affect the lawfulness of a previously imposed sentence, does not authorize a reduction in any other component of the sentence, and does not entitle a defendant to a reduced term of imprisonment as a matter of right.

The Commission has not included in this policy statement amendments that generally reduce the maximum of the guideline range by less than six months. This criterion is in accord with the legislative history of 28 U.S.C. § 994(u) (formerly § 994(t)), which states: "It should be noted that the Committee does not expect that the Commission will recommend adjusting existing sentences under the provision when guidelines are simply refined in a way that might cause isolated instances of existing sentences falling above the old guidelines* or when there is only a minor downward adjustment in the guidelines. The Committee does not believe the courts should be burdened with adjustments in these cases." S. Rep. 225, 98th Cong., 1st Sess. 180 (1983).

**So* in original. Probably should be "to fall above the amended guidelines".

Historical Note

Effective November 1, 1989 (amendment 306). Amended effective November 1, 1990 (amendment 360); November 1, 1991 (amendment 423); November 1, 1992 (amendment 469); November 1, 1993 (amendment 502); November 1, 1994 (amendment 504); November 1, 1995 (amendment 536); November 1, 1997 (amendment 548); November 1, 2000 (amendment 607); November 5, 2003 (amendment 662); November 1, 2007 (amendment 710); March 3, 2008 (amendments 712 and 713); May 1, 2008 (amendment 716); November 1, 2011 (amendment 759); November 1, 2012 (amendment 770); November 1, 2014 (amendments 780, 788, and 789).

§1B1.11. Use of Guidelines Manual in Effect on Date of Sentencing (Policy Statement)

(a) The court shall use the Guidelines Manual in effect on the date that the defendant is sentenced.

(b) (1) If the court determines that use of the Guidelines Manual in effect on the date that the defendant is sentenced would violate the *ex post facto* clause of the United States Constitution, the court shall use the Guidelines Manual in effect on the date that the offense of conviction was committed.

(2) The Guidelines Manual in effect on a particular date shall be applied in its entirety. The court shall not apply, for example, one guideline section from one edition of the Guidelines Manual and another guideline section from a different edition of the Guidelines Manual. However, if a court applies an earlier edition of the Guidelines Manual, the court shall consider subsequent amendments, to the extent that such amendments are clarifying rather than substantive changes.

(3) If the defendant is convicted of two offenses, the first committed before, and the second after, a revised edition of the Guidelines Manual became effective, the revised edition of the Guidelines Manual is to be applied to both offenses.

Commentary

Application Notes:

1. Subsection (b)(2) provides that if an earlier edition of the Guidelines Manual is used, it is to be used in its entirety, except that subsequent clarifying amendments are to be considered.

Example: A defendant is convicted of an antitrust offense committed in November 1989. He is to be sentenced in December 1992. Effective November 1, 1991, the Commission raised the base offense level for antitrust offenses. Effective November 1, 1992, the Commission lowered the guideline range in the Sentencing Table for cases with an offense level of 8 and criminal history category of I from 2–8 months to 0–6 months. Under the 1992 edition of the Guidelines Manual (effective November 1, 1992), the defendant has a guideline range of 4–10 months (final offense level of 9, criminal history category of I). Under the 1989 edition of the Guidelines Manual (effective November 1, 1989), the defendant has a guideline range of 2–8 months (final offense level of 8, criminal history category of I). If the court determines that application of the 1992 edition of the Guidelines Manual would violate the *ex post facto* clause of the United States Constitution, it shall apply the 1989 edition of the Guidelines Manual in its entirety. It shall not apply, for example, the offense level of 8 and criminal history category of I from the 1989 edition of the Guidelines Manual in conjunction with the amended guideline range of 0–6 months for this offense level and criminal history category from the 1992 edition of the Guidelines Manual.

2. Under subsection (b)(1), the last date of the offense of conviction is the controlling date for *ex post facto* purposes. For example, if the offense of conviction (*i.e.*, the conduct charged in the count of the indictment or information of which the defendant was convicted) was determined by the court to have been committed between October 15, 1991 and October 28, 1991, the date of October 28, 1991 is the controlling date for *ex post facto* purposes. This is true even if the defendant's conduct relevant to the determination of the guideline range under §1B1.3 (Relevant Conduct) included an act that occurred on November 2, 1991 (after a revised Guidelines Manual took effect).

Background: Subsections (a) and (b)(1) provide that the court should apply the Guidelines Manual in effect on the date the defendant is sentenced unless the court determines that doing so would violate the *ex post facto* clause in Article I, § 9 of the United States Constitution. Under 18 U.S.C. § 3553, the court is to apply the guidelines and policy statements in effect at the time of sentencing. However, the Supreme Court has held that the *ex post facto* clause applies to sentencing guideline amendments that subject the defendant to increased punishment. *See Peugh v. United States*, 133 S. Ct. 2072, 2078 (2013) (holding that "there is an *ex post facto* violation when a defendant is sentenced under Guidelines promulgated after he committed his criminal acts and the new version provides a higher applicable Guidelines sentencing range than the version in place at the time of the offense").

Subsection (b)(2) provides that the Guidelines Manual in effect on a particular date shall be applied in its entirety.

Subsection (b)(3) provides that where the defendant is convicted of two offenses, the first committed before, and the second after, a revised edition of the Guidelines Manual became effective, the revised edition of the Guidelines Manual is to be applied to both offenses, even if the revised edition results in an increased penalty for the first offense. Because the defendant completed the second offense after the amendment to the guidelines took effect, the *ex post facto* clause does not prevent determining the sentence for that count based on the amended guidelines. For example, if a defendant pleads guilty to a single count of embezzlement that occurred after the most recent edition of the Guidelines Manual became effective, the guideline range applicable in sentencing will encompass any relevant conduct (*e.g.*, related embezzlement offenses that may have occurred prior to the effective date of the guideline amendments) for the offense of conviction. The same would be true for a defendant convicted of two counts of embezzlement, one committed before the amendments were enacted, and the second after. In this example, the *ex post facto* clause would not bar application of the amended guideline to the first conviction; a contrary conclusion would mean that such defendant was subject to a lower guideline range than if convicted only of the second offense. Decisions from several appellate courts addressing the analogous situation of the constitutionality of counting pre-guidelines criminal activity as relevant conduct for a guidelines sentence support this approach. *See United States v. Ykema*, 887 F.2d 697 (6th Cir. 1989) (upholding inclusion of pre-November 1, 1987, drug quantities as relevant conduct for the count of conviction, noting that habitual offender statutes routinely augment punishment for an offense of conviction based on acts committed before a law is passed); *United States v. Allen*, 886 F.2d 143 (8th Cir. 1989) (similar); *see also United States v. Cusack*, 901 F.2d 29 (4th Cir. 1990) (similar).

Moreover, the approach set forth in subsection (b)(3) should be followed regardless of whether the offenses of conviction are the type in which the conduct is grouped under §3D1.2(d). The *ex post facto* clause does not distinguish between groupable and nongroupable offenses, and unless that clause would be violated, Congress's directive to apply the sentencing guidelines in effect at the time of sentencing must be followed. Under the guideline sentencing system, a single sentencing range is determined based on the defendant's overall conduct, even if there are multiple counts of conviction (*see* §§3D1.1–3D1.5, 5G1.2). Thus, if a defendant is sentenced in January 1992 for a bank robbery committed in October 1988 and one committed in November 1991, the November 1991 Guidelines Manual should be used to determine a combined guideline range for both counts. *See generally United States v. Stephenson*, 921 F.2d 438 (2d Cir. 1990) (holding that the Sentencing Commission and Congress intended that the applicable version of the guidelines be applied as a "cohesive and integrated whole" rather than in a piecemeal fashion).

Consequently, even in a complex case involving multiple counts that occurred under several different versions of the Guidelines Manual, it will not be necessary to compare more than two manuals to determine the applicable guideline range — the manual in effect at the time the last offense of conviction was completed and the manual in effect at the time of sentencing.

Historical Note

Effective November 1, 1992 (amendment 442). Amended effective November 1, 1993 (amendment 474); November

1, 2010 (amendment 746); November 1, 2013 (amendment 779); November 1, 2015 (amendment 796).

§1B1.12. Persons Sentenced Under the Federal Juvenile Delinquency Act (Policy Statement)

The sentencing guidelines do not apply to a defendant sentenced under the Federal Juvenile Delinquency Act (18 U.S.C. §§ 5031–5042). However, the sentence imposed upon a juvenile delinquent may not exceed the maximum of the guideline range applicable to an otherwise similarly situated adult defendant unless the court finds an aggravating factor sufficient to warrant an upward departure from that guideline range. *United States v. R.L.C.*, 503 U.S. 291 (1992). Therefore, a necessary step in ascertaining the maximum sentence that may be imposed upon a juvenile delinquent is the determination of the guideline range that would be applicable to a similarly situated adult defendant.

Historical Note
Effective November 1, 1993 (amendment 475).

§1B1.13. Reduction in Term of Imprisonment Under 18 U.S.C. § 3582(c)(1)(A) (Policy Statement)

Upon motion of the Director of the Bureau of Prisons under 18 U.S.C. § 3582(c)(1)(A), the court may reduce a term of imprisonment (and may impose a term of supervised release with or without conditions that does not exceed the unserved portion of the original term of imprisonment) if, after considering the factors set forth in 18 U.S.C. § 3553(a), to the extent that they are applicable, the court determines that—

(1) (A) extraordinary and compelling reasons warrant the reduction; or

(B) the defendant (i) is at least 70 years old; and (ii) has served at least 30 years in prison pursuant to a sentence imposed under 18 U.S.C. § 3559(c) for the offense or offenses for which the defendant is imprisoned;

(2) the defendant is not a danger to the safety of any other person or to the community, as provided in 18 U.S.C. § 3142(g); and

(3) the reduction is consistent with this policy statement.

Commentary

Application Notes:

1. **Extraordinary and Compelling Reasons.**—Provided the defendant meets the requirements of subdivision (2), extraordinary and compelling reasons exist under any of the circumstances set forth below:

(A) **Medical Condition of the Defendant.**—

(i) The defendant is suffering from a terminal illness (*i.e.*, a serious and advanced illness with an end of life trajectory). A specific prognosis of life expectancy (*i.e.*, a probability of death within a specific time period) is not required. Examples include metastatic solid-tumor cancer, amyotrophic lateral sclerosis (ALS), end-stage organ disease, and advanced dementia.

(ii) The defendant is—

(I) suffering from a serious physical or medical condition,

(II) suffering from a serious functional or cognitive impairment, or
(III) experiencing deteriorating physical or mental health because of the aging process,
that substantially diminishes the ability of the defendant to provide self-care within the environment of a correctional facility and from which he or she is not expected to recover.
(B) **Age of the Defendant.**—The defendant (i) is at least 65 years old; (ii) is experiencing a serious deterioration in physical or mental health because of the aging process; and (iii) has served at least 10 years or 75 percent of his or her term of imprisonment, whichever is less.
(C) **Family Circumstances.**—
(i) The death or incapacitation of the caregiver of the defendant's minor child or minor children.
(ii) The incapacitation of the defendant's spouse or registered partner when the defendant would be the only available caregiver for the spouse or registered partner.
(D) **Other Reasons.**—As determined by the Director of the Bureau of Prisons, there exists in the defendant's case an extraordinary and compelling reason other than, or in combination with, the reasons described in subdivisions (A) through (C).
2. **Foreseeability of Extraordinary and Compelling Reasons.**—For purposes of this policy statement, an extraordinary and compelling reason need not have been unforeseen at the time of sentencing in order to warrant a reduction in the term of imprisonment. Therefore, the fact that an extraordinary and compelling reason reasonably could have been known or anticipated by the sentencing court does not preclude consideration for a reduction under this policy statement.

3. **Rehabilitation of the Defendant.**—Pursuant to 28 U.S.C. § 994(t), rehabilitation of the defendant is not, by itself, an extraordinary and compelling reason for purposes of this policy statement.
4. **Motion by the Director of the Bureau of Prisons.**—A reduction under this policy statement may be granted only upon motion by the Director of the Bureau of Prisons pursuant to 18 U.S.C. § 3582(c)(1)(A). The Commission encourages the Director of the Bureau of Prisons to file such a motion if the defendant meets any of the circumstances set forth in Application Note 1. The court is in a unique position to determine whether the circumstances warrant a reduction (and, if so, the amount of reduction), after considering the factors set forth 18 U.S.C. § 3553(a) and the criteria set forth in this policy statement, such as the defendant's medical condition, the defendant's family circumstances, and whether the defendant is a danger to the safety of any other person or to the community.
This policy statement shall not be construed to confer upon the defendant any right not otherwise recognized in law.
5. **Application of Subdivision (3).**—Any reduction made pursuant to a motion by the Director of the Bureau of Prisons for the reasons set forth in subdivisions (1) and (2) is consistent with this policy statement.

Background: The Commission is required by 28 U.S.C. § 994(a)(2) to develop general policy statements regarding application of the guidelines or other aspects of sentencing that in the view of the Commission would further the purposes of sentencing (18 U.S.C. § 3553(a)(2)), including, among other things, the appropriate use of the sentence modification provisions set forth in 18 U.S.C. § 3582(c). In doing so, the Commission is authorized by 28 U.S.C. § 994(t) to "describe what should be considered extraordinary and compelling reasons for sentence reduction, including the criteria to be applied and a list of specific examples." This policy statement implements 28 U.S.C. § 994(a)(2) and (t).

Historical Note
Effective November 1, 2006 (amendment 683). Amended effective November 1, 2007 (amendment 698); November

CHAPTER TWO

OFFENSE CONDUCT

Introductory Commentary

Chapter Two pertains to offense conduct. The chapter is organized by offenses and divided into parts and related sections that may cover one statute or many. Each offense has a corresponding base offense level and may have one or more specific offense characteristics that adjust the offense level upward or downward. Certain factors relevant to the offense that are not covered in specific guidelines in Chapter Two are set forth in Chapter Three, Parts A (Victim-Related Adjustments), B (Role in the Offense), and C (Obstruction and Related Adjustments); Chapter Four, Part B (Career Offenders and Criminal Livelihood); and Chapter Five, Part K (Departures).

Historical
Note
Effective November 1, 1987. Amended effective November 1, 2011 (amendment 758).

PART A — OFFENSES AGAINST THE PERSON

1. HOMICIDE

§2A1.1. First Degree Murder

(a) Base Offense Level: **43**

Commentary

Statutory Provisions: 18 U.S.C. §§ 1111, 1841(a)(2)(C), 1992(a)(7), 2113(e), 2118(c)(2), 2199, 2282A, 2291, 2332b(a)(1), 2340A; 21 U.S.C. § 848(e). For additional statutory provision(s), *see* Appendix A (Statutory Index).

Application Notes:

1. **Applicability of Guideline.**—This guideline applies in cases of premeditated killing. This guideline also applies when death results from the commission of certain felonies. For example, this guideline may be applied as a result of a cross reference (*e.g.*, a kidnapping in which death occurs, *see* §2A4.1(c)(1)), or in cases in which the offense level of a guideline is calculated using the underlying crime (*e.g.*, murder in aid of racketeering, *see* §2E1.3(a)(2)).

2. **Imposition of Life Sentence.**—

(A) **Offenses Involving Premeditated Killing.**—In the case of premeditated killing, life imprisonment is the appropriate sentence if a sentence of death is not imposed. A downward departure would not be appropriate in such a case. A downward departure from a mandatory statutory term of life imprisonment is permissible only

in cases in which the government files a motion for a downward departure for the defendant's substantial assistance, as provided in 18 U.S.C. § 3553(e).

(B) **Felony Murder.**—If the defendant did not cause the death intentionally or knowingly, a downward departure may be warranted. For example, a downward departure may be warranted if in robbing a bank, the defendant merely passed a note to the teller, as a result of which the teller had a heart attack and died. The extent of the departure should be based upon the defendant's state of mind (*e.g.*, recklessness or negligence), the degree of risk inherent in the conduct, and the nature of the underlying offense conduct. However, departure below the minimum guideline sentence provided for second degree murder in §2A1.2 (Second Degree Murder) is not likely to be appropriate. Also, because death obviously is an aggravating factor, it necessarily would be inappropriate to impose a sentence at a level below that which the guideline for the underlying offense requires in the absence of death.

3. **Applicability of Guideline When Death Sentence Not Imposed.**—If the defendant is sentenced pursuant to 18 U.S.C. § 3591 *et seq.* or 21 U.S.C. § 848(e), a sentence of death may be imposed under the specific provisions contained in that statute. This guideline applies when a sentence of death is not imposed under those specific provisions.

Historical

Note
Effective November 1, 1987. Amended effective November 1, 1989 (amendment 82); November 1, 1990 (amendment 310); November 1, 1993 (amendment 476); November 1, 2002 (amendment 637); November 1, 2004 (amendment 663); November 1, 2006 (amendment 685); November 1, 2007 (amendments 699 and 700); November 1, 2010 (amendment 746).

§2A1.2. Second Degree Murder

(a) Base Offense Level: **38**

Commentary

Statutory Provisions: 18 U.S.C. §§ 1111, 1841(a)(2)(C), 2199, 2282A, 2291, 2332b(a)(1), 2340A. For additional statutory provision(s), *see* Appendix A (Statutory Index).

Application Note:

1. **Upward Departure Provision.**—If the defendant's conduct was exceptionally heinous, cruel, brutal, or degrading to the victim, an upward departure may be warranted. *See* §5K2.8 (Extreme Conduct).

Historical
Note
Effective November 1, 1987. Amended effective November 1, 2002 (amendment 637); November 1, 2004 (amendment 663); November 1, 2006 (amendment 685); November 1, 2007 (amendments 699 and 700).

§2A1.3. Voluntary Manslaughter

(a) Base Offense Level: **29**

Commentary

Statutory Provisions: 18 U.S.C. §§ 1112, 1841(a)(2)(C), 2199, 2291, 2332b(a)(1). For additional statutory provision(s), *see* Appendix A (Statutory Index).

Historical
Note
Effective November 1, 1987. Amended effective November 1, 2002 (amendment 637); November 1, 2004 (amendment 663); November 1, 2006 (amendment 685); November 1, 2007 (amendment 699).

§2A1.4. Involuntary Manslaughter

(a) Base Offense Level:

(1) **12**, if the offense involved criminally negligent conduct; or

(2) (Apply the greater):

(A) **18**, if the offense involved reckless conduct; or

(B) **22**, if the offense involved the reckless operation of a means of transportation.

(b) Special Instruction

(1) If the offense involved the involuntary manslaughter of more than one person, Chapter Three, Part D (Multiple Counts) shall be applied as if the involuntary manslaughter of each person had been contained in a separate count of conviction.

Commentary

Statutory Provisions: 18 U.S.C. §§ 1112, 1841(a)(2)(C), 2199, 2291, 2332b(a)(1). For additional statutory provision(s), *see* Appendix A (Statutory Index).

Application Note:

1. **Definitions.**—For purposes of this guideline:

"***Criminally negligent***" means conduct that involves a gross deviation from the standard of care that a reasonable person would exercise under the circumstances, but which is not reckless. Offenses with this characteristic usually will be encountered as assimilative crimes.

"***Means of transportation***" includes a motor vehicle (including an automobile or a boat) and a mass transportation vehicle. "Mass transportation" has the meaning given that term in 18 U.S.C. § 1992(d)(7).

"***Reckless***" means a situation in which the defendant was aware of the risk created by his conduct and the risk was of such a nature and degree that to disregard that risk constituted a gross deviation from the standard of care that a reasonable person would exercise in such a situation. "Reckless" includes all, or nearly all, convictions for involuntary manslaughter under 18 U.S.C. § 1112. A homicide resulting from driving a means of transportation, or similarly dangerous actions, while under the influence of alcohol or drugs ordinarily should be treated as reckless.

Historical Note

Effective November 1, 1987. Amended effective November 1, 2002 (amendment 637); November 1, 2003 (amendment 652); November 1, 2004 (amendment 663); November 1, 2006 (amendment 685); November 1, 2007 (amendment 699).

§2A1.5. Conspiracy or Solicitation to Commit Murder

(a) Base Offense Level: **33**

(b) Specific Offense Characteristic

(1) If the offense involved the offer or the receipt of anything of pecuniary value for undertaking the murder, increase by **4** levels.

(c) Cross References

(1) If the offense resulted in the death of a victim, apply §2A1.1 (First Degree Murder).

(2) If the offense resulted in an attempted murder or assault with intent to commit murder, apply §2A2.1 (Assault with Intent to Commit Murder; Attempted Murder).

Commentary

Statutory Provisions: 18 U.S.C. §§ 351(d), 371, 373, 1117, 1751(d).

Historical Note

Effective November 1, 1990 (amendment 311). Amended effective November 1, 2004 (amendment 663).

* * * * *

2. ASSAULT

§2A2.1. Assault with Intent to Commit Murder; Attempted Murder

(a) Base Offense Level:

(1) **33**, if the object of the offense would have constituted first degree murder; or

(2) **27**, otherwise.

(b) Specific Offense Characteristics

(1) If (A) the victim sustained permanent or life-threatening bodily injury, increase by **4** levels; (B) the victim sustained serious bodily injury, increase by **2** levels; or (C) the degree of injury is between that specified in subdivisions (A) and (B), increase by **3** levels.

(2) If the offense involved the offer or the receipt of anything of pecuniary value for undertaking the murder, increase by **4** levels.

Commentary

Statutory Provisions: 18 U.S.C. §§ 113(a)(1), 351(c), 1113, 1116(a), 1751(c), 1841(a)(2)(C), 1992(a)(7), 2199, 2291. For additional statutory provision(s), *see* Appendix A (Statutory Index).

Application Notes:

1. **Definitions.**—For purposes of this guideline:

"***First degree murder***" means conduct that, if committed within the special maritime and territorial jurisdiction of the United States, would constitute first degree murder under 18 U.S.C. § 1111.

"***Permanent or life-threatening bodily injury***" and "***serious bodily injury***" have the meaning given those terms in Application Note 1 of the Commentary to §1B1.1 (Application Instructions).

2. **Upward Departure Provision.**—If the offense created a substantial risk of death or serious bodily injury to more than one person, an upward departure may be warranted.

Background: This section applies to the offenses of assault with intent to commit murder and attempted murder. An attempted manslaughter, or assault with intent to commit manslaughter, is covered under §2A2.2 (Aggravated Assault).

Historical Note

Effective November 1, 1987. Amended effective November 1, 1989 (amendments 83 and 84); November 1, 1990 (amendment 311); November 1, 1991 (amendment 391); November 1, 1995 (amendment 534); November 1, 2002 (amendment 637); November 1, 2004 (amendment 663); November 1, 2006 (amendment 685); November 1, 2007 (amendment 699).

§2A2.2. Aggravated Assault

(a) Base Offense Level: **14**

(b) Specific Offense Characteristics

(1) If the assault involved more than minimal planning, increase by **2** levels.

(2) If (A) a firearm was discharged, increase by **5** levels; (B) a dangerous weapon (including a firearm) was otherwise used, increase by **4** levels; (C) a dangerous weapon (including a firearm) was brandished or its use was threatened, increase by **3** levels.

(3) If the victim sustained bodily injury, increase the offense level according to the seriousness of the injury:

DEGREE OF BODILY INJURY INCREASE IN LEVEL

(A) Bodily Injury add **3**

(B) Serious Bodily Injury add **5**

(C) Permanent or Life-Threatening Bodily Injury add **7**

(D) If the degree of injury is between that specified in subdivisions (A) and (B), add **4** levels; or

(E) If the degree of injury is between that specified in subdivisions (B) and (C), add **6** levels.

However, the cumulative adjustments from application of subdivisions (2) and (3) shall not exceed **10** levels.

(4) If the offense involved strangling, suffocating, or attempting to strangle or suffocate a spouse, intimate partner, or dating partner, increase by **3** levels.

However, the cumulative adjustments from application of subdivisions (2), (3), and (4) shall not exceed **12** levels.

(5) If the assault was motivated by a payment or offer of money or other thing of value, increase by **2** levels.

(6) If the offense involved the violation of a court protection order, increase by **2** levels.

(7) If the defendant was convicted under 18 U.S.C. § 111(b) or § 115, increase by **2** levels.

Commentary

Statutory Provisions: 18 U.S.C. §§ 111, 112, 113(a)(2), (3), (6), (8), 114, 115(a), (b)(1), 351(e), 1751(e), 1841(a)(2)(C), 1992(a)(7), 2199, 2291, 2332b(a)(1), 2340A. For additional statutory provision(s), *see* Appendix A (Statutory Index).

Application Notes:

1. **Definitions.**—For purposes of this guideline:

"***Aggravated assault***" means a felonious assault that involved (A) a dangerous weapon with intent to cause bodily injury (*i.e.*, not merely to frighten) with that weapon; (B) serious bodily injury; (C) strangling, suffocating, or attempting to strangle or suffocate; or (D) an intent to commit another felony.

"***Brandished,***" "***bodily injury,***" "***firearm,***" "***otherwise used,***" "***permanent or lifethreatening bodily injury,***" and "***serious bodily injury,***" have the meaning given those terms in §1B1.1 (Application Instructions), Application Note 1.

"***Dangerous weapon***" has the meaning given that term in §1B1.1, Application Note 1, and includes any instrument that is not ordinarily used as a weapon (*e.g.*, a car, a chair, or an ice pick) if such an instrument is involved in the offense with the intent to commit bodily injury.

"***Strangling***" and "***suffocating***" have the meaning given those terms in 18 U.S.C. § 113.

"***Spouse,***" "***intimate partner,***" and "***dating partner***" have the meaning given those terms in 18 U.S.C. § 2266.

2. **Application of Subsection (b)(1).**—For purposes of subsection (b)(1), "***more than minimal planning***" means more planning than is typical for commission of the offense in a simple form. "More than minimal planning" also exists if significant affirmative steps were taken to conceal the offense, other than conduct to which §3C1.1 (Obstructing or Impeding the Administration of Justice) applies. For example, waiting to commit the offense when no witnesses were present would not alone constitute more than minimal planning. By contrast, luring the victim to a specific location or wearing a ski mask to prevent identification would constitute more than minimal planning.

3. **Application of Subsection (b)(2).**—In a case involving a dangerous weapon with intent to cause bodily injury, the court shall apply both the base offense level and subsection (b)(2).

4. **Application of Official Victim Adjustment.**—If subsection (b)(7) applies, §3A1.2 (Official Victim) also shall apply.

Background: This guideline covers felonious assaults that are more serious than other assaults because of the presence of an aggravating factor, *i.e.*, serious bodily injury; the involvement of a dangerous weapon with intent to cause bodily injury; strangling, suffocating, or attempting to strangle or suffocate; or the intent to commit another felony. Such offenses occasionally may involve planning or be committed for hire. Consequently, the structure follows §2A2.1 (Assault with Intent to Commit Murder; Attempted Murder). This guideline also covers attempted manslaughter and assault with intent to commit manslaughter. Assault with intent to commit murder is covered by §2A2.1. Assault with intent to commit rape is covered by §2A3.1 (Criminal Sexual Abuse; Attempt to Commit Criminal Sexual Abuse).

An assault that involves the presence of a dangerous weapon is aggravated in form when the presence of the dangerous weapon is coupled with the intent to cause bodily injury. In such a case, the base offense level and the weapon enhancement in subsection (b)(2) take into account different aspects of the offense, even if application of the base offense level and the weapon enhancement is based on the same conduct.

Subsection (b)(7) implements the directive to the Commission in subsection 11008(e) of the 21st Century Department of Justice Appropriations Act (the "Act"), Public Law 107–273. The enhancement in subsection (b)(7) is cumulative to the adjustment in §3A1.2 (Official Victim) in order to address adequately the directive in section 11008(e)(2)(D) of the Act, which provides that the Commission shall consider "the extent to which sentencing enhancements within the Federal guidelines and the authority of the court to impose a sentence in excess of the applicable guideline range are adequate to ensure punishment at or near the maximum penalty for the most egregious conduct covered by" 18 U.S.C. §§ 111 and 115.

Historical Note

Effective November 1, 1987. Amended effective November 1, 1989 (amendments 85 and 86); November 1, 1990 (amendment 311); November 1, 1995 (amendment 534); November 1, 1997 (amendment 549); November 1, 2001 (amendment 614); November 1, 2002 (amendment 637); November 1, 2004 (amendment 663); November 1, 2006 (amendment 685); November 1, 2007 (amendment 699); November 1, 2014 (amendment 781).

§2A2.3. Assault

(a) Base Offense Level:

(1) **7**, if the offense involved physical contact, or if a dangerous weapon (including a firearm) was possessed and its use was threatened; or

(2) **4**, otherwise.

(b) Specific Offense Characteristic

(1) If (A) the victim sustained bodily injury, increase by **2** levels; or (B) the offense resulted in substantial bodily injury to a spouse, intimate partner, or dating partner, or an individual under the age of sixteen years, increase by **4** levels.

(c) Cross Reference

(1) If the conduct constituted aggravated assault, apply §2A2.2 (Aggravated Assault).

Commentary

Statutory Provisions: 18 U.S.C. §§ 112, 113(a)(4), (5), (7), 115(a), 115(b)(1), 351(e), 1751(e), 2199, 2291. For additional statutory provision(s), *see* Appendix A (Statutory Index).

Application Notes:

1. **Definitions.**—For purposes of this guideline:

"***Bodily injury***", "***dangerous weapon***", and "***firearm***" have the meaning given those terms in Application Note 1 of the Commentary to §1B1.1 (Application Instructions).

"***Spouse***," "***intimate partner***," and "***dating partner***" have the meaning given those terms in 18 U.S.C. § 2266.

"***Substantial bodily injury***" means "bodily injury which involves (A) a temporary but substantial disfigurement; or (B) a temporary but substantial loss or impairment of the function of any bodily member, organ, or mental faculty." *See* 18 U.S.C. § 113(b)(1).

2. **Application of Subsection (b)(1).**—Conduct that forms the basis for application of subsection (a)(1) also may form the basis for application of the enhancement in subsection (b)(1)(A) or (B).

Background: This section applies to misdemeanor assault and battery and to any felonious assault not covered by §2A2.2 (Aggravated Assault).

Historical Note

Effective November 1, 1987. Amended effective October 15, 1988 (amendment 64); November 1, 1989 (amendments 87 and 88); November 1, 1995 (amendment 510); November 1, 2004 (amendment 663); November 1, 2007 (amendment 699); November 1, 2014 (amendment 781).

§2A2.4. Obstructing or Impeding Officers

(a) Base Offense Level: **10**

(b) Specific Offense Characteristics

(1) If (A) the offense involved physical contact; or (B) a dangerous weapon (including a firearm) was possessed and its use was threatened, increase by **3** levels.

(2) If the victim sustained bodily injury, increase by **2** levels.

(c) Cross Reference
(1) If the conduct constituted aggravated assault, apply §2A2.2 (Aggravated Assault).

Commentary

Statutory Provisions: 18 U.S.C. §§ 111, 1501, 1502, 2237(a)(1), (a)(2)(A), 3056(d). For additional statutory provision(s), *see* Appendix A (Statutory Index).

Application Notes:

1. **Definitions.**—For purposes of this guideline, "***bodily injury***", "***dangerous weapon***", and "***firearm***" have the meaning given those terms in Application Note 1 of the Commentary to §1B1.1 (Application Instructions).
2. **Application of Certain Chapter Three Adjustments.**—The base offense level incorporates the fact that the victim was a governmental officer performing official duties. Therefore, do not apply §3A1.2 (Official Victim) unless, pursuant to subsection (c), the offense level is determined under §2A2.2 (Aggravated Assault). Conversely, the base offense level does not incorporate the possibility that the defendant may create a substantial risk of death or serious bodily injury to another person in the course of fleeing from a law enforcement official (although an offense under 18 U.S.C. § 758 for fleeing or evading a law enforcement checkpoint at high speed will often, but not always, involve the creation of that risk). If the defendant creates that risk and no higher guideline adjustment is applicable for the conduct creating the risk, apply §3C1.2 (Reckless Endangerment During Flight).
3. **Upward Departure Provision.**—The base offense level does not assume any significant disruption of governmental functions. In situations involving such disruption, an upward departure may be warranted. *See* §5K2.7 (Disruption of Governmental Function).

Historical Note
Effective October 15, 1988 (amendment 64). Amended effective November 1, 1989 (amendments 89 and 90); November 1, 1992 (amendment 443); November 1, 1997 (amendment 550); November 1, 2004 (amendment 663); November 1, 2005 (amendment 679); November 1, 2007 (amendment 699).

* * * * *

§2A3.1

3. CRIMINAL SEXUAL ABUSE AND OFFENSES RELATED TO REGISTRATION AS A SEX OFFENDER

Historical Note
Effective November 1, 1987. Amended effective November 1, 2007 (amendment 701).

§2A3.1. Criminal Sexual Abuse; Attempt to Commit Criminal Sexual Abuse

(a) Base Offense Level:
(1) **38**, if the defendant was convicted under 18 U.S.C. § 2241(c); or
(2) **30**, otherwise.
(b) Specific Offense Characteristics
(1) If the offense involved conduct described in 18 U.S.C. § 2241(a) or (b), increase by **4** levels.
(2) If subsection (a)(2) applies and (A) the victim had not attained the age of twelve years, increase by **4** levels; or (B) the victim had attained the age of twelve years but had not attained the age of sixteen years, increase by **2** levels.
(3) If the victim was (A) in the custody, care, or supervisory control of the defendant; or (B) a person held in the custody of a correctional facility, increase by **2** levels.
(4) (A) If the victim sustained permanent or life-threatening bodily

injury, increase by **4** levels; (B) if the victim sustained serious bodily injury, increase by **2** levels; or (C) if the degree of injury is between that specified in subdivisions (A) and (B), increase by **3** levels.

(5) If the victim was abducted, increase by **4** levels.

(6) If, to persuade, induce, entice, or coerce a minor to engage in prohibited sexual conduct, or if, to facilitate transportation or travel, by a minor or a participant, to engage in prohibited sexual conduct, the offense involved (A) the knowing misrepresentation of a participant's identity; or (B) the use of a computer or an interactive computer service, increase by **2** levels.

(c) Cross References

(1) If a victim was killed under circumstances that would constitute murder under 18 U.S.C. § 1111 had such killing taken place within the territorial or maritime jurisdiction of the United States, apply §2A1.1 (First Degree Murder), if the resulting offense level is greater than that determined above.

(2) If the offense involved causing, transporting, permitting, or offering or seeking by notice or advertisement, a minor to engage in sexually explicit conduct for the purpose of producing a visual depiction of such conduct, apply §2G2.1 (Sexually Exploiting a Minor by Production of Sexually Explicit Visual or Printed Material; Custodian Permitting Minor to Engage in Sexually Explicit Conduct; Advertisement for Minors to Engage in Production), if the resulting offense level is greater than that determined above.

(d) Special Instruction

(1) If the offense occurred in the custody or control of a prison or other correctional facility and the victim was a prison official, the offense shall be deemed to have an official victim for purposes of subsection (c)(2) of §3A1.2 (Official Victim).

Commentary

Statutory Provisions: 18 U.S.C. §§ 2241, 2242. For additional statutory provision(s), *see* Appendix A (Statutory Index).

Application Notes:

1. **Definitions.**—For purposes of this guideline:

"***Abducted***", "***permanent or life-threatening bodily injury***", and "***serious bodily injury***" have the meaning given those terms in Application Note 1 of the Commentary to §1B1.1 (Application Instructions). However, for purposes of this guideline, "***serious bodily injury***" means conduct other than criminal sexual abuse, which already is taken into account in the base offense level under subsection (a).

"***Custody or control***" and "***prison official***" have the meaning given those terms in Application Note 4 of the Commentary to §3A1.2 (Official Victim).

"***Child pornography***" has the meaning given that term in 18 U.S.C. § 2256(8).

"***Computer***" has the meaning given that term in 18 U.S.C. § 1030(e)(1).

"***Distribution***" means any act, including possession with intent to distribute, production, transportation, and advertisement, related to the transfer of material involving the sexual exploitation of a minor. Accordingly, distribution includes posting material involving the sexual exploitation of a minor on a website for public viewing, but does not include the mere solicitation of such material by a defendant.

"*Interactive computer service*" has the meaning given that term in section 230(e)(2) of the Communications Act of 1934 (47 U.S.C. § 230(f)(2)).

"*Minor*" means (A) an individual who had not attained the age of 18 years; (B) an individual, whether fictitious or not, who a law enforcement officer represented to a participant (i) had not attained the age of 18 years, and (ii) could be provided for the purposes of engaging in sexually explicit conduct; or (C) an undercover law enforcement officer who represented to a participant that the officer had not attained the age of 18 years.

"*Participant*" has the meaning given that term in Application Note 1 of the Commentary to §3B1.1 (Aggravating Role).

"*Prohibited sexual conduct*" (A) means any sexual activity for which a person can be charged with a criminal offense; (B) includes the production of child pornography; and (C) does not include trafficking in, or possession of, child pornography.

"*Victim*" includes an undercover law enforcement officer.

2. **Application of Subsection (b)(1).—**

(A) **Definitions.**—For purposes of subsection (b)(1), "***conduct described in 18 U.S.C. § 2241(a) or (b)***" is engaging in, or causing another person to engage in, a sexual act with another person by: (A) using force against the victim; (B) threatening or placing the victim in fear that any person will be subject to death, serious bodily injury, or kidnapping; (C) rendering the victim unconscious; or (D) administering by force or threat of force, or without the knowledge or permission of the victim, a drug, intoxicant, or other similar substance and thereby substantially impairing the ability of the victim to appraise or control conduct. This provision would apply, for example, if any dangerous weapon was used or brandished, or in a case in which the ability of the victim to appraise or control conduct was substantially impaired by drugs or alcohol.

(B) **Application in Cases Involving a Conviction under 18 U.S.C. § 2241(c).**—If the conduct that forms the basis for a conviction under 18 U.S.C. § 2241(c) is that the defendant engaged in conduct described in 18 U.S.C. § 2241(a) or (b), do not apply subsection (b)(1).

3. **Application of Subsection (b)(3).—**

(A) **Care, Custody, or Supervisory Control.**—Subsection (b)(3) is to be construed broadly and includes offenses involving a victim less than 18 years of age entrusted to the defendant, whether temporarily or permanently. For example, teachers, day care providers, baby-sitters, or other temporary caretakers are among those who would be subject to this enhancement. In determining whether to apply this enhancement, the court should look to the actual relationship that existed between the defendant and the minor and not simply to the legal status of the defendantminor relationship.

(B) **Inapplicability of Chapter Three Adjustment.**—If the enhancement in subsection (b)(3) applies, do not apply §3B1.3 (Abuse of Position of Trust or Use of Special Skill).

4. **Application of Subsection (b)(6).—**

(A) **Misrepresentation of Participant's Identity.**—The enhancement in subsection (b)(6)(A) applies in cases involving the misrepresentation of a participant's identity to (A) persuade, induce, entice, or coerce a minor to engage in prohibited sexual conduct; or (B) facilitate transportation or travel, by a minor or a participant, to engage in prohibited sexual conduct. Subsection (b)(6)(A) is intended to apply only to misrepresentations made directly to a minor or to a person who exercises custody, care, or supervisory control of the minor. Accordingly, the enhancement in subsection (b)(6)(A) would not apply to a misrepresentation made by a participant to an airline representative in the course of making travel arrangements for the minor. The misrepresentation to which the enhancement in subsection (b)(6)(A) may apply includes misrepresentation of a participant's name, age, occupation, gender, or status, as long as the misrepresentation was made with the intent to (A) persuade, induce, entice, or coerce a minor to engage in prohibited sexual conduct; or (B) facilitate transportation or travel, by a minor or a participant, to engage in prohibited sexual conduct. Accordingly, use of a computer screen name, without such intent, would not be a sufficient basis for application of the enhancement.

(B) **Use of a Computer or Interactive Computer Service.**—Subsection (b)(6)(B) provides an enhancement if a computer or an interactive computer service was used to (i) persuade, induce, entice, or coerce a minor to engage in prohibited sexual conduct; or (ii) facilitate transportation or travel, by a minor or a participant, to engage in prohibited sexual conduct. Subsection (b)(6)(B) is intended to apply only to the use of a computer or an interactive computer service to communicate directly with a minor or with a person who exercises custody, care, or supervisory control of the minor. Accordingly, the enhancement would not apply to the use of a computer or an interactive computer service to obtain airline tickets for the minor from an airline's Internet site.

5. **Application of Subsection (c)(2).**—

(A) **In General.**—The cross reference in subsection (c)(2) is to be construed broadly and includes all instances where the offense involved employing, using, persuading, inducing, enticing, coercing, transporting, permitting, or offering or seeking by notice or advertisement, a minor to engage in sexually explicit conduct for the purpose of producing any visual depiction of such conduct.

(B) **Definition.**—For purposes of subsection (c)(2), "***sexually explicit conduct***" has the meaning given that term in 18 U.S.C. § 2256(2).

6. **Upward Departure Provision.**—If a victim was sexually abused by more than one participant, an upward departure may be warranted. *See* §5K2.8 (Extreme Conduct).

Historical Note

Effective November 1, 1987. Amended effective November 1, 1989 (amendments 91 and 92); November 1, 1991 (amendment 392); November 1, 1992 (amendment 444); November 1, 1993 (amendment 477); November 1, 1995 (amendment 511); November 1, 1997 (amendment 545); November 1, 2000 (amendments 592 and 601); November 1, 2001 (amendment 615); November 1, 2003 (amendment 661); November 1, 2004 (amendment 664); November 1, 2007 (amendment 701); November 1, 2008 (amendment 725).

§2A3.2. Criminal Sexual Abuse of a Minor Under the Age of Sixteen Years (Statutory Rape) or Attempt to Commit Such Acts

(a) Base Offense Level: **18**

(b) Specific Offense Characteristics

(1) If the minor was in the custody, care, or supervisory control of the defendant, increase by **4** levels.

(2) If (A) subsection (b)(1) does not apply; and (B)(i) the offense involved the knowing misrepresentation of a participant's identity to persuade, induce, entice, or coerce the minor to engage in prohibited sexual conduct; or (ii) a participant otherwise unduly influenced the minor to engage in prohibited sexual conduct, increase by **4** levels.

(3) If a computer or an interactive computer service was used to persuade, induce, entice, or coerce the minor to engage in prohibited sexual conduct, increase by **2** levels.

(c) Cross Reference

(1) If the offense involved criminal sexual abuse or attempt to commit criminal sexual abuse (as defined in 18 U.S.C. § 2241 or § 2242), apply §2A3.1 (Criminal Sexual Abuse; Attempt to Commit Criminal Sexual Abuse). If the victim had not attained the age of 12 years, §2A3.1 shall apply, regardless of the "consent" of the victim.

Commentary

Statutory Provision: 18 U.S.C. § 2243(a). For additional statutory provision(s), *see* Appendix A (Statutory Index).

Application Notes:

1. **Definitions.**—For purposes of this guideline:

"***Computer***" has the meaning given that term in 18 U.S.C. § 1030(e)(1).

"***Interactive computer service***" has the meaning given that term in section 230(e)(2) of the Communications Act of 1934 (47 U.S.C. § 230(f)(2)).

"***Minor***" means (A) an individual who had not attained the age of 16 years; (B) an individual, whether fictitious or not, who a law enforcement officer represented to a participant (i) had not attained the age of 16 years, and (ii) could be provided for the purposes of engaging in sexually explicit conduct; or (C) an undercover law enforcement officer who represented to a participant that the officer had not attained the age of 16 years.

"***Participant***" has the meaning given that term in Application Note 1 of §3B1.1 (Aggravating Role).

"***Prohibited sexual conduct***" has the meaning given that term in Application Note 1 of §2A3.1 (Criminal Sexual Abuse; Attempt to Commit Criminal Sexual Abuse).

2. **Custody, Care, or Supervisory Control Enhancement.**—

(A) **In General.**—Subsection (b)(1) is intended to have broad application and is to be applied whenever the minor is entrusted to the defendant, whether temporarily or permanently. For example, teachers, day care providers, baby-sitters, or other temporary caretakers are among those who would be subject to this enhancement. In determining whether to apply this enhancement, the court should look to the actual relationship that existed between the defendant and the minor and not simply to the legal status of the defendant-minor relationship.

(B) **Inapplicability of Chapter Three Adjustment.**—If the enhancement in subsection (b)(1) applies, do not apply subsection (b)(2) or §3B1.3 (Abuse of Position of Trust or Use of Special Skill).

3. **Application of Subsection (b)(2).**—

(A) **Misrepresentation of Identity.**—The enhancement in subsection (b)(2)(B)(i) applies in cases involving the misrepresentation of a participant's identity to persuade, induce, entice, or coerce the minor to engage in prohibited sexual conduct. Subsection (b)(2)(B)(i) is intended to apply only to misrepresentations made directly to the minor or to a person who exercises custody, care, or supervisory control of the minor. Accordingly, the enhancement in subsection (b)(2)(B)(i) would not apply to a misrepresentation made by a participant to an airline representative in the course of making travel arrangements for the minor.

The misrepresentation to which the enhancement in subsection (b)(2)(B)(i) may apply includes misrepresentation of a participant's name, age, occupation, gender, or status, as long as the misrepresentation was made with the intent to persuade, induce, entice, or coerce the minor to engage in prohibited sexual conduct. Accordingly, use of a computer screen name, without such intent, would not be a sufficient basis for application of the enhancement.

(B) **Undue Influence.**—In determining whether subsection (b)(2)(B)(ii) applies, the court should closely consider the facts of the case to determine whether a participant's influence over the minor compromised the voluntariness of the minor's behavior.

The voluntariness of the minor's behavior may be compromised without prohibited sexual conduct occurring.

However, subsection (b)(2)(B)(ii) does not apply in a case in which the only "minor" (as defined in Application Note 1) involved in the offense is an undercover law enforcement officer.

In a case in which a participant is at least 10 years older than the minor, there shall be a rebuttable presumption that subsection (b)(2)(B)(ii) applies. In such a case, some degree of undue influence can be presumed because of the substantial difference in age between the participant and the minor.

4. **Application of Subsection (b)(3).**—Subsection (b)(3) provides an enhancement if a computer or an interactive computer service was used to persuade, induce, entice, or coerce the minor to engage in prohibited sexual conduct. Subsection (b)(3) is intended to apply only to the use of a computer or an interactive computer service to communicate directly with the minor or with a person who exercises custody, care, or supervisory control of the minor.

5. **Cross Reference.**—Subsection (c)(1) provides a cross reference to §2A3.1 (Criminal Sexual Abuse; Attempt to Commit Criminal Sexual Abuse) if the offense involved criminal sexual abuse or attempt to commit criminal sexual abuse, as defined in 18 U.S.C. § 2241 or § 2242. For example, the cross reference to §2A3.1 shall apply if (A) the victim had not attained the age of 12 years (*see* 18 U.S.C. § 2241(c)); (B) the victim had attained the age of 12 years but not attained the age of 16 years, and was placed in fear of death, serious bodily injury, or kidnapping (*see* 18 U.S.C. § 2241(a),(c)); or (C) the victim was threatened or placed in fear other than fear of death, serious bodily injury, or kidnapping (*see* 18 U.S.C. § 2242(1)).

6. **Upward Departure Consideration.**—There may be cases in which the offense level determined under this guideline substantially understates the seriousness of the offense. In such cases, an upward departure may be warranted. For example, an upward departure may be warranted if the defendant committed the criminal sexual act in furtherance of a commercial scheme such as pandering, transporting persons for the purpose of prostitution, or the production of pornography.

Background: This section applies to offenses involving the criminal sexual abuse of an individual who had not attained the age of 16 years. While this section applies to consensual sexual acts prosecuted under 18 U.S.C. § 2243(a) that would be lawful but for the age of the minor, it also applies to cases, prosecuted under 18 U.S.C. § 2243(a), in which a participant took active measure(s) to unduly influence the minor to engage in prohibited sexual conduct and, thus, the voluntariness of the minor's behavior was compromised. A four-level enhancement is provided in subsection (b)(2) for such cases. It is assumed that at least a four-year age difference exists between the minor and the defendant, as specified in 18 U.S.C. § 2243(a). A four-level enhancement is provided in subsection (b)(1) for a defendant who victimizes a minor under his supervision or care. However, if the minor had not attained the age of 12 years, §2A3.1 (Criminal Sexual Abuse; Attempt to Commit Criminal Sexual Abuse) will apply, regardless of the "consent" of the minor.

Historical Note

Effective November 1, 1987. Amended effective November 1, 1989 (amendment 93); November 1, 1991 (amendment 392); November 1, 1992 (amendment 444); November 1, 1995 (amendment 511); November 1, 2000 (amendment 592); November 1, 2001 (amendment 615); November 1, 2004 (amendment 664); November 1, 2009 (amendment 732); November 1, 2010 (amendment 746).

§2A3.3. Criminal Sexual Abuse of a Ward or Attempt to Commit Such Acts

(a) Base Offense Level: **14**

(b) Specific Offense Characteristics

(1) If the offense involved the knowing misrepresentation of a participant's identity to persuade, induce, entice, or coerce a minor to engage in prohibited sexual conduct, increase by **2** levels.
(2) If a computer or an interactive computer service was used to persuade, induce, entice, or coerce a minor to engage in prohibited sexual conduct, increase by **2** levels.

Commentary

Statutory Provision: 18 U.S.C. § 2243(b). For additional statutory provision(s), *see* Appendix A (Statutory Index).

Application Notes:

1. **Definitions.**—For purposes of this guideline:

"***Computer***" has the meaning given that term in 18 U.S.C. § 1030(e)(1).

"***Interactive computer service***" has the meaning given that term in section 230(e)(2) of the Communications Act of 1934 (47 U.S.C. § 230(f)(2)).

"***Minor***" means (A) an individual who had not attained the age of 18 years; (B) an individual, whether fictitious or not, who a law enforcement officer represented to a participant (i) had not attained the age of 18 years; and (ii) could be provided for the purposes of engaging in sexually explicit conduct; or (C) an undercover law enforcement officer who represented to a participant that the officer had not attained the age of 18 years.

"***Participant***" has the meaning given that term in Application Note 1 of the Commentary to §3B1.1 (Aggravating Role).

"***Prohibited sexual conduct***" has the meaning given that term in Application Note 1 of the Commentary to §2A3.1 (Criminal Sexual Abuse; Attempt to Commit Criminal Sexual Abuse).

"***Ward***" means a person in official detention under the custodial, supervisory, or disciplinary authority of the defendant.

2. **Application of Subsection (b)(1).**—The enhancement in subsection (b)(1) applies in cases involving the misrepresentation of a participant's identity to persuade, induce, entice, or coerce a minor to engage in prohibited sexual conduct. Subsection (b)(1) is intended to apply only to misrepresentations made directly to a minor or to a person who exercises custody, care, or supervisory control of the minor.

The misrepresentation to which the enhancement in subsection (b)(1) may apply includes misrepresentation of a participant's name, age, occupation, gender, or status, as long as the misrepresentation was made with the intent to persuade, induce, entice, or coerce a minor to engage in prohibited sexual conduct. Accordingly, use of a computer screen name, without such intent, would not be a sufficient basis for application of the enhancement.

3. **Application of Subsection (b)(2).**—Subsection (b)(2) provides an enhancement if a computer or an interactive computer service was used to persuade, induce, entice, or coerce a minor to engage in prohibited sexual conduct. Subsection (b)(2) is intended to apply only to the use of a computer or an interactive computer service to communicate directly with a minor or with a person who exercises custody, care, or supervisory control of the minor.

4. **Inapplicability of §3B1.3.**—Do not apply §3B1.3 (Abuse of Position of Trust or Use of Special Skill).

Historical Note

Effective November 1, 1987. Amended effective November 1, 1989 (amendment 94); November 1, 1995 (amendment 511); November 1, 2000 (amendment 592); November 1, 2001 (amendment 615); November 1, 2004 (amendment 664); November 1, 2007 (amendment 701); November 1, 2010 (amendment 746).

§2A3.4. Abusive Sexual Contact or Attempt to Commit Abusive Sexual Contact

(a) Base Offense Level:

(1) **20**, if the offense involved conduct described in 18 U.S.C.

§ 2241(a) or (b);
(2) **16**, if the offense involved conduct described in 18 U.S.C. § 2242; or
(3) **12**, otherwise.
(b) Specific Offense Characteristics
(1) If the victim had not attained the age of twelve years, increase by **4** levels; but if the resulting offense level is less than **22**, increase to level **22**.
(2) If the base offense level is determined under subsection (a)(1) or (2), and the victim had attained the age of twelve years but had not attained the age of sixteen years, increase by **2** levels.
(3) If the victim was in the custody, care, or supervisory control of the defendant, increase by **2** levels.
(4) If the offense involved the knowing misrepresentation of a participant's identity to persuade, induce, entice, or coerce a minor to engage in prohibited sexual conduct, increase by **2** levels.

(5) If a computer or an interactive computer service was used to persuade, induce, entice, or coerce a minor to engage in prohibited sexual conduct, increase by **2** levels.
(c) Cross References
(1) If the offense involved criminal sexual abuse or attempt to commit criminal sexual abuse (as defined in 18 U.S.C. § 2241 or § 2242), apply §2A3.1 (Criminal Sexual Abuse; Attempt to Commit Criminal Sexual Abuse).
(2) If the offense involved criminal sexual abuse of a minor or attempt to commit criminal sexual abuse of a minor (as defined in 18 U.S.C. § 2243(a)), apply §2A3.2 (Criminal Sexual Abuse of a Minor Under the Age of Sixteen Years (Statutory Rape) or Attempt to Commit Such Acts), if the resulting offense level is greater than that determined above.

Commentary

Statutory Provision: 18 U.S.C. § 2244. For additional statutory provision(s), *see* Appendix A (Statutory Index).

Application Notes:

1. **Definitions.**—For purposes of this guideline:
"***Computer***" has the meaning given that term in 18 U.S.C. § 1030(e)(1).
"***Interactive computer service***" has the meaning given that term in section 230(e)(2) of the Communications Act of 1934 (47 U.S.C. § 230(f)(2)).
"***Minor***" means (A) an individual who had not attained the age of 18 years; (B) an individual, whether fictitious or not, who a law enforcement officer represented to a participant (i) had not attained the age of 18 years, and (ii) could be provided for the purposes of engaging in sexually explicit conduct; or (C) an undercover law enforcement officer who represented to a participant that the officer had not attained the age of 18 years.
"***Participant***" has the meaning given that term in Application Note 1 of the Commentary to §3B1.1 (Aggravating Role).
"***Prohibited sexual conduct***" has the meaning given that term in Application Note 1 of the Commentary to §2A3.1 (Criminal Sexual Abuse; Attempt to Commit Criminal Sexual Abuse).
2. **Application of Subsection (a)(1).**—For purposes of subsection (a)(1), "***conduct described***

in 18 U.S.C. § 2241(a) or (b)" is engaging in, or causing sexual contact with, or by another person by: (A) using force against the victim; (B) threatening or placing the victim in fear that any person will be subjected to death, serious bodily injury, or kidnapping; (C) rendering the victim unconscious; or (D) administering by force or threat of force, or without the knowledge or permission of the victim, a drug, intoxicant, or other

similar substance and thereby substantially impairing the ability of the victim to appraise or control conduct.

3. **Application of Subsection (a)(2).**—For purposes of subsection (a)(2), "*conduct described in 18 U.S.C. § 2242*" is: (A) engaging in, or causing sexual contact with, or by another person by threatening or placing the victim in fear (other than by threatening or placing the victim in fear that any person will be subjected to death, serious bodily injury, or kidnapping); or (B) engaging in, or causing sexual contact with, or by another person who is incapable of appraising the nature of the conduct or physically incapable of declining participation in, or communicating unwillingness to engage in, the sexual act.

4. **Application of Subsection (b)(3).**—

(A) **Custody, Care, or Supervisory Control.**—Subsection (b)(3) is intended to have broad application and is to be applied whenever the victim is entrusted to the defendant, whether temporarily or permanently. For example, teachers, day care providers, baby-sitters, or other temporary caretakers are among those who would be subject to this enhancement. In determining whether to apply this enhancement, the court should look to the actual relationship that existed between the defendant and the victim and not simply to the legal status of the defendant-victim relationship.

(B) **Inapplicability of Chapter Three Adjustment.**—If the enhancement in subsection (b)(3) applies, do not apply §3B1.3 (Abuse of Position of Trust or Use of Special Skill).

5. **Misrepresentation of a Participant's Identity.**—The enhancement in subsection (b)(4) applies in cases involving the misrepresentation of a participant's identity to persuade, induce, entice, or coerce a minor to engage in prohibited sexual conduct. Subsection (b)(4) is intended to apply only to misrepresentations made directly to a minor or to a person who exercises custody, care, or supervisory control of the minor. Accordingly, the enhancement in subsection (b)(4) would not apply to a misrepresentation made by a participant to an airline representative in the course of making travel arrangements for the minor.

The misrepresentation to which the enhancement in subsection (b)(4) may apply includes misrepresentation of a participant's name, age, occupation, gender, or status, as long as the misrepresentation was made with the intent to persuade, induce, entice, or coerce a minor to engage in prohibited sexual conduct. Accordingly, use of a computer screen name, without such intent, would not be a sufficient basis for application of the enhancement.

6. **Application of Subsection (b)(5).**—Subsection (b)(5) provides an enhancement if a computer or an interactive computer service was used to persuade, induce, entice, or coerce a minor to engage in prohibited sexual conduct. Subsection (b)(5) is intended to apply only to the use of a computer or an interactive computer service to communicate directly with a minor or with a person who exercises custody, care, or supervisory control of the minor.

Background: This section covers abusive sexual contact not amounting to criminal sexual abuse (criminal sexual abuse is covered under §§2A3.1–3.3). Alternative base offense levels are provided to take account of the different means used to commit the offense.

Historical Note

Effective November 1, 1987. Amended effective November 1, 1989 (amendment 95); November 1, 1991 (amendment 392); November 1, 1992 (amendment 444); November 1, 1995 (amendment 511); November 1, 2000 (amendment 592); November 1, 2001 (amendment 615); November 1, 2004 (amendment 664); November

1, 2007 (amendments 701 and 711).

§2A3.5. Failure to Register as a Sex Offender

(a) Base Offense Level (Apply the greatest):
(1) **16**, if the defendant was required to register as a Tier III offender;
(2) **14**, if the defendant was required to register as a Tier II offender;
or
(3) **12**, if the defendant was required to register as a Tier I offender.
(b) Specific Offense Characteristics
(1) (Apply the greatest):
If, while in a failure to register status, the defendant committed—
(A) a sex offense against someone other than a minor, increase by **6** levels;
(B) a felony offense against a minor not otherwise covered by subdivision (C), increase by **6** levels; or
(C) a sex offense against a minor, increase by **8** levels.
(2) If the defendant voluntarily (A) corrected the failure to register; or (B) attempted to register but was prevented from registering by uncontrollable circumstances and the defendant did not contribute to the creation of those circumstances, decrease by **3** levels.

Commentary

Statutory Provision: 18 U.S.C. § 2250(a).

Application Notes:

1. **Definitions.**—For purposes of this guideline:

"***Minor***" means (A) an individual who had not attained the age of 18 years; (B) an individual, whether fictitious or not, who a law enforcement officer represented to a participant (i) had not attained the age of 18 years; and (ii) could be provided for the purposes of engaging in sexually explicit conduct; or (C) an undercover law enforcement officer who represented to a participant that the officer had not attained the age of 18 years.

"***Sex offense***" has the meaning given that term in 42 U.S.C. § 16911(5).

"***Tier I offender***", "***Tier II offender***", and "***Tier III offender***" have the meaning given the terms "tier I sex offender", "tier II sex offender", and "tier III sex offender", respectively, in 42 U.S.C. § 16911.

2. **Application of Subsection (b)(2).**—

(A) **In General.**—In order for subsection (b)(2) to apply, the defendant's voluntary attempt to register or to correct the failure to register must have occurred prior to the time the defendant knew or reasonably should have known a jurisdiction had detected the failure to register.

(B) **Interaction with Subsection (b)(1).**—Do not apply subsection (b)(2) if subsection (b)(1) also applies.

Historical Note

Effective November 1, 2007 (amendments 701 and 711). Amended effective November 1, 2010 (amendment 746).

§2A3.6. Aggravated Offenses Relating to Registration as a Sex Offender

If the defendant was convicted under—
(a) 18 U.S.C. § 2250(c), the guideline sentence is the minimum term of imprisonment required by statute; or
(b) 18 U.S.C. § 2260A, the guideline sentence is the term of imprisonment required by statute.
Chapters Three (Adjustments) and Four (Criminal History and Criminal

Livelihood) shall not apply to any count of conviction covered by this guideline.

Commentary

Statutory Provisions: 18 U.S.C. §§ 2250(c), 2260A.

Application Notes:

1. **In General.**—Section 2250(c) of title 18, United States Code, provides a mandatory minimum term of five years' imprisonment and a statutory maximum term of 30 years' imprisonment. The statute also requires a sentence to be imposed consecutively to any sentence imposed for a conviction under 18 U.S.C. § 2250(a). Section 2260A of title 18,

United States Code, provides a term of imprisonment of 10 years that is required to be imposed consecutively to any sentence imposed for an offense enumerated under that section.

2. **Inapplicability of Chapters Three and Four.**—Do not apply Chapters Three (Adjustments) and Four (Criminal History and Criminal Livelihood) to any offense sentenced under this guideline. Such offenses are excluded from application of those chapters because the guideline sentence for each offense is determined only by the relevant statute. *See* §§3D1.1 (Procedure for Determining Offense Level on Multiple Counts) and 5G1.2 (Sentencing on Multiple Counts of Conviction).

3. **Inapplicability of Chapter Two Enhancement.**—If a sentence under this guideline is imposed in conjunction with a sentence for an underlying offense, do not apply any specific offense characteristic that is based on the same conduct as the conduct comprising the conviction under 18 U.S.C. § 2250(c) or § 2260A.

4. **Upward Departure.**—In a case in which the guideline sentence is determined under subsection (a), a sentence above the minimum term required by 18 U.S.C. § 2250(c) is an upward departure from the guideline sentence. A departure may be warranted, for example, in a case involving a sex offense committed against a minor or if the offense resulted in serious bodily injury to a minor.

Historical Note

Effective November 1, 2007 (amendment 701).

* * * * *

4. KIDNAPPING, ABDUCTION, OR UNLAWFUL RESTRAINT

§2A4.1. Kidnapping, Abduction, Unlawful Restraint

(a) Base Offense Level: **32**

(b) Specific Offense Characteristics

(1) If a ransom demand or a demand upon government was made, increase by **6** levels.

(2) (A) If the victim sustained permanent or life-threatening bodily injury, increase by **4** levels; (B) if the victim sustained serious bodily injury, increase by **2** levels; or (C) if the degree of injury is between that specified in subdivisions (A) and (B), increase by **3** levels.

(3) If a dangerous weapon was used, increase by **2** levels.

(4) (A) If the victim was not released before thirty days had elapsed, increase by **2** levels.

(B) If the victim was not released before seven days had elapsed, increase by **1** level.

(5) If the victim was sexually exploited, increase by **6** levels.

(6) If the victim is a minor and, in exchange for money or other consideration, was placed in the care or custody of another person who had no legal right to such care or custody of the victim, increase by **3** levels.

(7) If the victim was kidnapped, abducted, or unlawfully restrained during the commission of, or in connection with, another offense or escape therefrom; or if another offense was committed during the kidnapping, abduction, or unlawful restraint, increase to—

(A) the offense level from the Chapter Two offense guideline applicable to that other offense if such offense guideline includes an adjustment for kidnapping, abduction, or unlawful restraint, or otherwise takes such conduct into account;

or

(B) **4** plus the offense level from the offense guideline applicable to that other offense, but in no event greater than level **43**, in any other case,

if the resulting offense level is greater than that determined above.

(c) Cross Reference

(1) If the victim was killed under circumstances that would constitute murder under 18 U.S.C. § 1111 had such killing taken place within the territorial or maritime jurisdiction of the United States, apply §2A1.1 (First Degree Murder).

Commentary

Statutory Provisions: 18 U.S.C. §§ 115(b)(2), 351(b), (d), 1201, 1203, 1751(b), 2340A. For additional statutory provision(s), *see* Appendix A (Statutory Index).

Application Notes:

1. For purposes of this guideline—

Definitions of "***serious bodily injury***" and "***permanent or life-threatening bodily injury***" are found in the Commentary to §1B1.1 (Application Instructions). However, for

purposes of this guideline, "***serious bodily injury***" means conduct other than criminal sexual abuse, which is taken into account in the specific offense characteristic under subsection (b)(5).

2. "***A dangerous weapon was used***" means that a firearm was discharged, or a "firearm" or "dangerous weapon" was "otherwise used" (as defined in the Commentary to §1B1.1 (Application Instructions)).

3. "***Sexually exploited***" includes offenses set forth in 18 U.S.C. §§ 2241–2244, 2251, and 2421–2423.

4. In the case of a conspiracy, attempt, or solicitation to kidnap, §2X1.1 (Attempt, Solicitation, or Conspiracy) requires that the court apply any adjustment that can be determined with reasonable certainty. Therefore, for example, if an offense involved conspiracy to kidnap for the purpose of committing murder, subsection (b)(7) would reference first degree murder (resulting in an offense level of 43, subject to a possible 3-level reduction under §2X1.1(b)).

Similarly, for example, if an offense involved a kidnapping during which a participant attempted to murder the victim under circumstances that would have constituted first degree murder had death occurred, the offense referenced under subsection (b)(7) would be the offense of first degree murder.

Background: Federal kidnapping cases generally encompass three categories of conduct: limited duration kidnapping where the victim is released unharmed; kidnapping that occurs as part of or to facilitate the commission of another offense (often, sexual assault); and kidnapping for ransom or political demand.

The guideline contains an adjustment for the length of time that the victim was detained. The adjustment recognizes the increased suffering involved in lengthy kidnappings and provides an incentive to release the victim.

An enhancement is provided when the offense is committed for ransom (subsection (b)(1)) or involves another federal, state, or local offense that results in a greater offense level (subsections (b)(7) and (c)(1)).

Section 401 of Public Law 101–647 amended 18 U.S.C. § 1201 to require that courts take into account certain specific offense characteristics in cases involving a victim under eighteen years of age and directed the Commission to include those specific offense characteristics within the guidelines. Where the guidelines did not already take into account the conduct identified by the Act, additional specific offense characteristics have been provided.

Subsections (a) and (b)(5), and the deletion of subsection (b)(4)(C), effective May 30, 2003, implement the directive to the Commission in section 104 of Public Law 108–21.

Historical Note

Effective November 1, 1987. Amended effective November 1, 1989 (amendment 96); November 1, 1991 (amendment 363); November 1, 1992 (amendment 445); November 1, 1993 (amendment 478); November 1, 1997 (amendment 545); November 1, 2002 (amendment 637); May 30, 2003 (amendment 650); October 27, 2003 (amendment 651).

§2A4.2. Demanding or Receiving Ransom Money

(a) Base Offense Level: **23**

(b) Cross Reference

(1) If the defendant was a participant in the kidnapping offense, apply §2A4.1 (Kidnapping, Abduction, Unlawful Restraint).

Commentary

Statutory Provisions: 18 U.S.C. §§ 876, 877, 1202. For additional statutory provision(s), *see* Appendix A (Statutory Index).

Application Note:

1. A "***participant***" is a person who is criminally responsible for the commission of the offense, but need not have been convicted.

Background: This section specifically includes conduct prohibited by 18 U.S.C. § 1202, requiring that ransom money be received, possessed, or disposed of with knowledge of its criminal origins. The actual demand for ransom under these circumstances is reflected in §2A4.1. This section additionally includes extortionate demands through the use of the United States Postal Service, behavior proscribed by 18 U.S.C. §§ 876–877.

Historical Note

Effective November 1, 1987. Amended effective November 1, 1993 (amendment 479).

* * * * *

5. AIR PIRACY AND OFFENSES AGAINST MASS TRANSPORTATION SYSTEMS

Historical Note

Effective November 1, 1987. Amended effective November 1, 2002 (amendment 637).

§2A5.1. Aircraft Piracy or Attempted Aircraft Piracy

(a) Base Offense Level: **38**

(b) Specific Offense Characteristic

(1) If death resulted, increase by **5** levels.

Commentary

Statutory Provisions: 49 U.S.C. § 46502(a), (b) (formerly 49 U.S.C. § 1472 (i), (n)). For additional

statutory provision(s), *see* Appendix A (Statutory Index).
Background: This section covers aircraft piracy both within the special aircraft jurisdiction of the United States, 49 U.S.C. § 46502(a), and aircraft piracy outside that jurisdiction when the defendant is later found in the United States, 49 U.S.C. § 46502(b). Seizure of control of an aircraft may be by force or violence, or threat of force or violence, or by any other form of intimidation. The presence of a weapon is assumed in the base offense level.
Historical
Note
Effective November 1, 1987. Amended effective November 1, 1995 (amendment 534).

§2A5.2. Interference with Flight Crew Member or Flight Attendant; Interference with Dispatch, Navigation, Operation, or Maintenance of Mass Transportation Vehicle

(a) Base Offense Level (Apply the greatest):
(1) **30**, if the offense involved intentionally endangering the safety of: (A) an airport or an aircraft; or (B) a mass transportation facility or a mass transportation vehicle;
(2) **18**, if the offense involved recklessly endangering the safety of: (A) an airport or an aircraft; or (B) a mass transportation facility or a mass transportation vehicle;
(3) if an assault occurred, the offense level from the most analogous assault guideline, §§2A2.1–2A2.4; or
(4) **9**.
(b) Specific Offense Characteristic
(1) If (A) subsection (a)(1) or (a)(2) applies; and (B)(i) a firearm was discharged, increase by **5** levels; (ii) a dangerous weapon was otherwise used, increase by **4** levels; or (iii) a dangerous weapon was brandished or its use was threatened, increase by **3** levels. If the resulting offense level is less than level **24**, increase to level **24**.

(c) Cross References
(1) If death resulted, apply the most analogous guideline from Chapter Two, Part A, Subpart 1 (Homicide), if the resulting offense level is greater than that determined above.
(2) If the offense involved possession of, or a threat to use (A) a nuclear weapon, nuclear material, or nuclear byproduct material; (B) a chemical weapon; (C) a biological agent, toxin, or delivery system; or (D) a weapon of mass destruction, apply §2M6.1 (Nuclear, Biological, and Chemical Weapons, and Other Weapons of Mass Destruction), if the resulting offense level is greater than that determined above.

Commentary

Statutory Provisions: 18 U.S.C. § 1992(a)(1), (a)(4), (a)(5), (a)(6); 49 U.S.C. §§ 46308, 46503, 46504 (formerly 49 U.S.C. § 1472(c), (j)). For additional statutory provision(s), *see* Appendix A (Statutory Index).
Application Note:
1. **Definitions.**—For purposes of this guideline:
"***Biological agent***", "***chemical weapon***", "***nuclear byproduct material***", "***nuclear material***", "***toxin***", and "***weapon of mass destruction***" have the meaning given those terms in Application Note 1 of the Commentary to §2M6.1 (Nuclear, Biological, and

Chemical Weapons, and Other Weapons of Mass Destruction).
"***Brandished***", "***dangerous weapon***", "***firearm***", and "***otherwise used***" have the meaning given those terms in Application Note 1 of the Commentary to §1B1.1 (Application Instructions).
"***Mass transportation***" has the meaning given that term in 18 U.S.C. § 1992(d)(7).
Historical
Note
Effective November 1, 1987. Amended effective November 1, 1989 (amendments 97 and 303); November 1, 1993 (amendment 480); November 1, 1995 (amendment 534); November 1, 2002 (amendment 637); November 1, 2007 (amendment 699).

§2A5.3. Committing Certain Crimes Aboard Aircraft

(a) Base Offense Level: The offense level applicable to the underlying offense.

Commentary

Statutory Provision: 49 U.S.C. § 46506 (formerly 49 U.S.C. § 1472(k)(1)).

Application Notes:

1. "***Underlying offense***" refers to the offense listed in 49 U.S.C. § 46506 of which the defendant is convicted.
2. If the conduct intentionally or recklessly endangered the safety of the aircraft or passengers, an upward departure may be warranted.

Historical
Note
Effective October 15, 1988 (amendment 65). Amended effective November 1, 1989 (amendment 98); November 1, 1995 (amendment 534).

* * * * *

6. THREATENING OR HARASSING COMMUNICATIONS, HOAXES, STALKING, AND DOMESTIC VIOLENCE

Historical
Note
Effective November 1, 1987. Amended effective November 1, 1997 (amendment 549); November 1, 2006 (amendment 686).

§2A6.1. Threatening or Harassing Communications; Hoaxes; False Liens

(a) Base Offense Level:
(1) **12**; or
(2) **6**, if the defendant is convicted of an offense under 47 U.S.C. § 223(a)(1)(C), (D), or (E) that did not involve a threat to injure a person or property.
(b) Specific Offense Characteristics
(1) If the offense involved any conduct evidencing an intent to carry out such threat, increase by **6** levels.
(2) If (A) the offense involved more than two threats; or (B) the defendant is convicted under 18 U.S.C. § 1521 and the offense involved more than two false liens or encumbrances, increase by **2** levels.
(3) If the offense involved the violation of a court protection order, increase by **2** levels.

(4) If the offense resulted in (A) substantial disruption of public, governmental, or business functions or services; or (B) a substantial expenditure of funds to clean up, decontaminate, or otherwise respond to the offense, increase by **4** levels.

(5) If the defendant (A) is convicted under 18 U.S.C. § 115, (B) made a public threatening communication, and (C) knew or should have known that the public threatening communication created a substantial risk of inciting others to violate 18 U.S.C. § 115, increase by **2** levels.

(6) If (A) subsection (a)(2) and subdivisions (1), (2), (3), (4), and (5) do not apply, and (B) the offense involved a single instance evidencing little or no deliberation, decrease by **4** levels.

(c) Cross Reference

(1) If the offense involved any conduct evidencing an intent to carry out a threat to use a weapon of mass destruction, as defined in 18 U.S.C. § 2332a(c)(2)(B), (C), and (D), apply §2M6.1 (Weapons of Mass Destruction), if the resulting offense level is greater than that determined under this guideline.

Commentary

Statutory Provisions: 18 U.S.C. §§ 32(c), 35(b), 871, 876, 877, 878(a), 879, 1038, 1521, 1992(a)(9), (a)(10), 2291(a)(8), 2291(e), 2292, 2332b(a)(2); 47 U.S.C. § 223(a)(1)(C)–(E); 49 U.S.C. § 46507. For additional statutory provision(s), *see* Appendix A (Statutory Index).

Application Notes:

1. **Scope of Conduct to Be Considered.**—In determining whether subsections (b)(1), (b)(2), and (b)(3) apply, the court shall consider both conduct that occurred prior to the offense and conduct that occurred during the offense; however, conduct that occurred prior to the offense must be substantially and directly connected to the offense, under the facts of the case taken as a whole. For example, if the defendant engaged in several acts of mailing threatening letters to the same victim over a period of years (including acts that occurred prior to the offense), then for purposes of determining whether subsections (b)(1), (b)(2), and (b)(3) apply, the court shall consider only those prior acts of threatening the victim that have a substantial and direct connection to the offense.

2. **Applicability of Chapter Three Adjustments.**—If the defendant is convicted under 18 U.S.C. § 1521, apply §3A1.2 (Official Victim).

3. **Grouping.**—For purposes of Chapter Three, Part D (Multiple Counts), multiple counts involving making a threatening or harassing communication to the same victim are grouped together under §3D1.2 (Groups of Closely Related Counts). Multiple counts involving different victims are not to be grouped under §3D1.2.

4. **Departure Provisions.**—

(A) **In General.**—The Commission recognizes that offenses covered by this guideline may include a particularly wide range of conduct and that it is not possible to include all of the potentially relevant circumstances in the offense level. Factors not incorporated in the guideline may be considered by the court in determining whether a departure from the guidelines is warranted. *See* Chapter Five, Part K (Departures).

(B) **Multiple Threats, False Liens or Encumbrances, or Victims; Pecuniary Harm.**—If the offense involved (i) substantially more than two threatening communications to the same victim, (ii) a prolonged period of making harassing communications to the same victim, (iii) substantially more than two false liens or encumbrances against the real or personal property of the same victim, (iv) multiple victims, or (v) substantial pecuniary harm to a victim, an upward departure may be warranted.

Background: These statutes cover a wide range of conduct, the seriousness of which depends upon the defendant's intent and the likelihood that the defendant would carry out the threat. The specific offense characteristics are intended to distinguish such cases.

Subsection (b)(5) implements, in a broader form, the directive to the Commission in section 209 of the Court Security Improvement Act of 2007, Public Law 110–177.

Historical Note

Effective November 1, 1987. Amended effective November 1, 1993 (amendment 480); November 1, 1997 (amendment 549); November 1, 2002 (amendment 637); November 1, 2006 (amendment 686); November 1, 2007 (amendment 699); November 1, 2008 (amendment 718); November 1, 2009 (amendment 729).

§2A6.2. Stalking or Domestic Violence

(a) Base Offense Level: **18**

(b) Specific Offense Characteristic

(1) If the offense involved one of the following aggravating factors: (A) the violation of a court protection order; (B) bodily injury; (C) strangling, suffocating, or attempting to strangle or suffocate; (D) possession, or threatened use, of a dangerous weapon; or (E) a pattern of activity involving stalking, threatening, harassing, or assaulting the same victim, increase by **2** levels. If the offense involved more than one of subdivisions (A), (B), (C), (D), or (E), increase by **4** levels.

(c) Cross Reference

(1) If the offense involved the commission of another criminal offense, apply the offense guideline from Chapter Two, Part A (Offenses Against the Person) most applicable to that other

criminal offense, if the resulting offense level is greater than that determined above.

Commentary

Statutory Provisions: 18 U.S.C. §§ 2261–2262.

Application Notes:

1. For purposes of this guideline:

"***Bodily injury***" and "***dangerous weapon***" are defined in the Commentary to §1B1.1 (Application Instructions).

"***Pattern of activity involving stalking, threatening, harassing, or assaulting the same victim***" means any combination of two or more separate instances of stalking, threatening, harassing, or assaulting the same victim, whether or not such conduct resulted in a conviction. For example, a single instance of stalking accompanied by a separate instance of threatening, harassing, or assaulting the same victim constitutes a pattern of activity for purposes of this guideline.

"***Stalking***" means conduct described in 18 U.S.C. § 2261A.

"***Strangling***" and "***suffocating***" have the meaning given those terms in 18 U.S.C. § 113.

2. Subsection (b)(1) provides for a two-level or four-level enhancement based on the degree to which the offense involved aggravating factors listed in that subsection. If the offense involved aggravating factors more serious than the factors listed in subsection (b)(1), the cross reference in subsection (c) most likely will apply, if the resulting offense level is greater, because the more serious conduct will be covered by another offense guideline from Chapter Two, Part A. For example, §2A2.2 (Aggravated Assault) most likely would apply pursuant to subsection (c) if the offense involved assaultive conduct in which injury more serious than bodily injury occurred or if a dangerous weapon was used rather than merely possessed.

3. In determining whether subsection (b)(1)(E) applies, the court shall consider, under the totality of the circumstances, any conduct that occurred prior to or during the offense; however, conduct that occurred prior to the offense must be substantially and directly connected to the offense. For example, if a defendant engaged in several acts of stalking the same victim over a period of years (including acts that occurred prior to the offense),

then for purposes of determining whether subsection (b)(1)(E) applies, the court shall look to the totality of the circumstances, considering only those prior acts of stalking the victim that have a substantial and direct connection to the offense.
Prior convictions taken into account under subsection (b)(1)(E) are also counted for purposes of determining criminal history points pursuant to Chapter Four, Part A (Criminal History).
4. For purposes of Chapter Three, Part D (Multiple Counts), multiple counts involving stalking, threatening, or harassing the same victim are grouped together (and with counts of other offenses involving the same victim that are covered by this guideline) under §3D1.2 (Groups of Closely Related Counts). For example, if the defendant is convicted of two counts of stalking the defendant's ex-spouse under 18 U.S.C. § 2261A and

one count of interstate domestic violence involving an assault of the ex-spouse under 18 U.S.C. § 2261, the stalking counts would be grouped together with the interstate domestic violence count. This grouping procedure avoids unwarranted "double counting" with the enhancement in subsection (b)(1)(E) (for multiple acts of stalking, threatening, harassing, or assaulting the same victim) and recognizes that the stalking and interstate domestic violence counts are sufficiently related to warrant grouping.
Multiple counts that are cross referenced to another offense guideline pursuant to subsection (c) are to be grouped together if §3D1.2 (Groups of Closely Related Counts) would require grouping of those counts under that offense guideline. Similarly, multiple counts cross referenced pursuant to subsection (c) are not to be grouped together if §3D1.2 would preclude grouping of the counts under that offense guideline. For example, if the defendant is convicted of multiple counts of threatening an ex-spouse in violation of a court protection order under 18 U.S.C. § 2262 and the counts are cross referenced to §2A6.1 (Threatening or Harassing Communications), the counts would group together because Application Note 3 of §2A6.1 specifically requires grouping. In contrast, if the defendant is convicted of multiple counts of assaulting the ex-spouse in violation of a court protection order under 18 U.S.C. § 2262 and the counts are cross referenced to §2A2.2 (Aggravated Assault), the counts probably would not group together inasmuch as §3D1.2(d) specifically precludes grouping of counts covered by §2A2.2 and no other provision of §3D1.2 would likely apply to require grouping.
Multiple counts involving different victims are not to be grouped under §3D1.2 (Groups of Closely Related Counts).
5. If the defendant received an enhancement under subsection (b)(1) but that enhancement does not adequately reflect the extent or seriousness of the conduct involved, an upward departure may be warranted. For example, an upward departure may be warranted if the defendant stalked the victim on many occasions over a prolonged period of time.

Historical Note

Effective November 1, 1997 (amendment 549). Amended effective November 1, 2001 (amendment 616); November 1, 2009 (amendment 737); November 1, 2014 (amendment 781).

PART B — BASIC ECONOMIC OFFENSES

1. THEFT, EMBEZZLEMENT, RECEIPT OF STOLEN PROPERTY, PROPERTY DESTRUCTION, AND OFFENSES INVOLVING FRAUD OR DECEIT

Introductory Commentary

These sections address basic forms of property offenses: theft, embezzlement, fraud, forgery, counterfeiting (other than offenses involving altered or counterfeit bearer obligations of the United States), insider trading, transactions in stolen goods, and simple property damage or destruction. (Arson is dealt with separately in Chapter Two, Part K (Offenses Involving Public Safety)). These guidelines apply to offenses prosecuted under a wide variety of federal statutes, as well as offenses that arise under the Assimilative Crimes Act.

Historical
Note
Effective November 1, 1987. Amended effective November 1, 1989 (amendment 303); November 1, 2001 (amendment 617).

§2B1.1. Larceny, Embezzlement, and Other Forms of Theft; Offenses Involving Stolen Property; Property Damage or Destruction; Fraud and Deceit; Forgery; Offenses Involving Altered or Counterfeit Instruments Other than Counterfeit Bearer Obligations of the United States

(a) Base Offense Level:
(1) **7**, if (A) the defendant was convicted of an offense referenced to this guideline; and (B) that offense of conviction has a statutory maximum term of imprisonment of 20 years or more; or
(2) **6**, otherwise.
(b) Specific Offense Characteristics
(1) If the loss exceeded $6,500, increase the offense level as follows:
LOSS (APPLY THE GREATEST) INCREASE IN LEVEL
(A) $6,500 or less no increase
(B) More than $6,500 add **2**
(C) More than $15,000 add **4**
(D) More than $40,000 add **6**
(E) More than $95,000 add **8**
(F) More than $150,000 add **10**
(G) More than $250,000 add **12**
(H) More than $550,000 add **14**
(I) More than $1,500,000 add **16**

(J) More than $3,500,000 add **18**
(K) More than $9,500,000 add **20**
(L) More than $25,000,000 add **22**
(M) More than $65,000,000 add **24**
(N) More than $150,000,000 add **26**
(O) More than $250,000,000 add **28**
(P) More than $550,000,000 add **30**.
(2) (Apply the greatest) If the offense—
(A) (i) involved 10 or more victims; (ii) was committed through mass-marketing; or (iii) resulted in substantial financial hardship to one or more victims, increase by **2** levels;
(B) resulted in substantial financial hardship to five or more victims, increase by **4** levels; or
(C) resulted in substantial financial hardship to 25 or more victims, increase by **6** levels.
(3) If the offense involved a theft from the person of another, increase by **2** levels.
(4) If the offense involved receiving stolen property, and the defendant was a person in the business of receiving and selling stolen property, increase by **2** levels.
(5) If the offense involved theft of, damage to, destruction of, or trafficking in, property from a national cemetery or veterans' memorial, increase by **2** levels.

(6) If (A) the defendant was convicted of an offense under 18 U.S.C. § 1037; and (B) the offense involved obtaining electronic mail addresses through improper means, increase by **2** levels.
(7) If (A) the defendant was convicted of a Federal health care offense involving a Government health care program; and (B) the loss under subsection (b)(1) to the Government health care program was (i) more than $1,000,000, increase by **2** levels; (ii) more than $7,000,000, increase by **3** levels; or (iii) more than $20,000,000, increase by **4** levels.
(8) (Apply the greater) If—
(A) the offense involved conduct described in 18 U.S.C. § 670, increase by **2** levels; or

(B) the offense involved conduct described in 18 U.S.C. § 670, and the defendant was employed by, or was an agent of, an organization in the supply chain for the pre-retail medical product, increase by **4** levels.
(9) If the offense involved (A) a misrepresentation that the defendant was acting on behalf of a charitable, educational, religious, or political organization, or a government agency; (B) a misrepresentation or other fraudulent action during the course of a bankruptcy proceeding; (C) a violation of any prior, specific judicial or administrative order, injunction, decree, or process not addressed elsewhere in the guidelines; or (D) a misrepresentation to a consumer in connection with obtaining, providing, or furnishing financial assistance for an institution of higher education, increase by **2** levels. If the resulting offense level is less than level **10**, increase to level **10**.
(10) If (A) the defendant relocated, or participated in relocating, a fraudulent scheme to another jurisdiction to evade law enforcement or regulatory officials; (B) a substantial part of a fraudulent scheme was committed from outside the United States; or (C) the offense otherwise involved sophisticated means and the defendant intentionally engaged in or caused the conduct constituting sophisticated means, increase by **2** levels. If the resulting offense level is less than level **12**, increase to level **12**.
(11) If the offense involved (A) the possession or use of any (i) device-making equipment, or (ii) authentication feature; (B) the production or trafficking of any (i) unauthorized access device or counterfeit access device, or (ii) authentication feature; or (C)(i) the unauthorized transfer or use of any means of identification unlawfully to produce or obtain any other means of identification, or (ii) the possession of 5 or more means of identification that unlawfully were produced from, or obtained by the use of, another means of identification, increase by **2** levels. If the resulting offense level is less than level **12**, increase to level **12**.

(12) If the offense involved conduct described in 18 U.S.C. § 1040, increase by **2** levels. If the resulting offense level is less than level **12**, increase to level **12**.
(13) (Apply the greater) If the offense involved misappropriation of a trade secret and the defendant knew or intended—
(A) that the trade secret would be transported or transmitted out of the United States, increase by **2** levels; or

(B) that the offense would benefit a foreign government, foreign instrumentality, or foreign agent, increase by **4** levels.
If subparagraph (B) applies and the resulting offense level is less than level **14**, increase to level **14**.
(14) If the offense involved an organized scheme to steal or to receive stolen (A) vehicles or vehicle parts; or (B) goods or chattels that are part of a cargo shipment, increase by **2** levels. If the resulting offense level is less than level **14**, increase to level **14**.
(15) If the offense involved (A) the conscious or reckless risk of death or serious bodily injury; or (B) possession of a dangerous weapon (including a firearm) in connection with the offense, increase by **2** levels. If the resulting offense level is less than level **14**, increase to level **14**.
(16) (Apply the greater) If—
(A) the defendant derived more than $1,000,000 in gross receipts from one or more financial institutions as a result of the offense, increase by **2** levels; or
(B) the offense (i) substantially jeopardized the safety and soundness of a financial institution; or (ii) substantially endangered the solvency or financial security of an organization that, at any time during the offense, (I) was a publicly traded company; or (II) had 1,000 or more employees, increase by **4** levels.
(C) The cumulative adjustments from application of both subsections (b)(2) and (b)(16)(B) shall not exceed **8** levels, except as provided in subdivision (D).
(D) If the resulting offense level determined under subdivision (A) or (B) is less than level **24**, increase to level **24**.
(17) If (A) the defendant was convicted of an offense under 18 U.S.C. § 1030, and the offense involved an intent to obtain personal information, or (B) the offense involved the unauthorized public dissemination of personal information, increase by **2** levels.

(18) (A) (Apply the greatest) If the defendant was convicted of an offense under:
(i) 18 U.S.C. § 1030, and the offense involved a computer system used to maintain or operate a critical infrastructure,

or used by or for a government entity in furtherance of the administration of justice, national defense, or national security, increase by **2** levels.
(ii) 18 U.S.C. § 1030(a)(5)(A), increase by **4** levels.
(iii) 18 U.S.C. § 1030, and the offense caused a substantial disruption of a critical infrastructure, increase by **6** levels.
(B) If subdivision (A)(iii) applies, and the offense level is less than level **24**, increase to level **24**.
(19) If the offense involved—
(A) a violation of securities law and, at the time of the offense, the defendant was (i) an officer or a director of a publicly traded company; (ii) a registered broker or dealer, or a person associated with a broker or dealer; or (iii) an investment adviser, or a person associated with an investment adviser; or
(B) a violation of commodities law and, at the time of the offense, the defendant was (i) an officer or a director of a futures commission merchant or an introducing broker; (ii) a commodities trading advisor; or (iii) a commodity pool operator,
increase by **4** levels.
(c) Cross References
(1) If (A) a firearm, destructive device, explosive material, or controlled substance was taken, or the taking of any such item was an object of the offense; or (B) the stolen property received, transported, transferred, transmitted, or possessed was a firearm, destructive device, explosive material, or controlled substance, apply §2D1.1 (Unlawful Manufacturing, Importing, Exporting, or Trafficking (Including Possession with Intent to Commit These Offenses); Attempt or Conspiracy), §2D2.1 (Unlawful Possession; Attempt or Conspiracy), §2K1.3 (Unlawful Receipt, Possession, or Transportation of Explosive Materials;

Prohibited Transactions Involving Explosive Materials), or §2K2.1 (Unlawful Receipt, Possession, or Transportation of Firearms or Ammunition; Prohibited Transactions Involving Firearms or Ammunition), as appropriate.
(2) If the offense involved arson, or property damage by use of explosives, apply §2K1.4 (Arson; Property Damage by Use of Explosives), if the resulting offense level is greater than that determined above.
(3) If (A) neither subdivision (1) nor (2) of this subsection applies; (B) the defendant was convicted under a statute proscribing false, fictitious, or fraudulent statements or representations generally (*e.g.*, 18 U.S.C. § 1001, § 1341, § 1342, or § 1343); and (C) the conduct set forth in the count of conviction establishes

an offense specifically covered by another guideline in Chapter Two (Offense Conduct), apply that other guideline.

(4) If the offense involved a cultural heritage resource or a paleontological resource, apply §2B1.5 (Theft of, Damage to, or Destruction of, Cultural Heritage Resources or Paleontological Resources; Unlawful Sale, Purchase, Exchange, Transportation, or Receipt of Cultural Heritage Resources or Paleontological Resources), if the resulting offense level is greater than that determined above.

Commentary

Statutory Provisions: 7 U.S.C. §§ 6, 6b, 6c, 6h, 6o, 13, 23; 15 U.S.C. §§ 50, 77e, 77q, 77x, 78j, 78ff, 80b-6, 1644, 6821; 18 U.S.C. §§ 38, 225, 285–289, 471–473, 500, 510, 553(a)(1), 641, 656, 657, 659, 662, 664, 1001–1008, 1010–1014, 1016–1022, 1025, 1026, 1028, 1029, 1030(a)(4)–(5), 1031, 1037, 1040, 1341–1344, 1348, 1350, 1361, 1363, 1369, 1702, 1703 (if vandalism or malicious mischief, including destruction of mail, is involved), 1708, 1831, 1832, 1992(a)(1), (a)(5), 2113(b), 2282A, 2282B, 2291, 2312–2317, 2332b(a)(1), 2701; 19 U.S.C. § 2401f; 29 U.S.C. § 501(c); 42 U.S.C. § 1011; 49 U.S.C. §§ 14915, 30170, 46317(a), 60123(b). For additional statutory provision(s), *see* Appendix A (Statutory Index).

Application Notes:

1. **Definitions.**—For purposes of this guideline:

"***Cultural heritage resource***" has the meaning given that term in Application Note 1 of the Commentary to §2B1.5 (Theft of, Damage to, or Destruction of, Cultural Heritage Resources or Paleontological Resources; Unlawful Sale, Purchase, Exchange, Transportation, or Receipt of Cultural Heritage Resources or Paleontological Resources).

"***Equity securities***" has the meaning given that term in section 3(a)(11) of the Securities Exchange Act of 1934 (15 U.S.C. § 78c(a)(11)).

"***Federal health care offense***" has the meaning given that term in 18 U.S.C. § 24.

"***Financial institution***" includes any institution described in 18 U.S.C. § 20, § 656, § 657, § 1005, § 1006, § 1007, or § 1014; any state or foreign bank, trust company, credit union, insurance company, investment company, mutual fund, savings (building and loan) association, union or employee pension fund; any health, medical, or hospital insurance association; brokers and dealers registered, or required to be registered, with the Securities and Exchange Commission; futures commodity merchants and commodity pool operators registered, or required to be registered, with the Commodity Futures Trading Commission; and any similar entity, whether or not insured by the federal government. "Union or employee pension fund" and "any health, medical, or hospital insurance association," primarily include large pension funds that serve many persons (*e.g.*, pension funds of large national and international organizations, unions, and corporations doing substantial interstate business), and associations that undertake to provide pension, disability, or other benefits (*e.g.*, medical or hospitalization insurance) to large numbers of persons.

"***Firearm***" and "***destructive device***" have the meaning given those terms in the Commentary to §1B1.1 (Application Instructions).

"***Foreign instrumentality***" and "***foreign agent***" have the meaning given those terms in 18 U.S.C. § 1839(1) and (2), respectively.

"***Government health care program***" means any plan or program that provides health benefits, whether directly, through insurance, or otherwise, which is funded directly, in whole or in part, by federal or state government. Examples of such programs are the Medicare program, the Medicaid program, and the CHIP program.

"***Means of identification***" has the meaning given that term in 18 U.S.C. § 1028(d)(7), except that such means of identification shall be of an actual (*i.e.*, not fictitious) individual, other than the defendant or a person for whose conduct the defendant is accountable

under §1B1.3 (Relevant Conduct).
"***National cemetery***" means a cemetery (A) established under section 2400 of title 38, United States Code; or (B) under the jurisdiction of the Secretary of the Army, the Secretary of the Navy, the Secretary of the Air Force, or the Secretary of the Interior.
"***Paleontological resource***" has the meaning given that term in Application Note 1 of the Commentary to §2B1.5 (Theft of, Damage to, or Destruction of, Cultural Heritage Resources or Paleontological Resources; Unlawful Sale, Purchase, Exchange, Transportation, or Receipt of Cultural Heritage Resources or Paleontological Resources).
"***Personal information***" means sensitive or private information involving an identifiable individual (including such information in the possession of a third party), including (A) medical records; (B) wills; (C) diaries; (D) private correspondence, including e-mail; (E) financial records; (F) photographs of a sensitive or private nature; or (G) similar information.
"***Pre-retail medical product***" has the meaning given that term in 18 U.S.C. § 670(e).
"***Publicly traded company***" means an issuer (A) with a class of securities registered under section 12 of the Securities Exchange Act of 1934 (15 U.S.C. § 78l); or (B) that is required to file reports under section 15(d) of the Securities Exchange Act of 1934 (15 U.S.C. § 78o(d)). "Issuer" has the meaning given that term in section 3 of the Securities Exchange Act of 1934 (15 U.S.C. § 78c).

"***Supply chain***" has the meaning given that term in 18 U.S.C. § 670(e).
"***Theft from the person of another***" means theft, without the use of force, of property that was being held by another person or was within arms' reach. Examples include pickpocketing and non-forcible purse-snatching, such as the theft of a purse from a shopping cart.
"***Trade secret***" has the meaning given that term in 18 U.S.C. § 1839(3).
"***Veterans' memorial***" means any structure, plaque, statue, or other monument described in 18 U.S.C. § 1369(a).
"***Victim***" means (A) any person who sustained any part of the actual loss determined under subsection (b)(1); or (B) any individual who sustained bodily injury as a result of the offense. "Person" includes individuals, corporations, companies, associations, firms, partnerships, societies, and joint stock companies.

2. **Application of Subsection (a)(1).—**

(A) **"Referenced to this Guideline".**—For purposes of subsection (a)(1), an offense is "***referenced to this guideline***" if (i) this guideline is the applicable Chapter Two guideline determined under the provisions of §1B1.2 (Applicable Guidelines) for the offense of conviction; or (ii) in the case of a conviction for conspiracy, solicitation, or attempt to which §2X1.1 (Attempt, Solicitation, or Conspiracy) applies, this guideline is the appropriate guideline for the offense the defendant was convicted of conspiring, soliciting, or attempting to commit.

(B) **Definition of "Statutory Maximum Term of Imprisonment".**—For purposes of this guideline, "***statutory maximum term of imprisonment***" means the maximum term of imprisonment authorized for the offense of conviction, including any increase in that maximum term under a statutory enhancement provision.

(C) **Base Offense Level Determination for Cases Involving Multiple Counts.**— In a case involving multiple counts sentenced under this guideline, the applicable base offense level is determined by the count of conviction that provides the highest statutory maximum term of imprisonment.

3. **Loss Under Subsection (b)(1).**—This application note applies to the determination of loss under subsection (b)(1).

(A) **General Rule.**—Subject to the exclusions in subdivision (D), loss is the greater of actual loss or intended loss.

(i) **Actual Loss.**—"***Actual loss***" means the reasonably foreseeable pecuniary harm that resulted from the offense.

(ii) **Intended Loss.**—"***Intended loss***" (I) means the pecuniary harm that the defendant purposely sought to inflict; and (II) includes intended pecuniary harm that would have been impossible or unlikely to occur (*e.g.*, as in a government sting operation, or an insurance fraud in which the claim exceeded the insured value).

(iii) **Pecuniary Harm.**—"***Pecuniary harm***" means harm that is monetary or that otherwise is readily measurable in money. Accordingly, pecuniary harm does not include emotional distress, harm to reputation, or other non-economic harm.

(iv) **Reasonably Foreseeable Pecuniary Harm.**—For purposes of this guideline, "***reasonably foreseeable pecuniary harm***" means pecuniary harm that the defendant knew or, under the circumstances, reasonably should have known, was a potential result of the offense.

(v) **Rules of Construction in Certain Cases.**—In the cases described in subdivisions (I) through (III), reasonably foreseeable pecuniary harm shall be considered to include the pecuniary harm specified for those cases as follows:

(I) **Product Substitution Cases.**—In the case of a product substitution offense, the reasonably foreseeable pecuniary harm includes the reasonably foreseeable costs of making substitute transactions and handling or disposing of the product delivered, or of retrofitting the product so that it can be used for its intended purpose, and the reasonably foreseeable costs of rectifying the actual or potential disruption to the victim's business operations caused by the product substitution.

(II) **Procurement Fraud Cases.**—In the case of a procurement fraud, such as a fraud affecting a defense contract award, reasonably foreseeable pecuniary harm includes the reasonably foreseeable administrative costs to the government and other participants of repeating or correcting the procurement action affected, plus any increased costs to procure the product or service involved that was reasonably foreseeable.

(III) **Offenses Under 18 U.S.C. § 1030.**—In the case of an offense under 18 U.S.C. § 1030, actual loss includes the following pecuniary harm, regardless of whether such pecuniary harm was reasonably foreseeable:
any reasonable cost to any victim, including the cost of responding to an offense, conducting a damage assessment, and restoring the data, program, system, or information to its condition prior to the offense, and
any revenue lost, cost incurred, or other damages incurred because of interruption of service.

(B) **Gain.**—The court shall use the gain that resulted from the offense as an alternative measure of loss only if there is a loss but it reasonably cannot be determined.

(C) **Estimation of Loss.**—The court need only make a reasonable estimate of the loss. The sentencing judge is in a unique position to assess the evidence and estimate the loss based upon that evidence. For this reason, the court's loss determination is entitled to appropriate deference. *See* 18 U.S.C. § 3742(e) and (f).
The estimate of the loss shall be based on available information, taking into account, as appropriate and practicable under the circumstances, factors such as the following:

(i) The fair market value of the property unlawfully taken, copied, or destroyed; or, if the fair market value is impracticable to determine or inadequately measures the harm, the cost to the victim of replacing that property.

(ii) In the case of proprietary information (*e.g.*, trade secrets), the cost of developing that information or the reduction in the value of that information that resulted from the offense.

(iii) The cost of repairs to damaged property.
(iv) The approximate number of victims multiplied by the average loss to each victim.
(v) The reduction that resulted from the offense in the value of equity securities or other corporate assets.
(vi) More general factors, such as the scope and duration of the offense and revenues generated by similar operations.
(D) **Exclusions from Loss.**—Loss shall not include the following:
(i) Interest of any kind, finance charges, late fees, penalties, amounts based on an agreed-upon return or rate of return, or other similar costs.
(ii) Costs to the government of, and costs incurred by victims primarily to aid the government in, the prosecution and criminal investigation of an offense.
(E) **Credits Against Loss.**—Loss shall be reduced by the following:
(i) The money returned, and the fair market value of the property returned and the services rendered, by the defendant or other persons acting jointly with the defendant, to the victim before the offense was detected. The time of detection of the offense is the earlier of (I) the time the offense was discovered by a victim or government agency; or (II) the time the defendant knew or reasonably should have known that the offense was detected or about to be detected by a victim or government agency.
(ii) In a case involving collateral pledged or otherwise provided by the defendant, the amount the victim has recovered at the time of sentencing from disposition of the collateral, or if the collateral has not been disposed of by that time, the fair market value of the collateral at the time of sentencing.
(iii) Notwithstanding clause (ii), in the case of a fraud involving a mortgage loan, if the collateral has not been disposed of by the time of sentencing, use the fair market value of the collateral as of the date on which the guilt of the defendant has been established, whether by guilty plea, trial, or plea of *nolo contendere*. In such a case, there shall be a rebuttable presumption that the most recent tax assessment value of the collateral is a reasonable estimate of the fair market value. In determining whether the most recent tax assessment value is a reasonable estimate of the fair market value, the court may consider, among other factors, the recency of the tax assessment and the extent to which the jurisdiction's tax assessment practices reflect factors not relevant to fair market value.
(F) **Special Rules.**—Notwithstanding subdivision (A), the following special rules shall be used to assist in determining loss in the cases indicated:

(i) **Stolen or Counterfeit Credit Cards and Access Devices; Purloined Numbers and Codes.**—In a case involving any counterfeit access device or unauthorized access device, loss includes any unauthorized charges made with the counterfeit access device or unauthorized access device and shall be not less than $500 per access device. However, if the unauthorized access device is a means of telecommunications access that identifies a specific telecommunications instrument or telecommunications account (including an electronic serial number/mobile identification number (ESN/MIN) pair), and that means was only possessed, and not used, during the commission of the offense, loss shall be not less than $100 per unused means. For purposes of this subdivision, "***counterfeit access device***" and "***unauthorized access device***" have the meaning given those terms in Application Note 10(A).
(ii) **Government Benefits.**—In a case involving government benefits (*e.g.*, grants, loans, entitlement program payments), loss shall be considered to be not less than the value of the benefits obtained by unintended recipients or diverted to unintended uses, as the case may be. For example, if the defendant

was the intended recipient of food stamps having a value of $100 but fraudulently received food stamps having a value of $150, loss is $50.

(iii) **Davis–Bacon Act Violations.**—In a case involving a Davis–Bacon Act violation (*i.e.*, a violation of 40 U.S.C. § 3142, criminally prosecuted under 18 U.S.C. § 1001), the value of the benefits shall be considered to be not less than the difference between the legally required wages and actual wages paid.

(iv) **Ponzi and Other Fraudulent Investment Schemes.**—In a case involving a fraudulent investment scheme, such as a Ponzi scheme, loss shall not be reduced by the money or the value of the property transferred to any individual investor in the scheme in excess of that investor's principal investment (*i.e.*, the gain to an individual investor in the scheme shall not be used to offset the loss to another individual investor in the scheme).

(v) **Certain Other Unlawful Misrepresentation Schemes.**—In a case involving a scheme in which (I) services were fraudulently rendered to the victim by persons falsely posing as licensed professionals; (II) goods were falsely represented as approved by a governmental regulatory agency; or (III) goods for which regulatory approval by a government agency was required but not obtained, or was obtained by fraud, loss shall include the amount paid for the property, services or goods transferred, rendered, or misrepresented, with no credit provided for the value of those items or services.

(vi) **Value of Controlled Substances.**—In a case involving controlled substances, loss is the estimated street value of the controlled substances.

(vii) **Value of Cultural Heritage Resources or Paleontological Resources.**—In a case involving a cultural heritage resource or paleontological resource, loss attributable to that resource shall be determined in accordance with the rules for determining the "value of the resource" set forth in Application Note 2 of the Commentary to §2B1.5.

(viii) **Federal Health Care Offenses Involving Government Health Care Programs.**—In a case in which the defendant is convicted of a Federal health care offense involving a Government health care program, the aggregate dol**§**

lar amount of fraudulent bills submitted to the Government health care program shall constitute prima facie evidence of the amount of the intended loss, *i.e.*, is evidence sufficient to establish the amount of the intended loss, if not rebutted.

(ix) **Fraudulent Inflation or Deflation in Value of Securities or Commodities.**—In a case involving the fraudulent inflation or deflation in the value of a publicly traded security or commodity, the court in determining loss may use any method that is appropriate and practicable under the circumstances. One such method the court may consider is a method under which the actual loss attributable to the change in value of the security or commodity is the amount determined by—

(I) calculating the difference between the average price of the security or commodity during the period that the fraud occurred and the average price of the security or commodity during the 90-day period after the fraud was disclosed to the market, and

(II) multiplying the difference in average price by the number of shares outstanding.

In determining whether the amount so determined is a reasonable estimate of the actual loss attributable to the change in value of the security or commodity, the court may consider, among other factors, the extent to which the amount so determined includes significant changes in value not resulting from the offense (*e.g.*, changes caused by external market forces, such as changed economic circumstances, changed investor expectations, and new industryspecific or firm-specific facts, conditions, or events).

4. **Application of Subsection (b)(2).—**
(A) **Definition.**—For purposes of subsection (b)(2), "***mass-marketing***" means a plan, program, promotion, or campaign that is conducted through solicitation by telephone, mail, the Internet, or other means to induce a large number of persons to
(i) purchase goods or services; (ii) participate in a contest or sweepstakes; or (iii) invest for financial profit. "Mass-marketing" includes, for example, a telemarketing campaign that solicits a large number of individuals to purchase fraudulent life insurance policies.
(B) **Applicability to Transmission of Multiple Commercial Electronic Mail Messages.**—For purposes of subsection (b)(2), an offense under 18 U.S.C. § 1037, or any other offense involving conduct described in 18 U.S.C. § 1037, shall be considered to have been committed through mass-marketing. Accordingly, the defendant shall receive at least a two-level enhancement under subsection (b)(2) and may, depending on the facts of the case, receive a greater enhancement under such subsection, if the defendant was convicted under, or the offense involved conduct described in, 18 U.S.C. § 1037.
(C) **Undelivered United States Mail.**—
(i) **In General.**—In a case in which undelivered United States mail was taken, or the taking of such item was an object of the offense, or in a case in which the stolen property received, transported, transferred, transmitted, or possessed was undelivered United States mail, "***victim***" means (I) any victim as

defined in Application Note 1; or (II) any person who was the intended recipient, or addressee, of the undelivered United States mail.
(ii) **Special Rule.**—A case described in subdivision (C)(i) of this note that involved—
(I) a United States Postal Service relay box, collection box, delivery vehicle, satchel, or cart, shall be considered to have involved at least 10 victims.
(II) a housing unit cluster box or any similar receptacle that contains multiple mailboxes, whether such receptacle is owned by the United States Postal Service or otherwise owned, shall, unless proven otherwise, be presumed to have involved the number of victims corresponding to the number of mailboxes in each cluster box or similar receptacle.
(iii) **Definition.**—"***Undelivered United States mail***" means mail that has not actually been received by the addressee or the addressee's agent (*e.g.*, mail taken from the addressee's mail box).
(D) **Vulnerable Victims.**—If subsection (b)(2)(B) or (C) applies, an enhancement under §3A1.1(b)(2) shall not apply.
(E) **Cases Involving Means of Identification.**—For purposes of subsection (b)(2), in a case involving means of identification "***victim***" means (i) any victim as defined in Application Note 1; or (ii) any individual whose means of identification was used unlawfully or without authority.
(F) **Substantial Financial Hardship.**—In determining whether the offense resulted in substantial financial hardship to a victim, the court shall consider, among other factors, whether the offense resulted in the victim—
(i) becoming insolvent;
(ii) filing for bankruptcy under the Bankruptcy Code (title 11, United States Code);
(iii) suffering substantial loss of a retirement, education, or other savings or investment fund;
(iv) making substantial changes to his or her employment, such as postponing his or her retirement plans;
(v) making substantial changes to his or her living arrangements, such as relocating to a less expensive home; and
(vi) suffering substantial harm to his or her ability to obtain credit.

5. **Enhancement for Business of Receiving and Selling Stolen Property under Subsection (b)(4).**—For purposes of subsection (b)(4), the court shall consider the following non-exhaustive list of factors in determining whether the defendant was in the business of receiving and selling stolen property:

(A) The regularity and sophistication of the defendant's activities.

(B) The value and size of the inventory of stolen property maintained by the defendant.

(C) The extent to which the defendant's activities encouraged or facilitated other crimes.

(D) The defendant's past activities involving stolen property.

6. **Application of Subsection (b)(6).**—For purposes of subsection (b)(6), "***improper means***" includes the unauthorized harvesting of electronic mail addresses of users of a website, proprietary service, or other online public forum.

7. **Application of Subsection (b)(8)(B).**—If subsection (b)(8)(B) applies, do not apply an adjustment under §3B1.3 (Abuse of Position of Trust or Use of Special Skill).

8. **Application of Subsection (b)(9).**—

(A) **In General.**—The adjustments in subsection (b)(9) are alternative rather than cumulative. If, in a particular case, however, more than one of the enumerated factors applied, an upward departure may be warranted.

(B) **Misrepresentations Regarding Charitable and Other Institutions.**—Subsection (b)(9)(A) applies in any case in which the defendant represented that the defendant was acting to obtain a benefit on behalf of a charitable, educational, religious, or political organization, or a government agency (regardless of whether the defendant actually was associated with the organization or government agency) when, in fact, the defendant intended to divert all or part of that benefit (*e.g.*, for the defendant's personal gain). Subsection (b)(9)(A) applies, for example, to the following:

(i) A defendant who solicited contributions for a non-existent famine relief organization.

(ii) A defendant who solicited donations from church members by falsely claiming to be a fundraiser for a religiously affiliated school.

(iii) A defendant, chief of a local fire department, who conducted a public fundraiser representing that the purpose of the fundraiser was to procure sufficient funds for a new fire engine when, in fact, the defendant intended to divert some of the funds for the defendant's personal benefit.

(C) **Fraud in Contravention of Prior Judicial Order.**—Subsection (b)(9)(C) provides an enhancement if the defendant commits a fraud in contravention of a prior, official judicial or administrative warning, in the form of an order, injunction, decree, or process, to take or not to take a specified action. A defendant who does not comply with such a prior, official judicial or administrative warning demonstrates aggravated criminal intent and deserves additional punishment. If it is established that an entity the defendant controlled was a party to the prior proceeding that resulted in the official judicial or administrative action, and the defendant had knowledge of that prior decree or order, this enhancement applies even if the defendant was not a specifically named party in that prior case. For example, a defendant whose business previously was enjoined from selling a dangerous product, but who nonetheless engaged in fraudulent conduct to sell the product, is subject to this enhancement. This enhancement does not apply if the same conduct resulted in an enhancement pursuant to a provision found elsewhere in the guidelines

(*e.g.*, a violation of a condition of release addressed in §3C1.3 (Commission of Offense While on Release) or a violation of probation addressed in §4A1.1 (Criminal History Category)).

(D) **College Scholarship Fraud.**—For purposes of subsection (b)(9)(D):

"***Financial assistance***" means any scholarship, grant, loan, tuition, discount,

award, or other financial assistance for the purpose of financing an education.
"***Institution of higher education***" has the meaning given that term in section 101 of the Higher Education Act of 1954 (20 U.S.C. § 1001).

(E) **Non-Applicability of Chapter Three Adjustments.—**

(i) **Subsection (b)(9)(A).—**If the conduct that forms the basis for an enhancement under subsection (b)(9)(A) is the only conduct that forms the basis for an adjustment under §3B1.3 (Abuse of Position of Trust or Use of Special Skill), do not apply that adjustment under §3B1.3.

(ii) **Subsection (b)(9)(B) and (C).—**If the conduct that forms the basis for an enhancement under subsection (b)(9)(B) or (C) is the only conduct that forms the basis for an adjustment under §3C1.1 (Obstructing or Impeding the Administration of Justice), do not apply that adjustment under §3C1.1.

9. **Application of Subsection (b)(10).—**

(A) **Definition of United States.—**For purposes of subsection (b)(10)(B), "***United States***" means each of the 50 states, the District of Columbia, the Commonwealth of Puerto Rico, the United States Virgin Islands, Guam, the Northern Mariana Islands, and American Samoa.

(B) **Sophisticated Means Enhancement under Subsection (b)(10)(C).—**For purposes of subsection (b)(10)(C), "***sophisticated means***" means especially complex or especially intricate offense conduct pertaining to the execution or concealment of an offense. For example, in a telemarketing scheme, locating the main office of the scheme in one jurisdiction but locating soliciting operations in another jurisdiction ordinarily indicates sophisticated means. Conduct such as hiding assets or transactions, or both, through the use of fictitious entities, corporate shells, or offshore financial accounts also ordinarily indicates sophisticated means.

(C) **Non-Applicability of Chapter Three Adjustment.—**If the conduct that forms the basis for an enhancement under subsection (b)(10) is the only conduct that forms the basis for an adjustment under §3C1.1, do not apply that adjustment under §3C1.1.

10. **Application of Subsection (b)(11).—**

(A) **Definitions.—**For purposes of subsection (b)(11):

"***Authentication feature***" has the meaning given that term in 18 U.S.C. § 1028(d)(1).

"***Counterfeit access device***" (i) has the meaning given that term in 18 U.S.C. § 1029(e)(2); and (ii) includes a telecommunications instrument that has been modified or altered to obtain unauthorized use of telecommunications service.

"***Device-making equipment***" (i) has the meaning given that term in 18 U.S.C. § 1029(e)(6); and (ii) includes (I) any hardware or software that has been configured as described in 18 U.S.C. § 1029(a)(9); and (II) a scanning receiver referred to in 18 U.S.C. § 1029(a)(8). "Scanning receiver" has the meaning given that term in 18 U.S.C. § 1029(e)(8).

"***Produce***" includes manufacture, design, alter, authenticate, duplicate, or assemble.

"***Production***" includes manufacture, design, alteration, authentication, duplication, or assembly.

"***Telecommunications service***" has the meaning given that term in 18 U.S.C. § 1029(e)(9).

"***Unauthorized access device***" has the meaning given that term in 18 U.S.C. § 1029(e)(3).

(B) **Authentication Features and Identification Documents.—**Offenses involving authentication features, identification documents, false identification documents, and means of identification, in violation of 18 U.S.C. § 1028, also are covered by this guideline. If the primary purpose of the offense, under 18 U.S.C. § 1028, was to violate, or assist another to violate, the law pertaining to naturalization, citizenship, or legal resident status, apply §2L2.1 (Trafficking in a Document Relating to Naturalization) or §2L2.2 (Fraudulently Acquiring Documents Relating to Naturalization), as appropriate, rather than this guideline.

(C) **Application of Subsection (b)(11)(C)(i).—**

(i) **In General.**—Subsection (b)(11)(C)(i) applies in a case in which a means of identification of an individual other than the defendant (or a person for whose conduct the defendant is accountable under §1B1.3 (Relevant Conduct)) is used without that individual's authorization unlawfully to produce or obtain another means of identification.

(ii) **Examples.**—Examples of conduct to which subsection (b)(11)(C)(i) applies are as follows:

(I) A defendant obtains an individual's name and social security number from a source (*e.g.*, from a piece of mail taken from the individual's mailbox) and obtains a bank loan in that individual's name. In this example, the account number of the bank loan is the other means of identification that has been obtained unlawfully.

(II) A defendant obtains an individual's name and address from a source (*e.g.*, from a driver's license in a stolen wallet) and applies for, obtains, and subsequently uses a credit card in that individual's name. In this example, the credit card is the other means of identification that has been obtained unlawfully.

(iii) **Non-Applicability of Subsection (b)(11)(C)(i).**—Examples of conduct to which subsection (b)(11)(C)(i) does not apply are as follows:

(I) A defendant uses a credit card from a stolen wallet only to make a purchase. In such a case, the defendant has not used the stolen credit card to obtain another means of identification.

(II) A defendant forges another individual's signature to cash a stolen check. Forging another individual's signature is not producing another means of identification.

(D) **Application of Subsection (b)(11)(C)(ii).**—Subsection (b)(11)(C)(ii) applies in any case in which the offense involved the possession of 5 or more means of identification that unlawfully were produced or obtained, regardless of the number of individuals in whose name (or other identifying information) the means of identification were so produced or so obtained.

11. **Application of Subsection (b)(14).**—Subsection (b)(14) provides a minimum offense level in the case of an ongoing, sophisticated operation (*e.g.*, an auto theft ring or "chop shop") to steal or to receive stolen (A) vehicles or vehicle parts; or (B) goods or chattels that are part of a cargo shipment. For purposes of this subsection, "***vehicle***" means motor vehicle, vessel, or aircraft. A "***cargo shipment***" includes cargo transported on a railroad car, bus, steamboat, vessel, or airplane.

12. **Gross Receipts Enhancement under Subsection (b)(16)(A).—**

(A) **In General.**—For purposes of subsection (b)(16)(A), the defendant shall be considered to have derived more than $1,000,000 in gross receipts if the gross receipts to the defendant individually, rather than to all participants, exceeded $1,000,000.

(B) **Definition.**—"***Gross receipts from the offense***" includes all property, real or personal, tangible or intangible, which is obtained directly or indirectly as a result of such offense. *See* 18 U.S.C. § 982(a)(4).

13. **Application of Subsection (b)(16)(B).—**

(A) **Application of Subsection (b)(16)(B)(i).**—The following is a non-exhaustive list of factors that the court shall consider in determining whether, as a result of the offense, the safety and soundness of a financial institution was substantially jeopardized:

(i) The financial institution became insolvent.

(ii) The financial institution substantially reduced benefits to pensioners or insureds.

(iii) The financial institution was unable on demand to refund fully any deposit, payment, or investment.
(iv) The financial institution was so depleted of its assets as to be forced to merge with another institution in order to continue active operations.
(v) One or more of the criteria in clauses (i) through (iv) was likely to result from the offense but did not result from the offense because of federal government intervention, such as a "bailout".

(B) **Application of Subsection (b)(16)(B)(ii).—**
(i) **Definition.—**For purposes of this subsection, "***organization***" has the meaning given that term in Application Note 1 of §8A1.1 (Applicability of Chapter Eight).
(ii) **In General.—**The following is a non-exhaustive list of factors that the court shall consider in determining whether, as a result of the offense, the solvency or financial security of an organization that was a publicly traded company or that had more than 1,000 employees was substantially endangered:
(I) The organization became insolvent or suffered a substantial reduction in the value of its assets.
(II) The organization filed for bankruptcy under Chapters 7, 11, or 13 of the Bankruptcy Code (title 11, United States Code).
(III) The organization suffered a substantial reduction in the value of its equity securities or the value of its employee retirement accounts.
(IV) The organization substantially reduced its workforce.
(V) The organization substantially reduced its employee pension benefits.
(VI) The liquidity of the equity securities of a publicly traded company was substantially endangered. For example, the company was delisted from its primary listing exchange, or trading of the company's securities was halted for more than one full trading day.
(VII) One or more of the criteria in subclauses (I) through (VI) was likely to result from the offense but did not result from the offense because of federal government intervention, such as a "bailout".

14. **Application of Subsection (b)(18).—**
(A) **Definitions.—**For purposes of subsection (b)(18):
"***Critical infrastructure***" means systems and assets vital to national defense, national security, economic security, public health or safety, or any combination of those matters. A critical infrastructure may be publicly or privately owned. Examples of critical infrastructures include gas and oil production, storage, and delivery systems, water supply systems, telecommunications networks, electrical power delivery systems, financing and banking systems, emergency services (including medical, police, fire, and rescue services), transportation systems and services (including highways, mass transit, airlines, and airports), and government operations that provide essential services to the public.
"***Government entity***" has the meaning given that term in 18 U.S.C. § 1030(e)(9).
(B) **Subsection (b)(18)(A)(iii).—**If the same conduct that forms the basis for an enhancement under subsection (b)(18)(A)(iii) is the only conduct that forms the basis for an enhancement under subsection (b)(16)(B), do not apply the enhancement under subsection (b)(16)(B).

15. **Application of Subsection (b)(19).—**
(A) **Definitions.—**For purposes of subsection (b)(19):
"***Commodities law***" means (i) the Commodity Exchange Act (7 U.S.C. § 1 *et seq.*) and 18 U.S.C. § 1348; and (ii) includes the rules, regulations, and orders issued by the Commodity Futures Trading Commission.

"***Commodity pool operator***" has the meaning given that term in section 1a(11) of the Commodity Exchange Act (7 U.S.C. § 1a(11)).
"***Commodity trading advisor***" has the meaning given that term in section 1a(12) of the Commodity Exchange Act (7 U.S.C. § 1a(12)).
"***Futures commission merchant***" has the meaning given that term in section 1a(28) of the Commodity Exchange Act (7 U.S.C. § 1a(28)).
"***Introducing broker***" has the meaning given that term in section 1a(31) of the Commodity Exchange Act (7 U.S.C. § 1a(31)).
"***Investment adviser***" has the meaning given that term in section 202(a)(11) of the Investment Advisers Act of 1940 (15 U.S.C. § 80b-2(a)(11)).
"***Person associated with a broker or dealer***" has the meaning given that term in section 3(a)(18) of the Securities Exchange Act of 1934 (15 U.S.C. § 78c(a)(18)).
"***Person associated with an investment adviser***" has the meaning given that term in section 202(a)(17) of the Investment Advisers Act of 1940 (15 U.S.C. § 80b-2(a)(17)).
"***Registered broker or dealer***" has the meaning given that term in section 3(a)(48) of the Securities Exchange Act of 1934 (15 U.S.C. § 78c(a)(48)).
"***Securities law***" (i) means 18 U.S.C. §§ 1348, 1350, and the provisions of law referred to in section 3(a)(47) of the Securities Exchange Act of 1934 (15 U.S.C. § 78c(a)(47)); and (ii) includes the rules, regulations, and orders issued by the Securities and Exchange Commission pursuant to the provisions of law referred to in such section.
(B) **In General.**—A conviction under a securities law or commodities law is not required in order for subsection (b)(19) to apply. This subsection would apply in the case of a defendant convicted under a general fraud statute if the defendant's conduct violated a securities law or commodities law. For example, this subsection would apply if an officer of a publicly traded company violated regulations issued by the Securities and Exchange Commission by fraudulently influencing an independent audit of the company's financial statements for the purposes of rendering such financial statements materially misleading, even if the officer is convicted only of wire fraud.
(C) **Nonapplicability of §3B1.3 (Abuse of Position of Trust or Use of Special Skill).**—If subsection (b)(19) applies, do not apply §3B1.3.
16. **Cross Reference in Subsection (c)(3).**—Subsection (c)(3) provides a cross reference to another guideline in Chapter Two (Offense Conduct) in cases in which the defendant is

convicted of a general fraud statute, and the count of conviction establishes an offense involving fraudulent conduct that is more aptly covered by another guideline. Sometimes, offenses involving fraudulent statements are prosecuted under 18 U.S.C. § 1001, or a similarly general statute, although the offense involves fraudulent conduct that is also covered by a more specific statute. Examples include false entries regarding currency transactions, for which §2S1.3 (Structuring Transactions to Evade Reporting Requirements) likely would be more apt, and false statements to a customs officer, for which §2T3.1 (Evading Import Duties or Restrictions (Smuggling); Receiving or Trafficking in Smuggled Property) likely would be more apt. In certain other cases, the mail or wire fraud statutes, or other relatively broad statutes, are used primarily as jurisdictional bases for the prosecution of other offenses. For example, a state employee who improperly influenced the award of a contract and used the mails to commit the offense may be prosecuted under 18 U.S.C. § 1341 for fraud involving the deprivation of the intangible right of honest services. Such a case would be more aptly sentenced pursuant to §2C1.1 (Offering, Giving, Soliciting, or Receiving a Bribe; Extortion Under Color of Official Right; Fraud involving the Deprivation of the Intangible Right to Honest Services of Public Officials; Conspiracy to Defraud by Interference with Governmental Functions).
17. **Continuing Financial Crimes Enterprise.**—If the defendant is convicted under

18 U.S.C. § 225 (relating to a continuing financial crimes enterprise), the offense level is that applicable to the underlying series of offenses comprising the "continuing financial crimes enterprise".

18. **Partially Completed Offenses.**—In the case of a partially completed offense (*e.g.*, an offense involving a completed theft or fraud that is part of a larger, attempted theft or fraud), the offense level is to be determined in accordance with the provisions of §2X1.1 (Attempt, Solicitation, or Conspiracy) whether the conviction is for the substantive offense, the inchoate offense (attempt, solicitation, or conspiracy), or both. *See* Application Note 4 of the Commentary to §2X1.1.

19. **Multiple-Count Indictments.**—Some fraudulent schemes may result in multiplecount indictments, depending on the technical elements of the offense. The cumulative loss produced by a common scheme or course of conduct should be used in determining the offense level, regardless of the number of counts of conviction. *See* Chapter Three, Part D (Multiple Counts).

20. **Departure Considerations.**—

(A) **Upward Departure Considerations.**—There may be cases in which the offense level determined under this guideline substantially understates the seriousness of the offense. In such cases, an upward departure may be warranted. The following is a non-exhaustive list of factors that the court may consider in determining whether an upward departure is warranted:

(i) A primary objective of the offense was an aggravating, non-monetary objective. For example, a primary objective of the offense was to inflict emotional harm.

(ii) The offense caused or risked substantial non-monetary harm. For example, the offense caused physical harm, psychological harm, or severe emotional trauma, or resulted in a substantial invasion of a privacy interest (through, for example, the theft of personal information such as medical, educational, or financial records). An upward departure would be warranted, for example, in an 18 U.S.C. § 1030 offense involving damage to a protected computer, if,

as a result of that offense, death resulted. An upward departure also would be warranted, for example, in a case involving animal enterprise terrorism under 18 U.S.C. § 43, if, in the course of the offense, serious bodily injury or death resulted, or substantial scientific research or information were destroyed. Similarly, an upward departure would be warranted in a case involving conduct described in 18 U.S.C. § 670 if the offense resulted in serious bodily injury or death, including serious bodily injury or death resulting from the use of the pre-retail medical product.

(iii) The offense involved a substantial amount of interest of any kind, finance charges, late fees, penalties, amounts based on an agreed-upon return or rate of return, or other similar costs, not included in the determination of loss for purposes of subsection (b)(1).

(iv) The offense created a risk of substantial loss beyond the loss determined for purposes of subsection (b)(1), such as a risk of a significant disruption of a national financial market.

(v) In a case involving stolen information from a "protected computer", as defined in 18 U.S.C. § 1030(e)(2), the defendant sought the stolen information to further a broader criminal purpose.

(vi) In a case involving access devices or unlawfully produced or unlawfully obtained means of identification:

(I) The offense caused substantial harm to the victim's reputation, or the victim suffered a substantial inconvenience related to repairing the victim's reputation.

(II) An individual whose means of identification the defendant used to obtain

unlawful means of identification is erroneously arrested or denied a job because an arrest record has been made in that individual's name.
(III) The defendant produced or obtained numerous means of identification with respect to one individual and essentially assumed that individual's identity.
(B) **Upward Departure for Debilitating Impact on a Critical Infrastructure.**—An upward departure would be warranted in a case in which subsection (b)(18)(A)(iii) applies and the disruption to the critical infrastructure(s) is so substantial as to have a debilitating impact on national security, national economic security, national public health or safety, or any combination of those matters.
(C) **Downward Departure Consideration.**—There may be cases in which the offense level determined under this guideline substantially overstates the seriousness of the offense. In such cases, a downward departure may be warranted.
For example, a securities fraud involving a fraudulent statement made publicly to the market may produce an aggregate loss amount that is substantial but diffuse, with relatively small loss amounts suffered by a relatively large number of victims.
In such a case, the loss table in subsection (b)(1) and the victims table in subsection (b)(2) may combine to produce an offense level that substantially overstates the seriousness of the offense. If so, a downward departure may be warranted.

(D) **Downward Departure for Major Disaster or Emergency Victims.**—If (i) the minimum offense level of level 12 in subsection (b)(12) applies; (ii) the defendant sustained damage, loss, hardship, or suffering caused by a major disaster or an emergency as those terms are defined in 42 U.S.C. § 5122; and (iii) the benefits received illegally were only an extension or overpayment of benefits received legitimately, a downward departure may be warranted.
Background: This guideline covers offenses involving theft, stolen property, property damage or destruction, fraud, forgery, and counterfeiting (other than offenses involving altered or counterfeit bearer obligations of the United States).
Because federal fraud statutes often are broadly written, a single pattern of offense conduct usually can be prosecuted under several code sections, as a result of which the offense of conviction may be somewhat arbitrary. Furthermore, most fraud statutes cover a broad range of conduct with extreme variation in severity. The specific offense characteristics and cross references contained in this guideline are designed with these considerations in mind.
The Commission has determined that, ordinarily, the sentences of defendants convicted of federal offenses should reflect the nature and magnitude of the loss caused or intended by their crimes. Accordingly, along with other relevant factors under the guidelines, loss serves as a measure of the seriousness of the offense and the defendant's relative culpability and is a principal factor in determining the offense level under this guideline.
Theft from the person of another, such as pickpocketing or non-forcible purse-snatching, receives an enhanced sentence because of the increased risk of physical injury. This guideline does not include an enhancement for thefts from the person by means of force or fear; such crimes are robberies and are covered under §2B3.1 (Robbery).
A minimum offense level of level 14 is provided for offenses involving an organized scheme to steal vehicles or vehicle parts. Typically, the scope of such activity is substantial, but the value of the property may be particularly difficult to ascertain in individual cases because the stolen property is rapidly resold or otherwise disposed of in the course of the offense.
Therefore, the specific offense characteristic of "organized scheme" is used as an alternative to "loss" in setting a minimum offense level.
Use of false pretenses involving charitable causes and government agencies enhances the sentences of defendants who take advantage of victims' trust in government or law enforcement agencies or the generosity and charitable motives of victims. Taking advantage of a victim's self-interest does not mitigate the seriousness of fraudulent conduct; rather, defendants who exploit victims' charitable impulses or trust in government create particular social harm.

In a similar vein, a defendant who has been subject to civil or administrative proceedings for the same or similar fraudulent conduct demonstrates aggravated criminal intent and is deserving of additional punishment for not conforming with the requirements of judicial process or orders issued by federal, state, or local administrative agencies.

Offenses that involve the use of financial transactions or financial accounts outside the United States in an effort to conceal illicit profits and criminal conduct involve a particularly high level of sophistication and complexity. These offenses are difficult to detect and require costly investigations and prosecutions. Diplomatic processes often must be used to secure testimony and evidence beyond the jurisdiction of United States courts. Consequently, a minimum offense level of level 12 is provided for these offenses.

Subsection (b)(5) implements the instruction to the Commission in section 2 of Public Law 105–101 and the directive to the Commission in section 3 of Public Law 110–384.

Subsection (b)(7) implements the directive to the Commission in section 10606 of Public Law 111–148.

Subsection (b)(8) implements the directive to the Commission in section 7 of Public Law 112–186.

Subsection (b)(9)(D) implements, in a broader form, the directive in section 3 of the College Scholarship Fraud Prevention Act of 2000, Public Law 106–420.

Subsection (b)(10) implements, in a broader form, the instruction to the Commission in section 6(c)(2) of Public Law 105–184.

Subsections (b)(11)(A)(i) and (B)(i) implement the instruction to the Commission in section 4 of the Wireless Telephone Protection Act, Public Law 105–172.

Subsection (b)(11)(C) implements the directive to the Commission in section 4 of the Identity Theft and Assumption Deterrence Act of 1998, Public Law 105–318. This subsection focuses principally on an aggravated form of identity theft known as "affirmative identity theft" or "breeding", in which a defendant uses another individual's name, social security number, or some other form of identification (the "means of identification") to "breed" (*i.e.*, produce or obtain) new or additional forms of identification. Because 18 U.S.C. § 1028(d) broadly defines "means of identification", the new or additional forms of identification can include items such as a driver's license, a credit card, or a bank loan. This subsection provides a minimum offense level of level 12, in part because of the seriousness of the offense. The minimum offense level accounts for the fact that the means of identification that were "bred" (*i.e.*, produced or obtained) often are within the defendant's exclusive control, making it difficult for the individual victim to detect that the victim's identity has been "stolen." Generally, the victim does not become aware of the offense until certain harms have already occurred (*e.g.*, a damaged credit rating or an inability to obtain a loan). The minimum offense level also accounts for the nonmonetary harm associated with these types of offenses, much of which may be difficult or impossible to quantify (*e.g.*, harm to the individual's reputation or credit rating, inconvenience, and other difficulties resulting from the offense). The legislative history of the Identity Theft and Assumption Deterrence Act of 1998 indicates that Congress was especially concerned with providing increased punishment for this type of harm.

Subsection (b)(12) implements the directive in section 5 of Public Law 110–179.

Subsection (b)(13) implements the directive in section 3 of Public Law 112–269.

Subsection (b)(15)(B) implements, in a broader form, the instruction to the Commission in section 110512 of Public Law 103–322.

Subsection (b)(16)(A) implements, in a broader form, the instruction to the Commission in section 2507 of Public Law 101–647.

Subsection (b)(16)(B)(i) implements, in a broader form, the instruction to the Commission in section 961(m) of Public Law 101–73.

Subsection (b)(17) implements the directive in section 209 of Public Law 110–326.

Subsection (b)(18) implements the directive in section 225(b) of Public Law 107–296. The minimum offense level of level 24 provided in subsection (b)(18)(B) for an offense that resulted in a substantial disruption of a critical infrastructure reflects the serious impact such an offense could have on national security, national economic security, national public health or safety, or a combination of any of these matters.

Historical Note

Effective November 1, 1987. Amended effective June 15, 1988 (amendment 7); November 1, 1989 (amendments 99–101 and 303); November 1, 1990 (amendments 312, 317, and 361); November 1, 1991 (amendments 364, and 393); November 1, 1993 (amendments 481 and 482); November 1, 1995 (amendment 512); November 1, 1997 (amendment 551); November 1, 1998 (amendment 576); November 1, 2000 (amendment 596); November 1, 2001 (amendment 617); November 1, 2002 (amendments 637, 638, and 646); January 25, 2003 (amendment 647); November 1, 2003 (amendments 653, 654, 655, and 661); November 1, 2004 (amendments 665, 666, and 674); November 1, 2005 (amendment 679); November 1, 2006 (amendments 685 and 696); November 1, 2007 (amendments 699, 700, and 702); February 6, 2008 (amendment 714); November 1, 2008 (amendments 719 and 725); November 1, 2009 (amendments 726, 733, and 737); November 1, 2010 (amendments 745 and 747); November 1, 2011 (amendment 749); November 1, 2012 (amendment 761); November 1, 2013 (amendments 771, 772, and 777); November 1, 2015 (amendments 791 and 792).

§2B1.2. [Deleted]

Historical Note

Section 2B1.2 (Receiving, Transporting, Transferring, Transmitting, or Possessing Stolen Property), effective November 1, 1987, amended effective January 15, 1988 (amendment 8), June 15, 1988 (amendment 9), November 1, 1989 (amendments 102–104), and November 1, 1990 (amendments 312 and 361), was deleted by consolidation with §2B1.1 effective November 1, 1993 (amendment 481).

§2B1.3. [Deleted]

Historical Note

Section 2B1.3 (Property Damage or Destruction), effective November 1, 1987, amended effective June 15, 1988 (amendment 10), November 1, 1990 (amendments 312 and 313), November 1, 1997 (amendment 551), November 1, 1998 (amendment 576), was deleted by consolidation with §2B1.1 effective November 1, 2001 (amendment 617).

§2B1.4. Insider Trading

(a) Base Offense Level: **8**

(b) Specific Offense Characteristics

(1) If the gain resulting from the offense exceeded $6,500, increase by the number of levels from the table in §2B1.1 (Theft, Property Destruction, and Fraud) corresponding to that amount.

(2) If the offense involved an organized scheme to engage in insider trading and the offense level determined above is less than level **14**, increase to level **14**.

Commentary

Statutory Provisions: 15 U.S.C. § 78j and 17 C.F.R. § 240.10b-5. For additional statutory provision(s), *see* Appendix A (Statutory Index).

Application Notes:

1. **Application of Subsection (b)(2).**—For purposes of subsection (b)(2), an "***organized scheme to engage in insider trading***" means a scheme to engage in insider trading that involves considered, calculated, systematic, or repeated efforts to obtain and trade on inside information, as distinguished from fortuitous or opportunistic instances of insider trading.

The following is a non-exhaustive list of factors that the court may consider in determining whether the offense involved an organized scheme to engage in insider trading:

(A) the number of transactions;

(B) the dollar value of the transactions;

(C) the number of securities involved;

(D) the duration of the offense;

(E) the number of participants in the scheme (although such a scheme may exist even in the absence of more than one participant);

(F) the efforts undertaken to obtain material, nonpublic information;
(G) the number of instances in which material, nonpublic information was obtained; and
(H) the efforts undertaken to conceal the offense.

2. **Application of §3B1.3.**—Section 3B1.3 (Abuse of Position of Trust or Use of Special Skill) should be applied if the defendant occupied and abused a position of special trust. Examples might include a corporate president or an attorney who misused information regarding a planned but unannounced takeover attempt. It typically would not apply to an ordinary "tippee".

Furthermore, §3B1.3 should be applied if the defendant's employment in a position that involved regular participation or professional assistance in creating, issuing, buying, selling, or trading securities or commodities was used to facilitate significantly the commission or concealment of the offense. It would apply, for example, to a hedge fund professional who regularly participates in securities transactions or to a lawyer who regularly provides professional assistance in securities transactions, if the defendant's employment in such a position was used to facilitate significantly the commission or concealment of the offense. It ordinarily would not apply to a position such as a clerical worker in an investment firm, because such a position ordinarily does not involve special skill. *See* §3B1.3, comment. (n.4).

Background: This guideline applies to certain violations of Rule 10b-5 that are commonly referred to as "insider trading". Insider trading is treated essentially as a sophisticated fraud. Because the victims and their losses are difficult if not impossible to identify, the gain, *i.e.*, the

total increase in value realized through trading in securities by the defendant and persons acting in concert with the defendant or to whom the defendant provided inside information, is employed instead of the victims' losses.

Certain other offenses, *e.g.*, 7 U.S.C. § 13(e), that involve misuse of inside information for personal gain also appropriately may be covered by this guideline.

Subsection (b)(2) implements the directive to the Commission in section 1079A(a)(1)(A) of Public Law 111–203.

Historical Note

Effective November 1, 2001 (amendment 617). Amended effective November 1, 2010 (amendment 746); November 1, 2012 (amendment 761); November 1, 2015 (amendment 791).

§2B1.5. Theft of, Damage to, or Destruction of, Cultural Heritage Resources or Paleontological Resources; Unlawful Sale, Purchase, Exchange, Transportation, or Receipt of Cultural Heritage Resources or Paleontological Resources

(a) Base Offense Level: **8**

(b) Specific Offense Characteristics

(1) If the value of the cultural heritage resource or paleontological resource (A) exceeded $2,500 but did not exceed $6,500, increase by **1** level; or (B) exceeded $6,500, increase by the number of levels from the table in §2B1.1 (Theft, Property Destruction, and Fraud) corresponding to that amount.

(2) If the offense involved a cultural heritage resource or paleontological resource from, or that, prior to the offense, was on, in, or in the custody of (A) the national park system; (B) a National Historic Landmark; (C) a national monument or national memorial; (D) a national marine sanctuary; (E) a national cemetery or veterans' memorial; (F) a museum; or (G) the World Heritage List, increase by **2** levels.

(3) If the offense involved a cultural heritage resource constituting (A) human remains; (B) a funerary object; (C) cultural patrimony; (D) a sacred object; (E) cultural property; (F) designated archaeological or ethnological material; or (G) a pre-Columbian monumental or architectural sculpture or mural, increase by **2** levels.

(4) If the offense was committed for pecuniary gain or otherwise involved a commercial purpose, increase by **2** levels.

(5) If the defendant engaged in a pattern of misconduct involving cultural heritage resources or paleontological resources, increase by **2** levels.

(6) If a dangerous weapon was brandished or its use was threatened, increase by **2** levels. If the resulting offense level is less than level **14**, increase to level **14**.

(c) Cross Reference

(1) If the offense involved arson, or property damage by the use of any explosive, explosive material, or destructive device, apply §2K1.4 (Arson; Property Damage by Use of Explosives), if the resulting offense level is greater than that determined above.

Commentary

Statutory Provisions: 16 U.S.C. §§ 470aaa–5, 470ee, 668(a), 707(b); 18 U.S.C. §§ 541–546, 554, 641, 661–662, 666, 668, 1163, 1168, 1170, 1361, 1369, 2232, 2314–2315.

Application Notes:

1. **Definitions.**—For purposes of this guideline:

(A) "***Cultural heritage resource***" means any of the following:

(i) A historic property, as defined in 16 U.S.C. § 470w(5) (*see also* section 16(l) of 36 C.F.R. pt. 800).

(ii) A historic resource, as defined in 16 U.S.C. § 470w(5).

(iii) An archaeological resource, as defined in 16 U.S.C. § 470bb(1) (*see also* section 3(a) of 43 C.F.R. pt. 7; 36 C.F.R. pt. 296; 32 C.F.R. pt. 229; 18 C.F.R. pt. 1312).

(iv) A cultural item, as defined in section 2(3) of the Native American Graves Protection and Repatriation Act, 25 U.S.C. § 3001(3) (*see also* 43 C.F.R. § 10.2(d)).

(v) A commemorative work. "***Commemorative work***" (I) has the meaning given that term in 40 U.S.C. § 8902(a)(1); and (II) includes any national monument or national memorial.

(vi) An object of cultural heritage, as defined in 18 U.S.C. § 668(a)(2).

(vii) Designated ethnological material, as described in 19 U.S.C. §§ 2601(2)(ii), 2601(7), and 2604.

(B) "***Paleontological resource***" has the meaning given such term in 16 U.S.C. § 470aaa.

2. **Value of the Resource Under Subsection (b)(1).**—This application note applies to the determination of the value of the resource under subsection (b)(1).

(A) **General Rule.**—For purposes of subsection (b)(1), the value of the resource shall include, as applicable to the particular resource involved, the following:

(i) The archaeological value. (Archaeological value shall be included in the case of any resource that is an archaeological resource.)

(ii) The commercial value.

(iii) The cost of restoration and repair.
(B) **Estimation of Value.**—For purposes of subsection (b)(1), the court need only make a reasonable estimate of the value of the resource based on available information.
(C) **Definitions.**—For purposes of this application note:
(i) "***Archaeological value***" of a resource means the cost of the retrieval of the scientific information which would have been obtainable prior to the offense, including the cost of preparing a research design, conducting field work, conducting laboratory analysis, and preparing reports, as would be necessary to realize the information potential. (*See, e.g.*, 43 C.F.R. § 7.14(a); 36 C.F.R. § 296.14(a); 32 C.F.R. § 229.14(a); 18 C.F.R. § 1312.14(a).)
(ii) "***Commercial value***" of a resource means the fair market value of the resource at the time of the offense. (*See, e.g.*, 43 C.F.R. § 7.14(b); 36 C.F.R. § 296.14(b); 32 C.F.R. § 229.14(b); 18 C.F.R. § 1312.14(b).)
(iii) "***Cost of restoration and repair***" includes all actual and projected costs of curation, disposition, and appropriate reburial of, and consultation with respect to, the resource; and any other actual and projected costs to complete restoration and repair of the resource, including (I) its reconstruction and stabilization; (II) reconstruction and stabilization of ground contour and surface; (III) research necessary to conduct reconstruction and stabilization; (IV) the construction of physical barriers and other protective devices; (V) examination and analysis of the resource as part of efforts to salvage remaining information about the resource; and (VI) preparation of reports. (*See, e.g.*, 43 C.F.R. § 7.14(c); 36 C.F.R. § 296.14(c); 32 C.F.R. § 229.14(c); 18 C.F.R. § 1312.14(c).)
(D) **Determination of Value in Cases Involving a Variety of Resources.**—In a case involving a variety of resources, the value of the resources is the sum of all calculations made for those resources under this application note.
3. **Enhancement in Subsection (b)(2).**—For purposes of subsection (b)(2):
(A) "***Museum***" has the meaning given that term in 18 U.S.C. § 668(a)(1) except that the museum may be situated outside the United States.
(B) "***National cemetery***" and "***veterans' memorial***" have the meaning given those terms in Application Note 1 of the Commentary to §2B1.1 (Theft, Property Destruction, and Fraud).
(C) "***National Historic Landmark***" means a property designated as such pursuant to 16 U.S.C. § 470a(a)(1)(B).

(D) "***National marine sanctuary***" means a national marine sanctuary designated as such by the Secretary of Commerce pursuant to 16 U.S.C. § 1433.
(E) "***National monument or national memorial***" means any national monument or national memorial established as such by Act of Congress or by proclamation pursuant to the Antiquities Act of 1906 (16 U.S.C. § 431).
(F) "***National park system***" has the meaning given that term in 16 U.S.C. § 1c(a).
(G) "***World Heritage List***" means the World Heritage List maintained by the World Heritage Committee of the United Nations Educational, Scientific, and Cultural Organization in accordance with the Convention Concerning the Protection of the World Cultural and Natural Heritage.
4. **Enhancement in Subsection (b)(3).**—For purposes of subsection (b)(3):
(A) "***Cultural patrimony***" has the meaning given that term in 25 U.S.C. § 3001(3)(D) (*see also* 43 C.F.R. 10.2(d)(4)).
(B) "***Cultural property***" has the meaning given that term in 19 U.S.C. § 2601(6).
(C) "***Designated archaeological or ethnological material***" means archaeological or ethnological material described in 19 U.S.C. § 2601(7) (*see also* 19 U.S.C. §§ 2601(2) and 2604).
(D) "***Funerary object***" means an object that, as a part of the death rite or ceremony of a culture, was placed intentionally, at the time of death or later, with or near human

remains.
(E) "***Human remains***" (i) means the physical remains of the body of a human; and (ii) does not include remains that reasonably may be determined to have been freely disposed of or naturally shed by the human from whose body the remains were obtained, such as hair made into ropes or nets.
(F) "***Pre-Columbian monumental or architectural sculpture or mural***" has the meaning given that term in 19 U.S.C. § 2095(3).
(G) "***Sacred object***" has the meaning given that term in 25 U.S.C. § 3001(3)(C) (*see also* 43 C.F.R. § 10.2(d)(3)).
5. **Pecuniary Gain and Commercial Purpose Enhancement Under Subsection (b)(4).—**
(A) **"For Pecuniary Gain".**—For purposes of subsection (b)(4), "***for pecuniary gain***" means for receipt of, or in anticipation of receipt of, anything of value, whether monetary or in goods or services. Therefore, offenses committed for pecuniary gain include both monetary and barter transactions, as well as activities designed to increase gross revenue.
(B) **Commercial Purpose.**—The acquisition of resources for display to the public, whether for a fee or donation and whether by an individual or an organization, including a governmental entity, a private non-profit organization, or a private forprofit organization, shall be considered to involve a "commercial purpose" for purposes of subsection (b)(4).

6. **Pattern of Misconduct Enhancement Under Subsection (b)(5).—**
(A) **Definition.**—For purposes of subsection (b)(5), "***pattern of misconduct involving cultural heritage resources or paleontological resources***" means two or more separate instances of offense conduct involving a resource that did not occur during the course of the offense (*i.e.*, that did not occur during the course of the instant offense of conviction and all relevant conduct under §1B1.3 (Relevant Conduct)). Offense conduct involving a resource may be considered for purposes of subsection (b)(5) regardless of whether the defendant was convicted of that conduct.
(B) **Computation of Criminal History Points.**—A conviction taken into account under subsection (b)(5) is not excluded from consideration of whether that conviction receives criminal history points pursuant to Chapter Four, Part A (Criminal History).
7. **Dangerous Weapons Enhancement Under Subsection (b)(6).**—For purposes of subsection (b)(6), "***brandished***" and "***dangerous weapon***" have the meaning given those terms in Application Note 1 of the Commentary to §1B1.1 (Application Instructions).
8. **Multiple Counts.**—For purposes of Chapter Three, Part D (Multiple Counts), multiple counts involving offenses covered by this guideline are grouped together under subsection (d) of §3D1.2 (Groups of Closely Related Counts). Multiple counts involving offenses covered by this guideline and offenses covered by other guidelines are not to be grouped under §3D1.2(d).
9. **Upward Departure Provision.**—There may be cases in which the offense level determined under this guideline substantially understates the seriousness of the offense. In such cases, an upward departure may be warranted. For example, an upward departure may be warranted if (A) in addition to cultural heritage resources or paleontological resources, the offense involved theft of, damage to, or destruction of, items that are not cultural heritage resources (such as an offense involving the theft from a national cemetery of lawnmowers and other administrative property in addition to historic gravemarkers or other cultural heritage resources) or paleontological resources; or (B) the offense involved a cultural heritage resource that has profound significance to cultural identity (*e.g.*, the Statue of Liberty or the Liberty Bell).

Historical Note

Effective November 1, 2002 (amendment 638). Amended effective November 1, 2006 (amendment 685); November 1, 2007 (amendment 700); November 1, 2010 (amendments 745 and 746); November 1, 2014 (amendment

781); November 1, 2015 (amendment 791).

§2B1.6. Aggravated Identity Theft

(a) If the defendant was convicted of violating 18 U.S.C. § 1028A, the guideline sentence is the term of imprisonment required by statute. Chapters Three (Adjustments) and Four (Criminal History and Criminal Livelihood) shall not apply to that count of conviction.

Commentary

Statutory Provision: 18 U.S.C. § 1028A. For additional statutory provision(s), *see* Appendix A (Statutory Index).

Application Notes:

1. **Imposition of Sentence.—**

(A) **In General.**—Section 1028A of title 18, United State Code, provides a mandatory term of imprisonment. Accordingly, the guideline sentence for a defendant convicted under 18 U.S.C. § 1028A is the term required by that statute. Except as provided in subdivision (B), 18 U.S.C. § 1028A also requires a term of imprisonment imposed under this section to run consecutively to any other term of imprisonment.

(B) **Multiple Convictions Under Section 1028A.**—Section 1028A(b)(4) of title 18, United State Code, provides that in the case of multiple convictions under 18 U.S.C. § 1028A, the terms of imprisonment imposed on such counts may, in the discretion of the court, run concurrently, in whole or in part, with each other. *See* the Commentary to §5G1.2 (Sentencing on Multiple Counts of Conviction) for guidance regarding imposition of sentence on multiple counts of 18 U.S.C. § 1028A.

2. **Inapplicability of Chapter Two Enhancement.**—If a sentence under this guideline is imposed in conjunction with a sentence for an underlying offense, do not apply any specific offense characteristic for the transfer, possession, or use of a means of identification when determining the sentence for the underlying offense. A sentence under this guideline accounts for this factor for the underlying offense of conviction, including any such enhancement that would apply based on conduct for which the defendant is accountable under §1B1.3 (Relevant Conduct). "***Means of identification***" has the meaning given that term in 18 U.S.C. § 1028(d)(7).

3. **Inapplicability of Chapters Three and Four.**—Do not apply Chapters Three (Adjustments) and Four (Criminal History and Criminal Livelihood) to any offense sentenced under this guideline. Such offenses are excluded from application of those chapters because the guideline sentence for each offense is determined only by the relevant statute. *See* §§3D1.1 (Procedure for Determining Offense Level on Multiple Counts) and 5G1.2.

Historical Note

Effective November 1, 2005 (amendment 677).

* * * * *

2. BURGLARY AND TRESPASS

§2B2.1. Burglary of a Residence or a Structure Other than a Residence

(a) Base Offense Level:

(1) **17**, if a residence; or

(2) **12**, if a structure other than a residence.

(b) Specific Offense Characteristics

(1) If the offense involved more than minimal planning, increase by **2** levels.

(2) If the loss exceeded $5,000, increase the offense level as follows:

LOSS (APPLY THE GREATEST) INCREASE IN LEVEL

(A) $5,000 or less no increase
(B) More than $5,000 add **1**
(C) More than $20,000 add **2**
(D) More than $95,000 add **3**
(E) More than $500,000 add **4**
(F) More than $1,500,000 add **5**
(G) More than $3,000,000 add **6**
(H) More than $5,000,000 add **7**
(I) More than $9,500,000 add **8**.
(3) If a firearm, destructive device, or controlled substance was taken, or if the taking of such item was an object of the offense, increase by **1** level.
(4) If a dangerous weapon (including a firearm) was possessed, increase by **2** levels.

Commentary

Statutory Provisions: 18 U.S.C. §§ 2113(a), 2115, 2117, 2118(b). For additional statutory provision(s), *see* Appendix A (Statutory Index).

Application Notes:

1. "***Firearm***," "***destructive device***," and "***dangerous weapon***" are defined in the Commentary to §1B1.1 (Application Instructions).
2. "***Loss***" means the value of the property taken, damaged, or destroyed.
3. Subsection (b)(4) does not apply to possession of a dangerous weapon (including a firearm) that was stolen during the course of the offense.
4. **More than Minimal Planning.**—"***More than minimal planning***" means more planning than is typical for commission of the offense in a simple form. "More than minimal planning" also exists if significant affirmative steps were taken to conceal the offense, other than conduct to which §3C1.1 (Obstructing or Impeding the Administration of Justice) applies. "More than minimal planning" shall be considered to be present in any case involving repeated acts over a period of time, unless it is clear that each instance was purely opportune. For example, checking the area to make sure no witnesses were present would not alone constitute more than minimal planning. By contrast, obtaining

building plans to plot a particular course of entry, or disabling an alarm system, would constitute more than minimal planning.

Background: The base offense level for residential burglary is higher than for other forms of burglary because of the increased risk of physical and psychological injury. Weapon possession, but not use, is a specific offense characteristic because use of a weapon (including to threaten) ordinarily would make the offense robbery. Weapon use would be a ground for upward departure.

Historical Note

Effective November 1, 1987. Amended effective January 15, 1988 (amendment 11); June 15, 1988 (amendment 12); November 1, 1989 (amendments 105 and 106); November 1, 1990 (amendments 315 and 361); November 1, 1993 (amendment 481); November 1, 2001 (amendment 617); November 1, 2014 (amendment 781); November 1, 2015 (amendment 791).

§2B2.2. [Deleted]

Historical Note

Section 2B2.2 (Burglary of Other Structures), effective November 1, 1987, amended effective June 15, 1988 (amendment 13), November 1, 1989 (amendment 107), and November 1, 1990 (amendments 315 and 361), was deleted by consolidation with §2B2.1 effective November 1, 1993 (amendment 481).

§2B2.3. Trespass

(a) Base Offense Level: **4**
(b) Specific Offense Characteristics
(1) (Apply the greater) If—

(A) the trespass occurred (i) at a secure government facility; (ii) at a nuclear energy facility; (iii) on a vessel or aircraft of the United States; (iv) in a secure area of an airport or a seaport; (v) at a residence; (vi) at Arlington National Cemetery or a cemetery under the control of the National Cemetery Administration; (vii) at any restricted building or grounds; or (viii) on a computer system used (I) to maintain or operate a critical infrastructure; or (II) by or for a government entity in furtherance of the administration of justice, national defense, or national security, increase by **2** levels; or

(B) the trespass occurred at the White House or its grounds, or the Vice President's official residence or its grounds, increase by **4** levels.

(2) If a dangerous weapon (including a firearm) was possessed, increase by **2** levels.

(3) If (A) the offense involved invasion of a protected computer; and (B) the loss resulting from the invasion (i) exceeded $2,500 but did not exceed $6,500, increase by **1** level; or (ii) exceeded $6,500, increase by the number of levels from the table in §2B1.1 (Theft, Property Destruction, and Fraud) corresponding to that amount.

(c) Cross Reference

(1) If the offense was committed with the intent to commit a felony offense, apply §2X1.1 (Attempt, Solicitation, or Conspiracy) in respect to that felony offense, if the resulting offense level is greater than that determined above.

Commentary

Statutory Provisions: 18 U.S.C. §§ 1030(a)(3), 1036, 2199; 38 U.S.C. § 2413; 42 U.S.C. § 7270b. For additional statutory provision(s), *see* Appendix A (Statutory Index).

Application Notes:

1. **Definitions.**—For purposes of this guideline:

"***Airport***" has the meaning given that term in section 47102 of title 49, United States Code.

"***Critical infrastructure***" means systems and assets vital to national defense, national security, economic security, public health or safety, or any combination of those matters. A critical infrastructure may be publicly or privately owned. Examples of critical infrastructures include gas and oil production, storage, and delivery systems, water supply systems, telecommunications networks, electrical power delivery systems, financing and banking systems, emergency services (including medical, police, fire, and rescue services), transportation systems and services (including highways, mass transit, airlines, and airports), and government operations that provide essential services to the public.

"***Felony offense***" means any offense (federal, state, or local) punishable by imprisonment for a term exceeding one year, whether or not a criminal charge was brought or a conviction was obtained.

"***Firearm***" and "***dangerous weapon***" are defined in the Commentary to §1B1.1 (Application Instructions).

"***Government entity***" has the meaning given that term in 18 U.S.C. § 1030(e)(9).

"***Protected computer***" means a computer described in 18 U.S.C. § 1030(e)(2)(A) or (B).

"***Restricted building or grounds***" has the meaning given that term in 18 U.S.C. § 1752.
"***Seaport***" has the meaning given that term in 18 U.S.C. § 26.

2. **Application of Subsection (b)(3).**—Valuation of loss is discussed in the Commentary to §2B1.1 (Theft, Property Destruction, and Fraud).

Background: Most trespasses punishable under federal law involve federal lands or property. The trespass section provides an enhancement for offenses involving trespass on secure government installations (such as nuclear facilities) and other locations (such as airports and seaports) to protect a significant federal interest. Additionally, an enhancement is provided for trespass at a residence.

Historical Note

Effective November 1, 1987. Amended effective November 1, 1989 (amendments 108 and 109); November 1, 1997 (amendment 551); November 1, 2001 (amendment 617); November 1, 2002 (amendment 637); November 1, 2003 (amendment 654); November 1, 2007 (amendments 699 and 703); November 1, 2013 (amendment 777); November 1, 2015 (amendment 791).

* * * * *

3. ROBBERY, EXTORTION, AND BLACKMAIL

§2B3.1. Robbery

(a) Base Offense Level: **20**

(b) Specific Offense Characteristics

(1) If the property of a financial institution or post office was taken, or if the taking of such property was an object of the offense, increase by **2** levels.

(2) (A) If a firearm was discharged, increase by **7** levels; (B) if a firearm was otherwise used, increase by **6** levels; (C) if a firearm was brandished or possessed, increase by **5** levels; (D) if a dangerous weapon was otherwise used, increase by **4** levels; (E) if a dangerous weapon was brandished or possessed, increase by **3** levels; or (F) if a threat of death was made, increase by **2** levels.

(3) If any victim sustained bodily injury, increase the offense level according to the seriousness of the injury:

Degree of Bodily Injury	Increase in Level
(A) Bodily Injury	add **2**
(B) Serious Bodily Injury	add **4**
(C) Permanent or Life-Threatening Bodily Injury	add **6**
(D) If the degree of injury is between that specified in subdivisions (A) and (B),	add **3** levels; or
(E) If the degree of injury is between that specified in subdivisions (B) and (C),	add **5** levels.

Provided, however, that the cumulative adjustments from (2) and (3) shall not exceed **11** levels.

(4) (A) If any person was abducted to facilitate commission of the offense or to facilitate escape, increase by **4** levels; or (B) if any person was physically restrained to facilitate commission of the offense or to facilitate escape, increase by **2** levels.

(5) If the offense involved carjacking, increase by **2** levels.
(6) If a firearm, destructive device, or controlled substance was taken, or if the taking of such item was an object of the offense, increase by **1** level.
(7) If the loss exceeded $20,000, increase the offense level as follows:
LOSS (APPLY THE GREATEST) INCREASE IN LEVEL
(A) $20,000 or less no increase
(B) More than $20,000 add **1**
(C) More than $95,000 add **2**
(D) More than $500,000 add **3**
(E) More than $1,500,000 add **4**
(F) More than $3,000,000 add **5**
(G) More than $5,000,000 add **6**
(H) More than $9,500,000 add 7.
(c) Cross Reference
(1) If a victim was killed under circumstances that would constitute murder under 18 U.S.C. § 1111 had such killing taken place within the territorial or maritime jurisdiction of the United States, apply §2A1.1 (First Degree Murder).

Commentary

Statutory Provisions: 18 U.S.C. §§ 1951, 2113, 2114, 2118(a), 2119. For additional statutory provision(s), *see* Appendix A (Statutory Index).

Application Notes:

1. "***Firearm,***" "***destructive device,***" "***dangerous weapon,***" "***otherwise used,***" "***brandished,***" "***bodily injury,***" "***serious bodily injury,***" "***permanent or life-threatening bodily injury,***" "***abducted,***" and "***physically restrained***" are defined in the Commentary to §1B1.1 (Application Instructions).
"***Carjacking***" means the taking or attempted taking of a motor vehicle from the person or presence of another by force and violence or by intimidation.

2. Consistent with Application Note 1(D)(ii) of §1B1.1 (Application Instructions), an object shall be considered to be a dangerous weapon for purposes of subsection (b)(2)(E) if (A) the object closely resembles an instrument capable of inflicting death or serious bodily injury; or (B) the defendant used the object in a manner that created the impression that the object was an instrument capable of inflicting death or serious bodily injury (*e.g.*, a defendant wrapped a hand in a towel during a bank robbery to create the appearance of a gun).
3. "***Loss***" means the value of the property taken, damaged, or destroyed.
4. The combined adjustments for weapon involvement and injury are limited to a maximum enhancement of 11 levels.
5. If the defendant intended to murder the victim, an upward departure may be warranted; *see* §2A2.1 (Assault with Intent to Commit Murder; Attempted Murder).
6. "A threat of death," as used in subsection (b)(2)(F), may be in the form of an oral or written statement, act, gesture, or combination thereof. Accordingly, the defendant does not have to state expressly his intent to kill the victim in order for the enhancement to apply. For example, an oral or written demand using words such as "Give me the money or I will kill you", "Give me the money or I will pull the pin on the grenade I have in my pocket", "Give me the money or I will shoot you", "Give me your money or else (where the defendant draws his hand across his throat in a slashing motion)", or "Give me the money or you are dead" would constitute a threat of death. The court should consider that the intent of this provision is to provide an increased offense level for cases in which the

offender(s) engaged in conduct that would instill in a reasonable person, who is a victim of the offense, a fear of death.

Background: Possession or use of a weapon, physical injury, and unlawful restraint sometimes occur during a robbery. The guideline provides for a range of enhancements where these factors are present.

Although in pre-guidelines practice the amount of money taken in robbery cases affected sentence length, its importance was small compared to that of the other harm involved. Moreover, because of the relatively high base offense level for robbery, an increase of 1 or 2 levels brings about a considerable increase in sentence length in absolute terms. Accordingly, the gradations for property loss increase more slowly than for simple property offenses.

The guideline provides an enhancement for robberies where a victim was forced to accompany the defendant to another location, or was physically restrained by being tied, bound, or locked up.

Historical Note

Effective November 1, 1987. Amended effective June 15, 1988 (amendments 14 and 15); November 1, 1989 (amendments 110 and 111); November 1, 1990 (amendments 314, 315, and 361); November 1, 1991 (amendment 365); November 1, 1993 (amendment 483); November 1, 1997 (amendments 545 and 552); November 1, 2000 (amendment 601); November 1, 2001 (amendment 617); November 1, 2010 (amendment 746); November 1, 2015 (amendment 791).

§2B3.2. Extortion by Force or Threat of Injury or Serious Damage

(a) Base Offense Level: **18**

(b) Specific Offense Characteristics

(1) If the offense involved an express or implied threat of death, bodily injury, or kidnapping, increase by **2** levels.

(2) If the greater of the amount demanded or the loss to the victim exceeded $20,000, increase by the corresponding number of levels from the table in §2B3.1(b)(7).

(3) (A)(i) If a firearm was discharged, increase by **7** levels; (ii) if a firearm was otherwise used, increase by **6** levels; (iii) if a firearm was brandished or possessed, increase by **5** levels; (iv) if a dangerous weapon was otherwise used, increase by **4** levels; or (v) if a dangerous weapon was brandished or possessed, increase by **3** levels; or

(B) If (i) the offense involved preparation to carry out a threat of (I) death; (II) serious bodily injury; (III) kidnapping; (IV) product tampering; or (V) damage to a computer system used to maintain or operate a critical infrastructure, or by or for a government entity in furtherance of the administration of justice, national defense, or national security; or (ii) the participant(s) otherwise demonstrated the ability to carry out a threat described in any of subdivisions (i)(I) through (i)(V), increase by **3** levels.

(4) If any victim sustained bodily injury, increase the offense level according to the seriousness of the injury:

Degree of Bodily Injury	Increase in Level
(A) Bodily Injury	add **2**
(B) Serious Bodily Injury	add **4**
(C) Permanent or Life-Threatening Bodily Injury	add **6**

(D) If the degree of injury is between that
specified in subdivisions (A) and (B), add **3** levels; or
(E) If the degree of injury is between that
specified in subdivisions (B) and (C), add **5** levels.
Provided, however, that the cumulative adjustments from (3)
and (4) shall not exceed **11** levels.

§2B3.2

(5) (A) If any person was abducted to facilitate commission of the offense or to facilitate escape, increase by **4** levels; or (B) if any person was physically restrained to facilitate commission of the offense or to facilitate escape, increase by **2** levels.
(c) Cross References
(1) If a victim was killed under circumstances that would constitute murder under 18 U.S.C. § 1111 had such killing taken place within the territorial or maritime jurisdiction of the United States, apply §2A1.1 (First Degree Murder).
(2) If the offense was tantamount to attempted murder, apply §2A2.1 (Assault with Intent to Commit Murder; Attempted Murder) if the resulting offense level is greater than that determined above.

Commentary

Statutory Provisions: 18 U.S.C. §§ 875(b), 876, 877, 1030(a)(7), 1951. For additional statutory provision(s), *see* Appendix A (Statutory Index).

Application Notes:

1. **Definitions.**—For purposes of this guideline:
"***Abducted***," "***bodily injury***," "***brandished***," "***dangerous weapon***," "***firearm***," "***otherwise used***," "***permanent or life-threatening bodily injury***," "***physically restrained***," and "***serious bodily injury***" have the meaning given those terms in Application Note 1 of the Commentary to §1B1.1 (Application Instructions).
"***Critical infrastructure***" means systems and assets vital to national defense, national security, economic security, public health or safety, or any combination of those matters. A critical infrastructure may be publicly or privately owned. Examples of critical infrastructures include gas and oil production, storage, and delivery systems, water supply systems, telecommunications networks, electrical power delivery systems, financing and banking systems, emergency services (including medical, police, fire, and rescue services), transportation systems and services (including highways, mass transit, airlines, and airports), and government operations that provide essential services to the public.
"***Government entity***" has the meaning given that term in 18 U.S.C. § 1030(e)(9).
2. This guideline applies if there was any threat, express or implied, that reasonably could be interpreted as one to injure a person or physically damage property, or any comparably serious threat, such as to drive an enterprise out of business. Even if the threat does not in itself imply violence, the possibility of violence or serious adverse consequences may be inferred from the circumstances of the threat or the reputation of the person making it. An ambiguous threat, such as "pay up or else," or a threat to cause labor problems, ordinarily should be treated under this section.

§2B3.3

3. Guidelines for bribery involving public officials are found in Part C, Offenses Involving Public Officials. "Extortion under color of official right," which usually is solicitation of a bribe by a public official, is covered under §2C1.1 unless there is use of force or a threat that qualifies for treatment under this section. Certain other extortion offenses are covered

under the provisions of Part E, Offenses Involving Criminal Enterprises and Racketeering.
4. The combined adjustments for weapon involvement and injury are limited to a maximum enhancement of 11 levels.
5. "***Loss to the victim***," as used in subsection (b)(2), means any demand paid plus any additional consequential loss from the offense (*e.g.*, the cost of defensive measures taken in direct response to the offense).
6. In certain cases, an extortionate demand may be accompanied by conduct that does not qualify as a display of a dangerous weapon under subsection (b)(3)(A)(v) but is nonetheless similar in seriousness, demonstrating the defendant's preparation or ability to carry out the threatened harm (*e.g.*, an extortionate demand containing a threat to tamper with a consumer product accompanied by a workable plan showing how the product's tamperresistant seals could be defeated, or a threat to kidnap a person accompanied by information showing study of that person's daily routine). Subsection (b)(3)(B) addresses such cases.
7. If the offense involved the threat of death or serious bodily injury to numerous victims (*e.g.*, in the case of a plan to derail a passenger train or poison consumer products), an upward departure may be warranted.
8. If the offense involved organized criminal activity, or a threat to a family member of the victim, an upward departure may be warranted.
Background: The Hobbs Act, 18 U.S.C. § 1951, prohibits extortion, attempted extortion, and conspiracy to extort. It provides for a maximum term of imprisonment of twenty years. 18 U.S.C. §§ 875–877 prohibit communication of extortionate demands through various means. The maximum penalty under these statutes varies from two to twenty years. Violations of 18 U.S.C. § 875 involve threats or demands transmitted by interstate commerce. Violations of 18 U.S.C. § 876 involve the use of the United States mails to communicate threats, while violations of 18 U.S.C. § 877 involve mailing threatening communications from foreign countries. This guideline also applies to offenses under 18 U.S.C. § 1030(a)(7) involving a threat to impair the operation of a "protected computer."

Historical Note

Effective November 1, 1987. Amended effective November 1, 1989 (amendments 112, 113, and 303); November 1, 1990 (amendment 316); November 1, 1991 (amendment 366); November 1, 1993 (amendment 479); November 1, 1997 (amendment 551); November 1, 1998 (amendment 586); November 1, 2000 (amendment 601); November 1, 2003 (amendment 654); November 1, 2015 (amendment 791).

§2B3.3. Blackmail and Similar Forms of Extortion

(a) Base Offense Level: **9**

(b) Specific Offense Characteristic

(1) If the greater of the amount obtained or demanded (A) exceeded $2,500 but did not exceed $6,500, increase by **1** level; or
(B) exceeded $6,500, increase by the number of levels from the table in §2B1.1 (Theft, Property Destruction, and Fraud) corresponding to that amount.

(c) Cross References

(1) If the offense involved extortion under color of official right, apply §2C1.1 (Offering, Giving, Soliciting, or Receiving a Bribe; Extortion Under Color of Official Right; Fraud Involving the Deprivation of the Intangible Right to Honest Services of Public Officials; Conspiracy to Defraud by Interference with Governmental Functions).

(2) If the offense involved extortion by force or threat of injury or serious damage, apply §2B3.2 (Extortion by Force or Threat of Injury or Serious Damage).

Commentary

Statutory Provisions: 18 U.S.C. §§ 873, 875–877, 1951. For additional statutory provision(s), *see* Appendix A (Statutory Index).

Application Note:

1. This section applies only to blackmail and similar forms of extortion where there clearly is no threat of violence to person or property. "***Blackmail***" (18 U.S.C. § 873) is defined as a threat to disclose a violation of United States law unless money or some other item of value is given.

Background: Under 18 U.S.C. § 873, the maximum term of imprisonment authorized for blackmail is one year. Extortionate threats to injure a reputation, or other threats that are less serious than those covered by §2B3.2, may also be prosecuted under 18 U.S.C. §§ 875–877, which carry higher maximum sentences.

Historical Note

Effective November 1, 1987. Amended effective November 1, 1989 (amendment 114); November 1, 1993 (amendment 479); November 1, 2001 (amendment 617); November 1, 2005 (amendment 679); November 1, 2015 (amendment 791).

* * * * *

4. COMMERCIAL BRIBERY AND KICKBACKS

§2B4.1. Bribery in Procurement of Bank Loan and Other Commercial Bribery

(a) Base Offense Level: **8**

(b) Specific Offense Characteristics

(1) If the greater of the value of the bribe or the improper benefit to be conferred (A) exceeded $2,500 but did not exceed $6,500, increase by **1** level; or (B) exceeded $6,500, increase by the number of levels from the table in §2B1.1 (Theft, Property Destruction, and Fraud) corresponding to that amount.

(2) (Apply the greater) If—

(A) the defendant derived more than $1,000,000 in gross receipts from one or more financial institutions as a result of the offense, increase by **2** levels; or

(B) the offense substantially jeopardized the safety and soundness of a financial institution, increase by **4** levels.

If the resulting offense level determined under subdivision (A) or (B) is less than level **24**, increase to level **24**.

(c) Special Instruction for Fines — Organizations

(1) In lieu of the pecuniary loss under subsection (a)(3) of §8C2.4 (Base Fine), use the greatest of: (A) the value of the unlawful payment; (B) the value of the benefit received or to be received in return for the unlawful payment; or (C) the consequential damages resulting from the unlawful payment.

Commentary

Statutory Provisions: 18 U.S.C. §§ 215, 224, 225; 26 U.S.C. §§ 9012(e), 9042(d); 41 U.S.C. §§ 8702, 8707; 42 U.S.C. §§ 1395nn(b)(1), (2), 1396h(b)(1),(2); 49 U.S.C. § 11902. For additional statutory provision(s), *see* Appendix A (Statutory Index).

Application Notes:

1. This guideline covers commercial bribery offenses and kickbacks that do not involve officials of federal, state, or local government, foreign governments, or public international organizations. *See* Part C, Offenses Involving Public Officials, if any such officials are involved.

2. The "***value of the improper benefit to be conferred***" refers to the value of the action to be taken or effected in return for the bribe. *See* Commentary to §2C1.1 (Offering, Giving, Soliciting, or Receiving a Bribe; Extortion Under Color of Official Right; Fraud Involving the Deprivation of the Intangible Right to Honest Services of Public Officials; Conspiracy to Defraud by Interference with Governmental Functions).
3. "***Financial institution,***" as used in this guideline, is defined to include any institution described in 18 U.S.C. §§ 20, 656, 657, 1005–1007, and 1014; any state or foreign bank, trust company, credit union, insurance company, investment company, mutual fund, savings (building and loan) association, union or employee pension fund; any health, medical or hospital insurance association; brokers and dealers registered, or required to be registered, with the Securities and Exchange Commission; futures commodity merchants and commodity pool operators registered, or required to be registered, with the Commodity Futures Trading Commission; and any similar entity, whether or not insured by the federal government. "Union or employee pension fund" and "any health, medical, or hospital insurance association," as used above, primarily include large pension funds that serve many individuals (*e.g.*, pension funds of large national and international organizations, unions, and corporations doing substantial interstate business), and associations that undertake to provide pension, disability, or other benefits (*e.g.*, medical or hospitalization insurance) to large numbers of persons.
4. **Gross Receipts Enhancement under Subsection (b)(2)(A).—**
(A) **In General.**—For purposes of subsection (b)(2)(A), the defendant shall be considered to have derived more than $1,000,000 in gross receipts if the gross receipts to the defendant individually, rather than to all participants, exceeded $1,000,000.
(B) **Definition.**—"***Gross receipts from the offense***" includes all property, real or personal, tangible or intangible, which is obtained directly or indirectly as a result of such offense. *See* 18 U.S.C. § 982(a)(4).
5. **Enhancement for Substantially Jeopardizing the Safety and Soundness of a Financial Institution under Subsection (b)(2)(B).**—For purposes of subsection (b)(2)(B), an offense shall be considered to have substantially jeopardized the safety and soundness of a financial institution if, as a consequence of the offense, the institution (A) became insolvent; (B) substantially reduced benefits to pensioners or insureds; (C) was unable on demand to refund fully any deposit, payment, or investment; (D) was so depleted of its assets as to be forced to merge with another institution in order to continue active operations; or (E) was placed in substantial jeopardy of any of subdivisions (A) through (D) of this note.
6. If the defendant is convicted under 18 U.S.C. § 225 (relating to a continuing financial crimes enterprise), the offense level is that applicable to the underlying series of offenses comprising the "continuing financial crimes enterprise."

Background: This guideline applies to violations of various federal bribery statutes that do not involve governmental officials. The base offense level is to be enhanced based upon the value of the unlawful payment or the value of the action to be taken or effected in return for the unlawful payment, whichever is greater.

One of the more commonly prosecuted offenses to which this guideline applies is offering or accepting a fee in connection with procurement of a loan from a financial institution in violation of 18 U.S.C. § 215.

As with non-commercial bribery, this guideline considers not only the amount of the bribe but also the value of the action received in return. Thus, for example, if a bank officer agreed to the offer of a $25,000 bribe to approve a $250,000 loan under terms for which the applicant would not otherwise qualify, the court, in increasing the offense level, would use the greater of the $25,000 bribe, and the savings in interest over the life of the loan compared with alternative loan terms. If a gambler paid a player $5,000 to shave points in a nationally televised basketball game, the value of the action to the gambler would be the amount that he and his confederates won or stood to gain. If that amount could not be estimated, the amount of the bribe would be used to determine the appropriate increase in offense level.

This guideline also applies to making prohibited payments to induce the award of subcontracts on federal projects for which the maximum term of imprisonment authorized is ten years. 41 U.S.C. §§ 8702, 8707. Violations of 42 U.S.C. § 1320a-7b involve the offer or acceptance of a payment to refer an individual for services or items paid for under a federal health care program (*e.g.*, the Medicare and Medicaid programs).

This guideline also applies to violations of law involving bribes and kickbacks in expenses incurred for a presidential nominating convention or presidential election campaign. These offenses are prohibited under 26 U.S.C. §§ 9012(e) and 9042(d), which apply to candidates for President and Vice President whose campaigns are eligible for federal matching funds.

This guideline also applies to violations of 18 U.S.C. § 224, sports bribery, as well as certain violations of the Interstate Commerce Act.

Subsection (b)(2)(A) implements, in a broader form, the instruction to the Commission in section 961(m) of Public Law 101–73.

Subsection (b)(2)(B) implements the instruction to the Commission in section 2507 of Public Law 101–647.

Historical
Note

Effective November 1, 1987. Amended effective November 1, 1990 (amendment 317); November 1, 1991 (amendments 364 and 422); November 1, 1992 (amendment 468); November 1, 1997 (amendment 553); November 1, 2001 (amendment 617); November 1, 2002 (amendments 639 and 646); November 1, 2004 (amendment 666); November 1, 2010 (amendment 746); November 1, 2015 (amendments 791 and 796).

* * * * *

5. COUNTERFEITING AND INFRINGEMENT OF COPYRIGHT OR TRADEMARK

Historical
Note

Effective November 1, 1987. Amended effective November 1, 1993 (amendment 481).

§2B5.1. Offenses Involving Counterfeit Bearer Obligations of the United States

(a) Base Offense Level: **9**

(b) Specific Offense Characteristics

(1) If the face value of the counterfeit items (A) exceeded $2,500 but did not exceed $6,500, increase by **1** level; or (B) exceeded $6,500, increase by the number of levels from the table in §2B1.1 (Theft, Property Destruction, and Fraud) corresponding to that amount.

(2) If the defendant (A) manufactured or produced any counterfeit obligation or security of the United States, or possessed or had custody of or control over a counterfeiting device or materials used for counterfeiting; or (B) controlled or possessed (i) counterfeiting paper similar to a distinctive paper; (ii) genuine United States currency paper from which the ink or other distinctive counterfeit deterrent has been completely or partially removed; or (iii) a feature or device essentially identical to a distinctive counterfeit deterrent, increase by **2** levels.

(3) If subsection (b)(2)(A) applies, and the offense level determined under that subsection is less than level **15**, increase to level **15**.

(4) If a dangerous weapon (including a firearm) was possessed in connection with the offense, increase by **2** levels. If the resulting offense level is less than level **13**, increase to level **13**.

(5) If any part of the offense was committed outside the United States, increase by **2** levels.

Commentary

Statutory Provisions: 18 U.S.C. §§ 470–474A, 476, 477, 500, 501, 1003. For additional statutory provision(s), *see* Appendix A (Statutory Index).

Application Notes:

1. **Definitions.**—For purposes of this guideline:

"***Counterfeit***" refers to an instrument that has been falsely made, manufactured, or altered. For example, an instrument that has been falsely made or manufactured in its entirety is "counterfeit", as is a genuine instrument that has been falsely altered (such as a genuine $5 bill that has been altered to appear to be a genuine $100 bill).

"***Distinctive counterfeit deterrent***" and "***distinctive paper***" have the meaning given those terms in 18 U.S.C. § 474A(c)(2) and (1), respectively.

"***United States***" means each of the fifty states, the District of Columbia, the Commonwealth of Puerto Rico, the United States Virgin Islands, Guam, the Northern Mariana Islands, and American Samoa.

2. **Applicability to Counterfeit Bearer Obligations of the United States.**—This guideline applies to counterfeiting of United States currency and coins, food stamps, postage stamps, treasury bills, bearer bonds and other items that generally could be described as bearer obligations of the United States, *i.e.*, that are not made out to a specific payee.

3. **Inapplicability to Certain Obviously Counterfeit Items.**—Subsection (b)(2)(A) does not apply to persons who produce items that are so obviously counterfeit that they are unlikely to be accepted even if subjected to only minimal scrutiny.

Background: Possession of counterfeiting devices to copy obligations (including securities) of the United States is treated as an aggravated form of counterfeiting because of the sophistication and planning involved in manufacturing counterfeit obligations and the public policy interest in protecting the integrity of government obligations. Similarly, an enhancement is provided for a defendant who produces, rather than merely passes, the counterfeit items.

Subsection (b)(4) implements, in a broader form, the instruction to the Commission in section 110512 of Public Law 103–322.

Historical Note

Effective November 1, 1987. Amended effective January 15, 1988 (amendment 16); November 1, 1989 (amendment 115); November 1, 1995 (amendment 513); November 1, 1997 (amendment 554); November 1, 1998 (amendment 587); November 1, 2000 (amendments 595 and 605); November 1, 2001 (amendments 617 and 618); November 1, 2009 (amendment 731); November 1, 2015 (amendment 791).

§2B5.2. [Deleted]

Historical Note

Section 2B5.2 (Forgery; Offenses Involving Altered or Counterfeit Instruments Other than Counterfeit Bearer Obligations of the United States), effective November 1, 1987, amended effective January 15, 1988 (amendment 17) and November 1, 1989 (amendment 116), was deleted by consolidation with §2F1.1 effective November 1, 1993 (amendment 481).

§2B5.3. Criminal Infringement of Copyright or Trademark

(a) Base Offense Level: **8**

(b) Specific Offense Characteristics

(1) If the infringement amount (A) exceeded $2,500 but did not exceed $6,500, increase by **1** level; or (B) exceeded $6,500, increase by the number of levels from the table in §2B1.1 (Theft, Property Destruction, and Fraud) corresponding to that amount.

(2) If the offense involved the display, performance, publication, reproduction, or distribution of a work being prepared for commercial distribution, increase by **2** levels.

(3) If the (A) offense involved the manufacture, importation, or uploading of infringing items; or (B) defendant was convicted under 17 U.S.C. §§ 1201 and 1204 for trafficking in circumvention devices, increase by **2** levels. If the resulting offense level is less than level **12**, increase to level **12.**

(4) If the offense was not committed for commercial advantage or private financial gain, decrease by **2** levels, but the resulting offense level shall be not less than level **8.**

(5) If the offense involved a counterfeit drug, increase by **2** levels.

(6) If the offense involved (A) the conscious or reckless risk of death or serious bodily injury; or (B) possession of a dangerous weapon (including a firearm) in connection with the offense, increase by **2** levels. If the resulting offense level is less than level **14**, increase to level **14.**

(7) If the offense involved a counterfeit military good or service the use, malfunction, or failure of which is likely to cause (A) the disclosure of classified information; (B) impairment of combat operations; or (C) other significant harm to (i) a combat operation, (ii) a member of the Armed Forces, or (iii) national security, increase by **2** levels. If the resulting offense level is less than level **14**, increase to level **14**.

Commentary

Statutory Provisions: 17 U.S.C. §§ 506(a), 1201, 1204; 18 U.S.C. §§ 2318–2320, 2511. For additional statutory provision(s), *see* Appendix A (Statutory Index).

Application Notes:

1. **Definitions.**—For purposes of this guideline:

"***Circumvention devices***" are devices used to perform the activity described in 17 U.S.C. §§ 1201(a)(3)(A) and 1201(b)(2)(A).

"***Commercial advantage or private financial gain***" means the receipt, or expectation of receipt, of anything of value, including other protected works.

"***Counterfeit drug***" has the meaning given that term in 18 U.S.C. § 2320(f)(6).

"***Counterfeit military good or service***" has the meaning given that term in 18 U.S.C. § 2320(f)(4).

"***Infringed item***" means the copyrighted or trademarked item with respect to which the crime against intellectual property was committed.

"***Infringing item***" means the item that violates the copyright or trademark laws.

"***Uploading***" means making an infringing item available on the Internet or a similar electronic bulletin board with the intent to enable other persons to (A) download or otherwise copy the infringing item; or (B) have access to the infringing item, including by storing the infringing item as an openly shared file. "Uploading" does not include merely downloading or installing an infringing item on a hard drive on a defendant's personal computer unless the infringing item is an openly shared file.

"***Work being prepared for commercial distribution***" has the meaning given that term in 17 U.S.C. § 506(a)(3).

2. **Determination of Infringement Amount.**—This note applies to the determination of the infringement amount for purposes of subsection (b)(1).

(A) **Use of Retail Value of Infringed Item.**—The infringement amount is the retail value of the infringed item, multiplied by the number of infringing items, in a case involving any of the following:

(i) The infringing item (I) is, or appears to a reasonably informed purchaser to

be, identical or substantially equivalent to the infringed item; or (II) is a digital or electronic reproduction of the infringed item.
(ii) The retail price of the infringing item is not less than 75% of the retail price of the infringed item.
(iii) The retail value of the infringing item is difficult or impossible to determine without unduly complicating or prolonging the sentencing proceeding.
(iv) The offense involves the illegal interception of a satellite cable transmission in violation of 18 U.S.C. § 2511. (In a case involving such an offense, the "retail value of the infringed item" is the price the user of the transmission would have paid to lawfully receive that transmission, and the "infringed item" is the satellite transmission rather than the intercepting device.)
(v) The retail value of the infringed item provides a more accurate assessment of the pecuniary harm to the copyright or trademark owner than does the retail value of the infringing item.
(vi) The offense involves the display, performance, publication, reproduction, or distribution of a work being prepared for commercial distribution. In a case involving such an offense, the "retail value of the infringed item" is the value of that item upon its initial commercial distribution.
(vii) A case under 18 U.S.C. § 2318 or § 2320 that involves a counterfeit label, patch, sticker, wrapper, badge, emblem, medallion, charm, box, container, can, case, hangtag, documentation, or packaging of any type or nature (I) that has not been affixed to, or does not enclose or accompany a good or service; and (II) which, had it been so used, would appear to a reasonably informed purchaser to be affixed to, enclosing or accompanying an identifiable, genuine good or service. In such a case, the "infringed item" is the identifiable, genuine good or service.
(viii) A case under 17 U.S.C. §§ 1201 and 1204 in which the defendant used a circumvention device. In such an offense, the "retail value of the infringed item"

is the price the user would have paid to access lawfully the copyrighted work, and the "infringed item" is the accessed work.
(B) **Use of Retail Value of Infringing Item.**—The infringement amount is the retail value of the infringing item, multiplied by the number of infringing items, in any case not covered by subdivision (A) of this Application Note, including a case involving the unlawful recording of a musical performance in violation of 18 U.S.C. § 2319A.
(C) **Retail Value Defined.**—For purposes of this Application Note, the "***retail value***" of an infringed item or an infringing item is the retail price of that item in the market in which it is sold.
(D) **Determination of Infringement Amount in Cases Involving a Variety of Infringing Items.**—In a case involving a variety of infringing items, the infringement amount is the sum of all calculations made for those items under subdivisions (A) and (B) of this Application Note. For example, if the defendant sold both counterfeit videotapes that are identical in quality to the infringed videotapes and obviously inferior counterfeit handbags, the infringement amount, for purposes of subsection (b)(1), is the sum of the infringement amount calculated with respect to the counterfeit videotapes under subdivision (A)(i) (*i.e.*, the quantity of the infringing videotapes multiplied by the retail value of the infringed videotapes) and the infringement amount calculated with respect to the counterfeit handbags under subdivision (B) (*i.e.*, the quantity of the infringing handbags multiplied by the retail value of the infringing handbags).
(E) **Indeterminate Number of Infringing Items.**—In a case in which the court cannot determine the number of infringing items, the court need only make a reasonable estimate of the infringement amount using any relevant information, including

financial records.

3. **Application of Subsection (b)(7).**—In subsection (b)(7), "***other significant harm to a member of the Armed Forces***" means significant harm other than serious bodily injury or death. In a case in which the offense involved a counterfeit military good or service the use, malfunction, or failure of which is likely to cause serious bodily injury or death, subsection (b)(6)(A) (conscious or reckless risk of serious bodily injury or death) would apply.

4. **Application of §3B1.3.**—If the defendant de-encrypted or otherwise circumvented a technological security measure to gain initial access to an infringed item, an adjustment under §3B1.3 (Abuse of Position of Trust or Use of Special Skill) may apply.

5. **Departure Considerations.**—If the offense level determined under this guideline substantially understates or overstates the seriousness of the offense, a departure may be warranted. The following is a non-exhaustive list of factors that the court may consider in determining whether a departure may be warranted:

(A) The offense involved substantial harm to the reputation of the copyright or trademark owner.

(B) The offense was committed in connection with, or in furtherance of, the criminal activities of a national, or international, organized criminal enterprise.

(C) The method used to calculate the infringement amount is based upon a formula or extrapolation that results in an estimated amount that may substantially exceed the actual pecuniary harm to the copyright or trademark owner.

(D) The offense resulted in death or serious bodily injury.

Background: This guideline treats copyright and trademark violations much like theft and fraud. Similar to the sentences for theft and fraud offenses, the sentences for defendants convicted of intellectual property offenses should reflect the nature and magnitude of the pecuniary harm caused by their crimes. Accordingly, similar to the loss enhancement in the theft and fraud guideline, the infringement amount in subsection (b)(1) serves as a principal factor in determining the offense level for intellectual property offenses.

Subsection (b)(1) implements section 2(g) of the No Electronic Theft (NET) Act of 1997, Pub. L. 105–147, by using the retail value of the infringed item, multiplied by the number of infringing items, to determine the pecuniary harm for cases in which use of the retail value of the infringed item is a reasonable estimate of that harm. For cases referred to in Application Note 2(B), the Commission determined that use of the retail value of the infringed item would overstate the pecuniary harm or otherwise be inappropriate. In these types of cases, use of the retail value of the infringing item, multiplied by the number of those items, is a more reasonable estimate of the resulting pecuniary harm.

Subsection (b)(5) implements the directive to the Commission in section 717 of Public Law 112–144.

Section 2511 of title 18, United States Code, as amended by the Electronic Communications Act of 1986, prohibits the interception of satellite transmission for purposes of direct or indirect commercial advantage or private financial gain. Such violations are similar to copyright offenses and are therefore covered by this guideline.

Historical
Note

Effective November 1, 1987. Amended effective November 1, 1993 (amendments 481 and 482); May 1, 2000 (amendment 590); November 1, 2000 (amendment 593); November 1, 2001 (amendment 617); October 24, 2005 (amendment 675); September 12, 2006 (amendment 682); November 1, 2006 (amendment 687); November 1, 2007 (amendment 704); November 1, 2009 (amendment 735); November 1, 2013 (amendment 773); November 1, 2015 (amendment 791).

§2B5.4. [Deleted]

Historical
Note

Section 2B5.4 (Criminal Infringement of Trademark), effective November 1, 1987, was deleted by consolidation with §2B5.3 effective November 1, 1993 (amendment 481).

* * * * *

6. MOTOR VEHICLE IDENTIFICATION NUMBERS

§2B6.1. Altering or Removing Motor Vehicle Identification Numbers, or Trafficking in Motor Vehicles or Parts with Altered or Obliterated Identification Numbers

(a) Base Offense Level: **8**

(b) Specific Offense Characteristics

(1) If the retail value of the motor vehicles or parts (A) exceeded $2,500 but did not exceed $6,500, increase by **1** level; or (B) exceeded $6,500, increase by the number of levels from the table in §2B1.1 (Theft, Property Destruction, and Fraud) corresponding to that amount.

(2) If the defendant was in the business of receiving and selling stolen property, increase by **2** levels.

(3) If the offense involved an organized scheme to steal vehicles or vehicle parts, or to receive stolen vehicles or vehicle parts, and the offense level as determined above is less than level **14**, increase to level **14**.

Commentary

Statutory Provisions: 18 U.S.C. §§ 511, 553(a)(2), 2321.

Application Notes:

1. Subsection (b)(3), referring to an "organized scheme to steal vehicles or vehicle parts, or to receive stolen vehicles or vehicle parts," provides an alternative minimum measure of loss in the case of an ongoing, sophisticated operation such as an auto theft ring or "chop shop." "***Vehicles***" refers to all forms of vehicles, including aircraft and watercraft. *See* Commentary to §2B1.1 (Theft, Property Destruction, and Fraud).

2. The term "***increase by the number of levels from the table in §2B1.1 (Theft, Property Destruction, and Fraud) corresponding to that amount***," as used in subsection (b)(1), refers to the number of levels corresponding to the retail value of the motor vehicles or parts involved.

Background: The statutes covered in this guideline prohibit altering or removing motor vehicle identification numbers, importing or exporting, or trafficking in motor vehicles or parts knowing that the identification numbers have been removed, altered, tampered with, or obliterated. Violations of 18 U.S.C. § 511 carry a maximum of five years imprisonment. Violations of 18 U.S.C. §§ 553(a)(2) and 2321 carry a maximum of ten years imprisonment.

Historical Note

Effective November 1, 1987. Amended effective November 1, 1989 (amendments 117–119); November 1, 1993 (amendment 482); November 1, 2001 (amendment 617); November 1, 2010 (amendment 746); November 1, 2015 (amendment 791).

PART C — OFFENSES INVOLVING PUBLIC OFFICIALS AND VIOLATIONS OF FEDERAL ELECTION CAMPAIGN LAWS

Historical Note

Effective November 1, 1987. Amended effective January 25, 2003 (amendment 648). Introductory Commentary to Part C, effective November 1, 1987, was deleted effective January 25, 2003 (amendment 648), and November 1, 2003 (amendment 656).

§2C1.1. Offering, Giving, Soliciting, or Receiving a Bribe; Extortion Under Color of Official Right; Fraud Involving the Deprivation of the Intangible Right to Honest Services of Public Officials; Conspiracy to

Defraud by Interference with Governmental Functions

(a) Base Offense Level:

(1) **14**, if the defendant was a public official; or

(2) **12**, otherwise.

(b) Specific Offense Characteristics

(1) If the offense involved more than one bribe or extortion, increase by **2** levels.

(2) If the value of the payment, the benefit received or to be received in return for the payment, the value of anything obtained or to be obtained by a public official or others acting with a public official, or the loss to the government from the offense, whichever is greatest, exceeded $6,500, increase by the number of levels from the table in §2B1.1 (Theft, Property Destruction, and Fraud) corresponding to that amount.

(3) If the offense involved an elected public official or any public official in a high-level decision-making or sensitive position, increase by **4** levels. If the resulting offense level is less than level **18**, increase to level **18**.

(4) If the defendant was a public official who facilitated (A) entry into the United States for a person, a vehicle, or cargo; (B) the obtaining of a passport or a document relating to naturalization, citizenship, legal entry, or legal resident status; or (C) the obtaining of a government identification document, increase by **2** levels.

§2C1.1

(c) Cross References

(1) If the offense was committed for the purpose of facilitating the commission of another criminal offense, apply the offense guideline applicable to a conspiracy to commit that other offense, if the resulting offense level is greater than that determined above.

(2) If the offense was committed for the purpose of concealing, or obstructing justice in respect to, another criminal offense, apply §2X3.1 (Accessory After the Fact) or §2J1.2 (Obstruction of Justice), as appropriate, in respect to that other offense, if the resulting offense level is greater than that determined above.

(3) If the offense involved a threat of physical injury or property destruction, apply §2B3.2 (Extortion by Force or Threat of Injury or Serious Damage), if the resulting offense level is greater than that determined above.

(d) Special Instruction for Fines — Organizations

(1) In lieu of the pecuniary loss under subsection (a)(3) of §8C2.4 (Base Fine), use the greatest of: (A) the value of the unlawful payment; (B) the value of the benefit received or to be received in return for the unlawful payment; or (C) the consequential damages resulting from the unlawful payment.

Commentary

Statutory Provisions: 15 U.S.C. §§ 78dd-1, 78dd-2, 78dd-3; 18 U.S.C. §§ 201(b)(1), (2), 226, 227, 371 (if conspiracy to defraud by interference with governmental functions), 872, 1341 (if the scheme or artifice to defraud was to deprive another of the intangible right of honest services of a public official), 1342 (if the scheme or artifice to defraud was to deprive another of the intangible right of honest services of a public official), 1343 (if the scheme or artifice to defraud was to deprive another of the intangible right of honest services of a public official), 1951. For additional statutory provision(s), *see* Appendix A (Statutory Index).

Application Notes:

1. **Definitions.**—For purposes of this guideline:

"***Government identification document***" means a document made or issued by or under the authority of the United States Government, a State, or a political subdivision of a State, which, when completed with information concerning a particular individual, is of a type intended or commonly accepted for the purpose of identification of individuals.

"***Payment***" means anything of value. A payment need not be monetary.

"***Public official***" shall be construed broadly and includes the following:

(A) "Public official" as defined in 18 U.S.C. § 201(a)(1).

(B) A member of a state or local legislature. "State" means a State of the United States, and any commonwealth, territory, or possession of the United States.

(C) An officer or employee or person acting for or on behalf of a state or local government, or any department, agency, or branch of government thereof, in any official function, under or by authority of such department, agency, or branch of government, or a juror in a state or local trial.

(D) Any person who has been selected to be a person described in subdivisions (A), (B), or (C), either before or after such person has qualified.

(E) An individual who, although not otherwise covered by subdivisions (A) through (D): (i) is in a position of public trust with official responsibility for carrying out a government program or policy; (ii) acts under color of law or official right; or (iii) participates so substantially in government operations as to possess de facto authority to make governmental decisions (*e.g.*, which may include a leader of a state or local political party who acts in the manner described in this subdivision).

2. **More than One Bribe or Extortion.**—Subsection (b)(1) provides an adjustment for offenses involving more than one incident of either bribery or extortion. Related payments that, in essence, constitute a single incident of bribery or extortion (*e.g.*, a number of installment payments for a single action) are to be treated as a single bribe or extortion, even if charged in separate counts.

In a case involving more than one incident of bribery or extortion, the applicable amounts under subsection (b)(2) (*i.e.*, the greatest of the value of the payment, the benefit received or to be received, the value of anything obtained or to be obtained by a public official or others acting with a public official, or the loss to the government) are determined separately for each incident and then added together.

3. **Application of Subsection (b)(2).**—"***Loss***", for purposes of subsection (b)(2), shall be determined in accordance with Application Note 3 of the Commentary to §2B1.1 (Theft, Property Destruction, and Fraud). The value of "***the benefit received or to be received***" means the net value of such benefit. **Examples:** (A) A government employee, in return for a $500 bribe, reduces the price of a piece of surplus property offered for sale by the government from $10,000 to $2,000; the value of the benefit received is $8,000. (B) A $150,000 contract on which $20,000 profit was made was awarded in return for a bribe; the value of the benefit received is $20,000. Do not deduct the value of the bribe itself in computing the value of the benefit received or to be received. In the preceding examples, therefore, the value of the benefit received would be the same regardless of the value of the bribe.

4. **Application of Subsection (b)(3).**—

(A) **Definition.**—"***High-level decision-making or sensitive position***" means a position characterized by a direct authority to make decisions for, or on behalf of, a government department, agency, or other government entity, or by a substantial influence over the decision-making process.

(B) **Examples.**—Examples of a public official in a high-level decision-making position include a prosecuting attorney, a judge, an agency administrator, and any other public official with a similar level of authority. Examples of a public official who holds a sensitive position include a juror, a law enforcement officer, an election official, and any other similarly situated individual.

5. **Application of Subsection (c).**—For the purposes of determining whether to apply the cross references in this section, the "***resulting offense level***" means the final offense level (*i.e.*, the offense level determined by taking into account both the Chapter Two offense level and any applicable adjustments from Chapter Three, Parts A–D).

See §1B1.5(d); Application Note 2 of the Commentary to §1B1.5 (Interpretation of References to Other Offense Guidelines).

6. **Inapplicability of §3B1.3.**—Do not apply §3B1.3 (Abuse of Position of Trust or Use of Special Skill).

7. **Upward Departure Provisions.**—In some cases the monetary value of the unlawful payment may not be known or may not adequately reflect the seriousness of the offense. For example, a small payment may be made in exchange for the falsification of inspection records for a shipment of defective parachutes or the destruction of evidence in a major narcotics case. In part, this issue is addressed by the enhancements in §2C1.1(b)(2) and (c)(1), (2), and (3). However, in cases in which the seriousness of the offense is still not adequately reflected, an upward departure is warranted. *See* Chapter Five, Part K (Departures).

In a case in which the court finds that the defendant's conduct was part of a systematic or pervasive corruption of a governmental function, process, or office that may cause loss of public confidence in government, an upward departure may be warranted. *See* §5K2.7 (Disruption of Governmental Function).

Background: This section applies to a person who offers or gives a bribe for a corrupt purpose, such as inducing a public official to participate in a fraud or to influence such individual's official actions, or to a public official who solicits or accepts such a bribe.

The object and nature of a bribe may vary widely from case to case. In some cases, the object may be commercial advantage (*e.g.*, preferential treatment in the award of a government contract). In others, the object may be issuance of a license to which the recipient is not entitled. In still others, the object may be the obstruction of justice. Consequently, a guideline for the offense must be designed to cover diverse situations.

In determining the net value of the benefit received or to be received, the value of the bribe is not deducted from the gross value of such benefit; the harm is the same regardless of value of the bribe paid to receive the benefit. In a case in which the value of the bribe exceeds the value of the benefit, or in which the value of the benefit cannot be determined, the value of the bribe is used because it is likely that the payer of such a bribe expected something in return that would be worth more than the value of the bribe. Moreover, for deterrence purposes, the punishment should be commensurate with the gain to the payer or the recipient of the bribe, whichever is greater.

Under §2C1.1(b)(3), if the payment was for the purpose of influencing an official act by certain officials, the offense level is increased by 4 levels.

Under §2C1.1(c)(1), if the payment was to facilitate the commission of another criminal offense, the guideline applicable to a conspiracy to commit that other offense will apply if the

result is greater than that determined above. For example, if a bribe was given to a law enforcement officer to allow the smuggling of a quantity of cocaine, the guideline for conspiracy to import cocaine would be applied if it resulted in a greater offense level.

Under §2C1.1(c)(2), if the payment was to conceal another criminal offense or obstruct justice in respect to another criminal offense, the guideline from §2X3.1 (Accessory After the Fact) or §2J1.2 (Obstruction of Justice), as appropriate, will apply if the result is greater than that determined above. For example, if a bribe was given for the purpose of concealing the offense of espionage, the guideline for accessory after the fact to espionage would be applied. Under §2C1.1(c)(3), if the offense involved forcible extortion, the guideline from §2B3.2 (Extortion by Force or Threat of Injury or Serious Damage) will apply if the result is greater than that determined above.

Section 2C1.1 also applies to offenses under 15 U.S.C. §§ 78dd-1, 78dd-2, and 78dd-3. Such offenses generally involve a payment to a foreign public official, candidate for public office, or agent or intermediary, with the intent to influence an official act or decision of a foreign government or political party. Typically, a case prosecuted under these provisions will involve an intent to influence governmental action.

Section 2C1.1 also applies to fraud involving the deprivation of the intangible right to honest services of government officials under 18 U.S.C. §§ 1341–1343 and conspiracy to defraud by interference with governmental functions under 18 U.S.C. § 371. Such fraud offenses typically involve an improper use of government influence that harms the operation of government in a manner similar to bribery offenses.

Offenses involving attempted bribery are frequently not completed because the offense is reported to authorities or an individual involved in the offense is acting in an undercover capacity. Failure to complete the offense does not lessen the defendant's culpability in attempting to use public position for personal gain. Therefore, solicitations and attempts are treated as equivalent to the underlying offense.

Historical Note

Effective November 1, 1987. Amended effective January 15, 1988 (amendment 18); November 1, 1989 (amendments 120–122); November 1, 1991 (amendments 367 and 422); November 1, 1997 (amendment 547); November 1, 2001 (amendment 617); November 1, 2002 (amendment 639); November 1, 2003 (amendment 653); November 1, 2004 (amendment 666); November 1, 2007 (amendment 699); November 1, 2008 (amendment 720); November 1, 2010 (amendment 746); November 1, 2015 (amendment 791).

§2C1.2. Offering, Giving, Soliciting, or Receiving a Gratuity

(a) Base Offense Level:

(1) **11**, if the defendant was a public official; or

(2) **9**, otherwise.

(b) Specific Offense Characteristics

(1) If the offense involved more than one gratuity, increase by **2** levels.

(2) If the value of the gratuity exceeded $6,500, increase by the number of levels from the table in §2B1.1 (Theft, Property Destruction, and Fraud) corresponding to that amount.

(3) If the offense involved an elected public official or any public official in a high-level decision-making or sensitive position, increase by **4** levels. If the resulting offense level is less than level **15**, increase to level **15**.

(4) If the defendant was a public official who facilitated (A) entry into the United States for a person, a vehicle, or cargo; (B) the obtaining of a passport or a document relating to naturalization, citizenship, legal entry, or legal resident status; or (C) the obtaining of a government identification document, increase by **2** levels.

(c) Special Instruction for Fines — Organizations

(1) In lieu of the pecuniary loss under subsection (a)(3) of §8C2.4

(Base Fine), use the value of the unlawful payment.

Commentary

Statutory Provisions: 18 U.S.C. §§ 201(c)(1), 212–214, 217. For additional statutory provision(s), *see* Appendix A (Statutory Index).

Application Notes:

1. **Definitions.**—For purposes of this guideline:

"***Government identification document***" means a document made or issued by or under the authority of the United States Government, a State, or a political subdivision of a State, which, when completed with information concerning a particular individual, is of a type intended or commonly accepted for the purpose of identification of individuals.

"***Public official***" shall be construed broadly and includes the following:

(A) "Public official" as defined in 18 U.S.C. § 201(a)(1).

(B) A member of a state or local legislature. "State" means a State of the United States, and any commonwealth, territory, or possession of the United States.

(C) An officer or employee or person acting for or on behalf of a state or local government, or any department, agency, or branch of government thereof, in any official function, under or by authority of such department, agency, or branch of government, or a juror.

(D) Any person who has been selected to be a person described in subdivisions (A), (B), or (C), either before or after such person has qualified.

(E) An individual who, although not otherwise covered by subdivisions (A) through (D): (i) is in a position of public trust with official responsibility for carrying out a government program or policy; (ii) acts under color of law or official right; or (iii) participates so substantially in government operations as to possess de facto authority to make governmental decisions (*e.g.*, which may include a leader of a state or local political party who acts in the manner described in this subdivision).

2. **Application of Subsection (b)(1).**—Related payments that, in essence, constitute a single gratuity (*e.g.*, separate payments for airfare and hotel for a single vacation trip) are to be treated as a single gratuity, even if charged in separate counts.

3. **Application of Subsection (b)(3).**—

(A) **Definition.**—"***High-level decision-making or sensitive position***" means a position characterized by a direct authority to make decisions for, or on behalf of, a government department, agency, or other government entity, or by a substantial influence over the decision-making process.

(B) **Examples.**—Examples of a public official in a high-level decision-making position include a prosecuting attorney, a judge, an agency administrator, a law enforcement officer, and any other public official with a similar level of authority. Examples of a public official who holds a sensitive position include a juror, a law enforcement officer, an election official, and any other similarly situated individual.

4. **Inapplicability of §3B1.3.**—Do not apply the adjustment in §3B1.3 (Abuse of Position of Trust or Use of Special Skill).

Background: This section applies to the offering, giving, soliciting, or receiving of a gratuity to a public official in respect to an official act. It also applies in cases involving (1) the offer to, or acceptance by, a bank examiner of a loan or gratuity; (2) the offer or receipt of anything of value for procuring a loan or discount of commercial bank paper from a Federal Reserve Bank; and (3) the acceptance of a fee or other consideration by a federal employee for adjusting or cancelling a farm debt.

Historical Note

Effective November 1, 1987. Amended effective November 1, 1989 (amendment 121); November 1, 1991 (amendment 422); November 1, 1995 (amendment 534); November 1, 2001 (amendment 617); November 1, 2004 (amendment 666); November 1, 2010 (amendment 746); November 1, 2015 (amendment 791).

§2C1.3. Conflict of Interest; Payment or Receipt of Unauthorized Compensation

(a) Base Offense Level: **6**

(b) Specific Offense Characteristic

(1) If the offense involved actual or planned harm to the government, increase by **4** levels.

(c) Cross Reference

(1) If the offense involved a bribe or gratuity, apply §2C1.1 (Offering, Giving, Soliciting, or Receiving a Bribe; Extortion Under Color of Official Right; Fraud Involving the Deprivation of the Intangible Right to Honest Services of Public Officials; Conspiracy to Defraud by Interference with Governmental Functions) or §2C1.2 (Offering, Giving, Soliciting, or Receiving a Gratuity), as appropriate, if the resulting offense level is greater than the offense level determined above.

Commentary

Statutory Provisions: 18 U.S.C. §§ 203, 205, 207, 208, 209, 1909; 40 U.S.C. § 14309(a), (b). For additional statutory provision(s), *see* Appendix A (Statutory Index).

Application Note:

1. **Abuse of Position of Trust.**—Do not apply the adjustment in §3B1.3 (Abuse of Position of Trust or Use of Special Skill).

Historical Note

Effective November 1, 1987. Amended effective November 1, 1995 (amendment 534); November 1, 2001 (amendment 619); November 1, 2003 (amendment 661); November 1, 2005 (amendment 679).

§2C1.4. [Deleted]

Historical Note

Section 2C1.4 (Payment or Receipt of Unauthorized Compensation), effective November 1, 1987, amended effective November 1, 1998 (amendment 588), was deleted by consolidation with §2C1.3 effective November 1, 2001 (amendment 619).

§2C1.5. Payments to Obtain Public Office

(a) Base Offense Level: **8**

Commentary

Statutory Provisions: 18 U.S.C. §§ 210, 211.

Application Note:

1. Do not apply the adjustment in §3B1.3 (Abuse of Position of Trust or Use of Special Skill).

Background: Under 18 U.S.C. § 210, it is unlawful to pay, offer, or promise anything of value to a person, firm, or corporation in consideration of procuring appointive office. Under

18 U.S.C. § 211, it is unlawful to solicit or accept anything of value in consideration of a promise of the use of influence in obtaining appointive federal office. Both offenses are misdemeanors for which the maximum term of imprisonment authorized by statute is one year.

Historical Note

Effective November 1, 1987.

§2C1.6. [Deleted]

Historical Note

Effective November 1, 1987. Amended effective November 1, 2001 (amendment 617); was deleted by consolidation with §2C1.2 effective November 1, 2004 (amendment 666).

§2C1.7. [Deleted]

Historical Note

Effective November 1, 1991 (amendment 368). Amended effective November 1, 1992 (amendment 468); November 1, 1997 (amendment 547); November 1, 2001 (amendment 617); November 1, 2003 (amendment

653); was deleted by consolidation with §2C1.1 effective November 1, 2004 (amendment 666).

§2C1.8. Making, Receiving, or Failing to Report a Contribution, Donation, or Expenditure in Violation of the Federal Election Campaign Act; Fraudulently Misrepresenting Campaign Authority; Soliciting or Receiving a Donation in Connection with an Election While on Certain Federal Property

(a) Base Offense Level: **8**

(b) Specific Offense Characteristics

(1) If the value of the illegal transactions exceeded $6,500, increase by the number of levels from the table in §2B1.1 (Theft, Property Destruction, and Fraud) corresponding to that amount.

(2) (Apply the greater) If the offense involved, directly or indirectly, an illegal transaction made by or received from—

(A) a foreign national, increase by **2** levels; or

(B) a government of a foreign country, increase by **4** levels.

(3) If (A) the offense involved the contribution, donation, solicitation, expenditure, disbursement, or receipt of governmental

funds; or (B) the defendant committed the offense for the purpose of obtaining a specific, identifiable non-monetary Federal benefit, increase by **2** levels.

(4) If the defendant engaged in 30 or more illegal transactions, increase by **2** levels.

(5) If the offense involved a contribution, donation, solicitation, or expenditure made or obtained through intimidation, threat of pecuniary or other harm, or coercion, increase by **4** levels.

(c) Cross Reference

(1) If the offense involved a bribe or gratuity, apply §2C1.1 (Offering, Giving, Soliciting, or Receiving a Bribe; Extortion Under Color of Official Right; Fraud Involving the Deprivation of the Intangible Right to Honest Services of Public Officials; Conspiracy to Defraud by Interference with Governmental Functions) or §2C1.2 (Offering, Giving, Soliciting, or Receiving a Gratuity), as appropriate, if the resulting offense level is greater than the offense level determined above.

Commentary

Statutory Provisions: 18 U.S.C. § 607; 52 U.S.C. §§ 30109(d), 30114, 30116, 30117, 30118, 30119, 30120, 30121, 30122, 30123, 30124(a), 30125, 30126. For additional provision(s), *see* Appendix A (Statutory Index).

Application Notes:

1. **Definitions.**—For purposes of this guideline:

"***Foreign national***" has the meaning given that term in section 319(b) of the Federal Election Campaign Act of 1971, 52 U.S.C. § 30121(b).

"***Government of a foreign country***" has the meaning given that term in section 1(e) of the Foreign Agents Registration Act of 1938 (22 U.S.C. § 611(e)).

"***Governmental funds***" means money, assets, or property, of the United States government, of a State government, or of a local government, including any branch, subdivision, department, agency, or other component of any such government. "State" means any of the fifty States, the District of Columbia, the Commonwealth of Puerto Rico, the United States Virgin Islands, Guam, the Northern Mariana Islands, or American Samoa. "Local government" means the government of a political subdivision of a State.

"***Illegal transaction***" means (A) any contribution, donation, solicitation, or expenditure of money or anything of value, or any other conduct, prohibited by the Federal Election Campaign Act of 1971, 52 U.S.C. § 30101 *et seq.*; (B) any contribution, donation, solicitation, or expenditure of money or anything of value made in excess of the amount of such contribution, donation, solicitation, or expenditure that may be made under such Act; and (C) in the case of a violation of 18 U.S.C. § 607, any solicitation or receipt of money

or anything of value under that section. The terms "***contribution***" and "***expenditure***" have the meaning given those terms in section 301(8) and (9) of the Federal Election Campaign Act of 1971 (52 U.S.C. § 30101(8) and (9)), respectively.

2. **Application of Subsection (b)(3)(B).**—Subsection (b)(3)(B) provides an enhancement for a defendant who commits the offense for the purpose of achieving a specific, identifiable non-monetary Federal benefit that does not rise to the level of a bribe or a gratuity. Subsection (b)(3)(B) is not intended to apply to offenses under this guideline in which the defendant's only motivation for commission of the offense is generally to achieve increased visibility with, or heightened access to, public officials. Rather, subsection (b)(3)(B) is intended to apply to defendants who commit the offense to obtain a specific, identifiable non-monetary Federal benefit, such as a Presidential pardon or information proprietary to the government.

3. **Application of Subsection (b)(4).**—Subsection (b)(4) shall apply if the defendant engaged in any combination of 30 or more illegal transactions during the course of the offense, whether or not the illegal transactions resulted in a conviction for such conduct.

4. **Departure Provision.**—In a case in which the defendant's conduct was part of a systematic or pervasive corruption of a governmental function, process, or office that may cause loss of public confidence in government, an upward departure may be warranted.

Historical Note

Effective January 25, 2003 (amendment 648). Amended effective November 1, 2003 (amendment 656); November 1, 2005 (amendment 679); November 1, 2015 (amendments 791 and 796).

PART D — OFFENSES INVOLVING DRUGS AND NARCOTERRORISM

Historical Note

Effective November 1, 1987. Amended effective November 1, 2007 (amendment 711).

1. UNLAWFUL MANUFACTURING, IMPORTING, EXPORTING, TRAFFICKING, OR POSSESSION; CONTINUING CRIMINAL ENTERPRISE

§2D1.1. Unlawful Manufacturing, Importing, Exporting, or Trafficking (Including Possession with Intent to Commit These Offenses); Attempt or Conspiracy

(a) Base Offense Level (Apply the greatest):

(1) **43**, if the defendant is convicted under 21 U.S.C. § 841(b)(1)(A), (b)(1)(B), or (b)(1)(C), or 21 U.S.C. § 960(b)(1), (b)(2), or (b)(3), and the offense of conviction establishes that death or serious bodily injury resulted from the use of the substance and that the defendant committed the offense after one or more prior convictions for a similar offense; or

(2) **38**, if the defendant is convicted under 21 U.S.C. § 841(b)(1)(A), (b)(1)(B), or (b)(1)(C), or 21 U.S.C. § 960(b)(1), (b)(2), or (b)(3), and the offense of conviction establishes that death or serious

bodily injury resulted from the use of the substance; or
(3) **30**, if the defendant is convicted under 21 U.S.C. § 841(b)(1)(E) or 21 U.S.C. § 960(b)(5), and the offense of conviction establishes that death or serious bodily injury resulted from the use of the substance and that the defendant committed the offense after one or more prior convictions for a similar offense; or
(4) **26**, if the defendant is convicted under 21 U.S.C. § 841(b)(1)(E) or 21 U.S.C. § 960(b)(5), and the offense of conviction establishes that death or serious bodily injury resulted from the use of the substance; or
(5) the offense level specified in the Drug Quantity Table set forth in subsection (c), except that if (A) the defendant receives an adjustment under §3B1.2 (Mitigating Role); and (B) the base offense level under subsection (c) is (i) level **32**, decrease by **2** levels; (ii) level **34** or level **36**, decrease by **3** levels; or (iii) level **38**, decrease by **4** levels. If the resulting offense level

is greater than level **32** and the defendant receives the **4**-level ("minimal participant") reduction in §3B1.2(a), decrease to level **32**.
(b) Specific Offense Characteristics
(1) If a dangerous weapon (including a firearm) was possessed, increase by **2** levels.
(2) If the defendant used violence, made a credible threat to use violence, or directed the use of violence, increase by **2** levels.
(3) If the defendant unlawfully imported or exported a controlled substance under circumstances in which (A) an aircraft other than a regularly scheduled commercial air carrier was used to import or export the controlled substance, (B) a submersible vessel or semi-submersible vessel as described in 18 U.S.C. § 2285 was used, or (C) the defendant acted as a pilot, copilot, captain, navigator, flight officer, or any other operation officer aboard any craft or vessel carrying a controlled substance, increase by **2** levels. If the resulting offense level is less than level **26**, increase to level **26**.
(4) If the object of the offense was the distribution of a controlled substance in a prison, correctional facility, or detention facility, increase by **2** levels.
(5) If (A) the offense involved the importation of amphetamine or methamphetamine or the manufacture of amphetamine or methamphetamine from listed chemicals that the defendant knew were imported unlawfully, and (B) the defendant is not subject to an adjustment under §3B1.2 (Mitigating Role), increase by **2** levels.
(6) If the defendant is convicted under 21 U.S.C. § 865, increase by **2** levels.
(7) If the defendant, or a person for whose conduct the defendant

is accountable under §1B1.3 (Relevant Conduct), distributed a controlled substance through mass-marketing by means of an interactive computer service, increase by **2** levels.

(8) If the offense involved the distribution of an anabolic steroid and a masking agent, increase by **2** levels.

(9) If the defendant distributed an anabolic steroid to an athlete, increase by **2** levels.

(10) If the defendant was convicted under 21 U.S.C. § 841(g)(1)(A), increase by **2** levels.

(11) If the defendant bribed, or attempted to bribe, a law enforcement officer to facilitate the commission of the offense, increase by **2** levels.

(12) If the defendant maintained a premises for the purpose of manufacturing or distributing a controlled substance, increase by **2** levels.

(13) (Apply the greatest):

(A) If the offense involved (i) an unlawful discharge, emission, or release into the environment of a hazardous or toxic substance; or (ii) the unlawful transportation, treatment, storage, or disposal of a hazardous waste, increase by **2** levels.

(B) If the defendant was convicted under 21 U.S.C. § 860a of distributing, or possessing with intent to distribute, methamphetamine on premises where a minor is present or resides, increase by **2** levels. If the resulting offense level is less than level **14**, increase to level **14**.

(C) If—

(i) the defendant was convicted under 21 U.S.C. § 860a of manufacturing, or possessing with intent to manufacture, methamphetamine on premises where a minor is present or resides; or

(ii) the offense involved the manufacture of amphetamine or methamphetamine and the offense created a substantial risk of harm to (I) human life other than a life described in subdivision (D); or (II) the environment, increase by **3** levels. If the resulting offense level is less than level **27**, increase to level **27**.

(D) If the offense (i) involved the manufacture of amphetamine or methamphetamine; and (ii) created a substantial risk of harm to the life of a minor or an incompetent, increase by **6** levels. If the resulting offense level is less than level **30**, increase to level **30**.

(14) If (A) the offense involved the cultivation of marihuana on state or federal land or while trespassing on tribal or private land;

and (B) the defendant receives an adjustment under §3B1.1 (Aggravating Role), increase by **2** levels.

(15) If the defendant receives an adjustment under §3B1.1 (Aggravating Role) and the offense involved 1 or more of the following factors:

(A) (i) the defendant used fear, impulse, friendship, affection, or some combination thereof to involve another individual in the illegal purchase, sale, transport, or storage of controlled substances, (ii) the individual received little or no compensation from the illegal purchase, sale, transport, or storage of controlled substances, and (iii) the individual had minimal knowledge of the scope and structure of the enterprise;

(B) the defendant, knowing that an individual was (i) less than 18 years of age, (ii) 65 or more years of age, (iii) pregnant, or (iv) unusually vulnerable due to physical or mental condition or otherwise particularly susceptible to the criminal conduct, distributed a controlled substance to that individual or involved that individual in the offense;

(C) the defendant was directly involved in the importation of a controlled substance;

(D) the defendant engaged in witness intimidation, tampered with or destroyed evidence, or otherwise obstructed justice in connection with the investigation or prosecution of the offense;

(E) the defendant committed the offense as part of a pattern of criminal conduct engaged in as a livelihood,

increase by **2** levels.

(16) If the defendant receives the **4**-level ("minimal participant") reduction in §3B1.2(a) and the offense involved all of the following factors:

(A) the defendant was motivated by an intimate or familial relationship or by threats or fear to commit the offense and was otherwise unlikely to commit such an offense;

(B) the defendant received no monetary compensation from the illegal purchase, sale, transport, or storage of controlled substances; and

(C) the defendant had minimal knowledge of the scope and structure of the enterprise,

decrease by **2** levels.

(17) If the defendant meets the criteria set forth in subdivisions (1)–(5) of subsection (a) of §5C1.2 (Limitation on Applicability of Statutory Minimum Sentences in Certain Cases), decrease by **2** levels.

[Subsection (c) (Drug Quantity Table) is set forth on the following pages.]

(d) Cross References

(1) If a victim was killed under circumstances that would constitute murder under 18 U.S.C. § 1111 had such killing taken place within the territorial or maritime jurisdiction of the United States, apply §2A1.1 (First Degree Murder) or §2A1.2 (Second Degree Murder), as appropriate, if the resulting offense level is greater than that determined under this guideline.
(2) If the defendant was convicted under 21 U.S.C. § 841(b)(7) (of distributing a controlled substance with intent to commit a crime of violence), apply §2X1.1 (Attempt, Solicitation, or Conspiracy) in respect to the crime of violence that the defendant committed, or attempted or intended to commit, if the resulting offense level is greater than that determined above.
(e) Special Instruction
(1) If (A) subsection (d)(2) does not apply; and (B) the defendant committed, or attempted to commit, a sexual offense against another individual by distributing, with or without that individual's knowledge, a controlled substance to that individual, an adjustment under §3A1.1(b)(1) shall apply.

(c) DRUG QUANTITY TABLE

CONTROLLED SUBSTANCES AND QUANTITY* BASE OFFENSE LEVEL

(1) • 90 KG or more of Heroin; **Level 38**

• 450 KG or more of Cocaine;

• 25.2 KG or more of Cocaine Base;

• 90 KG or more of PCP, or 9 KG or more of PCP (actual);

• 45 KG or more of Methamphetamine, or
4.5 KG or more of Methamphetamine (actual), or
4.5 KG or more of "Ice";

• 45 KG or more of Amphetamine, or
4.5 KG or more of Amphetamine (actual);

• 900 G or more of LSD;

• 36 KG or more of Fentanyl;

• 9 KG or more of a Fentanyl Analogue;

• 90,000 KG or more of Marihuana;

• 18,000 KG or more of Hashish;

• 1,800 KG or more of Hashish Oil;

• 90,000,000 units or more of Ketamine;

• 90,000,000 units or more of Schedule I or II Depressants;

• 5,625,000 units or more of Flunitrazepam.

(2) • At least 30 KG but less than 90 KG of Heroin; **Level 36**

• At least 150 KG but less than 450 KG of Cocaine;

• At least 8.4 KG but less than 25.2 KG of Cocaine Base;

- At least 30 KG but less than 90 KG of PCP, or
at least 3 KG but less than 9 KG of PCP (actual);
- At least 15 KG but less than 45 KG of Methamphetamine, or
at least 1.5 KG but less than 4.5 KG of Methamphetamine (actual), or
at least 1.5 KG but less than 4.5 KG of "Ice";
- At least 15 KG but less than 45 KG of Amphetamine, or
at least 1.5 KG but less than 4.5 KG of Amphetamine (actual);
- At least 300 G but less than 900 G of LSD;
- At least 12 KG but less than 36 KG of Fentanyl;
- At least 3 KG but less than 9 KG of a Fentanyl Analogue;
- At least 30,000 KG but less than 90,000 KG of Marihuana;
- At least 6,000 KG but less than 18,000 KG of Hashish;
- At least 600 KG but less than 1,800 KG of Hashish Oil;
- At least 30,000,000 units but less than 90,000,000 units of Ketamine;
- At least 30,000,000 units but less than 90,000,000 units of
Schedule I or II Depressants;
- At least 1,875,000 units but less than 5,625,000 units of Flunitrazepam.

(3) • At least 10 KG but less than 30 KG of Heroin; **Level 34**

- At least 50 KG but less than 150 KG of Cocaine;
- At least 2.8 KG but less than 8.4 KG of Cocaine Base;
- At least 10 KG but less than 30 KG of PCP, or
at least 1 KG but less than 3 KG of PCP (actual);
- At least 5 KG but less than 15 KG of Methamphetamine, or
at least 500 G but less than 1.5 KG of Methamphetamine (actual), or
at least 500 G but less than 1.5 KG of "Ice";
- At least 5 KG but less than 15 KG of Amphetamine, or

at least 500 G but less than 1.5 KG of Amphetamine (actual);

- At least 100 G but less than 300 G of LSD;
- At least 4 KG but less than 12 KG of Fentanyl;
- At least 1 KG but less than 3 KG of a Fentanyl Analogue;
- At least 10,000 KG but less than 30,000 KG of Marihuana;
- At least 2,000 KG but less than 6,000 KG of Hashish;
- At least 200 KG but less than 600 KG of Hashish Oil;
- At least 10,000,000 but less than 30,000,000 units of Ketamine;
- At least 10,000,000 but less than 30,000,000 units of Schedule I or II Depressants;
- At least 625,000 but less than 1,875,000 units of Flunitrazepam.

(4) • At least 3 KG but less than 10 KG of Heroin; **Level 32**

- At least 15 KG but less than 50 KG of Cocaine;

- At least 840 G but less than 2.8 KG of Cocaine Base;
- At least 3 KG but less than 10 KG of PCP, or
at least 300 G but less than 1 KG of PCP (actual);
- At least 1.5 KG but less than 5 KG of Methamphetamine, or
at least 150 G but less than 500 G of Methamphetamine (actual), or
at least 150 G but less than 500 G of "Ice";
- At least 1.5 KG but less than 5 KG of Amphetamine, or
at least 150 G but less than 500 G of Amphetamine (actual);
- At least 30 G but less than 100 G of LSD;
- At least 1.2 KG but less than 4 KG of Fentanyl;
- At least 300 G but less than 1 KG of a Fentanyl Analogue;
- At least 3,000 KG but less than 10,000 KG of Marihuana;
- At least 600 KG but less than 2,000 KG of Hashish;
- At least 60 KG but less than 200 KG of Hashish Oil;
- At least 3,000,000 but less than 10,000,000 units of Ketamine;
- At least 3,000,000 but less than 10,000,000 units of Schedule I or II Depressants;
- At least 187,500 but less than 625,000 units of Flunitrazepam.

(5) • At least 1 KG but less than 3 KG of Heroin; **Level 30**

- At least 5 KG but less than 15 KG of Cocaine;
- At least 280 G but less than 840 G of Cocaine Base;
- At least 1 KG but less than 3 KG of PCP, or
at least 100 G but less than 300 G of PCP (actual);
- At least 500 G but less than 1.5 KG of Methamphetamine, or
at least 50 G but less than 150 G of Methamphetamine (actual), or
at least 50 G but less than 150 G of "Ice";
- At least 500 G but less than 1.5 KG of Amphetamine, or
at least 50 G but less than 150 G of Amphetamine (actual);
- At least 10 G but less than 30 G of LSD;
- At least 400 G but less than 1.2 KG of Fentanyl;
- At least 100 G but less than 300 G of a Fentanyl Analogue;
- At least 1,000 KG but less than 3,000 KG of Marihuana;
- At least 200 KG but less than 600 KG of Hashish;
- At least 20 KG but less than 60 KG of Hashish Oil;
- At least 1,000,000 but less than 3,000,000 units of Ketamine;
- At least 1,000,000 but less than 3,000,000 units of Schedule I or II Depressants;
- At least 62,500 but less than 187,500 units of Flunitrazepam.

(6) • At least 700 G but less than 1 KG of Heroin; **Level 28**

- At least 3.5 KG but less than 5 KG of Cocaine;

- At least 196 G but less than 280 G of Cocaine Base;
- At least 700 G but less than 1 KG of PCP, or
at least 70 G but less than 100 G of PCP (actual);
- At least 350 G but less than 500 G of Methamphetamine, or
at least 35 G but less than 50 G of Methamphetamine (actual), or
at least 35 G but less than 50 G of "Ice";
- At least 350 G but less than 500 G of Amphetamine, or
at least 35 G but less than 50 G of Amphetamine (actual);
- At least 7 G but less than 10 G of LSD;
- At least 280 G but less than 400 G of Fentanyl;
- At least 70 G but less than 100 G of a Fentanyl Analogue;
- At least 700 KG but less than 1,000 KG of Marihuana;
- At least 140 KG but less than 200 KG of Hashish;
- At least 14 KG but less than 20 KG of Hashish Oil;
- At least 700,000 but less than 1,000,000 units of Ketamine;
- At least 700,000 but less than 1,000,000 units of Schedule I or II Depressants;
- At least 43,750 but less than 62,500 units of Flunitrazepam.

(7) · At least 400 G but less than 700 G of Heroin; **Level 26**

- At least 2 KG but less than 3.5 KG of Cocaine;
- At least 112 G but less than 196 G of Cocaine Base;
- At least 400 G but less than 700 G of PCP, or
at least 40 G but less than 70 G of PCP (actual);
- At least 200 G but less than 350 G of Methamphetamine, or
at least 20 G but less than 35 G of Methamphetamine (actual), or
at least 20 G but less than 35 G of "Ice";
- At least 200 G but less than 350 G of Amphetamine, or
at least 20 G but less than 35 G of Amphetamine (actual);
- At least 4 G but less than 7 G of LSD;
- At least 160 G but less than 280 G of Fentanyl;
- At least 40 G but less than 70 G of a Fentanyl Analogue;
- At least 400 KG but less than 700 KG of Marihuana;
- At least 80 KG but less than 140 KG of Hashish;
- At least 8 KG but less than 14 KG of Hashish Oil;
- At least 400,000 but less than 700,000 units of Ketamine;
- At least 400,000 but less than 700,000 units of Schedule I or II Depressants;
- At least 25,000 but less than 43,750 units of Flunitrazepam.

(8) · At least 100 G but less than 400 G of Heroin; **Level 24**

- At least 500 G but less than 2 KG of Cocaine;
- At least 28 G but less than 112 G of Cocaine Base;

- At least 100 G but less than 400 G of PCP, or
at least 10 G but less than 40 G of PCP (actual);
- At least 50 G but less than 200 G of Methamphetamine, or
at least 5 G but less than 20 G of Methamphetamine (actual), or
at least 5 G but less than 20 G of "Ice";
- At least 50 G but less than 200 G of Amphetamine, or
at least 5 G but less than 20 G of Amphetamine (actual);
- At least 1 G but less than 4 G of LSD;
- At least 40 G but less than 160 G of Fentanyl;
- At least 10 G but less than 40 G of a Fentanyl Analogue;

- At least 100 KG but less than 400 KG of Marihuana;
- At least 20 KG but less than 80 KG of Hashish;
- At least 2 KG but less than 8 KG of Hashish Oil;
- At least 100,000 but less than 400,000 units of Ketamine;
- At least 100,000 but less than 400,000 units of Schedule I or II Depressants;
- At least 6,250 but less than 25,000 units of Flunitrazepam.

(9) • At least 80 G but less than 100 G of Heroin; **Level 22**
- At least 400 G but less than 500 G of Cocaine;
- At least 22.4 G but less than 28 G of Cocaine Base;
- At least 80 G but less than 100 G of PCP, or
at least 8 G but less than 10 G of PCP (actual);
- At least 40 G but less than 50 G of Methamphetamine, or
at least 4 G but less than 5 G of Methamphetamine (actual), or
at least 4 G but less than 5 G of "Ice";
- At least 40 G but less than 50 G of Amphetamine, or
at least 4 G but less than 5 G of Amphetamine (actual);
- At least 800 MG but less than 1 G of LSD;
- At least 32 G but less than 40 G of Fentanyl;
- At least 8 G but less than 10 G of a Fentanyl Analogue;
- At least 80 KG but less than 100 KG of Marihuana;
- At least 16 KG but less than 20 KG of Hashish;
- At least 1.6 KG but less than 2 KG of Hashish Oil;
- At least 80,000 but less than 100,000 units of Ketamine;
- At least 80,000 but less than 100,000 units of Schedule I or II Depressants;
- At least 5,000 but less than 6,250 units of Flunitrazepam.

(10) • At least 60 G but less than 80 G of Heroin; **Level 20**
- At least 300 G but less than 400 G of Cocaine;
- At least 16.8 G but less than 22.4 G of Cocaine Base;

- At least 60 G but less than 80 G of PCP, or
at least 6 G but less than 8 G of PCP (actual);
- At least 30 G but less than 40 G of Methamphetamine, or
at least 3 G but less than 4 G of Methamphetamine (actual), or
at least 3 G but less than 4 G of "Ice";
- At least 30 G but less than 40 G of Amphetamine, or
at least 3 G but less than 4 G of Amphetamine (actual);
- At least 600 MG but less than 800 MG of LSD;
- At least 24 G but less than 32 G of Fentanyl;
- At least 6 G but less than 8 G of a Fentanyl Analogue;
- At least 60 KG but less than 80 KG of Marihuana;
- At least 12 KG but less than 16 KG of Hashish;
- At least 1.2 KG but less than 1.6 KG of Hashish Oil;
- At least 60,000 but less than 80,000 units of Ketamine;
- At least 60,000 but less than 80,000 units of Schedule I or II Depressants;
- 60,000 units or more of Schedule III substances (except Ketamine);
- At least 3,750 but less than 5,000 units of Flunitrazepam.

(11) • At least 40 G but less than 60 G of Heroin; **Level 18**

- At least 200 G but less than 300 G of Cocaine;
- At least 11.2 G but less than 16.8 G of Cocaine Base;
- At least 40 G but less than 60 G of PCP, or
at least 4 G but less than 6 G of PCP (actual);

- At least 20 G but less than 30 G of Methamphetamine, or
at least 2 G but less than 3 G of Methamphetamine (actual), or
at least 2 G but less than 3 G of "Ice";
- At least 20 G but less than 30 G of Amphetamine, or
at least 2 G but less than 3 G of Amphetamine (actual);
- At least 400 MG but less than 600 MG of LSD;
- At least 16 G but less than 24 G of Fentanyl;
- At least 4 G but less than 6 G of a Fentanyl Analogue;
- At least 40 KG but less than 60 KG of Marihuana;
- At least 8 KG but less than 12 KG of Hashish;
- At least 800 G but less than 1.2 KG of Hashish Oil;
- At least 40,000 but less than 60,000 units of Ketamine;
- At least 40,000 but less than 60,000 units of Schedule I or II Depressants;
- At least 40,000 but less than 60,000 units of Schedule III substances (except Ketamine);
- At least 2,500 but less than 3,750 units of Flunitrazepam.

(12) • At least 20 G but less than 40 G of Heroin; **Level 16**

• At least 100 G but less than 200 G of Cocaine;

• At least 5.6 G but less than 11.2 G of Cocaine Base;

• At least 20 G but less than 40 G of PCP, or
at least 2 G but less than 4 G of PCP (actual);

• At least 10 G but less than 20 G of Methamphetamine, or
at least 1 G but less than 2 G of Methamphetamine (actual), or
at least 1 G but less than 2 G of "Ice";

• At least 10 G but less than 20 G of Amphetamine, or
at least 1 G but less than 2 G of Amphetamine (actual);

• At least 200 MG but less than 400 MG of LSD;

• At least 8 G but less than 16 G of Fentanyl;

• At least 2 G but less than 4 G of a Fentanyl Analogue;

• At least 20 KG but less than 40 KG of Marihuana;

• At least 5 KG but less than 8 KG of Hashish;

• At least 500 G but less than 800 G of Hashish Oil;

• At least 20,000 but less than 40,000 units of Ketamine;

• At least 20,000 but less than 40,000 units of Schedule I or II Depressants;

• At least 20,000 but less than 40,000 units of Schedule III substances (except Ketamine);

• At least 1,250 but less than 2,500 units of Flunitrazepam.

(13) • At least 10 G but less than 20 G of Heroin; **Level 14**

• At least 50 G but less than 100 G of Cocaine;

• At least 2.8 G but less than 5.6 G of Cocaine Base;

• At least 10 G but less than 20 G of PCP, or
at least 1 G but less than 2 G of PCP (actual);

• At least 5 G but less than 10 G of Methamphetamine, or
at least 500 MG but less than 1 G of Methamphetamine (actual), or
at least 500 MG but less than 1 G of "Ice";

• At least 5 G but less than 10 G of Amphetamine, or
at least 500 MG but less than 1 G of Amphetamine (actual);

• At least 100 MG but less than 200 MG of LSD;

• At least 4 G but less than 8 G of Fentanyl;

• At least 1 G but less than 2 G of a Fentanyl Analogue;

• At least 10 KG but less than 20 KG of Marihuana;

• At least 2 KG but less than 5 KG of Hashish;

• At least 200 G but less than 500 G of Hashish Oil;

• At least 10,000 but less than 20,000 units of Ketamine;

• At least 10,000 but less than 20,000 units of Schedule I or II Depressants;

• At least 10,000 but less than 20,000 units of Schedule III substances (except Ketamine);

• At least 625 but less than 1,250 units of Flunitrazepam.

(14) • Less than 10 G of Heroin; **Level 12**

• Less than 50 G of Cocaine;

• Less than 2.8 G of Cocaine Base;

• Less than 10 G of PCP, or
less than 1 G of PCP (actual);

• Less than 5 G of Methamphetamine, or
less than 500 MG of Methamphetamine (actual), or
less than 500 MG of "Ice";

• Less than 5 G of Amphetamine, or
less than 500 MG of Amphetamine (actual);

• Less than 100 MG of LSD;

• Less than 4 G of Fentanyl;

• Less than 1 G of a Fentanyl Analogue;

• At least 5 KG but less than 10 KG of Marihuana;

• At least 1 KG but less than 2 KG of Hashish;

• At least 100 G but less than 200 G of Hashish Oil;

• At least 5,000 but less than 10,000 units of Ketamine;

• At least 5,000 but less than 10,000 units of Schedule I or II Depressants;

• At least 5,000 but less than 10,000 units of Schedule III substances (except Ketamine);

• At least 312 but less than 625 units of Flunitrazepam;

• 80,000 units or more of Schedule IV substances (except Flunitrazepam).

(15) • At least 2.5 KG but less than 5 KG of Marihuana; **Level 10**

• At least 500 G but less than 1 KG of Hashish;

• At least 50 G but less than 100 G of Hashish Oil;

• At least 2,500 but less than 5,000 units of Ketamine;

• At least 2,500 but less than 5,000 units of Schedule I or II Depressants;

• At least 2,500 but less than 5,000 units of Schedule III substances (except Ketamine);

• At least 156 but less than 312 units of Flunitrazepam;

• At least 40,000 but less than 80,000 units of Schedule IV substances (except Flunitrazepam).

(16) • At least 1 KG but less than 2.5 KG of Marihuana; **Level 8**

• At least 200 G but less than 500 G of Hashish;

• At least 20 G but less than 50 G of Hashish Oil;

- At least 1,000 but less than 2,500 units of Ketamine;
- At least 1,000 but less than 2,500 units of Schedule I or II Depressants;
- At least 1,000 but less than 2,500 units of Schedule III substances (except Ketamine);
- Less than 156 units of Flunitrazepam;
- At least 16,000 but less than 40,000 units of Schedule IV substances (except Flunitrazepam);
- 160,000 units or more of Schedule V substances.

(17) • Less than 1 KG of Marihuana; **Level 6**
- Less than 200 G of Hashish;
- Less than 20 G of Hashish Oil;
- Less than 1,000 units of Ketamine;
- Less than 1,000 units of Schedule I or II Depressants;
- Less than 1,000 units of Schedule III substances (except Ketamine);
- Less than 16,000 units of Schedule IV substances (except Flunitrazepam);
- Less than 160,000 units of Schedule V substances.

***Notes to Drug Quantity Table:**

(A) Unless otherwise specified, the weight of a controlled substance set forth in the table refers to the entire weight of any mixture or substance containing a detectable amount of the controlled substance. If a mixture or substance contains more than one controlled substance, the weight of the entire mixture or substance is assigned to the controlled substance that results in the greater offense level.

(B) The terms "***PCP (actual)***", "***Amphetamine (actual)***", and "***Methamphetamine (actual)***" refer to the weight of the controlled substance, itself, contained in the mixture or substance. For example, a mixture weighing 10 grams containing PCP at 50% purity contains 5 grams of PCP (actual). In the case of a mixture or substance containing PCP, amphetamine, or methamphetamine, use the offense level determined by the entire weight of the mixture or substance, or the offense level determined by the weight of the PCP (actual), amphetamine (actual), or methamphetamine (actual), whichever is greater.

The terms "***Hydrocodone (actual)***" and "***Oxycodone (actual)***" refer to the weight of the controlled substance, itself, contained in the pill, capsule, or mixture.

(C) "***Ice***," for the purposes of this guideline, means a mixture or substance containing d-methamphetamine hydrochloride of at least 80% purity.

(D) "***Cocaine base***," for the purposes of this guideline, means "crack." "***Crack***" is the street name for a form of cocaine base, usually prepared by processing cocaine hydrochloride and sodium bicarbonate, and usually appearing in a

lumpy, rocklike form.
(E) In the case of an offense involving marihuana plants, treat each plant, regardless of sex, as equivalent to 100 grams of marihuana. *Provided*, however, that if the actual weight of the marihuana is greater, use the actual weight of the marihuana.

(F) In the case of Schedule I or II Depressants (except gamma-hydroxybutyric acid), Schedule III substances, Schedule IV substances, and Schedule V substances, one "***unit***" means one pill, capsule, or tablet. If the substance (except gamma-hydroxybutyric acid) is in liquid form, one "***unit***" means 0.5 milliliters. For an anabolic steroid that is not in a pill, capsule, tablet, or liquid form (*e.g.*, patch, topical cream, aerosol), the court shall determine the base offense level using a reasonable estimate of the quantity of anabolic steroid involved in the offense. In making a reasonable estimate, the court shall consider that each 25 milligrams of an anabolic steroid is one "unit".
(G) In the case of LSD on a carrier medium (*e.g.*, a sheet of blotter paper), do not use the weight of the LSD/carrier medium. Instead, treat each dose of LSD on the carrier medium as equal to 0.4 milligrams of LSD for the purposes of the Drug Quantity Table.
(H) ***Hashish***, for the purposes of this guideline, means a resinous substance of cannabis that includes (i) one or more of the tetrahydrocannabinols (as listed in 21 C.F.R. § 1308.11(d)(31)), (ii) at least two of the following: cannabinol, cannabidiol, or cannabichromene, and (iii) fragments of plant material (such as cystolith fibers).
(I) ***Hashish oil***, for the purposes of this guideline, means a preparation of the soluble cannabinoids derived from cannabis that includes (i) one or more of the tetrahydrocannabinols (as listed in 21 C.F.R. § 1308.11(d)(31)), (ii) at least two of the following: cannabinol, cannabidiol, or cannabichromene, and (iii) is essentially free of plant material (*e.g.*, plant fragments). Typically, hashish oil is a viscous, dark colored oil, but it can vary from a dry resin to a colorless liquid.

Commentary

Statutory Provisions: 21 U.S.C. §§ 841(a), (b)(1)–(3), (7), (g), 860a, 865, 960(a), (b); 49 U.S.C. § 46317(b). For additional statutory provision(s), *see* Appendix A (Statutory Index).

Application Notes:

1. **"Mixture or Substance".**—"***Mixture or substance***" as used in this guideline has the same meaning as in 21 U.S.C. § 841, except as expressly provided. Mixture or substance does not include materials that must be separated from the controlled substance before the controlled substance can be used. Examples of such materials include the fiberglass in a cocaine/ fiberglass bonded suitcase, beeswax in a cocaine/beeswax statue, and waste water from an illicit laboratory used to manufacture a controlled substance. If such material cannot readily be separated from the mixture or substance that appropriately is counted in the Drug Quantity Table, the court may use any reasonable method to approximate the weight of the mixture or substance to be counted.
An upward departure nonetheless may be warranted when the mixture or substance counted in the Drug Quantity Table is combined with other, non-countable material in an unusually sophisticated manner in order to avoid detection.

Similarly, in the case of marihuana having a moisture content that renders the marihuana unsuitable for consumption without drying (this might occur, for example, with a bale of rain-soaked marihuana or freshly harvested marihuana that had not been dried), an approximation of the weight of the marihuana without such excess moisture content is to be used.

2. **"Plant".**—For purposes of the guidelines, a "***plant***" is an organism having leaves and a readily observable root formation (*e.g.*, a marihuana cutting having roots, a rootball, or root hairs is a marihuana plant).

3. **Classification of Controlled Substances.**—Certain pharmaceutical preparations are classified as Schedule III, IV, or V controlled substances by the Drug Enforcement Administration under 21 C.F.R. § 1308.13–15 even though they contain a small amount of a Schedule I or II controlled substance. For example, Tylenol 3 is classified as a Schedule III controlled substance even though it contains a small amount of codeine, a Schedule II opiate. For the purposes of the guidelines, the classification of the controlled substance under 21 C.F.R. § 1308.13–15 is the appropriate classification.

4. **Applicability to "Counterfeit" Substances.**—The statute and guideline also apply to ***"counterfeit" substances***, which are defined in 21 U.S.C. § 802 to mean controlled substances that are falsely labeled so as to appear to have been legitimately manufactured or distributed.

5. **Determining Drug Types and Drug Quantities.**—Types and quantities of drugs not specified in the count of conviction may be considered in determining the offense level. *See* §1B1.3(a)(2) (Relevant Conduct). Where there is no drug seizure or the amount seized does not reflect the scale of the offense, the court shall approximate the quantity of the controlled substance. In making this determination, the court may consider, for example, the price generally obtained for the controlled substance, financial or other records, similar transactions in controlled substances by the defendant, and the size or capability of any laboratory involved.

If the offense involved both a substantive drug offense and an attempt or conspiracy (*e.g.*, sale of five grams of heroin and an attempt to sell an additional ten grams of heroin), the total quantity involved shall be aggregated to determine the scale of the offense.

In an offense involving an agreement to sell a controlled substance, the agreed-upon quantity of the controlled substance shall be used to determine the offense level unless the sale is completed and the amount delivered more accurately reflects the scale of the offense. For example, a defendant agrees to sell 500 grams of cocaine, the transaction is completed by the delivery of the controlled substance — actually 480 grams of cocaine, and no further delivery is scheduled. In this example, the amount delivered more accurately reflects the scale of the offense. In contrast, in a reverse sting, the agreed-upon quantity of the controlled substance would more accurately reflect the scale of the offense because the amount actually delivered is controlled by the government, not by the defendant. If, however, the defendant establishes that the defendant did not intend to provide or purchase, or was not reasonably capable of providing or purchasing, the agreedupon quantity of the controlled substance, the court shall exclude from the offense level determination the amount of controlled substance that the defendant establishes that the defendant did not intend to provide or purchase or was not reasonably capable of providing or purchasing.

6. **Analogues and Controlled Substances Not Referenced in this Guideline.**—Any reference to a particular controlled substance in these guidelines includes all salts, isomers, all salts of isomers, and, except as otherwise provided, any analogue of that controlled substance. Any reference to cocaine includes ecgonine and coca leaves, except extracts of coca leaves from which cocaine and ecgonine have been removed. For purposes of this guideline "***analogue***" has the meaning given the term "controlled substance analogue" in 21 U.S.C. § 802(32). In determining the appropriate sentence, the court also may consider whether the same quantity of analogue produces a greater effect on the

central nervous system than the controlled substance for which it is an analogue.
In the case of a controlled substance that is not specifically referenced in this guideline, determine the base offense level using the marihuana equivalency of the most closely related controlled substance referenced in this guideline. In determining the most closely related controlled substance, the court shall, to the extent practicable, consider the following:
(A) Whether the controlled substance not referenced in this guideline has a chemical structure that is substantially similar to a controlled substance referenced in this guideline.
(B) Whether the controlled substance not referenced in this guideline has a stimulant, depressant, or hallucinogenic effect on the central nervous system that is substantially similar to the stimulant, depressant, or hallucinogenic effect on the central nervous system of a controlled substance referenced in this guideline.
(C) Whether a lesser or greater quantity of the controlled substance not referenced in this guideline is needed to produce a substantially similar effect on the central nervous system as a controlled substance referenced in this guideline.
7. **Multiple Transactions or Multiple Drug Types.**—Where there are multiple transactions or multiple drug types, the quantities of drugs are to be added. Tables for making the necessary conversions are provided below.
8. **Use of Drug Equivalency Tables.**—
(A) **Controlled Substances Not Referenced in Drug Quantity Table.**—The Commission has used the sentences provided in, and equivalences derived from, the statute (21 U.S.C. § 841(b)(1)), as the primary basis for the guideline sentences. The statute, however, provides direction only for the more common controlled substances, *i.e.*, heroin, cocaine, PCP, methamphetamine, fentanyl, LSD and marihuana.
In the case of a controlled substance that is not specifically referenced in the Drug Quantity Table, determine the base offense level as follows:
(i) Use the Drug Equivalency Tables to convert the quantity of the controlled substance involved in the offense to its equivalent quantity of marihuana.
(ii) Find the equivalent quantity of marihuana in the Drug Quantity Table.
(iii) Use the offense level that corresponds to the equivalent quantity of marihuana as the base offense level for the controlled substance involved in the offense.
(*See also* Application Note 6.) For example, in the Drug Equivalency Tables set forth in this Note, 1 gram of a substance containing oxymorphone, a Schedule I opiate,

converts to an equivalent quantity of 5 kilograms of marihuana. In a case involving 100 grams of oxymorphone, the equivalent quantity of marihuana would be 500 kilograms, which corresponds to a base offense level of 26 in the Drug Quantity Table.
(B) **Combining Differing Controlled Substances.**—The Drug Equivalency Tables also provide a means for combining differing controlled substances to obtain a single offense level. In each case, convert each of the drugs to its marihuana equivalent, add the quantities, and look up the total in the Drug Quantity Table to obtain the combined offense level.
For certain types of controlled substances, the marihuana equivalencies in the Drug Equivalency Tables are "capped" at specified amounts (*e.g.*, the combined equivalent weight of all Schedule V controlled substances shall not exceed 2.49 kilograms of marihuana). Where there are controlled substances from more than one schedule (*e.g.*, a quantity of a Schedule IV substance and a quantity of a Schedule V substance), determine the marihuana equivalency for each schedule separately (subject to the cap, if any, applicable to that schedule). Then add the marihuana equivalencies to determine the combined marihuana equivalency (subject to the cap, if any, applicable to the combined amounts).
Note: Because of the statutory equivalences, the ratios in the Drug Equivalency Tables do not necessarily reflect dosages based on pharmacological equivalents.

(C) **Examples for Combining Differing Controlled Substances.—**

(i) The defendant is convicted of selling 70 grams of a substance containing PCP (Level 20) and 250 milligrams of a substance containing LSD (Level 16). The PCP converts to 70 kilograms of marihuana; the LSD converts to 25 kilograms of marihuana. The total is therefore equivalent to 95 kilograms of marihuana, for which the Drug Quantity Table provides an offense level of 22.

(ii) The defendant is convicted of selling 500 grams of marihuana (Level 6) and 10,000 units of diazepam (Level 6). The diazepam, a Schedule IV drug, is equivalent to 625 grams of marihuana. The total, 1.125 kilograms of marihuana, has an offense level of 8 in the Drug Quantity Table.

(iii) The defendant is convicted of selling 80 grams of cocaine (Level 14) and 2 grams of cocaine base (Level 12). The cocaine is equivalent to 16 kilograms of marihuana, and the cocaine base is equivalent to 7.142 kilograms of marihuana. The total is therefore equivalent to 23.142 kilograms of marihuana, which has an offense level of 16 in the Drug Quantity Table.

(iv) The defendant is convicted of selling 76,000 units of a Schedule III substance, 200,000 units of a Schedule IV substance, and 600,000 units of a Schedule V substance. The marihuana equivalency for the Schedule III substance is 76 kilograms of marihuana (below the cap of 79.99 kilograms of marihuana set forth as the maximum equivalent weight for Schedule III substances). The marihuana equivalency for the Schedule IV substance is subject to a cap of 9.99 kilograms of marihuana set forth as the maximum equivalent weight for Schedule IV substances (without the cap it would have been 12.5 kilograms). The marihuana equivalency for the Schedule V substance is subject to the cap of 2.49 kilograms of marihuana set forth as the maximum equivalent weight for Schedule V substances (without the cap it would have been 3.75 kilograms). The combined equivalent weight, determined by adding together the

above amounts, is subject to the cap of 79.99 kilograms of marihuana set forth as the maximum combined equivalent weight for Schedule III, IV, and V substances. Without the cap, the combined equivalent weight would have been 88.48 (76 + 9.99 + 2.49) kilograms.

(D) **Drug Equivalency Tables.—**

SCHEDULE I OR II OPIATES*

1 gm of Heroin = 1 kg of marihuana
1 gm of Alpha-Methylfentanyl = 10 kg of marihuana
1 gm of Dextromoramide = 670 gm of marihuana
1 gm of Dipipanone = 250 gm of marihuana
1 gm of 3-Methylfentanyl = 10 kg of marihuana
1 gm of 1-Methyl-4-phenyl-4-propionoxypiperidine/MPPP = 700 gm of marihuana
1 gm of 1-(2-Phenylethyl)-4-phenyl-4-acetyloxypiperidine/PEPAP = 700 gm of marihuana
1 gm of Alphaprodine = 100 gm of marihuana
1 gm of Fentanyl (N-phenyl-N-[1-(2-phenylethyl)-4-piperidinyl] Propanamide) = 2.5 kg of marihuana
1 gm of Hydromorphone/Dihydromorphinone = 2.5 kg of marihuana
1 gm of Levorphanol = 2.5 kg of marihuana
1 gm of Meperidine/Pethidine = 50 gm of marihuana
1 gm of Methadone = 500 gm of marihuana
1 gm of 6-Monoacetylmorphine = 1 kg of marihuana
1 gm of Morphine = 500 gm of marihuana
1 gm of Oxycodone (actual) = 6700 gm of marihuana
1 gm of Oxymorphone = 5 kg of marihuana
1 gm of Racemorphan = 800 gm of marihuana
1 gm of Codeine = 80 gm of marihuana
1 gm of Dextropropoxyphene/Propoxyphene-Bulk = 50 gm of marihuana
1 gm of Ethylmorphine = 165 gm of marihuana
1 gm of Hydrocodone (actual) = 6700 gm of marihuana
1 gm of Mixed Alkaloids of Opium/Papaveretum = 250 gm of marihuana
1 gm of Opium = 50 gm of marihuana

1 gm of Levo-alpha-acetylmethadol (LAAM) = 3 kg of marihuana
*Provided, that the minimum offense level from the Drug Quantity Table for any of these controlled substances individually, or in combination with another controlled substance, is level 12.

COCAINE AND OTHER SCHEDULE I AND II STIMULANTS (AND THEIR IMMEDIATE PRECURSORS)*
1 gm of Cocaine = 200 gm of marihuana
1 gm of N-Ethylamphetamine = 80 gm of marihuana
1 gm of Fenethylline = 40 gm of marihuana
1 gm of Amphetamine = 2 kg of marihuana
1 gm of Amphetamine (Actual) = 20 kg of marihuana
1 gm of Methamphetamine = 2 kg of marihuana
1 gm of Methamphetamine (Actual) = 20 kg of marihuana
1 gm of "Ice" = 20 kg of marihuana
1 gm of Khat = .01 gm of marihuana
1 gm of 4-Methylaminorex ("Euphoria") = 100 gm of marihuana
1 gm of Methylphenidate (Ritalin) = 100 gm of marihuana
1 gm of Phenmetrazine = 80 gm of marihuana
1 gm Phenylacetone/P_2P (when possessed for the purpose of manufacturing methamphetamine) = 416 gm of marihuana
1 gm Phenylacetone/P_2P (in any other case) = 75 gm of marihuana
1 gm Cocaine Base ("Crack") = 3,571 gm of marihuana
1 gm of Aminorex = 100 gm of marihuana
1 gm of Methcathinone = 380 gm of marihuana
1 gm of N-N-Dimethylamphetamine = 40 gm of marihuana
1 gm of N-Benzylpiperazine = 100 gm of marihuana
*Provided, that the minimum offense level from the Drug Quantity Table for any of these controlled substances individually, or in combination with another controlled substance, is level 12.

LSD, PCP, AND OTHER SCHEDULE I AND II HALLUCINOGENS (AND THEIR IMMEDIATE PRECURSORS)*
1 gm of Bufotenine = 70 gm of marihuana
1 gm of D-Lysergic Acid Diethylamide/Lysergide/LSD = 100 kg of marihuana
1 gm of Diethyltryptamine/DET = 80 gm of marihuana
1 gm of Dimethyltryptamine/DM = 100 gm of marihuana
1 gm of Mescaline = 10 gm of marihuana
1 gm of Mushrooms containing Psilocin and/or Psilocybin (Dry) = 1 gm of marihuana
1 gm of Mushrooms containing Psilocin and/or Psilocybin (Wet) = 0.1 gm of marihuana
1 gm of Peyote (Dry) = 0.5 gm of marihuana
1 gm of Peyote (Wet) = 0.05 gm of marihuana
1 gm of Phencyclidine/PCP = 1 kg of marihuana
1 gm of Phencyclidine (actual) /PCP (actual) = 10 kg of marihuana
1 gm of Psilocin = 500 gm of marihuana
1 gm of Psilocybin = 500 gm of marihuana
1 gm of Pyrrolidine Analog of Phencyclidine/PHP = 1 kg of marihuana
1 gm of Thiophene Analog of Phencyclidine/TCP = 1 kg of marihuana
1 gm of 4-Bromo-2,5-Dimethoxyamphetamine/DOB = 2.5 kg of marihuana
1 gm of 2,5-Dimethoxy-4-methylamphetamine/DOM = 1.67 kg of marihuana
1 gm of 3,4-Methylenedioxyamphetamine/MDA = 500 gm of marihuana
1 gm of 3,4-Methylenedioxymethamphetamine/MDMA = 500 gm of marihuana
1 gm of 3,4-Methylenedioxy-N-ethylamphetamine/MDEA = 500 gm of marihuana
1 gm of Paramethoxymethamphetamine/PMA = 500 gm of marihuana
1 gm of 1-Piperidinocyclohexanecarbonitrile/PCC = 680 gm of marihuana
1 gm of N-ethyl-1-phenylcyclohexylamine (PCE) = 1 kg of marihuana
*Provided, that the minimum offense level from the Drug Quantity Table for any of these controlled substances individually, or in combination with another controlled substance, is level 12.

SCHEDULE I MARIHUANA
1 gm of Marihuana/Cannabis, granulated, powdered, etc. = 1 gm of marihuana
1 gm of Hashish Oil = 50 gm of marihuana
1 gm of Cannabis Resin or Hashish = 5 gm of marihuana
1 gm of Tetrahydrocannabinol, Organic = 167 gm of marihuana
1 gm of Tetrahydrocannabinol, Synthetic = 167 gm of marihuana

FLUNITRAZEPAM **
1 unit of Flunitrazepam = 16 gm of marihuana
**Provided, that the minimum offense level from the Drug Quantity Table for flunitrazepam individually, or in combination with any Schedule I or II depressants, Schedule III substances, Schedule IV substances, and Schedule V substances is level 8.

SCHEDULE I OR II DEPRESSANTS (EXCEPT GAMMA-HYDROXYBUTYRIC ACID)
1 unit of a Schedule I or II Depressant

(except gamma-hydroxybutyric acid) = 1 gm of marihuana
GAMMA-HYDROXYBUTYRIC ACID
1 ml of gamma-hydroxybutyric acid = 8.8 gm of marihuana

SCHEDULE III SUBSTANCES (EXCEPT KETAMINE)***
1 unit of a Schedule III Substance = 1 gm of marihuana
****Provided*, that the combined equivalent weight of all Schedule III substances (except ketamine), Schedule IV substances (except flunitrazepam), and Schedule V substances shall not exceed 79.99 kilograms of marihuana.
KETAMINE
1 unit of ketamine = 1 gm of marihuana
SCHEDULE IV SUBSTANCES (EXCEPT FLUNITRAZEPAM)*****
1 unit of a Schedule IV Substance
(except Flunitrazepam) = 0.0625 gm of marihuana
******Provided*, that the combined equivalent weight of all Schedule IV (except flunitrazepam) and V substances shall not exceed 9.99 kilograms of marihuana.
SCHEDULE V SUBSTANCES******
1 unit of a Schedule V Substance = 0.00625 gm of marihuana
*******Provided*, that the combined equivalent weight of Schedule V substances shall not exceed 2.49 kilograms of marihuana.
LIST I CHEMICALS (RELATING TO THE MANUFACTURE OF AMPHETAMINE OR METHAMPHETAMINE)*******
1 gm of Ephedrine = 10 kg of marihuana
1 gm of Phenylpropanolamine = 10 kg of marihuana
1 gm of Pseudoephedrine = 10 kg of marihuana
********Provided*, that in a case involving ephedrine, pseudoephedrine, or phenylpropanolamine tablets, use the weight of the ephedrine, pseudoephedrine, or phenylpropanolamine contained in the tablets, not the weight of the entire tablets, in calculating the base offense level.
DATE RAPE DRUGS (EXCEPT FLUNITRAZEPAM, GHB, OR KETAMINE)
1 ml of 1,4-butanediol = 8.8 gm marihuana
1 ml of gamma butyrolactone = 8.8 gm marihuana

To facilitate conversions to drug equivalencies, the following table is provided:

MEASUREMENT CONVERSION TABLE

1 oz = 28.35 gm
1 lb = 453.6 gm
1 lb = 0.4536 kg
1 gal = 3.785 liters
1 qt = 0.946 liters
1 gm = 1 ml (liquid)
1 liter = 1,000 ml
1 kg = 1,000 gm
1 gm = 1,000 mg
1 grain = 64.8 mg.

9. **Determining Quantity Based on Doses, Pills, or Capsules.**—If the number of doses, pills, or capsules but not the weight of the controlled substance is known, multiply the number of doses, pills, or capsules by the typical weight per dose in the table below to estimate the total weight of the controlled substance (*e.g.*, 100 doses of Mescaline at 500 milligrams per dose = 50 grams of mescaline). The Typical Weight Per Unit Table, prepared from information provided by the Drug Enforcement Administration, displays the typical weight per dose, pill, or capsule for certain controlled substances. Do not use this table if any more reliable estimate of the total weight is available from case-specific information.

TYPICAL WEIGHT PER UNIT (DOSE, PILL, OR CAPSULE) TABLE

HALLUCINOGENS
MDA 250 mg
MDMA 250 mg
Mescaline 500 mg
PCP* 5 mg

Peyote (dry) 12 gm
Peyote (wet) 120 gm
Psilocin* 10 mg
Psilocybe mushrooms (dry) 5 gm
Psilocybe mushrooms (wet) 50 gm
Psilocybin* 10 mg
2,5-Dimethoxy-4-methylamphetamine (STP, DOM)* 3 mg
MARIHUANA
1 marihuana cigarette 0.5 gm
STIMULANTS
Amphetamine* 10 mg
Methamphetamine* 5 mg
Phenmetrazine (Preludin)* 75 mg

*For controlled substances marked with an asterisk, the weight per unit shown is the weight of the actual controlled substance, and not generally the weight of the mixture or substance containing the controlled substance. Therefore, use of this table provides a very conservative estimate of the total weight.

10. **Determining Quantity of LSD.**—LSD on a blotter paper carrier medium typically is marked so that the number of doses ("hits") per sheet readily can be determined. When this is not the case, it is to be presumed that each 1/4 inch by 1/4 inch section of the blotter paper is equal to one dose.

In the case of liquid LSD (LSD that has not been placed onto a carrier medium), using the weight of the LSD alone to calculate the offense level may not adequately reflect the seriousness of the offense. In such a case, an upward departure may be warranted.

11. **Application of Subsections (b)(1) and (b)(2).**—

(A) **Application of Subsection (b)(1).**—Definitions of "***firearm***" and "***dangerous weapon***" are found in the Commentary to §1B1.1 (Application Instructions). The enhancement for weapon possession in subsection (b)(1) reflects the increased danger of violence when drug traffickers possess weapons. The enhancement should be

applied if the weapon was present, unless it is clearly improbable that the weapon was connected with the offense. For example, the enhancement would not be applied if the defendant, arrested at the defendant's residence, had an unloaded hunting rifle in the closet. The enhancement also applies to offenses that are referenced to §2D1.1; *see* §§2D1.2(a)(1) and (2), 2D1.5(a)(1), 2D1.6, 2D1.7(b)(1), 2D1.8, 2D1.11(c)(1), and 2D1.12(c)(1).

(B) **Interaction of Subsections (b)(1) and (b)(2).**—The enhancements in subsections (b)(1) and (b)(2) may be applied cumulatively (added together), as is generally the case when two or more specific offense characteristics each apply. *See* §1B1.1 (Application Instructions), Application Note 4(A). However, in a case in which the defendant merely possessed a dangerous weapon but did not use violence, make a credible threat to use violence, or direct the use of violence, subsection (b)(2) would not apply.

12. **Application of Subsection (b)(5).**—If the offense involved importation of amphetamine or methamphetamine, and an adjustment from subsection (b)(3) applies, do not apply subsection (b)(5).

13. **Application of Subsection (b)(7).**—For purposes of subsection (b)(7), "***mass-marketing by means of an interactive computer service***" means the solicitation, by means of an interactive computer service, of a large number of persons to induce those persons to purchase a controlled substance. For example, subsection (b)(7) would apply to a defendant who operated a web site to promote the sale of Gamma-hydroxybutyric Acid (GHB) but would not apply to coconspirators who use an interactive computer service only to communicate with one another in furtherance of the offense. "***Interactive computer service***", for purposes of subsection (b)(7) and this note, has the meaning given

that term in section 230(e)(2) of the Communications Act of 1934 (47 U.S.C. § 230(f)(2)).

14. **Application of Subsection (b)(8).**—For purposes of subsection (b)(8), "***masking agent***" means a substance that, when taken before, after, or in conjunction with an anabolic steroid, prevents the detection of the anabolic steroid in an individual's body.

15. **Application of Subsection (b)(9).**—For purposes of subsection (b)(9), "***athlete***" means an individual who participates in an athletic activity conducted by (A) an intercollegiate athletic association or interscholastic athletic association; (B) a professional athletic association; or (C) an amateur athletic organization.

16. **Application of Subsection (b)(11).**—Subsection (b)(11) does not apply if the purpose of the bribery was to obstruct or impede the investigation, prosecution, or sentencing of the defendant. Such conduct is covered by §3C1.1 (Obstructing or Impeding the Administration of Justice) and, if applicable, §2D1.1(b)(15)(D).

17. **Application of Subsection (b)(12).**—Subsection (b)(12) applies to a defendant who knowingly maintains a premises (*i.e.*, a building, room, or enclosure) for the purpose of manufacturing or distributing a controlled substance, including storage of a controlled substance for the purpose of distribution.

Among the factors the court should consider in determining whether the defendant "maintained" the premises are (A) whether the defendant held a possessory interest in (*e.g.*, owned or rented) the premises and (B) the extent to which the defendant controlled access to, or activities at, the premises.

Manufacturing or distributing a controlled substance need not be the sole purpose for which the premises was maintained, but must be one of the defendant's primary or principal uses for the premises, rather than one of the defendant's incidental or collateral uses for the premises. In making this determination, the court should consider how frequently the premises was used by the defendant for manufacturing or distributing a controlled substance and how frequently the premises was used by the defendant for lawful purposes.

18. **Application of Subsection (b)(13).**—

(A) **Hazardous or Toxic Substances (Subsection (b)(13)(A)).**—Subsection (b)(13)(A) applies if the conduct for which the defendant is accountable under §1B1.3 (Relevant Conduct) involved any discharge, emission, release, transportation, treatment, storage, or disposal violation covered by the Resource Conservation and Recovery Act, 42 U.S.C. § 6928(d); the Federal Water Pollution Control Act, 33 U.S.C. § 1319(c); the Comprehensive Environmental Response, Compensation, and Liability Act, 42 U.S.C. § 9603(b); or 49 U.S.C. § 5124 (relating to violations of laws and regulations enforced by the Department of Transportation with respect to the transportation of hazardous material). In some cases, the enhancement under subsection (b)(13)(A) may not account adequately for the seriousness of the environmental harm or other threat to public health or safety (including the health or safety of law enforcement and cleanup personnel). In such cases, an upward departure may be warranted. Additionally, in determining the amount of restitution under §5E1.1 (Restitution) and in fashioning appropriate conditions of probation and supervision under §§5B1.3 (Conditions of Probation) and 5D1.3 (Conditions of Supervised Release), respectively, any costs of environmental cleanup and harm to individuals or property shall be considered by the court in cases involving the manufacture of amphetamine or methamphetamine and should be considered by the court in cases involving the manufacture of a controlled substance other than amphetamine or methamphetamine. *See* 21 U.S.C. § 853(q) (mandatory restitution for cleanup costs relating to the manufacture of amphetamine and methamphetamine).

(B) **Substantial Risk of Harm Associated with the Manufacture of Amphetamine and Methamphetamine (Subsection (b)(13)(C)–(D)).**—

(i) **Factors to Consider.**—In determining, for purposes of subsection (b)(13)(C)(ii) or (D), whether the offense created a substantial risk of harm to human life or the environment, the court shall include consideration of the following factors:

(I) The quantity of any chemicals or hazardous or toxic substances found at the laboratory, and the manner in which the chemicals or substances were stored.

(II) The manner in which hazardous or toxic substances were disposed, and the likelihood of release into the environment of hazardous or toxic substances.

(III) The duration of the offense, and the extent of the manufacturing operation.

(IV) The location of the laboratory (*e.g.*, whether the laboratory is located in a residential neighborhood or a remote area), and the number of human lives placed at substantial risk of harm.

(ii) **Definitions.**—For purposes of subsection (b)(13)(D):

"***Incompetent***" means an individual who is incapable of taking care of the individual's self or property because of a mental or physical illness or disability, mental retardation, or senility.

"***Minor***" has the meaning given that term in Application Note 1 of the Commentary to §2A3.1 (Criminal Sexual Abuse).

19. **Application of Subsection (b)(14).**—Subsection (b)(14) applies to offenses that involve the cultivation of marihuana on state or federal land or while trespassing on tribal or private land. Such offenses interfere with the ability of others to safely access and use the area and also pose or risk a range of other harms, such as harms to the environment. The enhancements in subsection (b)(13)(A) and (b)(14) may be applied cumulatively (added together), as is generally the case when two or more specific offense characteristics each apply. *See* §1B1.1 (Application Instructions), Application Note 4(A).

20. **Application of Subsection (b)(15).**—

(A) **Distributing to a Specified Individual or Involving Such an Individual in the Offense (Subsection (b)(15)(B)).**—If the defendant distributes a controlled substance to an individual or involves an individual in the offense, as specified in subsection (b)(15)(B), the individual is not a "vulnerable victim" for purposes of §3A1.1(b).

(B) **Directly Involved in the Importation of a Controlled Substance (Subsection (b)(15)(C)).**—Subsection (b)(15)(C) applies if the defendant is accountable for the importation of a controlled substance under subsection (a)(1)(A) of §1B1.3 (Relevant Conduct (Factors that Determine the Guideline Range)), *i.e.*, the defendant committed, aided, abetted, counseled, commanded, induced, procured, or willfully caused the importation of a controlled substance.

If subsection (b)(3) or (b)(5) applies, do not apply subsection (b)(15)(C).

(C) **Pattern of Criminal Conduct Engaged in as a Livelihood (Subsection (b)(15)(E)).**—For purposes of subsection (b)(15)(E), "***pattern of criminal conduct***" and "***engaged in as a livelihood***" have the meaning given such terms in §4B1.3 (Criminal Livelihood).

21. **Applicability of Subsection (b)(17).**—The applicability of subsection (b)(17) shall be determined without regard to whether the defendant was convicted of an offense that subjects the defendant to a mandatory minimum term of imprisonment. Section §5C1.2(b), which provides a minimum offense level of level 17, is not pertinent to the determination of whether subsection (b)(17) applies.

22. **Application of Subsection (e)(1).**—

(A) **Definition.**—For purposes of this guideline, "***sexual offense***" means a "sexual act" or "sexual contact" as those terms are defined in 18 U.S.C. § 2246(2) and (3), respectively.

(B) **Upward Departure Provision.**—If the defendant committed a sexual offense against more than one individual, an upward departure would be warranted.

23. **Interaction with §3B1.3.**—A defendant who used special skills in the commission of the offense may be subject to an adjustment under §3B1.3 (Abuse of Position of Trust or Use of Special Skill). Certain professionals often occupy essential positions in drug trafficking schemes. These professionals include doctors, pilots, boat captains, financiers, bankers, attorneys, chemists, accountants, and others whose special skill, trade, profession, or position may be used to significantly facilitate the commission of a drug offense. Additionally, an enhancement under §3B1.3 ordinarily would apply in a case in which the defendant used his or her position as a coach to influence an athlete to use an anabolic steroid. Likewise, an adjustment under §3B1.3 ordinarily would apply in a case in which the defendant is convicted of a drug offense resulting from the authorization of the defendant to receive scheduled substances from an ultimate user or long-term care facility. *See* 21 U.S.C. § 822(g).
Note, however, that if an adjustment from subsection (b)(3)(C) applies, do not apply §3B1.3 (Abuse of Position of Trust or Use of Special Skill).
24. **Cases Involving Mandatory Minimum Penalties.**—Where a mandatory (statutory) minimum sentence applies, this mandatory minimum sentence may be "waived" and a lower sentence imposed (including a downward departure), as provided in 28 U.S.C. § 994(n), by reason of a defendant's "substantial assistance in the investigation or prosecution of another person who has committed an offense." *See* §5K1.1 (Substantial Assistance to Authorities). In addition, 18 U.S.C. § 3553(f) provides an exception to the applicability of mandatory minimum sentences in certain cases. *See* §5C1.2 (Limitation on Applicability of Statutory Minimum Sentences in Certain Cases).
25. **Imposition of Consecutive Sentence for 21 U.S.C. § 860a or § 865.**—Sections 860a and 865 of title 21, United States Code, require the imposition of a mandatory consecutive term of imprisonment of not more than 20 years and 15 years, respectively. In order to comply with the relevant statute, the court should determine the appropriate "total punishment" and divide the sentence on the judgment form between the sentence attributable to the underlying drug offense and the sentence attributable to 21 U.S.C. § 860a or § 865, specifying the number of months to be served consecutively for the conviction under 21 U.S.C. § 860a or § 865. For example, if the applicable adjusted guideline range is 151–188 months and the court determines a "total punishment" of 151 months is appropriate, a sentence of 130 months for the underlying offense plus 21 months for the conduct covered by 21 U.S.C. § 860a or § 865 would achieve the "total punishment" in a manner that satisfies the statutory requirement of a consecutive sentence.
26. **Cases Involving "Small Amount of Marihuana for No Remuneration".**—Distribution of "a small amount of marihuana for no remuneration", 21 U.S.C. § 841(b)(4), is treated as simple possession, to which §2D2.1 applies.
27. **Departure Considerations.**—
(A) **Downward Departure Based on Drug Quantity in Certain Reverse Sting Operations.**—If, in a reverse sting (an operation in which a government agent sells or negotiates to sell a controlled substance to a defendant), the court finds that the government agent set a price for the controlled substance that was substantially below the market value of the controlled substance, thereby leading to the defendant's purchase of a significantly greater quantity of the controlled substance than

his available resources would have allowed him to purchase except for the artificially low price set by the government agent, a downward departure may be warranted.
(B) **Upward Departure Based on Drug Quantity.**—In an extraordinary case, an upward departure above offense level 38 on the basis of drug quantity may be warranted. For example, an upward departure may be warranted where the quantity is at least ten times the minimum quantity required for level 38. Similarly, in the case of a controlled substance for which the maximum offense level is less than level 38, an upward departure may be warranted if the drug quantity substantially exceeds the quantity for the highest offense level established for that particular

controlled substance.

(C) **Upward Departure Based on Unusually High Purity.**—Trafficking in controlled substances, compounds, or mixtures of unusually high purity may warrant an upward departure, except in the case of PCP, amphetamine, methamphetamine, hydrocodone, or oxycodone for which the guideline itself provides for the consideration of purity (*see* the footnote to the Drug Quantity Table). The purity of the controlled substance, particularly in the case of heroin, may be relevant in the sentencing process because it is probative of the defendant's role or position in the chain of distribution. Since controlled substances are often diluted and combined with other substances as they pass down the chain of distribution, the fact that a defendant is in possession of unusually pure narcotics may indicate a prominent role in the criminal enterprise and proximity to the source of the drugs. As large quantities are normally associated with high purities, this factor is particularly relevant where smaller quantities are involved.

Background: Offenses under 21 U.S.C. §§ 841 and 960 receive identical punishment based upon the quantity of the controlled substance involved, the defendant's criminal history, and whether death or serious bodily injury resulted from the offense.

The base offense levels in §2D1.1 are either provided directly by the Anti-Drug Abuse Act of 1986 or are proportional to the levels established by statute, and apply to all unlawful trafficking. Levels 30 and 24 in the Drug Quantity Table are the distinctions provided by the Anti-Drug Abuse Act; however, further refinement of drug amounts is essential to provide a logical sentencing structure for drug offenses. To determine these finer distinctions, the Commission consulted numerous experts and practitioners, including authorities at the Drug Enforcement Administration, chemists, attorneys, probation officers, and members of the Organized Crime Drug Enforcement Task Forces, who also advocate the necessity of these distinctions. Where necessary, this scheme has been modified in response to specific congressional directives to the Commission.

The base offense levels at levels 24 and 30 establish guideline ranges such that the statutory minimum falls within the range; *e.g.*, level 30 ranges from 97 to 121 months, where the statutory minimum term is ten years or 120 months.

For marihuana plants, the Commission has adopted an equivalency of 100 grams per plant, or the actual weight of the usable marihuana, whichever is greater. The decision to treat each plant as equal to 100 grams is premised on the fact that the average yield from a mature marihuana plant equals 100 grams of marihuana. In controlled substance offenses, an attempt is assigned the same offense level as the object of the attempt. Consequently, the Commission adopted the policy that each plant is to be treated as the equivalent of an attempt to produce 100 grams of marihuana, except where the actual weight of the usable marihuana is greater.

Because the weights of LSD carrier media vary widely and typically far exceed the weight of the controlled substance itself, the Commission has determined that basing offense levels on the entire weight of the LSD and carrier medium would produce unwarranted disparity among offenses involving the same quantity of actual LSD (but different carrier weights), as well as sentences disproportionate to those for other, more dangerous controlled substances, such as PCP. Consequently, in cases involving LSD contained in a carrier medium, the Commission has established a weight per dose of 0.4 milligram for purposes of determining the base offense level.

The dosage weight of LSD selected exceeds the Drug Enforcement Administration's standard dosage unit for LSD of 0.05 milligram (*i.e.*, the quantity of actual LSD per dose) in order to assign some weight to the carrier medium. Because LSD typically is marketed and consumed orally on a carrier medium, the inclusion of some weight attributable to the carrier medium recognizes (A) that offense levels for most other controlled substances are based upon the weight of the mixture containing the controlled substance without regard to purity, and (B) the decision in *Chapman v. United States*, 500 U.S. 453 (1991) (holding that the term "mixture or substance" in 21 U.S.C. § 841(b)(1) includes the carrier medium in which LSD is absorbed).

At the same time, the weight per dose selected is less than the weight per dose that would equate the offense level for LSD on a carrier medium with that for the same number of doses of PCP, a controlled substance that comparative assessments indicate is more likely to induce violent acts and ancillary crime than is LSD. (Treating LSD on a carrier medium as weighing 0.5 milligram per dose would produce offense levels equivalent to those for PCP.) Thus, the approach decided upon by the Commission will harmonize offense levels for LSD offenses with those for other controlled substances and avoid an undue influence of varied carrier weight on the applicable offense level. Nonetheless, this approach does not override the applicability of "mixture or substance" for the purpose of applying any mandatory minimum sentence (*see Chapman*; §5G1.1(b)).

Frequently, a term of supervised release to follow imprisonment is required by statute for offenses covered by this guideline. Guidelines for the imposition, duration, and conditions of supervised release are set forth in Chapter Five, Part D (Supervised Release).

The last sentence of subsection (a)(5) implements the directive to the Commission in section 7(1) of Public Law 111–220.

Subsection (b)(2) implements the directive to the Commission in section 5 of Public Law 111–220.

Subsection (b)(3) is derived from Section 6453 of the Anti-Drug Abuse Act of 1988.

Subsection (b)(11) implements the directive to the Commission in section 6(1) of Public Law 111–220.

Subsection (b)(12) implements the directive to the Commission in section 6(2) of Public Law 111–220.

Subsection (b)(13)(A) implements the instruction to the Commission in section 303 of Public Law 103–237.

Subsections (b)(13)(C)(ii) and (D) implement, in a broader form, the instruction to the Commission in section 102 of Public Law 106–310.

Subsection (b)(15) implements the directive to the Commission in section 6(3) of Public Law 111–220.

Subsection (b)(16) implements the directive to the Commission in section 7(2) of Public Law 111–220.

Historical Note

Effective November 1, 1987. Amended effective January 15, 1988 (amendments 19, 20, and 21); November 1, 1989 (amendments 123–134, 302, and 303); November 1, 1990 (amendment 318); November 1, 1991 (amendments 369–371 and 394–396); November 1, 1992 (amendments 446 and 447); November 1, 1993 (amendments 479, 484–488, and 499); September 23, 1994 (amendment 509); November 1, 1994 (amendment 505); November 1, 1995 (amendments 514–518); November 1, 1997 (amendments 555 and 556); November 1, 2000 (amendments 594 and 605); December 16, 2000 (amendment 608); May 1, 2001 (amendments 609–611); November 1, 2001 (amendments 620–625); November 1, 2002 (amendment 640); November 1, 2003 (amendment 657); November 1, 2004 (amendments 667, 668, and 674); November 1, 2005 (amendment 679); March 27, 2006 (amendment 681); November 1, 2006 (amendments 684 and 688); November 1, 2007 (amendments 705, 706, and 711); May 1, 2008 (amendment 715); November 1, 2009 (amendments 727 and 728); November 1, 2010 (amendments 746 and 748); November 1, 2011 (amendments 750, 751, and 760); November 1, 2012 (amendments 762 and 770); November 1, 2013 (amendment 777); November 1, 2014 (amendments 782 and 783); November 1, 2015 (amendments 793 and 797).

§2D1.2. Drug Offenses Occurring Near Protected Locations or Involving Underage or Pregnant Individuals; Attempt or Conspiracy

(a) Base Offense Level (Apply the greatest):

(1) **2** plus the offense level from §2D1.1 applicable to the quantity of controlled substances directly involving a protected location or an underage or pregnant individual; or

(2) **1** plus the offense level from §2D1.1 applicable to the total quantity of controlled substances involved in the offense; or

(3) **26**, if the offense involved a person less than eighteen years of age; or

(4) **13**, otherwise.

Commentary

Statutory Provisions: 21 U.S.C. §§ 859 (formerly 21 U.S.C. § 845), 860 (formerly 21 U.S.C. § 845a), 861 (formerly 21 U.S.C. § 845b).

Application Note:

1. This guideline applies only in a case in which the defendant is convicted of a statutory violation of drug trafficking in a protected location or involving an underage or pregnant individual (including an attempt or conspiracy to commit such a violation) or in a case in which the defendant stipulated to such a statutory violation. *See* §1B1.2(a). In a case involving such a conviction but in which only part of the relevant offense conduct directly involved a protected location or an underage or pregnant individual, subsections (a)(1) and (a)(2) may result in different offense levels. For example, if the defendant, as part of the same course of conduct or common scheme or plan, sold 5 grams of heroin near a protected location and 10 grams of heroin elsewhere, the offense level from subsection

(a)(1) would be level 14 (2 plus the offense level for the sale of 5 grams of heroin, the amount sold near the protected location); the offense level from subsection (a)(2) would be level 15 (1 plus the offense level for the sale of 15 grams of heroin, the total amount of heroin involved in the offense).

Background: This section implements the direction to the Commission in Section 6454 of the Anti-Drug Abuse Act of 1988.

Historical
Note

Effective November 1, 1987. Amended effective January 15, 1988 (amendment 22); November 1, 1989 (amendment 135); November 1, 1990 (amendment 319); November 1, 1991 (amendment 421); November 1, 1992 (amendment 447); November 1, 2000 (amendment 591); November 1, 2014 (amendment 782).

§2D1.3. [Deleted]

Historical
Note

Section 2D1.3 (Distributing Controlled Substances to Individuals Younger than Twenty-One Years, to Pregnant Women, or Within 1000 Feet of a School or College), effective November 1, 1987, amended effective January 15, 1988 (amendment 23), was deleted by consolidation with §2D1.2 effective November 1, 1989 (amendment 135).

§2D1.4. [Deleted]

Historical
Note

Section 2D1.4 (Attempts and Conspiracies), effective November 1, 1987, amended effective November 1, 1989 (amendments 136–138), was deleted by consolidation with the guidelines applicable to the underlying substantive offenses effective November 1, 1992 (amendment 447).

§2D1.5. Continuing Criminal Enterprise; Attempt or Conspiracy

(a) Base Offense Level (Apply the greater):

(1) **4** plus the offense level from §2D1.1 applicable to the underlying offense; or

(2) **38**.

Commentary

Statutory Provision: 21 U.S.C. § 848.

Application Notes:

1. Do not apply any adjustment from Chapter Three, Part B (Role in the Offense).

2. If as part of the enterprise the defendant sanctioned the use of violence, or if the number of persons managed by the defendant was extremely large, an upward departure may be warranted.

3. Under 21 U.S.C. § 848, certain conduct for which the defendant has previously been sentenced may be charged as part of the instant offense to establish a "continuing series of violations." A sentence resulting from a conviction sustained prior to the last overt act of

the instant offense is to be considered a prior sentence under §4A1.2(a)(1) and not part of the instant offense.

4. Violations of 21 U.S.C. § 848 will be grouped with other drug offenses for the purpose of applying Chapter Three, Part D (Multiple Counts).

Background: Because a conviction under 21 U.S.C. § 848 establishes that a defendant controlled and exercised authority over one of the most serious types of ongoing criminal activity, this guideline provides a minimum base offense level of 38. An adjustment from Chapter Three, Part B is not authorized because the offense level of this guideline already reflects an adjustment for role in the offense.

Title 21 U.S.C. § 848 provides a 20-year minimum mandatory penalty for the first conviction, a 30-year minimum mandatory penalty for a second conviction, and a mandatory life sentence for principal administrators of extremely large enterprises. If the application of the guidelines results in a sentence below the minimum sentence required by statute, the statutory minimum shall be the guideline sentence. *See* §5G1.1(b).

Historical Note

Effective November 1, 1987. Amended effective October 15, 1988 (amendment 66); November 1, 1989 (amendment 139); November 1, 1992 (amendment 447).

§2D1.6. Use of Communication Facility in Committing Drug Offense; Attempt or Conspiracy

(a) Base Offense Level: the offense level applicable to the underlying offense.

Commentary

Statutory Provision: 21 U.S.C. § 843(b).

Application Note:

1. Where the offense level for the underlying offense is to be determined by reference to §2D1.1, *see* Application Note 5 of the Commentary to §2D1.1 for guidance in determining the scale of the offense. Note that the Drug Quantity Table in §2D1.1 provides a minimum offense level of 12 where the offense involves heroin (or other Schedule I or II opiates), cocaine (or other Schedule I or II stimulants), cocaine base, PCP, methamphetamine, LSD (or other Schedule I or II hallucinogens), fentanyl, or fentanyl analogue (§2D1.1(c)(14)); a minimum offense level of 8 where the offense involves flunitrazepam (§2D1.1(c)(16)); and a minimum offense level of 6 otherwise (§2D1.1(c)(17)).

Background: This section covers the use of a communication facility in committing a drug offense. A communication facility includes any public or private instrument used in the transmission of writing, signs, signals, pictures, and sound; *e.g.*, telephone, wire, radio.

Historical Note

Effective November 1, 1987. Amended effective November 1, 1990 (amendment 320); November 1, 1992 (amendment 447); November 1, 1994 (amendment 505); November 1, 2009 (amendment 737); November 1, 2012 (amendment 770).

§2D1.7. Unlawful Sale or Transportation of Drug Paraphernalia; Attempt or Conspiracy

(a) Base Offense Level: **12**

(b) Cross Reference

(1) If the offense involved a controlled substance, apply §2D1.1 (Unlawful Manufacturing, Importing, Exporting, or Trafficking) or §2D2.1 (Unlawful Possession), as appropriate, if the resulting offense level is greater than that determined above.

Commentary

Statutory Provision: 21 U.S.C. § 863 (formerly 21 U.S.C. § 857).

Application Note:

1. The typical case addressed by this guideline involves small-scale trafficking in drug paraphernalia (generally from a retail establishment that also sells items that are not unlawful).

In a case involving a large-scale dealer, distributor, or manufacturer, an upward departure may be warranted. Conversely, where the offense was not committed for pecuniary gain (*e.g.*, transportation for the defendant's personal use), a downward departure may be warranted.

Historical
Note
Effective November 1, 1987. Amended effective November 1, 1991 (amendment 397); November 1, 1992 (amendment 447).

§2D1.8. Renting or Managing a Drug Establishment; Attempt or Conspiracy

(a) Base Offense Level:

(1) The offense level from §2D1.1 applicable to the underlying controlled substance offense, except as provided below.

(2) If the defendant had no participation in the underlying controlled substance offense other than allowing use of the premises, the offense level shall be **4** levels less than the offense level from §2D1.1 applicable to the underlying controlled substance offense, but not greater than level **26**.

(b) Special Instruction

(1) If the offense level is determined under subsection (a)(2), do not apply an adjustment under §3B1.2 (Mitigating Role).

Commentary

Statutory Provision: 21 U.S.C. § 856.

Application Note:

1. Subsection (a)(2) does not apply unless the defendant had no participation in the underlying controlled substance offense other than allowing use of the premises. For example, subsection (a)(2) would not apply to a defendant who possessed a dangerous weapon in connection with the offense, a defendant who guarded the cache of controlled substances, a defendant who arranged for the use of the premises for the purpose of facilitating a drug transaction, a defendant who allowed the use of more than one premises, a defendant who made telephone calls to facilitate the underlying controlled substance offense, or a defendant who otherwise assisted in the commission of the underlying controlled substance offense. Furthermore, subsection (a)(2) does not apply unless the defendant initially leased, rented, purchased, or otherwise acquired a possessory interest in the premises for a legitimate purpose. Finally, subsection (a)(2) does not apply if the defendant had previously allowed any premises to be used as a drug establishment without regard to whether such prior misconduct resulted in a conviction.

Background: This section covers the offense of knowingly opening, maintaining, managing, or controlling any building, room, or enclosure for the purpose of manufacturing, distributing, storing, or using a controlled substance contrary to law (*e.g.*, a "crack house").

Historical
Note
Effective November 1, 1987. Amended effective November 1, 1991 (amendment 394); November 1, 1992 (amendments 447 and 448); November 1, 2002 (amendment 640).

§2D1.9. Placing or Maintaining Dangerous Devices on Federal Property to Protect the Unlawful Production of Controlled Substances; Attempt or Conspiracy

(a) Base Offense Level: **23**

Commentary

Statutory Provision: 21 U.S.C. § 841(d)(1).

Background: This section covers the offense of assembling, placing, or causing to be placed, or maintaining a "booby-trap" on federal property where a controlled substance is being manufactured or distributed.

Historical

Note
Effective November 1, 1987. Amended effective November 1, 1992 (amendment 447); November 1, 2002 (amendment 646).

§2D1.10. Endangering Human Life While Illegally Manufacturing a Controlled Substance; Attempt or Conspiracy

(a) Base Offense Level (Apply the greater):

(1) **3** plus the offense level from the Drug Quantity Table in §2D1.1; or

(2) **20**.

(b) Specific Offense Characteristic

(1) (Apply the greater):

(A) If the offense involved the manufacture of amphetamine or methamphetamine, increase by **3** levels. If the resulting offense level is less than level **27**, increase to level **27**.

(B) If the offense (i) involved the manufacture of amphetamine or methamphetamine; and (ii) created a substantial risk of harm to the life of a minor or an incompetent, increase by **6** levels. If the resulting offense level is less than level **30**, increase to level **30**.

Commentary

Statutory Provision: 21 U.S.C. § 858.

Application Note:

1. **Substantial Risk of Harm Associated with the Manufacture of Amphetamine and Methamphetamine.—**

(A) **Factors to Consider.**—In determining, for purposes of subsection (b)(1)(B), whether the offense created a substantial risk of harm to the life of a minor or an incompetent, the court shall include consideration of the following factors:

(i) The quantity of any chemicals or hazardous or toxic substances found at the laboratory, and the manner in which the chemicals or substances were stored.

(ii) The manner in which hazardous or toxic substances were disposed, and the likelihood of release into the environment of hazardous or toxic substances.

(iii) The duration of the offense, and the extent of the manufacturing operation.

(iv) The location of the laboratory (*e.g.*, whether the laboratory is located in a residential neighborhood or a remote area), and the number of human lives placed at substantial risk of harm.

(B) **Definitions.**—For purposes of subsection (b)(1)(B):

"***Incompetent***" means an individual who is incapable of taking care of the individual's self or property because of a mental or physical illness or disability, mental retardation, or senility.

"***Minor***" has the meaning given that term in Application Note 1 of the Commentary to §2A3.1 (Criminal Sexual Abuse).

Background: Subsection (b)(1) implements the instruction to the Commission in section 102 of Public Law 106–310.

Historical
Note
Effective November 1, 1989 (amendment 140). Amended effective November 1, 1992 (amendment 447); December 16, 2000 (amendment 608); November 1, 2001 (amendment 620).

§2D1.11. Unlawfully Distributing, Importing, Exporting or Possessing a Listed Chemical; Attempt or Conspiracy

(a) Base Offense Level: The offense level from the Chemical Quantity Table set forth in subsection (d) or (e), as appropriate, except that if (A) the defendant receives an adjustment under §3B1.2 (Mitigating Role); and (B) the base offense level under subsection (d) is (i) level **32**, decrease by **2** levels; (ii) level **34** or level **36**, decrease by **3** levels; or (iii) level **38**, decrease by **4** levels.

(b) Specific Offense Characteristics

(1) If a dangerous weapon (including a firearm) was possessed, increase by **2** levels.

(2) If the defendant is convicted of violating 21 U.S.C. § 841(c)(2) or (f)(1), or § 960(d)(2), (d)(3), or (d)(4), decrease by **3** levels, unless the defendant knew or believed that the listed chemical was to be used to manufacture a controlled substance unlawfully.

(3) If the offense involved (A) an unlawful discharge, emission, or release into the environment of a hazardous or toxic substance; or (B) the unlawful transportation, treatment, storage, or disposal of a hazardous waste, increase by **2** levels.

(4) If the defendant, or a person for whose conduct the defendant is accountable under §1B1.3 (Relevant Conduct), distributed a listed chemical through mass-marketing by means of an interactive computer service, increase by **2** levels.

(5) If the defendant is convicted under 21 U.S.C. § 865, increase by **2** levels.

(6) If the defendant meets the criteria set forth in subdivisions (1)–(5) of subsection (a) of §5C1.2 (Limitation on Applicability of Statutory Minimum Sentences in Certain Cases), decrease by **2** levels.

(c) Cross Reference

(1) If the offense involved unlawfully manufacturing a controlled substance, or attempting to manufacture a controlled substance unlawfully, apply §2D1.1 (Unlawful Manufacturing, Importing, Exporting, Trafficking) if the resulting offense level is greater than that determined above.

(d) EPHEDRINE, PSEUDOEPHEDRINE, AND PHENYLPROPANOLAMINE QUANTITY TABLE*

(Methamphetamine and Amphetamine Precursor Chemicals)

QUANTITY BASE OFFENSE LEVEL

(1) 9 KG or more of Ephedrine; **Level 38**
9 KG or more of Phenylpropanolamine;
9 KG or more of Pseudoephedrine.

(2) At least 3 KG but less than 9 KG of Ephedrine; **Level 36**
At least 3 KG but less than 9 KG of Phenylpropanolamine;
At least 3 KG but less than 9 KG of Pseudoephedrine.

(3) At least 1 KG but less than 3 KG of Ephedrine; **Level 34**
At least 1 KG but less than 3 KG of Phenylpropanolamine;
At least 1 KG but less than 3 KG of Pseudoephedrine.

(4) At least 300 G but less than 1 KG of Ephedrine; **Level 32**
At least 300 G but less than 1 KG of Phenylpropanolamine;
At least 300 G but less than 1 KG of Pseudoephedrine.

(5) At least 100 G but less than 300 G of Ephedrine; **Level 30**
At least 100 G but less than 300 G of Phenylpropanolamine;
At least 100 G but less than 300 G of Pseudoephedrine.

(6) At least 70 G but less than 100 G of Ephedrine; **Level 28**
At least 70 G but less than 100 G of Phenylpropanolamine;
At least 70 G but less than 100 G of Pseuodoephedrine.

(7) At least 40 G but less than 70 G of Ephedrine; **Level 26**
At least 40 G but less than 70 G of Phenylpropanolamine;
At least 40 G but less than 70 G of Pseudoephedrine.

(8) At least 10 G but less than 40 G of Ephedrine; **Level 24**
At least 10 G but less than 40 G of Phenylpropanolamine;
At least 10 G but less than 40 G of Pseudoephedrine.

(9) At least 8 G but less than 10 G of Ephedrine; **Level 22**
At least 8 G but less than 10 G of Phenylpropanolamine;
At least 8 G but less than 10 G of Pseudoephedrine.

(10) At least 6 G but less than 8 G of Ephedrine; **Level 20**
At least 6 G but less than 8 G of Phenylpropanolamine;
At least 6 G but less than 8 G of Pseudoephedrine.

(11) At least 4 G but less than 6 G of Ephedrine; **Level 18**
At least 4 G but less than 6 G of Phenylpropanolamine;
At least 4 G but less than 6 G of Pseudoephedrine.

(12) At least 2 G but less than 4 G of Ephedrine; **Level 16**
At least 2 G but less than 4 G of Phenylpropanolamine;
At least 2 G but less than 4 G of Pseudoephedrine.

(13) At least 1 G but less than 2 G of Ephedrine; **Level 14**
At least 1 G but less than 2 G of Phenylpropanolamine;
At least 1 G but less than 2 G of Pseudoephedrine.

(14) Less than 1 G of Ephedrine; **Level 12**
Less than 1 G of Phenylpropanolamine;
Less than 1 G of Pseudoephedrine.

(e) CHEMICAL QUANTITY TABLE*
(All Other Precursor Chemicals)

LISTED CHEMICALS AND QUANTITY BASE OFFENSE LEVEL

(1) **List I Chemicals Level 30**
2.7 KG or more of Benzaldehyde;
60 KG or more of Benzyl Cyanide;
600 G or more of Ergonovine;
1.2 KG or more of Ergotamine;
60 KG or more of Ethylamine;
6.6 KG or more of Hydriodic Acid;
3.9 KG or more of Iodine;
960 KG or more of Isosafrole;
600 G or more of Methylamine;
1500 KG or more of N-Methylephedrine;
1500 KG or more of N-Methylpseudoephedrine;

1.9 KG or more of Nitroethane;
30 KG or more of Norpseudoephedrine;
60 KG or more of Phenylacetic Acid;
30 KG or more of Piperidine;
960 KG or more of Piperonal;
4.8 KG or more of Propionic Anhydride;
960 KG or more of Safrole;
1200 KG or more of 3, 4-Methylenedioxyphenyl-2-propanone;
3406.5 L or more of Gamma-butyrolactone;
2.1 KG or more of Red Phosphorus, White Phosphorus, or Hypophosphorous Acid.

(2) **List I Chemicals Level 28**

At least 890 G but less than 2.7 KG of Benzaldehyde;
At least 20 KG but less than 60 KG of Benzyl Cyanide;
At least 200 G but less than 600 G of Ergonovine;
At least 400 G but less than 1.2 KG of Ergotamine;
At least 20 KG but less than 60 KG of Ethylamine;
At least 2.2 KG but less than 6.6 KG of Hydriodic Acid;
At least 1.3 KG but less than 3.9 KG of Iodine;
At least 320 KG but less than 960 KG of Isosafrole;
At least 200 G but less than 600 G of Methylamine;
At least 500 KG but less than 1500 KG of N-Methylephedrine;
At least 500 KG but less than 1500 KG of N-Methylpseudoephedrine;
At least 625 G but less than 1.9 KG of Nitroethane;
At least 10 KG but less than 30 KG of Norpseudoephedrine;
At least 20 KG but less than 60 KG of Phenylacetic Acid;
At least 10 KG but less than 30 KG of Piperidine;
At least 320 KG but less than 960 KG of Piperonal;
At least 1.6 KG but less than 4.8 KG of Propionic Anhydride;
At least 320 KG but less than 960 KG of Safrole;
At least 400 KG but less than 1200 KG of 3, 4-Methylenedioxyphenyl-2-propanone;
At least 1135.5 L but less than 3406.5 L of Gamma-butyrolactone;
At least 714 G but less than 2.1 KG of Red Phosphorus, White Phosphorus, or Hypophosphorous Acid.

List II Chemicals

33 KG or more of Acetic Anhydride;
3525 KG or more of Acetone;
60 KG or more of Benzyl Chloride;
3225 KG or more of Ethyl Ether;
3600 KG or more of Methyl Ethyl Ketone;
30 KG or more of Potassium Permanganate;
3900 KG or more of Toluene.

(3) **List I Chemicals Level 26**

At least 267 G but less than 890 G of Benzaldehyde;
At least 6 KG but less than 20 KG of Benzyl Cyanide;
At least 60 G but less than 200 G of Ergonovine;
At least 120 G but less than 400 G of Ergotamine;
At least 6 KG but less than 20 KG of Ethylamine;
At least 660 G but less than 2.2 KG of Hydriodic Acid;
At least 376.2 G but less than 1.3 KG of Iodine;
At least 96 KG but less than 320 KG of Isosafrole;

At least 60 G but less than 200 G of Methylamine;
At least 150 KG but less than 500 KG of N-Methylephedrine;
At least 150 KG but less than 500 KG of N-Methylpseudoephedrine;

At least 187.5 G but less than 625 G of Nitroethane;
At least 3 KG but less than 10 KG of Norpseudoephedrine;
At least 6 KG but less than 20 KG of Phenylacetic Acid;
At least 3 KG but less than 10 KG of Piperidine;
At least 96 KG but less than 320 KG of Piperonal;
At least 480 G but less than 1.6 KG of Propionic Anhydride;
At least 96 KG but less than 320 KG of Safrole;
At least 120 KG but less than 400 KG of 3, 4-Methylenedioxyphenyl-2-propanone;
At least 340.7 L but less than 1135.5 L of Gamma-butyrolactone;
At least 214 G but less than 714 G of Red Phosphorus, White Phosphorus, or Hypophosphorous Acid;

List II Chemicals

At least 11 KG but less than 33 KG of Acetic Anhydride;
At least 1175 KG but less than 3525 KG of Acetone;
At least 20 KG but less than 60 KG of Benzyl Chloride;
At least 1075 KG but less than 3225 KG of Ethyl Ether;
At least 1200 KG but less than 3600 KG of Methyl Ethyl Ketone;
At least 10 KG but less than 30 KG of Potassium Permanganate;
At least 1300 KG but less than 3900 KG of Toluene.

(4) **List I Chemicals Level 24**

At least 89 G but less than 267 G of Benzaldehyde;
At least 2 KG but less than 6 KG of Benzyl Cyanide;
At least 20 G but less than 60 G of Ergonovine;
At least 40 G but less than 120 G of Ergotamine;
At least 2 KG but less than 6 KG of Ethylamine;
At least 220 G but less than 660 G of Hydriodic Acid;
At least 125.4 G but less than 376.2 G of Iodine;
At least 32 KG but less than 96 KG of Isosafrole;
At least 20 G but less than 60 G of Methylamine;
At least 50 KG but less than 150 KG of N-Methylephedrine;
At least 50 KG but less than 150 KG of N-Methylpseudoephedrine;
At least 62.5 G but less than 187.5 G of Nitroethane;
At least 1 KG but less than 3 KG of Norpseudoephedrine;
At least 2 KG but less than 6 KG of Phenylacetic Acid;
At least 1 KG but less than 3 KG of Piperidine;
At least 32 KG but less than 96 KG of Piperonal;
At least 160 G but less than 480 G of Propionic Anhydride;
At least 32 KG but less than 96 KG of Safrole;
At least 40 KG but less than 120 KG of 3, 4-Methylenedioxyphenyl-2-propanone;
At least 113.6 L but less than 340.7 L of Gamma-butyrolactone;
At least 71 G but less than 214 G of Red Phosphorus, White Phosphorus, or Hypophosphorous Acid;

List II Chemicals

At least 3.3 KG but less than 11 KG of Acetic Anhydride;
At least 352.5 KG but less than 1175 KG of Acetone;
At least 6 KG but less than 20 KG of Benzyl Chloride;
At least 322.5 KG but less than 1075 KG of Ethyl Ether;
At least 360 KG but less than 1200 KG of Methyl Ethyl Ketone;

At least 3 KG but less than 10 KG of Potassium Permanganate;
At least 390 KG but less than 1300 KG of Toluene.

(5) **List I Chemicals Level 22**

At least 62.3 G but less than 89 G of Benzaldehyde;
At least 1.4 KG but less than 2 KG of Benzyl Cyanide;

At least 14 G but less than 20 G of Ergonovine;
At least 28 G but less than 40 G of Ergotamine;
At least 1.4 KG but less than 2 KG of Ethylamine;
At least 154 G but less than 220 G of Hydriodic Acid;
At least 87.8 G but less than 125.4 G of Iodine;
At least 22.4 KG but less than 32 KG of Isosafrole;
At least 14 G but less than 20 G of Methylamine;
At least 35 KG but less than 50 KG of N-Methylephedrine;
At least 35 KG but less than 50 KG of N-Methylpseudoephedrine;
At least 43.8 G but less than 62.5 G of Nitroethane;
At least 700 G but less than 1 KG of Norpseudoephedrine;
At least 1.4 KG but less than 2 KG of Phenylacetic Acid;
At least 700 G but less than 1 KG of Piperidine;
At least 22.4 KG but less than 32 KG of Piperonal;
At least 112 G but less than 160 G of Propionic Anhydride;
At least 22.4 KG but less than 32 KG of Safrole;
At least 28 KG but less than 40 KG of 3, 4-Methylenedioxyphenyl-2-propanone;
At least 79.5 L but less than 113.6 L of Gamma-butyrolactone;
At least 50 G but less than 71 G of Red Phosphorus, White Phosphorus, or Hypophosphorous Acid;

List II Chemicals

At least 1.1 KG but less than 3.3 KG of Acetic Anhydride;
At least 117.5 KG but less than 352.5 KG of Acetone;
At least 2 KG but less than 6 KG of Benzyl Chloride;
At least 107.5 KG but less than 322.5 KG of Ethyl Ether;
At least 120 KG but less than 360 KG of Methyl Ethyl Ketone;
At least 1 KG but less than 3 KG of Potassium Permanganate;
At least 130 KG but less than 390 KG of Toluene.

(6) **List I Chemicals Level 20**

At least 35.6 G but less than 62.3 G of Benzaldehyde;
At least 800 G but less than 1.4 KG of Benzyl Cyanide;
At least 8 G but less than 14 G of Ergonovine;
At least 16 G but less than 28 G of Ergotamine;
At least 800 G but less than 1.4 KG of Ethylamine;
At least 88 G but less than 154 G of Hydriodic Acid;
At least 50.2 G but less than 87.8 G of Iodine;
At least 12.8 KG but less than 22.4 KG of Isosafrole;
At least 8 G but less than 14 G of Methylamine;
At least 20 KG but less than 35 KG of N-Methylephedrine;
At least 20 KG but less than 35 KG of N-Methylpseudoephedrine;
At least 25 G but less than 43.8 G of Nitroethane;
At least 400 G but less than 700 G of Norpseudoephedrine;
At least 800 G but less than 1.4 KG of Phenylacetic Acid;
At least 400 G but less than 700 G of Piperidine;
At least 12.8 KG but less than 22.4 KG of Piperonal;

At least 64 G but less than 112 G of Propionic Anhydride;
At least 12.8 KG but less than 22.4 KG of Safrole;
At least 16 KG but less than 28 KG of 3, 4-Methylenedioxyphenyl-2-propanone;
At least 45.4 L but less than 79.5 L of Gamma-butyrolactone;
At least 29 G but less than 50 G of Red Phosphorus, White Phosphorus, or Hypophosphorous Acid;

List II Chemicals

At least 726 G but less than 1.1 KG of Acetic Anhydride;

At least 82.25 KG but less than 117.5 KG of Acetone;
At least 1.4 KG but less than 2 KG of Benzyl Chloride;
At least 75.25 KG but less than 107.5 KG of Ethyl Ether;
At least 84 KG but less than 120 KG of Methyl Ethyl Ketone;
At least 700 G but less than 1 KG of Potassium Permanganate;
At least 91 KG but less than 130 KG of Toluene.

(7) **List I Chemicals Level 18**

At least 8.9 G but less than 35.6 G of Benzaldehyde;
At least 200 G but less than 800 G of Benzyl Cyanide;
At least 2 G but less than 8 G of Ergonovine;
At least 4 G but less than 16 G of Ergotamine;
At least 200 G but less than 800 G of Ethylamine;
At least 22 G but less than 88 G of Hydriodic Acid;
At least 12.5 G but less than 50.2 G of Iodine;
At least 3.2 KG but less than 12.8 KG of Isosafrole;
At least 2 G but less than 8 G of Methylamine;
At least 5 KG but less than 20 KG of N-Methylephedrine;
At least 5 KG but less than 20 KG of N-Methylpseudoephedrine;
At least 6.3 G but less than 25 G of Nitroethane;
At least 100 G but less than 400 G of Norpseudoephedrine;
At least 200 G but less than 800 G of Phenylacetic Acid;
At least 100 G but less than 400 G of Piperidine;
At least 3.2 KG but less than 12.8 KG of Piperonal;
At least 16 G but less than 64 G of Propionic Anhydride;
At least 3.2 KG but less than 12.8 KG of Safrole;
At least 4 KG but less than 16 KG of 3, 4-Methylenedioxyphenyl-2-propanone;
At least 11.4 L but less than 45.4 L of Gamma-butyrolactone;
At least 7 G but less than 29 G of Red Phosphorus, White Phosphorus, or Hypophosphorous Acid;

List II Chemicals

At least 440 G but less than 726 G of Acetic Anhydride;
At least 47 KG but less than 82.25 KG of Acetone;
At least 800 G but less than 1.4 KG of Benzyl Chloride;
At least 43 KG but less than 75.25 KG of Ethyl Ether;
At least 48 KG but less than 84 KG of Methyl Ethyl Ketone;
At least 400 G but less than 700 G of Potassium Permanganate;
At least 52 KG but less than 91 KG of Toluene.

(8) **List I Chemicals Level 16**

At least 7.1 G but less than 8.9 G of Benzaldehyde;
At least 160 G but less than 200 G of Benzyl Cyanide;
At least 1.6 G but less than 2 G of Ergonovine;

At least 3.2 G but less than 4 G of Ergotamine;
At least 160 G but less than 200 G of Ethylamine;
At least 17.6 G but less than 22 G of Hydriodic Acid;
At least 10 G but less than 12.5 G of Iodine;
At least 2.56 KG but less than 3.2 KG of Isosafrole;
At least 1.6 G but less than 2 G of Methylamine;
At least 4 KG but less than 5 KG of N-Methylephedrine;
At least 4 KG but less than 5 KG of N-Methylpseudoephedrine;
At least 5 G but less than 6.3 G of Nitroethane;
At least 80 G but less than 100 G of Norpseudoephedrine;
At least 160 G but less than 200 G of Phenylacetic Acid;
At least 80 G but less than 100 G of Piperidine;

At least 2.56 KG but less than 3.2 KG of Piperonal;
At least 12.8 G but less than 16 G of Propionic Anhydride;
At least 2.56 KG but less than 3.2 KG of Safrole;
At least 3.2 KG but less than 4 KG of 3, 4-Methylenedioxyphenyl-2-propanone;
At least 9.1 L but less than 11.4 L of Gamma-butyrolactone;
At least 6 G but less than 7 G of Red Phosphorus, White Phosphorus, or Hypophosphorous Acid;

List II Chemicals

At least 110 G but less than 440 G of Acetic Anhydride;
At least 11.75 KG but less than 47 KG of Acetone;
At least 200 G but less than 800 G of Benzyl Chloride;
At least 10.75 KG but less than 43 KG of Ethyl Ether;
At least 12 KG but less than 48 KG of Methyl Ethyl Ketone;
At least 100 G but less than 400 G of Potassium Permanganate;
At least 13 KG but less than 52 KG of Toluene.

(9) **List I Chemicals Level 14**

3.6 KG or more of Anthranilic Acid;
At least 5.3 G but less than 7.1 G of Benzaldehyde;
At least 120 G but less than 160 G of Benzyl Cyanide;
At least 1.2 G but less than 1.6 G of Ergonovine;
At least 2.4 G but less than 3.2 G of Ergotamine;
At least 120 G but less than 160 G of Ethylamine;
At least 13.2 G but less than 17.6 G of Hydriodic Acid;
At least 7.5 G but less than 10 G of Iodine;
At least 1.92 KG but less than 2.56 KG of Isosafrole;
At least 1.2 G but less than 1.6 G of Methylamine;
4.8 KG or more of N-Acetylanthranilic Acid;
At least 3 KG but less than 4 KG of N-Methylephedrine;
At least 3 KG but less than 4 KG of N-Methylpseudoephedrine;
At least 3.8 G but less than 5 G of Nitroethane;
At least 60 G but less than 80 G of Norpseudoephedrine;
At least 120 G but less than 160 G of Phenylacetic Acid;
At least 60 G but less than 80 G of Piperidine;
At least 1.92 KG but less than 2.56 KG of Piperonal;
At least 9.6 G but less than 12.8 G of Propionic Anhydride;
At least 1.92 KG but less than 2.56 KG of Safrole;
At least 2.4 KG but less than 3.2 KG of 3, 4-Methylenedioxyphenyl-2-propanone;
At least 6.8 L but less than 9.1 L of Gamma-butyrolactone;
At least 4 G but less than 6 G of Red Phosphorus, White Phosphorus, or Hypophosphorous Acid;

List II Chemicals

At least 88 G but less than 110 G of Acetic Anhydride;
At least 9.4 KG but less than 11.75 KG of Acetone;
At least 160 G but less than 200 G of Benzyl Chloride;
At least 8.6 KG but less than 10.75 KG of Ethyl Ether;
At least 9.6 KG but less than 12 KG of Methyl Ethyl Ketone;
At least 80 G but less than 100 G of Potassium Permanganate;
At least 10.4 KG but less than 13 KG of Toluene.

(10) **List I Chemicals Level 12**

Less than 3.6 KG of Anthranilic Acid;
Less than 5.3 G of Benzaldehyde;
Less than 120 G of Benzyl Cyanide;
Less than 1.2 G of Ergonovine;

Less than 2.4 G of Ergotamine;
Less than 120 G of Ethylamine;
Less than 13.2 G of Hydriodic Acid;
Less than 7.5 G of Iodine;
Less than 1.92 KG of Isosafrole;
Less than 1.2 G of Methylamine;
Less than 4.8 KG of N-Acetylanthranilic Acid;
Less than 3 KG of N-Methylephedrine;
Less than 3 KG of N-Methylpseudoephedrine;
Less than 3.8 G of Nitroethane;
Less than 60 G of Norpseudoephedrine;
Less than 120 G of Phenylacetic Acid;
Less than 60 G of Piperidine;
Less than 1.92 KG of Piperonal;
Less than 9.6 G of Propionic Anhydride;
Less than 1.92 KG of Safrole;
Less than 2.4 KG of 3, 4-Methylenedioxyphenyl-2-propanone;
Less than 6.8 L of Gamma-butyrolactone;
Less than 4 G of Red Phosphorus, White Phosphorus, or Hypophosphorous Acid;

List II Chemicals

Less than 88 G of Acetic Anhydride;
Less than 9.4 KG of Acetone;
Less than 160 G of Benzyl Chloride;
Less than 8.6 KG of Ethyl Ether;
Less than 9.6 KG of Methyl Ethyl Ketone;
Less than 80 G of Potassium Permanganate;
Less than 10.4 KG of Toluene.

***Notes:**

(A) Except as provided in Note (B), to calculate the base offense level in an offense that involves two or more chemicals, use the quantity of the single chemical that results in the greatest offense level, regardless of whether the chemicals are set forth in different tables or in different categories (*i.e.*, list I or list II) under subsection (d) or (e) of this guideline, as appropriate.

(B) To calculate the base offense level in an offense that involves two or more chemicals each of which is set forth in the Ephedrine, Pseudoephedrine, and Phenylpropanolamine Quantity Table, (i) aggregate the quantities of all such chemicals, and (ii) determine the base offense level corresponding to the aggregate quantity.

(C) In a case involving ephedrine, pseudoephedrine, or phenylpropanolamine tablets, use the weight of the ephedrine, pseudoephedrine, or phenylpropanolamine contained in the tablets, not the weight of the entire tablets, in calculating the base offense level.

Commentary

Statutory Provisions: 21 U.S.C. §§ 841(c)(1), (2), (f)(1), 865, 960(d)(1), (2), (3), (4).

Application Notes:

1. **Cases Involving Multiple Chemicals.—**

(A) **Determining the Base Offense Level for Two or More Chemicals.—**Except as provided in subdivision (B), if the offense involves two or more chemicals, use the quantity of the single chemical that results in the greatest offense level, regardless of whether the chemicals are set forth in different tables or in different categories (*i.e.*, list I or list II) under this guideline.

Example: The defendant was in possession of five kilograms of ephedrine and 300 grams of hydriodic acid. Ephedrine and hydriodic acid typically are used together in the same manufacturing process to manufacture methamphetamine. The base offense level for each chemical is calculated separately and the chemical with the higher base offense level is used. Five kilograms of ephedrine result in a base offense level of level 36; 300 grams of hydriodic acid result in a base offense level of level 24. In this case, the base offense level would be level 36.

(B) **Determining the Base Offense Level for Offenses involving Ephedrine, Pseudoephedrine, or Phenylpropanolamine.**—If the offense involves two or more chemicals each of which is set forth in the Ephedrine, Pseudoephedrine, and Phenylpropanolamine Quantity Table, (i) aggregate the quantities of all such chemicals, and (ii) determine the base offense level corresponding to the aggregate quantity.

Example: The defendant was in possession of 80 grams of ephedrine and 50 grams of phenylpropanolamine, an aggregate quantity of 130 grams of such chemicals. The base offense level corresponding to that aggregate quantity is level 30.

(C) **Upward Departure.**—In a case involving two or more chemicals used to manufacture different controlled substances, or to manufacture one controlled substance by different manufacturing processes, an upward departure may be warranted if the offense level does not adequately address the seriousness of the offense.

2. **Application of Subsection (b)(1).**—"***Firearm***" and "***dangerous weapon***" are defined in the Commentary to §1B1.1 (Application Instructions). The adjustment in subsection

(b)(1) should be applied if the weapon was present, unless it is improbable that the weapon was connected with the offense.

3. **Application of Subsection (b)(2).**—Convictions under 21 U.S.C. §§ 841(c)(2) and (f)(1), and 960(d)(2), (d)(3), and (d)(4) do not require that the defendant have knowledge or an actual belief that the listed chemical was to be used to manufacture a controlled substance unlawfully. In a case in which the defendant possessed or distributed the listed chemical without such knowledge or belief, a 3-level reduction is provided to reflect that the defendant is less culpable than one who possessed or distributed listed chemicals knowing or believing that they would be used to manufacture a controlled substance unlawfully.

4. **Application of Subsection (b)(3).**—Subsection (b)(3) applies if the conduct for which the defendant is accountable under §1B1.3 (Relevant Conduct) involved any discharge, emission, release, transportation, treatment, storage, or disposal violation covered by the Resource Conservation and Recovery Act, 42 U.S.C. § 6928(d), the Federal Water Pollution Control Act, 33 U.S.C. § 1319(c), the Comprehensive Environmental Response, Compensation, and Liability Act, 42 U.S.C. § 9603(b), and 49 U.S.C. § 5124 (relating to violations of laws and regulations enforced by the Department of Transportation with respect to the transportation of hazardous material). In some cases, the enhancement under subsection (b)(3) may not adequately account for the seriousness of the environmental harm or other threat to public health or safety (including the health or safety of law enforcement and cleanup personnel). In such cases, an upward departure may be warranted. Additionally, any costs of environmental cleanup and harm to persons or property should be considered by the court in determining the amount of restitution under §5E1.1 (Restitution) and in fashioning appropriate conditions of supervision under §§5B1.3 (Conditions of Probation) and 5D1.3 (Conditions of Supervised Release).

5. **Application of Subsection (b)(4).**—For purposes of subsection (b)(4), "***mass-marketing by means of an interactive computer service***" means the solicitation, by means of an interactive computer service, of a large number of persons to induce those persons to purchase a controlled substance. For example, subsection (b)(4) would apply to a defendant who operated a web site to promote the sale of Gamma-butyrolactone (GBL) but would not apply to coconspirators who use an interactive computer service only to communicate with one another in furtherance of the offense. "***Interactive computer service***", for purposes of subsection (b)(4) and this note, has the meaning given that term in

section 230(e)(2) of the Communications Act of 1934 (47 U.S.C. § 230(f)(2)).

6. **Imposition of Consecutive Sentence for 21 U.S.C. § 865.**—Section 865 of title 21, United States Code, requires the imposition of a mandatory consecutive term of imprisonment of not more than 15 years. In order to comply with the relevant statute, the court should determine the appropriate "total punishment" and, on the judgment form, divide the sentence between the sentence attributable to the underlying drug offense and the sentence attributable to 21 U.S.C. § 865, specifying the number of months to be served consecutively for the conviction under 21 U.S.C. § 865. For example, if the applicable adjusted guideline range is 151–188 months and the court determines a "total punishment" of 151 months is appropriate, a sentence of 130 months for the underlying offense plus 21 months for the conduct covered by 21 U.S.C. § 865 would achieve the "total punishment" in a manner that satisfies the statutory requirement of a consecutive sentence.

7. **Applicability of Subsection (b)(6).**—The applicability of subsection (b)(6) shall be determined without regard to the offense of conviction. If subsection (b)(6) applies, §5C1.2(b) does not apply. *See* §5C1.2(b)(2)(requiring a minimum offense level of level 17 if the "statutorily required minimum sentence is at least five years").

8. **Application of Subsection (c)(1).**—"***Offense involved unlawfully manufacturing a controlled substance or attempting to manufacture a controlled substance unlawfully***," as used in subsection (c)(1), means that the defendant, or a person for whose conduct the defendant is accountable under §1B1.3 (Relevant Conduct), completed the actions sufficient to constitute the offense of unlawfully manufacturing a controlled substance or attempting to manufacture a controlled substance unlawfully.

9. **Offenses Involving Immediate Precursors or Other Controlled Substances Covered Under §2D1.1.**—In certain cases, the defendant will be convicted of an offense involving a listed chemical covered under this guideline, and a related offense involving an immediate precursor or other controlled substance covered under §2D1.1 (Unlawfully Manufacturing, Importing, Exporting, or Trafficking). For example, P2P (an immediate precursor) and methylamine (a listed chemical) are used together to produce methamphetamine. Determine the offense level under each guideline separately. The offense level for methylamine is determined by using §2D1.11. The offense level for P2P is determined by using §2D1.1 (P2P is listed in the Drug Equivalency Table under Cocaine and Other Schedule I and II Stimulants (and their immediate precursors)). Under the grouping rules of §3D1.2(b), the counts will be grouped together. Note that in determining the scale of the offense under §2D1.1, the quantity of both the controlled substance and listed chemical should be considered (*see* Application Note 5 in the Commentary to §2D1.1).

Background: Offenses covered by this guideline involve list I chemicals (including ephedrine, pseudoephedrine, and phenylpropanolamine) and list II chemicals. List I chemicals are important to the manufacture of a controlled substance and usually become part of the final product. For example, ephedrine reacts with other chemicals to form methamphetamine. The amount of ephedrine directly affects the amount of methamphetamine produced. List II chemicals are generally used as solvents, catalysts, and reagents.

Historical Note

Effective November 1, 1991 (amendment 371). Amended effective November 1, 1992 (amendment 447); November 1, 1995 (amendment 519); May 1, 1997 (amendment 541); November 1, 1997 (amendment 557); November 1, 2000 (amendments 605 and 606); May 1, 2001 (amendment 611); November 1, 2001 (amendment 625); November 1, 2002 (amendment 646); November 1, 2003 (amendment 661); November 1, 2004 (amendments 667 and 668); November 1, 2005 (amendment 679); November 1, 2007 (amendments 705 and 707); November 1, 2010 (amendments 745 and 746); November 1, 2012 (amendments 763 and 770); November 1, 2014 (amendment 782); November 1, 2015 (amendment 796).

§2D1.12. Unlawful Possession, Manufacture, Distribution, Transportation, Exportation, or Importation of Prohibited Flask, Equipment, Chemical, Product, or Material; Attempt or Conspiracy

(a) Base Offense Level (Apply the greater):

(1) **12**, if the defendant intended to manufacture a controlled substance

or knew or believed the prohibited flask, equipment, chemical, product, or material was to be used to manufacture a controlled substance; or

(2) **9**, if the defendant had reasonable cause to believe the prohibited flask, equipment, chemical, product, or material was to be used to manufacture a controlled substance.

(b) Specific Offense Characteristics

(1) If the defendant (A) intended to manufacture methamphetamine, or (B) knew, believed, or had reasonable cause to believe that prohibited flask, equipment, chemical, product, or material was to be used to manufacture methamphetamine, increase by **2** levels.

(2) If the offense involved (A) an unlawful discharge, emission, or release into the environment of a hazardous or toxic substance; or (B) the unlawful transportation, treatment, storage, or disposal of a hazardous waste, increase by **2** levels.

(3) If the defendant, or a person for whose conduct the defendant is accountable under §1B1.3 (Relevant Conduct), distributed any prohibited flask, equipment, chemical, product, or material through mass-marketing by means of an interactive computer service, increase by **2** levels.

(4) If the offense involved stealing anhydrous ammonia or transporting stolen anhydrous ammonia, increase by **6** levels.

(c) Cross Reference

(1) If the offense involved unlawfully manufacturing a controlled substance, or attempting to manufacture a controlled substance unlawfully, apply §2D1.1 (Unlawful Manufacturing, Importing, Exporting, or Trafficking) if the resulting offense level is greater than that determined above.

Commentary

Statutory Provisions: 21 U.S.C. §§ 843(a)(6), (7), 864.

Application Notes:

1. If the offense involved the large-scale manufacture, distribution, transportation, exportation, or importation of prohibited flasks, equipment, chemicals, products, or material, an upward departure may be warranted.

2. "***Offense involved unlawfully manufacturing a controlled substance or attempting to manufacture a controlled substance unlawfully***," as used in subsection (c)(1), means that the defendant, or a person for whose conduct the defendant is accountable

under §1B1.3 (Relevant Conduct), completed the actions sufficient to constitute the offense of unlawfully manufacturing a controlled substance or attempting to manufacture a controlled substance unlawfully.

3. Subsection (b)(2) applies if the conduct for which the defendant is accountable under §1B1.3 (Relevant Conduct) involved any discharge, emission, release, transportation, treatment, storage, or disposal violation covered by the Resource Conservation and Recovery Act, 42 U.S.C. § 6928(d), the Federal Water Pollution Control Act, 33 U.S.C. § 1319(c), the Comprehensive Environmental Response, Compensation, and Liability

Act, 42 U.S.C. § 9603(b), and 49 U.S.C. § 5124 (relating to violations of laws and regulations enforced by the Department of Transportation with respect to the transportation of hazardous material). In some cases, the enhancement under subsection (b)(2) may not adequately account for the seriousness of the environmental harm or other threat to public health or safety (including the health or safety of law enforcement and cleanup personnel). In such cases, an upward departure may be warranted. Additionally, any costs of environmental cleanup and harm to persons or property should be considered by the court in determining the amount of restitution under §5E1.1 (Restitution) and in fashioning appropriate conditions of supervision under §§5B1.3 (Conditions of Probation) and 5D1.3 (Conditions of Supervised Release).

4. **Application of Subsection (b)(3).**—For purposes of subsection (b)(3), "***mass-marketing by means of an interactive computer service***" means the solicitation, by means of an interactive computer service, of a large number of persons to induce those persons to purchase a controlled substance. For example, subsection (b)(3) would apply to a defendant who operated a web site to promote the sale of prohibited flasks but would not apply to coconspirators who use an interactive computer service only to communicate with one another in furtherance of the offense. "***Interactive computer service***", for purposes of subsection (b)(3) and this note, has the meaning given that term in section 230(e)(2) of the Communications Act of 1934 (47 U.S.C. § 230(f)(2)).

Historical Note

Effective November 1, 1991 (amendment 371). Amended effective November 1, 1992 (amendment 447); November 1, 1995 (amendment 520); November 1, 1997 (amendment 558); November 1, 2000 (amendment 605); November 1, 2001 (amendment 626); November 1, 2004 (amendment 667); November 1, 2010 (amendment 746).

§2D1.13. Structuring Chemical Transactions or Creating a Chemical Mixture to Evade Reporting or Recordkeeping Requirements; Presenting False or Fraudulent Identification to Obtain a Listed Chemical; Attempt or Conspiracy

(a) Base Offense Level (Apply the greatest):

(1) The offense level from §2D1.11 (Unlawfully Distributing, Importing, Exporting, or Possessing a Listed Chemical) if the defendant knew or believed that the chemical was to be used to manufacture a controlled substance unlawfully; or

(2) The offense level from §2D1.11 (Unlawfully Distributing, Importing, Exporting or Possessing a Listed Chemical) reduced

by **3** levels if the defendant had reason to believe that the chemical was to be used to manufacture a controlled substance unlawfully; or

(3) **6**, otherwise.

Commentary

Statutory Provisions: 21 U.S.C. §§ 841(c)(3), (f)(1), 843(a)(4)(B), (a)(8).

Application Note:

1. "***The offense level from §2D1.11***" includes the base offense level and any applicable specific offense characteristic or cross reference; *see* §1B1.5 (Interpretation of References to Other Offense Guidelines).

Historical Note

Effective November 1, 1991 (amendment 371). Amended effective November 1, 1992 (amendment 447); November 1, 2002 (amendment 646).

§2D1.14. Narco-Terrorism

(a) Base Offense Level:

(1) The offense level from §2D1.1 (Unlawful Manufacturing, Importing,

Exporting, or Trafficking (Including Possession with Intent to Commit These Offenses); Attempt or Conspiracy) applicable to the underlying offense, except that §2D1.1(a)(5)(A), (a)(5)(B), and (b)(17) shall not apply.

(b) Specific Offense Characteristic

(1) If §3A1.4 (Terrorism) does not apply, increase by **6** levels.

Commentary

Statutory Provision: 21 U.S.C. § 960a.

Historical Note

Effective November 1, 2007 (amendment 700). Amended effective November 1, 2010 (amendments 746 and 748); November 1, 2011 (amendment 750); November 1, 2014 (amendment 783).

* * * * *

2. UNLAWFUL POSSESSION

§2D2.1. Unlawful Possession; Attempt or Conspiracy

(a) Base Offense Level:

(1) **8**, if the substance is heroin or any Schedule I or II opiate, an analogue of these, or cocaine base; or

(2) **6**, if the substance is cocaine, flunitrazepam, LSD, or PCP; or

(3) **4**, if the substance is any other controlled substance or a list I chemical.

(b) Cross Reference

(1) If the offense involved possession of a controlled substance in a prison, correctional facility, or detention facility, apply §2P1.2 (Providing or Possessing Contraband in Prison).

Commentary

Statutory Provision: 21 U.S.C. § 844(a). For additional statutory provision(s), *see* Appendix A (Statutory Index).

Application Note:

1. The typical case addressed by this guideline involves possession of a controlled substance by the defendant for the defendant's own consumption. Where the circumstances establish intended consumption by a person other than the defendant, an upward departure may be warranted.

Background: Mandatory (statutory) minimum penalties for several categories of cases, ranging from fifteen days' to three years' imprisonment, are set forth in 21 U.S.C. § 844(a). When a mandatory minimum penalty exceeds the guideline range, the mandatory minimum becomes the guideline sentence. *See* §5G1.1(b). Note, however, that 18 U.S.C. § 3553(f) provides an exception to the applicability of mandatory minimum sentences in certain cases. *See* §5C1.2 (Limitation on Applicability of Statutory Minimum Sentences in Certain Cases).

Historical Note

Effective November 1, 1987. Amended effective January 15, 1988 (amendment 24); November 1, 1989 (amendment 304); November 1, 1990 (amendment 321); November 1, 1992 (amendment 447); September 23, 1994 (amendment 509); November 1, 1995 (amendment 514); November 1, 1997 (amendments 556 and 558); November 1, 2010 (amendments 746 and 748); November 1, 2011 (amendment 750).

§2D2.2. Acquiring a Controlled Substance by Forgery, Fraud, Deception, or Subterfuge; Attempt or Conspiracy

(a) Base Offense Level: **8**

Commentary

Statutory Provision: 21 U.S.C. § 843(a)(3).

Historical
Note
Effective November 1, 1987. Amended effective November 1, 1992 (amendment 447).

§2D2.3. Operating or Directing the Operation of a Common Carrier Under the Influence of Alcohol or Drugs

(a) Base Offense Level (Apply the greatest):
(1) **26**, if death resulted; or
(2) **21**, if serious bodily injury resulted; or
(3) **13**, otherwise.
(b) Special Instruction:
(1) If the defendant is convicted of a single count involving the death or serious bodily injury of more than one person, apply Chapter Three, Part D (Multiple Counts) as if the defendant had been convicted of a separate count for each such victim.

Commentary

Statutory Provision: 18 U.S.C. § 342.

Background: This section implements the direction to the Commission in Section 6482 of the Anti-Drug Abuse Act of 1988. Offenses covered by this guideline may vary widely with regard to harm and risk of harm. The offense levels assume that the offense involved the operation of a common carrier carrying a number of passengers, *e.g.*, a bus. If no or only a few passengers were placed at risk, a downward departure may be warranted. If the offense resulted in the death or serious bodily injury of a large number of persons, such that the resulting offense level under subsection (b) would not adequately reflect the seriousness of the offense, an upward departure may be warranted.

Historical
Note
Effective November 1, 1987. Amended effective January 15, 1988 (amendment 25); November 1, 1989 (amendment 141).

* * * * *

3. REGULATORY VIOLATIONS

§2D3.1. Regulatory Offenses Involving Registration Numbers; Unlawful Advertising Relating to Scheduled Substances; Attempt or Conspiracy

(a) Base Offense Level: **6**

Commentary

Statutory Provisions: 21 U.S.C. §§ 842(a)(1), 843(a)(1), (2). For additional statutory provision(s), *see* Appendix A (Statutory Index).

Historical
Note
Effective November 1, 1987. Amended effective November 1, 1991 (amendment 421); November 1, 1992 (amendment 447); November 1, 1995 (amendment 534); November 1, 2009 (amendment 727).

§2D3.2. Regulatory Offenses Involving Controlled Substances or Listed Chemicals; Attempt or Conspiracy

(a) Base Offense Level: **4**

Commentary

Statutory Provisions: 21 U.S.C. §§ 842(a)(2), (9), (10), (b), 954, 961. For additional statutory provision(s), *see* Appendix A (Statutory Index).

Historical
Note
Effective November 1, 1987. Amended effective November 1, 1991 (amendment 421); November 1, 1992 (amendment 447); November 1, 1993 (amendment 481); November 1, 1995 (amendment 534).

§2D3.3. [Deleted]

Historical
Note
Section 2D3.3 (Illegal Use of Registration Number to Distribute or Dispense a Controlled Substance to Another

Registrant or Authorized Person; Attempt or Conspiracy), effective November 1, 1987, amended effective November 1, 1991 (amendment 421) and November 1, 1992 (amendment 447), was deleted by consolidation with §2D3.2 effective November 1, 1993 (amendment 481).

§2D3.4. [Deleted]

Historical
Note
Section 2D3.4 (Illegal Transfer or Transshipment of a Controlled Substance; Attempt or Conspiracy), effective November 1, 1987, amended effective November 1, 1990 (amendment 359) and November 1, 1992 (amendment 447), was deleted by consolidation with §2D3.2 effective November 1, 1993 (amendment 481).

§2D3.5. [Deleted]

Historical
Note
Section 2D3.5 (Violation of Recordkeeping or Reporting Requirements for Listed Chemicals and Certain Machines; Attempt or Conspiracy), effective November 1, 1991 (amendment 371), amended effective November 1, 1992 (amendment 447), was deleted by consolidation with §2D3.2 effective November 1, 1993 (amendment 481).

PART E — OFFENSES INVOLVING CRIMINAL ENTERPRISES AND RACKETEERING

1. RACKETEERING

Introductory Commentary

Because of the jurisdictional nature of the offenses included, this subpart covers a wide variety of criminal conduct. The offense level usually will be determined by the offense level of the underlying conduct.

Historical
Note
Effective November 1, 1987.

§2E1.1. Unlawful Conduct Relating to Racketeer Influenced and Corrupt Organizations

(a) Base Offense Level (Apply the greater):

(1) **19**; or

(2) the offense level applicable to the underlying racketeering activity.

Commentary

Statutory Provisions: 18 U.S.C. §§ 1962, 1963.

Application Notes:

1. Where there is more than one underlying offense, treat each underlying offense as if contained in a separate count of conviction for the purposes of subsection (a)(2). To determine whether subsection (a)(1) or (a)(2) results in the greater offense level, apply Chapter Three, Parts A, B, C, and D to both (a)(1) and (a)(2). Use whichever subsection results in the greater offense level.

2. If the underlying conduct violates state law, the offense level corresponding to the most analogous federal offense is to be used.

3. If the offense level for the underlying racketeering activity is less than the alternative minimum level specified (*i.e.*, 19), the alternative minimum base offense level is to be used.

4. Certain conduct may be charged in the count of conviction as part of a "pattern of racketeering activity" even though the defendant has previously been sentenced for that conduct. Where such previously imposed sentence resulted from a conviction prior to the last overt act of the instant offense, treat as a prior sentence under §4A1.2(a)(1) and not as part of the instant offense. This treatment is designed to produce a result consistent with

the distinction between the instant offense and criminal history found throughout the guidelines. If this treatment produces an anomalous result in a particular case, a guideline departure may be warranted.

Historical Note

Effective November 1, 1987. Amended effective June 15, 1988 (amendment 26); November 1, 1989 (amendment 142).

§2E1.2. Interstate or Foreign Travel or Transportation in Aid of a Racketeering Enterprise

(a) Base Offense Level (Apply the greater):

(1) **6**; or

(2) the offense level applicable to the underlying crime of violence or other unlawful activity in respect to which the travel or transportation was undertaken.

Commentary

Statutory Provision: 18 U.S.C. § 1952.

Application Notes:

1. Where there is more than one underlying offense, treat each underlying offense as if contained in a separate count of conviction for the purposes of subsection (a)(2). To determine whether subsection (a)(1) or (a)(2) results in the greater offense level, apply Chapter Three, Parts A, B, C, and D to both (a)(1) and (a)(2). Use whichever subsection results in the greater offense level.
2. If the underlying conduct violates state law, the offense level corresponding to the most analogous federal offense is to be used.
3. If the offense level for the underlying conduct is less than the alternative minimum base offense level specified (*i.e.*, 6), the alternative minimum base offense level is to be used.

Historical Note

Effective November 1, 1987. Amended effective June 15, 1988 (amendment 27).

§2E1.3. Violent Crimes in Aid of Racketeering Activity

(a) Base Offense Level (Apply the greater):

(1) **12**; or

(2) the offense level applicable to the underlying crime or racketeering activity.

Commentary

Statutory Provision: 18 U.S.C. § 1959 (formerly 18 U.S.C. § 1952B).

Application Notes:

1. If the underlying conduct violates state law, the offense level corresponding to the most analogous federal offense is to be used.
2. If the offense level for the underlying conduct is less than the alternative minimum base offense level specified (*i.e.*, 12), the alternative minimum base offense level is to be used.

Background: The conduct covered under this section ranges from threats to murder. The maximum term of imprisonment authorized by statute ranges from three years to life imprisonment.

Historical Note

Effective November 1, 1987. Amended effective November 1, 1989 (amendment 143).

§2E1.4. Use of Interstate Commerce Facilities in the Commission of Murder-For-Hire

(a) Base Offense Level (Apply the greater):

(1) **32**; or

(2) the offense level applicable to the underlying unlawful conduct.

Commentary

Statutory Provision: 18 U.S.C. § 1958 (formerly 18 U.S.C. § 1952A).

Application Note:

1. If the underlying conduct violates state law, the offense level corresponding to the most analogous federal offense is to be used.

Background: This guideline and the statute to which it applies do not require that a murder actually have been committed.

Historical
Note
Effective November 1, 1987. Amended effective November 1, 1989 (amendment 144); November 1, 1990 (amendment 311); November 1, 1992 (amendment 449).

§2E1.5. [Deleted]

Historical
Note
Section 2E1.5 (Hobbs Act Extortion or Robbery), effective November 1, 1987, amended effective November 1, 1989 (amendment 145), was deleted by consolidation with §§2B3.1, 2B3.2, 2B3.3, and 2C1.1 effective November 1, 1993 (amendment 481).

* * * * *

2. EXTORTIONATE EXTENSION OF CREDIT

§2E2.1. Making or Financing an Extortionate Extension of Credit; Collecting an Extension of Credit by Extortionate Means

(a) Base Offense Level: **20**

(b) Specific Offense Characteristics

(1) (A) If a firearm was discharged increase by **5** levels; or

(B) if a dangerous weapon (including a firearm) was otherwise used, increase by **4** levels; or

(C) if a dangerous weapon (including a firearm) was brandished or possessed, increase by **3** levels.

(2) If any victim sustained bodily injury, increase the offense level according to the seriousness of the injury:

DEGREE OF BODILY INJURY INCREASE IN LEVEL

(A) Bodily Injury add **2**

(B) Serious Bodily Injury add **4**

(C) Permanent or Life-Threatening Bodily Injury add **6**

(D) If the degree of injury is between that specified in subdivisions (A) and (B), add **3** levels; or

(E) If the degree of injury is between that specified in subdivisions (B) and (C), add **5** levels.

Provided, however, that the combined increase from (1) and (2) shall not exceed **9** levels.

(3) (A) If any person was abducted to facilitate commission of the offense or to facilitate escape, increase by **4** levels; or

(B) if any person was physically restrained to facilitate commission of the offense or to facilitate escape, increase by **2** levels.

(c) Cross Reference

(1) If a victim was killed under circumstances that would constitute murder under 18 U.S.C. § 1111 had such killing taken place within the territorial or maritime jurisdiction of the United States, apply §2A1.1 (First Degree Murder).

Commentary

Statutory Provisions: 18 U.S.C. §§ 892–894.

Application Notes:

1. Definitions of "***firearm***," "***dangerous weapon***," "***otherwise used***," "***brandished***," "***bodily injury***," "***serious bodily injury***," "***permanent or life-threatening bodily injury***," "***abducted***," and "***physically restrained***" are found in the Commentary to §1B1.1 (Application Instructions).

2. *See also* Commentary to §2B3.2 (Extortion by Force or Threat of Injury or Serious Damage) regarding the interpretation of the specific offense characteristics.

Background: This section refers to offenses involving the making or financing of extortionate extensions of credit, or the collection of loans by extortionate means. These "loan-sharking" offenses typically involve threats of violence and provide economic support for organized crime. The base offense level for these offenses is higher than the offense level for extortion because loan sharking is in most cases a continuing activity. In addition, the guideline does not include the amount of money involved because the amount of money in such cases is often difficult to determine. Other enhancements parallel those in §2B3.2 (Extortion by Force or Threat of Injury or Serious Damage).

Historical Note

Effective November 1, 1987. Amended effective November 1, 1989 (amendments 146–148); November 1, 1991 (amendment 398); November 1, 1993 (amendment 479); November 1, 2000 (amendment 601).

* * * * *

3. GAMBLING

Introductory Commentary

This subpart covers a variety of proscribed conduct. The adjustments in Chapter Three, Part B (Role in the Offense) are particularly relevant in providing a measure of the scope of the offense and the defendant's participation.

Historical Note

Effective November 1, 1987.

§2E3.1. Gambling Offenses; Animal Fighting Offenses

(a) Base Offense Level: (Apply the greatest)

(1) **16**, if the offense involved an animal fighting venture, except as provided in subdivision (3) below;

(2) **12**, if the offense was (A) engaging in a gambling business; (B) transmission of wagering information; or (C) committed as part of, or to facilitate, a commercial gambling operation;

(3) **10**, if the defendant was convicted under 7 U.S.C. § 2156(a)(2)(B); or

(4) **6**, otherwise.

Commentary

Statutory Provisions: 7 U.S.C. § 2156 (felony provisions only); 15 U.S.C. §§ 1172–1175; 18 U.S.C. §§ 1082, 1301–1304, 1306, 1511, 1953, 1955; 31 U.S.C. § 5363. For additional statutory provision(s), *see* Appendix A (Statutory Index).

Application Notes:

1. **Definition.**—For purposes of this guideline, "***animal fighting venture***" has the meaning given that term in 7 U.S.C. § 2156(g).

2. **Upward Departure Provision.**—The base offense levels provided for animal fighting ventures in subsection (a)(1) and (a)(3) reflect that an animal fighting venture involves one or more violent fights between animals and that a defeated animal often is severely injured in the fight, dies as a result of the fight, or is killed afterward. Nonetheless, there may be cases in which the offense level determined under this guideline substantially understates the seriousness of the offense. In such a case, an upward departure may be

warranted. For example, an upward departure may be warranted if (A) the offense involved extraordinary cruelty to an animal beyond the violence inherent in such a venture (such as by killing an animal in a way that prolongs the suffering of the animal); or (B) the offense involved animal fighting on an exceptional scale (such as an offense involving an unusually large number of animals).

Historical Note

Effective November 1, 1987. Amended effective November 1, 1993 (amendment 481); November 1, 2007 (amendment 703); November 1, 2008 (amendment 721); November 1, 2016 (amendment 800).

§2E3.2. [Deleted]

Historical Note

Section 2E3.2 (Transmission of Wagering Information), effective November 1, 1987, was deleted by consolidation with §2E3.1 effective November 1, 1993 (amendment 481).

§2E3.3. [Deleted]

Historical Note

Section 2E3.3 (Other Gambling Offenses), effective November 1, 1987, was deleted by consolidation with §2E3.1 effective November 1, 1993 (amendment 481).

* * * * *

4. TRAFFICKING IN CONTRABAND CIGARETTES AND SMOKELESS TOBACCO

Historical Note

Effective November 1, 1987. Amended effective November 1, 2007 (amendment 700).

§2E4.1. Unlawful Conduct Relating to Contraband Cigarettes and Smokeless Tobacco

(a) Base Offense Level (Apply the greater):

(1) **9**; or

(2) the offense level from the table in §2T4.1 (Tax Table) corresponding to the amount of the tax evaded.

Commentary

Statutory Provisions: 18 U.S.C. §§ 2342(a), 2344(a).

Application Note:

1. "***Tax evaded***" refers to state and local excise taxes.

Background: The conduct covered by this section generally involves evasion of state and local excise taxes. At least 10,000 cigarettes must be involved. Because this offense is basically a tax matter, it is graded by use of the tax table in §2T4.1.

Historical Note

Effective November 1, 1987. Amended effective November 1, 2007 (amendment 700); November 1, 2008 (amendment 724).

* * * * *

5. LABOR RACKETEERING

Introductory Commentary

The statutes included in this subpart protect the rights of employees under the Taft–Hartley Act, members of labor organizations under the Labor-Management Reporting and Disclosure Act of 1959, and participants of employee pension and welfare benefit plans covered under the Employee Retirement Income Security Act.

The base offense levels for many of the offenses in this subpart have been determined by reference to analogous sections of the guidelines. Thus, the base offense levels for bribery, theft, and fraud in this subpart generally correspond to similar conduct under other parts of the guidelines. The base offense levels for bribery and graft have been set higher than the level for commercial bribery due to the particular vulnerability to exploitation of the organizations covered by this subpart.

Historical
Note
Effective November 1, 1987.

§2E5.1. Offering, Accepting, or Soliciting a Bribe or Gratuity Affecting the Operation of an Employee Welfare or Pension Benefit Plan; Prohibited Payments or Lending of Money by Employer or Agent to Employees, Representatives, or Labor Organizations

(a) Base Offense Level:
(1) **10**, if a bribe; or
(2) **6**, if a gratuity.
(b) Specific Offense Characteristics
(1) If the defendant was a fiduciary of the benefit plan or labor organization, increase by **2** levels.
(2) If the value of the prohibited payment or the value of the improper benefit to the payer, whichever is greater (A) exceeded $2,500 but did not exceed $6,500, increase by **1** level; or (B) exceeded $6,500, increase by the number of levels from the table in §2B1.1 (Theft, Property Destruction, and Fraud) corresponding to that amount.
(c) Special Instruction for Fines — Organizations
(1) In lieu of the pecuniary loss under subsection (a)(3) of §8C2.4 (Base Fine), use the greatest of: (A) the value of the unlawful

payment; (B) if a bribe, the value of the benefit received or to be received in return for the unlawful payment; or (C) if a bribe, the consequential damages resulting from the unlawful payment.

Commentary

Statutory Provisions: 18 U.S.C. § 1954; 29 U.S.C. § 186.

Application Notes:

1. "***Bribe***" refers to the offer or acceptance of an unlawful payment with the specific understanding that it will corruptly affect an official action of the recipient.
2. "***Gratuity***" refers to the offer or acceptance of an unlawful payment other than a bribe.
3. "***Fiduciary of the benefit plan***" is defined in 29 U.S.C. § 1002(21)(A) to mean a person who exercises any discretionary authority or control in respect to the management of such plan or exercises authority or control in respect to management or disposition of its assets, or who renders investment advice for a fee or other direct or indirect compensation with respect to any moneys or other property of such plan, or has any authority or responsibility to do so, or who has any discretionary authority or responsibility in the administration of such plan.
4. "***Value of the improper benefit to the payer***" is explained in the Commentary to §2C1.1 (Offering, Giving, Soliciting, or Receiving a Bribe; Extortion Under Color of Official Right; Fraud Involving the Deprivation of the Intangible Right to Honest Services of Public Officials; Conspiracy to Defraud by Interference with Governmental Functions).
5. If the adjustment for a fiduciary at §2E5.1(b)(1) applies, do not apply the adjustment at §3B1.3 (Abuse of Position of Trust or Use of Special Skill).

Background: This section covers the giving or receipt of bribes and other unlawful gratuities involving employee welfare or pension benefit plans, or labor organizations. The seriousness of the offense is determined by several factors, including the value of the bribe or gratuity and the magnitude of the loss resulting from the transaction.

Historical

Note
Effective November 1, 1987. Amended effective November 1, 1989 (amendment 149); November 1, 1991 (amendment 422); November 1, 1993 (amendment 481); November 1, 2001 (amendment 617); November 1, 2004 (amendment 666); November 1, 2015 (amendment 791).

§2E5.2. [Deleted]

Historical
Note
Section 2E5.2 (Theft or Embezzlement from Employee Pension and Welfare Benefit Plans), effective November 1, 1987, amended effective June 15, 1988 (amendment 28), November 1, 1989 (amendment 150), and November 1, 1991 (amendment 399), was deleted by consolidation with §2B1.1 effective November 1, 1993 (amendment 481).

§2E5.3. False Statements and Concealment of Facts in Relation to Documents Required by the Employee Retirement Income Security Act; Failure to Maintain and Falsification of Records Required by the Labor Management Reporting and Disclosure Act; Destruction and Failure to Maintain Corporate Audit Records

(a) Base Offense Level (Apply the greater):
(1) **6**; or
(2) If the offense was committed to facilitate or conceal (A) an offense involving a theft, a fraud, or an embezzlement; (B) an offense involving a bribe or a gratuity; or (C) an obstruction of justice offense, apply §2B1.1 (Theft, Property Destruction, and Fraud), §2E5.1 (Offering, Accepting, or Soliciting a Bribe or Gratuity Affecting the Operation of an Employee Welfare or Pension Benefit Plan; Prohibited Payments or Lending of Money by Employer or Agent to Employees, Representatives, or Labor Organizations), or §2J1.2 (Obstruction of Justice), as applicable.

Commentary

Statutory Provisions: 18 U.S.C. §§ 1027, 1520; 29 U.S.C. §§ 439, 461, 1131. For additional statutory provision(s), *see* Appendix A (Statutory Index).

Background: This section covers the falsification of documents or records relating to a benefit plan covered by ERISA. It also covers failure to maintain proper documents required by the LMRDA or falsification of such documents. Such violations sometimes occur in connection with the criminal conversion of plan funds or schemes involving bribery or graft. Where a violation under this section occurs in connection with another offense, the offense level is determined by reference to the offense facilitated by the false statements or documents.

Historical
Note
Effective November 1, 1987. Amended effective November 1, 1989 (amendment 151); November 1, 1993 (amendment 481); January 25, 2003 (amendment 647); November 1, 2003 (amendment 653).

§2E5.4. [Deleted]

Historical
Note
Section 2E5.4 (Embezzlement or Theft from Labor Unions in the Private Sector), effective November 1, 1987, amended effective June 15, 1988 (amendment 29) and November 1, 1989 (amendment 152), was deleted by consolidation with §2B1.1 effective November 1, 1993 (amendment 481).

§2E5.5. [Deleted]

Historical
Note
Section 2E5.5 (Failure to Maintain and Falsification of Records Required by the Labor Management Reporting and Disclosure Act), effective November 1, 1987, amended effective November 1, 1989 (amendment 153), was deleted by consolidation with §2E5.3 effective November 1, 1993 (amendment 481).

§2E5.6. [Deleted]

Historical
Note
Section 2E5.6 (Prohibited Payments or Lending of Money by Employer or Agent to Employees, Representatives, or Labor Organizations), effective November 1, 1987, amended effective November 1, 1991 (amendment 422), was deleted by consolidation with §2E5.1 effective November 1, 1993 (amendment 481).

PART F — [DELETED]

Historical
Note
The heading to Part F — Offenses Involving Fraud or Deceit, effective November 1, 1987, was deleted due to the deletion of §§2F1.1 and 2F1.2 effective November 1, 2001 (amendment 617).

§2F1.1. [Deleted]

Historical
Note
Section 2F1.1 (Fraud and Deceit; Forgery; Offenses Involving Altered or Counterfeit Instruments Other than Counterfeit Bearer Obligations of the United States), effective November 1, 1987, amended effective June 15, 1988 (amendment 30), November 1, 1989 (amendments 154–156 and 303), November 1, 1990 (amendment 317), November 1, 1991 (amendments 364 and 393), November 1, 1992 (amendment 470), November 1, 1993 (amendments 481 and 482), November 1, 1995 (amendment 513), November 1, 1997 (amendment 551), November 1, 1998 (amendments 577 and 587), November 1, 2000 (amendments 595, 596, and 597), was deleted by consolidation with §2B1.1 effective November 1, 2001 (amendment 617).

§2F1.2. [Deleted]

Historical
Note
Section 2F1.2 (Insider Trading), effective November 1, 1987, was deleted by consolidation with §2B1.1 effective November 1, 2001 (amendment 617).

PART G — OFFENSES INVOLVING COMMERCIAL SEX ACTS, SEXUAL EXPLOITATION OF MINORS, AND OBSCENITY

Historical
Note
Effective November 1, 1987. Amended effective November 1, 2002 (amendment 641).

1. PROMOTING A COMMERCIAL SEX ACT OR PROHIBITED SEXUAL CONDUCT

Historical
Note
Effective November 1, 1987. Amended effective November 1, 2000 (amendment 592); November 1, 2002 (amendment 641).

§2G1.1. Promoting a Commercial Sex Act or Prohibited Sexual Conduct with an Individual Other than a Minor

(a) Base Offense Level:

(1) **34**, if the offense of conviction is 18 U.S.C. § 1591(b)(1); or

(2) **14**, otherwise.

(b) Specific Offense Characteristic

(1) If (A) subsection (a)(2) applies; and (B) the offense involved fraud or coercion, increase by **4** levels.

(c) Cross Reference

(1) If the offense involved conduct described in 18 U.S.C. § 2241(a) or (b) or 18 U.S.C. § 2242, apply §2A3.1 (Criminal Sexual Abuse; Attempt to Commit Criminal Sexual Abuse).

(d) Special Instruction

(1) If the offense involved more than one victim, Chapter Three, Part D (Multiple Counts) shall be applied as if the promoting of a commercial sex act or prohibited sexual conduct in respect to each victim had been contained in a separate count of conviction.

Commentary

Statutory Provisions: 8 U.S.C. § 1328 (only if the offense involved a victim other than a minor); 18 U.S.C. §§ 1591 (only if the offense involved a victim other than a minor), 2421 (only if the offense involved a victim other than a minor), 2422(a) (only if the offense involved a victim other than a minor).

Application Notes:

1. **Definitions.**—For purposes of this guideline:

"***Commercial sex act***" has the meaning given that term in 18 U.S.C. § 1591(e)(3).

"***Prohibited sexual conduct***" has the meaning given that term in Application Note 1 of §2A3.1 (Criminal Sexual Abuse; Attempt to Commit Criminal Sexual Abuse).

"***Promoting a commercial sex act***" means persuading, inducing, enticing, or coercing a person to engage in a commercial sex act, or to travel to engage in, a commercial sex act.

"***Victim***" means a person transported, persuaded, induced, enticed, or coerced to engage in, or travel for the purpose of engaging in, a commercial sex act or prohibited sexual conduct, whether or not the person consented to the commercial sex act or prohibited sexual conduct. Accordingly, "victim" may include an undercover law enforcement officer.

2. **Application of Subsection (b)(1).**—Subsection (b)(1) provides an enhancement for fraud or coercion that occurs as part of the offense and anticipates no bodily injury. If bodily injury results, an upward departure may be warranted. *See* Chapter Five, Part K (Departures). For purposes of subsection (b)(1), "***coercion***" includes any form of conduct that negates the voluntariness of the victim. This enhancement would apply, for example, in a case in which the ability of the victim to appraise or control conduct was substantially impaired by drugs or alcohol. This characteristic generally will not apply if the drug or alcohol was voluntarily taken.

3. **Application of Chapter Three Adjustment.**—For the purposes of §3B1.1 (Aggravating Role), a victim, as defined in this guideline, is considered a participant only if that victim assisted in the promoting of a commercial sex act or prohibited sexual conduct in respect to another victim.

4. **Application of Subsection (c)(1).**—

(A) **Conduct Described in 18 U.S.C. § 2241(a) or (b).**—For purposes of subsection (c)(1), conduct described in 18 U.S.C. § 2241(a) or (b) is engaging in, or causing another person to engage in, a sexual act with another person by: (i) using force against the victim; (ii) threatening or placing the victim in fear that any person will be subject to death, serious bodily injury, or kidnapping; (iii) rendering the victim unconscious; or (iv) administering by force or threat of force, or without the knowledge or permission of the victim, a drug, intoxicant, or other similar substance and thereby substantially impairing the ability of the victim to appraise or control conduct. This provision would apply, for example, if any dangerous weapon was used or brandished, or in a case in which the ability of the victim to appraise or control conduct was substantially impaired by drugs or alcohol.

(B) **Conduct Described in 18 U.S.C. § 2242.**—For purposes of subsection (c)(1), conduct described in 18 U.S.C. § 2242 is: (i) engaging in, or causing another person to engage in, a sexual act with another person by threatening or placing the victim in fear (other than by threatening or placing the victim in fear that any person will be subject to death, serious bodily injury, or kidnapping); or (ii) engaging in, or causing

another person to engage in, a sexual act with a victim who is incapable of appraising the nature of the conduct or who is physically incapable of declining participation in, or communicating unwillingness to engage in, the sexual act.

5. **Special Instruction at Subsection (d)(1).**—For the purposes of Chapter Three, Part D (Multiple Counts), each person transported, persuaded, induced, enticed, or coerced to engage in, or travel to engage in, a commercial sex act or prohibited sexual conduct is to be treated as a separate victim. Consequently, multiple counts involving more than one victim are not to be grouped together under §3D1.2 (Groups of Closely Related Counts).

In addition, subsection (d)(1) directs that if the relevant conduct of an offense of conviction includes the promoting of a commercial sex act or prohibited sexual conduct in respect to more than one victim, whether specifically cited in the count of conviction, each such victim shall be treated as if contained in a separate count of conviction.

6. **Upward Departure Provision.**—If the offense involved more than ten victims, an upward departure may be warranted.

Historical Note

Effective November 1, 1987. Amended effective November 1, 1989 (amendments 157 and 158); November 1, 1990 (amendment 322); November 1, 1996 (amendment 538); November 1, 2000 (amendment 592); May 1, 2001 (amendment 612); November 1, 2001 (amendment 627); November 1, 2002 (amendment 641); November 1, 2004 (amendment 664); November 1, 2007 (amendment 701); November 1, 2009 (amendment 737).

§2G1.2. [Deleted]

Historical Note

Section 2G1.2 (Transportation of a Minor for the Purpose of Prostitution or Prohibited Sexual Conduct), effective November 1, 1987, amended effective November 1, 1989 (amendments 159 and 160), November 1, 1990 (amendment 323), November 1, 1991 (amendment 400), and November 1, 1992 (amendment 444), was deleted by consolidation with §2G1.1 effective November 1, 1996 (amendment 538).

2G1.3. Promoting a Commercial Sex Act or Prohibited Sexual Conduct with a Minor; Transportation of Minors to Engage in a Commercial Sex Act or Prohibited Sexual Conduct; Travel to Engage in Commercial Sex Act or Prohibited Sexual Conduct with a Minor; Sex Trafficking of Children; Use of Interstate Facilities to Transport Information about a Minor

(a) Base Offense Level:

(1) **34**, if the defendant was convicted under 18 U.S.C. § 1591(b)(1);

(2) **30**, if the defendant was convicted under 18 U.S.C. § 1591(b)(2);

(3) **28**, if the defendant was convicted under 18 U.S.C. § 2422(b) or § 2423(a); or

(4) **24**, otherwise.

(b) Specific Offense Characteristics

(1) If (A) the defendant was a parent, relative, or legal guardian of the minor; or (B) the minor was otherwise in the custody, care, or supervisory control of the defendant, increase by **2** levels.

(2) If (A) the offense involved the knowing misrepresentation of a participant's identity to persuade, induce, entice, coerce, or facilitate the travel of, a minor to engage in prohibited sexual conduct; or (B) a participant otherwise unduly influenced a minor to engage in prohibited sexual conduct, increase by **2** levels.

(3) If the offense involved the use of a computer or an interactive computer service to (A) persuade, induce, entice, coerce, or facilitate the travel of, the minor to engage in prohibited sexual conduct; or (B) entice, encourage, offer, or solicit a person to engage in prohibited sexual conduct with the minor, increase by **2** levels.

(4) If (A) the offense involved the commission of a sex act or sexual contact; or (B) subsection (a)(3) or (a)(4) applies and the offense involved a commercial sex act, increase by **2** levels.

(5) If (A) subsection (a)(3) or (a)(4) applies; and (B) the offense involved a minor who had not attained the age of 12 years, increase

by **8** levels.
(c) Cross References
(1) If the offense involved causing, transporting, permitting, or offering or seeking by notice or advertisement, a minor to engage in sexually explicit conduct for the purpose of producing a visual depiction of such conduct, apply §2G2.1 (Sexually Exploiting a Minor by Production of Sexually Explicit Visual or Printed Material; Custodian Permitting Minor to Engage in Sexually Explicit Conduct; Advertisement for Minors to Engage in Production), if the resulting offense level is greater than that determined above.
(2) If a minor was killed under circumstances that would constitute murder under 18 U.S.C. § 1111 had such killing taken place within the territorial or maritime jurisdiction of the United States, apply §2A1.1 (First Degree Murder), if the resulting offense level is greater than that determined above.

(3) If the offense involved conduct described in 18 U.S.C. § 2241 or § 2242, apply §2A3.1 (Criminal Sexual Abuse; Attempt to Commit Criminal Sexual Abuse), if the resulting offense level is greater than that determined above. If the offense involved interstate travel with intent to engage in a sexual act with a minor who had not attained the age of 12 years, or knowingly engaging in a sexual act with a minor who had not attained the age of 12 years, §2A3.1 shall apply, regardless of the "consent" of the minor.
(d) Special Instruction
(1) If the offense involved more than one minor, Chapter Three, Part D (Multiple Counts) shall be applied as if the persuasion, enticement, coercion, travel, or transportation to engage in a commercial sex act or prohibited sexual conduct of each victim had been contained in a separate count of conviction.

Commentary

Statutory Provisions: 8 U.S.C. § 1328 (only if the offense involved a minor); 18 U.S.C. §§ 1591 (only if the offense involved a minor), 2421 (only if the offense involved a minor), 2422 (only if the offense involved a minor), 2423, 2425.

Application Notes:

1. **Definitions.**—For purposes of this guideline:
"***Commercial sex act***" has the meaning given that term in 18 U.S.C. § 1591(e)(3).
"***Computer***" has the meaning given that term in 18 U.S.C. § 1030(e)(1).
"***Illicit sexual conduct***" has the meaning given that term in 18 U.S.C. § 2423(f).
"***Interactive computer service***" has the meaning given that term in section 230(e)(2) of the Communications Act of 1934 (47 U.S.C. § 230(f)(2)).
"***Minor***" means (A) an individual who had not attained the age of 18 years; (B) an individual, whether fictitious or not, who a law enforcement officer represented to a participant (i) had not attained the age of 18 years, and (ii) could be provided for the purposes of engaging in sexually explicit conduct; or (C) an undercover law enforcement officer who represented to a participant that the officer had not attained the age of 18 years.
"***Participant***" has the meaning given that term in Application Note 1 of the Commentary to §3B1.1 (Aggravating Role).

"***Prohibited sexual conduct***" has the meaning given that term in Application Note 1 of the Commentary to §2A3.1 (Criminal Sexual Abuse; Attempt to Commit Criminal Sexual Abuse).
"***Sexual act***" has the meaning given that term in 18 U.S.C. § 2246(2).

"***Sexual contact***" has the meaning given that term in 18 U.S.C. § 2246(3).

2. **Application of Subsection (b)(1).**—

(A) **Custody, Care, or Supervisory Control.**—Subsection (b)(1) is intended to have broad application and includes offenses involving a victim less than 18 years of age entrusted to the defendant, whether temporarily or permanently. For example, teachers, day care providers, baby-sitters, or other temporary caretakers are among those who would be subject to this enhancement. In determining whether to apply this enhancement, the court should look to the actual relationship that existed between the defendant and the minor and not simply to the legal status of the defendant-minor relationship.

(B) **Inapplicability of Chapter Three Adjustment.**—If the enhancement under subsection (b)(1) applies, do not apply §3B1.3 (Abuse of Position of Trust or Use of Special Skill).

3. **Application of Subsection (b)(2).**—

(A) **Misrepresentation of Participant's Identity.**—The enhancement in subsection (b)(2)(A) applies in cases involving the misrepresentation of a participant's identity to persuade, induce, entice, coerce, or facilitate the travel of, a minor to engage in prohibited sexual conduct. Subsection (b)(2)(A) is intended to apply only to misrepresentations made directly to a minor or to a person who exercises custody, care, or supervisory control of the minor. Accordingly, the enhancement in subsection (b)(2)(A) would not apply to a misrepresentation made by a participant to an airline representative in the course of making travel arrangements for the minor.

The misrepresentation to which the enhancement in subsection (b)(2)(A) may apply includes misrepresentation of a participant's name, age, occupation, gender, or status, as long as the misrepresentation was made with the intent to persuade, induce, entice, coerce, or facilitate the travel of, a minor to engage in prohibited sexual conduct. Accordingly, use of a computer screen name, without such intent, would not be a sufficient basis for application of the enhancement.

(B) **Undue Influence.**—In determining whether subsection (b)(2)(B) applies, the court should closely consider the facts of the case to determine whether a participant's influence over the minor compromised the voluntariness of the minor's behavior. The voluntariness of the minor's behavior may be compromised without prohibited sexual conduct occurring.

However, subsection (b)(2)(B) does not apply in a case in which the only "minor" (as defined in Application Note 1) involved in the offense is an undercover law enforcement officer.

In a case in which a participant is at least 10 years older than the minor, there shall be a rebuttable presumption that subsection (b)(2)(B) applies. In such a case, some degree of undue influence can be presumed because of the substantial difference in age between the participant and the minor.

4. **Application of Subsection (b)(3).**—Subsection (b)(3) is intended to apply only to the use of a computer or an interactive computer service to communicate directly with a minor or with a person who exercises custody, care, or supervisory control of the minor.

Accordingly, the enhancement in subsection (b)(3) would not apply to the use of a computer or an interactive computer service to obtain airline tickets for the minor from an airline's Internet site.

5. **Application of Subsection (c).**—

(A) **Application of Subsection (c)(1).**—The cross reference in subsection (c)(1) is to be construed broadly and includes all instances in which the offense involved employing, using, persuading, inducing, enticing, coercing, transporting, permitting, or offering or seeking by notice, advertisement or other method, a minor to engage in sexually explicit conduct for the purpose of producing any visual depiction of such conduct. For purposes of subsection (c)(1), "***sexually explicit conduct***" has the meaning given that term in 18 U.S.C. § 2256(2).

(B) **Application of Subsection (c)(3).**—For purposes of subsection (c)(3), conduct described in 18 U.S.C. § 2241 means conduct described in 18 U.S.C. § 2241(a), (b), or (c). Accordingly, for purposes of subsection (c)(3):

(i) Conduct described in 18 U.S.C. § 2241(a) or (b) is engaging in, or causing another person to engage in, a sexual act with another person: (I) using force against the minor; (II) threatening or placing the minor in fear that any person will be subject to death, serious bodily injury, or kidnapping; (III) rendering the minor unconscious; or (IV) administering by force or threat of force, or without the knowledge or permission of the minor, a drug, intoxicant, or other similar substance and thereby substantially impairing the ability of the minor to appraise or control conduct. This provision would apply, for example, if any dangerous weapon was used or brandished, or in a case in which the ability of the minor to appraise or control conduct was substantially impaired by drugs or alcohol.

(ii) Conduct described in 18 U.S.C. § 2241(c) is: (I) interstate travel with intent to engage in a sexual act with a minor who has not attained the age of 12 years; (II) knowingly engaging in a sexual act with a minor who has not attained the age of 12 years; or (III) knowingly engaging in a sexual act under the circumstances described in 18 U.S.C. § 2241(a) and (b) with a minor who has attained the age of 12 years but has not attained the age of 16 years (and is at least 4 years younger than the person so engaging).

(iii) Conduct described in 18 U.S.C. § 2242 is: (I) engaging in, or causing another person to engage in, a sexual act with another person by threatening or placing the minor in fear (other than by threatening or placing the minor in fear that any person will be subject to death, serious bodily injury, or kidnapping); or (II) engaging in, or causing another person to engage in, a sexual act with a minor who is incapable of appraising the nature of the conduct or who is physically incapable of declining participation in, or communicating unwillingness to engage in, the sexual act.

6. **Application of Subsection (d)(1).**—For the purposes of Chapter Three, Part D (Multiple Counts), each minor transported, persuaded, induced, enticed, or coerced to engage in, or travel to engage in, a commercial sex act or prohibited sexual conduct is to be treated as a separate minor. Consequently, multiple counts involving more than one minor are not to be grouped together under §3D1.2 (Groups of Closely Related Counts). In addition, subsection (d)(1) directs that if the relevant conduct of an offense of conviction includes travel or transportation to engage in a commercial sex act or prohibited sexual

conduct in respect to more than one minor, whether specifically cited in the count of conviction, each such minor shall be treated as if contained in a separate count of conviction.

7. **Upward Departure Provision.**—If the offense involved more than ten minors, an upward departure may be warranted.

Historical
Note

Effective November 1, 2004 (amendment 664). Amended effective November 1, 2007 (amendment 701); November 1, 2009 (amendments 732 and 737).

* * * * *

2. SEXUAL EXPLOITATION OF A MINOR

§2G2.1. Sexually Exploiting a Minor by Production of Sexually Explicit Visual

or Printed Material; Custodian Permitting Minor to Engage in Sexually Explicit Conduct; Advertisement for Minors to Engage in Production

(a) Base Offense Level: **32**

(b) Specific Offense Characteristics

(1) If the offense involved a minor who had (A) not attained the age of twelve years, increase by **4** levels; or (B) attained the age of twelve years but not attained the age of sixteen years, increase by **2** levels.

(2) (Apply the greater) If the offense involved—

(A) the commission of a sexual act or sexual contact, increase by **2** levels; or

(B) (i) the commission of a sexual act; and (ii) conduct described in 18 U.S.C. § 2241(a) or (b), increase by **4** levels.

(3) If the defendant knowingly engaged in distribution, increase by **2** levels.

(4) If the offense involved material that portrays (A) sadistic or masochistic conduct or other depictions of violence; or (B) an infant or toddler, increase by **4** levels.

(5) If the defendant was a parent, relative, or legal guardian of the minor involved in the offense, or if the minor was otherwise in the custody, care, or supervisory control of the defendant, increase by **2** levels.

(6) If, for the purpose of producing sexually explicit material or for the purpose of transmitting such material live, the offense involved (A) the knowing misrepresentation of a participant's identity to persuade, induce, entice, coerce, or facilitate the travel of, a minor to engage sexually explicit conduct; or (B) the use of a computer or an interactive computer service to (i) persuade, induce, entice, coerce, or facilitate the travel of, a minor to engage in sexually explicit conduct, or to otherwise solicit participation by a minor in such conduct; or (ii) solicit participation with a minor in sexually explicit conduct, increase by **2** levels.

(c) Cross Reference

(1) If the victim was killed in circumstances that would constitute murder under 18 U.S.C. § 1111 had such killing taken place within the territorial or maritime jurisdiction of the United States, apply §2A1.1 (First Degree Murder), if the resulting offense level is greater than that determined above.

(d) Special Instruction

(1) If the offense involved the exploitation of more than one minor, Chapter Three, Part D (Multiple Counts) shall be applied as if the exploitation of each minor had been contained in a separate count of conviction.

Commentary

Statutory Provisions: 18 U.S.C. §§ 1591, 2251(a)–(c), 2251(d)(1)(B), 2260(a). For additional statutory provision(s), *see* Appendix A (Statutory Index).

Application Notes:

1. **Definitions.**—For purposes of this guideline:

"***Computer***" has the meaning given that term in 18 U.S.C. § 1030(e)(1).

"***Distribution***" means any act, including possession with intent to distribute, production, transmission, advertisement, and transportation, related to the transfer of material involving the sexual exploitation of a minor. Accordingly, distribution includes posting material involving the sexual exploitation of a minor on a website for public viewing but does not include the mere solicitation of such material by a defendant.

"***Interactive computer service***" has the meaning given that term in section 230(e)(2) of the Communications Act of 1934 (47 U.S.C. § 230(f)(2)).

"***Material***" includes a visual depiction, as defined in 18 U.S.C. § 2256.

"***Minor***" means (A) an individual who had not attained the age of 18 years; (B) an individual, whether fictitious or not, who a law enforcement officer represented to a participant (i) had not attained the age of 18 years, and (ii) could be provided for the purposes of engaging in sexually explicit conduct; or (C) an undercover law enforcement officer who represented to a participant that the officer had not attained the age of 18 years.

"***Sexually explicit conduct***" has the meaning given that term in 18 U.S.C. § 2256(2).

2. **Application of Subsection (b)(2).**—For purposes of subsection (b)(2):

"***Conduct described in 18 U.S.C. § 2241(a) or (b)***" is: (i) using force against the minor; (ii) threatening or placing the minor in fear that any person will be subject to death, serious bodily injury, or kidnapping; (iii) rendering the minor unconscious; or (iv) administering by force or threat of force, or without the knowledge or permission of the minor, a drug, intoxicant, or other similar substance and thereby substantially impairing the ability of the minor to appraise or control conduct. This provision would apply, for example, if any dangerous weapon was used or brandished, or in a case in which the ability of the minor to appraise or control conduct was substantially impaired by drugs or alcohol.

"***Sexual act***" has the meaning given that term in 18 U.S.C. § 2246(2).

"***Sexual contact***" has the meaning given that term in 18 U.S.C. § 2246(3).

3. **Application of Subsection (b)(3).**—For purposes of subsection (b)(3), the defendant "knowingly engaged in distribution" if the defendant (A) knowingly committed the distribution, (B) aided, abetted, counseled, commanded, induced, procured, or willfully caused the distribution, or (C) conspired to distribute.

4. **Interaction of Subsection (b)(4)(B) and Vulnerable Victim (§3A1.1(b)).**—If subsection (b)(4)(B) applies, do not apply §3A1.1(b).

5. **Application of Subsection (b)(5).**—

(A) **In General.**—Subsection (b)(5) is intended to have broad application and includes offenses involving a minor entrusted to the defendant, whether temporarily or permanently. For example, teachers, day care providers, baby-sitters, or other temporary caretakers are among those who would be subject to this enhancement. In determining whether to apply this adjustment, the court should look to the actual relationship that existed between the defendant and the minor and not simply to the legal status of the defendant-minor relationship.

(B) **Inapplicability of Chapter Three Adjustment.**—If the enhancement in subsection (b)(5) applies, do not apply §3B1.3 (Abuse of Position of Trust or Use of Special Skill).

6. **Application of Subsection (b)(6).**—

(A) **Misrepresentation of Participant's Identity.**—The enhancement in subsection (b)(6)(A) applies in cases involving the misrepresentation of a participant's identity to persuade, induce, entice, coerce, or facilitate the travel of, a minor to engage in sexually explicit conduct for the purpose of producing sexually explicit material or for the purpose of transmitting such material live. Subsection (b)(6)(A) is intended to apply only to misrepresentations made directly to a minor or to a person who exercises custody, care, or supervisory control of the minor. Accordingly, the enhancement in subsection (b)(6)(A) would not apply to a misrepresentation made by a participant to an airline representative in the course of making travel arrangements for the minor.

The misrepresentation to which the enhancement in subsection (b)(6)(A) may apply includes misrepresentation of a participant's name, age, occupation, gender, or status, as long as the misrepresentation was made with the intent to persuade, induce, entice, coerce, or facilitate the travel of, a minor to engage in sexually explicit conduct for the purpose of producing sexually explicit material or for the purpose of transmitting such material live. Accordingly, use of a computer screen name, without such intent, would not be a sufficient basis for application of the enhancement.

(B) **Use of a Computer or an Interactive Computer Service.**—Subsection (b)(6)(B) provides an enhancement if the offense involved the use of a computer or an interactive computer service to persuade, induce, entice, coerce, or facilitate the travel of, a minor to engage in sexually explicit conduct for the purpose of producing sexually explicit material or for the purpose of transmitting such material live or otherwise to solicit participation by a minor in such conduct for such purposes. Subsection (b)(6)(B) is intended to apply only to the use of a computer or an interactive computer service to communicate directly with a minor or with a person who exercises custody, care, or supervisory control of the minor. Accordingly, the enhancement would not apply to the use of a computer or an interactive computer service to obtain airline tickets for the minor from an airline's Internet site.

7. **Application of Subsection (d)(1).**—For the purposes of Chapter Three, Part D (Multiple Counts), each minor exploited is to be treated as a separate minor. Consequently, multiple counts involving the exploitation of different minors are not to be grouped together under §3D1.2 (Groups of Closely Related Counts). Subsection (d)(1) directs that if the relevant conduct of an offense of conviction includes more than one minor being exploited, whether specifically cited in the count of conviction or not, each such minor shall be treated as if contained in a separate count of conviction.

8. **Upward Departure Provision.**—An upward departure may be warranted if the offense involved more than 10 minors.

Historical Note

Effective November 1, 1987. Amended effective November 1, 1989 (amendment 161); November 1, 1990 (amendment 324); November 1, 1991 (amendment 400); November 1, 1996 (amendment 537); November 1, 1997 (amendment 575); November 1, 2000 (amendment 592); May 1, 2001 (amendment 612); November 1, 2001 (amendment 627); November 1, 2003 (amendment 661); November 1, 2004 (amendment 664); November 1, 2009 (amendments 733, 736, and 737); November 1, 2016 (amendment 801).

§2G2.2. Trafficking in Material Involving the Sexual Exploitation of a Minor; Receiving, Transporting, Shipping, Soliciting, or Advertising Material Involving the Sexual Exploitation of a Minor; Possessing Material Involving the Sexual Exploitation of a Minor with Intent to Traffic; Possessing Material Involving the Sexual Exploitation of a Minor

(a) Base Offense Level:

(1) **18**, if the defendant is convicted of 18 U.S.C. § 1466A(b), § 2252(a)(4), § 2252A(a)(5), or § 2252A(a)(7).

(2) **22**, otherwise.

(b) Specific Offense Characteristics

(1) If (A) subsection (a)(2) applies; (B) the defendant's conduct was limited to the receipt or solicitation of material involving the sexual exploitation of a minor; and (C) the defendant did not

intend to traffic in, or distribute, such material, decrease by
2 levels.
(2) If the material involved a prepubescent minor or a minor who had not attained the age of 12 years, increase by **2** levels.
(3) (Apply the greatest):
(A) If the offense involved distribution for pecuniary gain, increase by the number of levels from the table in §2B1.1 (Theft, Property Destruction, and Fraud) corresponding to the retail value of the material, but by not less than **5** levels.
(B) If the defendant distributed in exchange for any valuable consideration, but not for pecuniary gain, increase by **5** levels.
(C) If the offense involved distribution to a minor, increase by **5** levels.
(D) If the offense involved distribution to a minor that was intended to persuade, induce, entice, or coerce the minor to engage in any illegal activity, other than illegal activity covered under subdivision (E), increase by **6** levels.
(E) If the offense involved distribution to a minor that was intended to persuade, induce, entice, coerce, or facilitate the

travel of, the minor to engage in prohibited sexual conduct, increase by **7** levels.
(F) If the defendant knowingly engaged in distribution, other than distribution described in subdivisions (A) through (E), increase by **2** levels.
(4) If the offense involved material that portrays (A) sadistic or masochistic conduct or other depictions of violence; or (B) sexual abuse or exploitation of an infant or toddler, increase by **4** levels.
(5) If the defendant engaged in a pattern of activity involving the sexual abuse or exploitation of a minor, increase by **5** levels.
(6) If the offense involved the use of a computer or an interactive computer service for the possession, transmission, receipt, or distribution of the material, or for accessing with intent to view the material, increase by **2** levels.
(7) If the offense involved—
(A) at least 10 images, but fewer than 150, increase by **2** levels;
(B) at least 150 images, but fewer than 300, increase by **3** levels;
(C) at least 300 images, but fewer than 600, increase by **4** levels; and
(D) 600 or more images, increase by **5** levels.
(c) Cross Reference
(1) If the offense involved causing, transporting, permitting, or offering or seeking by notice or advertisement, a minor to engage

in sexually explicit conduct for the purpose of producing a visual depiction of such conduct or for the purpose of transmitting a live visual depiction of such conduct, apply §2G2.1 (Sexually Exploiting a Minor by Production of Sexually Explicit Visual or Printed Material; Custodian Permitting Minor to Engage in Sexually Explicit Conduct; Advertisement for Minors to Engage in Production), if the resulting offense level is greater than that determined above.

Commentary

Statutory Provisions: 18 U.S.C. §§ 1466A, 2252, 2252A(a)–(b), 2260(b). For additional statutory provision(s), *see* Appendix A (Statutory Index).

Application Notes:

1. **Definitions.**—For purposes of this guideline:

"***Computer***" has the meaning given that term in 18 U.S.C. § 1030(e)(1).

"***Distribution***" means any act, including possession with intent to distribute, production, transmission, advertisement, and transportation, related to the transfer of material involving the sexual exploitation of a minor. Accordingly, distribution includes posting material involving the sexual exploitation of a minor on a website for public viewing but does not include the mere solicitation of such material by a defendant.

"***Distribution for pecuniary gain***" means distribution for profit.

"***The defendant distributed in exchange for any valuable consideration***" means the defendant agreed to an exchange with another person under which the defendant knowingly distributed to that other person for the specific purpose of obtaining something of valuable consideration from that other person, such as other child pornographic material, preferential access to child pornographic material, or access to a child.

"***Distribution to a minor***" means the knowing distribution to an individual who is a minor at the time of the offense.

"***Interactive computer service***" has the meaning given that term in section 230(e)(2) of the Communications Act of 1934 (47 U.S.C. § 230(f)(2)).

"***Material***" includes a visual depiction, as defined in 18 U.S.C. § 2256.

"***Minor***" means (A) an individual who had not attained the age of 18 years; (B) an individual, whether fictitious or not, who a law enforcement officer represented to a participant (i) had not attained the age of 18 years, and (ii) could be provided for the purposes of engaging in sexually explicit conduct; or (C) an undercover law enforcement officer who represented to a participant that the officer had not attained the age of 18 years.

"***Pattern of activity involving the sexual abuse or exploitation of a minor***" means any combination of two or more separate instances of the sexual abuse or sexual exploitation of a minor by the defendant, whether or not the abuse or exploitation (A) occurred during the course of the offense; (B) involved the same minor; or (C) resulted in a conviction for such conduct.

"***Prohibited sexual conduct***" has the meaning given that term in Application Note 1 of the Commentary to §2A3.1 (Criminal Sexual Abuse; Attempt to Commit Criminal Sexual Abuse).

"***Sexual abuse or exploitation***" means any of the following: (A) conduct described in 18 U.S.C. § 2241, § 2242, § 2243, § 2251(a)–(c), § 2251(d)(1)(B), § 2251A, § 2260(b), § 2421, § 2422, or § 2423; (B) an offense under state law, that would have been an offense under any such section if the offense had occurred within the special maritime or territorial jurisdiction of the United States; or (C) an attempt or conspiracy to commit any of

the offenses under subdivisions (A) or (B). "Sexual abuse or exploitation" does not include possession, accessing with intent to view, receipt, or trafficking in material relating to the sexual abuse or exploitation of a minor.

2. **Application of Subsection (b)(3)(F).**—For purposes of subsection (b)(3)(F), the defendant "knowingly engaged in distribution" if the defendant (A) knowingly committed the distribution, (B) aided, abetted, counseled, commanded, induced, procured, or willfully caused the distribution, or (C) conspired to distribute.

3. **Application of Subsection (b)(4)(A).**—Subsection (b)(4)(A) applies if the offense involved material that portrays sadistic or masochistic conduct or other depictions of violence, regardless of whether the defendant specifically intended to possess, access with intent to view, receive, or distribute such materials.

4. **Interaction of Subsection (b)(4)(B) and Vulnerable Victim (§3A1.1(b)).**—If subsection (b)(4)(B) applies, do not apply §3A1.1(b).

5. **Application of Subsection (b)(5).**—A conviction taken into account under subsection (b)(5) is not excluded from consideration of whether that conviction receives criminal history points pursuant to Chapter Four, Part A (Criminal History).

6. **Application of Subsection (b)(7).**—

(A) **Definition of "Images".**—"***Images***" means any visual depiction, as defined in 18 U.S.C. § 2256(5), that constitutes child pornography, as defined in 18 U.S.C. § 2256(8).

(B) **Determining the Number of Images.**—For purposes of determining the number of images under subsection (b)(7):

(i) Each photograph, picture, computer or computer-generated image, or any similar visual depiction shall be considered to be one image. If the number of images substantially underrepresents the number of minors depicted, an upward departure may be warranted.

(ii) Each video, video-clip, movie, or similar visual depiction shall be considered to have 75 images. If the length of the visual depiction is substantially more than 5 minutes, an upward departure may be warranted.

7. **Application of Subsection (c)(1).**—

(A) **In General.**—The cross reference in subsection (c)(1) is to be construed broadly and includes all instances where the offense involved employing, using, persuading, inducing, enticing, coercing, transporting, permitting, or offering or seeking by notice or advertisement, a minor to engage in sexually explicit conduct for the purpose of producing any visual depiction of such conduct or for the purpose of transmitting live any visual depiction of such conduct.

(B) **Definition.**—"***Sexually explicit conduct***" has the meaning given that term in 18 U.S.C. § 2256(2).

8. **Cases Involving Adapted or Modified Depictions.**—If the offense involved material that is an adapted or modified depiction of an identifiable minor (*e.g.*, a case in which the

defendant is convicted under 18 U.S.C. § 2252A(a)(7)), the term "material involving the sexual exploitation of a minor" includes such material.

9. **Upward Departure Provision.**—If the defendant engaged in the sexual abuse or exploitation of a minor at any time (whether or not such abuse or exploitation occurred during the course of the offense or resulted in a conviction for such conduct) and subsection (b)(5) does not apply, an upward departure may be warranted. In addition, an upward departure may be warranted if the defendant received an enhancement under subsection (b)(5) but that enhancement does not adequately reflect the seriousness of the sexual abuse or exploitation involved.

Background: Section 401(i)(1)(C) of Public Law 108–21 directly amended subsection (b) to add subdivision (7), effective April 30, 2003.

Historical Note

Effective November 1, 1987. Amended effective June 15, 1988 (amendment 31); November 1, 1990 (amendment 325); November 1, 1991 (amendment 372); November 27, 1991 (amendment 435); November 1, 1996 (amendment 537); November 1, 1997 (amendment 575); November 1, 2000 (amendment 592); November 1, 2001 (amendment 615); April 30, 2003 (amendment 649); November 1, 2003 (amendment 661); November 1, 2004 (amendment 664); November 1, 2009 (amendments 733 and 736); November 1, 2016 (amendment 801).

§2G2.3. Selling or Buying of Children for Use in the Production of Pornography

(a) Base Offense Level: **38**

Commentary

Statutory Provision: 18 U.S.C. § 2251A.

Background: The statutory minimum sentence for a defendant convicted under 18 U.S.C. § 2251A is thirty years imprisonment.

Historical Note

Effective November 1, 1989 (amendment 162). Amended effective November 1, 2009 (amendment 736).

§2G2.4. [Deleted]

Historical Note

Effective November 1, 1991 (amendment 372). Amended effective November 27, 1991 (amendment 436); November 1, 1996 (amendment 537); November 1, 2000 (amendment 592); April 30, 2003 (amendment 649); was deleted by consolidation with §2G2.2 effective November 1, 2004 (amendment 664).

§2G2.5. Recordkeeping Offenses Involving the Production of Sexually Explicit Materials; Failure to Provide Required Marks in Commercial Electronic Email

(a) Base Offense Level: **6**

(b) Cross References

(1) If the offense reflected an effort to conceal a substantive offense that involved causing, transporting, permitting, or offering or seeking by notice or advertisement, a minor to engage in sexually explicit conduct for the purpose of producing a visual depiction of such conduct, apply §2G2.1 (Sexually Exploiting a Minor by Production of Sexually Explicit Visual or Printed Material; Custodian Permitting Minor to Engage in Sexually Explicit Conduct; Advertisement for Minors to Engage in Production).

(2) If the offense reflected an effort to conceal a substantive offense that involved trafficking in material involving the sexual exploitation of a minor (including receiving, transporting, advertising, or possessing material involving the sexual exploitation of a minor with intent to traffic), apply §2G2.2 (Trafficking in Material Involving the Sexual Exploitation of a Minor; Receiving, Transporting, Advertising, or Possessing Material Involving the Sexual Exploitation of a Minor with Intent to Traffic).

Commentary

Statutory Provisions: 15 U.S.C. § 7704(d); 18 U.S.C. §§ 2257, 2257A.

Historical Note

Effective November 1, 1991 (amendment 372). Amended effective November 1, 2006 (amendment 689); November 1, 2007 (amendment 701).

§2G2.6. Child Exploitation Enterprises

(a) Base Offense Level: **35**

(b) Specific Offense Characteristics

(1) If a victim (A) had not attained the age of 12 years, increase by **4** levels; or (B) had attained the age of 12 years but had not attained the age of 16 years, increase by **2** levels.

(2) If (A) the defendant was a parent, relative, or legal guardian of a minor victim; or (B) a minor victim was otherwise in the custody, care, or supervisory control of the defendant, increase by **2** levels.

(3) If the offense involved conduct described in 18 U.S.C. § 2241(a) or (b), increase by **2** levels.

(4) If a computer or an interactive computer service was used in furtherance of the offense, increase by **2** levels.

Commentary

Statutory Provision: 18 U.S.C. § 2252A(g).

Application Notes:

1. **Definitions.**—For purposes of this guideline:

"***Computer***" has the meaning given that term in 18 U.S.C. § 1030(e)(1).

"***Interactive computer service***" has the meaning given that term in section 230(e)(2) of the Communications Act of 1934 (47 U.S.C. § 230(f)(2)).

"***Minor***" means (A) an individual who had not attained the age of 18 years; (B) an individual, whether fictitious or not, who a law enforcement officer represented to a participant (i) had not attained the age of 18 years; and (ii) could be provided for the purposes of engaging in sexually explicit conduct; or (C) an undercover law enforcement officer who represented to a participant that the officer had not attained the age of 18 years.

2. **Application of Subsection (b)(2).**—

(A) **Custody, Care, or Supervisory Control.**—Subsection (b)(2) is intended to have broad application and includes offenses involving a victim less than 18 years of age entrusted to the defendant, whether temporarily or permanently. For example, teachers, day care providers, baby-sitters, or other temporary caretakers are among those who would be subject to this enhancement. In determining whether to apply this enhancement, the court should look to the actual relationship that existed between the defendant and the minor and not simply to the legal status of the defendant-minor relationship.

(B) **Inapplicability of Chapter Three Adjustment.**—If the enhancement under subsection (b)(2) applies, do not apply §3B1.3 (Abuse of Position of Trust or Use of Special Skill).

3. **Application of Subsection (b)(3).**—For purposes of subsection (b)(3), "***conduct described in 18 U.S.C. § 2241(a) or (b)***" is: (i) using force against the minor; (ii) threatening or placing the minor in fear that any person will be subject to death, serious bodily injury, or kidnapping; (iii) rendering the minor unconscious; or (iv) administering by force or threat of force, or without the knowledge or permission of the minor, a drug, intoxicant, or other similar substance and thereby substantially impairing the ability of the minor to appraise or control conduct. This provision would apply, for example, if any dangerous

weapon was used or brandished, or in a case in which the ability of the minor to appraise or control conduct was substantially impaired by drugs or alcohol.

Historical Note

Effective November 1, 2007 (amendment 701).

* * * * *

3. OBSCENITY

§2G3.1. Importing, Mailing, or Transporting Obscene Matter; Transferring Obscene Matter to a Minor; Misleading Domain Names

(a) Base Offense Level: **10**

(b) Specific Offense Characteristics

(1) (Apply the Greatest):
(A) If the offense involved distribution for pecuniary gain, increase by the number of levels from the table in §2B1.1 (Theft, Property Destruction, and Fraud) corresponding to the retail value of the material, but by not less than **5** levels.
(B) If the defendant distributed in exchange for any valuable consideration, but not for pecuniary gain, increase by **5** levels.
(C) If the offense involved distribution to a minor, increase by **5** levels.
(D) If the offense involved distribution to a minor that was intended to persuade, induce, entice, or coerce the minor to engage in any illegal activity, other than illegal activity covered under subdivision (E), increase by **6** levels.
(E) If the offense involved distribution to a minor that was intended to persuade, induce, entice, coerce, or facilitate the travel of, the minor to engage in prohibited sexual conduct, increase by **7** levels.
(F) If the defendant knowingly engaged in distribution, other than distribution described in subdivisions (A) through (E), increase by **2** levels.

(2) If, with the intent to deceive a minor into viewing material that is harmful to minors, the offense involved the use of (A) a misleading domain name on the Internet; or (B) embedded words or digital images in the source code of a website, increase by **2** levels.
(3) If the offense involved the use of a computer or an interactive computer service, increase by **2** levels.
(4) If the offense involved material that portrays sadistic or masochistic conduct or other depictions of violence, increase by **4** levels.
(c) Cross Reference
(1) If the offense involved transporting, distributing, receiving, possessing, or advertising to receive material involving the sexual exploitation of a minor, apply §2G2.2 (Trafficking in Material Involving the Sexual Exploitation of a Minor; Receiving, Transporting, Shipping, Soliciting, or Advertising Material Involving the Sexual Exploitation of a Minor; Possessing Material Involving the Sexual Exploitation of a Minor with Intent to Traffic; Possessing Material Involving the Sexual Exploitation of a Minor).

Commentary

Statutory Provisions: 18 U.S.C. §§ 1460–1463, 1465, 1466, 1470, 2252B, 2252C. For additional statutory provision(s), *see* Appendix A (Statutory Index).

Application Notes:

1. **Definitions.**—For purposes of this guideline:
"***Computer***" has the meaning given that term in 18 U.S.C. § 1030(e)(1).
"***Distribution***" means any act, including possession with intent to distribute, production,

transmission, advertisement, and transportation, related to the transfer of obscene matter. Accordingly, distribution includes posting material involving the sexual exploitation of a minor on a website for public viewing but does not include the mere solicitation of such material by a defendant.

"***Distribution for pecuniary gain***" means distribution for profit.

"***The defendant distributed in exchange for any valuable consideration***" means the defendant agreed to an exchange with another person under which the defendant knowingly distributed to that other person for the specific purpose of obtaining something of valuable consideration from that other person, such as other obscene material, preferential access to obscene material, or access to a child.

"***Distribution to a minor***" means the knowing distribution to an individual who is a minor at the time of the offense.

"***Interactive computer service***" has the meaning given that term in section 230(e)(2) of the Communications Act of 1934 (47 U.S.C. § 230(f)(2)).

"***Material that is harmful to minors***" has the meaning given that term in 18 U.S.C. § 2252B(d).

"***Minor***" means (A) an individual who had not attained the age of 18 years; (B) an individual, whether fictitious or not, who a law enforcement officer represented to a participant (i) had not attained the age of 18 years, and (ii) could be provided for the purposes of engaging in sexually explicit conduct; or (C) an undercover law enforcement officer who represented to a participant that the officer had not attained the age of 18 years.

"***Prohibited sexual conduct***" has the meaning given that term in Application Note 1 of the Commentary to §2A3.1 (Criminal Sexual Abuse; Attempt to Commit Criminal Sexual Abuse).

"***Sexually explicit conduct***" has the meaning given that term in 18 U.S.C. § 2256(2).

2. **Application of Subsection (b)(1)(F).**—For purposes of subsection (b)(1)(F), the defendant "knowingly engaged in distribution" if the defendant (A) knowingly committed the distribution, (B) aided, abetted, counseled, commanded, induced, procured, or willfully caused the distribution, or (C) conspired to distribute.

3. **Inapplicability of Subsection (b)(3).**—If the defendant is convicted of 18 U.S.C. § 2252B or § 2252C, subsection (b)(3) shall not apply.

4. **Application of Subsection (b)(4).**—Subsection (b)(4) applies if the offense involved material that portrays sadistic or masochistic conduct or other depictions of violence, regardless of whether the defendant specifically intended to possess, receive, or distribute such materials.

Background: Most federal prosecutions for offenses covered in this guideline are directed to offenses involving distribution for pecuniary gain. Consequently, the offense level under this section generally will be at least 15.

Historical Note

Effective November 1, 1987. Amended effective November 1, 1989 (amendment 163); November 1, 1990 (amendment 326); November 1, 1991 (amendment 372); November 27, 1991 (amendment 437); November 1, 2000 (amendment 592); November 1, 2001 (amendment 617); November 1, 2004 (amendment 664); November 1, 2007 (amendment 701); November 1, 2009 (amendment 736); November 1, 2010 (amendment 746); November 1, 2016 (amendment 801).

§2G3.2. Obscene Telephone Communications for a Commercial Purpose; Broadcasting Obscene Material

(a) Base Offense Level: **12**

(b) Specific Offense Characteristics

(1) If a person who received the telephonic communication was less than eighteen years of age, or if a broadcast was made between

six o'clock in the morning and eleven o'clock at night, increase by **4** levels.

(2) If **6** plus the offense level from the table in §2B1.1 (Theft, Property Destruction, and Fraud) corresponding to the volume of commerce attributable to the defendant is greater than the offense level determined above, increase to that offense level.

Commentary

Statutory Provisions: 18 U.S.C. §§ 1464, 1468; 47 U.S.C. § 223(b)(1)(A).

Background: Subsection (b)(1) provides an enhancement where an obscene telephonic communication was received by a minor less than 18 years of age or where a broadcast was made during a time when such minors were likely to receive it. Subsection (b)(2) provides an enhancement for large-scale "dial-a-porn" or obscene broadcasting operations that results in an offense level comparable to the offense level for such operations under §2G3.1 (Importing, Mailing, or Transporting Obscene Matter; Transferring Obscene Matter to a Minor). The extent to which the obscene material was distributed is approximated by the volume of commerce attributable to the defendant.

Historical Note

Effective November 1, 1989 (amendment 164). Amended effective November 1, 2000 (amendment 592); November 1, 2001 (amendment 617). A former §2G3.2 (Obscene or Indecent Telephone Communications), effective November 1, 1987, was deleted effective November 1, 1989 (amendment 164).

PART H — OFFENSES INVOLVING INDIVIDUAL RIGHTS

1. CIVIL RIGHTS

Historical Note

Introductory Commentary to Part H, Subpart 1, effective November 1, 1987, was deleted effective November 1, 1995 (amendment 521).

§2H1.1. Offenses Involving Individual Rights

(a) Base Offense Level (Apply the Greatest):

(1) the offense level from the offense guideline applicable to any underlying offense;

(2) **12**, if the offense involved two or more participants;

(3) **10**, if the offense involved (A) the use or threat of force against a person; or (B) property damage or the threat of property damage; or

(4) **6**, otherwise.

(b) Specific Offense Characteristic

(1) If (A) the defendant was a public official at the time of the offense; or (B) the offense was committed under color of law, increase by **6** levels.

Commentary

Statutory Provisions: 18 U.S.C. §§ 241, 242, 245(b), 246, 247, 248, 249, 1091; 42 U.S.C. § 3631.

Application Notes:

1. "***Offense guideline applicable to any underlying offense***" means the offense guideline applicable to any conduct established by the offense of conviction that constitutes an offense under federal, state, or local law (other than an offense that is itself covered under Chapter Two, Part H, Subpart 1).

In certain cases, conduct set forth in the count of conviction may constitute more than one underlying offense (*e.g.*, two instances of assault, or one instance of assault and one instance of arson). In such cases, use the following comparative procedure to determine the applicable base offense level: (i) determine the underlying offenses encompassed within the count of conviction as if the defendant had been charged with a conspiracy to commit multiple offenses. *See* Application Note 4 of §1B1.2 (Applicable Guidelines);

(ii) determine the Chapter Two offense level (*i.e.*, the base offense level, specific offense characteristics, cross references, and special instructions) for each such underlying offense; and (iii) compare each of the Chapter Two offense levels determined above with the alternative base offense level under subsection (a)(2), (3), or (4). The determination of the applicable alternative base offense level is to be based on the entire conduct underlying the count of conviction (*i.e.*, the conduct taken as a whole). Use the alternative base offense level only if it is greater than each of the Chapter Two offense levels determined above. Otherwise, use the Chapter Two offense levels for each of the underlying offenses (with each underlying offense treated as if contained in a separate count of conviction). Then apply subsection (b) to the alternative base offense level, or to the Chapter Two offense levels for each of the underlying offenses, as appropriate.

2. "***Participant***" is defined in the Commentary to §3B1.1 (Aggravating Role).

3. The burning or defacement of a religious symbol with an intent to intimidate shall be deemed to involve the threat of force against a person for the purposes of subsection (a)(3)(A).

4. If the finder of fact at trial or, in the case of a plea of guilty or *nolo contendere*, the court at sentencing determines beyond a reasonable doubt that the defendant intentionally selected any victim or any property as the object of the offense because of the actual or perceived race, color, religion, national origin, ethnicity, gender, gender identity, disability, or sexual orientation of any person, an additional 3-level enhancement from §3A1.1(a) will apply. An adjustment from §3A1.1(a) will not apply, however, if a 6-level adjustment from §2H1.1(b) applies. *See* §3A1.1(c).

5. If subsection (b)(1) applies, do not apply §3B1.3 (Abuse of Position of Trust or Use of Special Skill).

Historical Note

Effective November 1, 1987. Amended effective November 1, 1989 (amendment 303); November 1, 1990 (amendments 313 and 327); November 1, 1991 (amendment 430); November 1, 1995 (amendment 521); November 1, 2000 (amendment 591); November 1, 2010 (amendment 743).

§2H1.2. [Deleted]

Historical Note

Section 2H1.2 (Conspiracy to Interfere with Civil Rights), effective November 1, 1987, amended effective November 1, 1989 (amendment 303), was deleted by consolidation with §2H1.1 effective November 1, 1990 (amendment 327).

§2H1.3. [Deleted]

Historical Note

Section 2H1.3 (Use of Force or Threat of Force to Deny Benefits or Rights in Furtherance of Discrimination; Damage to Religious Real Property), effective November 1, 1987, amended effective November 1, 1989 (amendment 165), was deleted by consolidation with §2H1.1 effective November 1, 1995 (amendment 521).

§2H1.4. [Deleted]

Historical Note

Section 2H1.4 (Interference with Civil Rights Under Color of Law), effective November 1, 1987, amended effective November 1, 1989 (amendment 166), was deleted by consolidation with §2H1.1 effective November 1, 1995 (amendment 521).

§2H1.5. [Deleted]

Historical Note

Section 2H1.5 (Other Deprivations of Rights or Benefits in Furtherance of Discrimination), effective November 1, 1987, amended effective November 1, 1989 (amendment 167) and November 1, 1990 (amendment 328), was deleted by consolidation with §2H1.1 effective November 1, 1995 (amendment 521).

* * * * *

2. POLITICAL RIGHTS

§2H2.1. Obstructing an Election or Registration

(a) Base Offense Level (Apply the greatest):

(1) **18**, if the obstruction occurred by use of force or threat of force against person(s) or property; or

(2) **12**, if the obstruction occurred by forgery, fraud, theft, bribery, deceit, or other means, except as provided in (3) below; or

(3) **6**, if the defendant (A) solicited, demanded, accepted, or agreed to accept anything of value to vote, refrain from voting, vote for or against a particular candidate, or register to vote, (B) gave false information to establish eligibility to vote, or (C) voted more than once in a federal election.

Commentary

Statutory Provisions: 18 U.S.C. §§ 241, 242, 245(b)(1)(A), 592, 593, 594, 597, 1015(f); 52 U.S.C. §§ 10307, 10308(a), (b). For additional statutory provision(s), *see* Appendix A (Statutory Index).

Application Note:

1. If the offense resulted in bodily injury or significant property damage, or involved corrupting a public official, an upward departure may be warranted. *See* Chapter Five, Part K (Departures).

Background: Alternative base offense levels cover three major ways of obstructing an election: by force, by deceptive or dishonest conduct, or by bribery. A defendant who is a public official or who directs others to engage in criminal conduct is subject to an enhancement from Chapter Three, Part B (Role in the Offense).

Historical Note

Effective November 1, 1987. Amended effective November 1, 1989 (amendment 168); November 1, 1995 (amendment 534); November 1, 2003 (amendment 661); November 1, 2015 (amendment 796).

* * * * *

3. PRIVACY AND EAVESDROPPING

§2H3.1. Interception of Communications; Eavesdropping; Disclosure of Certain Private or Protected Information

(a) Base Offense Level (Apply the greater):

(1) **9**; or

(2) **6**, if the offense of conviction has a statutory maximum term of imprisonment of one year or less but more than six months.

(b) Specific Offense Characteristics

(1) If (A) the defendant is convicted under 18 U.S.C. § 1039(d) or (e); or (B) the purpose of the offense was to obtain direct or indirect commercial advantage or economic gain, increase by **3** levels.

(2) (Apply the greater) If—

(A) the defendant is convicted under 18 U.S.C. § 119, increase by **8** levels; or

(B) the defendant is convicted under 18 U.S.C. § 119, and the offense involved the use of a computer or an interactive computer service to make restricted personal information about a covered person publicly available, increase by **10** levels.

(c) Cross Reference

(1) If the purpose of the offense was to facilitate another offense, apply the guideline applicable to an attempt to commit that

other offense, if the resulting offense level is greater than that determined above.

Commentary

Statutory Provisions: 8 U.S.C. § 1375a(d)(5)(B)(i), (ii); 18 U.S.C. §§ 119, 1039, 1905, 2511; 26 U.S.C. §§ 7213(a)(1)–(3), (a)(5), (d), 7213A, 7216; 42 U.S.C. §§ 16962, 16984; 47 U.S.C. § 605. For additional statutory provision(s), *see* Appendix A (Statutory Index).

Application Notes:

1. **Satellite Cable Transmissions.**—If the offense involved interception of satellite cable transmissions for purposes of commercial advantage or private financial gain (including avoiding payment of fees), apply §2B5.3 (Criminal Infringement of Copyright) rather than this guideline.

2. **Imposition of Sentence for 18 U.S.C. § 1039(d) and (e).**—Subsections 1039(d) and (e) of title 18, United States Code, require a term of imprisonment of not more than 5 years to be imposed in addition to any sentence imposed for a conviction under 18 U.S.C. § 1039(a), (b), or (c). In order to comply with the statute, the court should determine the appropriate "total punishment" and divide the sentence on the judgment form between the sentence attributable to the conviction under 18 U.S.C. § 1039(d) or (e) and the sentence attributable to the conviction under 18 U.S.C. § 1039(a), (b), or (c), specifying the number of months to be served for the conviction under 18 U.S.C. § 1039(d) or (e). For example, if the applicable adjusted guideline range is 15–21 months and the court determines a "total punishment" of 21 months is appropriate, a sentence of 9 months for conduct under 18 U.S.C. § 1039(a) plus 12 months for 18 U.S.C. § 1039(d) conduct would achieve the "total punishment" in a manner that satisfies the statutory requirement.

3. **Inapplicability of Chapter Three (Adjustments).**—If the enhancement under subsection (b)(2) applies, do not apply §3A1.2 (Official Victim).

4. **Definitions.**—For purposes of this guideline:

"***Computer***" has the meaning given that term in 18 U.S.C. § 1030(e)(1).

"***Covered person***" has the meaning given that term in 18 U.S.C. § 119(b).

"***Interactive computer service***" has the meaning given that term in section 230(e)(2) of the Communications Act of 1934 (47 U.S.C. § 230(f)(2)).

"***Means of identification***" has the meaning given that term in 18 U.S.C. § 1028(d)(7), except that such means of identification shall be of an actual (*i.e.*, not fictitious) individual, other than the defendant or a person for whose conduct the defendant is accountable under §1B1.3 (Relevant Conduct).

"***Personal information***" means sensitive or private information involving an identifiable individual (including such information in the possession of a third party), including (A) medical records; (B) wills; (C) diaries; (D) private correspondence, including e-mail; (E) financial records; (F) photographs of a sensitive or private nature; or (G) similar information.

"***Restricted personal information***" has the meaning given that term in 18 U.S.C. § 119(b).

5. **Upward Departure.**—There may be cases in which the offense level determined under this guideline substantially understates the seriousness of the offense. In such a case, an upward departure may be warranted. The following are examples of cases in which an upward departure may be warranted:

(A) The offense involved personal information, means of identification, confidential phone records information, or tax return information of a substantial number of individuals.

(B) The offense caused or risked substantial non-monetary harm *(e.g.* physical harm, psychological harm, or severe emotional trauma, or resulted in a substantial invasion of privacy interest) to individuals whose private or protected information was obtained.

Historical
Note
Effective November 1, 1987. Amended effective November 1, 1989 (amendment 169); November 1, 2001 (amendment 628); May 1, 2007 (amendment 697); November 1, 2007 (amendment 708); November 1, 2008 (amendment 718); November 1, 2009 (amendments 726 and 737); November 1, 2104 (amendment 781).

§2H3.2. Manufacturing, Distributing, Advertising, or Possessing an Eavesdropping Device

(a) Base Offense Level: **6**

(b) Specific Offense Characteristic

(1) If the offense was committed for pecuniary gain, increase by **3** levels.

Commentary

Statutory Provision: 18 U.S.C. § 2512.

Historical
Note
Effective November 1, 1987.

§2H3.3. Obstructing Correspondence

(a) Base Offense Level:

(1) **6**; or

(2) if the conduct was theft or destruction of mail, apply §2B1.1 (Theft, Property Destruction, and Fraud).

Commentary

Statutory Provision: 18 U.S.C. § 1702. For additional statutory provision(s), *see* Appendix A (Statutory Index).

Background: The statutory provision covered by this guideline is sometimes used to prosecute offenses more accurately described as theft or destruction of mail. In such cases, §2B1.1 (Theft, Property Destruction, and Fraud) is to be applied.

Historical
Note
Effective November 1, 1987. Amended effective November 1, 1990 (amendment 313); November 1, 2001 (amendment 617).

* * * * *

4. PEONAGE, INVOLUNTARY SERVITUDE, SLAVE TRADE, AND CHILD SOLDIERS

Historical
Note
Effective November 1, 1987. Amended effective November 1, 2009 (amendment 733).

§2H4.1. Peonage, Involuntary Servitude, Slave Trade, and Child Soldiers

(a) Base Offense Level:

(1) **22**; or

(2) **18**, if (A) the defendant was convicted of an offense under 18 U.S.C. § 1592, or (B) the defendant was convicted of an offense under 18 U.S.C. § 1593A based on an act in violation of 18 U.S.C. § 1592.

(b) Specific Offense Characteristics

(1) (A) If any victim sustained permanent or life-threatening bodily injury, increase by **4** levels; or (B) if any victim sustained serious bodily injury, increase by **2** levels.

(2) If (A) a dangerous weapon was used, increase by **4** levels; or (B) a dangerous weapon was brandished, or the use of a dangerous

weapon was threatened, increase by **2** levels.
(3) If any victim was held in a condition of peonage or involuntary servitude for (A) more than one year, increase by **3** levels;
(B) between 180 days and one year, increase by **2** levels; or

(C) more than 30 days but less than 180 days, increase by **1** level.
(4) If any other felony offense was committed during the commission of, or in connection with, the peonage or involuntary servitude offense, increase to the greater of:
(A) **2** plus the offense level as determined above, or
(B) **2** plus the offense level from the offense guideline applicable to that other offense, but in no event greater than level **43**.

Commentary

Statutory Provisions: 18 U.S.C. §§ 241, 1581–1590, 1592, 1593A, 2442.

Application Notes:

1. For purposes of this guideline—

"***A dangerous weapon was used***" means that a firearm was discharged, or that a firearm or other dangerous weapon was otherwise used. "***The use of a dangerous weapon was threatened***" means that the use of a dangerous weapon was threatened regardless of whether a dangerous weapon was present.

Definitions of "***firearm***," "***dangerous weapon***," "***otherwise used***," "***serious bodily injury***," and "***permanent or life-threatening bodily injury***" are found in the Commentary to §1B1.1 (Application Instructions).

"***Peonage or involuntary servitude***" includes forced labor, slavery, and recruitment or use of a child soldier.

2. Under subsection (b)(4), "***any other felony offense***" means any conduct that constitutes a felony offense under federal, state, or local law (other than an offense that is itself covered by this subpart). When there is more than one such other offense, the most serious such offense (or group of closely related offenses in the case of offenses that would be grouped together under §3D1.2(d)) is to be used. *See* Application Note 3 of §1B1.5 (Interpretation of References to other Offense Guidelines).

3. If the offense involved the holding of more than ten victims in a condition of peonage or involuntary servitude, an upward departure may be warranted.

4. In a case in which the defendant was convicted under 18 U.S.C. §§ 1589(b) or 1593A, a downward departure may be warranted if the defendant benefitted from participating in a venture described in those sections without knowing that (*i.e.*, in reckless disregard of the fact that) the venture had engaged in the criminal activity described in those sections.

Historical Note

Effective November 1, 1987. Amended effective November 1, 1995 (amendment 521); May 1, 1997 (amendment 542); November 1, 1997 (amendment 559); May 1, 2001 (amendment 612); November 1, 2001 (amendment 627); November 1, 2009 (amendments 730 and 733).

§2H4.2. Willful Violations of the Migrant and Seasonal Agricultural Worker Protection Act

(a) Base Offense Level: **6**
(b) Specific Offense Characteristics
(1) If the offense involved (A) serious bodily injury, increase by **4** levels; or (B) bodily injury, increase by **2** levels.

(2) If the defendant committed any part of the instant offense subsequent to sustaining a civil or administrative adjudication for similar misconduct, increase by **2** levels.

Commentary

Statutory Provision: 29 U.S.C. § 1851.

Application Notes:

1. **Definitions.**—For purposes of subsection (b)(1), "***bodily injury***" and "***serious bodily injury***" have the meaning given those terms in Application Note 1 of the Commentary to §1B1.1 (Application Instructions).
2. **Application of Subsection (b)(2).**—Section 1851 of title 29, United States Code, covers a wide range of conduct. Accordingly, the enhancement in subsection (b)(2) applies only if the instant offense is similar to previous misconduct that resulted in a civil or administrative adjudication under the provisions of the Migrant and Seasonal Agricultural Worker Protection Act (29 U.S.C. § 1801 *et seq.*).

Historical Note

Effective May 1, 2001 (amendment 612). Amended effective November 1, 2001 (amendment 627); November 1, 2010 (amendment 746); November 1, 2015 (amendment 796).

PART I — [NOT USED]

PART J — OFFENSES INVOLVING THE ADMINISTRATION OF JUSTICE

§2J1.1. Contempt

Apply §2X5.1 (Other Offenses).

Commentary

Statutory Provisions: 18 U.S.C. §§ 401, 228. For additional statutory provision(s), *see* Appendix A (Statutory Index).

Application Notes:

1. **In General.**—Because misconduct constituting contempt varies significantly and the nature of the contemptuous conduct, the circumstances under which the contempt was committed, the effect the misconduct had on the administration of justice, and the need to vindicate the authority of the court are highly context-dependent, the Commission has not provided a specific guideline for this offense. In certain cases, the offense conduct will be sufficiently analogous to §2J1.2 (Obstruction of Justice) for that guideline to apply.
2. **Willful Failure to Pay Court-Ordered Child Support.**—For offenses involving the willful failure to pay court-ordered child support (violations of 18 U.S.C. § 228), the most analogous guideline is §2B1.1 (Theft, Property Destruction, and Fraud). The amount of the loss is the amount of child support that the defendant willfully failed to pay. In such a case, do not apply §2B1.1(b)(9)(C) (pertaining to a violation of a prior, specific judicial order). *Note*: This guideline applies to second and subsequent offenses under 18 U.S.C. § 228(a)(1) and to any offense under 18 U.S.C. § 228(a)(2) and (3). A first offense under 18 U.S.C. § 228(a)(1) is not covered by this guideline because it is a Class B misdemeanor.
3. **Violation of Judicial Order Enjoining Fraudulent Behavior.**—In a case involving a violation of a judicial order enjoining fraudulent behavior, the most analogous guideline is §2B1.1. In such a case, §2B1.1(b)(9)(C) (pertaining to a violation of a prior, specific judicial order) ordinarily would apply.

Historical Note

Effective November 1, 1987. Amended effective November 1, 1989 (amendments 170 and 171); November 1, 1993 (amendment 496); November 1, 1998 (amendment 588); November 1, 2001 (amendment 617); November 1, 2003 (amendment 653); November 1, 2009 (amendment 736); November 1, 2011 (amendments 752 and 760).

§2J1.2. Obstruction of Justice

(a) Base Offense Level: **14**

(b) Specific Offense Characteristics
(1) (Apply the greatest):
(A) If the (i) defendant was convicted under 18 U.S.C. § 1001; and (ii) statutory maximum term of eight years' imprisonment applies because the matter relates to sex offenses under 18 U.S.C. § 1591 or chapters 109A, 109B, 110, or 117 of title 18, United States Code, increase by **4** levels.
(B) If the offense involved causing or threatening to cause physical injury to a person, or property damage, in order to obstruct the administration of justice, increase by **8** levels.
(C) If the (i) defendant was convicted under 18 U.S.C. § 1001 or § 1505; and (ii) statutory maximum term of eight years' imprisonment applies because the matter relates to international terrorism or domestic terrorism, increase by **12** levels.
(2) If the offense resulted in substantial interference with the administration of justice, increase by **3** levels.
(3) If the offense (A) involved the destruction, alteration, or fabrication of a substantial number of records, documents, or tangible objects; (B) involved the selection of any essential or especially probative record, document, or tangible object, to destroy or alter; or (C) was otherwise extensive in scope, planning, or preparation, increase by **2** levels.
(c) Cross Reference
(1) If the offense involved obstructing the investigation or prosecution of a criminal offense, apply §2X3.1 (Accessory After the Fact) in respect to that criminal offense, if the resulting offense level is greater than that determined above.

Commentary

Statutory Provisions: 18 U.S.C. §§ 1001 (when the statutory maximum term of eight years' imprisonment applies because the matter relates to international terrorism or domestic terrorism, or to sex offenses under 18 U.S.C. § 1591 or chapters 109A, 109B, 110, or 117 of title 18, United States Code), 1503, 1505–1513, 1516, 1519. For additional statutory provision(s), *see* Appendix A (Statutory Index).

Application Notes:

1. **Definitions.**—For purposes of this guideline:

"***Domestic terrorism***" has the meaning given that term in 18 U.S.C. § 2331(5).

"***International terrorism***" has the meaning given that term in 18 U.S.C. § 2331(1).

"***Records, documents, or tangible objects***" includes (A) records, documents, or tangible objects that are stored on, or that are, magnetic, optical, digital, other electronic, or other storage mediums or devices; and (B) wire or electronic communications.

"***Substantial interference with the administration of justice***" includes a premature or improper termination of a felony investigation; an indictment, verdict, or any judicial determination based upon perjury, false testimony, or other false evidence; or the unnecessary expenditure of substantial governmental or court resources.

2. **Chapter Three Adjustments.**—

(A) **Inapplicability of §3C1.1.**—For offenses covered under this section, §3C1.1 (Obstructing or Impeding the Administration of Justice) does not apply, unless the defendant obstructed the investigation, prosecution, or sentencing of the obstruction of justice count.

(B) **Interaction with Terrorism Adjustment.**—If §3A1.4 (Terrorism) applies, do not apply subsection (b)(1)(C).

3. **Convictions for the Underlying Offense.**—In the event that the defendant is convicted of an offense sentenced under this section as well as for the underlying offense (*i.e.*, the offense that is the object of the obstruction), *see* the Commentary to Chapter Three, Part C (Obstruction and Related Adjustments), and to §3D1.2(c) (Groups of Closely Related Counts).

4. **Upward Departure Considerations.**—If a weapon was used, or bodily injury or significant property damage resulted, an upward departure may be warranted. *See* Chapter Five, Part K (Departures). In a case involving an act of extreme violence (for example, retaliating against a government witness by throwing acid in the witness's face) or a particularly serious sex offense, an upward departure would be warranted.

5. **Subsection (b)(1)(B).**—The inclusion of "property damage" under subsection (b)(1)(B) is designed to address cases in which property damage is caused or threatened as a means of intimidation or retaliation (*e.g.*, to intimidate a witness from, or retaliate against a witness for, testifying). Subsection (b)(1)(B) is not intended to apply, for example, where the offense consisted of destroying a ledger containing an incriminating entry.

Background: This section addresses offenses involving the obstruction of justice generally prosecuted under the above-referenced statutory provisions. Numerous offenses of varying seriousness may constitute obstruction of justice: using threats or force to intimidate or influence a juror or federal officer; obstructing a civil or administrative proceeding; stealing or altering court records; unlawfully intercepting grand jury deliberations; obstructing a criminal investigation; obstructing a state or local investigation of illegal gambling; using intimidation or force to influence testimony, alter evidence, evade legal process, or obstruct the communication of a judge or law enforcement officer; or causing a witness bodily injury or property damage in

retaliation for providing testimony, information or evidence in a federal proceeding. The conduct that gives rise to the violation may, therefore, range from a mere threat to an act of extreme violence.

The specific offense characteristics reflect the more serious forms of obstruction. Because the conduct covered by this guideline is frequently part of an effort to avoid punishment for an offense that the defendant has committed or to assist another person to escape punishment for an offense, a cross reference to §2X3.1 (Accessory After the Fact) is provided. Use of this cross reference will provide an enhanced offense level when the obstruction is in respect to a particularly serious offense, whether such offense was committed by the defendant or another person.

Historical
Note

Effective November 1, 1987. Amended effective November 1, 1989 (amendments 172–174); November 1, 1991 (amendment 401); January 25, 2003 (amendment 647); November 1, 2003 (amendment 653); October 24, 2005 (amendment 676); November 1, 2006 (amendment 690); November 1, 2007 (amendment 701); November 1, 2011 (amendment 758); November 1, 2013 (amendment 777).

§2J1.3. Perjury or Subornation of Perjury; Bribery of Witness

(a) Base Offense Level: **14**

(b) Specific Offense Characteristics

(1) If the offense involved causing or threatening to cause physical injury to a person, or property damage, in order to suborn perjury, increase by **8** levels.

(2) If the perjury, subornation of perjury, or witness bribery resulted in substantial interference with the administration of justice, increase by **3** levels.

(c) Cross Reference
(1) If the offense involved perjury, subornation of perjury, or witness bribery in respect to a criminal offense, apply §2X3.1 (Accessory After the Fact) in respect to that criminal offense, if the resulting offense level is greater than that determined above.
(d) Special Instruction
(1) In the case of counts of perjury or subornation of perjury arising from testimony given, or to be given, in separate proceedings, do not group the counts together under §3D1.2 (Groups of Closely Related Counts).

Commentary
Statutory Provisions: 18 U.S.C. §§ 201(b)(3), (4), 1621–1623. For additional statutory provision(s), *see* Appendix A (Statutory Index).
Application Notes:
1. "***Substantial interference with the administration of justice***" includes a premature or improper termination of a felony investigation; an indictment, verdict, or any judicial determination based upon perjury, false testimony, or other false evidence; or the unnecessary expenditure of substantial governmental or court resources.
2. For offenses covered under this section, §3C1.1 (Obstructing or Impeding the Administration of Justice) does not apply, unless the defendant obstructed the investigation or trial of the perjury count.
3. In the event that the defendant is convicted under this section as well as for the underlying offense (*i.e.*, the offense with respect to which he committed perjury, subornation of perjury, or witness bribery), *see* the Commentary to §3C1.1, and to §3D1.2(c) (Groups of Closely Related Counts).
4. If a weapon was used, or bodily injury or significant property damage resulted, an upward departure may be warranted. *See* Chapter Five, Part K (Departures).
5. "***Separate proceedings***," as used in subsection (d)(1), includes different proceedings in the same case or matter (*e.g.*, a grand jury proceeding and a trial, or a trial and retrial), and proceedings in separate cases or matters (*e.g.*, separate trials of codefendants), but does not include multiple grand jury proceedings in the same case.
Background: This section applies to perjury, subornation of perjury, and witness bribery, generally prosecuted under the referenced statutes. The guidelines provide a higher penalty for perjury than the pre-guidelines practice estimate of ten months imprisonment. The Commission believes that perjury should be treated similarly to obstruction of justice. Therefore, the same considerations for enhancing a sentence are applied in the specific offense characteristics, and an alternative reference to the guideline for accessory after the fact is made.
Historical Note
Effective November 1, 1987. Amended effective November 1, 1989 (amendment 175); November 1, 1991 (amendments 401 and 402); November 1, 1993 (amendment 481); November 1, 2003 (amendment 653); November 1, 2011 (amendment 758); November 1, 2013 (amendment 777).
§2J1.4. Impersonation
(a) Base Offense Level: **6**
(b) Specific Offense Characteristic
(1) If the impersonation was committed for the purpose of conducting an unlawful arrest, detention, or search, increase by **6** levels.

(c) Cross Reference
(1) If the impersonation was to facilitate another offense, apply the

guideline for an attempt to commit that offense, if the resulting offense level is greater than the offense level determined above.

Commentary

Statutory Provisions: 18 U.S.C. §§ 912, 913.

Background: This section applies to impersonation of a federal officer, agent, or employee; and impersonation to conduct an unlawful search or arrest.

Historical Note

Effective November 1, 1987. Amended effective November 1, 1989 (amendment 176).

§2J1.5. Failure to Appear by Material Witness

(a) Base Offense Level:

(1) **6**, if in respect to a felony; or

(2) **4**, if in respect to a misdemeanor.

(b) Specific Offense Characteristic

(1) If the offense resulted in substantial interference with the administration of justice, increase by **3** levels.

Commentary

Statutory Provisions: 18 U.S.C. § 3146(b)(1)(B). For additional statutory provision(s), *see* Appendix A (Statutory Index).

Application Notes:

1. "***Substantial interference with the administration of justice***" includes a premature or improper termination of a felony investigation; an indictment, verdict, or any judicial determination based upon perjury, false testimony, or other false evidence; or the unnecessary expenditure of substantial governmental or court resources.

2. By statute, a term of imprisonment imposed for an offense under 18 U.S.C. § 3146(b)(1)(B) runs consecutively to any other term of imprisonment imposed. 18 U.S.C. § 3146(b)(2).

Background: This section applies to a failure to appear by a material witness. The base offense level incorporates a distinction as to whether the failure to appear was in respect to a

felony or misdemeanor prosecution. The offense under 18 U.S.C. § 3146(b)(1)(B) is a misdemeanor for which the maximum period of imprisonment authorized by statute is one year.

Historical Note

Effective November 1, 1987. Amended effective November 1, 1989 (amendment 177); November 1, 1991 (amendment 401); November 1, 2009 (amendment 737).

§2J1.6. Failure to Appear by Defendant

(a) Base Offense Level:

(1) **11**, if the offense constituted a failure to report for service of sentence; or

(2) **6**, otherwise.

(b) Specific Offense Characteristics

(1) If the base offense level is determined under subsection (a)(1), and the defendant—

(A) voluntarily surrendered within 96 hours of the time he was originally scheduled to report, decrease by **5** levels; or

(B) was ordered to report to a community corrections center, community treatment center, "halfway house," or similar facility, and subdivision (A) above does not apply, decrease by **2** levels.

Provided, however, that this reduction shall not apply if the defendant, while away from the facility, committed any federal, state, or local offense punishable by a term of imprisonment of one year or more.

(2) If the base offense level is determined under subsection (a)(2), and the underlying offense is—

(A) punishable by death or imprisonment for a term of fifteen years or more, increase by **9** levels; or

(B) punishable by a term of imprisonment of five years or more, but less than fifteen years, increase by **6** levels; or

(C) a felony punishable by a term of imprisonment of less than five years, increase by **3** levels.

§2J1.6

Commentary

Statutory Provision: 18 U.S.C. § 3146(b)(1).

Application Notes:

1. "***Underlying offense***" means the offense in respect to which the defendant failed to appear.
2. For offenses covered under this section, §3C1.1 (Obstructing or Impeding the Administration of Justice) does not apply, unless the defendant obstructed the investigation or trial of the failure to appear count.
3. In the case of a failure to appear for service of sentence, any term of imprisonment imposed on the failure to appear count is to be imposed consecutively to any term of imprisonment imposed for the underlying offense. *See* §5G1.3(a). The guideline range for the failure to appear count is to be determined independently and the grouping rules of §§3D1.1–3D1.5 do not apply.

However, in the case of a conviction on both the underlying offense and the failure to appear, other than a case of failure to appear for service of sentence, the failure to appear is treated under §3C1.1 (Obstructing or Impeding the Administration of Justice) as an obstruction of the underlying offense, and the failure to appear count and the count or counts for the underlying offense are grouped together under §3D1.2(c). (Note that 18 U.S.C. § 3146(b)(2) does not require a sentence of imprisonment on a failure to appear count, although if a sentence of imprisonment on the failure to appear count is imposed, the statute requires that the sentence be imposed to run consecutively to any other sentence of imprisonment. Therefore, unlike a count in which the statute mandates both a minimum and a consecutive sentence of imprisonment, the grouping rules of §§3D1.1–3D1.5 apply. *See* §3D1.1(b)(1), comment. (n.1), and §3D1.2, comment. (n.1).) The combined sentence will then be constructed to provide a "total punishment" that satisfies the requirements both of §5G1.2 (Sentencing on Multiple Counts of Conviction) and 18 U.S.C. § 3146(b)(2). For example, if the combined applicable guideline range for both counts is 30–37 months and the court determines that a "total punishment" of 36 months is appropriate, a sentence of 30 months for the underlying offense plus a consecutive six months' sentence for the failure to appear count would satisfy these requirements. (Note that the combination of this instruction and increasing the offense level for the obstructive, failure to appear conduct has the effect of ensuring an incremental, consecutive punishment for the failure to appear count, as required by 18 U.S.C. § 3146(b)(2).)

4. If a defendant is convicted of both the underlying offense and the failure to appear count, and the defendant committed additional acts of obstructive behavior (*e.g.*, perjury) during the investigation, prosecution, or sentencing of the instant offense, an upward departure may be warranted. The upward departure will ensure an enhanced sentence for obstructive conduct for which no adjustment under §3C1.1 (Obstructing or Impeding the Administration of Justice) is made because of the operation of the rules set out in Application Note 3.
5. In some cases, the defendant may be sentenced on the underlying offense (the offense in respect to which the defendant failed to appear) before being sentenced on the failure to appear offense. In such cases, criminal history points for the sentence imposed on the

underlying offense are to be counted in determining the guideline range on the failure to appear offense only where the offense level is determined under subsection (a)(1) (*i.e.*, where the offense constituted a failure to report for service of sentence).

Background: This section applies to a failure to appear by a defendant who was released pending trial, sentencing, appeal, or surrender for service of sentence. Where the base offense level is determined under subsection (a)(2), the offense level increases in relation to the statutory maximum of the underlying offense.

Historical Note

Effective November 1, 1987. Amended effective November 1, 1990 (amendment 329); November 1, 1991 (amendment 403); November 1, 1998 (amendment 579); November 1, 2001 (amendment 636); November 1, 2005 (amendment 680); November 1, 2011 (amendment 758); November 1, 2013 (amendment 777).

§2J1.7. [Deleted]

Historical Note

Effective November 1, 1987. Amended effective January 15, 1988 (amendment 32); November 1, 1989 (amendment 178); November 1, 1991 (amendment 431); was deleted from Chapter Two and replaced by §3C1.3 effective November 1, 2006 (amendment 684).

§2J1.8. [Deleted]

Historical Note

Section 2J1.8 (Bribery of Witness), effective November 1, 1987, amended effective January 15, 1988 (amendment 33), November 1, 1989 (amendment 179), and November 1, 1991 (amendment 401), was deleted by consolidation with §2J1.3 effective November 1, 1993 (amendment 481).

§2J1.9. Payment to Witness

(a) Base Offense Level: **6**

(b) Specific Offense Characteristic

(1) If the payment was made or offered for refusing to testify or for the witness absenting himself to avoid testifying, increase by **4** levels.

Commentary

Statutory Provisions: 18 U.S.C. § 201(c)(2), (3).

Application Notes:

1. For offenses covered under this section, §3C1.1 (Obstructing or Impeding the Administration of Justice) does not apply unless the defendant obstructed the investigation or trial of the payment to witness count.

2. In the event that the defendant is convicted under this section as well as for the underlying offense (*i.e.*, the offense with respect to which the payment was made), *see* the Commentary to §3C1.1, and to §3D1.2(c) (Groups of Closely Related Counts).

Background: This section applies to witness gratuities in federal proceedings.

Historical Note

Effective November 1, 1987. Amended effective November 1, 1989 (amendments 180 and 181); November 1, 2011 (amendment 758); November 1, 2013 (amendment 777).

PART K — OFFENSES INVOLVING PUBLIC SAFETY

1. EXPLOSIVES AND ARSON

§2K1.1. Failure to Report Theft of Explosive Materials; Improper Storage of Explosive Materials

(a) Base Offense Level: **6**

Commentary

Statutory Provisions: 18 U.S.C. §§ 842(j), (k), 844(b). For additional statutory provision(s), *see* Appendix A (Statutory Index).
Background: The above-referenced provisions are misdemeanors. The maximum term of imprisonment authorized by statute is one year.
Historical
Note
Effective November 1, 1987. Amended effective November 1, 1991 (amendment 404); November 1, 1993 (amendment 481).

§2K1.2. [Deleted]

Historical
Note
Section 2K1.2 (Improper Storage of Explosive Materials), effective November 1, 1987, amended effective November 1, 1991 (amendment 404), was deleted by consolidation with §2K1.1 effective November 1, 1993 (amendment 481).

§2K1.3. Unlawful Receipt, Possession, or Transportation of Explosive Materials; Prohibited Transactions Involving Explosive Materials

(a) Base Offense Level (Apply the Greatest):
(1) **24**, if the defendant committed any part of the instant offense subsequent to sustaining at least two felony convictions of either a crime of violence or a controlled substance offense;
(2) **20**, if the defendant committed any part of the instant offense subsequent to sustaining one felony conviction of either a crime of violence or a controlled substance offense;
(3) **18**, if the defendant was convicted under 18 U.S.C. § 842(p)(2);

(4) **16**, if the defendant (A) was a prohibited person at the time the defendant committed the instant offense; or (B) knowingly distributed explosive materials to a prohibited person; or
(5) **12**, otherwise.
(b) Specific Offense Characteristics
(1) If the offense involved twenty-five pounds or more of explosive materials, increase as follows:
WEIGHT OF EXPLOSIVE MATERIAL INCREASE IN LEVEL
(A) At least 25 but less than 100 lbs. add **1**
(B) At least 100 but less than 250 lbs. add **2**
(C) At least 250 but less than 500 lbs. add **3**
(D) At least 500 but less than 1000 lbs. add **4**
(E) 1000 lbs. or more add **5**.
(2) If the offense involved any explosive material that the defendant knew or had reason to believe was stolen, increase by **2** levels. *Provided,* that the cumulative offense level determined above shall not exceed level **29**.
(3) If the defendant (A) was convicted under 18 U.S.C. § 842(p)(2); or (B) used or possessed any explosive material in connection with another felony offense; or possessed or transferred any explosive material with knowledge, intent, or reason to believe that it would be used or possessed in connection with another felony offense, increase by **4** levels. If the resulting offense level is less than level **18**, increase to level **18**.
(c) Cross Reference
(1) If the defendant (A) was convicted under 18 U.S.C. § 842(p)(2);

or (B) used or possessed any explosive material in connection with the commission or attempted commission of another offense, or possessed or transferred any explosive material with knowledge or intent that it would be used or possessed in connection with another offense, apply—

(A) §2X1.1 (Attempt, Solicitation, or Conspiracy) in respect to that other offense if the resulting offense level is greater than that determined above; or

(B) if death resulted, the most analogous offense guideline from Chapter Two, Part A, Subpart 1 (Homicide), if the resulting offense level is greater than that determined above.

Commentary

Statutory Provisions: 18 U.S.C. §§ 842(a)–(e), (h), (i), (l)–(o), (p)(2), 844(d), (g), 1716, 2283; 26 U.S.C. § 5685.

Application Notes:

1. "***Explosive material(s)***" include explosives, blasting agents, and detonators. *See* 18 U.S.C. § 841(c). "Explosives" is defined at 18 U.S.C. § 844(j). A destructive device, defined in the Commentary to §1B1.1 (Application Instructions), may contain explosive materials. Where the conduct charged in the count of which the defendant was convicted establishes that the offense involved a destructive device, apply §2K2.1 (Unlawful Receipt, Possession, or Transportation of Firearms or Ammunition; Prohibited Transactions Involving Firearms or Ammunition) if the resulting offense level is greater.

2. For purposes of this guideline:

"***Controlled substance offense***" has the meaning given that term in §4B1.2(b) and Application Note 1 of the Commentary to §4B1.2 (Definitions of Terms Used in Section 4B1.1).

"***Crime of violence***" has the meaning given that term in §4B1.2(a) and Application Note 1 of the Commentary to §4B1.2.

"***Felony conviction***" means a prior adult federal or state conviction for an offense punishable by death or imprisonment for a term exceeding one year, regardless of whether such offense is specifically designated as a felony and regardless of the actual sentence imposed. A conviction for an offense committed at age eighteen years or older is an adult conviction. A conviction for an offense committed prior to age eighteen years is an adult conviction if it is classified as an adult conviction under the laws of the jurisdiction in which the defendant was convicted (*e.g.*, a federal conviction for an offense committed prior to the defendant's eighteenth birthday is an adult conviction if the defendant was expressly proceeded against as an adult).

3. For purposes of subsection (a)(4), "***prohibited person***" means any person described in 18 U.S.C. § 842(i).

4. "***Felony offense***," as used in subsection (b)(3), means any offense (federal, state, or local) punishable by imprisonment for a term exceeding one year, whether or not a criminal charge was brought, or conviction obtained.

5. For purposes of calculating the weight of explosive materials under subsection (b)(1), include only the weight of the actual explosive material and the weight of packaging material that is necessary for the use or detonation of the explosives. Exclude the weight of any other shipping or packaging materials. For example, the paper and fuse on a stick of dynamite would be included; the box that the dynamite was shipped in would not be included.

6. For purposes of calculating the weight of explosive materials under subsection (b)(1), count only those explosive materials that were unlawfully sought to be obtained, unlawfully possessed, or unlawfully distributed, including any explosive material that a defendant attempted to obtain by making a false statement.

7. If the defendant is convicted under 18 U.S.C. § 842(h) (offense involving stolen explosive materials), and is convicted of no other offenses subject to this guideline, do not apply the adjustment in subsection (b)(2) because the base offense level itself takes such conduct into account.

8. Under subsection (c)(1), the offense level for the underlying offense (which may be a federal, state, or local offense) is to be determined under §2X1.1 (Attempt, Solicitation, or Conspiracy) or, if death results, under the most analogous guideline from Chapter Two, Part A, Subpart 1 (Homicide).

9. For purposes of applying subsection (a)(1) or (2), use only those felony convictions that receive criminal history points under §4A1.1(a), (b), or (c). In addition, for purposes of applying subsection (a)(1), use only those felony convictions that are counted separately under §4A1.1(a), (b), or (c). *See* §4A1.2(a)(2).

Prior felony conviction(s) resulting in an increased base offense level under subsection (a)(1), (a)(2), or (a)(4) are also counted for purposes of determining criminal history points pursuant to Chapter Four, Part A (Criminal History).

10. An upward departure may be warranted in any of the following circumstances: (A) the quantity of explosive materials significantly exceeded 1000 pounds; (B) the explosive materials were of a nature more volatile or dangerous than dynamite or conventional powder explosives (*e.g.*, plastic explosives); (C) the defendant knowingly distributed explosive materials to a person under twenty-one years of age; or (D) the offense posed a substantial risk of death or bodily injury to multiple individuals.

11. As used in subsections (b)(3) and (c)(1), "***another felony offense***" and "***another offense***" refer to offenses other than explosives or firearms possession or trafficking offenses. However, where the defendant used or possessed a firearm or explosive to facilitate another firearms or explosives offense (*e.g.*, the defendant used or possessed a firearm to protect the delivery of an unlawful shipment of explosives), an upward departure under §5K2.6 (Weapons and Dangerous Instrumentalities) may be warranted.

In addition, for purposes of subsection (c)(1)(A), "***that other offense***" means, with respect to an offense under 18 U.S.C. § 842(p)(2), the underlying Federal crime of violence.

Historical Note

Effective November 1, 1987. Amended effective November 1, 1989 (amendment 183); November 1, 1991 (amendment 373); November 1, 1992 (amendment 471); November 1, 1993 (amendment 478); November 1, 1995 (amendment 534); November 1, 1997 (amendment 568); November 1, 2001 (amendments 629 and 630); November 1, 2002 (amendment 646); November 1, 2003 (amendment 655); November 1, 2007 (amendment 700); November 1, 2010 (amendments 746 and 747).

§2K1.4. Arson; Property Damage by Use of Explosives

(a) Base Offense Level (Apply the Greatest):

(1) **24**, if the offense (A) created a substantial risk of death or serious bodily injury to any person other than a participant in the offense, and that risk was created knowingly; or (B) involved the destruction or attempted destruction of a dwelling, an airport, an aircraft, a mass transportation facility, a mass transportation vehicle, a maritime facility, a vessel, or a vessel's cargo, a public transportation system, a state or government facility, an infrastructure facility, or a place of public use;

(2) **20**, if the offense (A) created a substantial risk of death or serious bodily injury to any person other than a participant in the offense; (B) involved the destruction or attempted destruction

of a structure other than (i) a dwelling, or (ii) an airport, an aircraft, a mass transportation facility, a mass transportation vehicle, a maritime facility, a vessel, or a vessel's cargo, a public transportation system, a state or government facility, an infrastructure facility, or a place of public use; or (C) endangered
(i) a dwelling, (ii) a structure other than a dwelling, or (iii) an airport, an aircraft, a mass transportation facility, a mass transportation vehicle, a maritime facility, a vessel, or a vessel's cargo, a public transportation system, a state or government facility, an infrastructure facility, or a place of public use;
(3) **16**, if the offense involved the destruction of or tampering with aids to maritime navigation; or
(4) **2** plus the offense level from §2B1.1 (Theft, Property Destruction, and Fraud).
(b) Specific Offense Characteristics
(1) If the offense was committed to conceal another offense, increase by **2** levels.
(2) If the base offense level is not determined under (a)(4), and the offense occurred on a national cemetery, increase by **2** levels.
(c) Cross Reference
(1) If death resulted, or the offense was intended to cause death or serious bodily injury, apply the most analogous guideline from

Chapter Two, Part A (Offenses Against the Person) if the resulting offense level is greater than that determined above.

Commentary

Statutory Provisions: 18 U.S.C. §§ 32(a), (b), 33, 81, 844(f), (h) (only in the case of an offense committed prior to November 18, 1988), (i), 1855, 1992(a)(1), (a)(2), (a)(4), 2275, 2282A, 2282B, 2291, 2332a, 2332f; 49 U.S.C. § 60123(b). For additional statutory provision(s), *see* Appendix A (Statutory Index).

Application Notes:

1. **Definitions.**—For purposes of this guideline:

"***Aids to maritime navigation***" means any device external to a vessel intended to assist the navigator to determine position or save course, or to warn of dangers or obstructions to navigation.

"***Explosives***" includes any explosive, explosive material, or destructive device.

"***Maritime facility***" means any structure or facility of any kind located in, on, under, or adjacent to any waters subject to the jurisdiction of the United States and used, operated, or maintained by a public or private entity, including any contiguous or adjoining property under common ownership or operation.

"***National cemetery***" means a cemetery (A) established under section 2400 of title 38, United States Code; or (B) under the jurisdiction of the Secretary of the Army, the Secretary of the Navy, the Secretary of the Air Force, or the Secretary of the Interior.

"***Mass transportation***" has the meaning given that term in 18 U.S.C. § 1992(d)(7).

"***State or government facility***", "***infrastructure facility***", "***place of public use***", and "***public transportation system***" have the meaning given those terms in 18 U.S.C. § 2332f(e)(3), (5), (6), and (7), respectively.

"***Vessel***" includes every description of watercraft or other artificial contrivance used, or capable of being used, as a means of transportation on water.

2. **Risk of Death or Serious Bodily Injury.**—Creating a substantial risk of death or serious bodily injury includes creating that risk to fire fighters and other emergency and

law enforcement personnel who respond to or investigate an offense.

3. **Upward Departure Provision.**—If bodily injury resulted, an upward departure may be warranted. *See* Chapter Five, Part K (Departures).

Background: Subsection (b)(2) implements the directive to the Commission in section 2 of Public Law 105–101.

Historical
Note

Effective November 1, 1987. Amended effective November 1, 1989 (amendments 182, 184, and 185); November 1, 1990 (amendment 330); November 1, 1991 (amendment 404); November 1, 1998 (amendment 576); November 1, 2001 (amendment 617); November 1, 2002 (amendment 637); November 1, 2003 (amendment 655); November 1, 2007 (amendments 699 and 700); November 1, 2014 (amendment 781).

§2K1.5. Possessing Dangerous Weapons or Materials While Boarding or Aboard an Aircraft

(a) Base Offense Level: **9**

(b) Specific Offense Characteristics

If more than one applies, use the greatest:

(1) If the offense was committed willfully and without regard for the safety of human life, or with reckless disregard for the safety of human life, increase by **15** levels.

(2) If the defendant was prohibited by another federal law from possessing the weapon or material, increase by **2** levels.

(3) If the defendant's possession of the weapon or material would have been lawful but for 49 U.S.C. § 46505 and he acted with mere negligence, decrease by **3** levels.

(c) Cross Reference

(1) If the defendant used or possessed the weapon or material in committing or attempting another offense, apply the guideline for such other offense, or §2X1.1 (Attempt, Solicitation, or Conspiracy), as appropriate, if the resulting offense level is greater than that determined above.

Commentary

Statutory Provision: 49 U.S.C. § 46505 (formerly 49 U.S.C. § 1472(l)).

Background: This guideline provides an enhancement where the defendant was a person prohibited by federal law from possession of the weapon or material. A decrease is provided in a case of mere negligence where the defendant was otherwise authorized to possess the weapon or material.

Historical
Note

Effective November 1, 1987. Amended effective November 1, 1989 (amendments 182, 186, 187, and 303); November 1, 1991 (amendment 404); November 1, 1992 (amendment 443); November 1, 1995 (amendment 534); November 1, 1997 (amendment 560).

§2K1.6. Licensee Recordkeeping Violations Involving Explosive Materials

(a) Base Offense Level: **6**

(b) Cross Reference

(1) If a recordkeeping offense reflected an effort to conceal a substantive explosive materials offense, apply §2K1.3 (Unlawful Receipt, Possession, or Transportation of Explosives Materials; Prohibited Transactions Involving Explosive Materials).

Commentary

Statutory Provisions: 18 U.S.C. § 842(f), (g).
Background: The above-referenced provisions are recordkeeping offenses applicable only to "***licensees***," who are defined at 18 U.S.C. § 841(m).

Historical
Note
Effective November 1, 1991 (amendment 373). A former §2K1.6 (Shipping, Transporting, or Receiving Explosives with Felonious Intent or Knowledge; Using or Carrying Explosives in Certain Crimes), effective November 1, 1987, amended effective November 1, 1989 (amendment 303) and November 1, 1990 (amendment 331), was deleted by consolidation with §2K1.3 effective November 1, 1991 (amendment 373).

§2K1.7. [Deleted]

Historical
Note
Section 2K1.7 (Use of Fire or Explosives to Commit a Federal Felony), effective November 1, 1989 (amendment 188), amended effective November 1, 1990 (amendment 332), was deleted by consolidation with §2K2.4 effective November 1, 1993 (amendment 481).

* * * * *

2. FIREARMS

§2K2.1. Unlawful Receipt, Possession, or Transportation of Firearms or Ammunition; Prohibited Transactions Involving Firearms or Ammunition

(a) Base Offense Level (Apply the Greatest):

(1) **26**, if (A) the offense involved a (i) semiautomatic firearm that is capable of accepting a large capacity magazine; or (ii) firearm that is described in 26 U.S.C. § 5845(a); and (B) the defendant committed any part of the instant offense subsequent to sustaining at least two felony convictions of either a crime of violence or a controlled substance offense;

(2) **24**, if the defendant committed any part of the instant offense subsequent to sustaining at least two felony convictions of either a crime of violence or a controlled substance offense;

(3) **22**, if (A) the offense involved a (i) semiautomatic firearm that is capable of accepting a large capacity magazine; or (ii) firearm that is described in 26 U.S.C. § 5845(a); and (B) the defendant committed any part of the instant offense subsequent to sustaining one felony conviction of either a crime of violence or a controlled substance offense;

(4) **20**, if—

(A) the defendant committed any part of the instant offense subsequent to sustaining one felony conviction of either a crime of violence or a controlled substance offense; or

(B) the (i) offense involved a (I) semiautomatic firearm that is capable of accepting a large capacity magazine; or (II) firearm that is described in 26 U.S.C. § 5845(a); and (ii) defendant (I) was a prohibited person at the time the defendant committed the instant offense; (II) is convicted under 18 U.S.C. § 922(d); or (III) is convicted under 18 U.S.C. § 922(a)(6) or § 924(a)(1)(A) and committed the offense with knowledge, intent, or reason to believe that the offense would result in the transfer of a firearm or ammunition to a prohibited person;

(5) **18**, if the offense involved a firearm described in 26 U.S.C. § 5845(a);
(6) **14**, if the defendant (A) was a prohibited person at the time the defendant committed the instant offense; (B) is convicted under 18 U.S.C. § 922(d); or (C) is convicted under 18 U.S.C. § 922(a)(6) or § 924(a)(1)(A) and committed the offense with knowledge, intent, or reason to believe that the offense would result in the transfer of a firearm or ammunition to a prohibited person;
(7) **12**, except as provided below; or
(8) **6**, if the defendant is convicted under 18 U.S.C. § 922(c), (e), (f), (m), (s), (t), or (x)(1), or 18 U.S.C. § 1715.

(b) Specific Offense Characteristics
(1) If the offense involved three or more firearms, increase as follows:

NUMBER OF FIREARMS	INCREASE IN LEVEL
(A) 3–7	add **2**
(B) 8–24	add **4**
(C) 25–99	add **6**
(D) 100–199	add **8**
(E) 200 or more	add **10**.

(2) If the defendant, other than a defendant subject to subsection (a)(1), (a)(2), (a)(3), (a)(4), or (a)(5), possessed all ammunition and firearms solely for lawful sporting purposes or collection, and did not unlawfully discharge or otherwise unlawfully use such firearms or ammunition, decrease the offense level determined above to level **6**.
(3) If the offense involved—
(A) a destructive device that is a portable rocket, a missile, or a device for use in launching a portable rocket or a missile, increase by **15** levels; or
(B) a destructive device other than a destructive device referred to in subdivision (A), increase by **2** levels.
(4) If any firearm (A) was stolen, increase by **2** levels; or (B) had an altered or obliterated serial number, increase by **4** levels.
The cumulative offense level determined from the application of subsections (b)(1) through (b)(4) may not exceed level **29**, except if subsection (b)(3)(A) applies.
(5) If the defendant engaged in the trafficking of firearms, increase by **4** levels.
(6) If the defendant—
(A) possessed any firearm or ammunition while leaving or attempting to leave the United States, or possessed or transferred any firearm or ammunition with knowledge, intent, or reason to believe that it would be transported out of the United States; or

(B) used or possessed any firearm or ammunition in connection with another felony offense; or possessed or transferred any firearm or ammunition with knowledge, intent, or reason to believe that it would be used or possessed in connection with another felony offense,
increase by **4** levels. If the resulting offense level is less than level **18**, increase to level **18**.
(7) If a recordkeeping offense reflected an effort to conceal a substantive offense involving firearms or ammunition, increase to the offense level for the substantive offense.
(c) Cross Reference
(1) If the defendant used or possessed any firearm or ammunition cited in the offense of conviction in connection with the commission or attempted commission of another offense, or possessed or transferred a firearm or ammunition cited in the offense of conviction with knowledge or intent that it would be used or possessed in connection with another offense, apply—
(A) §2X1.1 (Attempt, Solicitation, or Conspiracy) in respect to that other offense, if the resulting offense level is greater than that determined above; or
(B) if death resulted, the most analogous offense guideline from Chapter Two, Part A, Subpart 1 (Homicide), if the resulting offense level is greater than that determined above.

Commentary

Statutory Provisions: 18 U.S.C. §§ 922(a)–(p), (r)–(w), (x)(1), 924(a), (b), (e)–(i), (k)–(o), 1715, 2332g; 26 U.S.C. § 5861(a)–(l). For additional statutory provisions, *see* Appendix A (Statutory Index).

Application Notes:

1. **Definitions.**—For purposes of this guideline:
"***Ammunition***" has the meaning given that term in 18 U.S.C. § 921(a)(17)(A).
"***Controlled substance offense***" has the meaning given that term in §4B1.2(b) and Application Note 1 of the Commentary to §4B1.2 (Definitions of Terms Used in Section 4B1.1).
"***Crime of violence***" has the meaning given that term in §4B1.2(a) and Application Note 1 of the Commentary to §4B1.2.

"***Destructive device***" has the meaning given that term in 26 U.S.C. § 5845(f).
"***Felony conviction***" means a prior adult federal or state conviction for an offense punishable by death or imprisonment for a term exceeding one year, regardless of whether such offense is specifically designated as a felony and regardless of the actual sentence imposed. A conviction for an offense committed at age eighteen years or older is an adult conviction. A conviction for an offense committed prior to age eighteen years is an adult conviction if it is classified as an adult conviction under the laws of the jurisdiction in which the defendant was convicted (*e.g.*, a federal conviction for an offense committed prior to the defendant's eighteenth birthday is an adult conviction if the defendant was expressly proceeded against as an adult).
"***Firearm***" has the meaning given that term in 18 U.S.C. § 921(a)(3).

2. **Semiautomatic Firearm That Is Capable of Accepting a Large Capacity Magazine.**—

For purposes of subsections (a)(1), (a)(3), and (a)(4), a "***semiautomatic firearm that is capable of accepting a large capacity magazine***" means a semiautomatic firearm that has the ability to fire many rounds without reloading because at the time of the offense (A) the firearm had attached to it a magazine or similar device that could accept more than 15 rounds of ammunition; or (B) a magazine or similar device that could accept more than 15 rounds of ammunition was in close proximity to the firearm. This definition does not include a semiautomatic firearm with an attached tubular device capable of operating only with .22 caliber rim fire ammunition.

3. **Definition of "Prohibited Person".**—For purposes of subsections (a)(4)(B) and (a)(6), "***prohibited person***" means any person described in 18 U.S.C. § 922(g) or § 922(n).

4. **Application of Subsection (a)(7).**—Subsection (a)(7) includes the interstate transportation or interstate distribution of firearms, which is frequently committed in violation of state, local, or other federal law restricting the possession of firearms, or for some other underlying unlawful purpose. In the unusual case in which it is established that neither avoidance of state, local, or other federal firearms law, nor any other underlying unlawful purpose was involved, a reduction in the base offense level to no lower than level 6 may be warranted to reflect the less serious nature of the violation.

5. **Application of Subsection (b)(1).**—For purposes of calculating the number of firearms under subsection (b)(1), count only those firearms that were unlawfully sought to be obtained, unlawfully possessed, or unlawfully distributed, including any firearm that a defendant obtained or attempted to obtain by making a false statement to a licensed dealer.

6. **Application of Subsection (b)(2).**—Under subsection (b)(2), "lawful sporting purposes or collection" as determined by the surrounding circumstances, provides for a reduction to an offense level of 6. Relevant surrounding circumstances include the number and type of firearms, the amount and type of ammunition, the location and circumstances of possession and actual use, the nature of the defendant's criminal history (*e.g.*, prior convictions for offenses involving firearms), and the extent to which possession was restricted by local law. Note that where the base offense level is determined under subsections (a)(1)–(a)(5), subsection (b)(2) is not applicable.

7. **Destructive Devices.**—A defendant whose offense involves a destructive device receives both the base offense level from the subsection applicable to a firearm listed in 26 U.S.C. § 5845(a) (*e.g.*, subsection (a)(1), (a)(3), (a)(4)(B), or (a)(5)), and the applicable

enhancement under subsection (b)(3). Such devices pose a considerably greater risk to the public welfare than other National Firearms Act weapons.

Offenses involving such devices cover a wide range of offense conduct and involve different degrees of risk to the public welfare depending on the type of destructive device involved and the location or manner in which that destructive device was possessed or transported. For example, a pipe bomb in a populated train station creates a substantially greater risk to the public welfare, and a substantially greater risk of death or serious bodily injury, than an incendiary device in an isolated area. In a case in which the cumulative result of the increased base offense level and the enhancement under subsection (b)(3) does not adequately capture the seriousness of the offense because of the type of destructive device involved, the risk to the public welfare, or the risk of death or serious bodily injury that the destructive device created, an upward departure may be warranted. *See also* §§5K2.1 (Death), 5K2.2 (Physical Injury), and 5K2.14 (Public Welfare).

8. **Application of Subsection (b)(4).**—

(A) **Interaction with Subsection (a)(7).**—If the only offense to which §2K2.1 applies is 18 U.S.C. § 922(i), (j), or (u), or 18 U.S.C. § 924(l) or (m) (offenses involving a stolen firearm or stolen ammunition) and the base offense level is determined under subsection (a)(7), do not apply the enhancement in subsection (b)(4)(A). This is because the base offense level takes into account that the firearm or ammunition was stolen. However, if the offense involved a firearm with an altered or obliterated serial number, apply subsection (b)(4)(B).

Similarly, if the offense to which §2K2.1 applies is 18 U.S.C. § 922(k) or 26 U.S.C. § 5861(g) or (h) (offenses involving an altered or obliterated serial number) and the base offense level is determined under subsection (a)(7), do not apply the enhancement in subsection (b)(4)(B). This is because the base offense level takes into account that the firearm had an altered or obliterated serial number. However, it the offense involved a stolen firearm or stolen ammunition, apply subsection (b)(4)(A).

(B) **Knowledge or Reason to Believe.**—Subsection (b)(4) applies regardless of whether the defendant knew or had reason to believe that the firearm was stolen or had an altered or obliterated serial number.

9. **Application of Subsection (b)(7).**—Under subsection (b)(7), if a record-keeping offense was committed to conceal a substantive firearms or ammunition offense, the offense level is increased to the offense level for the substantive firearms or ammunition offense (*e.g.*, if the defendant falsifies a record to conceal the sale of a firearm to a prohibited person, the offense level is increased to the offense level applicable to the sale of a firearm to a prohibited person).

10. **Prior Felony Convictions.**—For purposes of applying subsection (a)(1), (2), (3), or (4)(A), use only those felony convictions that receive criminal history points under §4A1.1(a), (b), or (c). In addition, for purposes of applying subsection (a)(1) and (a)(2), use only those felony convictions that are counted separately under §4A1.1(a), (b), or (c). *See* §4A1.2(a)(2).

Prior felony conviction(s) resulting in an increased base offense level under subsection (a)(1), (a)(2), (a)(3), (a)(4)(A), (a)(4)(B), or (a)(6) are also counted for purposes of determining criminal history points pursuant to Chapter Four, Part A (Criminal History).

11. **Upward Departure Provisions.**—An upward departure may be warranted in any of the following circumstances: (A) the number of firearms substantially exceeded 200; (B) the offense involved multiple National Firearms Act weapons (*e.g.*, machineguns, destructive devices), military type assault rifles, non-detectable ("plastic") firearms (defined at 18 U.S.C. § 922(p)); (C) the offense involved large quantities of armor-piercing ammunition (defined at 18 U.S.C. § 921(a)(17)(B)); or (D) the offense posed a substantial risk of death or bodily injury to multiple individuals (*see* Application Note 7).

12. **Armed Career Criminal.**—A defendant who is subject to an enhanced sentence under the provisions of 18 U.S.C. § 924(e) is an Armed Career Criminal. *See* §4B1.4.

13. **Application of Subsection (b)(5).**—

(A) **In General.**—Subsection (b)(5) applies, regardless of whether anything of value was exchanged, if the defendant—

(i) transported, transferred, or otherwise disposed of two or more firearms to another individual, or received two or more firearms with the intent to transport, transfer, or otherwise dispose of firearms to another individual; and

(ii) knew or had reason to believe that such conduct would result in the transport, transfer, or disposal of a firearm to an individual—

(I) whose possession or receipt of the firearm would be unlawful; or

(II) who intended to use or dispose of the firearm unlawfully.

(B) **Definitions.**—For purposes of this subsection:

"***Individual whose possession or receipt of the firearm would be unlawful***" means an individual who (i) has a prior conviction for a crime of violence, a controlled substance offense, or a misdemeanor crime of domestic violence; or (ii) at the time of the offense was under a criminal justice sentence, including probation, parole, supervised release, imprisonment, work release, or escape status. "Crime of violence" and "controlled substance offense" have the meaning given those terms in §4B1.2 (Definitions of Terms Used in Section 4B1.1). "Misdemeanor crime of domestic violence" has the meaning given that term in 18 U.S.C. § 921(a)(33)(A).

The term "***defendant***", consistent with §1B1.3 (Relevant Conduct), limits the accountability of the defendant to the defendant's own conduct and conduct that the defendant aided or abetted, counseled, commanded, induced, procured, or willfully caused.

(C) **Upward Departure Provision.**—If the defendant trafficked substantially more than 25 firearms, an upward departure may be warranted.

(D) **Interaction with Other Subsections.**—In a case in which three or more firearms were both possessed and trafficked, apply both subsections (b)(1) and (b)(5). If the defendant used or transferred one of such firearms in connection with another felony offense (*i.e.*, an offense other than a firearms possession or trafficking offense) an enhancement under subsection (b)(6)(B) also would apply.

14. **Application of Subsections (b)(6)(B) and (c)(1).**—

(A) **In General.**—Subsections (b)(6)(B) and (c)(1) apply if the firearm or ammunition facilitated, or had the potential of facilitating, another felony offense or another offense, respectively. However, subsection (c)(1) contains the additional requirement that the firearm or ammunition be cited in the offense of conviction.

(B) **Application When Other Offense is Burglary or Drug Offense.**—Subsections (b)(6)(B) and (c)(1) apply (i) in a case in which a defendant who, during the course of a burglary, finds and takes a firearm, even if the defendant did not engage in any other conduct with that firearm during the course of the burglary; and (ii) in the case of a drug trafficking offense in which a firearm is found in close proximity to drugs, drug-manufacturing materials, or drug paraphernalia. In these cases, application of subsections (b)(6)(B) and, if the firearm was cited in the offense of conviction, (c)(1) is warranted because the presence of the firearm has the potential of facilitating another felony offense or another offense, respectively.

(C) **Definitions.**—

"***Another felony offense***", for purposes of subsection (b)(6)(B), means any federal, state, or local offense, other than the explosive or firearms possession or trafficking offense, punishable by imprisonment for a term exceeding one year, regardless of whether a criminal charge was brought, or a conviction obtained.

"***Another offense***", for purposes of subsection (c)(1), means any federal, state, or local offense, other than the explosive or firearms possession or trafficking offense, regardless of whether a criminal charge was brought, or a conviction obtained.

(D) **Upward Departure Provision.**—In a case in which the defendant used or possessed a firearm or explosive to facilitate another firearms or explosives offense (*e.g.*, the defendant used or possessed a firearm to protect the delivery of an unlawful shipment of explosives), an upward departure under §5K2.6 (Weapons and Dangerous Instrumentalities) may be warranted.

(E) **Relationship Between the Instant Offense and the Other Offense.**—In determining whether subsections (b)(6)(B) and (c)(1) apply, the court must consider the relationship between the instant offense and the other offense, consistent with relevant conduct principles. *See* §1B1.3(a)(1)–(4) and accompanying commentary.
In determining whether subsection (c)(1) applies, the court must also consider whether the firearm used in the other offense was a firearm cited in the offense of conviction.

For example:

(i) **Firearm Cited in the Offense of Conviction.** Defendant A's offense of conviction is for unlawfully possessing a shotgun on October 15. The court determines that, on the preceding February 10, Defendant A used the shotgun in connection with a robbery. Ordinarily, under these circumstances, subsection (b)(6)(B) applies, and the cross reference in subsection (c)(1) also applies if it results in a greater offense level.

Ordinarily, the unlawful possession of the shotgun on February 10 will be "part of the same course of conduct or common scheme or plan" as the unlawful possession of the same shotgun on October 15. *See* §1B1.3(a)(2) and accompanying commentary (including, in particular, the factors discussed in Application Note 5(B) to §1B1.3). The use of the shotgun "in connection with" the robbery is relevant conduct because it is a factor specified in subsections (b)(6)(B) and (c)(1). *See* §1B1.3(a)(4) ("any other information specified in the applicable guideline").

(ii) **Firearm Not Cited in the Offense of Conviction.** Defendant B's offense of conviction is for unlawfully possessing a shotgun on October 15. The court determines that, on the preceding February 10, Defendant B unlawfully possessed a handgun (not cited in the offense of conviction) and used the handgun in connection with a robbery.

Subsection (b)(6)(B). In determining whether subsection (b)(6)(B) applies, the threshold question for the court is whether the two unlawful possession offenses (the shotgun on October 15 and the handgun on February 10) were "part of the same course of conduct or common scheme or plan". *See* §1B1.3(a)(2) and accompanying commentary (including, in particular, the factors discussed in Application Note 5(B) to §1B1.3).

If they were, then the handgun possession offense is relevant conduct to the shotgun possession offense, and the use of the handgun "in connection with" the robbery is relevant conduct because it is a factor specified in subsection (b)(6)(B). *See* §1B1.3(a)(4) ("any other information specified in the applicable guideline"). Accordingly, subsection (b)(6)(B) applies.

On the other hand, if the court determines that the two unlawful possession offenses were not "part of the same course of conduct or common scheme or plan," then the handgun possession offense is not relevant conduct to the shotgun possession offense and subsection (b)(6)(B) does not apply.

Subsection (c)(1). Under these circumstances, the cross reference in subsection (c)(1) does not apply, because the handgun was not cited in the offense of conviction.

15. **Certain Convictions Under 18 U.S.C. §§ 922(a)(6), 922(d), and 924(a)(1)(A).**—In a case in which the defendant is convicted under 18 U.S.C. §§ 922(a)(6), 922(d), or 924(a)(1)(A), a downward departure may be warranted if (A) none of the enhancements in subsection (b) apply, (B) the defendant was motivated by an intimate or familial relationship or by threats or fear to commit the offense and was otherwise unlikely to commit such an offense, and (C) the defendant received no monetary compensation from the offense.

Historical Note

Effective November 1, 1987. Amended effective November 1, 1989 (amendment 189); November 1, 1990 (amendment 333); November 1, 1991 (amendment 374); November 1, 1992 (amendment 471); November 1, 1993 (amendment 478); November 1, 1995 (amendment 522); November 1, 1997 (amendments 568 and 575); November 1, 1998 (amendments 578 and 586); November 1, 2000 (amendment 605); November 1, 2001 (amendments 629–631); November 1, 2004 (amendment 669); November 1, 2005 (amendments 679 and 680); November 1, 2006 (amendments 686, 691, and 696); November 1, 2007 (amendment 707); November 1, 2010 (amendment 746); November 1, 2011 (amendment 753); November 1, 2014 (amendment 784); November 1, 2015 (amendments 790 and 797); November 1, 2016 (amendment 804).

§2K2.2. [Deleted]

Historical Note

Section 2K2.2 (Unlawful Trafficking and Other Prohibited Transactions Involving Firearms), effective November 1, 1987, amended effective January 15, 1988 (amendment 34), November 1, 1989 (amendment 189), and November 1, 1990 (amendment 333), was deleted by consolidation with §2K2.1 effective November 1, 1991 (amendment 374).

§2K2.3. [Deleted]

Historical Note

Section 2K2.3 (Receiving, Transporting, Shipping or Transferring a Firearm or Ammunition With Intent to Commit Another Offense, or With Knowledge that It Will Be Used in Committing Another Offense), effective

November 1, 1989 (amendment 189), was deleted by consolidation with §2K2.1 effective November 1, 1991 (amendment 374). A former §2K2.3 (Prohibited Transactions in or Shipment of Firearms and Other Weapons), effective November 1, 1987, was deleted by consolidation with §2K2.2 effective November 1, 1989 (amendment 189).

§2K2.4. Use of Firearm, Armor-Piercing Ammunition, or Explosive During or in Relation to Certain Crimes

(a) If the defendant, whether or not convicted of another crime, was convicted of violating section 844(h) of title 18, United States Code, the guideline sentence is the term of imprisonment required by statute. Chapters Three (Adjustments) and Four (Criminal History and Criminal Livelihood) shall not apply to that count of conviction.

(b) Except as provided in subsection (c), if the defendant, whether or not convicted of another crime, was convicted of violating section 924(c) or section 929(a) of title 18, United States Code, the guideline sentence is the minimum term of imprisonment required by statute. Chapters Three and Four shall not apply to that count of conviction.

(c) If the defendant (1) was convicted of violating section 924(c) or section 929(a) of title 18, United States Code; and (2) as a result of that conviction (alone or in addition to another offense of conviction), is determined to be a career offender under §4B1.1 (Career Offender), the guideline sentence shall be determined under §4B1.1(c). Except for §§3E1.1 (Acceptance of Responsibility), 4B1.1, and 4B1.2 (Definitions of Terms Used in Section 4B1.1), Chapters Three and Four shall not apply to that count of conviction.

(d) Special Instructions for Fines

(1) Where there is a federal conviction for the underlying offense, the fine guideline shall be the fine guideline that would have

been applicable had there only been a conviction for the underlying offense. This guideline shall be used as a consolidated fine guideline for both the underlying offense and the conviction underlying this section.

Commentary

Statutory Provisions: 18 U.S.C. §§ 844(h), 924(c), 929(a).

Application Notes:

1. **Application of Subsection (a).**—Section 844(h) of title 18, United State Code, provides a mandatory term of imprisonment of 10 years (or 20 years for the second or subsequent offense). Accordingly, the guideline sentence for a defendant convicted under 18 U.S.C. § 844(h) is the term required by that statute. Section 844(h) of title 18, United State Code, also requires a term of imprisonment imposed under this section to run consecutively to any other term of imprisonment.

2. **Application of Subsection (b).**—

(A) **In General.**—Sections 924(c) and 929(a) of title 18, United States Code, provide mandatory minimum terms of imprisonment (*e.g.*, not less than five years). Except as provided in subsection (c), in a case in which the defendant is convicted under 18 U.S.C. § 924(c) or § 929(a), the guideline sentence is the minimum term required by the relevant statute. Each of 18 U.S.C. §§ 924(c) and 929(a) also requires that a term of imprisonment imposed under that section shall run consecutively to any other term of imprisonment.

(B) **Upward Departure Provision.**—In a case in which the guideline sentence is determined under subsection (b), a sentence above the minimum term required by

18 U.S.C. § 924(c) or § 929(a) is an upward departure from the guideline sentence. A departure may be warranted, for example, to reflect the seriousness of the defendant's criminal history in a case in which the defendant is convicted of an 18 U.S.C. § 924(c) or § 929(a) offense but is not determined to be a career offender under §4B1.1.

3. **Application of Subsection (c).**—In a case in which the defendant (A) was convicted of violating 18 U.S.C. § 924(c) or 18 U.S.C. § 929(a); and (B) as a result of that conviction (alone or in addition to another offense of conviction), is determined to be a career offender under §4B1.1 (Career Offender), the guideline sentence shall be determined under §4B1.1(c). In a case involving multiple counts, the sentence shall be imposed according to the rules in subsection (e) of §5G1.2 (Sentencing on Multiple Counts of Conviction)

4. **Weapon Enhancement.**—If a sentence under this guideline is imposed in conjunction with a sentence for an underlying offense, do not apply any specific offense characteristic for possession, brandishing, use, or discharge of an explosive or firearm when determining the sentence for the underlying offense. A sentence under this guideline accounts for any explosive or weapon enhancement for the underlying offense of conviction, including any such enhancement that would apply based on conduct for which the defendant is accountable under §1B1.3 (Relevant Conduct). Do not apply any weapon enhancement in the guideline for the underlying offense, for example, if (A) a co-defendant, as part of the jointly undertaken criminal activity, possessed a firearm different from the one for which

the defendant was convicted under 18 U.S.C. § 924(c); or (B) in an ongoing drug trafficking offense, the defendant possessed a firearm other than the one for which the defendant was convicted under 18 U.S.C. § 924(c). However, if a defendant is convicted of two armed bank robberies, but is convicted under 18 U.S.C. § 924(c) in connection with only one of the robberies, a weapon enhancement would apply to the bank robbery which was not the basis for the 18 U.S.C. § 924(c) conviction.

A sentence under this guideline also accounts for conduct that would subject the defendant to an enhancement under §2D1.1(b)(2) (pertaining to use of violence, credible threat to use violence, or directing the use of violence). Do not apply that enhancement when determining the sentence for the underlying offense.

If the explosive or weapon that was possessed, brandished, used, or discharged in the course of the underlying offense also results in a conviction that would subject the defendant to an enhancement under §2K1.3(b)(3) (pertaining to possession of explosive material in connection with another felony offense) or §2K2.1(b)(6)(B) (pertaining to possession of any firearm or ammunition in connection with another felony offense), do not apply that enhancement. A sentence under this guideline accounts for the conduct covered by these enhancements because of the relatedness of that conduct to the conduct that forms the basis for the conviction under 18 U.S.C. § 844(h), § 924(c) or § 929(a). For example, if in addition to a conviction for an underlying offense of armed bank robbery, the defendant was convicted of being a felon in possession under 18 U.S.C. § 922(g), the enhancement under §2K2.1(b)(6)(B) would not apply.

In a few cases in which the defendant is determined not to be a career offender, the offense level for the underlying offense determined under the preceding paragraphs may result in a guideline range that, when combined with the mandatory consecutive sentence under 18 U.S.C. § 844(h), § 924(c), or § 929(a), produces a total maximum penalty that is less than the maximum of the guideline range that would have resulted had there not been a count of conviction under 18 U.S.C. § 844(h), § 924(c), or § 929(a) (*i.e.*, the guideline range that would have resulted if the enhancements for possession, use, or discharge of a firearm had been applied). In such a case, an upward departure may be warranted so that the conviction under 18 U.S.C. § 844(h), § 924(c), or § 929(a) does not result in a decrease in the total punishment. An upward departure under this paragraph shall not exceed the maximum of the guideline range that would have resulted had there not been a count of conviction under 18 U.S.C. § 844(h), § 924(c), or § 929(a).

5. **Chapters Three and Four.**—Except for those cases covered by subsection (c), do not apply Chapter Three (Adjustments) and Chapter Four (Criminal History and Criminal Livelihood) to any offense sentenced under this guideline. Such offenses are excluded from application of those chapters because the guideline sentence for each offense is determined only by the relevant statute. *See* §§3D1.1 (Procedure for Determining Offense Level on Multiple Counts) and 5G1.2. In determining the guideline sentence for those cases covered by subsection (c): (A) the adjustment in §3E1.1 (Acceptance of Responsibility) may apply, as provided in §4B1.1(c); and (B) no other adjustments in Chapter Three and no provisions of Chapter Four, other than §§4B1.1 and 4B1.2, shall apply.

6. **Terms of Supervised Release.**—Imposition of a term of supervised release is governed by the provisions of §5D1.1 (Imposition of a Term of Supervised Release).

7. **Fines.**—Subsection (d) sets forth special provisions concerning the imposition of fines. Where there is also a conviction for the underlying offense, a consolidated fine guideline is determined by the offense level that would have applied to the underlying offense absent a conviction under 18 U.S.C. § 844(h), § 924(c), or § 929(a). This is required because

the offense level for the underlying offense may be reduced when there is also a conviction under 18 U.S.C. § 844(h), § 924(c), or § 929(a) in that any specific offense characteristic for possession, brandishing, use, or discharge of a firearm is not applied (*see* Application Note 4). The Commission has not established a fine guideline range for the unusual case in which there is no conviction for the underlying offense, although a fine is authorized under 18 U.S.C. § 3571.

Background: Section 844(h) of title 18, United States Code, provides a mandatory term of imprisonment. Sections 924(c) and 929(a) of title 18, United States Code, provide mandatory minimum terms of imprisonment. A sentence imposed pursuant to any of these statutes must be imposed to run consecutively to any other term of imprisonment. To avoid double counting, when a sentence under this section is imposed in conjunction with a sentence for an underlying offense, any specific offense characteristic for explosive or firearm discharge, use, brandishing, or possession is not applied in respect to such underlying offense.

Historical
Note

Effective November 1, 1987. Amended effective November 1, 1989 (amendment 190); November 1, 1990 (amendment 332); November 1, 1991 (amendment 405); November 1, 1993 (amendments 481 and 489); November 1, 2000 (amendments 598, 599, and 600); November 1, 2002 (amendment 642); November 1, 2006 (amendment 696); November 1, 2010 (amendment 748); November 1, 2011 (amendments 750 and 760).

§2K2.5. Possession of Firearm or Dangerous Weapon in Federal Facility; Possession or Discharge of Firearm in School Zone

(a) Base Offense Level: **6**

(b) Specific Offense Characteristic

(1) If—

(A) the defendant unlawfully possessed or caused any firearm or dangerous weapon to be present in a federal court facility;

or

(B) the defendant unlawfully possessed or caused any firearm to be present in a school zone,

increase by **2** levels.

(c) Cross Reference

(1) If the defendant used or possessed any firearm or dangerous weapon in connection with the commission or attempted commission of another offense, or possessed or transferred a firearm or dangerous weapon with knowledge or intent that it would be used or possessed in connection with another offense, apply—

(A) §2X1.1 (Attempt, Solicitation, or Conspiracy) in respect to that other offense if the resulting offense level is greater than that determined above; or

(B) if death resulted, the most analogous offense guideline from Chapter Two, Part A, Subpart 1 (Homicide), if the resulting offense level is greater than that determined above.

Commentary

Statutory Provisions: 18 U.S.C. §§ 922(q), 930; 40 U.S.C. § 5104(e)(1).

Application Notes:

1. "***Dangerous weapon***" and "***firearm***" are defined in the Commentary to §1B1.1 (Application Instructions).

2. "***Federal court facility***" includes the courtroom; judges' chambers; witness rooms; jury deliberation rooms; attorney conference rooms; prisoner holding cells; offices and parking facilities of the court clerks, the United States attorney, and the United States marshal; probation and parole offices; and adjoining corridors and parking facilities of any court of the United States. *See* 18 U.S.C. § 930(g)(3).

3. "***School zone***" is defined at 18 U.S.C. § 922(q). A sentence of imprisonment under 18 U.S.C. § 922(q) must run consecutively to any sentence of imprisonment imposed for any other offense. *See* 18 U.S.C. § 924(a)(4). In order to comply with the statute, when the guideline range is based on the underlying offense, and the defendant is convicted both of the underlying offense and 18 U.S.C. § 922(q), the court should apportion the sentence between the count for the underlying offense and the count under 18 U.S.C. § 922(q). For example, if the guideline range is 30–37 months and the court determines "total punishment" of 36 months is appropriate, a sentence of 30 months for the underlying offense, plus 6 months under 18 U.S.C. § 922(q) would satisfy this requirement.

4. Where the firearm was brandished, discharged, or otherwise used, in a federal facility, federal court facility, or school zone, and the cross reference from subsection (c)(1) does not apply, an upward departure may be warranted.

Historical Note

Effective November 1, 1989 (amendment 191). Amended effective November 1, 1991 (amendment 374); November 1, 2003 (amendment 661); November 1, 2010 (amendment 746).

§2K2.6. Possessing, Purchasing, or Owning Body Armor by Violent Felons

(a) Base Offense Level: **10**

(b) Specific Offense Characteristic

(1) If the defendant used the body armor in connection with another felony offense, increase by **4** levels.

Commentary

Statutory Provision: 18 U.S.C. § 931.

Application Notes:

1. **Application of Subsection (b)(1).**—

(A) **Meaning of "Defendant".**—Consistent with §1B1.3 (Relevant Conduct), the term "***defendant***", for purposes of subsection (b)(1), limits the accountability of the defendant to the defendant's own conduct and conduct that the defendant aided or abetted, counseled, commanded, induced, procured, or willfully caused.

(B) **Meaning of "Felony Offense".**—For purposes of subsection (b)(1), "***felony offense***" means any offense (federal, state, or local) punishable by imprisonment for a term exceeding one year, regardless of whether a criminal charge was brought, or a conviction obtained.

(C) **Meaning of "Used".**—For purposes of subsection (b)(1), "***used***" means the body armor was (i) actively employed in a manner to protect the person from gunfire; or (ii) used as a means of bartering. Subsection (b)(1) does not apply if the body armor was merely possessed. For example, subsection (b)(1) would not apply if the body armor was found in the trunk of a car but was not being actively used as protection.

2. **Inapplicability of §3B1.5.**—If subsection (b)(1) applies, do not apply the adjustment in §3B1.5 (Use of Body Armor in Drug Trafficking Crimes and Crimes of Violence).

3. **Grouping of Multiple Counts.**—If subsection (b)(1) applies (because the defendant used the body armor in connection with another felony offense) and the instant offense of conviction includes a count of conviction for that other felony offense, the counts of conviction for the 18 U.S.C. § 931 offense and that other felony offense shall be grouped pursuant to subsection (c) of §3D1.2 (Groups of Closely Related Counts).

Historical
Note
Effective November 1, 2004 (amendment 670).

* * * * *

3. MAILING INJURIOUS ARTICLES

Historical
Note
Effective November 1, 1987. Amended effective November 1, 1993 (amendment 481).

§2K3.1. [Deleted]

Historical
Note
Section 2K3.1 (Unlawfully Transporting Hazardous Materials in Commerce), effective November 1, 1987, was deleted by consolidation with §2Q1.2 effective November 1, 1993 (amendment 481).

§2K3.2. Feloniously Mailing Injurious Articles

(a) Base Offense Level (Apply the greater):

(1) If the offense was committed with intent (A) to kill or injure any person, or (B) to injure the mails or other property, apply §2X1.1 (Attempt, Solicitation, or Conspiracy) in respect to the intended offense; or

(2) If death resulted, apply the most analogous offense guideline from Chapter Two, Part A, Subpart 1 (Homicide).

Commentary

Statutory Provision: 18 U.S.C. § 1716 (felony provisions only).

Background: This guideline applies only to the felony provisions of 18 U.S.C. § 1716. The Commission has not promulgated a guideline for the misdemeanor provisions of this statute.

Historical
Note
Effective November 1, 1990 (amendment 334).

PART L — OFFENSES INVOLVING IMMIGRATION, NATURALIZATION, AND PASSPORTS

1. IMMIGRATION

§2L1.1. Smuggling, Transporting, or Harboring an Unlawful Alien

(a) Base Offense Level:

(1) **25**, if the defendant was convicted under 8 U.S.C. § 1327 of a violation involving an alien who was inadmissible under 8 U.S.C. § 1182(a)(3);

(2) **23**, if the defendant was convicted under 8 U.S.C. § 1327 of a violation involving an alien who previously was deported after

a conviction for an aggravated felony; or
(3) **12**, otherwise.
(b) Specific Offense Characteristics
(1) If (A) the offense was committed other than for profit, or the offense involved the smuggling, transporting, or harboring only of the defendant's spouse or child (or both the defendant's spouse and child), and (B) the base offense level is determined under subsection (a)(3), decrease by **3** levels.
(2) If the offense involved the smuggling, transporting, or harboring of six or more unlawful aliens, increase as follows:

Number of Unlawful Aliens Smuggled, Transported, or Harbored	Increase in Level
(A) 6–24	add **3**
(B) 25–99	add **6**
(C) 100 or more	add **9**.

(3) If the defendant committed any part of the instant offense after sustaining (A) a conviction for a felony immigration and naturalization offense, increase by **2** levels; or (B) two (or more) convictions for felony immigration and naturalization offenses, each such conviction arising out of a separate prosecution, increase by **4** levels.

(4) If the offense involved the smuggling, transporting, or harboring of a minor who was unaccompanied by the minor's parent, adult relative, or legal guardian, increase by **4** levels.
(5) (Apply the Greatest):
(A) If a firearm was discharged, increase by **6** levels, but if the resulting offense level is less than level **22**, increase to level **22**.
(B) If a dangerous weapon (including a firearm) was brandished or otherwise used, increase by **4** levels, but if the resulting offense level is less than level **20**, increase to level **20**.
(C) If a dangerous weapon (including a firearm) was possessed, increase by **2** levels, but if the resulting offense level is less than level **18**, increase to level **18**.
(6) If the offense involved intentionally or recklessly creating a substantial risk of death or serious bodily injury to another person, increase by **2** levels, but if the resulting offense level is less than level **18**, increase to level **18**.
(7) If any person died or sustained bodily injury, increase the offense level according to the seriousness of the injury:

Death or Degree of Injury	Increase in Level
(A) Bodily Injury	add **2** levels
(B) Serious Bodily Injury	add **4** levels
(C) Permanent or Life-Threatening	

Bodily Injury add **6** levels
(D) Death add **10** levels.
(8) (Apply the greater):
(A) If an alien was involuntarily detained through coercion or threat, or in connection with a demand for payment, (i) after the alien was smuggled into the United States; or (ii) while the alien was transported or harbored in the United States, increase by **2** levels. If the resulting offense level is less than level **18**, increase to level **18**.
(B) If (i) the defendant was convicted of alien harboring, (ii) the alien harboring was for the purpose of prostitution, and (iii) the defendant receives an adjustment under

§3B1.1 (Aggravating Role), increase by **2** levels, but if the alien engaging in the prostitution had not attained the age of 18 years, increase by **6** levels.
(9) If the defendant was convicted under 8 U.S.C. § 1324(a)(4), increase by **2** levels.
(c) Cross Reference
(1) If death resulted, apply the appropriate homicide guideline from Chapter Two, Part A, Subpart 1, if the resulting offense level is greater than that determined under this guideline.

Commentary

Statutory Provisions: 8 U.S.C. §§ 1324(a), 1327. For additional statutory provision(s), *see* Appendix A (Statutory Index).

Application Notes:

1. **Definitions.**—For purposes of this guideline:

"***The offense was committed other than for profit***" means that there was no payment or expectation of payment for the smuggling, transporting, or harboring of any of the unlawful aliens.

"***Number of unlawful aliens smuggled, transported, or harbored***" does not include the defendant.

"***Aggravated felony***" has the meaning given that term in section 101(a)(43) of the Immigration and Nationality Act (8 U.S.C. § 1101(a)(43)), without regard to the date of conviction for the aggravated felony.

"***Child***" has the meaning set forth in section 101(b)(1) of the Immigration and Nationality Act (8 U.S.C. § 1101(b)(1)).

"***Spouse***" has the meaning set forth in 101(a)(35) of the Immigration and Nationality Act (8 U.S.C. § 1101(a)(35)).

"***Immigration and naturalization offense***" means any offense covered by Chapter Two, Part L.

"***Minor***" means an individual who had not attained the age of 18 years.

"***Parent***" means (A) a natural mother or father; (B) a stepmother or stepfather; or (C) an adoptive mother or father.

"***Bodily injury***," "***serious bodily injury***," and "***permanent or life-threatening bodily injury***" have the meaning given those terms in the Commentary to §1B1.1 (Application Instructions).

2. **Prior Convictions Under Subsection (b)(3).**—Prior felony conviction(s) resulting in

an adjustment under subsection (b)(3) are also counted for purposes of determining criminal history points pursuant to Chapter Four, Part A (Criminal History).

3. **Application of Subsection (b)(6).**—Reckless conduct to which the adjustment from subsection (b)(6) applies includes a wide variety of conduct (*e.g.*, transporting persons in the trunk or engine compartment of a motor vehicle; carrying substantially more passengers than the rated capacity of a motor vehicle or vessel; harboring persons in a crowded, dangerous, or inhumane condition; or guiding persons through, or abandoning persons in, a dangerous or remote geographic area without adequate food, water, clothing, or protection from the elements). If subsection (b)(6) applies solely on the basis of conduct related to fleeing from a law enforcement officer, do not apply an adjustment from §3C1.2 (Reckless Endangerment During Flight). Additionally, do not apply the adjustment in subsection (b)(6) if the only reckless conduct that created a substantial risk of death or serious bodily injury is conduct for which the defendant received an enhancement under subsection (b)(5).

4. **Application of Subsection (b)(7) to Conduct Constituting Criminal Sexual Abuse.**—Consistent with Application Note 1(L) of §1B1.1 (Application Instructions), "serious bodily injury" is deemed to have occurred if the offense involved conduct constituting criminal sexual abuse under 18 U.S.C. § 2241 or § 2242 or any similar offense under state law.

5. **Inapplicability of §3A1.3.**—If an enhancement under subsection (b)(8)(A) applies, do not apply §3A1.3 (Restraint of Victim).

6. **Interaction with §3B1.1.**—For the purposes of §3B1.1 (Aggravating Role), the aliens smuggled, transported, or harbored are not considered participants unless they actively assisted in the smuggling, transporting, or harboring of others. In large scale smuggling, transporting, or harboring cases, an additional adjustment from §3B1.1 typically will apply.

7. **Upward Departure Provisions.**—An upward departure may be warranted in any of the following cases:

(A) The defendant smuggled, transported, or harbored an alien knowing that the alien intended to enter the United States to engage in subversive activity, drug trafficking, or other serious criminal behavior.

(B) The defendant smuggled, transported, or harbored an alien the defendant knew was inadmissible for reasons of security and related grounds, as set forth under 8 U.S.C. § 1182(a)(3).

(C) The offense involved substantially more than 100 aliens.

Background: This section includes the most serious immigration offenses covered under the Immigration Reform and Control Act of 1986.

Historical Note

Effective November 1, 1987. Amended effective January 15, 1988 (amendments 35, 36, and 37); November 1, 1989 (amendment 192); November 1, 1990 (amendment 335); November 1, 1991 (amendment 375); November 1, 1992 (amendment 450); May 1, 1997 (amendment 543); November 1, 1997 (amendment 561); November 1, 2006 (amendments 686 and 692); November 1, 2007 (amendment 702); November 1, 2009 (amendment 730); November 1, 2014 (amendment 785); November 1, 2016 (amendment 802).

§2L1.2. Unlawfully Entering or Remaining in the United States

(a) Base Offense Level: **8**

(b) Specific Offense Characteristics

(1) (Apply the Greater) If the defendant committed the instant offense after sustaining—

(A) a conviction for a felony that is an illegal reentry offense, increase by **4** levels; or

(B) two or more convictions for misdemeanors under 8 U.S.C. § 1325(a), increase by **2** levels.

(2) (Apply the Greatest) If, before the defendant was ordered deported

or ordered removed from the United States for the first time, the defendant sustained—

(A) a conviction for a felony offense (other than an illegal reentry offense) for which the sentence imposed was five years or more, increase by **10** levels;

(B) a conviction for a felony offense (other than an illegal reentry offense) for which the sentence imposed was two years or more, increase by **8** levels;

(C) a conviction for a felony offense (other than an illegal reentry offense) for which the sentence imposed exceeded one year and one month, increase by **6** levels;

(D) a conviction for any other felony offense (other than an illegal reentry offense), increase by **4** levels; or

(E) three or more convictions for misdemeanors that are crimes of violence or drug trafficking offenses, increase by **2** levels.

(3) (Apply the Greatest) If, at any time after the defendant was ordered deported or ordered removed from the United States for the first time, the defendant engaged in criminal conduct resulting in—

(A) a conviction for a felony offense (other than an illegal reentry offense) for which the sentence imposed was five years or more, increase by **10** levels;

(B) a conviction for a felony offense (other than an illegal reentry offense) for which the sentence imposed was two years or more, increase by **8** levels;

(C) a conviction for a felony offense (other than an illegal reentry offense) for which the sentence imposed exceeded one year and one month, increase by **6** levels;

(D) a conviction for any other felony offense (other than an illegal reentry offense), increase by **4** levels; or

(E) three or more convictions for misdemeanors that are crimes of violence or drug trafficking offenses, increase by **2** levels.

Commentary

Statutory Provisions: 8 U.S.C. § 1253, § 1325(a) (second or subsequent offense only), § 1326. For additional statutory provision(s), *see* Appendix A (Statutory Index).

Application Notes:

1. **In General.**—

(A) **"Ordered Deported or Ordered Removed from the United States for the First Time".**—For purposes of this guideline, a defendant shall be considered "ordered deported or ordered removed from the United States" if the defendant was ordered deported or ordered removed from the United States based on a final order of exclusion, deportation, or removal, regardless of whether the order was in response to a conviction. "For the first time" refers to the first time the defendant was ever the subject of such an order.

(B) **Offenses Committed Prior to Age Eighteen.**—Subsections (b)(1), (b)(2), and (b)(3) do not apply to a conviction for an offense committed before the defendant was eighteen years of age unless such conviction is classified as an adult conviction under the laws of the jurisdiction in which the defendant was convicted.

2. **Definitions.**—For purposes of this guideline:

"***Crime of violence***" means any of the following offenses under federal, state, or local law: murder, voluntary manslaughter, kidnapping, aggravated assault, a forcible sex offense, robbery, arson, extortion, the use or unlawful possession of a firearm described in 26 U.S.C. § 5845(a) or explosive material as defined in 18 U.S.C. § 841(c), or any other offense under federal, state, or local law that has as an element the use, attempted use, or threatened use of physical force against the person of another. "Forcible sex offense" includes where consent to the conduct is not given or is not legally valid, such as where consent to the conduct is involuntary, incompetent, or coerced. The offenses of sexual abuse of a minor and statutory rape are included only if the sexual abuse of a minor or statutory rape was (A) an offense described in 18 U.S.C. § 2241(c) or (B) an offense under state law that would have been an offense under section 2241(c) if the offense had oc

curred within the special maritime and territorial jurisdiction of the United States. "Extortion" is obtaining something of value from another by the wrongful use of (A) force, (B) fear of physical injury, or (C) threat of physical injury.

"***Drug trafficking offense***" means an offense under federal, state, or local law that prohibits the manufacture, import, export, distribution, or dispensing of, or offer to sell a controlled substance (or a counterfeit substance) or the possession of a controlled substance (or a counterfeit substance) with intent to manufacture, import, export, distribute, or dispense.

"***Felony***" means any federal, state, or local offense punishable by imprisonment for a term exceeding one year.

"***Illegal reentry offense***" means (A) an offense under 8 U.S.C. § 1253 or § 1326, or (B) a second or subsequent offense under 8 U.S.C. § 1325(a).

"***Misdemeanor***" means any federal, state, or local offense punishable by a term of imprisonment of one year or less.

"***Sentence imposed***" has the meaning given the term "sentence of imprisonment" in Application Note 2 and subsection (b) of §4A1.2 (Definitions and Instructions for Computing Criminal History). The length of the sentence imposed includes any term of imprisonment given upon revocation of probation, parole, or supervised release.

3. **Criminal History Points.**—For purposes of applying subsections (b)(1), (b)(2), and (b)(3), use only those convictions that receive criminal history points under §4A1.1(a), (b), or (c). In addition, for purposes of subsections (b)(1)(B), (b)(2)(E), and (b)(3)(E), use only those convictions that are counted separately under §4A1.2(a)(2).

A conviction taken into account under subsection (b)(1), (b)(2), or (b)(3) is not excluded from consideration of whether that conviction receives criminal history points pursuant to Chapter Four, Part A (Criminal History).

4. **Cases in Which Sentences for An Illegal Reentry Offense and Another Felony Offense were Imposed at the Same Time.**—There may be cases in which the sentences for an illegal reentry offense and another felony offense were imposed at the same time and treated as a single sentence for purposes of calculating the criminal history score under §4A1.1(a), (b), and (c). In such a case, use the illegal reentry offense in determining the appropriate enhancement under subsection (b)(1), if it independently would have received criminal history points. In addition, use the prior sentence for the other felony offense in determining the appropriate enhancement under subsection (b)(3), if it independently would have received criminal history points.

5. **Departure Based on Seriousness of a Prior Offense.**—There may be cases in which the offense level provided by an enhancement in subsection (b)(2) or (b)(3) substantially understates or overstates the seriousness of the conduct underlying the prior offense, because (A) the length of the sentence imposed does not reflect the seriousness of the prior offense; (B) the prior conviction is too remote to receive criminal history points

(*see* §4A1.2(e)); or (C) the time actually served was substantially less than the length of the sentence imposed for the prior offense. In such a case, a departure may be warranted.

6. **Departure Based on Time Served in State Custody.**—In a case in which the defendant is located by immigration authorities while the defendant is serving time in state custody, whether pre- or post-conviction, for a state offense, the time served is not covered

by an adjustment under §5G1.3(b) and, accordingly, is not covered by a departure under §5K2.23 (Discharged Terms of Imprisonment). *See* §5G1.3(a). In such a case, the court may consider whether a departure is appropriate to reflect all or part of the time served in state custody, from the time immigration authorities locate the defendant until the service of the federal sentence commences, that the court determines will not be credited to the federal sentence by the Bureau of Prisons. Any such departure should be fashioned to achieve a reasonable punishment for the instant offense.

Such a departure should be considered only in cases where the departure is not likely to increase the risk to the public from further crimes of the defendant. In determining whether such a departure is appropriate, the court should consider, among other things, (A) whether the defendant engaged in additional criminal activity after illegally reentering the United States; (B) the seriousness of any such additional criminal activity, including (1) whether the defendant used violence or credible threats of violence or possessed a firearm or other dangerous weapon (or induced another person to do so) in connection with the criminal activity, (2) whether the criminal activity resulted in death or serious bodily injury to any person, and (3) whether the defendant was an organizer, leader, manager, or supervisor of others in the criminal activity; and (C) the seriousness of the defendant's other criminal history.

7. **Departure Based on Cultural Assimilation.**—There may be cases in which a downward departure may be appropriate on the basis of cultural assimilation. Such a departure should be considered only in cases where (A) the defendant formed cultural ties primarily with the United States from having resided continuously in the United States from childhood, (B) those cultural ties provided the primary motivation for the defendant's illegal reentry or continued presence in the United States, and (C) such a departure is not likely to increase the risk to the public from further crimes of the defendant. In determining whether such a departure is appropriate, the court should consider, among other things, (1) the age in childhood at which the defendant began residing continuously in the United States, (2) whether and for how long the defendant attended school in the United States, (3) the duration of the defendant's continued residence in the United States, (4) the duration of the defendant's presence outside the United States, (5) the nature and extent of the defendant's familial and cultural ties inside the United States, and the nature and extent of such ties outside the United States, (6) the seriousness of the defendant's criminal history, and (7) whether the defendant engaged in additional criminal activity after illegally reentering the United States.

Historical Note

Effective November 1, 1987. Amended effective January 15, 1988 (amendment 38); November 1, 1989 (amendment 193); November 1, 1991 (amendment 375); November 1, 1995 (amendment 523); November 1, 1997 (amendment 562); November 1, 2001 (amendment 632); November 1, 2002 (amendment 637); November 1, 2003 (amendment 658); November 1, 2007 (amendment 709); November 1, 2008 (amendment 722); November 1, 2010 (amendment 740); November 1, 2011 (amendment 754); November 1, 2012 (amendment 764); November 1, 2014 (amendment 787); November 1, 2015 (amendment 795); November 1, 2016 (amendment 802).

§2L1.3. [Deleted]

Historical Note

Section 2L1.3 (Engaging in a Pattern of Unlawful Employment of Aliens), effective November 1, 1987, was deleted effective November 1, 1989 (amendment 194).

* * * * *

§2L1.3

2. NATURALIZATION AND PASSPORTS

§2L2.1. Trafficking in a Document Relating to Naturalization, Citizenship, or Legal Resident Status, or a United States Passport; False Statement in Respect to the Citizenship or Immigration Status of Another; Fraudulent Marriage to Assist Alien to Evade Immigration Law

(a) Base Offense Level: **11**

(b) Specific Offense Characteristics

(1) If the offense was committed other than for profit, or the offense involved the smuggling, transporting, or harboring only of the defendant's spouse or child (or both the defendant's spouse and child), decrease by **3** levels.

(2) If the offense involved six or more documents or passports, increase as follows:

NUMBER OF DOCUMENTS/PASSPORTS	INCREASE IN LEVEL
(A) 6–24	add **3**
(B) 25–99	add **6**
(C) 100 or more	add **9**.

(3) If the defendant knew, believed, or had reason to believe that a passport or visa was to be used to facilitate the commission of a felony offense, other than an offense involving violation of the immigration laws, increase by **4** levels.

(4) If the defendant committed any part of the instant offense after sustaining (A) a conviction for a felony immigration and naturalization offense, increase by **2** levels; or (B) two (or more) convictions for felony immigration and naturalization offenses, each such conviction arising out of a separate prosecution, increase by **4** levels.

(5) If the defendant fraudulently obtained or used (A) a United States passport, increase by **4** levels; or (B) a foreign passport, increase by **2** levels.

Commentary

Statutory Provisions: 8 U.S.C. §§ 1160(b)(7)(A), 1185(a)(3), (4), 1325(c), (d); 18 U.S.C. §§ 1015, 1028, 1425–1427, 1542, 1544, 1546. For additional statutory provision(s), *see* Appendix A (Statutory Index).

Application Notes:

1. For purposes of this guideline—

"***The offense was committed other than for profit***" means that there was no payment or expectation of payment for the smuggling, transporting, or harboring of any of the unlawful aliens.

"***Immigration and naturalization offense***" means any offense covered by Chapter Two, Part L.

"***Child***" has the meaning set forth in section 101(b)(1) of the Immigration and Nationality Act (8 U.S.C. § 1101(b)(1)).

"***Spouse***" has the meaning set forth in section 101(a)(35) of the Immigration and Nationality Act (8 U.S.C. § 1101(a)(35)).

2. Where it is established that multiple documents are part of a set of documents intended

for use by a single person, treat the set as one document.

3. Subsection (b)(3) provides an enhancement if the defendant knew, believed, or had reason to believe that a passport or visa was to be used to facilitate the commission of a felony offense, other than an offense involving violation of the immigration laws. If the defendant knew, believed, or had reason to believe that the felony offense to be committed was of an especially serious type, an upward departure may be warranted.

4. Prior felony conviction(s) resulting in an adjustment under subsection (b)(4) are also counted for purposes of determining criminal history points pursuant to Chapter Four, Part A (Criminal History).

5. If the offense involved substantially more than 100 documents, an upward departure may be warranted.

Historical Note

Effective November 1, 1987. Amended effective November 1, 1989 (amendment 195); November 1, 1992 (amendment 450); November 1, 1993 (amendment 481); November 1, 1995 (amendment 524); May 1, 1997 (amendment 544); November 1, 1997 (amendment 563); November 1, 2006 (amendment 692); November 1, 2010 (amendment 746).

§2L2.2. Fraudulently Acquiring Documents Relating to Naturalization, Citizenship, or Legal Resident Status for Own Use; False Personation or Fraudulent Marriage by Alien to Evade Immigration Law; Fraudulently Acquiring or Improperly Using a United States Passport

(a) Base Offense Level: **8**

(b) Specific Offense Characteristics

(1) If the defendant is an unlawful alien who has been deported (voluntarily or involuntarily) on one or more occasions prior to the instant offense, increase by **2** levels.

(2) If the defendant committed any part of the instant offense after sustaining (A) a conviction for a felony immigration and naturalization offense, increase by **2** levels; or (B) two (or more) convictions for felony immigration and naturalization offenses, each such conviction arising out of a separate prosecution, increase by **4** levels.

(3) If the defendant fraudulently obtained or used (A) a United States passport, increase by **4** levels; or (B) a foreign passport, increase by **2** levels.

(4) (Apply the Greater):

(A) If the defendant committed any part of the instant offense to conceal the defendant's membership in, or authority over, a military, paramilitary, or police organization that was involved in a serious human rights offense during the period in which the defendant was such a member or had such authority, increase by **2** levels. If the resulting offense level is less than level **13**, increase to level **13**.

(B) If the defendant committed any part of the instant offense to conceal the defendant's participation in (i) the offense of incitement to genocide, increase by **6** levels; or (ii) any other serious human rights offense, increase by **10** levels. If clause (ii) applies and the resulting offense level is less than level **25**, increase to level **25**.

(c) Cross Reference

(1) If the defendant used a passport or visa in the commission or attempted commission of a felony offense, other than an offense involving violation of the immigration laws, apply—

(A) §2X1.1 (Attempt, Solicitation, or Conspiracy) in respect to that felony offense, if the resulting offense level is greater than that determined above; or

(B) if death resulted, the most analogous offense guideline from Chapter Two, Part A, Subpart 1 (Homicide), if the

resulting offense level is greater than that determined above.

Commentary

Statutory Provisions: 8 U.S.C. §§ 1160(b)(7)(A), 1185(a)(3), (5), 1325(c), (d); 18 U.S.C. §§ 911, 1015, 1028, 1423–1426, 1542–1544, 1546.

Application Notes:

1. **Definition.**—For purposes of this guideline, "***immigration and naturalization offense***" means any offense covered by Chapter Two, Part L.

2. **Application of Subsection (b)(2).**—Prior felony conviction(s) resulting in an adjustment under subsection (b)(2) are also counted for purposes of determining criminal history points pursuant to Chapter Four, Part A (Criminal History).

3. **Application of Subsection (b)(3).**—The term "***used***" is to be construed broadly and includes the attempted renewal of previously-issued passports.

4. **Application of Subsection (b)(4).**—For purposes of subsection (b)(4):

"***Serious human rights offense***" means (A) violations of federal criminal laws relating to genocide, torture, war crimes, and the use or recruitment of child soldiers under sections 1091, 2340, 2340A, 2441, and 2442 of title 18, United States Code, *see* 28 U.S.C. § 509B(e); and (B) conduct that would have been a violation of any such law if the offense had occurred within the jurisdiction of the United States or if the defendant or the victim had been a national of the United States.

"***The offense of incitement to genocide***" means (A) violations of 18 U.S.C. § 1091(c); and (B) conduct that would have been a violation of such section if the offense had occurred within the jurisdiction of the United States or if the defendant or the victim had been a national of the United States.

5. **Multiple Counts.**—For the purposes of Chapter Three, Part D (Multiple Counts), a count of conviction for unlawfully entering or remaining in the United States covered by §2L1.2 (Unlawfully Entering or Remaining in the United States) arising from the same course of conduct as the count of conviction covered by this guideline shall be considered a closely related count to the count of conviction covered by this guideline, and therefore is to be grouped with the count of conviction covered by this guideline.

6. **Upward Departure Provision.**—If the defendant fraudulently obtained or used a United States passport for the purpose of entering the United States to engage in terrorist activity, an upward departure may be warranted. *See* Application Note 4 of the Commentary to §3A1.4 (Terrorism).

Historical
Note

Effective November 1, 1987. Amended effective January 15, 1988 (amendment 39); November 1, 1989 (amendment 196); November 1, 1992 (amendment 450); November 1, 1993 (amendment 481); November 1, 1995 (amendment 524); May 1, 1997 (amendment 544); November 1, 1997 (amendment 563); November 1, 2004 (amendment 671); November 1, 2006 (amendment 692); November 1, 2010 (amendment 746); November 1, 2012 (amendment 765).

§2L2.3. [Deleted]

Historical

Note
Section 2L2.3 (Trafficking in a United States Passport), effective November 1, 1987, amended effective November 1, 1989 (amendment 197) and November 1, 1992 (amendment 450), was deleted by consolidation with §2L2.1 effective November 1, 1993 (amendment 481).

§2L2.4. [Deleted]

Historical
Note
Section 2L2.4 (Fraudulently Acquiring or Improperly Using a United States Passport), effective November 1, 1987, amended effective January 15, 1988 (amendment 40) and November 1, 1989 (amendment 198), was deleted by consolidation with §2L2.2 effective November 1, 1993 (amendment 481).

§2L2.5. Failure to Surrender Canceled Naturalization Certificate

(a) Base Offense Level: **6**

Commentary

Statutory Provision: 18 U.S.C. § 1428.
Historical
Note
Effective November 1, 1987.

PART M — OFFENSES INVOLVING NATIONAL DEFENSE AND WEAPONS OF MASS DESTRUCTION

Historical
Note
Effective November 1, 1987. Amended effective November 1, 2001 (amendment 633).

1. TREASON

§2M1.1. Treason

(a) Base Offense Level:
(1) **43**, if the conduct is tantamount to waging war against the United States;
(2) the offense level applicable to the most analogous offense, otherwise.

Commentary

Statutory Provision: 18 U.S.C. § 2381.
Background: Treason is a rarely prosecuted offense that could encompass a relatively broad range of conduct, including many of the more specific offenses in this Part. The guideline contemplates imposition of the maximum penalty in the most serious cases, with reference made to the most analogous offense guideline in lesser cases.
Historical
Note
Effective November 1, 1987.
* * * * *

2. SABOTAGE

§2M2.1. Destruction of, or Production of Defective, War Material, Premises, or Utilities

(a) Base Offense Level: **32**

Commentary

Statutory Provisions: 18 U.S.C. § 2153, 2154; 42 U.S.C. § 2284; 49 U.S.C. § 60123(b).

Application Note:
1. Violations of 42 U.S.C. § 2284 are included in this section where the defendant was convicted of acting with intent to injure the United States or aid a foreign nation.
Historical
Note
Effective November 1, 1987. Amended effective November 1, 1993 (amendment 481); November 1, 2002 (amendment 637).

§2M2.2. [Deleted]

Historical

Note
Section 2M2.2 (Production of Defective War Material, Premises, or Utilities), effective November 1, 1987, was deleted by consolidation with §2M2.1 effective November 1, 1993 (amendment 481).

§2M2.3. Destruction of, or Production of Defective, National Defense Material, Premises, or Utilities

(a) Base Offense Level: **26**

Commentary

Statutory Provisions: 18 U.S.C. §§ 2155, 2156; 42 U.S.C. § 2284; 49 U.S.C. § 60123(b).

Application Note:

1. Violations of 42 U.S.C. § 2284 not included in §2M2.1 are included in this section.

Historical
Note
Effective November 1, 1987. Amended effective November 1, 1993 (amendment 481); November 1, 2002 (amendment 637).

§2M2.4. [Deleted]

Historical
Note
Section 2M2.4 (Production of Defective National Defense Material, Premises, or Utilities), effective November 1, 1987, was deleted by consolidation with §2M2.3 effective November 1, 1993 (amendment 481).

* * * * *

3. ESPIONAGE AND RELATED OFFENSES

§2M3.1. Gathering or Transmitting National Defense Information to Aid a Foreign Government

(a) Base Offense Level:

(1) **42**, if top secret information was gathered or transmitted; or

(2) **37**, otherwise.

Commentary

Statutory Provisions: 18 U.S.C. § 794; 42 U.S.C. §§ 2274(a), (b), 2275.

Application Notes:

1. "***Top secret information***" is information that, if disclosed, "reasonably could be expected to cause exceptionally grave damage to the national security." Executive Order 13526 (50 U.S.C. § 3161 note).

2. The Commission has set the base offense level in this subpart on the assumption that the information at issue bears a significant relation to the nation's security, and that the revelation will significantly and adversely affect security interests. When revelation is likely to cause little or no harm, a downward departure may be warranted. *See* Chapter Five, Part K (Departures).

3. The court may depart from the guidelines upon representation by the President or his duly authorized designee that the imposition of a sanction other than authorized by the guideline is necessary to protect national security or further the objectives of the nation's foreign policy.

Background: Offense level distinctions in this subpart are generally based on the classification of the information gathered or transmitted. This classification, in turn, reflects the importance of the information to the national security.

Historical
Note
Effective November 1, 1987. Amended effective November 1, 2010 (amendment 746); November 1, 2013 (amendment 778); November 1, 2014 (amendment 789).

§2M3.2. Gathering National Defense Information

(a) Base Offense Level:

(1) **35**, if top secret information was gathered; or

(2) **30**, otherwise.

Commentary

Statutory Provisions: 18 U.S.C. §§ 793(a), (b), (c), (d), (e), (g), 1030(a)(1). For additional statutory provision(s), *see* Appendix A (Statutory Index).

Application Notes:

1. *See* Commentary to §2M3.1.

2. If the defendant is convicted under 18 U.S.C. § 793(d) or (e), §2M3.3 may apply. *See* Commentary to §2M3.3.

Background: The statutes covered in this section proscribe diverse forms of obtaining and transmitting national defense information with intent or reason to believe the information would injure the United States or be used to the advantage of a foreign government.

Historical Note

Effective November 1, 1987. Amended effective November 1, 2003 (amendment 654).

§2M3.3. Transmitting National Defense Information; Disclosure of Classified Cryptographic Information; Unauthorized Disclosure to a Foreign Government or a Communist Organization of Classified Information by Government Employee; Unauthorized Receipt of Classified Information

(a) Base Offense Level:

(1) **29**, if top secret information; or

(2) **24**, otherwise.

Commentary

Statutory Provisions: 18 U.S.C. §§ 793(d), (e), (g), 798; 50 U.S.C. § 783.

Application Notes:

1. *See* Commentary to §2M3.1.

2. If the defendant was convicted of 18 U.S.C. § 793(d) or (e) for the willful transmission or communication of intangible information with reason to believe that it could be used to the injury of the United States or the advantage of a foreign nation, apply §2M3.2.

Background: The statutes covered in this section proscribe willfully transmitting or communicating to a person not entitled to receive it a document, writing, code book, signal book, sketch, photograph, photographic negative, blueprint, plan, map, model, instrument, appliance, or note relating to the national defense. Proof that the item was communicated with reason to believe that it could be used to the injury of the United States or the advantage of a

foreign nation is required only where intangible information is communicated under 18 U.S.C. § 793(d) or (e).

This section also covers statutes that proscribe the disclosure of classified information concerning cryptographic or communication intelligence to the detriment of the United States or for the benefit of a foreign government, the unauthorized disclosure to a foreign government or a communist organization of classified information by a government employee, and the unauthorized receipt of classified information.

Historical Note

Effective November 1, 1987. Amended effective November 1, 1993 (amendment 481); November 1, 2010 (amendment 746).

§2M3.4. Losing National Defense Information

(a) Base Offense Level:

(1) **18**, if top secret information was lost; or

(2) **13**, otherwise.

Commentary

Statutory Provision: 18 U.S.C. § 793(f).

Application Note:

1. *See* Commentary to §2M3.1.

Background: Offenses prosecuted under this statute generally do not involve subversive conduct on behalf of a foreign power, but rather the loss of classified information by the gross negligence of an employee of the federal government or a federal contractor.

Historical Note

Effective November 1, 1987.

§2M3.5. Tampering with Restricted Data Concerning Atomic Energy

(a) Base Offense Level: **24**

Commentary

Statutory Provision: 42 U.S.C. § 2276.

Application Note:

1. *See* Commentary to §2M3.1.

Historical Note

Effective November 1, 1987.

§2M3.6. [Deleted]

Historical Note

Section 2M3.6 (Disclosure of Classified Cryptographic Information), effective November 1, 1987, was deleted by consolidation with §2M3.3 effective November 1, 1993 (amendment 481).

§2M3.7. [Deleted]

Historical Note

Section 2M3.7 (Unauthorized Disclosure to Foreign Government or a Communist Organization of Classified Information by Government Employee), effective November 1, 1987, was deleted by consolidation with §2M3.3 effective November 1, 1993 (amendment 481).

§2M3.8. [Deleted]

Historical Note

Section 2M3.8 (Receipt of Classified Information), effective November 1, 1987, was deleted by consolidation with §2M3.3 effective November 1, 1993 (amendment 481).

§2M3.9. Disclosure of Information Identifying a Covert Agent

(a) Base Offense Level:

(1) **30**, if the information was disclosed by a person with, or who had authorized access to classified information identifying a covert agent; or

(2) **25**, if the information was disclosed by a person with authorized access only to other classified information.

Commentary

Statutory Provision: 50 U.S.C. § 3121.

Application Notes:

1. *See* Commentary to §2M3.1.

2. This guideline applies only to violations of 50 U.S.C. § 3121 by persons who have or previously had authorized access to classified information. This guideline does not apply to violations of 50 U.S.C. § 3121 by defendants, including journalists, who disclosed such

information without having or having had authorized access to classified information. Violations of 50 U.S.C. § 3121 not covered by this guideline may vary in the degree of harm they inflict, and the court should impose a sentence that reflects such harm. *See* §2X5.1 (Other Offenses).

3. A term of imprisonment imposed for a conviction under 50 U.S.C. § 3121 shall be imposed consecutively to any other term of imprisonment. *See* 50 U.S.C. § 3121(d).

Background: The alternative base offense levels reflect a statutory distinction by providing a greater base offense level for a violation of 50 U.S.C. § 3121 by an official who has or had authorized access to classified information identifying a covert agent than for a violation by an official with authorized access only to other classified information. This guideline does not apply to violations of 50 U.S.C. § 3121 by defendants who disclosed such information without having, or having had, authorized access to classified information.

Historical
Note
Effective November 1, 1987. Amended effective November 1, 2001 (amendment 636); November 1, 2010 (amendment 746); November 1, 2015 (amendment 796).

* * * * *

4. EVASION OF MILITARY SERVICE

§2M4.1. Failure to Register and Evasion of Military Service

(a) Base Offense Level: **6**

(b) Specific Offense Characteristic

(1) If the offense occurred at a time when persons were being inducted for compulsory military service, increase by **6** levels.

Commentary

Statutory Provision: 50 U.S.C. App. § 462.

Application Note:

1. Subsection (b)(1) does not distinguish between whether the offense was committed in peacetime or during time of war or armed conflict. If the offense was committed when persons were being inducted for compulsory military service during time of war or armed conflict, an upward departure may be warranted.

Historical
Note
Effective November 1, 1987. Amended effective November 1, 1990 (amendment 336).

* * * * *

5. PROHIBITED FINANCIAL TRANSACTIONS AND EXPORTS, AND PROVIDING MATERIAL SUPPORT TO DESIGNATED FOREIGN TERRORIST ORGANIZATIONS

Historical
Note
Effective November 1, 1987. Amended effective November 1, 2002 (amendment 637).

§2M5.1. Evasion of Export Controls; Financial Transactions with Countries Supporting International Terrorism

(a) Base Offense Level (Apply the greater):

(1) **26**, if (A) national security controls or controls relating to the proliferation of nuclear, biological, or chemical weapons or materials were evaded; or (B) the offense involved a financial transaction with a country supporting international terrorism;

or

(2) **14**, otherwise.

Commentary

Statutory Provisions: 18 U.S.C. § 2332d; 22 U.S.C. § 8512; 50 U.S.C. § 1705; 50 U.S.C. App. §§ 2401–2420.

Application Notes:

1. In the case of a violation during time of war or armed conflict, an upward departure may be warranted.

2. In determining the sentence within the applicable guideline range, the court may consider the degree to which the violation threatened a security interest of the United States, the volume of commerce involved, the extent of planning or sophistication, and whether there were multiple occurrences. Where such factors are present in an extreme form, a departure from the guidelines may be warranted. *See* Chapter Five, Part K (Departures).

3. In addition to the provisions for imprisonment, 50 U.S.C. App. § 2410 contains provisions for criminal fines and forfeiture as well as civil penalties. The maximum fine for individual defendants is $250,000. In the case of corporations, the maximum fine is five times

the value of the exports involved or $1 million, whichever is greater. When national security controls are violated, in addition to any other sanction, the defendant is subject to forfeiture of any interest in, security of, or claim against: any goods or tangible items that were the subject of the violation; property used to export or attempt to export that was the subject of the violation; and any proceeds obtained directly or indirectly as a result of the violation.

4. For purposes of subsection (a)(1)(B), "***a country supporting international terrorism***" means a country designated under section 6(j) of the Export Administration Act (50 U.S.C. App. 2405).

Historical Note

Effective November 1, 1987. Amended effective November 1, 2001 (amendment 633); November 1, 2002 (amendment 637); November 1, 2011 (amendment 753).

§2M5.2. Exportation of Arms, Munitions, or Military Equipment or Services Without Required Validated Export License

(a) Base Offense Level:

(1) **26**, except as provided in subdivision (2) below;

(2) **14**, if the offense involved only (A) non-fully automatic small arms (rifles, handguns, or shotguns), and the number of weapons did not exceed two, (B) ammunition for non-fully automatic small arms, and the number of rounds did not exceed 500, or (C) both.

Commentary

Statutory Provisions: 18 U.S.C. § 554; 22 U.S.C. §§ 2778, 2780, 8512; 50 U.S.C. § 1705.

Application Notes:

1. Under 22 U.S.C. § 2778, the President is authorized, through a licensing system administered by the Department of State, to control exports of defense articles and defense services that he deems critical to a security or foreign policy interest of the United States. The items subject to control constitute the United States Munitions List, which is set out in 22 C.F.R. Part 121.1. Included in this list are such things as military aircraft, helicopters, artillery, shells, missiles, rockets, bombs, vessels of war, explosives, military and space electronics, and certain firearms.

The base offense level assumes that the offense conduct was harmful or had the potential to be harmful to a security or foreign policy interest of the United States. In the unusual case where the offense conduct posed no such risk, a downward departure may be warranted. In the case of a violation during time of war or armed conflict, an upward departure may be warranted. *See* Chapter Five, Part K (Departures).

2. In determining the sentence within the applicable guideline range, the court may consider the degree to which the violation threatened a security or foreign policy interest of the United States, the volume of commerce involved, the extent of planning or sophistication, and whether there were multiple occurrences. Where such factors are present in an extreme form, a departure from the guidelines may be warranted.

Historical Note

Effective November 1, 1987. Amended effective November 1, 1990 (amendment 337); November 1, 2001 (amendment 633); November 1, 2007 (amendment 700); November 1, 2011 (amendment 753).

§2M5.3. Providing Material Support or Resources to Designated Foreign Terrorist Organizations or Specially Designated Global Terrorists, or For a Terrorist Purpose

(a) Base Offense Level: **26**

(b) Specific Offense Characteristic
(1) If the offense involved the provision of (A) dangerous weapons; (B) firearms; (C) explosives; (D) funds with the intent, knowledge, or reason to believe such funds would be used to purchase any of the items described in subdivisions (A) through (C); or (E) funds or other material support or resources with the intent, knowledge, or reason to believe they are to be used to commit or assist in the commission of a violent act, increase by **2** levels.
(c) Cross References
(1) If the offense resulted in death, apply §2A1.1 (First Degree Murder) if the death was caused intentionally or knowingly, or §2A1.2 (Second Degree Murder) otherwise, if the resulting offense level is greater than that determined above.
(2) If the offense was tantamount to attempted murder, apply §2A2.1 (Assault with Intent to Commit Murder; Attempted Murder), if the resulting offense level is greater than that determined above.
(3) If the offense involved the provision of (A) a nuclear weapon, nuclear material, or nuclear byproduct material; (B) a chemical weapon; (C) a biological agent, toxin, or delivery system; or (D) a weapon of mass destruction, apply §2M6.1 (Nuclear, Biological, and Chemical Weapons, and Other Weapons of Mass Destruction), if the resulting offense level is greater than that determined above.

Commentary

Statutory Provisions: 18 U.S.C. §§ 2283, 2284, 2339B, 2339C(a)(1)(B), (c)(2)(B) (but only with respect to funds known or intended to have been provided or collected in violation of 18 U.S.C. § 2339C(a)(1)(B)); 22 U.S.C. § 8512; 50 U.S.C. § 1705.

Application Notes:

1. **Definitions.**—For purposes of this guideline:

"***Biological agent***", "***chemical weapon***", "***nuclear byproduct material***", "***nuclear material***", "***toxin***", and "***weapon of mass destruction***" have the meaning given those terms in Application Note 1 of the Commentary to §2M6.1 (Nuclear, Biological, and Chemical Weapons, and Other Weapons of Mass Destruction).

"***Dangerous weapon***", "***firearm***", and "***destructive device***" have the meaning given those terms in Application Note 1 of the Commentary to §1B1.1 (Application Instructions).

"***Explosives***" has the meaning given that term in Application Note 1 of the Commentary to §2K1.4 (Arson; Property Damage by Use of Explosives).

"***Foreign terrorist organization***" has the meaning given the term "terrorist organization" in 18 U.S.C. § 2339B(g)(6).

"***Material support or resources***" has the meaning given that term in 18 U.S.C. § 2339B(g)(4).

"***Specially designated global terrorist***" has the meaning given that term in 31 C.F.R. § 594.513.

2. **Departure Provisions.**—

(A) **In General.**—In determining the sentence within the applicable guideline range, the court may consider the degree to which the violation threatened a security interest of the United States, the volume of the funds or other material support or resources involved, the extent of planning or sophistication, and whether there were multiple occurrences. In a case in which such factors are present in an extreme form, a departure from the guidelines may be warranted. *See* Chapter Five, Part K (Departures).

(B) **War or Armed Conflict.**—In the case of a violation during time of war or armed conflict, an upward departure may be warranted.

Historical Note

Effective November 1, 2002 (amendment 637). Amended effective November 1, 2003 (amendment 655); November 1, 2007 (amendment 700); November 1, 2011 (amendment 753).

* * * * *

6. NUCLEAR, BIOLOGICAL, AND CHEMICAL WEAPONS AND MATERIALS, AND OTHER WEAPONS OF MASS DESTRUCTION

Historical Note

Effective November 1, 1987. Amended effective November 1, 2001 (amendment 633).

§2M6.1. Unlawful Activity Involving Nuclear Material, Weapons, or Facilities, Biological Agents, Toxins, or Delivery Systems, Chemical Weapons, or Other Weapons of Mass Destruction; Attempt or Conspiracy

(a) Base Offense Level (Apply the Greatest):

(1) **42**, if the offense was committed with intent (A) to injure the United States; or (B) to aid a foreign nation or a foreign terrorist organization;

(2) **28**, if subsections (a)(1), (a)(3), and (a)(4) do not apply;

(3) **22**, if the defendant is convicted under 18 U.S.C. § 175b; or

(4) **20**, if (A) the defendant is convicted under 18 U.S.C. § 175(b); or (B) the offense (i) involved a threat to use a nuclear weapon, nuclear material, or nuclear byproduct material, a chemical weapon, a biological agent, toxin, or delivery system, or a weapon of mass destruction; but (ii) did not involve any conduct evidencing an intent or ability to carry out the threat.

(b) Specific Offense Characteristics

(1) If (A) subsection (a)(2) or (a)(4)(A) applies; and (B) the offense involved a threat to use, or otherwise involved (i) a select biological agent; (ii) a listed precursor or a listed toxic chemical; (iii) nuclear material or nuclear byproduct material; or (iv) a weapon of mass destruction that contains any agent, precursor, toxic chemical, or material referred to in subdivision (i), (ii), or (iii), increase by **2** levels.

(2) If (A) subsection (a)(2), (a)(3), or (a)(4)(A) applies; and (B)(i) any victim died or sustained permanent or life-threatening bodily injury, increase by **4** levels; (ii) any victim sustained serious bodily injury, increase by **2** levels; or (iii) the degree of injury is between that specified in subdivisions (i) and (ii), increase by **3** levels.

(3) If (A) subsection (a)(2), (a)(3), or (a)(4) applies; and (B) the offense resulted in (i) substantial disruption of public, governmental,

or business functions or services; or (ii) a substantial expenditure of funds to clean up, decontaminate, or otherwise respond to the offense, increase by **4** levels.

(c) Cross References

(1) If the offense resulted in death, apply §2A1.1 (First Degree Murder) if the death was caused intentionally or knowingly, or §2A1.2 (Second Degree Murder) otherwise, if the resulting offense level is greater than that determined above.

(2) If the offense was tantamount to attempted murder, apply §2A2.1 (Assault with Intent to Commit Murder; Attempted Murder), if the resulting offense level is greater than that determined above.

(d) Special Instruction

(1) If the defendant is convicted of a single count involving (A) conduct that resulted in the death or permanent, life-threatening, or serious bodily injury of more than one victim, or (B) conduct tantamount to the attempted murder of more than one victim, Chapter Three, Part D (Multiple Counts) shall be applied as if such conduct in respect to each victim had been contained in a separate count of conviction.

Commentary

Statutory Provisions: 18 U.S.C. §§ 175, 175b, 175c, 229, 831, 832, 842(p)(2) (only with respect to weapons of mass destruction as defined in 18 U.S.C. § 2332a(c)(2)(B), (C), and (D)), 1992(a)(2), (a)(3), (a)(4), (b)(2), 2283, 2291, 2332h; 42 U.S.C. §§ 2077(b), 2122, 2131. For additional statutory provision(s), *see* Appendix A (Statutory Index).

Application Notes:

1. **Definitions.**—For purposes of this guideline:

"***Biological agent***" has the meaning given that term in 18 U.S.C. § 178(1).

"***Chemical weapon***" has the meaning given that term in 18 U.S.C. § 229F(1).

"***Foreign terrorist organization***" (A) means an organization that engages in terrorist activity that threatens the security of a national of the United States or the national security of the United States; and (B) includes an organization designated by the Secretary of State as a foreign terrorist organization pursuant to section 219 of the Immigration and Nationality Act (8 U.S.C. § 1189). "National of the United States" has the meaning given that term in section 101(a)(22) of the Immigration and Nationality Act (8 U.S.C. § 1101(a)(22)).

"***Listed precursor or a listed toxic chemical***" means a precursor or a toxic chemical, respectively, listed in Schedule I of the Annex on Chemicals to the Chemical Weapons Convention. *See* 18 U.S.C. § 229F(6)(B), (8)(B). "Precursor" has the meaning given that term in 18 U.S.C. § 229F(6)(A). "Toxic chemical" has the meaning given that term in 18 U.S.C. § 229F(8)(A).

"***Nuclear byproduct material***" has the meaning given that term in 18 U.S.C. § 831(g)(2).

"***Nuclear material***" has the meaning given that term in 18 U.S.C. § 831(g)(1).

"***Restricted person***" has the meaning given that term in 18 U.S.C. § 175b(d)(2).

"***Select biological agent***" means a biological agent or toxin identified (A) by the Secretary of Health and Human Services on the select agent list established and maintained pursuant to section 351A of the Public Health Service Act (42 U.S.C. § 262a); or (B) by the Secretary of Agriculture on the list established and maintained pursuant to section 212 of the Agricultural Bioterrorism Protection Act of 2002 (7 U.S.C. § 8401).

"***Toxin***" has the meaning given that term in 18 U.S.C. § 178(2).
"***Vector***" has the meaning given that term in 18 U.S.C. § 178(4).
"***Weapon of mass destruction***" has the meaning given that term in 18 U.S.C. § 2332a(c)(2)(B), (C), and (D).

2. **Threat Cases.**—Subsection (a)(4)(B) applies in cases that involved a threat to use a weapon, agent, or material covered by this guideline but that did not involve any conduct evidencing an intent or ability to carry out the threat. For example, subsection (a)(4)(B) would apply in a case in which the defendant threatened to contaminate an area with anthrax and also dispersed into the area a substance that appeared to be anthrax but that the defendant knew to be harmless talcum powder. In such a case, the dispersal of talcum powder does not evidence an intent on the defendant's part to carry out the threat. In contrast, subsection (a)(4)(B) would not apply in a case in which the defendant threatened to contaminate an area with anthrax and also dispersed into the area a substance that the defendant believed to be anthrax but that in fact was harmless talcum powder. In such a case, the dispersal of talcum powder was conduct evidencing an intent to carry out the threat because of the defendant's belief that the talcum powder was anthrax. Subsection (a)(4)(B) shall not apply in any case involving both a threat to use any weapon, agent, or material covered by this guideline and the possession of that weapon, agent, or material. In such a case, possession of the weapon, agent, or material is conduct evidencing an intent to use that weapon, agent, or material.

3. **Application of Special Instruction.**—Subsection (d) applies in any case in which the defendant is convicted of a single count involving (A) the death or permanent, life-threatening, or serious bodily injury of more than one victim, or (B) conduct tantamount to the attempted murder of more than one victim, regardless of whether the offense level is determined under this guideline or under another guideline in Chapter Two (Offense Conduct) by use of a cross reference under subsection (c).

Historical Note

Effective November 1, 1987. Amended effective November 1, 2001 (amendment 633); November 1, 2002 (amendment 637); November 1, 2003 (amendment 655); November 1, 2005 (amendment 679); November 1, 2006 (amendment 686); November 1, 2007 (amendments 699 and 700); November 1, 2010 (amendment 746); November 1, 2016 (amendment 804).

§2M6.2. Violation of Other Federal Atomic Energy Agency Statutes, Rules, and Regulations

(a) Base Offense Level (Apply the greater):

(1) **30**, if the offense was committed with intent to injure the United States or to aid a foreign nation; or

(2) **6**.

Commentary

Statutory Provision: 42 U.S.C. § 2273.

Background: This section applies to offenses related to nuclear energy not specifically addressed elsewhere. This provision covers, for example, violations of statutes dealing with rules and regulations, license conditions, and orders of the Nuclear Regulatory Commission and the Department of Energy.

Historical Note

Effective November 1, 1987. Amended effective November 1, 1990 (amendment 359).

PART N — OFFENSES INVOLVING FOOD, DRUGS, AGRICULTURAL PRODUCTS, CONSUMER PRODUCTS, AND ODOMETER LAWS

Historical

Note
Effective November 1, 1987. Amended effective November 1, 2009 (amendment 733).

1. TAMPERING WITH CONSUMER PRODUCTS

§2N1.1. Tampering or Attempting to Tamper Involving Risk of Death or Bodily Injury

(a) Base Offense Level: **25**
(b) Specific Offense Characteristic
(1) (A) If any victim sustained permanent or life-threatening bodily injury, increase by **4** levels; (B) if any victim sustained serious bodily injury, increase by **2** levels; or (C) if the degree of injury is between that specified in subdivisions (A) and (B), increase by **3** levels.
(c) Cross References
(1) If the offense resulted in death, apply §2A1.1 (First Degree Murder) if the death was caused intentionally or knowingly, or §2A1.2 (Second Degree Murder) in any other case.
(2) If the offense was tantamount to attempted murder, apply §2A2.1 (Assault with Intent to Commit Murder; Attempted Murder) if the resulting offense level is greater than that determined above.
(3) If the offense involved extortion, apply §2B3.2 (Extortion by Force or Threat of Injury or Serious Damage) if the resulting offense level is greater than that determined above.
(d) Special Instruction
(1) If the defendant is convicted of a single count involving (A) the death or permanent, life-threatening, or serious bodily injury of more than one victim, or (B) conduct tantamount to the attempted murder of more than one victim, Chapter Three,

Part D (Multiple Counts) shall be applied as if the defendant had been convicted of a separate count for each such victim.

Commentary

Statutory Provisions: 18 U.S.C. § 1365(a), (e).

Application Notes:

1. The base offense level reflects that this offense typically poses a risk of death or serious bodily injury to one or more victims; or causes, or is intended to cause, bodily injury. Where the offense posed a substantial risk of death or serious bodily injury to numerous victims, or caused extreme psychological injury or substantial property damage or monetary loss, an upward departure may be warranted. In the unusual case in which the offense did not cause a risk of death or serious bodily injury, and neither caused nor was intended to cause bodily injury, a downward departure may be warranted.
2. The special instruction in subsection (d)(1) applies whether the offense level is determined under subsection (b)(1) or by use of a cross reference in subsection (c).

Historical
Note
Effective November 1, 1987. Amended effective November 1, 1990 (amendment 338); November 1, 1991 (amendment 376).

§2N1.2. Providing False Information or Threatening to Tamper with Consumer Products

(a) Base Offense Level: **16**
(b) Cross Reference

(1) If the offense involved extortion, apply §2B3.2 (Extortion by Force or Threat of Injury or Serious Damage).

Commentary

Statutory Provisions: 18 U.S.C. § 1365(c), (d).

Application Note:

1. If death or bodily injury, extreme psychological injury, or substantial property damage or monetary loss resulted, an upward departure may be warranted. *See* Chapter Five, Part K (Departures).

Historical Note

Effective November 1, 1987. Amended effective November 1, 1990 (amendment 339).

§2N1.3. Tampering With Intent to Injure Business

(a) Base Offense Level: **12**

Commentary

Statutory Provision: 18 U.S.C. § 1365(b).

Application Note:

1. If death or bodily injury, extreme psychological injury, or substantial property damage or monetary loss resulted, an upward departure may be warranted. *See* Chapter Five, Part K (Departures).

Historical Note

Effective November 1, 1987.

* * * * *

2. FOOD, DRUGS, AGRICULTURAL PRODUCTS, AND CONSUMER PRODUCTS

Historical Note

Effective November 1, 1987. Amended effective November 1, 2009 (amendment 733).

§2N2.1. Violations of Statutes and Regulations Dealing With Any Food, Drug, Biological Product, Device, Cosmetic, Agricultural Product, or Consumer Product

(a) Base Offense Level: **6**

(b) Specific Offense Characteristic

(1) If the defendant was convicted under 21 U.S.C. § 331 after sustaining a prior conviction under 21 U.S.C. § 331, increase by **4** levels.

(c) Cross References

(1) If the offense involved fraud, apply §2B1.1 (Theft, Property Destruction, and Fraud).

(2) If the offense was committed in furtherance of, or to conceal, an offense covered by another offense guideline, apply that other offense guideline if the resulting offense level is greater than that determined above.

Commentary

Statutory Provisions: 7 U.S.C. §§ 150bb, 150gg, 6810, 7734, 8313; 21 U.S.C. §§ 115, 117, 122, 134–134e, 151–158, 331, 333(a)(1), (a)(2), (b), 458–461, 463, 466, 610, 611, 614, 617, 619, 620, 642–644, 676; 42 U.S.C. § 262. For additional statutory provision(s), *see* Appendix A (Statutory Index).

Application Notes:

1. This guideline assumes a regulatory offense that involved knowing or reckless conduct. Where only negligence was involved, a downward departure may be warranted.

See Chapter Five, Part K (Departures).

2. The cross reference at subsection (c)(1) addresses cases in which the offense involved fraud. The cross reference at subsection (c)(2) addresses cases in which the offense was committed in furtherance of, or to conceal, an offense covered by another offense guideline (*e.g.*, bribery).

3. **Upward Departure Provisions.**—The following are circumstances in which an upward departure may be warranted:

(A) The offense created a substantial risk of bodily injury or death; or bodily injury, death, extreme psychological injury, property damage, or monetary loss resulted from the offense. *See* Chapter Five, Part K (Departures).

(B) The defendant was convicted under 7 U.S.C. § 7734.

4. The Commission has not promulgated a guideline for violations of 21 U.S.C. § 333(e) (offenses involving human growth hormones). Offenses involving anabolic steroids are covered by Chapter Two, Part D (Offenses Involving Drugs and Narco-Terrorism). In the case of an offense involving a substance purported to be an anabolic steroid, but not containing any active ingredient, apply §2B1.1 (Theft, Property Destruction, and Fraud) with "loss" measured by the amount paid, or to be paid, by the victim for such substance.

Historical Note

Effective November 1, 1987. Amended effective November 1, 1990 (amendment 340); November 1, 1991 (amendment 432); November 1, 1992 (amendment 451); November 1, 2001 (amendment 617); November 1, 2002 (amendment 646); November 1, 2003 (amendment 661); November 1, 2006 (amendment 685); November 1, 2007 (amendment 711); November 1, 2008 (amendment 723); November 1, 2009 (amendment 733).

* * * * *

3. ODOMETER LAWS AND REGULATIONS

§2N3.1. Odometer Laws and Regulations

(a) Base Offense Level: **6**

(b) Cross Reference

(1) If the offense involved more than one vehicle, apply §2B1.1 (Theft, Property Destruction, and Fraud).

Commentary

Statutory Provisions: 49 U.S.C. §§ 32703–32705, 32709(b).

Background: The base offense level takes into account the deceptive aspect of the offense assuming a single vehicle was involved. If more than one vehicle was involved, §2B1.1 (Theft, Property Destruction, and Fraud) is to be applied because it is designed to deal with a pattern or scheme.

Historical Note

Effective November 1, 1987. Amended effective November 1, 1989 (amendment 199); November 1, 1997 (amendment 553); November 1, 2001 (amendment 617).

PART O — [NOT USED]

PART P — OFFENSES INVOLVING PRISONS AND CORRECTIONAL FACILITIES

§2P1.1. Escape, Instigating or Assisting Escape

(a) Base Offense Level:

(1) **13**, if the custody or confinement is by virtue of an arrest on a charge of felony, or conviction of any offense;

(2) **8**, otherwise.

(b) Specific Offense Characteristics

(1) If the use or the threat of force against any person was involved,

increase by **5** levels.

(2) If the defendant escaped from non-secure custody and returned voluntarily within ninety-six hours, decrease the offense level under §2P1.1(a)(1) by **7** levels or the offense level under §2P1.1(a)(2) by **4** levels. *Provided*, however, that this reduction shall not apply if the defendant, while away from the facility, committed any federal, state, or local offense punishable by a term of imprisonment of one year or more.

(3) If the defendant escaped from the non-secure custody of a community corrections center, community treatment center, "halfway house," or similar facility, and subsection (b)(2) is not applicable, decrease the offense level under subsection (a)(1) by **4** levels or the offense level under subsection (a)(2) by **2** levels. *Provided*, however, that this reduction shall not apply if the defendant, while away from the facility, committed any federal, state, or local offense punishable by a term of imprisonment of one year or more.

(4) If the defendant was a law enforcement or correctional officer or employee, or an employee of the Department of Justice, at the time of the offense, increase by **2** levels.

Commentary

Statutory Provisions: 18 U.S.C. §§ 751, 752, 755; 28 U.S.C. § 1826. For additional statutory provision(s), *see* Appendix A (Statutory Index).

Application Notes:

1. "***Non-secure custody***" means custody with no significant physical restraint (*e.g.*, where a defendant walked away from a work detail outside the security perimeter of an institution; where a defendant failed to return to any institution from a pass or unescorted furlough; or where a defendant escaped from an institution with no physical perimeter barrier).
2. "***Returned voluntarily***" includes voluntarily returning to the institution or turning one's self in to a law enforcement authority as an escapee (not in connection with an arrest or other charges).
3. If the adjustment in subsection (b)(4) applies, no adjustment is to be made under §3B1.3 (Abuse of Position of Trust or Use of Special Skill).
4. If death or bodily injury resulted, an upward departure may be warranted. *See* Chapter Five, Part K (Departures).
5. Criminal history points under Chapter Four, Part A (Criminal History) are to be determined independently of the application of this guideline. For example, in the case of a defendant serving a one-year sentence of imprisonment at the time of the escape, criminal history points from §4A1.1(b) (for the sentence being served at the time of the escape) and §4A1.1(d) (custody status) would be applicable.
6. If the adjustment in subsection (b)(1) applies as a result of conduct that involves an official victim, do not apply §3A1.2 (Official Victim).

Historical Note

Effective November 1, 1987. Amended effective November 1, 1989 (amendments 200 and 201); November 1, 1990 (amendment 341); November 1, 1991 (amendment 406); November 1, 2010 (amendment 747).

§2P1.2. Providing or Possessing Contraband in Prison

(a) Base Offense Level:

(1) **23**, if the object was a firearm or destructive device.

(2) **13**, if the object was a weapon (other than a firearm or a destructive

device), any object that might be used as a weapon or
as a means of facilitating escape, ammunition, LSD, PCP, methamphetamine, or a narcotic drug.

(3) **6**, if the object was an alcoholic beverage, United States or foreign currency, a mobile phone or similar device, or a controlled substance (other than LSD, PCP, methamphetamine, or a narcotic drug).

(4) **4**, if the object was any other object that threatened the order, discipline, or security of the institution or the life, health, or safety of an individual.

(b) Specific Offense Characteristic

(1) If the defendant was a law enforcement or correctional officer or employee, or an employee of the Department of Justice, at the time of the offense, increase by **2** levels.

(c) Cross Reference

(1) If the object of the offense was the distribution of a controlled substance, apply the offense level from §2D1.1 (Unlawful Manufacturing, Importing, Exporting, or Trafficking; Attempt or Conspiracy). *Provided*, that if the defendant is convicted under 18 U.S.C. § 1791(a)(1) and is punishable under 18 U.S.C. § 1791(b)(1), and the resulting offense level is less than level **26**, increase to level **26**.

Commentary

Statutory Provision: 18 U.S.C. § 1791.

Application Notes:

1. In this guideline, the term "***mobile phone or similar device***" means a phone or other device as described in 18 U.S.C. § 1791(d)(1)(F).

2. If the adjustment in §2P1.2(b)(1) applies, no adjustment is to be made under §3B1.3 (Abuse of Position of Trust or Use of Special Skill).

3. In a case in which the defendant is convicted of the underlying offense and an offense involving providing or possessing a controlled substance in prison, group the offenses together under §3D1.2(c). (Note that 18 U.S.C. § 1791(b) does not require a sentence of imprisonment, although if a sentence of imprisonment is imposed on a count involving providing or possessing a controlled substance in prison, section 1791(c) requires that the sentence be imposed to run consecutively to any other sentence of imprisonment for the controlled substance. Therefore, unlike a count in which the statute mandates both a minimum and a consecutive sentence of imprisonment, the grouping rules of §§3D1.1–3D1.5 apply. *See* §3D1.1(b)(1), comment. (n.1), and §3D1.2, comment. (n.1).) The combined sentence will then be constructed to provide a "total punishment" that satisfies the requirements both of §5G1.2 (Sentencing on Multiple Counts of Conviction) and 18 U.S.C. § 1791(c). For example, if the combined applicable guideline range for both counts is 30–37 months and the court determines a "total punishment" of 36 months is appropriate, a sentence of 30 months for the underlying offense plus a consecutive six months' sentence for the providing or possessing a controlled substance in prison count would satisfy these requirements.

Pursuant to 18 U.S.C. § 1791(c), a sentence imposed upon an inmate for a violation of 18 U.S.C. § 1791 shall be consecutive to the sentence being served by the inmate at the time of the violation.

Historical
Note
Effective November 1, 1987. Amended effective November 1, 1989 (amendments 202 and 203); November 1, 1995 (amendment 525); November 1, 1998 (amendment 579); November 1, 2005 (amendment 680); November 1, 2012 (amendment 769).

§2P1.3. Engaging In, Inciting or Attempting to Incite a Riot Involving Persons in a Facility for Official Detention

(a) Base Offense Level:

(1) **22**, if the offense was committed under circumstances creating a substantial risk of death or serious bodily injury to any person.

(2) **16**, if the offense involved a major disruption to the operation of an institution.

(3) **10**, otherwise.

Commentary

Statutory Provision: 18 U.S.C. § 1792.

Application Note:

1. If death or bodily injury resulted, an upward departure may be warranted. *See* Chapter Five, Part K (Departures).

Historical
Note
Effective November 1, 1987.

§2P1.4. [Deleted]

Historical
Note
Section 2P1.4 (Trespass on Bureau of Prisons Facilities), effective November 1, 1987, was deleted effective November 1, 1989 (amendment 204).

PART Q — OFFENSES INVOLVING THE ENVIRONMENT

1. ENVIRONMENT

§2Q1.1. Knowing Endangerment Resulting From Mishandling Hazardous or Toxic Substances, Pesticides or Other Pollutants

(a) Base Offense Level: **24**

Commentary

Statutory Provisions: 18 U.S.C. § 1992(b)(3); 33 U.S.C. § 1319(c)(3); 42 U.S.C. § 6928(e).

Application Note:

1. If death or serious bodily injury resulted, an upward departure may be warranted. *See* Chapter Five, Part K (Departures).

Background: This section applies to offenses committed with knowledge that the violation placed another person in imminent danger of death or serious bodily injury.

Historical
Note
Effective November 1, 1987. Amended effective November 1, 2007 (amendment 699).

§2Q1.2. Mishandling of Hazardous or Toxic Substances or Pesticides; Recordkeeping, Tampering, and Falsification; Unlawfully Transporting Hazardous Materials in Commerce

(a) Base Offense Level: **8**

(b) Specific Offense Characteristics

(1) (A) If the offense resulted in an ongoing, continuous, or repetitive discharge, release, or emission of a hazardous or toxic substance or pesticide into the environment, increase by **6** levels; or

(B) if the offense otherwise involved a discharge, release, or emission of a hazardous or toxic substance or pesticide, increase

by **4** levels.
(2) If the offense resulted in a substantial likelihood of death or serious bodily injury, increase by **9** levels.

(3) If the offense resulted in disruption of public utilities or evacuation of a community, or if cleanup required a substantial expenditure, increase by **4** levels.
(4) If the offense involved transportation, treatment, storage, or disposal without a permit or in violation of a permit, increase by **4** levels.
(5) If a recordkeeping offense reflected an effort to conceal a substantive environmental offense, use the offense level for the substantive offense.
(6) If the offense involved a simple recordkeeping or reporting violation only, decrease by **2** levels.
(7) If the defendant was convicted under 49 U.S.C. § 5124 or § 46312, increase by **2** levels.

Commentary

Statutory Provisions: 7 U.S.C. §§ 136j–136l; 15 U.S.C. §§ 2614 and 2615; 33 U.S.C. §§ 1319(c)(1), (2), 1321(b)(5), 1517(b); 42 U.S.C. §§ 300h-2, 6928(d), 7413, 9603(b), (c), (d); 43 U.S.C. §§ 1350, 1816(a), 1822(b); 49 U.S.C. §§ 5124, 46312. For additional statutory provision(s), *see* Appendix A (Statutory Index).

Application Notes:

1. "***Recordkeeping offense***" includes both recordkeeping and reporting offenses. The term is to be broadly construed as including failure to report discharges, releases, or emissions where required; the giving of false information; failure to file other required reports or provide necessary information; and failure to prepare, maintain, or provide records as prescribed.
2. "***Simple recordkeeping or reporting violation***" means a recordkeeping or reporting offense in a situation where the defendant neither knew nor had reason to believe that the recordkeeping offense would significantly increase the likelihood of any substantive environmental harm.
3. This section applies to offenses involving pesticides or substances designated toxic or hazardous at the time of the offense by statute or regulation. A listing of hazardous and toxic substances in the guidelines would be impractical. Several federal statutes (or regulations promulgated thereunder) list toxics, hazardous wastes and substances, and pesticides. These lists, such as those of toxic pollutants for which effluent standards are published under the Federal Water Pollution Control Act (*e.g.*, 33 U.S.C. § 1317) as well as the designation of hazardous substances under the Comprehensive Environmental Response, Compensation and Liability Act (*e.g.*, 42 U.S.C. § 9601(14)), are revised from time to time. "Toxic" and "hazardous" are defined differently in various statutes, but the common dictionary meanings of the words are not significantly different.

4. Except when the adjustment in subsection (b)(6) for simple recordkeeping offenses applies, this section assumes knowing conduct. In cases involving negligent conduct, a downward departure may be warranted.
5. Subsection (b)(1) assumes a discharge or emission into the environment resulting in actual environmental contamination. A wide range of conduct, involving the handling of different quantities of materials with widely differing propensities, potentially is covered. Depending upon the harm resulting from the emission, release or discharge, the quantity

and nature of the substance or pollutant, the duration of the offense and the risk associated with the violation, a departure of up to two levels in either direction from the offense levels prescribed in these specific offense characteristics may be appropriate.

6. Subsection (b)(2) applies to offenses where the public health is seriously endangered. Depending upon the nature of the risk created and the number of people placed at risk, a departure of up to three levels upward or downward may be warranted. If death or serious bodily injury results, a departure would be called for. *See* Chapter Five, Part K (Departures).

7. Subsection (b)(3) provides an enhancement where a public disruption, evacuation or cleanup at substantial expense has been required. Depending upon the nature of the contamination involved, a departure of up to two levels either upward or downward could be warranted.

8. Subsection (b)(4) applies where the offense involved violation of a permit, or where there was a failure to obtain a permit when one was required. Depending upon the nature and quantity of the substance involved and the risk associated with the offense, a departure of up to two levels either upward or downward may be warranted.

9. **Other Upward Departure Provisions.—**

(A) **Civil Adjudications and Failure to Comply with Administrative Order.**—In a case in which the defendant has previously engaged in similar misconduct established by a civil adjudication or has failed to comply with an administrative order, an upward departure may be warranted. *See* §4A1.3 (Departures Based on Inadequacy of Criminal History Category).

(B) **Extreme Psychological Injury.**—If the offense caused extreme psychological injury, an upward departure may be warranted. *See* §5K2.3 (Extreme Psychological Injury).

(C) **Terrorism.**—If the offense was calculated to influence or affect the conduct of government by intimidation or coercion, or to retaliate against government conduct, an upward departure would be warranted. *See* Application Note 4 of the Commentary to §3A1.4 (Terrorism).

Background: This section applies both to substantive violations of the statute governing the handling of pesticides and toxic and hazardous substances and to recordkeeping offenses. The first four specific offense characteristics provide enhancements when the offense involved a substantive violation. The fifth and sixth specific offense characteristics apply to recordkeeping offenses. Although other sections of the guidelines generally prescribe a base offense level of 6 for regulatory violations, §2Q1.2 prescribes a base offense level of 8 because of the inherently dangerous nature of hazardous and toxic substances and pesticides. A decrease of 2 levels is provided, however, for "simple recordkeeping or reporting violations" under §2Q1.2(b)(6).

Historical Note

Effective November 1, 1987. Amended effective November 1, 1993 (amendment 481); November 1, 1997 (amendment 553); November 1, 2004 (amendment 672); November 1, 2010 (amendment 746).

§2Q1.3. Mishandling of Other Environmental Pollutants; Recordkeeping, Tampering, and Falsification

(a) Base Offense Level: **6**

(b) Specific Offense Characteristics

(1) (A) If the offense resulted in an ongoing, continuous, or repetitive discharge, release, or emission of a pollutant into the environment, increase by **6** levels; or

(B) if the offense otherwise involved a discharge, release, or emission of a pollutant, increase by **4** levels.

(2) If the offense resulted in a substantial likelihood of death or serious bodily injury, increase by **11** levels.

(3) If the offense resulted in disruption of public utilities or evacuation

of a community, or if cleanup required a substantial expenditure, increase by **4** levels.

(4) If the offense involved a discharge without a permit or in violation of a permit, increase by **4** levels.

(5) If a recordkeeping offense reflected an effort to conceal a substantive environmental offense, use the offense level for the substantive offense.

Commentary

Statutory Provisions: 33 U.S.C. §§ 403, 406, 407, 411, 1319(c)(1), (c)(2), 1415(b), 1907, 1908; 42 U.S.C. § 7413. For additional statutory provision(s), *see* Appendix A (Statutory Index).

Application Notes:

1. "***Recordkeeping offense***" includes both recordkeeping and reporting offenses. The term is to be broadly construed as including failure to report discharges, releases, or emissions where required; the giving of false information; failure to file other required reports or provide necessary information; and failure to prepare, maintain, or provide records as prescribed.

2. If the offense involved mishandling of nuclear material, apply §2M6.2 (Violation of Other Federal Atomic Energy Agency Statutes, Rules, and Regulations) rather than this guideline.

3. The specific offense characteristics in this section assume knowing conduct. In cases involving negligent conduct, a downward departure may be warranted.

4. Subsection (b)(1) assumes a discharge or emission into the environment resulting in actual environmental contamination. A wide range of conduct, involving the handling of different quantities of materials with widely differing propensities, potentially is covered. Depending upon the harm resulting from the emission, release or discharge, the quantity and nature of the substance or pollutant, the duration of the offense and the risk associated with the violation, a departure of up to two levels in either direction from that prescribed in these specific offense characteristics may be appropriate.

5. Subsection (b)(2) applies to offenses where the public health is seriously endangered. Depending upon the nature of the risk created and the number of people placed at risk, a departure of up to three levels upward or downward may be warranted. If death or serious bodily injury results, a departure would be called for. *See* Chapter Five, Part K (Departures).

6. Subsection (b)(3) provides an enhancement where a public disruption, evacuation or cleanup at substantial expense has been required. Depending upon the nature of the contamination involved, a departure of up to two levels in either direction could be warranted.

7. Subsection (b)(4) applies where the offense involved violation of a permit, or where there was a failure to obtain a permit when one was required. Depending upon the nature and quantity of the substance involved and the risk associated with the offense, a departure of up to two levels in either direction may be warranted.

8. Where a defendant has previously engaged in similar misconduct established by a civil adjudication or has failed to comply with an administrative order, an upward departure may be warranted. *See* §4A1.3 (Adequacy of Criminal History Category).

Background: This section parallels §2Q1.2 but applies to offenses involving substances which are not pesticides and are not designated as hazardous or toxic.

Historical Note

Effective November 1, 1987. Amended effective November 1, 1989 (amendment 205).

§2Q1.4. Tampering or Attempted Tampering with a Public Water System; Threatening to Tamper with a Public Water System

(a) Base Offense Level (Apply the greatest):

(1) **26**;

(2) **22**, if the offense involved (A) a threat to tamper with a public water system; and (B) any conduct evidencing an intent to

carry out the threat; or

§2Q1.4

(3) **16**, if the offense involved a threat to tamper with a public water system but did not involve any conduct evidencing an intent to carry out the threat.

(b) Specific Offense Characteristics

(1) If (A) any victim sustained permanent or life-threatening bodily injury, increase by **4** levels; (B) any victim sustained serious bodily injury, increase by **2** levels; or (C) the degree of injury is between that specified in subdivisions (A) and (B), increase by **3** levels.

(2) If the offense resulted in (A) a substantial disruption of public, governmental, or business functions or services; or (B) a substantial expenditure of funds to clean up, decontaminate, or otherwise respond to the offense, increase by **4** levels.

(3) If the offense resulted in an ongoing, continuous, or repetitive release of a contaminant into a public water system or lasted for a substantial period of time, increase by **2** levels.

(c) Cross References

(1) If the offense resulted in death, apply §2A1.1 (First Degree Murder) if the death was caused intentionally or knowingly, or §2A1.2 (Second Degree Murder) in any other case, if the resulting offense level is greater than that determined above.

(2) If the offense was tantamount to attempted murder, apply §2A2.1 (Assault with Intent to Commit Murder; Attempted Murder) if the resulting offense level is greater than that determined above.

(3) If the offense involved extortion, apply §2B3.2 (Extortion by Force or Threat of Injury or Serious Damage) if the resulting offense level is greater than that determined above.

(d) Special Instruction

(1) If the defendant is convicted of a single count involving (A) the death or permanent, life-threatening, or serious bodily injury of more than one victim; or (B) conduct tantamount to the attempted murder of more than one victim, Chapter Three, Part D (Multiple Counts) shall be applied as if the defendant had been convicted of a separate count for each such victim.

§2Q1.5

Commentary

Statutory Provision: 42 U.S.C. § 300i-1.

Application Notes:

1. **Definitions.**—For purposes of this guideline, "***permanent or life-threatening bodily injury***" and "***serious bodily injury***" have the meaning given those terms in Note 1 of the Commentary to §1B1.1 (Application Instructions).

2. **Application of Special Instruction.**—Subsection (d) applies in any case in which the defendant is convicted of a single count involving (A) the death or permanent, life-threatening, or serious bodily injury of more than one victim; or (B) conduct tantamount to the

attempted murder of more than one victim, regardless of whether the offense level is determined under this guideline or under another guideline in Chapter Two (Offense Conduct) by use of a cross reference under subsection (c).

3. **Departure Provisions.—**

(A) **Downward Departure Provision.**—The base offense level in subsection (a)(1) reflects that offenses covered by that subsection typically pose a risk of death or serious bodily injury to one or more victims, or cause, or are intended to cause, bodily injury. In the unusual case in which such an offense did not cause a risk of death or serious bodily injury, and neither caused nor was intended to cause bodily injury, a downward departure may be warranted.

(B) **Upward Departure Provisions.**—If the offense caused extreme psychological injury, or caused substantial property damage or monetary loss, an upward departure may be warranted.

If the offense was calculated to influence or affect the conduct of government by intimidation or coercion, or to retaliate against government conduct, an upward departure would be warranted. *See* Application Note 4 of §3A1.4 (Terrorism).

Historical
Note
Effective November 1, 1987. Amended effective November 1, 1989 (amendment 206); November 1, 2003 (amendment 655).

§2Q1.5. [Deleted]

Historical
Note
Effective November 1, 1987. Amended effective November 1, 1989 (amendment 207), was deleted by consolidation with §2Q1.4 effective November 1, 2003 (amendment 655).

§2Q1.6. Hazardous or Injurious Devices on Federal Lands

(a) Base Offense Level (Apply the greatest):

(1) If the intent was to violate the Controlled Substances Act, apply §2D1.9 (Placing or Maintaining Dangerous Devices on Federal Property to Protect the Unlawful Production of Controlled Substances; Attempt or Conspiracy);

(2) If the intent was to obstruct the harvesting of timber, and property destruction resulted, apply §2B1.1 (Theft, Property Destruction, and Fraud);

(3) If the offense involved reckless disregard to the risk that another person would be placed in danger of death or serious bodily injury under circumstances manifesting extreme indifference to such risk, the offense level from §2A2.2 (Aggravated Assault); or

(4) **6**, otherwise.

Commentary

Statutory Provision: 18 U.S.C. § 1864.

Background: The statute covered by this guideline proscribes a wide variety of conduct, ranging from placing nails in trees to interfere with harvesting equipment to placing anti-personnel devices capable of causing death or serious bodily injury to protect the unlawful production of a controlled substance. Subsections (a)(1)–(a)(3) cover the more serious forms of this offense. Subsection (a)(4) provides a minimum offense level of 6 where the intent was to obstruct the harvesting of timber and little or no property damage resulted.

Historical
Note
Effective November 1, 1989 (amendment 208). Amended effective November 1, 1990 (amendment 313); November 1, 2001 (amendment 617); November 1, 2002 (amendment 646); November 1, 2010 (amendment 746).

* * * * *

2. CONSERVATION AND WILDLIFE

§2Q2.1. Offenses Involving Fish, Wildlife, and Plants

(a) Base Offense Level: **6**

(b) Specific Offense Characteristics

(1) If the offense (A) was committed for pecuniary gain or otherwise involved a commercial purpose; or (B) involved a pattern of similar violations, increase by **2** levels.

(2) If the offense (A) involved fish, wildlife, or plants that were not quarantined as required by law; or (B) otherwise created a significant risk of infestation or disease transmission potentially harmful to humans, fish, wildlife, or plants, increase by **2** levels.

(3) (If more than one applies, use the greater):

(A) If the market value of the fish, wildlife, or plants (i) exceeded $2,500 but did not exceed $6,500, increase by **1** level; or (ii) exceeded $6,500, increase by the number of levels from the table in §2B1.1 (Theft, Property Destruction, and Fraud) corresponding to that amount; or

(B) If the offense involved (i) marine mammals that are listed as depleted under the Marine Mammal Protection Act (as set forth in 50 C.F.R. § 216.15); (ii) fish, wildlife, or plants that are listed as endangered or threatened by the Endangered Species Act (as set forth in 50 C.F.R. Part 17); or (iii) fish, wildlife, or plants that are listed in Appendix I to the Convention on International Trade in Endangered Species of Wild Fauna or Flora (as set forth in 50 C.F.R. Part 23), increase by **4** levels.

(c) Cross Reference

(1) If the offense involved a cultural heritage resource or paleontological resource, apply §2B1.5 (Theft of, Damage to, or Destruction of, Cultural Heritage Resources or Paleontological Resources; Unlawful Sale, Purchase, Exchange, Transportation, or Receipt of Cultural Heritage Resources or Paleontological Resources), if the resulting offense level is greater than that determined above.

Commentary

Statutory Provisions: 16 U.S.C. §§ 668(a), 707(b), 1174(a), 1338(a), 1375(b), 1540(b), 3373(d); 18 U.S.C. §§ 545, 554. For additional statutory provision(s), *see* Appendix A (Statutory Index).

Application Notes:

1. "***For pecuniary gain***" means for receipt of, or in anticipation of receipt of, anything of value, whether monetary or in goods or services. Thus, offenses committed for pecuniary gain include both monetary and barter transactions. Similarly, activities designed to increase gross revenue are considered to be committed for pecuniary gain.

2. The acquisition of fish, wildlife, or plants for display to the public, whether for a fee or donation and whether by an individual or an organization, including a governmental entity,

a private non-profit organization, or a private for-profit organization, shall be considered to involve a "commercial purpose."

3. For purposes of subsection (b)(2), the quarantine requirements include those set forth in 9 C.F.R. Part 92, and 7 C.F.R., Subtitle B, Chapter III. State quarantine laws are included as well.

4. When information is reasonably available, "***market value***" under subsection (b)(3)(A) shall be based on the fair-market retail price. Where the fair-market retail price is difficult to ascertain, the court may make a reasonable estimate using any reliable information, such as the reasonable replacement or restitution cost or the acquisition and preservation (*e.g.*, taxidermy) cost. Market value, however, shall not be based on measurement of aesthetic loss (so called "contingent valuation" methods).

5. If the offense involved the destruction of a substantial quantity of fish, wildlife, or plants, and the seriousness of the offense is not adequately measured by the market value, an upward departure may be warranted.

6. For purposes of subsection (c)(1), "***cultural heritage resource***" has the meaning given that term in Application Note 1 of the Commentary to §2B1.5 (Theft of, Damage to, or Destruction of, Cultural Heritage Resources; Unlawful Sale, Purchase, Exchange, Transportation, or Receipt of Cultural Heritage Resources).

Background: This section applies to violations of the Endangered Species Act, the Bald Eagle Protection Act, the Migratory Bird Treaty, the Marine Mammal Protection Act, the Wild Free-Roaming Horses and Burros Act, the Fur Seal Act, the Lacey Act, and to violations of 18 U.S.C. §§ 545 and 554 if the smuggling activity involved fish, wildlife, or plants.

Historical Note

Effective November 1, 1987. Amended effective January 15, 1988 (amendment 41); November 1, 1989 (amendments 209 and 210); November 1, 1991 (amendment 407); November 1, 1992 (amendment 452); November 1, 1995 (amendment 534); November 1, 2001 (amendment 617); November 1, 2002 (amendment 638); November 1, 2007 (amendment 700); November 1, 2010 (amendment 746); November 1, 2011 (amendment 758); November 1, 2015 (amendment 791).

§2Q2.2. [Deleted]

Historical Note

Section 2Q2.2 (Lacey Act; Smuggling and Otherwise Unlawfully Dealing in Fish, Wildlife, and Plants), effective November 1, 1987, was deleted by consolidation with §2Q2.1 effective November 1, 1989 (amendment 209).

PART R — ANTITRUST OFFENSES

§2R1.1. Bid-Rigging, Price-Fixing or Market-Allocation Agreements Among Competitors

(a) Base Offense Level: **12**

(b) Specific Offense Characteristics

(1) If the conduct involved participation in an agreement to submit non-competitive bids, increase by **1** level.

(2) If the volume of commerce attributable to the defendant was more than $1,000,000, adjust the offense level as follows:

VOLUME OF COMMERCE (APPLY THE GREATEST)	ADJUSTMENT TO OFFENSE LEVEL
(A) More than $1,000,000	add **2**
(B) More than $10,000,000	add **4**
(C) More than $50,000,000	add **6**
(D) More than $100,000,000	add **8**
(E) More than $300,000,000	add **10**
(F) More than $600,000,000	add **12**
(G) More than $1,200,000,000	add **14**

(H) More than $1,850,000,000 add **16**.
For purposes of this guideline, the volume of commerce attributable to an individual participant in a conspiracy is the volume of commerce done by him or his principal in goods or services that were affected by the violation. When multiple counts or conspiracies are involved, the volume of commerce should be treated cumulatively to determine a single, combined offense level.
(c) Special Instruction for Fines
(1) For an individual, the guideline fine range shall be from one to five percent of the volume of commerce, but not less than $20,000.
(d) Special Instructions for Fines — Organizations
(1) In lieu of the pecuniary loss under subsection (a)(3) of §8C2.4 (Base Fine), use 20 percent of the volume of affected commerce.

(2) When applying §8C2.6 (Minimum and Maximum Multipliers), neither the minimum nor maximum multiplier shall be less than 0.75.
(3) In a bid-rigging case in which the organization submitted one or more complementary bids, use as the organization's volume of commerce the greater of (A) the volume of commerce done by the organization in the goods or services that were affected by the violation, or (B) the largest contract on which the organization submitted a complementary bid in connection with the bidrigging conspiracy.

Commentary

Statutory Provisions: 15 U.S.C. §§ 1, 3(b). For additional statutory provision(s), *see* Appendix A (Statutory Index).

Application Notes:

1. **Application of Chapter Three (Adjustments).**—Sections 3B1.1 (Aggravating Role), 3B1.2 (Mitigating Role), 3B1.3 (Abuse of Position of Trust or Use of Special Skill), and 3C1.1 (Obstructing or Impeding the Administration of Justice) may be relevant in determining the seriousness of the defendant's offense. For example, if a sales manager organizes or leads the price-fixing activity of five or more participants, the 4-level increase at §3B1.1(a) should be applied to reflect the defendant's aggravated role in the offense. For purposes of applying §3B1.2, an individual defendant should be considered for a mitigating role adjustment only if he were responsible in some minor way for his firm's participation in the conspiracy.
2. **Considerations in Setting Fine for Individuals.**—In setting the fine for individuals, the court should consider the extent of the defendant's participation in the offense, the defendant's role, and the degree to which the defendant personally profited from the offense (including salary, bonuses, and career enhancement). If the court concludes that the defendant lacks the ability to pay the guideline fine, it should impose community service in lieu of a portion of the fine. The community service should be equally as burdensome as a fine.
3. The fine for an organization is determined by applying Chapter Eight (Sentencing of Organizations). In selecting a fine for an organization within the guideline fine range, the court should consider both the gain to the organization from the offense and the loss caused by the organization. It is estimated that the average gain from price-fixing is

10 percent of the selling price. The loss from price-fixing exceeds the gain because, among other things, injury is inflicted upon consumers who are unable or for other reasons do not buy the product at the higher prices. Because the loss from price-fixing exceeds the gain, subsection (d)(1) provides that 20 percent of the volume of affected commerce is to be used in lieu of the pecuniary loss under §8C2.4(a)(3). The purpose for specifying a percent of the volume of commerce is to avoid the time and expense that would be required for the court to determine the actual gain or loss. In cases in which the actual monopoly overcharge appears to be either substantially more or substantially less than 10 percent, this factor should be considered in setting the fine within the guideline fine range.

4. Another consideration in setting the fine is that the average level of mark-up due to pricefixing may tend to decline with the volume of commerce involved.
5. It is the intent of the Commission that alternatives such as community confinement not be used to avoid imprisonment of antitrust offenders.
6. Understatement of seriousness is especially likely in cases involving complementary bids. If, for example, the defendant participated in an agreement not to submit a bid, or to submit an unreasonably high bid, on one occasion, in exchange for his being allowed to win a subsequent bid that he did not in fact win, his volume of commerce would be zero, although he would have contributed to harm that possibly was quite substantial. The court should consider sentences near the top of the guideline range in such cases.
7. In the case of a defendant with previous antitrust convictions, a sentence at the maximum of the applicable guideline range, or an upward departure, may be warranted. *See* §4A1.3 (Adequacy of Criminal History Category).

Background: These guidelines apply to violations of the antitrust laws. Although they are not unlawful in all countries, there is near universal agreement that restrictive agreements among competitors, such as horizontal price-fixing (including bid-rigging) and horizontal market-allocation, can cause serious economic harm. There is no consensus, however, about the harmfulness of other types of antitrust offenses, which furthermore are rarely prosecuted and may involve unsettled issues of law. Consequently, only one guideline, which deals with horizontal agreements in restraint of trade, has been promulgated.

The agreements among competitors covered by this section are almost invariably covert conspiracies that are intended to, and serve no purpose other than to, restrict output and raise prices, and that are so plainly anticompetitive that they have been recognized as illegal *per se*, *i.e.*, without any inquiry in individual cases as to their actual competitive effect.

Under the guidelines, prison terms for these offenders should be much more common, and usually somewhat longer, than typical under pre-guidelines practice. Absent adjustments, the guidelines require some period of confinement in the great majority of cases that are prosecuted, including all bid-rigging cases. The court will have the discretion to impose considerably longer sentences within the guideline ranges. Adjustments from Chapter Three, Part E (Acceptance of Responsibility) and, in rare instances, Chapter Three, Part B (Role in the Offense), may decrease these minimum sentences; nonetheless, in very few cases will the guidelines not require that some confinement be imposed. Adjustments will not affect the level of fines.

Tying the offense level to the scale or scope of the offense is important in order to ensure that the sanction is in fact punitive and that there is an incentive to desist from a violation once it has begun. The offense levels are not based directly on the damage caused or profit made by the defendant because damages are difficult and time consuming to establish. The volume of commerce is an acceptable and more readily measurable substitute. The limited empirical data available as to pre-guidelines practice showed that fines increased with the volume of commerce and the term of imprisonment probably did as well.

The Commission believes that the volume of commerce is liable to be an understated measure of seriousness in some bid-rigging cases. For this reason, and consistent with preguidelines practice, the Commission has specified a 1-level increase for bid-rigging.

Substantial fines are an essential part of the sentence. For an individual, the guideline fine range is from one to five percent of the volume of commerce, but not less than $20,000.

For an organization, the guideline fine range is determined under Chapter Eight (Sentencing of Organizations), but pursuant to subsection (d)(2), the minimum multiplier is at least 0.75. This multiplier, which requires a minimum fine of 15 percent of the volume of commerce for the least serious case, was selected to provide an effective deterrent to antitrust offenses. At the same time, this minimum multiplier maintains incentives for desired organizational behavior. Because the Department of Justice has a well-established amnesty program for organizations that self-report antitrust offenses, no lower minimum multiplier is needed as an incentive for self-reporting. A minimum multiplier of at least 0.75 ensures that fines imposed in antitrust cases will exceed the average monopoly overcharge.

The Commission believes that most antitrust defendants have the resources and earning capacity to pay the fines called for by this guideline, at least over time on an installment basis.

Historical Note

Effective November 1, 1987. Amended effective November 1, 1989 (amendments 211 and 303); November 1, 1991 (amendments 377 and 422); November 1, 2003 (amendment 661); November 1, 2004 (amendment 674); November 1, 2005 (amendment 678); November 1, 2015 (amendment 791).

PART S — MONEY LAUNDERING AND MONETARY TRANSACTION REPORTING

Historical Note

Introductory Commentary to this Part, effective November 1, 1987, was deleted effective November 1, 1990 (amendment 342).

§2S1.1. Laundering of Monetary Instruments; Engaging in Monetary Transactions in Property Derived from Unlawful Activity

(a) Base Offense Level:

(1) The offense level for the underlying offense from which the laundered funds were derived, if (A) the defendant committed the underlying offense (or would be accountable for the underlying offense under subsection (a)(1)(A) of §1B1.3 (Relevant Conduct)); and (B) the offense level for that offense can be determined; or

(2) **8** plus the number of offense levels from the table in §2B1.1 (Theft, Property Destruction, and Fraud) corresponding to the value of the laundered funds, otherwise.

(b) Specific Offense Characteristics

(1) If (A) subsection (a)(2) applies; and (B) the defendant knew or believed that any of the laundered funds were the proceeds of, or were intended to promote (i) an offense involving the manufacture, importation, or distribution of a controlled substance or a listed chemical; (ii) a crime of violence; or (iii) an offense involving firearms, explosives, national security, or the sexual exploitation of a minor, increase by **6** levels.

(2) (Apply the Greatest):

(A) If the defendant was convicted under 18 U.S.C. § 1957, increase by **1** level.

(B) If the defendant was convicted under 18 U.S.C. § 1956, increase

by **2** levels.
(C) If (i) subsection (a)(2) applies; and (ii) the defendant was in the business of laundering funds, increase by **4** levels.

(3) If (A) subsection (b)(2)(B) applies; and (B) the offense involved sophisticated laundering, increase by **2** levels.

Commentary

Statutory Provisions: 18 U.S.C. §§ 1956, 1957, 1960 (but only with respect to unlicensed money transmitting businesses as defined in 18 U.S.C. § 1960(b)(1)(C)). For additional statutory provision(s), *see* Appendix A (Statutory Index).

Application Notes:

1. **Definitions.**—For purposes of this guideline:

"***Crime of violence***" has the meaning given that term in subsection (a)(1) of §4B1.2 (Definitions of Terms Used in Section 4B1.1).

"***Criminally derived funds***" means any funds derived, or represented by a law enforcement officer, or by another person at the direction or approval of an authorized Federal official, to be derived from conduct constituting a criminal offense.

"***Laundered funds***" means the property, funds, or monetary instrument involved in the transaction, financial transaction, monetary transaction, transportation, transfer, or transmission in violation of 18 U.S.C. § 1956 or § 1957.

"***Laundering funds***" means making a transaction, financial transaction, monetary transaction, or transmission, or transporting or transferring property, funds, or a monetary instrument in violation of 18 U.S.C. § 1956 or § 1957.

"***Sexual exploitation of a minor***" means an offense involving (A) promoting prostitution by a minor; (B) sexually exploiting a minor by production of sexually explicit visual or printed material; (C) distribution of material involving the sexual exploitation of a minor, or possession of material involving the sexual exploitation of a minor with intent to distribute; or (D) aggravated sexual abuse, sexual abuse, or abusive sexual contact involving a minor. "Minor" means an individual under the age of 18 years.

2. **Application of Subsection (a)(1).**—

(A) **Multiple Underlying Offenses.**—In cases in which subsection (a)(1) applies and there is more than one underlying offense, the offense level for the underlying offense is to be determined under the procedures set forth in Application Note 3 of the Commentary to §1B1.5 (Interpretation of References to Other Offense Guidelines).

(B) **Defendants Accountable for Underlying Offense.**—In order for subsection (a)(1) to apply, the defendant must have committed the underlying offense or be accountable for the underlying offense under §1B1.3(a)(1)(A). The fact that the defendant was involved in laundering criminally derived funds after the commission of the underlying offense, without additional involvement in the underlying offense, does not establish that the defendant committed, aided, abetted, counseled, commanded, induced, procured, or willfully caused the underlying offense.

(C) **Application of Chapter Three Adjustments.**—Notwithstanding §1B1.5(c), in cases in which subsection (a)(1) applies, application of any Chapter Three adjustment shall be determined based on the offense covered by this guideline (*i.e.*, the laundering of criminally derived funds) and not on the underlying offense from which the laundered funds were derived.

3. **Application of Subsection (a)(2).**—

(A) **In General.**—Subsection (a)(2) applies to any case in which (i) the defendant did not commit the underlying offense; or (ii) the defendant committed the underlying offense (or would be accountable for the underlying offense under §1B1.3(a)(1)(A)), but the offense level for the underlying offense is impossible or impracticable to

determine.
(B) **Commingled Funds.**—In a case in which a transaction, financial transaction, monetary transaction, transportation, transfer, or transmission results in the commingling of legitimately derived funds with criminally derived funds, the value of the laundered funds, for purposes of subsection (a)(2), is the amount of the criminally derived funds, not the total amount of the commingled funds, if the defendant provides sufficient information to determine the amount of criminally derived funds without unduly complicating or prolonging the sentencing process. If the amount of the criminally derived funds is difficult or impracticable to determine, the value of the laundered funds, for purposes of subsection (a)(2), is the total amount of the commingled funds.
(C) **Non-Applicability of Enhancement.**—Subsection (b)(2)(B) shall not apply if the defendant was convicted of a conspiracy under 18 U.S.C. § 1956(h) and the sole object of that conspiracy was to commit an offense set forth in 18 U.S.C. § 1957.
4. **Enhancement for Business of Laundering Funds.**—
(A) **In General.**—The court shall consider the totality of the circumstances to determine whether a defendant who did not commit the underlying offense was in the business of laundering funds, for purposes of subsection (b)(2)(C).
(B) **Factors to Consider.**—The following is a non-exhaustive list of factors that may indicate the defendant was in the business of laundering funds for purposes of subsection (b)(2)(C):
(i) The defendant regularly engaged in laundering funds.
(ii) The defendant engaged in laundering funds during an extended period of time.
(iii) The defendant engaged in laundering funds from multiple sources.
(iv) The defendant generated a substantial amount of revenue in return for laundering funds.
(v) At the time the defendant committed the instant offense, the defendant had one or more prior convictions for an offense under 18 U.S.C. § 1956 or § 1957, or under 31 U.S.C. § 5313, § 5314, § 5316, § 5324 or § 5326, or any similar offense under state law, or an attempt or conspiracy to commit any such fed§

eral or state offense. A conviction taken into account under subsection (b)(2)(C) is not excluded from consideration of whether that conviction receives criminal history points pursuant to Chapter Four, Part A (Criminal History).
(vi) During the course of an undercover government investigation, the defendant made statements that the defendant engaged in any of the conduct described in subdivisions (i) through (iv).
5. (A) **Sophisticated Laundering under Subsection (b)(3).**—For purposes of subsection (b)(3), "***sophisticated laundering***" means complex or intricate offense conduct pertaining to the execution or concealment of the 18 U.S.C. § 1956 offense. Sophisticated laundering typically involves the use of—
(i) fictitious entities;
(ii) shell corporations;
(iii) two or more levels (*i.e.*, layering) of transactions, transportation, transfers, or transmissions, involving criminally derived funds that were intended to appear legitimate; or
(iv) offshore financial accounts.
(B) **Non-Applicability of Enhancement.**—If subsection (b)(3) applies, and the conduct that forms the basis for an enhancement under the guideline applicable to the underlying offense is the only conduct that forms the basis for application of subsection (b)(3) of this guideline, do not apply subsection (b)(3) of this guideline.
6. **Grouping of Multiple Counts.**—In a case in which the defendant is convicted of a

count of laundering funds and a count for the underlying offense from which the laundered funds were derived, the counts shall be grouped pursuant to subsection (c) of §3D1.2 (Groups of Closely-Related Counts).

Historical
Note

Effective November 1, 1987. Amended effective November 1, 1989 (amendments 212–214); November 1, 1991 (amendments 378 and 422); November 1, 2001 (amendment 634); November 1, 2003 (amendment 655).

§2S1.2. [Deleted]

Historical
Note

Section 2S1.2 (Engaging in Monetary Transactions in Property Derived from Specified Unlawful Activity), effective November 1, 1987, amended effective November 1, 1989 (amendment 215), and November 1, 1991 (amendment 422), was deleted by consolidation with §2S1.1 effective November 1, 2001 (amendment 634).

§2S1.3. Structuring Transactions to Evade Reporting Requirements; Failure to Report Cash or Monetary Transactions; Failure to File Currency and Monetary Instrument Report; Knowingly Filing False Reports; Bulk Cash Smuggling; Establishing or Maintaining Prohibited Accounts

(a) Base Offense Level:

(1) **8**, if the defendant was convicted under 31 U.S.C. § 5318 or § 5318A; or

(2) **6** plus the number of offense levels from the table in §2B1.1 (Theft, Property Destruction, and Fraud) corresponding to the value of the funds, if subsection (a)(1) does not apply.

(b) Specific Offense Characteristics

(1) If (A) the defendant knew or believed that the funds were proceeds of unlawful activity, or were intended to promote unlawful activity; or (B) the offense involved bulk cash smuggling, increase by **2** levels.

(2) If the defendant (A) was convicted of an offense under subchapter II of chapter 53 of title 31, United States Code; and (B) committed the offense as part of a pattern of unlawful activity involving more than $100,000 in a 12-month period, increase by **2** levels.

(3) If (A) subsection (a)(2) applies and subsections (b)(1) and (b)(2) do not apply; (B) the defendant did not act with reckless disregard of the source of the funds; (C) the funds were the proceeds of lawful activity; and (D) the funds were to be used for a lawful purpose, decrease the offense level to level **6**.

(c) Cross Reference

(1) If the offense was committed for the purposes of violating the Internal Revenue laws, apply the most appropriate guideline from Chapter Two, Part T (Offenses Involving Taxation) if the resulting offense level is greater than that determined above.

Commentary

Statutory Provisions: 18 U.S.C. § 1960 (but only with respect to unlicensed money transmitting businesses as defined in 18 U.S.C. § 1960(b)(1)(A) and (B)); 26 U.S.C. §§ 7203 (if a violation based upon 26 U.S.C. § 6050I), 7206 (if a violation based upon 26 U.S.C. § 6050I); 31 U.S.C. §§ 5313, 5314, 5316, 5318, 5318A(b), 5322, 5324, 5326, 5331, 5332. For additional statutory provision(s), *see* Appendix A (Statutory Index).

Application Notes:

1. **Definition of "Value of the Funds".**—For purposes of this guideline, "***value of the funds***" means the amount of the funds involved in the structuring or reporting conduct. The relevant statutes require monetary reporting without regard to whether the funds were lawfully or unlawfully obtained.
2. **Bulk Cash Smuggling.**—For purposes of subsection (b)(1)(B), "***bulk cash smuggling***" means (A) knowingly concealing, with the intent to evade a currency reporting requirement under 31 U.S.C. § 5316, more than $10,000 in currency or other monetary instruments; and (B) transporting or transferring (or attempting to transport or transfer) such currency or monetary instruments into or outside of the United States. "United States" has the meaning given that term in Application Note 1 of the Commentary to §2B5.1 (Offenses Involving Counterfeit Bearer Obligations of the United States).
3. **Enhancement for Pattern of Unlawful Activity.**—For purposes of subsection (b)(2), "***pattern of unlawful activity***" means at least two separate occasions of unlawful activity involving a total amount of more than $100,000 in a 12-month period, without regard to whether any such occasion occurred during the course of the offense or resulted in a conviction for the conduct that occurred on that occasion.

Background: Some of the offenses covered by this guideline relate to records and reports of certain transactions involving currency and monetary instruments. These reports include Currency Transaction Reports, Currency and Monetary Instrument Reports, Reports of Foreign Bank and Financial Accounts, and Reports of Cash Payments Over $10,000 Received in a Trade or Business.

This guideline also covers offenses under 31 U.S.C. §§ 5318 and 5318A, pertaining to records, reporting and identification requirements, prohibited accounts involving certain foreign jurisdictions, foreign institutions, and foreign banks, and other types of transactions and types of accounts.

Historical Note

Effective November 1, 1987. Amended effective November 1, 1989 (amendments 216–218); November 1, 1991 (amendments 379 and 422); November 1, 1993 (amendment 490); November 1, 2001 (amendments 617 and 634); November 1, 2002 (amendment 637); November 1, 2003 (amendment 655).

§2S1.4. [Deleted]

Historical Note

Section 2S1.4 (Failure to File Currency and Monetary Instrument Report), effective November 1, 1991 (amendments 379 and 422), was deleted by consolidation with §2S1.3 effective November 1, 1993 (amendment 490).

PART T — OFFENSES INVOLVING TAXATION

1. INCOME TAXES, EMPLOYMENT TAXES, ESTATE TAXES, GIFT TAXES, AND EXCISE TAXES (OTHER THAN ALCOHOL, TOBACCO, AND CUSTOMS TAXES)

Historical Note

Effective November 1, 1987. Amended effective November 1, 1993 (amendment 491).

Introductory Commentary

The criminal tax laws are designed to protect the public interest in preserving the integrity of the nation's tax system. Criminal tax prosecutions serve to punish the violator and promote respect for the tax laws. Because of the limited number of criminal tax prosecutions relative to the estimated incidence of such violations, deterring others from violating the tax laws is a primary consideration underlying these guidelines. Recognition that the sentence for a criminal tax case will be commensurate with the gravity of the offense should act as a deterrent to would-be violators.

Historical Note

Effective November 1, 1987.

§2T1.1. Tax Evasion; Willful Failure to File Return, Supply Information, or Pay Tax; Fraudulent or False Returns, Statements, or Other Documents

(a) Base Offense Level:

(1) Level from §2T4.1 (Tax Table) corresponding to the tax loss; or

(2) **6**, if there is no tax loss.

(b) Specific Offense Characteristics

(1) If the defendant failed to report or to correctly identify the source of income exceeding $10,000 in any year from criminal activity, increase by **2** levels. If the resulting offense level is less than level **12**, increase to level **12**.

(2) If the offense involved sophisticated means, increase by **2** levels. If the resulting offense level is less than level **12**, increase to level **12**.

(c) Special Instructions

For the purposes of this guideline—

(1) If the offense involved tax evasion or a fraudulent or false return, statement, or other document, the tax loss is the total amount of loss that was the object of the offense (*i.e.*, the loss that would have resulted had the offense been successfully completed).

Notes:

(A) If the offense involved filing a tax return in which gross income was underreported, the tax loss shall be treated as equal to 28% of the unreported gross income (34% if the taxpayer is a corporation) plus 100% of any false credits claimed against tax, unless a more accurate determination of the tax loss can be made.

(B) If the offense involved improperly claiming a deduction or an exemption, the tax loss shall be treated as equal to 28% of the amount of the improperly claimed deduction or exemption (34% if the taxpayer is a corporation) plus 100% of any false credits claimed against tax, unless a more accurate determination of the tax loss can be made.

(C) If the offense involved improperly claiming a deduction to provide a basis for tax evasion in the future, the tax loss shall be treated as equal to 28% of the amount of the improperly claimed deduction (34% if the taxpayer is a corporation) plus 100% of any false credits claimed against tax, unless a more accurate determination of the tax loss can be made.

(D) If the offense involved (i) conduct described in subdivision (A), B), or (C) of these Notes; and (ii) both individual and corporate tax returns, the tax loss is the aggregate tax loss from the offenses added together.

(2) If the offense involved failure to file a tax return, the tax loss is the amount of tax that the taxpayer owed and did not pay.

Notes:
(A) If the offense involved failure to file a tax return, the tax loss shall be treated as equal to 20% of the gross income (25% if the taxpayer is a corporation) less any tax withheld

or otherwise paid, unless a more accurate determination of the tax loss can be made.
(B) If the offense involved (i) conduct described in subdivision (A) of these Notes; and (ii) both individual and corporate tax returns, the tax loss is the aggregate tax loss from the offenses added together.
(3) If the offense involved willful failure to pay tax, the tax loss is the amount of tax that the taxpayer owed and did not pay.
(4) If the offense involved improperly claiming a refund to which the claimant was not entitled, the tax loss is the amount of the claimed refund to which the claimant was not entitled.
(5) The tax loss is not reduced by any payment of the tax subsequent to the commission of the offense.

Commentary

Statutory Provisions: 26 U.S.C. §§ 7201, 7203 (other than a violation based upon 26 U.S.C. § 6050I), 7206 (other than a violation based upon 26 U.S.C. § 6050I or § 7206(2)), and 7207. For additional statutory provision(s), *see* Appendix A (Statutory Index).

Application Notes:

1. **Tax Loss.**—"***Tax loss***" is defined in subsection (c). The tax loss does not include interest or penalties, except in willful evasion of payment cases under 26 U.S.C. § 7201 and willful failure to pay cases under 26 U.S.C. § 7203. Although the definition of tax loss corresponds to what is commonly called the "criminal figures," its amount is to be determined by the same rules applicable in determining any other sentencing factor. In some instances, such as when indirect methods of proof are used, the amount of the tax loss may be uncertain; the guidelines contemplate that the court will simply make a reasonable estimate based on the available facts.

Notes under subsections (c)(1) and (c)(2) address certain situations in income tax cases in which the tax loss may not be reasonably ascertainable. In these situations, the "presumptions" set forth are to be used unless the government or defense provides sufficient information for a more accurate assessment of the tax loss. In cases involving other types of taxes, the presumptions in the notes under subsections (c)(1) and (c)(2) do not apply.

Example 1: A defendant files a tax return reporting income of $40,000 when his income was actually $90,000. Under Note (A) to subsection (c)(1), the tax loss is treated as $14,000 ($90,000 of actual gross income minus $40,000 of reported gross income = $50,000 x 28%) unless sufficient information is available to make a more accurate assessment of the tax loss.

Example 2: A defendant files a tax return reporting income of $60,000 when his income was actually $130,000. In addition, the defendant claims $10,000 in false tax credits. Under Note (A) to subsection (c)(1), the tax loss is treated as $29,600 ($130,000 of actual gross income minus $60,000 of reported gross income = $70,000 x 28% = $19,600, plus

$10,000 of false tax credits) unless sufficient information is available to make a more accurate assessment of the tax loss.

Example 3: A defendant fails to file a tax return for a year in which his salary was $24,000, and $2,600 in income tax was withheld by his employer. Under the note to subsection (c)(2), the tax loss is treated as $2,200 ($24,000 of gross income x 20% = $4,800, minus $2,600 of tax withheld) unless sufficient information is available to make a more accurate assessment of the tax loss.

In determining the tax loss attributable to the offense, the court should use as many methods set forth in subsection (c) and this commentary as are necessary given the circumstances of the particular case. If none of the methods of determining the tax loss set forth fit the circumstances of the particular case, the court should use any method of determining the tax loss that appears appropriate to reasonably calculate the loss that would have resulted had the offense been successfully completed.

2. **Total Tax Loss Attributable to the Offense.**—In determining the total tax loss attributable to the offense (*see* §1B1.3(a)(2)), all conduct violating the tax laws should be considered as part of the same course of conduct or common scheme or plan unless the evidence demonstrates that the conduct is clearly unrelated. The following examples are illustrative of conduct that is part of the same course of conduct or common scheme or plan: (A) there is a continuing pattern of violations of the tax laws by the defendant; (B) the defendant uses a consistent method to evade or camouflage income, *e.g.*, backdating documents or using off-shore accounts; (C) the violations involve the same or a related series of transactions; (D) the violation in each instance involves a false or inflated claim of a similar deduction or credit; and (E) the violation in each instance involves a failure to report or an understatement of a specific source of income, *e.g.*, interest from savings accounts or income from a particular business activity. These examples are not intended to be exhaustive.

3. **Unclaimed Credits, Deductions, and Exemptions.**—In determining the tax loss, the court should account for the standard deduction and personal and dependent exemptions to which the defendant was entitled. In addition, the court should account for any unclaimed credit, deduction, or exemption that is needed to ensure a reasonable estimate of the tax loss, but only to the extent that (A) the credit, deduction, or exemption was related to the tax offense and could have been claimed at the time the tax offense was committed; (B) the credit, deduction, or exemption is reasonably and practicably ascertainable; and (C) the defendant presents information to support the credit, deduction, or exemption sufficiently in advance of sentencing to provide an adequate opportunity to evaluate whether it has sufficient indicia of reliability to support its probable accuracy (*see* §6A1.3 (Resolution of Disputed Factors) (Policy Statement)).

However, the court shall not account for payments to third parties made in a manner that encouraged or facilitated a separate violation of law (*e.g.*, "under the table" payments to employees or expenses incurred to obstruct justice).

The burden is on the defendant to establish any such credit, deduction, or exemption by a preponderance of the evidence. *See* §6A1.3, comment.

4. **Application of Subsection (b)(1) (Criminal Activity).**—"***Criminal activity***" means any conduct constituting a criminal offense under federal, state, local, or foreign law.

5. **Application of Subsection (b)(2) (Sophisticated Means).**—For purposes of subsection (b)(2), "***sophisticated means***" means especially complex or especially intricate offense conduct pertaining to the execution or concealment of an offense. Conduct such as hiding assets or transactions, or both, through the use of fictitious entities, corporate shells, or offshore financial accounts ordinarily indicates sophisticated means.

6. **Other Definitions.**—For purposes of this section:

A "***credit claimed against tax***" is an item that reduces the amount of tax directly. In contrast, a "***deduction***" is an item that reduces the amount of taxable income.

"***Gross income***" has the same meaning as it has in 26 U.S.C. § 61 and 26 C.F.R. § 1.61.

7. **Aggregation of Individual and Corporate Tax Loss.**—If the offense involved both individual and corporate tax returns, the tax loss is the aggregate tax loss from the individual tax offense and the corporate tax offense added together. Accordingly, in a case in which a defendant fails to report income derived from a corporation on both the defendant's

individual tax return and the defendant's corporate tax return, the tax loss is the sum of (A) the unreported or diverted amount multiplied by (i) 28%; or (ii) the tax rate for the individual tax offense, if sufficient information is available to make a more accurate assessment of that tax rate; and (B) the unreported or diverted amount multiplied by (i) 34%; or (ii) the tax rate for the corporate tax offense, if sufficient information is available to make a more accurate assessment of that tax rate. For example, the defendant, the sole owner of a Subchapter C corporation, fraudulently understates the corporation's income in the amount of $100,000 on the corporation's tax return, diverts the funds to the defendant's own use, and does not report these funds on the defendant's individual tax return. For purposes of this example, assume the use of 34% with respect to the corporate tax loss and the use of 28% with respect to the individual tax loss. The tax loss attributable to the defendant's corporate tax return is $34,000 ($100,000 multiplied by 34%). The tax loss attributable to the defendant's individual tax return is $28,000 ($100,000 multiplied by 28%). The tax loss for the offenses are added together to equal $62,000 ($34,000 + $28,000).

Background: This guideline relies most heavily on the amount of loss that was the object of the offense. Tax offenses, in and of themselves, are serious offenses; however, a greater tax loss is obviously more harmful to the treasury and more serious than a smaller one with otherwise similar characteristics. Furthermore, as the potential benefit from the offense increases, the sanction necessary to deter also increases.

Under pre-guidelines practice, roughly half of all tax evaders were sentenced to probation without imprisonment, while the other half received sentences that required them to serve an average prison term of twelve months. This guideline is intended to reduce disparity in sentencing for tax offenses and to somewhat increase average sentence length. As a result, the number of purely probationary sentences will be reduced. The Commission believes that any additional costs of imprisonment that may be incurred as a result of the increase in the average term of imprisonment for tax offenses are inconsequential in relation to the potential increase in revenue. According to estimates current at the time this guideline was originally developed (1987), income taxes are underpaid by approximately $90 billion annually. Guideline sentences should result in small increases in the average length of imprisonment for most tax cases that involve less than $100,000 in tax loss. The increase is expected to be somewhat larger for cases involving more taxes.

Failure to report criminally derived income is included as a factor for deterrence purposes. Criminally derived income is generally difficult to establish, so that the tax loss in such

cases will tend to be substantially understated. An enhancement for offenders who violate the tax laws as part of a pattern of criminal activity from which they derive a substantial portion of their income also serves to implement the mandate of 28 U.S.C. § 994(i)(2).

Although tax offenses always involve some planning, unusually sophisticated efforts to conceal the offense decrease the likelihood of detection and therefore warrant an additional sanction for deterrence purposes.

The guideline does not make a distinction for an employee who prepares fraudulent returns on behalf of his employer. The adjustments in Chapter Three, Part B (Role in the Offense) should be used to make appropriate distinctions.

Historical Note

Effective November 1, 1987. Amended effective November 1, 1989 (amendments 219–223); November 1, 1990 (amendment 343); November 1, 1992 (amendment 468); November 1, 1993 (amendment 491); November 1, 1998 (amendment 577); November 1, 2001 (amendment 617); November 1, 2002 (amendment 646); November 1, 2013 (amendment 774).

§2T1.2. [Deleted]

Historical Note

Section 2T1.2 (Willful Failure To File Return, Supply Information, or Pay Tax), effective November 1, 1987, amended effective November 1, 1989 (amendments 224–227), November 1, 1990 (amendment 343), and November 1, 1991 (amendment 408), was deleted by consolidation with §2T1.1 effective November 1, 1993 (amendment 491).

§2T1.3. [Deleted]

Historical
Note
Section 2T1.3 (Fraud and False Statements Under Penalty of Perjury), effective November 1, 1987, amended effective November 1, 1989 (amendments 228–230), November 1, 1990 (amendment 343), and November 1, 1991 (amendment 426), was deleted by consolidation with §2T1.1 effective November 1, 1993 (amendment 491).

§2T1.4. Aiding, Assisting, Procuring, Counseling, or Advising Tax Fraud

(a) Base Offense Level:

(1) Level from §2T4.1 (Tax Table) corresponding to the tax loss; or

(2) **6**, if there is no tax loss.

For purposes of this guideline, the "tax loss" is the tax loss, as defined in §2T1.1, resulting from the defendant's aid, assistance, procurance or advice.

(b) Specific Offense Characteristics

(1) If (A) the defendant committed the offense as part of a pattern or scheme from which he derived a substantial portion of his income; or (B) the defendant was in the business of preparing or assisting in the preparation of tax returns, increase by **2** levels.

(2) If the offense involved sophisticated means, increase by **2** levels. If the resulting offense level is less than level **12**, increase to level **12**.

Commentary

Statutory Provision: 26 U.S.C. § 7206(2) (other than a violation based upon 26 U.S.C. § 6050I).

Application Notes:

1. For the general principles underlying the determination of tax loss, *see* §2T1.1(c) and Application Note 1 of the Commentary to §2T1.1 (Tax Evasion; Willful Failure to File Return, Supply Information, or Pay Tax; Fraudulent or False Returns, Statements, or Other Documents). In certain instances, such as promotion of a tax shelter scheme, the defendant may advise other persons to violate their tax obligations through filing returns that find no support in the tax laws. If this type of conduct can be shown to have resulted in the filing of false returns (regardless of whether the principals were aware of their falsity), the misstatements in all such returns will contribute to one aggregate "tax loss."

2. Subsection (b)(1) has two prongs. The first prong applies to persons who derive a substantial portion of their income through the promotion of tax schemes, *e.g.*, through promoting fraudulent tax shelters. The second prong applies to persons who regularly prepare or assist in the preparation of tax returns for profit. If an enhancement from this subsection applies, do not apply §3B1.3 (Abuse of Position of Trust or Use of Special Skill).

3. **Sophisticated Means.**—For purposes of subsection (b)(2), "***sophisticated means***" means especially complex or especially intricate offense conduct pertaining to the execution or concealment of an offense. Conduct such as hiding assets or transactions, or both, through the use of fictitious entities, corporate shells, or offshore financial accounts ordinarily indicates sophisticated means.

Background: An increased offense level is specified for those in the business of preparing or assisting in the preparation of tax returns and those who make a business of promoting tax fraud because their misconduct poses a greater risk of revenue loss and is more clearly willful. Other considerations are similar to those in §2T1.1.

Historical
Note
Effective November 1, 1987. Amended effective November 1, 1989 (amendments 231 and 303); November 1, 1990 (amendment 343); November 1, 1993 (amendment 491); November 1, 1998 (amendment 577); November 1, 2001 (amendment 617).

§2T1.5. [Deleted]

Historical
Note
Section 2T1.5 (Fraudulent Returns, Statements, or Other Documents), effective November 1, 1987, was deleted by consolidation with §2T1.1 effective November 1, 1993 (amendment 491).

§2T1.6. Failing to Collect or Truthfully Account for and Pay Over Tax

(a) Base Offense Level: Level from §2T4.1 (Tax Table) corresponding to the tax not collected or accounted for and paid over.

(b) Cross Reference

(1) Where the offense involved embezzlement by withholding tax from an employee's earnings and willfully failing to account to the employee for it, apply §2B1.1 (Theft, Property Destruction, and Fraud) if the resulting offense level is greater than that determined above.

Commentary

Statutory Provision: 26 U.S.C. § 7202.

Application Note:

1. In the event that the employer not only failed to account to the Internal Revenue Service and pay over the tax, but also collected the tax from employees and did not account to them for it, it is both tax evasion and a form of embezzlement. Subsection (b)(1) addresses such cases.

Background: The failure to collect or truthfully account for the tax must be willful, as must the failure to pay. Where no effort is made to defraud the employee, the offense is a form of tax evasion, and is treated as such in the guidelines.

Historical
Note
Effective November 1, 1987. Amended effective November 1, 1989 (amendment 232); November 1, 1991 (amendment 409); November 1, 2001 (amendment 617); November 1, 2016 (amendment 804).

§2T1.7. Failing to Deposit Collected Taxes in Trust Account as Required After Notice

(a) Base Offense Level (Apply the greater):

(1) **4**; or

(2) **5** less than the level from §2T4.1 (Tax Table) corresponding to the amount not deposited.

Commentary

Statutory Provisions: 26 U.S.C. §§ 7215, 7512(b).

Application Notes:

1. If funds are deposited and withdrawn without being paid to the Internal Revenue Service, they should be treated as never having been deposited.

2. It is recommended that the fine be based on the total amount of funds not deposited.

Background: This offense is a misdemeanor that does not require any intent to evade taxes, nor even that taxes have not been paid. The more serious offense is 26 U.S.C. § 7202 (*see* §2T1.6).

This offense should be relatively easy to detect and fines may be feasible. Accordingly, the offense level has been set considerably lower than for tax evasion, although some effort has been made to tie the offense level to the level of taxes that were not deposited.

Historical
Note
Effective November 1, 1987.

§2T1.8. Offenses Relating to Withholding Statements

(a) Base Offense Level: **4**

Commentary

Statutory Provisions: 26 U.S.C. §§ 7204, 7205.

Application Note:

1. If the defendant was attempting to evade, rather than merely delay, payment of taxes, an upward departure may be warranted.

Background: The offenses are misdemeanors. Under pre-guidelines practice, imprisonment was unusual.

Historical Note

Effective November 1, 1987. Amended effective November 1, 2004 (amendment 674).

§2T1.9. Conspiracy to Impede, Impair, Obstruct, or Defeat Tax

(a) Base Offense Level (Apply the greater):

(1) Offense level determined from §2T1.1 or §2T1.4, as appropriate; or

(2) **10**.

(b) Specific Offense Characteristics

If more than one applies, use the greater:

(1) If the offense involved the planned or threatened use of violence to impede, impair, obstruct, or defeat the ascertainment, computation, assessment, or collection of revenue, increase by **4** levels.

(2) If the conduct was intended to encourage persons other than or in addition to co-conspirators to violate the internal revenue laws or impede, impair, obstruct, or defeat the ascertainment, computation, assessment, or collection of revenue, increase by **2** levels. Do not, however, apply this adjustment if an adjustment from §2T1.4(b)(1) is applied.

Commentary

Statutory Provision: 18 U.S.C. § 371.

Application Notes:

1. This section applies to conspiracies to "defraud the United States by impeding, impairing, obstructing and defeating . . . the collection of revenue." *United States v. Carruth*, 699 F.2d 1017, 1021 (9th Cir. 1983), *cert. denied*, 464 U.S. 1038 (1984). *See also United States v. Browning*, 723 F.2d 1544 (11th Cir. 1984); *United States v. Klein*, 247 F.2d 908, 915 (2d Cir. 1957), *cert. denied*, 355 U.S. 924 (1958). It does not apply to taxpayers, such as a husband and wife, who merely evade taxes jointly or file a fraudulent return.

2. The base offense level is the offense level (base offense level plus any applicable specific offense characteristics) from §2T1.1 or §2T1.4 (whichever guideline most closely addresses the harm that would have resulted had the conspirators succeeded in impeding, impairing, obstructing, or defeating the Internal Revenue Service) if that offense level is greater than 10. Otherwise, the base offense level is 10.

3. Specific offense characteristics from §2T1.9(b) are to be applied to the base offense level determined under §2T1.9(a)(1) or (2).

4. Subsection (b)(2) provides an enhancement where the conduct was intended to encourage persons, other than the participants directly involved in the offense, to violate the tax

laws (*e.g.*, an offense involving a "tax protest" group that encourages persons to violate the tax laws, or an offense involving the marketing of fraudulent tax shelters or schemes).

Background: This type of conspiracy generally involves substantial sums of money. It also typically is complex and may be far-reaching, making it quite difficult to evaluate the extent of the revenue loss caused. Additional specific offense characteristics are included because of the potential for these tax conspiracies to subvert the revenue system and the danger to law enforcement agents and the public.

Historical
Note
Effective November 1, 1987. Amended effective November 1, 1989 (amendments 233 and 234); November 1, 1993 (amendment 491).

* * * * *

2. ALCOHOL AND TOBACCO TAXES

Introductory Commentary

This subpart deals with offenses contained in Parts I–IV of Subchapter J of Chapter 51 of Subtitle E of Title 26, chiefly 26 U.S.C. §§ 5601–5605, 5607, 5608, 5661, 5671, 5691, and 5762, where the essence of the conduct is tax evasion or a regulatory violation. No effort has been made to provide a section-by-section set of guidelines. Rather, the conduct is dealt with by dividing offenses into two broad categories: tax evasion offenses and regulatory offenses.

Historical
Note
Effective November 1, 1987. Amended effective November 1, 2010 (amendment 746); November 1, 2016 (amendment 804).

§2T2.1. Non-Payment of Taxes

(a) Base Offense Level: Level from §2T4.1 (Tax Table) corresponding to the tax loss.

For purposes of this guideline, the "tax loss" is the amount of taxes that the taxpayer failed to pay or attempted not to pay.

Commentary

Statutory Provisions: 15 U.S.C. § 377, 26 U.S.C. §§ 5601–5605, 5607, 5608, 5661, 5671, 5691, 5762, provided the conduct constitutes non-payment, evasion or attempted evasion of taxes. For additional statutory provision(s), *see* Appendix A (Statutory Index).

Application Notes:

1. The tax loss is the total amount of unpaid taxes that were due on the alcohol and/or tobacco, or that the defendant was attempting to evade.

2. Offense conduct directed at more than tax evasion (*e.g.*, theft or fraud) may warrant an upward departure.

Historical
Note
Effective November 1, 1987. Amended effective November 1, 2012 (amendment 769); November 1, 2016 (amendment 804).

§2T2.2. Regulatory Offenses

(a) Base Offense Level: **4**

Commentary

Statutory Provisions: 15 U.S.C. § 377, 26 U.S.C. §§ 5601, 5603–5605, 5661, 5671, 5762, provided the conduct is tantamount to a record-keeping violation rather than an effort to evade payment of taxes. For additional statutory provision(s), *see* Appendix A (Statutory Index).

Historical
Note
Effective November 1, 1987. Amended effective November 1, 1990 (amendment 359); November 1, 2012 (amendment 769); November 1, 2016 (amendment 804).

* * * * *

3. CUSTOMS TAXES

Introductory Commentary

This Subpart deals with violations of 18 U.S.C. §§ 496, 541–545, 547, 548, 550, 551, 1915 and 19 U.S.C. §§ 283, 1436, 1464, 1465, 1586(e), 1708(b), and 3907, and is designed to address violations involving revenue collection or trade regulation. It is intended to deal with some types of contraband, such as certain uncertified diamonds, but is not intended to deal with the importation of other types of contraband, such as drugs, or other items such as obscene material, firearms or pelts of endangered species, the importation of which is prohibited or restricted for non-economic reasons. Other, more specific criminal statutes apply to most of these offenses. Importation of contraband or stolen goods not specifically covered by this Subpart would be a reason for referring to another, more specific guideline, if applicable, or for departing upward if there is not another more specific applicable guideline.

Historical
Note
Effective November 1, 1987. Amended effective November 1, 1992 (amendment 453); November 1, 2004 (amendment 674); November 1, 2006 (amendment 685).

§2T3.1. Evading Import Duties or Restrictions (Smuggling); Receiving or Trafficking in Smuggled Property

(a) Base Offense Level:

(1) The level from §2T4.1 (Tax Table) corresponding to the tax loss, if the tax loss exceeded $1,500; or

(2) **5**, if the tax loss exceeded $200 but did not exceed $1,500; or

(3) **4**, if the tax loss did not exceed $200.

For purposes of this guideline, the "tax loss" is the amount of the duty.

(b) Specific Offense Characteristic

(1) If the offense involved sophisticated means, increase by **2** levels. If the resulting offense level is less than level **12**, increase to level **12**.

(c) Cross Reference

(1) If the offense involves a contraband item covered by another offense guideline, apply that offense guideline if the resulting offense level is greater than that determined above.

Commentary

Statutory Provisions: 18 U.S.C. §§ 496, 541–545, 547, 548, 550, 551, 1915; 19 U.S.C. §§ 283, 1436, 1464, 1465, 1586(e), 1708(b), 3907. For additional statutory provision(s), *see* Appendix A (Statutory Index).

Application Notes:

1. A sentence at or near the minimum of the guideline range typically would be appropriate for cases involving tourists who bring in items for their own use. Such conduct generally poses a lesser threat to revenue collection.

2. Particular attention should be given to those items for which entry is prohibited, limited, or restricted. Especially when such items are harmful or protective quotas are in effect, the duties evaded on such items may not adequately reflect the harm to society or protected industries resulting from their importation. In such instances, an upward departure may be warranted. A sentence based upon an alternative measure of the "duty" evaded, such as the increase in market value due to importation, or 25 percent of the items' fair market value in the United States if the increase in market value due to importation is not readily ascertainable, might be considered.

3. **Sophisticated Means.**—For purposes of subsection (b)(1), "***sophisticated means***" means especially complex or especially intricate offense conduct pertaining to the execution or concealment of an offense. Conduct such as hiding assets or transactions, or both, through the use of fictitious entities, corporate shells, or offshore financial accounts ordinarily indicates sophisticated means.

Historical
Note
Effective November 1, 1987. Amended effective November 1, 1989 (amendment 235); November 1, 1991 (amendment 410); November 1, 1992 (amendment 453); November 1, 1998 (amendment 577); November 1,

2001 (amendment 617); November 1, 2006 (amendment 685); November 1, 2015 (amendment 791).

§2T3.2. [Deleted]

Historical
Note

Section 2T3.2 (Receiving or Trafficking in Smuggled Property), effective November 1, 1987, amended effective November 1, 1989 (amendment 236) and November 1, 1991 (amendment 410), was deleted by consolidation with §2T3.1 effective November 1, 1992 (amendment 453).

* * * * *

4. TAX TABLE

§2T4.1. Tax Table

TAX LOSS (APPLY THE GREATEST) OFFENSE LEVEL

(A) $2,500 or less **6**
(B) More than $2,500 **8**
(C) More than $6,500 **10**
(D) More than $15,000 **12**
(E) More than $40,000 **14**
(F) More than $100,000 **16**
(G) More than $250,000 **18**
(H) More than $550,000 **20**
(I) More than $1,500,000 **22**
(J) More than $3,500,000 **24**
(K) More than $9,500,000 **26**
(L) More than $25,000,000 **28**
(M) More than $65,000,000 **30**
(N) More than $150,000,000 **32**
(O) More than $250,000,000 **34**
(P) More than $550,000,000 **36**.

Historical
Note

Effective November 1, 1987. Amended effective November 1, 1989 (amendment 237); November 1, 1993 (amendment 491); November 1, 2001 (amendment 617); January 25, 2003 (amendment 647); November 1, 2003 (amendment 653); November 1, 2015 (amendment 791).

PART U — [NOT USED]

PART V — [NOT USED]

PART W — [NOT USED]

PART X — OTHER OFFENSES

1. CONSPIRACIES, ATTEMPTS, SOLICITATIONS

§2X1.1. Attempt, Solicitation, or Conspiracy (Not Covered by a Specific Offense Guideline)

(a) Base Offense Level: The base offense level from the guideline for the substantive offense, plus any adjustments from such guideline for any intended offense conduct that can be established with reasonable certainty.

(b) Specific Offense Characteristics

(1) If an attempt, decrease by **3** levels, unless the defendant completed all the acts the defendant believed necessary for successful completion of the substantive offense or the circumstances demonstrate that the defendant was about to complete all such acts but for apprehension or interruption by some similar event

beyond the defendant's control.
(2) If a conspiracy, decrease by **3** levels, unless the defendant or a co-conspirator completed all the acts the conspirators believed necessary on their part for the successful completion of the substantive offense or the circumstances demonstrate that the conspirators were about to complete all such acts but for apprehension or interruption by some similar event beyond their control.
(3) (A) If a solicitation, decrease by **3** levels unless the person solicited to commit or aid the substantive offense completed all the acts he believed necessary for successful completion of the substantive offense or the circumstances demonstrate that the person was about to complete all such acts but for apprehension or interruption by some similar event beyond such person's control.
(B) If the statute treats solicitation of the substantive offense identically with the substantive offense, do not apply subdivision (A) above; *i.e.*, the offense level for solicitation is the same as that for the substantive offense.

(c) Cross Reference
(1) When an attempt, solicitation, or conspiracy is expressly covered by another offense guideline section, apply that guideline section.
(d) Special Instruction
(1) Subsection (b) shall not apply to:
(A) Any of the following offenses, if such offense involved, or was intended to promote, a federal crime of terrorism as defined in 18 U.S.C. § 2332b(g)(5):
18 U.S.C. § 81;
18 U.S.C. § 930(c);
18 U.S.C. § 1362;
18 U.S.C. § 1363;
18 U.S.C. § 1992(a)(1)–(a)(7), (a)(9), (a)(10);
18 U.S.C. § 2339A;
18 U.S.C. § 2340A;
49 U.S.C. § 46504;
49 U.S.C. § 46505; and
49 U.S.C. § 60123(b).
(B) Any of the following offenses:
18 U.S.C. § 32; and
18 U.S.C. § 2332a.

Commentary

Statutory Provisions: 18 U.S.C. §§ 371, 372, 2271, 2282A, 2282B. For additional statutory provision(s), *see* Appendix A (Statutory Index).

Application Notes:

1. Certain attempts, conspiracies, and solicitations are expressly covered by other offense guidelines.

Offense guidelines that expressly cover attempts include:
§§2A2.1, 2A3.1, 2A3.2, 2A3.3, 2A3.4, 2A4.2, 2A5.1;
§§2C1.1, 2C1.2;
§§2D1.1, 2D1.2, 2D1.5, 2D1.6, 2D1.7, 2D1.8, 2D1.9, 2D1.10, 2D1.11, 2D1.12, 2D1.13, 2D2.1, 2D2.2, 2D3.1, 2D3.2;
§2E5.1;
§2M6.1;
§2N1.1;
§2Q1.4.

Offense guidelines that expressly cover conspiracies include:
§2A1.5;
§§2D1.1, 2D1.2, 2D1.5, 2D1.6, 2D1.7, 2D1.8, 2D1.9, 2D1.10, 2D1.11, 2D1.12, 2D1.13, 2D2.1, 2D2.2, 2D3.1, 2D3.2;
§2H1.1;
§2M6.1;
§2T1.9.

Offense guidelines that expressly cover solicitations include:
§2A1.5;
§§2C1.1, 2C1.2;
§2E5.1.

2. "***Substantive offense***," as used in this guideline, means the offense that the defendant was convicted of soliciting, attempting, or conspiring to commit. Under §2X1.1(a), the base offense level will be the same as that for the substantive offense. But the only specific offense characteristics from the guideline for the substantive offense that apply are those that are determined to have been specifically intended or actually occurred. Speculative specific offense characteristics will not be applied. For example, if two defendants are arrested during the conspiratorial stage of planning an armed bank robbery, the offense level ordinarily would not include aggravating factors regarding possible injury to others, hostage taking, discharge of a weapon, or obtaining a large sum of money, because such factors would be speculative. The offense level would simply reflect the level applicable to robbery of a financial institution, with the enhancement for possession of a weapon. If it was established that the defendants actually intended to physically restrain the teller, the specific offense characteristic for physical restraint would be added. In an attempted theft, the value of the items that the defendant attempted to steal would be considered.

3. If the substantive offense is not covered by a specific guideline, *see* §2X5.1 (Other Offenses).

4. In certain cases, the participants may have completed (or have been about to complete but for apprehension or interruption) all of the acts necessary for the successful completion of part, but not all, of the intended offense. In such cases, the offense level for the count (or group of closely related multiple counts) is whichever of the following is greater: the offense level for the intended offense minus 3 levels (under §2X1.1(b)(1), (b)(2), or (b)(3)(A)), or the offense level for the part of the offense for which the necessary acts were completed (or about to be completed but for apprehension or interruption). For example, where the intended offense was the theft of $800,000 but the participants completed (or were about to complete) only the acts necessary to steal $30,000, the offense level is the offense level for the theft of $800,000 minus 3 levels, or the offense level for the theft of $30,000, whichever is greater.

In the case of multiple counts that are not closely related counts, whether the 3-level reduction under §2X1.1(b)(1), (b)(2), or (b)(3)(A) applies is determined separately for each count.

Background: In most prosecutions for conspiracies or attempts, the substantive offense was substantially completed or was interrupted or prevented on the verge of completion by the intercession of law enforcement authorities or the victim. In such cases, no reduction of the offense level is warranted. Sometimes, however, the arrest occurs well before the defendant or

any co-conspirator has completed the acts necessary for the substantive offense. Under such circumstances, a reduction of 3 levels is provided under §2X1.1(b)(1) or (2).

Historical Note

Effective November 1, 1987. Amended effective January 15, 1988 (amendment 42); November 1, 1989 (amendments 238–242); November 1, 1990 (amendments 311 and 327); November 1, 1991 (amendment 411); November 1, 1992 (amendments 444 and 447); November 1, 1993 (amendment 496); November 1, 2001 (amendment 633); November 1, 2002 (amendment 637); November 1, 2004 (amendment 669); November 1, 2007 (amendments 699 and 700).

* * * * *

2. AIDING AND ABETTING

§2X2.1. Aiding and Abetting

The offense level is the same level as that for the underlying offense.

Commentary

Statutory Provisions: 18 U.S.C. §§ 2, 2284, 2339, 2339A, 2339C(a)(1)(A).

Application Note:

1. **Definition.**—For purposes of this guideline, "***underlying offense***" means the offense the defendant is convicted of aiding or abetting, or in the case of a violation of 18 U.S.C. § 2339A or § 2339C(a)(1)(A), "underlying offense" means the offense the defendant is convicted of having materially supported or provided or collected funds for, prior to or during its commission.

Background: A defendant convicted of aiding and abetting is punishable as a principal. 18 U.S.C. § 2. This section provides that aiding and abetting the commission of an offense has the same offense level as the underlying offense. An adjustment for a mitigating role (§3B1.2) may be applicable.

Historical Note

Effective November 1, 1987. Amended effective November 1, 1990 (amendment 359); November 1, 2002 (amendment 637); November 1, 2003 (amendment 655); November 1, 2007 (amendment 700).

* * * * *

3. ACCESSORY AFTER THE FACT

§2X3.1. Accessory After the Fact

(a) Base Offense Level:

(1) **6** levels lower than the offense level for the underlying offense, except as provided in subdivisions (2) and (3).

(2) The base offense level under this guideline shall be not less than level **4**.

(3) (A) The base offense level under this guideline shall be not more than level **30**, except as provided in subdivision (B).

(B) In any case in which the conduct is limited to harboring a fugitive, other than a case described in subdivision (C), the base offense level under this guideline shall be not more than level **20**.

(C) The limitation in subdivision (B) shall not apply in any case in which (i) the defendant is convicted under 18 U.S.C. § 2339 or § 2339A; or (ii) the conduct involved harboring a person who committed any offense listed in 18 U.S.C. § 2339 or § 2339A or who committed any offense involving or intending to promote a federal crime of terrorism, as defined in 18 U.S.C. § 2332b(g)(5). In such a case, the base offense level under this guideline shall be not more than level **30**, as provided in subdivision (A).

Commentary

Statutory Provisions: 18 U.S.C. §§ 3, 757, 1071, 1072, 2284, 2339, 2339A, 2339C(c)(2)(A), (c)(2)(B) (but only with respect to funds known or intended to have been provided or collected in violation of 18 U.S.C. § 2339C(a)(1)(A)).

Application Notes:

1. **Definition.**—For purposes of this guideline, "***underlying offense***" means the offense as to which the defendant is convicted of being an accessory, or in the case of a violation of 18 U.S.C. § 2339A, "***underlying offense***" means the offense the defendant is convicted of having materially supported after its commission (*i.e.*, in connection with the concealment of or an escape from that offense), or in the case of a violation of 18 U.S.C. § 2339C(c)(2)(A), "***underlying offense***" means the violation of 18 U.S.C. § 2339B with respect to which the material support or resources were concealed or disguised. Apply the base offense level plus any applicable specific offense characteristics that were known, or reasonably should have been known, by the defendant; *see* Application Note 9 of the Commentary to §1B1.3 (Relevant Conduct).
2. **Application of Mitigating Role Adjustment.**—The adjustment from §3B1.2 (Mitigating Role) normally would not apply because an adjustment for reduced culpability is incorporated in the base offense level.

Historical
Note
Effective November 1, 1987. Amended effective November 1, 1989 (amendment 243); November 1, 1991 (amendment 380); November 1, 1993 (amendment 496); November 1, 2002 (amendment 637); November 1, 2003 (amendment 655); November 1, 2007 (amendment 700); November 1, 2015 (amendments 790 and 797).

* * * * *

4. MISPRISION OF FELONY

§2X4.1. Misprision of Felony

(a) Base Offense Level: **9** levels lower than the offense level for the underlying offense, but in no event less than **4**, or more than **19**.

Commentary

Statutory Provision: 18 U.S.C. § 4.

Application Notes:

1. "***Underlying offense***" means the offense as to which the defendant is convicted of committing the misprision. Apply the base offense level plus any applicable specific offense characteristics that were known, or reasonably should have been known, by the defendant; *see* Application Note 9 of the Commentary to §1B1.3 (Relevant Conduct).
2. The adjustment from §3B1.2 (Mitigating Role) normally would not apply because an adjustment for reduced culpability is incorporated in the base offense level.

Historical
Note
Effective November 1, 1987. Amended effective November 1, 1989 (amendment 244); November 1, 1993 (amendment 496); November 1, 2015 (amendments 790 and 797).

* * * * *

5. ALL OTHER FELONY OFFENSES AND CLASS A MISDEMEANORS

Historical
Note
Effective November 1, 1987. Amended effective November 1, 2006 (amendment 685).

§2X5.1. Other Felony Offenses

If the offense is a felony for which no guideline expressly has been promulgated, apply the most analogous offense guideline. If there is not a sufficiently analogous guideline, the provisions of 18 U.S.C. § 3553 shall control, except that any guidelines and policy statements that can be applied meaningfully in the absence of a Chapter Two offense guideline shall remain applicable.

If the defendant is convicted under 18 U.S.C. § 1841(a)(1), apply the guideline that covers the conduct the defendant is convicted of having engaged in, as that conduct is described in 18 U.S.C. § 1841(a)(1) and listed in 18 U.S.C. § 1841(b).

§2X5.1

Commentary

Statutory Provision: 18 U.S.C. § 1841(a)(1).

Application Notes:

1. **In General.**—Guidelines and policy statements that can be applied meaningfully in the absence of a Chapter Two offense guideline include: §5B1.3 (Conditions of Probation); §5D1.1 (Imposition of a Term of Supervised Release); §5D1.2 (Term of Supervised Release); §5D1.3 (Conditions of Supervised Release); §5E1.1 (Restitution); §5E1.3 (Special Assessments); §5E1.4 (Forfeiture); Chapter Five, Part F (Sentencing Options); §5G1.3 (Imposition of a Sentence on a Defendant Subject to an Undischarged Term of Imprisonment or Anticipated State Term of Imprisonment); Chapter Five, Part H (Specific Offender Characteristics); Chapter Five, Part J (Relief from Disability); Chapter Five, Part K (Departures); Chapter Six, Part A (Sentencing Procedures); Chapter Six, Part B (Plea Agreements).

2. **Convictions under 18 U.S.C. § 1841(a)(1).**—

(A) **In General.**—If the defendant is convicted under 18 U.S.C. § 1841(a)(1), the Chapter Two offense guideline that applies is the guideline that covers the conduct the defendant is convicted of having engaged in, *i.e.*, the conduct of which the defendant is convicted that violates a specific provision listed in 18 U.S.C. § 1841(b) and that results in the death of, or bodily injury to, a child in utero at the time of the offense of conviction. For example, if the defendant committed aggravated sexual abuse against the unborn child's mother and it caused the death of the child in utero, the applicable Chapter Two guideline would be §2A3.1 (Criminal Sexual Abuse; Attempt to Commit Criminal Sexual Abuse).

(B) **Upward Departure Provision.**—For offenses under 18 U.S.C. § 1841(a)(1), an upward departure may be warranted if the offense level under the applicable guideline does not adequately account for the death of, or serious bodily injury to, the child in utero.

3. **Application of §2X5.2.**—This guideline applies only to felony offenses not referenced in Appendix A (Statutory Index). For Class A misdemeanor offenses that have not been referenced in Appendix A, apply §2X5.2 (Class A Misdemeanors (Not Covered by Another Specific Offense Guideline)).

Background: Many offenses, especially assimilative crimes, are not listed in the Statutory Index or in any of the lists of Statutory Provisions that follow each offense guideline. Nonetheless, the specific guidelines that have been promulgated cover the type of criminal behavior that most such offenses proscribe. The court is required to determine if there is a sufficiently analogous offense guideline, and, if so, to apply the guideline that is most analogous. In a case in which there is no sufficiently analogous guideline, the provisions of 18 U.S.C. § 3553 control. The sentencing guidelines apply to convictions under 18 U.S.C. § 13 (Assimilative Crimes Act) and 18 U.S.C. § 1153 (Indian Major Crimes Act); *see* 18 U.S.C. § 3551(a), as amended by section 1602 of Public Law 101–647.

Historical Note

Effective November 1, 1987. Amended effective June 15, 1988 (amendment 43); November 1, 1991 (amendment 412); November 1, 1997 (amendment 569); November 1, 2006 (amendment 685); November 1, 2014 (amendment 787).

§2X6.1

§2X5.2. Class A Misdemeanors (Not Covered by Another Specific Offense Guideline)

(a) Base Offense Level: **6**

Commentary

Statutory Provisions: 18 U.S.C. §§ 1365(f), 1801; 42 U.S.C. § 14133; 49 U.S.C. § 31310.

Application Note:

1. **In General.**—This guideline applies to Class A misdemeanor offenses that are specifically referenced in Appendix A (Statutory Index) to this guideline. This guideline also applies to Class A misdemeanor offenses that have not been referenced in Appendix A. Do not apply this guideline to a Class A misdemeanor that has been specifically referenced in Appendix A to another Chapter Two guideline.

Historical Note

Effective November 1, 2006 (amendment 685). Amended effective November 1, 2007 (amendment 699); November 1, 2008 (amendment 721); November 1, 2010 (amendment 746).

* * * * *

6. OFFENSES INVOLVING USE OF A MINOR IN A CRIME OF VIOLENCE

Historical Note

Effective November 1, 2004 (amendment 674).

§2X6.1. Use of a Minor in a Crime of Violence

(a) Base Offense Level: **4** plus the offense level from the guideline applicable to the underlying crime of violence.

Commentary

Statutory Provision: 18 U.S.C. § 25.

Application Notes:

1. **Definition.**—For purposes of this guideline, "***underlying crime of violence***" means the crime of violence as to which the defendant is convicted of using a minor.

2. **Inapplicability of §3B1.4.**—Do not apply the adjustment under §3B1.4 (Using a Minor to Commit a Crime).

3. **Multiple Counts.**—

(A) In a case in which the defendant is convicted under both 18 U.S.C. § 25 and the underlying crime of violence, the counts shall be grouped pursuant to subsection (a) of §3D1.2 (Groups of Closely Related Counts).

(B) Multiple counts involving the use of a minor in a crime of violence shall not be grouped under §3D1.2.

Historical Note

Effective November 1, 2004 (amendment 674).

* * * * *

7. OFFENSES INVOLVING BORDER TUNNELS AND SUBMERSIBLE AND SEMI-SUBMERSIBLE VESSELS

Historical Note

Effective November 1, 2007 (amendment 700). Amended effective November 1, 2009 (amendment 728).

§2X7.1. Border Tunnels and Subterranean Passages

(a) Base Offense Level:

(1) If the defendant was convicted under 18 U.S.C. § 555(c), **4** plus the offense level applicable to the underlying smuggling offense. If the resulting offense level is less than level **16**, increase to level **16**.

(2) **16**, if the defendant was convicted under 18 U.S.C. § 555(a); or

(3) **8**, if the defendant was convicted under 18 U.S.C. § 555(b).

Commentary

Statutory Provision: 18 U.S.C. § 555.

Application Note:

1. **Definition.**—For purposes of this guideline, "***underlying smuggling offense***" means the smuggling offense the defendant committed through the use of the tunnel or subterranean passage.

Historical Note

Effective November 1, 2007 (amendment 700). Amended effective November 1, 2008 (amendment 724).

§2X7.2. Submersible and Semi-Submersible Vessels

(a) Base Offense Level: **26**

(b) Specific Offense Characteristic

(1) (Apply the greatest) If the offense involved—

(A) a failure to heave to when directed by law enforcement officers, increase by **2** levels;

(B) an attempt to sink the vessel, increase by **4** levels; or

(C) the sinking of the vessel, increase by **8** levels.

Commentary

Statutory Provision: 18 U.S.C. § 2285.

Application Note:

1. **Upward Departure Provisions.**—An upward departure may be warranted in any of the following cases:

(A) The defendant engaged in a pattern of activity involving use of a submersible vessel or semi-submersible vessel described in 18 U.S.C. § 2285 to facilitate other felonies.

(B) The offense involved use of the vessel as part of an ongoing criminal organization or enterprise.

Background: This guideline implements the directive to the Commission in section 103 of Public Law 110–407.

Historical Note

Effective November 1, 2009 (amendment 728).

PART Y — [NOT USED]

PART Z — [NOT USED]

CHAPTER THREE

ADJUSTMENTS

PART A — VICTIM-RELATED ADJUSTMENTS

Introductory Commentary

The following adjustments are included in this Part because they may apply to a wide variety of offenses.

Historical Note

Effective November 1, 1987. Amended effective November 1, 1990 (amendment 344).

§3A1.1. Hate Crime Motivation or Vulnerable Victim

(a) If the finder of fact at trial or, in the case of a plea of guilty or *nolo contendere*, the court at sentencing determines beyond a reasonable doubt that the defendant intentionally selected any victim or any property as the object of the offense of conviction because of the actual or perceived race, color, religion, national origin, ethnicity, gender, gender identity, disability, or sexual orientation of any person, increase by **3** levels.

(b) (1) If the defendant knew or should have known that a victim of the offense was a vulnerable victim, increase by **2** levels.

(2) If (A) subdivision (1) applies; and (B) the offense involved a large number of vulnerable victims, increase the offense level determined under subdivision (1) by **2** additional levels.

(c) Special Instruction

(1) Subsection (a) shall not apply if an adjustment from §2H1.1(b)(1) applies.

Commentary

Application Notes:

1. Subsection (a) applies to offenses that are hate crimes. Note that special evidentiary requirements govern the application of this subsection.

Do not apply subsection (a) on the basis of gender in the case of a sexual offense. In such cases, this factor is taken into account by the offense level of the Chapter Two offense

guideline. Moreover, do not apply subsection (a) if an adjustment from §2H1.1(b)(1) applies.

2. For purposes of subsection (b), "***vulnerable victim***" means a person (A) who is a victim of the offense of conviction and any conduct for which the defendant is accountable under §1B1.3 (Relevant Conduct); and (B) who is unusually vulnerable due to age, physical or mental condition, or who is otherwise particularly susceptible to the criminal conduct.

Subsection (b) applies to offenses involving an unusually vulnerable victim in which the defendant knows or should have known of the victim's unusual vulnerability. The adjustment would apply, for example, in a fraud case in which the defendant marketed an ineffective cancer cure or in a robbery in which the defendant selected a handicapped victim.

But it would not apply in a case in which the defendant sold fraudulent securities by mail to the general public and one of the victims happened to be senile. Similarly, for example, a bank teller is not an unusually vulnerable victim solely by virtue of the teller's position in a bank.

Do not apply subsection (b) if the factor that makes the person a vulnerable victim is incorporated in the offense guideline. For example, if the offense guideline provides an enhancement for the age of the victim, this subsection would not be applied unless the victim was unusually vulnerable for reasons unrelated to age.

3. The adjustments from subsections (a) and (b) are to be applied cumulatively. Do not, however, apply subsection (b) in a case in which subsection (a) applies unless a victim of

the offense was unusually vulnerable for reasons unrelated to race, color, religion, national origin, ethnicity, gender, gender identity, disability, or sexual orientation.

4. If an enhancement from subsection (b) applies and the defendant's criminal history includes a prior sentence for an offense that involved the selection of a vulnerable victim, an upward departure may be warranted.

5. For purposes of this guideline, "***gender identity***" means actual or perceived gender-related characteristics. *See* 18 U.S.C. § 249(c)(4).

Background: Subsection (a) reflects the directive to the Commission, contained in Section 280003 of the Violent Crime Control and Law Enforcement Act of 1994, to provide an enhancement of not less than three levels for an offense when the finder of fact at trial determines beyond a reasonable doubt that the defendant had a hate crime motivation. To avoid unwarranted sentencing disparity based on the method of conviction, the Commission has broadened the application of this enhancement to include offenses that, in the case of a plea of guilty or *nolo contendere*, the court at sentencing determines are hate crimes. In section 4703(a) of Public Law 111–84, Congress broadened the scope of that directive to include gender identity; to reflect that congressional action, the Commission has broadened the scope of this enhancement to include gender identity.

Subsection (b)(2) implements, in a broader form, the instruction to the Commission in section 6(c)(3) of Public Law 105–184.

Historical Note

Effective November 1, 1987. Amended effective November 1, 1989 (amendment 245); November 1, 1990 (amendment 344); November 1, 1992 (amendment 454); November 1, 1995 (amendment 521); November 1, 1997 (amendment 564); November 1, 1998 (amendment 587); November 1, 2000 (amendment 595); November 1, 2010 (amendment 743).

§3A1.2. Official Victim

(Apply the greatest):

(a) If (1) the victim was (A) a government officer or employee; (B) a former government officer or employee; or (C) a member of the immediate family of a person described in subdivision (A) or (B); and

(2) the offense of conviction was motivated by such status, increase by **3** levels.

(b) If subsection (a)(1) and (2) apply, and the applicable Chapter Two guideline is from Chapter Two, Part A (Offenses Against the Person), increase by **6** levels.

(c) If, in a manner creating a substantial risk of serious bodily injury, the defendant or a person for whose conduct the defendant is otherwise accountable—

(1) knowing or having reasonable cause to believe that a person was a law enforcement officer, assaulted such officer during the course of the offense or immediate flight therefrom; or

(2) knowing or having reasonable cause to believe that a person was a prison official, assaulted such official while the defendant (or a person for whose conduct the defendant is otherwise accountable) was in the custody or control of a prison or other correctional facility,

increase by **6** levels.

Commentary

Application Notes:

1. **Applicability to Certain Victims.**—This guideline applies when specified individuals are victims of the offense. This guideline does not apply when the only victim is an organization,

agency, or the government.

2. **Nonapplicability in Case of Incorporation of Factor in Chapter Two.**—Do not apply this adjustment if the offense guideline specifically incorporates this factor. The only offense guideline in Chapter Two that specifically incorporates this factor is §2A2.4 (Obstructing or Impeding Officers).

3. **Application of Subsections (a) and (b).**—"***Motivated by such status***", for purposes of subsections (a) and (b), means that the offense of conviction was motivated by the fact that the victim was a government officer or employee, or a member of the immediate family thereof. This adjustment would not apply, for example, where both the defendant and victim were employed by the same government agency and the offense was motivated by a personal dispute. This adjustment also would not apply in the case of a robbery of a

postal employee because the offense guideline for robbery contains an enhancement (§2B3.1(b)(1)) that takes such conduct into account.

4. **Application of Subsection (c).**—

(A) **In General.**—Subsection (c) applies in circumstances tantamount to aggravated assault (i) against a law enforcement officer, committed in the course of, or in immediate flight following, another offense; or (ii) against a prison official, while the defendant (or a person for whose conduct the defendant is otherwise accountable) was in the custody or control of a prison or other correctional facility. While subsection (c) may apply in connection with a variety of offenses that are not by nature targeted against official victims, its applicability is limited to assaultive conduct against such official victims that is sufficiently serious to create at least a "substantial risk of serious bodily injury".

(B) **Definitions.**—For purposes of subsection (c):

"***Custody or control***" includes "non-secure custody", *i.e.*, custody with no significant physical restraint. For example, a defendant is in the custody or control of a prison or other correctional facility if the defendant (i) is on a work detail outside the security perimeter of the prison or correctional facility; (ii) is physically away from the prison or correctional facility while on a pass or furlough; or (iii) is in custody at a community corrections center, community treatment center, "halfway house", or similar facility. The defendant also shall be deemed to be in the custody or control of a prison or other correctional facility while the defendant is in the status of having escaped from that prison or correctional facility.

"***Prison official***" means any individual (including a director, officer, employee, independent contractor, or volunteer, but not including an inmate) authorized to act on behalf of a prison or correctional facility. For example, this enhancement would be applicable to any of the following: (i) an individual employed by a prison as a corrections officer; (ii) an individual employed by a prison as a work detail supervisor; and (iii) a nurse who, under contract, provides medical services to prisoners in a prison health facility.

"***Substantial risk of serious bodily injury***" includes any more serious injury that was risked, as well as actual serious bodily injury (or more serious injury) if it occurs.

5. **Upward Departure Provision.**—If the official victim is an exceptionally high-level official, such as the President or the Vice President of the United States, an upward departure may be warranted due to the potential disruption of the governmental function.

Historical Note

Effective November 1, 1987. Amended effective January 15, 1988 (amendment 44); November 1, 1989 (amendments 246–248); November 1, 1992 (amendment 455); November 1, 2002 (amendment 643); November 1, 2004 (amendment 663); November 1, 2010 (amendment 747).

§3A1.3. Restraint of Victim

If a victim was physically restrained in the course of the offense, increase by **2** levels.

Commentary

Application Notes:

1. "***Physically restrained***" is defined in the Commentary to §1B1.1 (Application Instructions).
2. Do not apply this adjustment where the offense guideline specifically incorporates this factor, or where the unlawful restraint of a victim is an element of the offense itself (*e.g.*, this adjustment does not apply to offenses covered by §2A4.1 (Kidnapping, Abduction, Unlawful Restraint)).
3. If the restraint was sufficiently egregious, an upward departure may be warranted. *See* §5K2.4 (Abduction or Unlawful Restraint).

Historical Note

Effective November 1, 1987. Amended effective November 1, 1989 (amendments 249 and 250); November 1, 1991 (amendment 413).

§3A1.4. Terrorism

(a) If the offense is a felony that involved, or was intended to promote, a federal crime of terrorism, increase by **12** levels; but if the resulting offense level is less than level **32**, increase to level **32**.

(b) In each such case, the defendant's criminal history category from Chapter Four (Criminal History and Criminal Livelihood) shall be Category VI.

Commentary

Application Notes:

1. **"Federal Crime of Terrorism" Defined.**—For purposes of this guideline, "***federal crime of terrorism***" has the meaning given that term in 18 U.S.C. § 2332b(g)(5).
2. **Harboring, Concealing, and Obstruction Offenses.**—For purposes of this guideline, an offense that involved (A) harboring or concealing a terrorist who committed a federal crime of terrorism (such as an offense under 18 U.S.C. § 2339 or § 2339A); or (B) obstructing an investigation of a federal crime of terrorism, shall be considered to have involved, or to have been intended to promote, that federal crime of terrorism.
3. **Computation of Criminal History Category.**—Under subsection (b), if the defendant's criminal history category as determined under Chapter Four (Criminal History and Criminal Livelihood) is less than Category VI, it shall be increased to Category VI.
4. **Upward Departure Provision.**—By the terms of the directive to the Commission in section 730 of the Antiterrorism and Effective Death Penalty Act of 1996, the adjustment provided by this guideline applies only to federal crimes of terrorism. However, there may be cases in which (A) the offense was calculated to influence or affect the conduct of government by intimidation or coercion, or to retaliate against government conduct but the offense involved, or was intended to promote, an offense other than one of the offenses specifically enumerated in 18 U.S.C. § 2332b(g)(5)(B); or (B) the offense involved, or was

intended to promote, one of the offenses specifically enumerated in 18 U.S.C. § 2332b(g)(5)(B), but the terrorist motive was to intimidate or coerce a civilian population, rather than to influence or affect the conduct of government by intimidation or coercion, or to retaliate against government conduct. In such cases an upward departure would be warranted, except that the sentence resulting from such a departure may not exceed the top of the guideline range that would have resulted if the adjustment under this guideline had been applied.

Historical Note

Effective November 1, 1995 (amendment 526). Amended effective November 1, 1996 (amendment 539); November 1, 1997 (amendment 565); November 1, 2002 (amendment 637).

§3A1.5. Serious Human Rights Offense

If the defendant was convicted of a serious human rights offense, increase

the offense level as follows:
(a) If the defendant was convicted of an offense under 18 U.S.C. § 1091(c), increase by **2** levels.
(b) If the defendant was convicted of any other serious human rights offense, increase by **4** levels. If (1) death resulted, and (2) the resulting offense level is less than level **37**, increase to level **37**.

Commentary

Application Notes:

1. **Definition.**—For purposes of this guideline, "***serious human rights offense***" means violations of federal criminal laws relating to genocide, torture, war crimes, and the use or recruitment of child soldiers under sections 1091, 2340, 2340A, 2441, and 2442 of title 18, United States Code. *See* 28 U.S.C. § 509B(e).
2. **Application of Minimum Offense Level in Subsection (b).**—The minimum offense level in subsection (b) is cumulative with any other provision in the guidelines. For example, if death resulted and this factor was specifically incorporated into the Chapter Two offense guideline, the minimum offense level in subsection (b) may also apply.

Background: This guideline covers a range of conduct considered to be serious human rights offenses, including genocide, war crimes, torture, and the recruitment or use of child soldiers. *See* generally 28 U.S.C. § 509B(e).
Serious human rights offenses generally have a statutory maximum term of imprisonment of 20 years, but if death resulted, a higher statutory maximum term of imprisonment of any term of years or life applies. *See* 18 U.S.C. §§ 1091(b), 2340A(a), 2442(b). For the offense of war crimes, a statutory maximum term of imprisonment of any term of years or life always applies. *See* 18 U.S.C. § 2441(a). For the offense of incitement to genocide, the statutory maximum term of imprisonment is five years. *See* 18 U.S.C. § 1091(c).

Historical Note
Effective November 1, 2012 (amendment 765).

PART B — ROLE IN THE OFFENSE

Introductory Commentary

This Part provides adjustments to the offense level based upon the role the defendant played in committing the offense. The determination of a defendant's role in the offense is to be made on the basis of all conduct within the scope of §1B1.3 (Relevant Conduct), *i.e.*, all conduct included under §1B1.3(a)(1)–(4), and not solely on the basis of elements and acts cited in the count of conviction.
When an offense is committed by more than one participant, §3B1.1 or §3B1.2 (or neither) may apply. Section 3B1.3 may apply to offenses committed by any number of participants.

Historical Note
Effective November 1, 1987. Amended effective November 1, 1990 (amendment 345); November 1, 1992 (amendment 456).

§3B1.1. Aggravating Role

Based on the defendant's role in the offense, increase the offense level as follows:
(a) If the defendant was an organizer or leader of a criminal activity that involved five or more participants or was otherwise extensive, increase by **4** levels.
(b) If the defendant was a manager or supervisor (but not an organizer or leader) and the criminal activity involved five or more participants or was otherwise extensive, increase by **3** levels.
(c) If the defendant was an organizer, leader, manager, or supervisor in any criminal activity other than described in (a) or (b), increase

by **2** levels.

Commentary

Application Notes:

1. A "***participant***" is a person who is criminally responsible for the commission of the offense, but need not have been convicted. A person who is not criminally responsible for the commission of the offense (*e.g.*, an undercover law enforcement officer) is not a participant.

2. To qualify for an adjustment under this section, the defendant must have been the organizer, leader, manager, or supervisor of one or more other participants. An upward departure may be warranted, however, in the case of a defendant who did not organize, lead, manage, or supervise another participant, but who nevertheless exercised management responsibility over the property, assets, or activities of a criminal organization.

3. In assessing whether an organization is "otherwise extensive," all persons involved during the course of the entire offense are to be considered. Thus, a fraud that involved only three participants but used the unknowing services of many outsiders could be considered extensive.

4. In distinguishing a leadership and organizational role from one of mere management or supervision, titles such as "kingpin" or "boss" are not controlling. Factors the court should consider include the exercise of decision making authority, the nature of participation in the commission of the offense, the recruitment of accomplices, the claimed right to a larger share of the fruits of the crime, the degree of participation in planning or organizing the offense, the nature and scope of the illegal activity, and the degree of control and authority exercised over others. There can, of course, be more than one person who qualifies as a leader or organizer of a criminal association or conspiracy. This adjustment does not apply to a defendant who merely suggests committing the offense.

Background: This section provides a range of adjustments to increase the offense level based upon the size of a criminal organization (*i.e.*, the number of participants in the offense) and the degree to which the defendant was responsible for committing the offense. This adjustment is included primarily because of concerns about relative responsibility. However, it is also likely that persons who exercise a supervisory or managerial role in the commission of an offense tend to profit more from it and present a greater danger to the public and/or are more likely to recidivate. The Commission's intent is that this adjustment should increase with both the size of the organization and the degree of the defendant's responsibility.

In relatively small criminal enterprises that are not otherwise to be considered as extensive in scope or in planning or preparation, the distinction between organization and leadership, and that of management or supervision, is of less significance than in larger enterprises that tend to have clearly delineated divisions of responsibility. This is reflected in the inclusiveness of §3B1.1(c).

Historical Note

Effective November 1, 1987. Amended effective November 1, 1991 (amendment 414); November 1, 1993 (amendment 500).

§3B1.2. Mitigating Role

Based on the defendant's role in the offense, decrease the offense level as follows:

(a) If the defendant was a minimal participant in any criminal activity, decrease by **4** levels.

(b) If the defendant was a minor participant in any criminal activity, decrease by **2** levels.

In cases falling between (a) and (b), decrease by **3** levels.

Commentary

Application Notes:
1. **Definition.**—For purposes of this guideline, "***participant***" has the meaning given that term in Application Note 1 of §3B1.1 (Aggravating Role).
2. **Requirement of Multiple Participants.**—This guideline is not applicable unless more than one participant was involved in the offense. *See* the Introductory Commentary to this Part (Role in the Offense). Accordingly, an adjustment under this guideline may not apply to a defendant who is the only defendant convicted of an offense unless that offense involved other participants in addition to the defendant and the defendant otherwise qualifies for such an adjustment.
3. **Applicability of Adjustment.**—
(A) **Substantially Less Culpable than Average Participant.**—This section provides a range of adjustments for a defendant who plays a part in committing the offense that makes him substantially less culpable than the average participant in the criminal activity.
A defendant who is accountable under §1B1.3 (Relevant Conduct) only for the conduct in which the defendant personally was involved and who performs a limited function in the criminal activity may receive an adjustment under this guideline.
For example, a defendant who is convicted of a drug trafficking offense, whose participation in that offense was limited to transporting or storing drugs and who is accountable under §1B1.3 only for the quantity of drugs the defendant personally transported or stored may receive an adjustment under this guideline.
Likewise, a defendant who is accountable under §1B1.3 for a loss amount under §2B1.1 (Theft, Property Destruction, and Fraud) that greatly exceeds the defendant's personal gain from a fraud offense or who had limited knowledge of the scope of the scheme may receive an adjustment under this guideline. For example, a defendant in a health care fraud scheme, whose participation in the scheme was limited to serving as a nominee owner and who received little personal gain relative to the loss amount, may receive an adjustment under this guideline.
(B) **Conviction of Significantly Less Serious Offense.**—If a defendant has received a lower offense level by virtue of being convicted of an offense significantly less serious than warranted by his actual criminal conduct, a reduction for a mitigating role under this section ordinarily is not warranted because such defendant is not substantially less culpable than a defendant whose only conduct involved the less serious offense. For example, if a defendant whose actual conduct involved a minimal role in the distribution of 25 grams of cocaine (an offense having a Chapter Two offense level of level 12 under §2D1.1 (Unlawful Manufacturing, Importing, Exporting, or Trafficking (Including Possession with Intent to Commit These Offenses); Attempt or Conspiracy)) is convicted of simple possession of cocaine (an offense having a Chapter Two offense level of level 6 under §2D2.1 (Unlawful Possession; Attempt or Conspiracy)), no reduction for a mitigating role is warranted because the defendant is not substantially less culpable than a defendant whose only conduct involved the simple possession of cocaine.

(C) **Fact-Based Determination.**—The determination whether to apply subsection (a) or subsection (b), or an intermediate adjustment, is based on the totality of the circumstances and involves a determination that is heavily dependent upon the facts of the particular case.
In determining whether to apply subsection (a) or (b), or an intermediate adjustment, the court should consider the following non-exhaustive list of factors:
(i) the degree to which the defendant understood the scope and structure of the criminal activity;
(ii) the degree to which the defendant participated in planning or organizing the criminal activity;
(iii) the degree to which the defendant exercised decision-making authority or influenced

the exercise of decision-making authority;
(iv) the nature and extent of the defendant's participation in the commission of the criminal activity, including the acts the defendant performed and the responsibility and discretion the defendant had in performing those acts;
(v) the degree to which the defendant stood to benefit from the criminal activity.
For example, a defendant who does not have a proprietary interest in the criminal activity and who is simply being paid to perform certain tasks should be considered for an adjustment under this guideline.
The fact that a defendant performs an essential or indispensable role in the criminal activity is not determinative. Such a defendant may receive an adjustment under this guideline if he or she is substantially less culpable than the average participant in the criminal activity.
4. **Minimal Participant.**—Subsection (a) applies to a defendant described in Application Note 3(A) who plays a minimal role in the criminal activity. It is intended to cover defendants who are plainly among the least culpable of those involved in the conduct of a group. Under this provision, the defendant's lack of knowledge or understanding of the scope and structure of the enterprise and of the activities of others is indicative of a role as minimal participant.
5. **Minor Participant.**—Subsection (b) applies to a defendant described in Application Note 3(A) who is less culpable than most other participants in the criminal activity, but whose role could not be described as minimal.
6. **Application of Role Adjustment in Certain Drug Cases.**—In a case in which the court applied §2D1.1 and the defendant's base offense level under that guideline was reduced by operation of the maximum base offense level in §2D1.1(a)(5), the court also shall apply the appropriate adjustment under this guideline.
Historical
Note
Effective November 1, 1987. Amended effective November 1, 1992 (amendment 456); November 1, 2001 (amendment 635); November 1, 2002 (amendment 640); November 1, 2009 (amendment 737); November 1, 2011 (amendments 749 and 755); November 1, 2014 (amendment 782); November 1, 2015 (amendment 794).

§3B1.3. Abuse of Position of Trust or Use of Special Skill
If the defendant abused a position of public or private trust, or used a special skill, in a manner that significantly facilitated the commission or concealment of the offense, increase by **2** levels. This adjustment may not be employed if an abuse of trust or skill is included in the base offense level or specific offense characteristic. If this adjustment is based upon an abuse of a position of trust, it may be employed in addition to an adjustment under §3B1.1 (Aggravating Role); if this adjustment is based solely on the use of a special skill, it may not be employed in addition to an adjustment under §3B1.1 (Aggravating Role).
Commentary
Application Notes:
1. **Definition of "Public or Private Trust".**—"***Public or private trust***" refers to a position of public or private trust characterized by professional or managerial discretion (*i.e.*, substantial discretionary judgment that is ordinarily given considerable deference). Persons holding such positions ordinarily are subject to significantly less supervision than employees whose responsibilities are primarily non-discretionary in nature. For this adjustment to apply, the position of public or private trust must have contributed in some significant way to facilitating the commission or concealment of the offense (*e.g.*, by making the detection of the offense or the defendant's responsibility for the offense more difficult). This adjustment, for example, applies in the case of an embezzlement of a client's funds by an attorney serving as a guardian, a bank executive's fraudulent loan scheme, or the criminal sexual abuse of a patient by a physician under the guise of an examination.

This adjustment does not apply in the case of an embezzlement or theft by an ordinary bank teller or hotel clerk because such positions are not characterized by the abovedescribed factors.

2. **Application of Adjustment in Certain Circumstances.**—Notwithstanding Application Note 1, or any other provision of this guideline, an adjustment under this guideline shall apply to the following:

(A) An employee of the United States Postal Service who engages in the theft or destruction of undelivered United States mail.

(B) A defendant who exceeds or abuses the authority of his or her position in order to obtain, transfer, or issue unlawfully, or use without authority, any means of identification. "***Means of identification***" has the meaning given that term in 18 U.S.C. § 1028(d)(7). The following are examples to which this subdivision would apply: (i) an employee of a state motor vehicle department who exceeds or abuses the authority of his or her position by knowingly issuing a driver's license based on false, incomplete, or misleading information; (ii) a hospital orderly who exceeds or abuses the authority of his or her position by obtaining or misusing patient identification information from a patient chart; and (iii) a volunteer at a charitable organization who exceeds or abuses the authority of his or her position by obtaining or misusing identification information from a donor's file.

3. This adjustment also applies in a case in which the defendant provides sufficient indicia to the victim that the defendant legitimately holds a position of private or public trust when, in fact, the defendant does not. For example, the adjustment applies in the case of

a defendant who (A) perpetrates a financial fraud by leading an investor to believe the defendant is a legitimate investment broker; or (B) perpetrates a fraud by representing falsely to a patient or employer that the defendant is a licensed physician. In making the misrepresentation, the defendant assumes a position of trust, relative to the victim, that provides the defendant with the same opportunity to commit a difficult-to-detect crime that the defendant would have had if the position were held legitimately.

4. "***Special skill***" refers to a skill not possessed by members of the general public and usually requiring substantial education, training or licensing. Examples would include pilots, lawyers, doctors, accountants, chemists, and demolition experts.

5. The following additional illustrations of an abuse of a position of trust pertain to theft or embezzlement from employee pension or welfare benefit plans or labor unions:

(A) If the offense involved theft or embezzlement from an employee pension or welfare benefit plan and the defendant was a fiduciary of the benefit plan, an adjustment under this section for abuse of a position of trust will apply. "***Fiduciary of the benefit plan***" is defined in 29 U.S.C. § 1002(21)(A) to mean a person who exercises any discretionary authority or control in respect to the management of such plan or exercises authority or control in respect to management or disposition of its assets, or who renders investment advice for a fee or other direct or indirect compensation with respect to any moneys or other property of such plan, or has any authority or responsibility to do so, or who has any discretionary authority or responsibility in the administration of such plan.

(B) If the offense involved theft or embezzlement from a labor union and the defendant was a union officer or occupied a position of trust in the union (as set forth in 29 U.S.C. § 501(a)), an adjustment under this section for an abuse of a position of trust will apply.

Background: This adjustment applies to persons who abuse their positions of trust or their special skills to facilitate significantly the commission or concealment of a crime. The adjustment also applies to persons who provide sufficient indicia to the victim that they legitimately hold a position of public or private trust when, in fact, they do not. Such persons generally are viewed as more culpable.

Historical Note

Effective November 1, 1987. Amended effective November 1, 1990 (amendment 346); November 1, 1993 (amendment 492); November 1, 1998 (amendment 580); November 1, 2001 (amendment 617); November 1, 2005 (amendment 677); November 1, 2009 (amendment 726).

§3B1.4. Using a Minor To Commit a Crime

If the defendant used or attempted to use a person less than eighteen years of age to commit the offense or assist in avoiding detection of, or apprehension for, the offense, increase by **2** levels.

Commentary

Application Notes:

1. "***Used or attempted to use***" includes directing, commanding, encouraging, intimidating, counseling, training, procuring, recruiting, or soliciting.
2. Do not apply this adjustment if the Chapter Two offense guideline incorporates this factor. For example, if the defendant receives an enhancement under §2D1.1(b)(15)(B) for involving an individual less than 18 years of age in the offense, do not apply this adjustment.
3. If the defendant used or attempted to use more than one person less than eighteen years of age, an upward departure may be warranted.

Historical Note

Effective November 1, 1995 (amendment 527). Amended effective November 1, 1996 (amendment 540); November 1, 2010 (amendment 748); November 1, 2011 (amendment 750). A former §3B1.4 (untitled), effective November 1, 1987, amended effective November 1, 1989 (amendment 303), was deleted effective November 1, 1995 (amendment 527); November 1, 2014 (amendment 783).

§3B1.5. Use of Body Armor in Drug Trafficking Crimes and Crimes of Violence

If—

(1) the defendant was convicted of a drug trafficking crime or a crime of violence; and

(2) (apply the greater)—

(A) the offense involved the use of body armor, increase by **2** levels; or

(B) the defendant used body armor during the commission of the offense, in preparation for the offense, or in an attempt to avoid apprehension for the offense, increase by **4** levels.

Commentary

Application Notes:

1. **Definitions.**—For purposes of this guideline:

"***Body armor***" means any product sold or offered for sale, in interstate or foreign commerce, as personal protective body covering intended to protect against gunfire, regardless of whether the product is to be worn alone or is sold as a complement to another product or garment. *See* 18 U.S.C. § 921(a)(35).

"***Crime of violence***" has the meaning given that term in 18 U.S.C. § 16.

"***Drug trafficking crime***" has the meaning given that term in 18 U.S.C. § 924(c)(2).

"***Offense***" has the meaning given that term in Application Note 1 of the Commentary to §1B1.1 (Application Instructions).

"***Use***" means (A) active employment in a manner to protect the person from gunfire; or (B) use as a means of bartering. "Use" does not mean mere possession (*e.g.*, "use" does not mean that the body armor was found in the trunk of the car but not used actively as protection). "***Used***" means put into "use" as defined in this paragraph.

2. **Application of Subdivision (2)(B).**—Consistent with §1B1.3 (Relevant Conduct), the term "***defendant***", for purposes of subdivision (2)(B), limits the accountability of the defendant to the defendant's own conduct and conduct that the defendant aided or abetted, counseled, commanded, induced, procured, or willfully caused.

3. **Interaction with §2K2.6 and Other Counts of Conviction.**—If the defendant is convicted only of 18 U.S.C. § 931 and receives an enhancement under subsection (b)(1) of §2K2.6 (Possessing, Purchasing, or Owning Body Armor by Violent Felons), do not apply an adjustment under this guideline. However, if, in addition to the count of conviction under 18 U.S.C. § 931, the defendant (A) is convicted of an offense that is a drug trafficking crime or a crime of violence; and (B) used the body armor with respect to that offense, an adjustment under this guideline shall apply with respect to that offense.

Background: This guideline implements the directive in the James Guelff and Chris McCurley Body Armor Act of 2002 (section 11009(d) of the 21st Century Department of Justice Appropriations Authorization Act, Pub. L. 107–273).

Historical
Note
Effective November 1, 2003 (amendment 659). Amended effective November 1, 2004 (amendment 670).

PART C — OBSTRUCTION AND RELATED ADJUSTMENTS

Historical
Note
Effective November 1, 1987. Amended effective November 1, 2006 (amendment 684).

§3C1.1. Obstructing or Impeding the Administration of Justice

If (1) the defendant willfully obstructed or impeded, or attempted to obstruct or impede, the administration of justice with respect to the investigation, prosecution, or sentencing of the instant offense of conviction, and (2) the obstructive conduct related to (A) the defendant's offense of conviction and any relevant conduct; or (B) a closely related offense, increase the offense level by **2** levels.

Commentary

Application Notes:

1. **In General.**—This adjustment applies if the defendant's obstructive conduct (A) occurred with respect to the investigation, prosecution, or sentencing of the defendant's instant offense of conviction, and (B) related to (i) the defendant's offense of conviction and any relevant conduct; or (ii) an otherwise closely related case, such as that of a codefendant. Obstructive conduct that occurred prior to the start of the investigation of the instant offense of conviction may be covered by this guideline if the conduct was purposefully calculated, and likely, to thwart the investigation or prosecution of the offense of conviction.

2. **Limitations on Applicability of Adjustment.**—This provision is not intended to punish a defendant for the exercise of a constitutional right. A defendant's denial of guilt (other than a denial of guilt under oath that constitutes perjury), refusal to admit guilt or provide information to a probation officer, or refusal to enter a plea of guilty is not a basis for application of this provision. In applying this provision in respect to alleged false testimony or statements by the defendant, the court should be cognizant that inaccurate testimony or statements sometimes may result from confusion, mistake, or faulty memory and, thus, not all inaccurate testimony or statements necessarily reflect a willful attempt to obstruct justice.

3. **Covered Conduct Generally.**—Obstructive conduct can vary widely in nature, degree of planning, and seriousness. Application Note 4 sets forth examples of the types of conduct to which this adjustment is intended to apply. Application Note 5 sets forth examples of less serious forms of conduct to which this enhancement is not intended to apply, but that ordinarily can appropriately be sanctioned by the determination of the particular sentence within the otherwise applicable guideline range. Although the conduct to which this adjustment applies is not subject to precise definition, comparison of the examples set forth in Application Notes 4 and 5 should assist the court in determining whether application of this adjustment is warranted in a particular case.

4. **Examples of Covered Conduct.**—The following is a non-exhaustive list of examples of the types of conduct to which this adjustment applies:

(A) threatening, intimidating, or otherwise unlawfully influencing a co-defendant, witness, or juror, directly or indirectly, or attempting to do so;

(B) committing, suborning, or attempting to suborn perjury, including during the course of a civil proceeding if such perjury pertains to conduct that forms the basis of the offense of conviction;

(C) producing or attempting to produce a false, altered, or counterfeit document or record during an official investigation or judicial proceeding;

(D) destroying or concealing or directing or procuring another person to destroy or conceal evidence that is material to an official investigation or judicial proceeding (*e.g.*, shredding a document or destroying ledgers upon learning that an official investigation has commenced or is about to commence), or attempting to do so; however, if such conduct occurred contemporaneously with arrest (*e.g.*, attempting to swallow or throw away a controlled substance), it shall not, standing alone, be sufficient to warrant an adjustment for obstruction unless it resulted in a material hindrance to the official investigation or prosecution of the instant offense or the sentencing of the offender;

(E) escaping or attempting to escape from custody before trial or sentencing; or willfully failing to appear, as ordered, for a judicial proceeding;

(F) providing materially false information to a judge or magistrate judge;

(G) providing a materially false statement to a law enforcement officer that significantly obstructed or impeded the official investigation or prosecution of the instant offense;

(H) providing materially false information to a probation officer in respect to a presentence or other investigation for the court;

(I) other conduct prohibited by obstruction of justice provisions under Title 18, United States Code (*e.g.*, 18 U.S.C. §§ 1510, 1511);

(J) failing to comply with a restraining order or injunction issued pursuant to 21 U.S.C. § 853(e) or with an order to repatriate property issued pursuant to 21 U.S.C. § 853(p);

(K) threatening the victim of the offense in an attempt to prevent the victim from reporting the conduct constituting the offense of conviction.

This adjustment also applies to any other obstructive conduct in respect to the official investigation, prosecution, or sentencing of the instant offense where there is a separate count of conviction for such conduct.

5. **Examples of Conduct Ordinarily Not Covered.**—Some types of conduct ordinarily do not warrant application of this adjustment but may warrant a greater sentence within the otherwise applicable guideline range or affect the determination of whether other guideline adjustments apply (*e.g.*, §3E1.1 (Acceptance of Responsibility)). However, if the defendant is convicted of a separate count for such conduct, this adjustment will apply

and increase the offense level for the underlying offense (*i.e.*, the offense with respect to which the obstructive conduct occurred). *See* Application Note 8, below.

The following is a non-exhaustive list of examples of the types of conduct to which this application note applies:

(A) providing a false name or identification document at arrest, except where such conduct actually resulted in a significant hindrance to the investigation or prosecution of the instant offense;

(B) making false statements, not under oath, to law enforcement officers, unless Application Note 4(G) above applies;

(C) providing incomplete or misleading information, not amounting to a material falsehood, in respect to a presentence investigation;

(D) avoiding or fleeing from arrest (*see, however*, §3C1.2 (Reckless Endangerment During

Flight));
(E) lying to a probation or pretrial services officer about defendant's drug use while on pre-trial release, although such conduct may be a factor in determining whether to reduce the defendant's sentence under §3E1.1 (Acceptance of Responsibility).

6. **"Material" Evidence Defined.**—"***Material***" evidence, fact, statement, or information, as used in this section, means evidence, fact, statement, or information that, if believed, would tend to influence or affect the issue under determination.

7. **Inapplicability of Adjustment in Certain Circumstances.**—If the defendant is convicted of an offense covered by §2J1.1 (Contempt), §2J1.2 (Obstruction of Justice), §2J1.3 (Perjury or Subornation of Perjury; Bribery of Witness), §2J1.5 (Failure to Appear by Material Witness), §2J1.6 (Failure to Appear by Defendant), §2J1.9 (Payment to Witness), §2X3.1 (Accessory After the Fact), or §2X4.1 (Misprision of Felony), this adjustment is not to be applied to the offense level for that offense except if a significant further obstruction occurred during the investigation, prosecution, or sentencing of the obstruction offense itself (*e.g.*, if the defendant threatened a witness during the course of the prosecution for the obstruction offense).
Similarly, if the defendant receives an enhancement under §2D1.1(b)(15)(D), do not apply this adjustment.

8. **Grouping Under §3D1.2(c).**—If the defendant is convicted both of an obstruction offense (*e.g.*, 18 U.S.C. § 3146 (Penalty for failure to appear); 18 U.S.C. § 1621 (Perjury generally)) and an underlying offense (the offense with respect to which the obstructive conduct occurred), the count for the obstruction offense will be grouped with the count for the underlying offense under subsection (c) of §3D1.2 (Groups of Closely Related Counts). The offense level for that group of closely related counts will be the offense level for the underlying offense increased by the 2-level adjustment specified by this section, or the offense level for the obstruction offense, whichever is greater.

9. **Accountability for §1B1.3(a)(1)(A) Conduct.**—Under this section, the defendant is accountable for the defendant's own conduct and for conduct that the defendant aided or abetted, counseled, commanded, induced, procured, or willfully caused.

Historical Note
Effective November 1, 1987. Amended effective November 1, 1989 (amendments 251 and 252); November 1, 1990 (amendment 347); November 1, 1991 (amendment 415); November 1, 1992 (amendment 457); November 1, 1993 (amendment 496); November 1, 1997 (amendment 566); November 1, 1998 (amendments 579, 581, and 582); November 1, 2002 (amendment 637); November 1, 2004 (amendment 674); November 1, 2006 (amendment 693); November 1, 2010 (amendments 746, 747, and 748); November 1, 2011 (amendments 750 and 758); November 1, 2014 (amendment 783).

§3C1.2. Reckless Endangerment During Flight

If the defendant recklessly created a substantial risk of death or serious bodily injury to another person in the course of fleeing from a law enforcement officer, increase by **2** levels.

Commentary

Application Notes:

1. Do not apply this enhancement where the offense guideline in Chapter Two, or another adjustment in Chapter Three, results in an equivalent or greater increase in offense level solely on the basis of the same conduct.

2. "***Reckless***" is defined in the Commentary to §2A1.4 (Involuntary Manslaughter). For the purposes of this guideline, "reckless" means that the conduct was at least reckless and includes any higher level of culpability. However, where a higher degree of culpability was involved, an upward departure above the 2-level increase provided in this section may be warranted.

3. "***During flight***" is to be construed broadly and includes preparation for flight. Therefore, this adjustment also is applicable where the conduct occurs in the course of resisting arrest.

4. "***Another person***" includes any person, except a participant in the offense who willingly

participated in the flight.
5. Under this section, the defendant is accountable for the defendant's own conduct and for conduct that the defendant aided or abetted, counseled, commanded, induced, procured, or willfully caused.
6. If death or bodily injury results or the conduct posed a substantial risk of death or bodily injury to more than one person, an upward departure may be warranted. *See* Chapter Five, Part K (Departures).
Historical
Note
Effective November 1, 1990 (amendment 347). Amended effective November 1, 1991 (amendment 416); November 1, 1992 (amendment 457); November 1, 2010 (amendment 747).

§3C1.3. Commission of Offense While on Release

If a statutory sentencing enhancement under 18 U.S.C. § 3147 applies, increase the offense level by **3** levels.

Commentary

Application Note:
1. Under 18 U.S.C. § 3147, a sentence of imprisonment must be imposed in addition to the sentence for the underlying offense, and the sentence of imprisonment imposed under 18 U.S.C. § 3147 must run consecutively to any other sentence of imprisonment. Therefore, the court, in order to comply with the statute, should divide the sentence on the judgment form between the sentence attributable to the underlying offense and the sentence attributable to the enhancement. The court will have to ensure that the "total punishment" (*i.e.*, the sentence for the offense committed while on release plus the statutory sentencing enhancement under 18 U.S.C. § 3147) is in accord with the guideline range for the offense committed while on release, including, as in any other case in which a Chapter Three adjustment applies (*see* §1B1.1 (Application Instructions)), the adjustment provided by the enhancement in this section. For example, if the applicable adjusted guideline range is 30–37 months and the court determines a "total punishment" of 36 months is appropriate, a sentence of 30 months for the underlying offense plus 6 months under 18 U.S.C. § 3147 would satisfy this requirement. Similarly, if the applicable adjusted guideline range is 30–37 months and the court determines a "total punishment" of 30 months is appropriate, a sentence of 24 months for the underlying offense plus 6 months under 18 U.S.C. § 3147 would satisfy this requirement.
Background: An enhancement under 18 U.S.C. § 3147 applies, after appropriate sentencing notice, when a defendant is sentenced for an offense committed while released in connection with another federal offense.
This guideline enables the court to determine and implement a combined "total punishment" consistent with the overall structure of the guidelines, while at the same time complying with the statutory requirement.
Historical
Note
Effective November 1, 2006 (amendment 684). Amended effective November 1, 2009 (amendment 734).

§3C1.4. False Registration of Domain Name

If a statutory enhancement under 18 U.S.C. § 3559(g)(1) applies, increase by **2** levels.

Commentary

Background: This adjustment implements the directive to the Commission in section 204(b) of Pub. L. 108–482.
Historical
Note
Effective November 1, 2006 (amendment 689). Amended effective November 1, 2008 (amendment 724).

PART D — MULTIPLE COUNTS

Introductory Commentary

This Part provides rules for determining a single offense level that encompasses all the counts of which the defendant is convicted. These rules apply to multiple counts of conviction (A) contained in the same indictment or information; or (B) contained in different indictments or informations for which sentences are to be imposed at the same time or in a consolidated proceeding. The single, "combined" offense level that results from applying these rules is used, after adjustment pursuant to the guidelines in subsequent parts, to determine the sentence. These rules have been designed primarily with the more commonly prosecuted federal offenses in mind.

The rules in this Part seek to provide incremental punishment for significant additional criminal conduct. The most serious offense is used as a starting point. The other counts determine how much to increase the offense level. The amount of the additional punishment declines as the number of additional offenses increases.

Some offenses that may be charged in multiple-count indictments are so closely intertwined with other offenses that conviction for them ordinarily would not warrant increasing the guideline range. For example, embezzling money from a bank and falsifying the related records, although legally distinct offenses, represent essentially the same type of wrongful conduct with the same ultimate harm, so that it would be more appropriate to treat them as a single offense for purposes of sentencing. Other offenses, such as an assault causing bodily injury to a teller during a bank robbery, are so closely related to the more serious offense that it would be appropriate to treat them as part of the more serious offense, leaving the sentence enhancement to result from application of a specific offense characteristic.

In order to limit the significance of the formal charging decision and to prevent multiple punishment for substantially identical offense conduct, this Part provides rules for grouping offenses together. Convictions on multiple counts do not result in a sentence enhancement unless they represent additional conduct that is not otherwise accounted for by the guidelines. In essence, counts that are grouped together are treated as constituting a single offense for purposes of the guidelines.

Some offense guidelines, such as those for theft, fraud and drug offenses, contain provisions that deal with repetitive or ongoing behavior. Other guidelines, such as those for assault and robbery, are oriented more toward single episodes of criminal behavior. Accordingly, different rules are required for dealing with multiple-count convictions involving these two different general classes of offenses. More complex cases involving different types of offenses may require application of one rule to some of the counts and another rule to other counts.

Some offenses, *e.g.*, racketeering and conspiracy, may be "composite" in that they involve a pattern of conduct or scheme involving multiple underlying offenses. The rules in this Part are to be used to determine the offense level for such composite offenses from the offense level for the underlying offenses.

Essentially, the rules in this Part can be summarized as follows: (1) If the offense guidelines in Chapter Two base the offense level primarily on the amount of money or quantity of substance involved (*e.g.*, theft, fraud, drug trafficking, firearms dealing), or otherwise contain provisions dealing with repetitive or ongoing misconduct (*e.g.*, many environmental offenses), add the numerical quantities and apply the pertinent offense guideline, including any specific

offense characteristics for the conduct taken as a whole. (2) When offenses are closely interrelated, group them together for purposes of the multiple-count rules, and use only the offense level for the most serious offense in that group. (3) As to other offenses (*e.g.*, independent instances of assault or robbery), start with the offense level for the most serious count and use the number and severity of additional counts to determine the amount by which to increase that offense level.

Historical Note

Effective November 1, 1987. Amended effective November 1, 1989 (amendment 121); November 1, 2007 (amendment 707).

§3D1.1. Procedure for Determining Offense Level on Multiple Counts

(a) When a defendant has been convicted of more than one count, the court shall:
(1) Group the counts resulting in conviction into distinct Groups of Closely Related Counts ("Groups") by applying the rules specified in §3D1.2.
(2) Determine the offense level applicable to each Group by applying the rules specified in §3D1.3.
(3) Determine the combined offense level applicable to all Groups taken together by applying the rules specified in §3D1.4.
(b) Exclude from the application of §§3D1.2–3D1.5 the following:
(1) Any count for which the statute (A) specifies a term of imprisonment to be imposed; and (B) requires that such term of imprisonment be imposed to run consecutively to any other term of imprisonment. Sentences for such counts are governed by the provisions of §5G1.2(a).
(2) Any count of conviction under 18 U.S.C. § 1028A. *See* Application Note 2(B) of the Commentary to §5G1.2 (Sentencing on Multiple Counts of Conviction) for guidance on how sentences for multiple counts of conviction under 18 U.S.C. § 1028A should be imposed.

Commentary

Application Notes:

1. **In General.**—For purposes of sentencing multiple counts of conviction, counts can be (A) contained in the same indictment or information; or (B) contained in different indictments or informations for which sentences are to be imposed at the same time or in a consolidated proceeding.

2. Subsection (b)(1) applies if a statute (A) specifies a term of imprisonment to be imposed; and (B) requires that such term of imprisonment be imposed to run consecutively to any other term of imprisonment. *See, e.g.*, 18 U.S.C. § 924(c) (requiring mandatory minimum terms of imprisonment, based on the conduct involved, to run consecutively). The multiple count rules set out under this Part do not apply to a count of conviction covered by subsection (b). However, a count covered by subsection (b)(1) may affect the offense level determination for other counts. For example, a defendant is convicted of one count of bank robbery (18 U.S.C. § 2113), and one count of use of a firearm in the commission of a crime of violence (18 U.S.C. § 924(c)). The two counts are not grouped together pursuant to this guideline, and, to avoid unwarranted double counting, the offense level for the bank robbery count under §2B3.1 (Robbery) is computed without application of the enhancement for weapon possession or use as otherwise required by subsection (b)(2) of that guideline. Pursuant to 18 U.S.C. § 924(c), the mandatory minimum five-year sentence on the weapon-use count runs consecutively to the guideline sentence imposed on the bank robbery count. *See* §5G1.2(a).

Unless specifically instructed, subsection (b)(1) does not apply when imposing a sentence under a statute that requires the imposition of a consecutive term of imprisonment only if a term of imprisonment is imposed (*i.e.*, the statute does not otherwise require a term of imprisonment to be imposed). *See, e.g.*, 18 U.S.C. § 3146 (Penalty for failure to appear); 18 U.S.C. § 924(a)(4) (regarding penalty for 18 U.S.C. § 922(q) (possession or discharge of a firearm in a school zone)); 18 U.S.C. § 1791(c) (penalty for providing or possessing a controlled substance in prison). Accordingly, the multiple count rules set out under this Part do apply to a count of conviction under this type of statute.

Background: This section outlines the procedure to be used for determining the combined offense level. After any adjustments from Chapter 3, Part E (Acceptance of Responsibility) and Chapter 4, Part B (Career Offenders and Criminal Livelihood) are made, this combined offense level is used to determine the guideline sentence range. Chapter Five (Determining the Sentence) discusses how to determine the sentence from the (combined) offense level; §5G1.2 deals specifically with determining the sentence of imprisonment when convictions on multiple counts are involved. References in Chapter Five (Determining the Sentence) to the "offense level" should be treated as referring to the combined offense level after all subsequent adjustments have been made.

Historical Note

Effective November 1, 1987. Amended effective November 1, 1990 (amendment 348); November 1, 1998 (amendment 579); November 1, 2000 (amendment 598); November 1, 2005 (amendments 677 and 680); November 1, 2007 (amendment 707).

§3D1.2. Groups of Closely Related Counts

All counts involving substantially the same harm shall be grouped together into a single Group. Counts involve substantially the same harm within the meaning of this rule:

(a) When counts involve the same victim and the same act or transaction.

(b) When counts involve the same victim and two or more acts or transactions connected by a common criminal objective or constituting part of a common scheme or plan.

(c) When one of the counts embodies conduct that is treated as a specific offense characteristic in, or other adjustment to, the guideline applicable to another of the counts.

(d) When the offense level is determined largely on the basis of the total amount of harm or loss, the quantity of a substance involved, or some other measure of aggregate harm, or if the offense behavior is ongoing or continuous in nature and the offense guideline is written to cover such behavior.

Offenses covered by the following guidelines are to be grouped under this subsection:

§2A3.5;
§§2B1.1, 2B1.4, 2B1.5, 2B4.1, 2B5.1, 2B5.3, 2B6.1;
§§2C1.1, 2C1.2, 2C1.8;
§§2D1.1, 2D1.2, 2D1.5, 2D1.11, 2D1.13;
§§2E4.1, 2E5.1;
§§2G2.2, 2G3.1;
§2K2.1;
§§2L1.1, 2L2.1;
§2N3.1;
§2Q2.1;
§2R1.1;
§§2S1.1, 2S1.3;
§§2T1.1, 2T1.4, 2T1.6, 2T1.7, 2T1.9, 2T2.1, 2T3.1.

Specifically excluded from the operation of this subsection are:

all offenses in Chapter Two, Part A (except §2A3.5);
§§2B2.1, 2B2.3, 2B3.1, 2B3.2, 2B3.3;
§2C1.5;
§§2D2.1, 2D2.2, 2D2.3;

§§2E1.3, 2E1.4, 2E2.1;
§§2G1.1, 2G2.1;
§§2H1.1, 2H2.1, 2H4.1;
§§2L2.2, 2L2.5;
§§2M2.1, 2M2.3, 2M3.1, 2M3.2, 2M3.3, 2M3.4, 2M3.5, 2M3.9;
§§2P1.1, 2P1.2, 2P1.3;
§2X6.1.

For multiple counts of offenses that are not listed, grouping under this subsection may or may not be appropriate; a case-by-case determination must be made based upon the facts of the case and the applicable guidelines (including specific offense characteristics and other adjustments) used to determine the offense level.

Exclusion of an offense from grouping under this subsection does not necessarily preclude grouping under another subsection.

Commentary

Application Notes:

1. Subsections (a)–(d) set forth circumstances in which counts are to be grouped together into a single Group. Counts are to be grouped together into a single Group if any one or more of the subsections provide for such grouping. Counts for which the statute (A) specifies a term of imprisonment to be imposed; and (B) requires that such term of imprisonment be imposed to run consecutively to any other term of imprisonment are excepted from application of the multiple count rules. *See* §3D1.1(b)(1); *id.*, comment. (n.1).

2. The term "***victim***" is not intended to include indirect or secondary victims. Generally, there will be one person who is directly and most seriously affected by the offense and is therefore identifiable as the victim. For offenses in which there are no identifiable victims (*e.g.*, drug or immigration offenses, where society at large is the victim), the "victim" for purposes of subsections (a) and (b) is the societal interest that is harmed. In such cases, the counts are grouped together when the societal interests that are harmed are closely related. Where one count, for example, involves unlawfully entering the United States and the other involves possession of fraudulent evidence of citizenship, the counts are grouped together because the societal interests harmed (the interests protected by laws governing immigration) are closely related. In contrast, where one count involves the sale of controlled substances and the other involves an immigration law violation, the counts are not grouped together because different societal interests are harmed. Ambiguities should be resolved in accordance with the purpose of this section as stated in the lead paragraph, *i.e.*, to identify and group "counts involving substantially the same harm."

3. Under subsection (a), counts are to be grouped together when they represent essentially a single injury or are part of a single criminal episode or transaction involving the same victim.

When one count charges an attempt to commit an offense and the other charges the commission of that offense, or when one count charges an offense based on a general prohibition and the other charges violation of a specific prohibition encompassed in the general prohibition, the counts will be grouped together under subsection (a).

Examples: (1) The defendant is convicted of forging and uttering the same check. The counts are to be grouped together. (2) The defendant is convicted of kidnapping and assaulting the victim during the course of the kidnapping. The counts are to be grouped together. (3) The defendant is convicted of bid rigging (an antitrust offense) and of mail fraud for signing and mailing a false statement that the bid was competitive. The counts are to be grouped together. (4) The defendant is convicted of two counts of assault on a federal officer for shooting at the same officer twice while attempting to prevent apprehension as part of a single criminal episode. The counts are to be grouped together.

(5) The defendant is convicted of three counts of unlawfully bringing aliens into the United States, all counts arising out of a single incident. The three counts are to be

grouped together. *But*: (6) The defendant is convicted of two counts of assault on a federal officer for shooting at the officer on two separate days. The counts *are not* to be grouped together.

4. Subsection (b) provides that counts that are part of a single course of conduct with a single criminal objective and represent essentially one composite harm to the same victim are to be grouped together, even if they constitute legally distinct offenses occurring at different times. This provision does not authorize the grouping of offenses that cannot be considered to represent essentially one composite harm (*e.g.*, robbery of the same victim on different occasions involves multiple, separate instances of fear and risk of harm, not one composite harm).

When one count charges a conspiracy or solicitation and the other charges a substantive offense that was the sole object of the conspiracy or solicitation, the counts will be grouped together under subsection (b).

Examples: (1) The defendant is convicted of one count of conspiracy to commit extortion and one count of extortion for the offense he conspired to commit. The counts are to be grouped together. (2) The defendant is convicted of two counts of mail fraud and one count of wire fraud, each in furtherance of a single fraudulent scheme. The counts are to be grouped together, even if the mailings and telephone call occurred on different days.

(3) The defendant is convicted of one count of auto theft and one count of altering the vehicle identification number of the car he stole. The counts are to be grouped together.

(4) The defendant is convicted of two counts of distributing a controlled substance, each count involving a separate sale of 10 grams of cocaine that is part of a common scheme or plan. In addition, a finding is made that there are two other sales, also part of the common scheme or plan, each involving 10 grams of cocaine. The total amount of all four sales (40 grams of cocaine) will be used to determine the offense level for each count under §1B1.3(a)(2). The two counts will then be grouped together under either this subsection or subsection (d) to avoid double counting. *But*: (5) The defendant is convicted of two counts of rape for raping the same person on different days. The counts *are not* to be grouped together.

5. Subsection (c) provides that when conduct that represents a separate count, *e.g.*, bodily injury or obstruction of justice, is also a specific offense characteristic in or other adjustment to another count, the count represented by that conduct is to be grouped with the count to which it constitutes an aggravating factor. This provision prevents "double counting" of offense behavior. Of course, this rule applies only if the offenses are closely related. It is not, for example, the intent of this rule that (assuming they could be joined together) a bank robbery on one occasion and an assault resulting in bodily injury on another occasion be grouped together. The bodily injury (the harm from the assault) would not be a specific offense characteristic to the robbery and would represent a different harm. On the other hand, use of a firearm in a bank robbery and unlawful possession of that firearm are sufficiently related to warrant grouping of counts under this subsection. Frequently, this provision will overlap subsection (a), at least with respect to specific offense characteristics. However, a count such as obstruction of justice, which represents a Chapter Three adjustment and involves a different harm or societal interest than the underlying offense, is covered by subsection (c) even though it is not covered by subsection (a).

Sometimes there may be several counts, each of which could be treated as an aggravating factor to another more serious count, but the guideline for the more serious count provides an adjustment for only one occurrence of that factor. In such cases, only the count representing the most serious of those factors is to be grouped with the other count. For example, if in a robbery of a credit union on a military base the defendant is also convicted of assaulting two employees, one of whom is injured seriously, the assault with serious bodily injury would be grouped with the robbery count, while the remaining assault conviction would be treated separately.

A cross reference to another offense guideline does not constitute "a specific offense characteristic . . . or other adjustment" within the meaning of subsection (c). For example, the guideline for bribery of a public official contains a cross reference to the guideline for a conspiracy to commit the offense that the bribe was to facilitate. Nonetheless, if the defendant were convicted of one count of securities fraud and one count of bribing a public official to facilitate the fraud, the two counts would not be grouped together by virtue of the cross reference. If, however, the bribe was given for the purpose of hampering a criminal investigation into the offense, it would constitute obstruction and under §3C1.1 would result in a 2-level enhancement to the offense level for the fraud. Under the latter circumstances, the counts would be grouped together.

6. Subsection (d) likely will be used with the greatest frequency. It provides that most property crimes (except robbery, burglary, extortion and the like), drug offenses, firearms offenses, and other crimes where the guidelines are based primarily on quantity or contemplate continuing behavior are to be grouped together. The list of instances in which this subsection should be applied is not exhaustive. Note, however, that certain guidelines are specifically excluded from the operation of subsection (d).

A conspiracy, attempt, or solicitation to commit an offense is covered under subsection (d) if the offense that is the object of the conspiracy, attempt, or solicitation is covered under subsection (d).

Counts involving offenses to which different offense guidelines apply are grouped together under subsection (d) if the offenses are of the same general type and otherwise meet the criteria for grouping under this subsection. In such cases, the offense guideline that results in the highest offense level is used; *see* §3D1.3(b). The "same general type" of offense is to be construed broadly.

Examples: (1) The defendant is convicted of five counts of embezzling money from a bank. The five counts are to be grouped together. (2) The defendant is convicted of two counts of theft of social security checks and three counts of theft from the mail, each from a different victim. All five counts are to be grouped together. (3) The defendant is convicted of five counts of mail fraud and ten counts of wire fraud. Although the counts arise from various schemes, each involves a monetary objective. All fifteen counts are to be grouped together. (4) The defendant is convicted of three counts of unlicensed dealing in firearms. All three counts are to be grouped together. (5) The defendant is convicted of one count of selling heroin, one count of selling PCP, and one count of selling cocaine. The counts are to be grouped together. The Commentary to §2D1.1 provides rules for combining (adding) quantities of different drugs to determine a single combined offense level.

(6) The defendant is convicted of three counts of tax evasion. The counts are to be grouped together. (7) The defendant is convicted of three counts of discharging toxic substances from a single facility. The counts are to be grouped together. (8) The defendant is convicted on two counts of check forgery and one count of uttering the first of the forged checks. All three counts are to be grouped together. Note, however, that the uttering count is first grouped with the first forgery count under subsection (a) of this guideline, so that the monetary amount of that check counts only once when the rule in §3D1.3(b) is applied. *But*: (9) The defendant is convicted of three counts of bank robbery. The counts *are not* to be grouped together, nor are the amounts of money involved to be added.

7. A single case may result in application of several of the rules in this section. Thus, for example, example (8) in the discussion of subsection (d) involves an application of §3D1.2(a) followed by an application of §3D1.2(d). Note also that a Group may consist of a single count; conversely, all counts may form a single Group.

8. A defendant may be convicted of conspiring to commit several substantive offenses and

also of committing one or more of the substantive offenses. In such cases, treat the conspiracy count as if it were several counts, each charging conspiracy to commit one of the substantive offenses. *See* §1B1.2(d) and accompanying commentary. Then apply the ordinary grouping rules to determine the combined offense level based upon the substantive counts of which the defendant is convicted and the various acts cited by the conspiracy count that would constitute behavior of a substantive nature. **Example:** The defendant is convicted of two counts: conspiring to commit offenses A, B, and C, and committing offense A. Treat this as if the defendant was convicted of (1) committing offense A; (2) conspiracy to commit offense A; (3) conspiracy to commit offense B; and (4) conspiracy to commit offense C. Count (1) and count (2) are grouped together under §3D1.2(b). Group the remaining counts, including the various acts cited by the conspiracy count that would constitute behavior of a substantive nature, according to the rules in this section.

Background: Ordinarily, the first step in determining the combined offense level in a case involving multiple counts is to identify those counts that are sufficiently related to be placed in the same Group of Closely Related Counts ("Group"). This section specifies four situations in which counts are to be grouped together. Although it appears last for conceptual reasons, subsection (d) probably will be used most frequently.

A primary consideration in this section is whether the offenses involve different victims. For example, a defendant may stab three prison guards in a single escape attempt. Some would argue that all counts arising out of a single transaction or occurrence should be grouped together even when there are distinct victims. Although such a proposal was considered, it was rejected because it probably would require departure in many cases in order to capture adequately the criminal behavior. Cases involving injury to distinct victims are sufficiently comparable, whether or not the injuries are inflicted in distinct transactions, so that each such count should be treated separately rather than grouped together. Counts involving different victims (or societal harms in the case of "victimless" crimes) are grouped together only as provided in subsection (c) or (d).

Even if counts involve a single victim, the decision as to whether to group them together may not always be clear cut. For example, how contemporaneous must two assaults on the same victim be in order to warrant grouping together as constituting a single transaction or occurrence? Existing case law may provide some guidance as to what constitutes distinct offenses, but such decisions often turn on the technical language of the statute and cannot be controlling. In interpreting this Part and resolving ambiguities, the court should look to the underlying policy of this Part as stated in the Introductory Commentary.

Historical Note

Effective November 1, 1987. Amended effective June 15, 1988 (amendment 45); November 1, 1989 (amendments 121, 253–256, and 303); November 1, 1990 (amendments 309, 348, and 349); November 1, 1991 (amendment 417); November 1, 1992 (amendment 458); November 1, 1993 (amendment 496); November 1, 1995 (amendment 534); November 1, 1996 (amendment 538); November 1, 1998 (amendment 579); November 1, 2001 (amendments 615, 617, and 634); November 1, 2002 (amendment 638); January 25, 2003 (amendment 648); November 1, 2003 (amendment 656); November 1, 2004 (amendment 664); November 1, 2005 (amendments 679 and 680); November 1, 2007 (amendment 701).

§3D1.3. Offense Level Applicable to Each Group of Closely Related Counts

Determine the offense level applicable to each of the Groups as follows:

(a) In the case of counts grouped together pursuant to §3D1.2(a)–(c), the offense level applicable to a Group is the offense level, determined in accordance with Chapter Two and Parts A, B, and C of Chapter Three, for the most serious of the counts comprising the Group, *i.e.*, the highest offense level of the counts in the Group.

(b) In the case of counts grouped together pursuant to §3D1.2(d), the offense level applicable to a Group is the offense level corresponding to the aggregated quantity, determined in accordance with Chapter Two and Parts A, B and C of Chapter Three. When the counts involve offenses of the same general type to which different guidelines apply, apply the offense guideline that produces the highest offense level.

Commentary

Application Notes:

1. The "***offense level***" for a count refers to the offense level from Chapter Two after all adjustments from Parts A, B, and C of Chapter Three.

2. When counts are grouped pursuant to §3D1.2(a)–(c), the highest offense level of the counts in the group is used. Ordinarily, it is necessary to determine the offense level for each of the counts in a Group in order to ensure that the highest is correctly identified. Sometimes, it will be clear that one count in the Group cannot have a higher offense level than another, as with a count for an attempt or conspiracy to commit the completed offense. The formal determination of the offense level for such a count may be unnecessary.

3. When counts are grouped pursuant to §3D1.2(d), the offense guideline applicable to the aggregate behavior is used. If the counts in the Group are covered by different guidelines, use the guideline that produces the highest offense level. Determine whether the specific offense characteristics or adjustments from Chapter Three, Parts A, B, and C apply based upon the combined offense behavior taken as a whole. Note that guidelines for similar property offenses have been coordinated to produce identical offense levels, at least when substantial property losses are involved. However, when small sums are involved the differing specific offense characteristics that require increasing the offense level to a certain minimum may affect the outcome.

4. Sometimes the rule specified in this section may not result in incremental punishment for additional criminal acts because of the grouping rules. For example, if the defendant commits forcible criminal sexual abuse (rape), aggravated assault, and robbery, all against the same victim on a single occasion, all of the counts are grouped together under §3D1.2. The aggravated assault will increase the guideline range for the rape. The robbery, however, will not. This is because the offense guideline for rape (§2A3.1) includes the most common aggravating factors, including injury, that data showed to be significant in actual practice. The additional factor of property loss ordinarily can be taken into account adequately within the guideline range for rape, which is fairly wide. However,

an exceptionally large property loss in the course of the rape would provide grounds for an upward departure. *See* §5K2.5 (Property Damage or Loss).

Background: This section provides rules for determining the offense level associated with each Group of Closely Related Counts. Summary examples of the application of these rules are provided at the end of the Commentary to this Part.

Historical Note

Effective November 1, 1987. Amended effective November 1, 1989 (amendments 257 and 303); November 1, 2001 (amendment 617); November 1, 2004 (amendment 674).

§3D1.4. Determining the Combined Offense Level

The combined offense level is determined by taking the offense level applicable to the Group with the highest offense level and increasing that offense level by the amount indicated in the following table:

NUMBER OF UNITS	INCREASE IN OFFENSE LEVEL
1	none
1 1/2	add **1** level
2	add **2** levels
2 1/2 – 3	add **3** levels
3 1/2 – 5	add **4** levels
More than 5	add **5** levels.

In determining the number of Units for purposes of this section:

(a) Count as one Unit the Group with the highest offense level. Count one additional Unit for each Group that is equally serious or from **1** to **4** levels less serious.

(b) Count as one-half Unit any Group that is **5** to **8** levels less serious than the Group with the highest offense level.

(c) Disregard any Group that is **9** or more levels less serious than the Group with the highest offense level. Such Groups will not increase the applicable offense level but may provide a reason for sentencing at the higher end of the sentencing range for the applicable offense level.

Commentary

Application Notes:

1. Application of the rules in §§3D1.2 and 3D1.3 may produce a single Group of Closely Related Counts. In such cases, the combined offense level is the level corresponding to the Group determined in accordance with §3D1.3.

§3D1.5

2. The procedure for calculating the combined offense level when there is more than one Group of Closely Related Counts is as follows: First, identify the offense level applicable to the most serious Group; assign it one Unit. Next, determine the number of Units that the remaining Groups represent. Finally, increase the offense level for the most serious Group by the number of levels indicated in the table corresponding to the total number of Units.

Background: When Groups are of roughly comparable seriousness, each Group will represent one Unit. When the most serious Group carries an offense level substantially higher than that applicable to the other Groups, however, counting the lesser Groups fully for purposes of the table could add excessive punishment, possibly even more than those offenses would carry if prosecuted separately. To avoid this anomalous result and produce declining marginal punishment, Groups 9 or more levels less serious than the most serious Group should not be counted for purposes of the table, and that Groups 5 to 8 levels less serious should be treated as equal to one-half of a Group. Thus, if the most serious Group is at offense level 15 and if two other Groups are at level 10, there would be a total of two Units for purposes of the table (one plus one-half plus one-half) and the combined offense level would be 17. Inasmuch as the maximum increase provided in the guideline is 5 levels, departure would be warranted in the unusual case where the additional offenses resulted in a total of significantly more than 5 Units.
In unusual circumstances, the approach adopted in this section could produce adjustments for the additional counts that are inadequate or excessive. If there are several groups and the most serious offense is considerably more serious than all of the others, there will be no increase in the offense level resulting from the additional counts. Ordinarily, the court will have latitude to impose added punishment by sentencing toward the upper end of the range authorized for the most serious offense. Situations in which there will be inadequate scope for ensuring appropriate additional punishment for the additional crimes are likely to be unusual and can be handled by departure from the guidelines. Conversely, it is possible that if there are several minor offenses that are not grouped together, application of the rules in this Part could result in an excessive increase in the sentence range. Again, such situations should be infrequent and can be handled through departure. An alternative method for ensuring more precise adjustments would have been to determine the appropriate offense level adjustment through a more complicated mathematical formula; that approach was not adopted because of its complexity.

Historical
Note
Effective November 1, 1987. Amended effective November 1, 1990 (amendment 350).

§3D1.5. Determining the Total Punishment

Use the combined offense level to determine the appropriate sentence in accordance with the provisions of Chapter Five.

Commentary

This section refers the court to Chapter Five (Determining the Sentence) in order to determine the total punishment to be imposed based upon the combined offense level. The combined offense level is subject to adjustments from Chapter Three, Part E (Acceptance of Responsibility) and Chapter Four, Part B (Career Offenders and Criminal Livelihood).

Historical
Note
Effective November 1, 1987.

* * * * *

Concluding Commentary to Part D of Chapter Three
Illustrations of the Operation of the Multiple-Count Rules

The following examples, drawn from presentence reports in the Commission's files, illustrate the operation of the guidelines for multiple counts. The examples are discussed summarily; a more thorough, step-by-step approach is recommended until the user is thoroughly familiar with the guidelines.

1. Defendant A was convicted of four counts, each charging robbery of a different bank. Each would represent a distinct Group. §3D1.2. In each of the first three robberies, the offense level was 22 (20 plus a 2-level increase because a financial institution was robbed) (§2B3.1(b)). In the fourth robbery $21,000 was taken and a firearm was displayed; the offense level was therefore 28. As the first three counts are 6 levels lower than the fourth, each of the first three represents one-half unit for purposes of §3D1.4. Altogether there are 2 1/2 Units, and the offense level for the most serious (28) is therefore increased by 3 levels under the table. The combined offense level is 31.

2. Defendant B was convicted of four counts: (1) distribution of 230 grams of cocaine; (2) distribution of 150 grams of cocaine; (3) distribution of 75 grams of heroin; (4) offering a DEA agent $20,000 to avoid prosecution. The combined offense level for drug offenses is determined by the total quantity of drugs, converted to marihuana equivalents (using the Drug Equivalency Tables in the Commentary to §2D1.1 (Unlawful Manufacturing, Importing, Exporting, or Trafficking)). The first count translates into 46 kilograms of marihuana; the second count translates into 30 kilograms of marihuana; and the third count translates into 75 kilograms of marihuana. The total is 151 kilograms of marihuana. Under §2D1.1, the combined offense level for the drug offenses is 24. In addition, because of the attempted bribe of the DEA agent, this offense level is increased by 2 levels to 26 under §3C1.1 (Obstructing or Impeding the Administration of Justice). Because the conduct constituting the bribery offense is accounted for by §3C1.1, it becomes part of the same Group as the drug offenses pursuant to §3D1.2(c). The combined offense level is 26 pursuant to §3D1.3(a), because the offense level for bribery (20) is less than the offense level for the drug offenses (26).

3. Defendant C was convicted of four counts arising out of a scheme pursuant to which the defendant received kickbacks from subcontractors. The counts were as follows: (1) The defendant received $1,000 from subcontractor A relating to contract X (Mail Fraud). (2) The defendant received $1,000 from subcontractor A relating to contract X (Commercial Bribery). (3) The defendant received $1,000 from subcontractor A relating to contract Y (Mail Fraud). (4) The defendant received $1,000 from subcontractor B relating to contract Z (Commercial Bribery). The mail fraud counts are covered by §2B1.1 (Theft, Property Destruction, and Fraud). The bribery counts are covered by §2B4.1 (Bribery in Procurement of Bank Loan and Other Commercial Bribery), which treats the offense as a sophisticated fraud. The total money involved is $4,000, which results in an offense level of 9 under either §2B1.1 (assuming the application of the "sophisticated means" enhancement in §2B1.1(b)(10)) or §2B4.1. Since these two guidelines produce identical offense levels, the combined offense level is 9.

Historical
Note
Effective November 1, 1987. Amended effective November 1, 1989 (amendment 303); November 1, 1990 (amendment 350); November 1, 1991 (amendment 417); November 1, 1995 (amendment 534); November 1, 2001 (amendment 617); November 1, 2009 (amendment 737); November 1, 2011 (amendment 760); November 1, 2014 (amendment 782); November 1, 2015 (amendment 796).

PART E — ACCEPTANCE OF RESPONSIBILITY

§3E1.1. Acceptance of Responsibility

(a) If the defendant clearly demonstrates acceptance of responsibility for his offense, decrease the offense level by **2** levels.

(b) If the defendant qualifies for a decrease under subsection (a), the offense level determined prior to the operation of subsection (a) is level **16** or greater, and upon motion of the government stating that the defendant has assisted authorities in the investigation or prosecution of his own misconduct by timely notifying authorities of his intention to enter a plea of guilty, thereby permitting the government to avoid preparing for trial and permitting the government and the court to allocate their resources efficiently, decrease the offense level by **1** additional level.

Commentary

Application Notes:

1. In determining whether a defendant qualifies under subsection (a), appropriate considerations include, but are not limited to, the following:

(A) truthfully admitting the conduct comprising the offense(s) of conviction, and truthfully admitting or not falsely denying any additional relevant conduct for which the defendant is accountable under §1B1.3 (Relevant Conduct). Note that a defendant is not required to volunteer, or affirmatively admit, relevant conduct beyond the offense of conviction in order to obtain a reduction under subsection (a). A defendant may remain silent in respect to relevant conduct beyond the offense of conviction without affecting his ability to obtain a reduction under this subsection. However, a defendant who falsely denies, or frivolously contests, relevant conduct that the court determines to be true has acted in a manner inconsistent with acceptance of responsibility;

(B) voluntary termination or withdrawal from criminal conduct or associations;

(C) voluntary payment of restitution prior to adjudication of guilt;

(D) voluntary surrender to authorities promptly after commission of the offense;

(E) voluntary assistance to authorities in the recovery of the fruits and instrumentalities of the offense;

(F) voluntary resignation from the office or position held during the commission of the offense;

(G) post-offense rehabilitative efforts (*e.g.*, counseling or drug treatment); and

(H) the timeliness of the defendant's conduct in manifesting the acceptance of responsibility.

2. This adjustment is not intended to apply to a defendant who puts the government to its burden of proof at trial by denying the essential factual elements of guilt, is convicted, and only then admits guilt and expresses remorse. Conviction by trial, however, does not automatically preclude a defendant from consideration for such a reduction. In rare situations a defendant may clearly demonstrate an acceptance of responsibility for his criminal conduct even though he exercises his constitutional right to a trial. This may occur,

for example, where a defendant goes to trial to assert and preserve issues that do not relate to factual guilt (*e.g.*, to make a constitutional challenge to a statute or a challenge to the applicability of a statute to his conduct). In each such instance, however, a determination that a defendant has accepted responsibility will be based primarily upon pretrial statements and conduct.

3. Entry of a plea of guilty prior to the commencement of trial combined with truthfully admitting the conduct comprising the offense of conviction, and truthfully admitting or not falsely denying any additional relevant conduct for which he is accountable under §1B1.3 (Relevant Conduct) (*see* Application Note 1(A)), will constitute significant evidence of acceptance of responsibility for the purposes of subsection (a). However, this evidence may be outweighed by conduct of the defendant that is inconsistent with such acceptance of responsibility. A defendant who enters a guilty plea is not entitled to an adjustment under this section as a matter of right.

4. Conduct resulting in an enhancement under §3C1.1 (Obstructing or Impeding the Administration of Justice) ordinarily indicates that the defendant has not accepted responsibility for his criminal conduct. There may, however, be extraordinary cases in which adjustments under both §§3C1.1 and 3E1.1 may apply.

5. The sentencing judge is in a unique position to evaluate a defendant's acceptance of responsibility. For this reason, the determination of the sentencing judge is entitled to great deference on review.

6. Subsection (a) provides a 2-level decrease in offense level. Subsection (b) provides an additional 1-level decrease in offense level for a defendant at offense level 16 or greater prior to the operation of subsection (a) who both qualifies for a decrease under subsection (a) and who has assisted authorities in the investigation or prosecution of his own misconduct by taking the steps set forth in subsection (b). The timeliness of the defendant's acceptance of responsibility is a consideration under both subsections, and is context specific. In general, the conduct qualifying for a decrease in offense level under subsection (b) will occur particularly early in the case. For example, to qualify under subsection (b), the defendant must have notified authorities of his intention to enter a plea of guilty at a sufficiently early point in the process so that the government may avoid preparing for trial and the court may schedule its calendar efficiently.

Because the Government is in the best position to determine whether the defendant has assisted authorities in a manner that avoids preparing for trial, an adjustment under subsection (b) may only be granted upon a formal motion by the Government at the time of sentencing. *See* section 401(g)(2)(B) of Public Law 108–21. The government should not withhold such a motion based on interests not identified in §3E1.1, such as whether the defendant agrees to waive his or her right to appeal.

If the government files such a motion, and the court in deciding whether to grant the motion also determines that the defendant has assisted authorities in the investigation

or prosecution of his own misconduct by timely notifying authorities of his intention to enter a plea of guilty, thereby permitting the government to avoid preparing for trial and permitting the government and the court to allocate their resources efficiently, the court should grant the motion.

Background: The reduction of offense level provided by this section recognizes legitimate societal interests. For several reasons, a defendant who clearly demonstrates acceptance of responsibility for his offense by taking, in a timely fashion, the actions listed above (or some equivalent action) is appropriately given a lower offense level than a defendant who has not demonstrated acceptance of responsibility.

Subsection (a) provides a 2-level decrease in offense level. Subsection (b) provides an additional 1-level decrease for a defendant at offense level 16 or greater prior to operation of subsection (a) who both qualifies for a decrease under subsection (a) and has assisted authorities in the investigation or prosecution of his own misconduct by taking the steps specified in subsection (b). Such a defendant has accepted responsibility in a way that ensures the certainty of his just punishment in a timely manner, thereby appropriately meriting an additional reduction. Subsection (b) does not apply, however, to a defendant whose offense level is level 15 or lower prior to application of subsection (a). At offense level 15 or lower, the reduction in the guideline range provided by a 2-level decrease in offense level under subsection (a) (which is a greater proportional reduction in the guideline range than at higher offense levels due to the structure of the Sentencing Table) is adequate for the court to take into account the factors set forth in subsection (b) within the applicable guideline range.

Section 401(g) of Public Law 108–21 directly amended subsection (b), Application Note 6 (including adding the first sentence of the second paragraph of that application note), and the Background Commentary, effective April 30, 2003.

Historical Note

Effective November 1, 1987. Amended effective January 15, 1988 (amendment 46); November 1, 1989 (amendment 258); November 1, 1990 (amendment 351); November 1, 1992 (amendment 459); April 30, 2003 (amendment 649); November 1, 2010 (amendments 746 and 747); November 1, 2013 (amendment 775).

CHAPTER FOUR

CRIMINAL HISTORY AND CRIMINAL LIVELIHOOD

PART A — CRIMINAL HISTORY

Introductory Commentary

The Comprehensive Crime Control Act sets forth four purposes of sentencing. (*See* 18 U.S.C. § 3553(a)(2).) A defendant's record of past criminal conduct is directly relevant to those purposes. A defendant with a record of prior criminal behavior is more culpable than a first offender and thus deserving of greater punishment. General deterrence of criminal conduct dictates that a clear message be sent to society that repeated criminal behavior will aggravate the need for punishment with each recurrence. To protect the public from further crimes of the particular defendant, the likelihood of recidivism and future criminal behavior must be considered. Repeated criminal behavior is an indicator of a limited likelihood of successful rehabilitation.

The specific factors included in §4A1.1 and §4A1.3 are consistent with the extant empirical research assessing correlates of recidivism and patterns of career criminal behavior. While empirical research has shown that other factors are correlated highly with the likelihood of recidivism, *e.g.*, age and drug abuse, for policy reasons they were not included here at this time. The Commission has made no definitive judgment as to the reliability of the existing data. However, the Commission will review additional data insofar as they become available in the future.

Historical Note

Effective November 1, 1987.

§4A1.1. Criminal History Category

The total points from subsections (a) through (e) determine the criminal history category in the Sentencing Table in Chapter Five, Part A.

(a) Add **3** points for each prior sentence of imprisonment exceeding one year and one month.

(b) Add **2** points for each prior sentence of imprisonment of at least sixty days not counted in (a).

(c) Add **1** point for each prior sentence not counted in (a) or (b), up to a total of **4** points for this subsection.

(d) Add **2** points if the defendant committed the instant offense while under any criminal justice sentence, including probation, parole, supervised release, imprisonment, work release, or escape status.

(e) Add **1** point for each prior sentence resulting from a conviction of a crime of violence that did not receive any points under (a), (b), or (c) above because such sentence was treated as a single sentence, up to a total of **3** points for this subsection.

Commentary

The total criminal history points from §4A1.1 determine the criminal history category (I–VI) in the Sentencing Table in Chapter Five, Part A. The definitions and instructions in §4A1.2 govern the computation of the criminal history points. Therefore, §§4A1.1 and 4A1.2 must be read together. The following notes highlight the interaction of §§4A1.1 and 4A1.2.

Application Notes:

1. **§4A1.1(a).** Three points are added for each prior sentence of imprisonment exceeding one year and one month. There is no limit to the number of points that may be counted under this subsection. The term "***prior sentence***" is defined at §4A1.2(a). The term "***sentence***

of imprisonment" is defined at §4A1.2(b). Where a prior sentence of imprisonment resulted from a revocation of probation, parole, or a similar form of release, *see* §4A1.2(k).
Certain prior sentences are not counted or are counted only under certain conditions:
A sentence imposed more than fifteen years prior to the defendant's commencement of the instant offense is not counted unless the defendant's incarceration extended into this fifteen-year period. *See* §4A1.2(e).
A sentence imposed for an offense committed prior to the defendant's eighteenth birthday is counted under this subsection only if it resulted from an adult conviction. *See* §4A1.2(d).
A sentence for a foreign conviction, a conviction that has been expunged, or an invalid conviction is not counted. *See* §4A1.2(h) and (j) and the Commentary to §4A1.2.
2. **§4A1.1(b).** Two points are added for each prior sentence of imprisonment of at least sixty days not counted in §4A1.1(a). There is no limit to the number of points that may be counted under this subsection. The term "***prior sentence***" is defined at §4A1.2(a). The term "***sentence of imprisonment***" is defined at §4A1.2(b). Where a prior sentence of imprisonment resulted from a revocation of probation, parole, or a similar form of release, *see* §4A1.2(k).
Certain prior sentences are not counted or are counted only under certain conditions:
A sentence imposed more than ten years prior to the defendant's commencement of the instant offense is not counted. *See* §4A1.2(e).

An adult or juvenile sentence imposed for an offense committed prior to the defendant's eighteenth birthday is counted only if confinement resulting from such sentence extended into the five-year period preceding the defendant's commencement of the instant offense. *See* §4A1.2(d).
Sentences for certain specified non-felony offenses are never counted. *See* §4A1.2(c)(2).
A sentence for a foreign conviction or a tribal court conviction, an expunged conviction, or an invalid conviction is not counted. *See* §4A1.2(h), (i), (j), and the Commentary to §4A1.2.
A military sentence is counted only if imposed by a general or special court-martial. *See* §4A1.2(g).
3. **§4A1.1(c).** One point is added for each prior sentence not counted under §4A1.1(a) or (b). A maximum of four points may be counted under this subsection. The term "***prior sentence***" is defined at §4A1.2(a).
Certain prior sentences are not counted or are counted only under certain conditions:
A sentence imposed more than ten years prior to the defendant's commencement of the instant offense is not counted. *See* §4A1.2(e).
An adult or juvenile sentence imposed for an offense committed prior to the defendant's eighteenth birthday is counted only if imposed within five years of the defendant's commencement of the current offense. *See* §4A1.2(d).
Sentences for certain specified non-felony offenses are counted only if they meet certain requirements. *See* §4A1.2(c)(1).
Sentences for certain specified non-felony offenses are never counted. *See* §4A1.2(c)(2).
A diversionary disposition is counted only where there is a finding or admission of guilt in a judicial proceeding. *See* §4A1.2(f).
A sentence for a foreign conviction, a tribal court conviction, an expunged conviction, or an invalid conviction, is not counted. *See* §4A1.2(h), (i), (j), and the Commentary to §4A1.2.
A military sentence is counted only if imposed by a general or special court-martial. *See* §4A1.2(g).
4. **§4A1.1(d).** Two points are added if the defendant committed any part of the instant offense

(*i.e.*, any relevant conduct) while under any criminal justice sentence, including probation, parole, supervised release, imprisonment, work release, or escape status. Failure to report for service of a sentence of imprisonment is to be treated as an escape from such sentence. *See* §4A1.2(n). For the purposes of this subsection, a "***criminal justice sentence***" means a sentence countable under §4A1.2 (Definitions and Instructions for Computing Criminal History) having a custodial or supervisory component, although active supervision is not required for this subsection to apply. For example, a term of unsupervised probation would be included; but a sentence to pay a fine, by itself, would not be included. A defendant who commits the instant offense while a violation warrant from

a prior sentence is outstanding (*e.g.*, a probation, parole, or supervised release violation warrant) shall be deemed to be under a criminal justice sentence for the purposes of this provision if that sentence is otherwise countable, even if that sentence would have expired absent such warrant. *See* §4A1.2(m).

5. **§4A1.1(e).** In a case in which the defendant received two or more prior sentences as a result of convictions for crimes of violence that are treated as a single sentence (*see* §4A1.2(a)(2)), one point is added under §4A1.1(e) for each such sentence that did not result in any additional points under §4A1.1(a), (b), or (c). A total of up to 3 points may be added under §4A1.1(e). For purposes of this guideline, "***crime of violence***" has the meaning given that term in §4B1.2(a). *See* §4A1.2(p).

For example, a defendant's criminal history includes two robbery convictions for offenses committed on different occasions. The sentences for these offenses were imposed on the same day and are treated as a single prior sentence. *See* §4A1.2(a)(2). If the defendant received a five-year sentence of imprisonment for one robbery and a four-year sentence of imprisonment for the other robbery (consecutively or concurrently), a total of 3 points is added under §4A1.1(a). An additional point is added under §4A1.1(e) because the second sentence did not result in any additional point(s) (under §4A1.1(a), (b), or (c)). In contrast, if the defendant received a one-year sentence of imprisonment for one robbery and a nine-month consecutive sentence of imprisonment for the other robbery, a total of 3 points also is added under §4A1.1(a) (a one-year sentence of imprisonment and a consecutive nine-month sentence of imprisonment are treated as a combined one-year-ninemonth sentence of imprisonment). But no additional point is added under §4A1.1(e) because the sentence for the second robbery already resulted in an additional point under §4A1.1(a). Without the second sentence, the defendant would only have received two points under §4A1.1(b) for the one-year sentence of imprisonment.

Background: Prior convictions may represent convictions in the federal system, fifty state systems, the District of Columbia, territories, and foreign, tribal, and military courts. There are jurisdictional variations in offense definitions, sentencing structures, and manner of sentence pronouncement. To minimize problems with imperfect measures of past crime seriousness, criminal history categories are based on the maximum term imposed in previous sentences rather than on other measures, such as whether the conviction was designated a felony or misdemeanor. In recognition of the imperfection of this measure however, §4A1.3 authorizes the court to depart from the otherwise applicable criminal history category in certain circumstances.

Subsections (a), (b), and (c) of §4A1.1 distinguish confinement sentences longer than one year and one month, shorter confinement sentences of at least sixty days, and all other sentences, such as confinement sentences of less than sixty days, probation, fines, and residency in a halfway house.

Section 4A1.1(d) adds two points if the defendant was under a criminal justice sentence during any part of the instant offense.

Historical Note

Effective November 1, 1987. Amended effective November 1, 1989 (amendments 259–261); November 1, 1991 (amendments 381 and 382); October 27, 2003 (amendment 651); November 1, 2007 (amendment 709); November 1, 2010 (amendment 742); November 1, 2013 (amendment 777); November 1, 2015 (amendment 795).

§4A1.2. Definitions and Instructions for Computing Criminal History

(a) PRIOR SENTENCE

(1) The term "prior sentence" means any sentence previously imposed upon adjudication of guilt, whether by guilty plea, trial, or plea of *nolo contendere*, for conduct not part of the instant offense.

(2) If the defendant has multiple prior sentences, determine whether those sentences are counted separately or treated as a single sentence. Prior sentences always are counted separately if the sentences were imposed for offenses that were separated by an intervening arrest (*i.e.*, the defendant is arrested for the first offense prior to committing the second offense). If there is no intervening arrest, prior sentences are counted separately unless (A) the sentences resulted from offenses contained in the same charging instrument; or (B) the sentences were imposed on the same day. Treat any prior sentence covered by (A) or (B) as a single sentence. *See also* §4A1.1(e).

For purposes of applying §4A1.1(a), (b), and (c), if prior sentences are treated as a single sentence, use the longest sentence of imprisonment if concurrent sentences were imposed. If consecutive sentences were imposed, use the aggregate sentence of imprisonment.

(3) A conviction for which the imposition or execution of sentence was totally suspended or stayed shall be counted as a prior sentence under §4A1.1(c).

(4) Where a defendant has been convicted of an offense, but not yet sentenced, such conviction shall be counted as if it constituted a prior sentence under §4A1.1(c) if a sentence resulting from that conviction otherwise would be countable. In the case of a conviction for an offense set forth in §4A1.2(c)(1), apply this provision only where the sentence for such offense would be countable regardless of type or length.

"Convicted of an offense," for the purposes of this provision, means that the guilt of the defendant has been established, whether by guilty plea, trial, or plea of *nolo contendere*.

(b) SENTENCE OF IMPRISONMENT DEFINED

(1) The term "sentence of imprisonment" means a sentence of incarceration and refers to the maximum sentence imposed.

(2) If part of a sentence of imprisonment was suspended, "sentence of imprisonment" refers only to the portion that was not suspended.

(c) SENTENCES COUNTED AND EXCLUDED

Sentences for all felony offenses are counted. Sentences for misdemeanor and petty offenses are counted, except as follows:

(1) Sentences for the following prior offenses and offenses similar

to them, by whatever name they are known, are counted only if (A) the sentence was a term of probation of more than one year or a term of imprisonment of at least thirty days, or (B) the prior offense was similar to an instant offense:
Careless or reckless driving
Contempt of court
Disorderly conduct or disturbing the peace
Driving without a license or with a revoked or suspended license
False information to a police officer
Gambling
Hindering or failure to obey a police officer
Insufficient funds check
Leaving the scene of an accident
Non-support
Prostitution
Resisting arrest
Trespassing.
(2) Sentences for the following prior offenses and offenses similar to them, by whatever name they are known, are never counted:
Fish and game violations
Hitchhiking
Juvenile status offenses and truancy
Local ordinance violations (except those violations that are also violations under state criminal law)
Loitering
Minor traffic infractions (*e.g.*, speeding)
Public intoxication
Vagrancy.

(d) OFFENSES COMMITTED PRIOR TO AGE EIGHTEEN
(1) If the defendant was convicted as an adult and received a sentence of imprisonment exceeding one year and one month, add **3** points under §4A1.1(a) for each such sentence.
(2) In any other case,
(A) add **2** points under §4A1.1(b) for each adult or juvenile sentence to confinement of at least sixty days if the defendant was released from such confinement within five years of his commencement of the instant offense;
(B) add **1** point under §4A1.1(c) for each adult or juvenile sentence imposed within five years of the defendant's commencement of the instant offense not covered in (A).
(e) APPLICABLE TIME PERIOD
(1) Any prior sentence of imprisonment exceeding one year and one month that was imposed within fifteen years of the defendant's commencement of the instant offense is counted. Also count any prior sentence of imprisonment exceeding one year

and one month, whenever imposed, that resulted in the defendant being incarcerated during any part of such fifteen-year period.
(2) Any other prior sentence that was imposed within ten years of the defendant's commencement of the instant offense is counted.
(3) Any prior sentence not within the time periods specified above is not counted.
(4) The applicable time period for certain sentences resulting from offenses committed prior to age eighteen is governed by §4A1.2(d)(2).
(f) DIVERSIONARY DISPOSITIONS
Diversion from the judicial process without a finding of guilt (*e.g.*, deferred prosecution) is not counted. A diversionary disposition resulting from a finding or admission of guilt, or a plea of *nolo contendere*, in a judicial proceeding is counted as a sentence under §4A1.1(c) even if a conviction is not formally entered, except that diversion from juvenile court is not counted.

(g) MILITARY SENTENCES
Sentences resulting from military offenses are counted if imposed by a general or special court-martial. Sentences imposed by a summary court-martial or Article 15 proceeding are not counted.
(h) FOREIGN SENTENCES
Sentences resulting from foreign convictions are not counted, but may be considered under §4A1.3 (Adequacy of Criminal History Category).
(i) TRIBAL COURT SENTENCES
Sentences resulting from tribal court convictions are not counted, but may be considered under §4A1.3 (Adequacy of Criminal History Category).
(j) EXPUNGED CONVICTIONS
Sentences for expunged convictions are not counted, but may be considered under §4A1.3 (Adequacy of Criminal History Category).
(k) REVOCATIONS OF PROBATION, PAROLE, MANDATORY RELEASE, OR SUPERVISED RELEASE
(1) In the case of a prior revocation of probation, parole, supervised release, special parole, or mandatory release, add the original term of imprisonment to any term of imprisonment imposed upon revocation. The resulting total is used to compute the criminal history points for §4A1.1(a), (b), or (c), as applicable.
(2) Revocation of probation, parole, supervised release, special parole, or mandatory release may affect the time period under which certain sentences are counted as provided in §4A1.2(d)(2) and (e). For the purposes of determining the applicable time period, use the following: (A) in the case of an adult term of imprisonment totaling more than one year and one month, the date of last release from incarceration on such

sentence (*see* §4A1.2(e)(1)); (B) in the case of any other confinement sentence for an offense committed prior to the defendant's eighteenth birthday, the date of the defendant's last release from confinement on such sentence (*see* §4A1.2(d)(2)(A)); and (C) in any other case, the date of the original sentence (*see* §4A1.2(d)(2)(B) and (e)(2)).

(l) SENTENCES ON APPEAL

Prior sentences under appeal are counted except as expressly provided below. In the case of a prior sentence, the execution of which has been stayed pending appeal, §4A1.1(a), (b), (c), (d), and (e) shall apply as if the execution of such sentence had not been stayed.

(m) EFFECT OF A VIOLATION WARRANT

For the purposes of §4A1.1(d), a defendant who commits the instant offense while a violation warrant from a prior sentence is outstanding (*e.g.*, a probation, parole, or supervised release violation warrant) shall be deemed to be under a criminal justice sentence if that sentence is otherwise countable, even if that sentence would have expired absent such warrant.

(n) FAILURE TO REPORT FOR SERVICE OF SENTENCE OF IMPRISONMENT

For the purposes of §4A1.1(d), failure to report for service of a sentence of imprisonment shall be treated as an escape from such sentence.

(o) FELONY OFFENSE

For the purposes of §4A1.2(c), a "felony offense" means any federal, state, or local offense punishable by death or a term of imprisonment exceeding one year, regardless of the actual sentence imposed.

(p) CRIME OF VIOLENCE DEFINED

For the purposes of §4A1.1(e), the definition of "crime of violence" is that set forth in §4B1.2(a).

Commentary

Application Notes:

1. **Prior Sentence.**—"***Prior sentence***" means a sentence imposed prior to sentencing on the instant offense, other than a sentence for conduct that is part of the instant offense. *See* §4A1.2(a). A sentence imposed after the defendant's commencement of the instant offense, but prior to sentencing on the instant offense, is a prior sentence if it was for conduct other than conduct that was part of the instant offense. Conduct that is part of the instant offense means conduct that is relevant conduct to the instant offense under the provisions of §1B1.3 (Relevant Conduct).

Under §4A1.2(a)(4), a conviction for which the defendant has not yet been sentenced is treated as if it were a prior sentence under §4A1.1(c) if a sentence resulting from such conviction otherwise would have been counted. In the case of an offense set forth in §4A1.2(c)(1) (which lists certain misdemeanor and petty offenses), a conviction for which the defendant has not yet been sentenced is treated as if it were a prior sentence under

§4A1.2(a)(4) only where the offense is similar to the instant offense (because sentences for other offenses set forth in §4A1.2(c)(1) are counted only if they are of a specified type and length).

2. **Sentence of Imprisonment.**—To qualify as a sentence of imprisonment, the defendant

must have actually served a period of imprisonment on such sentence (or, if the defendant escaped, would have served time). *See* §4A1.2(a)(3) and (b)(2). For the purposes of applying §4A1.1(a), (b), or (c), the length of a sentence of imprisonment is the stated maximum (*e.g.*, in the case of a determinate sentence of five years, the stated maximum is five years; in the case of an indeterminate sentence of one to five years, the stated maximum is five years; in the case of an indeterminate sentence for a term not to exceed five years, the stated maximum is five years; in the case of an indeterminate sentence for a term not to exceed the defendant's twenty-first birthday, the stated maximum is the amount of time in pre-trial detention plus the amount of time between the date of sentence and the defendant's twenty-first birthday). That is, criminal history points are based on the sentence pronounced, not the length of time actually served. *See* §4A1.2(b)(1) and (2). A sentence of probation is to be treated as a sentence under §4A1.1(c) unless a condition of probation requiring imprisonment of at least sixty days was imposed.

3. **Application of "Single Sentence" Rule (Subsection (a)(2)).—**

(A) **Predicate Offenses.**—In some cases, multiple prior sentences are treated as a single sentence for purposes of calculating the criminal history score under §4A1.1(a), (b), and (c). However, for purposes of determining predicate offenses, a prior sentence included in the single sentence should be treated as if it received criminal history points, if it independently would have received criminal history points. Therefore, an individual prior sentence may serve as a predicate under the career offender guideline (*see* §4B1.2(c)) or other guidelines with predicate offenses, if it independently would have received criminal history points. However, because predicate offenses may be used only if they are counted "separately" from each other (*see* §4B1.2(c)), no more than one prior sentence in a given single sentence may be used as a predicate offense.

For example, a defendant's criminal history includes one robbery conviction and one theft conviction. The sentences for these offenses were imposed on the same day, eight years ago, and are treated as a single sentence under §4A1.2(a)(2). If the defendant received a one-year sentence of imprisonment for the robbery and a twoyear sentence of imprisonment for the theft, to be served concurrently, a total of 3 points is added under §4A1.1(a). Because this particular robbery met the definition of a felony crime of violence and independently would have received 2 criminal history points under §4A1.1(b), it may serve as a predicate under the career offender guideline.

Note, however, that if the sentences in the example above were imposed thirteen years ago, the robbery independently would have received no criminal history points under §4A1.1(b), because it was not imposed within ten years of the defendant's commencement of the instant offense. *See* §4A1.2(e)(2). Accordingly, it may not serve as a predicate under the career offender guideline.

(B) **Upward Departure Provision.**—Treating multiple prior sentences as a single sentence may result in a criminal history score that underrepresents the seriousness of the defendant's criminal history and the danger that the defendant presents to the public. In such a case, an upward departure may be warranted. For example, if a defendant was convicted of a number of serious non-violent offenses committed

on different occasions, and the resulting sentences were treated as a single sentence because either the sentences resulted from offenses contained in the same charging instrument or the defendant was sentenced for these offenses on the same day, the assignment of a single set of points may not adequately reflect the seriousness of the defendant's criminal history or the frequency with which the defendant has committed crimes.

4. **Sentences Imposed in the Alternative.**—A sentence which specifies a fine or other non-incarcerative disposition as an alternative to a term of imprisonment (*e.g.*, $1,000 fine or ninety days' imprisonment) is treated as a non-imprisonment sentence.

5. **Sentences for Driving While Intoxicated or Under the Influence.**—Convictions for driving while intoxicated or under the influence (and similar offenses by whatever name they are known) are always counted, without regard to how the offense is classified. Paragraphs (1) and (2) of §4A1.2(c) do not apply.

6. **Reversed, Vacated, or Invalidated Convictions.**—Sentences resulting from convictions that (A) have been reversed or vacated because of errors of law or because of subsequently discovered evidence exonerating the defendant, or (B) have been ruled constitutionally invalid in a prior case are not to be counted. With respect to the current sentencing proceeding, this guideline and commentary do not confer upon the defendant any right to attack collaterally a prior conviction or sentence beyond any such rights otherwise recognized in law (*e.g.*, 21 U.S.C. § 851 expressly provides that a defendant may collaterally attack certain prior convictions).

Nonetheless, the criminal conduct underlying any conviction that is not counted in the criminal history score may be considered pursuant to §4A1.3 (Adequacy of Criminal History Category).

7. **Offenses Committed Prior to Age Eighteen.**—Section 4A1.2(d) covers offenses committed prior to age eighteen. Attempting to count every juvenile adjudication would have the potential for creating large disparities due to the differential availability of records. Therefore, for offenses committed prior to age eighteen, only those that resulted in adult sentences of imprisonment exceeding one year and one month, or resulted in imposition of an adult or juvenile sentence or release from confinement on that sentence within five years of the defendant's commencement of the instant offense are counted. To avoid disparities from jurisdiction to jurisdiction in the age at which a defendant is considered a "juvenile," this provision applies to all offenses committed prior to age eighteen.

8. **Applicable Time Period.**—Section 4A1.2(d)(2) and (e) establishes the time period within which prior sentences are counted. As used in §4A1.2(d)(2) and (e), the term "***commencement of the instant offense***" includes any relevant conduct. *See* §1B1.3 (Relevant Conduct). If the court finds that a sentence imposed outside this time period is evidence of similar, or serious dissimilar, criminal conduct, the court may consider this information in determining whether an upward departure is warranted under §4A1.3 (Adequacy of Criminal History Category).

9. **Diversionary Dispositions.**—Section 4A1.2(f) requires counting prior adult diversionary dispositions if they involved a judicial determination of guilt or an admission of guilt in open court. This reflects a policy that defendants who receive the benefit of a rehabilitative sentence and continue to commit crimes should not be treated with further leniency.

10. **Convictions Set Aside or Defendant Pardoned.**—A number of jurisdictions have various procedures pursuant to which previous convictions may be set aside or the defendant may be pardoned for reasons unrelated to innocence or errors of law, *e.g.*, in order to restore civil rights or to remove the stigma associated with a criminal conviction. Sentences resulting from such convictions are to be counted. However, expunged convictions are not counted. §4A1.2(j).

11. **Revocations to be Considered.**—Section 4A1.2(k) covers revocations of probation and other conditional sentences where the original term of imprisonment imposed, if any, did not exceed one year and one month. Rather than count the original sentence and the resentence after revocation as separate sentences, the sentence given upon revocation should be added to the original sentence of imprisonment, if any, and the total should be counted as if it were one sentence. By this approach, no more than three points will be assessed for a single conviction, even if probation or conditional release was subsequently revoked. If the sentence originally imposed, the sentence imposed upon revocation, or the total of both sentences exceeded one year and one month, the maximum three points would be assigned. If, however, at the time of revocation another sentence was imposed for a new criminal conviction, that conviction would be computed separately from the sentence imposed for the revocation.

Where a revocation applies to multiple sentences, and such sentences are counted separately under §4A1.2(a)(2), add the term of imprisonment imposed upon revocation to the sentence that will result in the greatest increase in criminal history points. **Example:** A defendant was serving two probationary sentences, each counted separately under §4A1.2(a)(2); probation was revoked on both sentences as a result of the same violation conduct; and the defendant was sentenced to a total of 45 days of imprisonment. If one sentence had been a "straight" probationary sentence and the other had been a probationary sentence that had required service of 15 days of imprisonment, the revocation term of imprisonment (45 days) would be added to the probationary sentence that had the 15-day term of imprisonment. This would result in a total of 2 criminal history points under §4A1.1(b) (for the combined 60-day term of imprisonment) and 1 criminal history point under §4A1.1(c) (for the other probationary sentence).

12. **Application of Subsection (c).—**

(A) **In General.**—In determining whether an unlisted offense is similar to an offense listed in subsection (c)(1) or (c)(2), the court should use a common sense approach that includes consideration of relevant factors such as (i) a comparison of punishments imposed for the listed and unlisted offenses; (ii) the perceived seriousness of the offense as indicated by the level of punishment; (iii) the elements of the offense; (iv) the level of culpability involved; and (v) the degree to which the commission of the offense indicates a likelihood of recurring criminal conduct.

(B) **Local Ordinance Violations.**—A number of local jurisdictions have enacted ordinances covering certain offenses (*e.g.*, larceny and assault misdemeanors) that are also violations of state criminal law. This enables a local court (*e.g.*, a municipal court) to exercise jurisdiction over such offenses. Such offenses are excluded from the definition of local ordinance violations in §4A1.2(c)(2) and, therefore, sentences for such offenses are to be treated as if the defendant had been convicted under state law.

(C) **Insufficient Funds Check.**—"***Insufficient funds check***," as used in §4A1.2(c)(1), does not include any conviction establishing that the defendant used a false name or non-existent account.

Background: Prior sentences, not otherwise excluded, are to be counted in the criminal history score, including uncounseled misdemeanor sentences where imprisonment was not imposed.

Historical Note

Effective November 1, 1987. Amended effective November 1, 1989 (amendments 262–265); November 1, 1990 (amendments 352 and 353); November 1, 1991 (amendments 381 and 382); November 1, 1992 (amendment 472); November 1, 1993 (amendment 493); November 1, 2007 (amendment 709); November 1, 2010 (amendment 742); November 1, 2011 (amendment 758); November 1, 2012 (amendment 766); November 1, 2013 (amendment 777); November 1, 2015 (amendment 795).

§4A1.3. Departures Based on Inadequacy of Criminal History Category (Policy Statement)

(a) UPWARD DEPARTURES.—

(1) STANDARD FOR UPWARD DEPARTURE.—If reliable information indicates that the defendant's criminal history category substantially under-represents the seriousness of the defendant's criminal history or the likelihood that the defendant will commit other crimes, an upward departure may be warranted.

(2) TYPES OF INFORMATION FORMING THE BASIS FOR UPWARD DEPARTURE.— The information described in subsection (a) may include information concerning the following:

(A) Prior sentence(s) not used in computing the criminal history category (*e.g.*, sentences for foreign and tribal offenses).

(B) Prior sentence(s) of substantially more than one year imposed as a result of independent crimes committed on different occasions.

(C) Prior similar misconduct established by a civil adjudication or by a failure to comply with an administrative order.

(D) Whether the defendant was pending trial or sentencing on another charge at the time of the instant offense.

(E) Prior similar adult criminal conduct not resulting in a criminal conviction.

(3) PROHIBITION.—A prior arrest record itself shall not be considered for purposes of an upward departure under this policy statement.

(4) DETERMINATION OF EXTENT OF UPWARD DEPARTURE.—

(A) IN GENERAL.—Except as provided in subdivision (B), the court shall determine the extent of a departure under this subsection by using, as a reference, the criminal history category applicable to defendants whose criminal history or likelihood to recidivate most closely resembles that of the defendant's.

(B) UPWARD DEPARTURES FROM CATEGORY VI.—In a case in which the court determines that the extent and nature of the defendant's criminal history, taken together, are sufficient to warrant an upward departure from Criminal History Category VI, the court should structure the departure by moving incrementally down the sentencing table to the next higher offense level in Criminal History Category VI until it finds a guideline range appropriate to the case.

(b) DOWNWARD DEPARTURES.—

(1) STANDARD FOR DOWNWARD DEPARTURE.—If reliable information indicates that the defendant's criminal history category substantially over-represents the seriousness of the defendant's criminal history or the likelihood that the defendant will commit other crimes, a downward departure may be warranted.

(2) PROHIBITIONS.—

(A) CRIMINAL HISTORY CATEGORY I.—A departure below the lower limit of the applicable guideline range for Criminal History Category I is prohibited.

(B) ARMED CAREER CRIMINAL AND REPEAT AND DANGEROUS SEX OFFENDER.—A downward departure under this subsection is prohibited for (i) an armed career criminal within the meaning of §4B1.4 (Armed Career Criminal); and (ii) a repeat and dangerous sex offender against minors within the meaning of §4B1.5 (Repeat and Dangerous Sex Offender Against Minors).

(3) LIMITATIONS.—

(A) LIMITATION ON EXTENT OF DOWNWARD DEPARTURE FOR CAREER

OFFENDER.—The extent of a downward departure

under this subsection for a career offender within the meaning of §4B1.1 (Career Offender) may not exceed one criminal history category.

(B) LIMITATION ON APPLICABILITY OF §5C1.2 IN EVENT OF DOWNWARD DEPARTURE TO CATEGORY I.—A defendant whose criminal history category is Category I after receipt of a downward departure under this subsection does not meet the criterion of subsection (a)(1) of §5C1.2 (Limitation on Applicability of Statutory Maximum Sentences in Certain Cases) if, before receipt of the downward departure, the defendant had more than one criminal history point under §4A1.1 (Criminal History Category).

(c) WRITTEN SPECIFICATION OF BASIS FOR DEPARTURE.—In departing from the otherwise applicable criminal history category under this policy statement, the court shall specify in writing the following:

(1) In the case of an upward departure, the specific reasons why the applicable criminal history category substantially underrepresents the seriousness of the defendant's criminal history or the likelihood that the defendant will commit other crimes.

(2) In the case of a downward departure, the specific reasons why the applicable criminal history category substantially over-represents the seriousness of the defendant's criminal history or the likelihood that the defendant will commit other crimes.

Commentary

Application Notes:

1. **Definitions.**—For purposes of this policy statement, the terms "***depart***", "***departure***", "***downward departure***", and "***upward departure***" have the meaning given those terms in Application Note 1 of the Commentary to §1B1.1 (Application Instructions).

2. **Upward Departures.**—

(A) **Examples.**—An upward departure from the defendant's criminal history category may be warranted based on any of the following circumstances:

(i) A previous foreign sentence for a serious offense.

(ii) Receipt of a prior consolidated sentence of ten years for a series of serious assaults.

(iii) A similar instance of large scale fraudulent misconduct established by an adjudication in a Securities and Exchange Commission enforcement proceeding.

(iv) Commission of the instant offense while on bail or pretrial release for another serious offense.

(B) **Upward Departures from Criminal History Category VI.**—In the case of an egregious, serious criminal record in which even the guideline range for Criminal History Category VI is not adequate to reflect the seriousness of the defendant's criminal history, a departure above the guideline range for a defendant with Criminal History Category VI may be warranted. In determining whether an upward departure from Criminal History Category VI is warranted, the court should consider that the nature of the prior offenses rather than simply their number is often more indicative of the seriousness of the defendant's criminal record. For example, a defendant with five prior sentences for very large-scale fraud offenses may have 15 criminal history points, within the range of points typical for Criminal History Category VI, yet have a substantially more serious criminal history overall because of the nature of the prior offenses.

3. **Downward Departures.**—A downward departure from the defendant's criminal history category may be warranted if, for example, the defendant had two minor misdemeanor convictions close to ten years prior to the instant offense and no other evidence of prior criminal behavior in the intervening period. A departure below the lower limit of the applicable guideline range for Criminal History Category I is prohibited under subsection (b)(2)(B), due to the fact that the lower limit of the guideline range for Criminal History Category I is set for a first offender with the lowest risk of recidivism.

Background: This policy statement recognizes that the criminal history score is unlikely to take into account all the variations in the seriousness of criminal history that may occur. For example, a defendant with an extensive record of serious, assaultive conduct who had received what might now be considered extremely lenient treatment in the past might have the same criminal history category as a defendant who had a record of less serious conduct. Yet, the first defendant's criminal history clearly may be more serious. This may be particularly true in the case of younger defendants (*e.g.*, defendants in their early twenties or younger) who are more likely to have received repeated lenient treatment, yet who may actually pose a greater risk of serious recidivism than older defendants. This policy statement authorizes the consideration of a departure from the guidelines in the limited circumstances where reliable information indicates that the criminal history category does not adequately reflect the seriousness of the defendant's criminal history or likelihood of recidivism, and provides guidance for the consideration of such departures.

Historical Note

Effective November 1, 1987. Amended effective November 1, 1991 (amendment 381); November 1, 1992 (amendment 460); October 27, 2003 (amendment 651).

PART B — CAREER OFFENDERS AND CRIMINAL LIVELIHOOD

§4B1.1. Career Offender

(a) A defendant is a career offender if (1) the defendant was at least eighteen years old at the time the defendant committed the instant offense of conviction; (2) the instant offense of conviction is a felony that is either a crime of violence or a controlled substance offense; and (3) the defendant has at least two prior felony convictions of either a crime of violence or a controlled substance offense.

(b) Except as provided in subsection (c), if the offense level for a career offender from the table in this subsection is greater than the offense level otherwise applicable, the offense level from the table in this subsection shall apply. A career offender's criminal history category in every case under this subsection shall be Category VI.

Offense Statutory Maximum	Offense Level*
(1) Life	**37**
(2) 25 years or more	**34**
(3) 20 years or more, but less than 25 years	**32**
(4) 15 years or more, but less than 20 years	**29**
(5) 10 years or more, but less than 15 years	**24**
(6) 5 years or more, but less than 10 years	**17**
(7) More than 1 year, but less than 5 years	**12**.

*If an adjustment from §3E1.1 (Acceptance of Responsibility) applies, decrease the offense level by the number of levels corresponding to that adjustment.

(c) If the defendant is convicted of 18 U.S.C. § 924(c) or § 929(a), and the defendant is determined to be a career offender under subsection (a), the applicable guideline range shall be determined as follows:

(1) If the only count of conviction is 18 U.S.C. § 924(c) or § 929(a), the applicable guideline range shall be determined using the table in subsection (c)(3).

(2) In the case of multiple counts of conviction in which at least one of the counts is a conviction other than a conviction for 18 U.S.C. § 924(c) or § 929(a), the guideline range shall be the greater of—

(A) the guideline range that results by adding the mandatory minimum consecutive penalty required by the 18 U.S.C. § 924(c) or § 929(a) count(s) to the minimum and the maximum of the otherwise applicable guideline range determined for the count(s) of conviction other than the 18 U.S.C. § 924(c) or § 929(a) count(s); and

(B) the guideline range determined using the table in subsection (c)(3).

(3) CAREER OFFENDER TABLE FOR 18 U.S.C. § 924(C) OR § 929(A) OFFENDERS

§3E1.1 REDUCTION	GUIDELINE RANGE FOR THE 18 U.S.C. §924(C) OR § 929(A) COUNT(S)
No reduction	360–life
2-level reduction	292–365
3-level reduction	262–327.

Commentary

Application Notes:

1. **Definitions.**—"***Crime of violence***," "***controlled substance offense***," and "***two prior felony convictions***" are defined in §4B1.2.

2. **"Offense Statutory Maximum".**—"***Offense Statutory Maximum***," for the purposes of this guideline, refers to the maximum term of imprisonment authorized for the offense of conviction that is a crime of violence or controlled substance offense, including any increase in that maximum term under a sentencing enhancement provision that applies because of the defendant's prior criminal record (such sentencing enhancement provisions are contained, for example, in 21 U.S.C. § 841(b)(1)(A), (B), (C), and (D)). For example, in a case in which the statutory maximum term of imprisonment under 21 U.S.C. § 841(b)(1)(C) is increased from twenty years to thirty years because the defendant has one or more qualifying prior drug convictions, the "Offense Statutory Maximum" for that defendant for the purposes of this guideline is thirty years and not twenty years. If more than one count of conviction is of a crime of violence or controlled substance offense, use the maximum authorized term of imprisonment for the count that has the greatest offense statutory maximum.

3. **Application of Subsection (c).**—

(A) **In General.**—Subsection (c) applies in any case in which the defendant (i) was convicted of violating 18 U.S.C. § 924(c) or § 929(a); and (ii) as a result of that conviction (alone or in addition to another offense of conviction), is determined to be a career offender under §4B1.1(a).

(B) **Subsection (c)(2).**—To determine the greater guideline range under subsection (c)(2), the court shall use the guideline range with the highest minimum term of imprisonment.

(C) **"Otherwise Applicable Guideline Range".**—For purposes of subsection (c)(2)(A), "otherwise applicable guideline range" for the count(s) of conviction other than the 18 U.S.C. § 924(c) or 18 U.S.C. § 929(a) count(s) is determined as follows:

(i) If the count(s) of conviction other than the 18 U.S.C. § 924(c) or 18 U.S.C. § 929(a) count(s) does not qualify the defendant as a career offender, the otherwise applicable guideline range for that count(s) is the guideline range determined using: (I) the Chapter Two and Three offense level for that count(s); and (II) the appropriate criminal history category determined under §§4A1.1 (Criminal History Category) and 4A1.2 (Definitions and Instructions for Computing Criminal History).

(ii) If the count(s) of conviction other than the 18 U.S.C. § 924(c) or 18 U.S.C. § 929(a) count(s) qualifies the defendant as a career offender, the otherwise applicable guideline range for that count(s) is the guideline range determined for that count(s) under §4B1.1(a) and (b).

(D) **Imposition of Consecutive Term of Imprisonment.**—In a case involving multiple counts, the sentence shall be imposed according to the rules in subsection (e) of §5G1.2 (Sentencing on Multiple Counts of Conviction).

(E) **Example.**—The following example illustrates the application of subsection (c)(2) in a multiple count situation:

The defendant is convicted of one count of violating 18 U.S.C. § 924(c) for possessing a firearm in furtherance of a drug trafficking offense (5 year mandatory minimum), and one count of violating 21 U.S.C. § 841(b)(1)(B) (5 year mandatory minimum, 40 year statutory maximum). Applying subsection (c)(2)(A), the court determines that the drug count (without regard to the 18 U.S.C. § 924(c) count) qualifies the defendant as a career offender under §4B1.1(a). Under §4B1.1(a), the otherwise applicable guideline range for the drug count is 188–235 months (using offense level 34 (because the statutory maximum for the drug count is 40 years), minus 3 levels for acceptance of responsibility, and criminal history category VI). The court adds 60 months (the minimum required by 18 U.S.C. § 924(c)) to the minimum and the maximum of that range, resulting in a guideline range of 248–295 months. Applying subsection (c)(2)(B), the court then determines the career offender guideline range from the table in subsection (c)(3) is 262–327 months. The range with the greatest minimum, 262–327 months, is used to impose the sentence in accordance with §5G1.2(e).

4. **Departure Provision for State Misdemeanors.**—In a case in which one or both of the defendant's "two prior felony convictions" is based on an offense that was classified as a misdemeanor at the time of sentencing for the instant federal offense, application of the career offender guideline may result in a guideline range that substantially overrepresents the seriousness of the defendant's criminal history or substantially overstates the seriousness of the instant offense. In such a case, a downward departure may be warranted without regard to the limitation in §4A1.3(b)(3)(A).

Background: Section 994(h) of Title 28, United States Code, mandates that the Commission assure that certain "career" offenders receive a sentence of imprisonment "at or near the maximum term authorized." Section 4B1.1 implements this directive, with the definition of a career offender tracking in large part the criteria set forth in 28 U.S.C. § 994(h). However, in accord with its general guideline promulgation authority under 28 U.S.C. § 994(a)–(f), and its

amendment authority under 28 U.S.C. § 994(o) and (p), the Commission has modified this definition in several respects to focus more precisely on the class of recidivist offenders for whom a lengthy term of imprisonment is appropriate and to avoid "unwarranted sentencing disparities among defendants with similar records who have been found guilty of similar criminal conduct . . . ." 28 U.S.C. § 991(b)(1)(B). The Commission's refinement of this definition over time is consistent with Congress's choice of a directive to the Commission rather than a mandatory minimum sentencing statute ("The [Senate Judiciary] Committee believes that such a directive to the Commission will be more effective; the guidelines development process can assure consistent and rational implementation for the Committee's view that substantial prison terms should be imposed on repeat violent offenders and repeat drug traffickers." S. Rep. No. 225, 98th Cong., 1st Sess. 175 (1983)).

Subsection (c) provides rules for determining the sentence for career offenders who have been convicted of 18 U.S.C. § 924(c) or § 929(a). The Career Offender Table in subsection (c)(3) provides a sentence at or near the statutory maximum for these offenders by using guideline ranges that correspond to criminal history category VI and offense level 37 (assuming §3E.1.1 (Acceptance of Responsibility) does not apply), offense level 35 (assuming a 2-level reduction under §3E.1.1 applies), and offense level 34 (assuming a 3-level reduction under §3E1.1 applies).

Historical Note

Effective November 1, 1987. Amended effective January 15, 1988 (amendments 47 and 48); November 1, 1989 (amendments 266 and 267); November 1, 1992 (amendment 459); November 1, 1994 (amendment 506); November 1, 1995 (amendment 528); November 1, 1997 (amendments 546 and 567); November 1, 2002 (amendment 642); November 1, 2011 (amendment 758); August 1, 2016 (amendment 798).

§4B1.2. Definitions of Terms Used in Section 4B1.1

(a) The term "crime of violence" means any offense under federal or state law, punishable by imprisonment for a term exceeding one year, that—

(1) has as an element the use, attempted use, or threatened use of physical force against the person of another, or

(2) is murder, voluntary manslaughter, kidnapping, aggravated assault, a forcible sex offense, robbery, arson, extortion, or the use or unlawful possession of a firearm described in 26 U.S.C. § 5845(a) or explosive material as defined in 18 U.S.C. § 841(c).

(b) The term "controlled substance offense" means an offense under federal or state law, punishable by imprisonment for a term exceeding one year, that prohibits the manufacture, import, export, distribution, or dispensing of a controlled substance (or a counterfeit substance) or the possession of a controlled substance (or a counterfeit substance) with intent to manufacture, import, export, distribute, or dispense.

(c) The term "two prior felony convictions" means (1) the defendant committed the instant offense of conviction subsequent to sustaining at least two felony convictions of either a crime of violence or a controlled substance offense (*i.e.*, two felony convictions of a crime of violence, two felony convictions of a controlled substance offense, or one felony conviction of a crime of violence and one felony conviction of a controlled substance offense), and (2) the sentences for at least two of the aforementioned felony convictions are counted separately under the provisions of §4A1.1(a), (b), or (c). The date that a defendant sustained a conviction shall be the date that the guilt of the defendant has been established, whether by guilty plea, trial, or plea of *nolo contendere*.

Commentary

Application Notes:

1. **Definitions.**—For purposes of this guideline—

"***Crime of violence***" and "***controlled substance offense***" include the offenses of aiding and abetting, conspiring, and attempting to commit such offenses.

"***Forcible sex offense***" includes where consent to the conduct is not given or is not legally valid, such as where consent to the conduct is involuntary, incompetent, or coerced. The offenses of sexual abuse of a minor and statutory rape are included only if the sexual abuse of a minor or statutory rape was (A) an offense described in 18 U.S.C. § 2241(c) or (B) an offense under state law that would have been an offense under section 2241(c) if the offense had occurred within the special maritime and territorial jurisdiction of the United States.

"***Extortion***" is obtaining something of value from another by the wrongful use of (A) force, (B) fear of physical injury, or (C) threat of physical injury.

Unlawfully possessing a listed chemical with intent to manufacture a controlled substance (21 U.S.C. § 841(c)(1)) is a "controlled substance offense."

Unlawfully possessing a prohibited flask or equipment with intent to manufacture a controlled substance (21 U.S.C. § 843(a)(6)) is a "controlled substance offense."

Maintaining any place for the purpose of facilitating a drug offense (21 U.S.C. § 856) is a "controlled substance offense" if the offense of conviction established that the underlying offense (the offense facilitated) was a "controlled substance offense."

Using a communications facility in committing, causing, or facilitating a drug offense (21 U.S.C. § 843(b)) is a "controlled substance offense" if the offense of conviction established that the underlying offense (the offense committed, caused, or facilitated) was a "controlled substance offense."

A violation of 18 U.S.C. § 924(c) or § 929(a) is a "crime of violence" or a "controlled substance offense" if the offense of conviction established that the underlying offense was a "crime of violence" or a "controlled substance offense". (Note that in the case of a prior

18 U.S.C. § 924(c) or § 929(a) conviction, if the defendant also was convicted of the underlying offense, the sentences for the two prior convictions will be treated as a single sentence under §4A1.2 (Definitions and Instructions for Computing Criminal History).)

"***Prior felony conviction***" means a prior adult federal or state conviction for an offense punishable by death or imprisonment for a term exceeding one year, regardless of whether such offense is specifically designated as a felony and regardless of the actual sentence imposed. A conviction for an offense committed at age eighteen or older is an adult conviction. A conviction for an offense committed prior to age eighteen is an adult conviction if it is classified as an adult conviction under the laws of the jurisdiction in which the defendant was convicted (*e.g.*, a federal conviction for an offense committed prior to the defendant's eighteenth birthday is an adult conviction if the defendant was expressly proceeded against as an adult).

2. **Offense of Conviction as Focus of Inquiry.**—Section 4B1.1 (Career Offender) expressly provides that the instant and prior offenses must be crimes of violence or controlled substance offenses of which the defendant was convicted. Therefore, in determining whether an offense is a crime of violence or controlled substance for the purposes of §4B1.1 (Career Offender), the offense of conviction (*i.e.*, the conduct of which the defendant was convicted) is the focus of inquiry.

3. **Applicability of §4A1.2.**—The provisions of §4A1.2 (Definitions and Instructions for Computing Criminal History) are applicable to the counting of convictions under §4B1.1.

4. **Upward Departure for Burglary Involving Violence.**—There may be cases in which a burglary involves violence, but does not qualify as a "crime of violence" as defined in §4B1.2(a) and, as a result, the defendant does not receive a higher offense level or higher Criminal History Category that would have applied if the burglary qualified as a "crime of violence." In such a case, an upward departure may be appropriate.

Historical
Note
Effective November 1, 1987. Amended effective January 15, 1988 (amendment 49); November 1, 1989 (amendment 268); November 1, 1991 (amendment 433); November 1, 1992 (amendment 461); November 1, 1995 (amendment 528); November 1, 1997 (amendments 546 and 568); November 1, 2000 (amendment 600); November 1, 2002 (amendments 642 and 646); November 1, 2004 (amendment 674); November 1, 2007 (amendment 709); November 1, 2009 (amendment 736); November 1, 2015 (amendment 795); August 1, 2016 (amendment 798).

§4B1.3. Criminal Livelihood

If the defendant committed an offense as part of a pattern of criminal conduct engaged in as a livelihood, his offense level shall be not less than **13**, unless §3E1.1 (Acceptance of Responsibility) applies, in which event his offense level shall be not less than **11**.

Commentary

Application Notes:

1. "***Pattern of criminal conduct***" means planned criminal acts occurring over a substantial period of time. Such acts may involve a single course of conduct or independent offenses.

2. "***Engaged in as a livelihood***" means that (A) the defendant derived income from the pattern of criminal conduct that in any twelve-month period exceeded 2,000 times the then existing hourly minimum wage under federal law; and (B) the totality of circumstances shows that such criminal conduct was the defendant's primary occupation in that twelve-month period (*e.g.*, the defendant engaged in criminal conduct rather than regular, legitimate employment; or the defendant's legitimate employment was merely a front for the defendant's criminal conduct).

Background: Section 4B1.3 implements 28 U.S.C. § 994(i)(2), which directs the Commission to ensure that the guidelines specify a "substantial term of imprisonment" for a defendant who committed an offense as part of a pattern of criminal conduct from which the defendant derived a substantial portion of the defendant's income.

Historical
Note
Effective November 1, 1987. Amended effective June 15, 1988 (amendment 50); November 1, 1989 (amendment 269); November 1, 1990 (amendment 354); November 1, 2010 (amendment 747).

§4B1.4. Armed Career Criminal

(a) A defendant who is subject to an enhanced sentence under the provisions of 18 U.S.C. § 924(e) is an armed career criminal.

(b) The offense level for an armed career criminal is the greatest of:

(1) the offense level applicable from Chapters Two and Three; or

(2) the offense level from §4B1.1 (Career Offender) if applicable; or

(3) (A) **34**, if the defendant used or possessed the firearm or ammunition in connection with either a crime of violence, as defined in §4B1.2(a), or a controlled substance offense, as defined in §4B1.2(b), or if the firearm possessed by the defendant was of a type described in 26 U.S.C. § 5845(a)*; or

(B) **33**, otherwise.*

*If an adjustment from §3E1.1 (Acceptance of Responsibility) applies, decrease the offense level by the number of levels corresponding to that adjustment.

(c) The criminal history category for an armed career criminal is the greatest of:

(1) the criminal history category from Chapter Four, Part A (Criminal History), or §4B1.1 (Career Offender) if applicable; or

(2) Category VI, if the defendant used or possessed the firearm or ammunition in connection with either a crime of violence, as defined in §4B1.2(a), or a controlled substance offense, as defined in §4B1.2(b), or if the firearm possessed by the defendant was of a type described in 26 U.S.C. § 5845(a); or

(3) Category IV.

Commentary

Application Notes:

1. This guideline applies in the case of a defendant subject to an enhanced sentence under 18 U.S.C. § 924(e). Under 18 U.S.C. § 924(e)(1), a defendant is subject to an enhanced sentence if the instant offense of conviction is a violation of 18 U.S.C. § 922(g) and the defendant has at least three prior convictions for a "violent felony" or "serious drug offense," or both, committed on occasions different from one another. The terms "***violent felony***" and "***serious drug offense***" are defined in 18 U.S.C. § 924(e)(2). It is to be noted that the definitions of "violent felony" and "serious drug offense" in 18 U.S.C. § 924(e)(2) are not identical to the definitions of "crime of violence" and "controlled substance offense" used in §4B1.1 (Career Offender), nor are the time periods for the counting of prior sentences under §4A1.2 (Definitions and Instructions for Computing Criminal History) applicable to the determination of whether a defendant is subject to an enhanced sentence under 18 U.S.C. § 924(e).

It is also to be noted that the procedural steps relative to the imposition of an enhanced sentence under 18 U.S.C. § 924(e) are not set forth by statute and may vary to some extent from jurisdiction to jurisdiction.

2. **Application of §4B1.4 in Cases Involving Convictions Under 18 U.S.C. § 844(h), § 924(c), or § 929(a).**—If a sentence under this guideline is imposed in conjunction with a sentence for a conviction under 18 U.S.C. § 844(h), § 924(c), or § 929(a), do not apply either subsection (b)(3)(A) or (c)(2). A sentence under 18 U.S.C. § 844(h), § 924(c), or § 929(a) accounts for the conduct covered by subsections (b)(3)(A) and (c)(2) because of the relatedness of the conduct covered by these subsections to the conduct that forms the basis for the conviction under 18 U.S.C. § 844(h), § 924(c), or § 929(a).

In a few cases, the rule provided in the preceding paragraph may result in a guideline range that, when combined with the mandatory consecutive sentence under 18 U.S.C. § 844(h), § 924(c), or § 929(a), produces a total maximum penalty that is less than the maximum of the guideline range that would have resulted had there not been a count of conviction under 18 U.S.C. § 844(h), § 924(c), or § 929(a) (*i.e.*, the guideline range that would have resulted if subsections (b)(3)(A) and (c)(2) had been applied). In such a case, an upward departure may be warranted so that the conviction under 18 U.S.C. § 844(h), § 924(c), or § 929(a) does not result in a decrease in the total punishment. An upward departure under this paragraph shall not exceed the maximum of the guideline range that would have resulted had there not been a count of conviction under 18 U.S.C. § 844(h), § 924(c), or § 929(a).

Background: This section implements 18 U.S.C. § 924(e), which requires a minimum sentence of imprisonment of fifteen years for a defendant who violates 18 U.S.C. § 922(g) and has three previous convictions for a violent felony or a serious drug offense. If the offense level determined under this section is greater than the offense level otherwise applicable, the offense level determined under this section shall be applied. A minimum criminal history category

(Category IV) is provided, reflecting that each defendant to whom this section applies will have at least three prior convictions for serious offenses. In some cases, the criminal history category may not adequately reflect the defendant's criminal history; *see* §4A1.3 (Adequacy of Criminal History Category).

Historical

Note
Effective November 1, 1990 (amendment 355). Amended effective November 1, 1992 (amendment 459); November 1, 2002 (amendment 646); November 1, 2004 (amendment 674).

§4B1.5. Repeat and Dangerous Sex Offender Against Minors

(a) In any case in which the defendant's instant offense of conviction is a covered sex crime, §4B1.1 (Career Offender) does not apply, and the defendant committed the instant offense of conviction subsequent to sustaining at least one sex offense conviction:

(1) The offense level shall be the greater of:

(A) the offense level determined under Chapters Two and Three; or

(B) the offense level from the table below decreased by the number of levels corresponding to any applicable adjustment from §3E1.1 (Acceptance of Responsibility):

Offense Statutory Maximum	Offense Level
(i) Life	**37**
(ii) 25 years or more	**34**
(iii) 20 years or more, but less than 25 years	**32**
(iv) 15 years or more, but less than 20 years	**29**
(v) 10 years or more, but less than 15 years	**24**
(vi) 5 years or more, but less than 10 years	**17**
(vii) More than 1 year, but less than 5 years	**12**.

(2) The criminal history category shall be the greater of: (A) the criminal history category determined under Chapter Four, Part A (Criminal History); or (B) criminal history Category V.

(b) In any case in which the defendant's instant offense of conviction is a covered sex crime, neither §4B1.1 nor subsection (a) of this guideline applies, and the defendant engaged in a pattern of activity involving prohibited sexual conduct:

(1) The offense level shall be **5** plus the offense level determined under Chapters Two and Three. However, if the resulting offense level is less than level **22**, the offense level shall be

level **22**, decreased by the number of levels corresponding to any applicable adjustment from §3E1.1.

(2) The criminal history category shall be the criminal history category determined under Chapter Four, Part A.

Commentary

Application Notes:

1. **Definition.**—For purposes of this guideline, "***minor***" means (A) an individual who had not attained the age of 18 years; (B) an individual, whether fictitious or not, who a law enforcement officer represented to a participant (i) had not attained the age of 18 years; and (ii) could be provided for the purposes of engaging in sexually explicit conduct; or (C) an undercover law enforcement officer who represented to a participant that the officer had not attained the age of 18 years.

2. **Covered Sex Crime as Instant Offense of Conviction.**—For purposes of this guideline, the instant offense of conviction must be a covered sex crime, *i.e.*: (A) an offense, perpetrated against a minor, under (i) chapter 109A of title 18, United States Code; (ii) chapter 110 of such title, not including trafficking in, receipt of, or possession of, child pornography, or a recordkeeping offense; (iii) chapter 117 of such title, not including

transmitting information about a minor or filing a factual statement about an alien individual; or (iv) 18 U.S.C. § 1591; or (B) an attempt or a conspiracy to commit any offense described in subdivisions (A)(i) through (iv) of this note.

3. **Application of Subsection (a).—**

(A) **Definitions.**—For purposes of subsection (a):

(i) "***Offense statutory maximum***" means the maximum term of imprisonment authorized for the instant offense of conviction that is a covered sex crime, including any increase in that maximum term under a sentencing enhancement provision (such as a sentencing enhancement provision contained in 18 U.S.C. § 2247(a) or § 2426(a)) that applies to that covered sex crime because of the defendant's prior criminal record.

(ii) "***Sex offense conviction***" (I) means any offense described in 18 U.S.C. § 2426(b)(1)(A) or (B), if the offense was perpetrated against a minor; and (II) does not include trafficking in, receipt of, or possession of, child pornography. "***Child pornography***" has the meaning given that term in 18 U.S.C. § 2256(8).

(B) **Determination of Offense Statutory Maximum in the Case of Multiple Counts of Conviction.**—In a case in which more than one count of the instant offense of conviction is a felony that is a covered sex crime, the court shall use the maximum authorized term of imprisonment for the count that has the greatest offense statutory maximum, for purposes of determining the offense statutory maximum under subsection (a).

4. **Application of Subsection (b).—**

(A) **Definition.**—For purposes of subsection (b), "***prohibited sexual conduct***" means any of the following: (i) any offense described in 18 U.S.C. § 2426(b)(1)(A) or (B);

(ii) the production of child pornography; or (iii) trafficking in child pornography only if, prior to the commission of the instant offense of conviction, the defendant sustained a felony conviction for that trafficking in child pornography. It does not include receipt or possession of child pornography. "***Child pornography***" has the meaning given that term in 18 U.S.C. § 2256(8).

(B) **Determination of Pattern of Activity.—**

(i) **In General.**—For purposes of subsection (b), the defendant engaged in a pattern of activity involving prohibited sexual conduct if on at least two separate occasions, the defendant engaged in prohibited sexual conduct with a minor.

(ii) **Occasion of Prohibited Sexual Conduct.**—An occasion of prohibited sexual conduct may be considered for purposes of subsection (b) without regard to whether the occasion (I) occurred during the course of the instant offense; or (II) resulted in a conviction for the conduct that occurred on that occasion.

5. **Treatment and Monitoring.—**

(A) **Recommended Maximum Term of Supervised Release.**—The statutory maximum term of supervised release is recommended for offenders sentenced under this guideline.

(B) **Recommended Conditions of Probation and Supervised Release.**—Treatment and monitoring are important tools for supervising offenders and should be considered as special conditions of any term of probation or supervised release that is imposed.

Background: This guideline applies to offenders whose instant offense of conviction is a sex offense committed against a minor and who present a continuing danger to the public. The relevant criminal provisions provide for increased statutory maximum penalties for repeat sex offenders and make those increased statutory maximum penalties available if the defendant previously was convicted of any of several federal and state sex offenses (*see* 18 U.S.C. §§ 2247, 2426). In addition, section 632 of Public Law 102–141 and section 505 of Public Law 105–314 directed the Commission to ensure lengthy incarceration for offenders who engage in a pattern of activity involving the sexual abuse or exploitation of minors.

Section 401(i)(1)(A) of Public Law 108–21 directly amended Application Note 4(b)(i), effective April 30, 2003.

Historical Note

Effective November 1, 2001 (amendment 615). Amended effective April 30, 2003 (amendment 649); November 1, 2003 (amendment 661); November 1, 2007 (amendment 701).

CHAPTER FIVE
DETERMINING THE SENTENCE

Introductory Commentary

For certain categories of offenses and offenders, the guidelines permit the court to impose either imprisonment or some other sanction or combination of sanctions. In determining the type of sentence to impose, the sentencing judge should consider the nature and seriousness of the conduct, the statutory purposes of sentencing, and the pertinent offender characteristics. A sentence is within the guidelines if it complies with each applicable section of this chapter. The court should impose a sentence sufficient, but not greater than necessary, to comply with the statutory purposes of sentencing. 18 U.S.C. § 3553(a).

Historical Note

Effective November 1, 1987.

PART A — SENTENCING TABLE

The Sentencing Table used to determine the guideline range follows:

SENTENCING TABLE
(in months of imprisonment)

Criminal History Category (Criminal History Points)

Offense Level	I (0 or 1)	II (2 or 3)	III (4, 5, 6)	IV (7, 8, 9)	V (10, 11, 12)	VI (13 or more)
Zone A						
1	0–6	0–6	0–6	0–6	0–6	0–6
2	0–6	0–6	0–6	0–6	0–6	1–7
3	0–6	0–6	0–6	0–6	2–8	3–9
4	0–6	0–6	0–6	2–8	4–10	6–12
5	0–6	0–6	1–7	4–10	6–12	9–15
6	0–6	1–7	2–8	6–12	9–15	12–18
7	0–6	2–8	4–10	8–14	12–18	15–21
8	0–6	4–10	6–12	10–16	15–21	18–24
Zone B						
9	4–10	6–12	8–14	12–18	18–24	21–27
10	6–12	8–14	10–16	15–21	21–27	24–30
11	8–14	10–16	12–18	18–24	24–30	27–33
Zone C						
12	10–16	12–18	15–21	21–27	27–33	30–37
13	12–18	15–21	18–24	24–30	30–37	33–41
Zone D						
14	15–21	18–24	21–27	27–33	33–41	37–46
15	18–24	21–27	24–30	30–37	37–46	41–51
16	21–27	24–30	27–33	33–41	41–51	46–57
17	24–30	27–33	30–37	37–46	46–57	51–63

18 27–33 30–37 33–41 41–51 51–63 57–71
19 30–37 33–41 37–46 46–57 57–71 63–78
20 33–41 37–46 41–51 51–63 63–78 70–87
21 37–46 41–51 46–57 57–71 70–87 77–96
22 41–51 46–57 51–63 63–78 77–96 84–105
23 46–57 51–63 57–71 70–87 84–105 92–115
24 51–63 57–71 63–78 77–96 92–115 100–125
25 57–71 63–78 70–87 84–105 100–125 110–137
26 63–78 70–87 78–97 92–115 110–137 120–150
27 70–87 78–97 87–108 100–125 120–150 130–162
28 78–97 87–108 97–121 110–137 130–162 140–175
29 87–108 97–121 108–135 121–151 140–175 151–188
30 97–121 108–135 121–151 135–168 151–188 168–210
31 108–135 121–151 135–168 151–188 168–210 188–235
32 121–151 135–168 151–188 168–210 188–235 210–262
33 135–168 151–188 168–210 188–235 210–262 235–293
34 151–188 168–210 188–235 210–262 235–293 262–327
35 168–210 188–235 210–262 235–293 262–327 292–365
36 188–235 210–262 235–293 262–327 292–365 324–405
37 210–262 235–293 262–327 292–365 324–405 360–life
38 235–293 262–327 292–365 324–405 360–life 360–life
39 262–327 292–365 324–405 360–life 360–life 360–life
40 292–365 324–405 360–life 360–life 360–life 360–life
41 324–405 360–life 360–life 360–life 360–life 360–life
42 360–life 360–life 360–life 360–life 360–life 360–life
43 life life life life life life

Commentary to Sentencing Table

Application Notes:

1. The Offense Level (1–43) forms the vertical axis of the Sentencing Table. The Criminal History Category (I–VI) forms the horizontal axis of the Table. The intersection of the Offense Level and Criminal History Category displays the Guideline Range in months of imprisonment. "***Life***" means life imprisonment. For example, the guideline range applicable to a defendant with an Offense Level of 15 and a Criminal History Category of III is 24–30 months of imprisonment.
2. In rare cases, a total offense level of less than 1 or more than 43 may result from application of the guidelines. A total offense level of less than 1 is to be treated as an offense level of 1. An offense level of more than 43 is to be treated as an offense level of 43.
3. The Criminal History Category is determined by the total criminal history points from Chapter Four, Part A, except as provided in §§4B1.1 (Career Offender) and 4B1.4 (Armed Career Criminal). The total criminal history points associated with each Criminal History Category are shown under each Criminal History Category in the Sentencing Table.

Historical Note

Effective November 1, 1987. Amended effective November 1, 1989 (amendment 270); November 1, 1991 (amendment 418); November 1, 1992 (amendment 462); November 1, 2010 (amendment 738).

PART B — PROBATION

Introductory Commentary

The Comprehensive Crime Control Act of 1984 makes probation a sentence in and of itself. 18 U.S.C. § 3561. Probation may be used as an alternative to incarceration, provided that the terms and conditions of probation can be fashioned so as to meet fully the statutory purposes of sentencing, including promoting respect for law, providing just punishment for the offense, achieving general deterrence, and protecting the public from further crimes by the

defendant.
Historical
Note
Effective November 1, 1987.

§5B1.1. Imposition of a Term of Probation

(a) Subject to the statutory restrictions in subsection (b) below, a sentence of probation is authorized if:
(1) the applicable guideline range is in Zone A of the Sentencing Table; or
(2) the applicable guideline range is in Zone B of the Sentencing Table and the court imposes a condition or combination of conditions requiring intermittent confinement, community confinement, or home detention as provided in subsection (c)(3) of §5C1.1 (Imposition of a Term of Imprisonment).
(b) A sentence of probation may not be imposed in the event:
(1) the offense of conviction is a Class A or B felony, 18 U.S.C. § 3561(a)(1);
(2) the offense of conviction expressly precludes probation as a sentence, 18 U.S.C. § 3561(a)(2);
(3) the defendant is sentenced at the same time to a sentence of imprisonment for the same or a different offense, 18 U.S.C. § 3561(a)(3).

Commentary

Application Notes:

1. Except where prohibited by statute or by the guideline applicable to the offense in Chapter Two, the guidelines authorize, but do not require, a sentence of probation in the following circumstances:

(A) **Where the applicable guideline range is in Zone A of the Sentencing Table (*i.e.*, the minimum term of imprisonment specified in the applicable guideline range is zero months).** In such cases, a condition requiring a period of community confinement, home detention, or intermittent confinement may be imposed but is not required.
(B) **Where the applicable guideline range is in Zone B of the Sentencing Table (*i.e.*, the minimum term of imprisonment specified in the applicable guideline range is at least one but not more than nine months).** In such cases, the court may impose probation only if it imposes a condition or combination of conditions requiring a period of community confinement, home detention, or intermittent confinement sufficient to satisfy the minimum term of imprisonment specified in the guideline range. For example, where the offense level is 7 and the criminal history category is II, the guideline range from the Sentencing Table is 2–8 months. In such a case, the court may impose a sentence of probation only if it imposes a condition or conditions requiring at least two months of community confinement, home detention, or intermittent confinement, or a combination of community confinement, home detention, and intermittent confinement totaling at least two months.

2. Where the applicable guideline range is in Zone C or D of the Sentencing Table (*i.e.*, the minimum term of imprisonment specified in the applicable guideline range is ten months or more), the guidelines do not authorize a sentence of probation. *See* §5C1.1 (Imposition of a Term of Imprisonment).

Background: This section provides for the imposition of a sentence of probation. The court may sentence a defendant to a term of probation in any case unless (1) prohibited by statute, or (2) where a term of imprisonment is required under §5C1.1 (Imposition of a Term of Imprisonment).

Under 18 U.S.C. § 3561(a)(3), the imposition of a sentence of probation is prohibited where the defendant is sentenced at the same time to a sentence of imprisonment for the same or a different offense. Although this provision has effectively abolished the use of "split sentences" imposable pursuant to the former 18 U.S.C. § 3651, the drafters of the Sentencing Reform Act noted that the functional equivalent of the split sentence could be "achieved by a more direct and logically consistent route" by providing that a defendant serve a term of imprisonment followed by a period of supervised release. (S. Rep. No. 225, 98th Cong., 1st Sess. 89 (1983)). Section 5B1.1(a)(2) provides a transition between the circumstances under which a "straight" probationary term is authorized and those where probation is prohibited.

Historical Note

Effective November 1, 1987. Amended effective November 1, 1989 (amendment 302); November 1, 1992 (amendment 462); November 1, 2010 (amendments 738 and 747).

§5B1.2. Term of Probation

(a) When probation is imposed, the term shall be:

(1) at least one year but not more than five years if the offense level is **6** or greater;

(2) no more than three years in any other case.

Commentary

Background: This section governs the length of a term of probation. Subject to statutory restrictions, the guidelines provide that a term of probation may not exceed three years if the offense level is less than 6. If a defendant has an offense level of 6 or greater, the guidelines provide that a term of probation be at least one year but not more than five years. Although some distinction in the length of a term of probation is warranted based on the circumstances of the case, a term of probation may also be used to enforce conditions such as fine or restitution payments, or attendance in a program of treatment such as drug rehabilitation. Often, it may not be possible to determine the amount of time required for the satisfaction of such payments or programs in advance. This issue has been resolved by setting forth two broad ranges for the duration of a term of probation depending upon the offense level. Within the guidelines set forth in this section, the determination of the length of a term of probation is within the discretion of the sentencing judge.

Historical Note

Effective November 1, 1987

§5B1.3. Conditions of Probation

(a) MANDATORY CONDITIONS

(1) For any offense, the defendant shall not commit another federal, state or local offense (*see* 18 U.S.C. § 3563(a)).

(2) For a felony, the defendant shall (A) make restitution, (B) work in community service, or (C) both, unless the court has imposed a fine, or unless the court finds on the record that extraordinary circumstances exist that would make such a condition plainly unreasonable, in which event the court shall impose one or more of the discretionary conditions set forth under 18 U.S.C. § 3563(b) (*see* 18 U.S.C. § 3563(a)(2)).

(3) For any offense, the defendant shall not unlawfully possess a controlled substance (*see* 18 U.S.C. § 3563(a)).

(4) For a domestic violence crime as defined in 18 U.S.C. § 3561(b) by a defendant convicted of such an offense for the first time, the defendant shall attend a public, private, or non-profit offender rehabilitation program that has been approved by the

court, in consultation with a State Coalition Against Domestic Violence or other appropriate experts, if an approved program is available within a 50-mile radius of the legal residence of the defendant (*see* 18 U.S.C. § 3563(a)).

(5) For any offense, the defendant shall refrain from any unlawful use of a controlled substance and submit to one drug test within 15 days of release on probation and at least two periodic drug tests thereafter (as determined by the court) for use of a controlled substance, but the condition stated in this paragraph may be ameliorated or suspended by the court for any individual defendant if the defendant's presentence report or other reliable information indicates a low risk of future substance abuse by the defendant (*see* 18 U.S.C. § 3563(a)).

(6) The defendant shall (A) make restitution in accordance with 18 U.S.C. §§ 2248, 2259, 2264, 2327, 3663, 3663A, and 3664; and (B) pay the assessment imposed in accordance with 18 U.S.C. § 3013. If there is a court-established payment schedule for making restitution or paying the assessment (*see* 18 U.S.C. § 3572(d)), the defendant shall adhere to the schedule.

(7) The defendant shall notify the court of any material change in the defendant's economic circumstances that might affect the defendant's ability to pay restitution, fines, or special assessments (*see* 18 U.S.C. § 3563(a)).

(8) If the court has imposed a fine, the defendant shall pay the fine or adhere to a court-established payment schedule (*see* 18 U.S.C. § 3563(a)).

(9) If the defendant is required to register under the Sex Offender Registration and Notification Act, the defendant shall comply with the requirements of that Act (*see* 18 U.S.C. § 3563(a)).

(10) The defendant shall submit to the collection of a DNA sample from the defendant at the direction of the United States Probation Office if the collection of such a sample is authorized pursuant to section 3 of the DNA Analysis Backlog Elimination Act of 2000 (42 U.S.C. § 14135a).

(b) DISCRETIONARY CONDITIONS

The court may impose other conditions of probation to the extent that such conditions (1) are reasonably related to (A) the nature and circumstances of the offense and the history and characteristics of the defendant; (B) the need for the sentence imposed to reflect the seriousness of the offense, to promote respect for the law, and to provide just punishment for the offense; (C) the need for the sentence imposed to afford adequate deterrence to criminal conduct;

(D) the need to protect the public from further crimes of the defendant;

and (E) the need to provide the defendant with needed educational or vocational training, medical care, or other correctional treatment in the most effective manner; and (2) involve only such deprivations of liberty or property as are reasonably necessary for the purposes of sentencing indicated in 18 U.S.C. § 3553(a) (*see* 18 U.S.C. § 3563(b)).

(c) "STANDARD" CONDITIONS (POLICY STATEMENT)

The following "standard" conditions are recommended for probation. Several of the conditions are expansions of the conditions required by statute:

(1) The defendant shall report to the probation office in the federal judicial district where he or she is authorized to reside within 72 hours of the time the defendant was sentenced, unless the probation officer instructs the defendant to report to a different probation office or within a different time frame.

(2) After initially reporting to the probation office, the defendant will receive instructions from the court or the probation officer about how and when to report to the probation officer, and the defendant shall report to the probation officer as instructed.

(3) The defendant shall not knowingly leave the federal judicial district where he or she is authorized to reside without first getting permission from the court or the probation officer.

(4) The defendant shall answer truthfully the questions asked by the probation officer.

(5) The defendant shall live at a place approved by the probation officer. If the defendant plans to change where he or she lives or anything about his or her living arrangements (such as the people the defendant lives with), the defendant shall notify the probation officer at least 10 days before the change. If notifying the probation officer at least 10 days in advance is not possible due to unanticipated circumstances, the defendant shall notify the probation officer within 72 hours of becoming aware of a change or expected change.

(6) The defendant shall allow the probation officer to visit the defendant at any time at his or her home or elsewhere, and the defendant shall permit the probation officer to take any items prohibited by the conditions of the defendant's supervision that he or she observes in plain view.

(7) The defendant shall work full time (at least 30 hours per week) at a lawful type of employment, unless the probation officer excuses the defendant from doing so. If the defendant does not have full-time employment he or she shall try to find full-time employment, unless the probation officer excuses the defendant from doing so. If the defendant plans to change where the defendant works or anything about his or her work (such as the position or the job responsibilities), the defendant shall notify

the probation officer at least 10 days before the change. If notifying the probation officer at least 10 days in advance is not possible due to unanticipated circumstances, the defendant shall notify the probation officer within 72 hours of becoming aware of a change or expected change.

(8) The defendant shall not communicate or interact with someone the defendant knows is engaged in criminal activity. If the defendant knows someone has been convicted of a felony, the defendant shall not knowingly communicate or interact with that person without first getting the permission of the probation officer.

(9) If the defendant is arrested or questioned by a law enforcement officer, the defendant shall notify the probation officer within 72 hours.

(10) The defendant shall not own, possess, or have access to a firearm, ammunition, destructive device, or dangerous weapon (*i.e.*, anything that was designed, or was modified for, the specific purpose of causing bodily injury or death to another person, such as nunchakus or tasers).

(11) The defendant shall not act or make any agreement with a law enforcement agency to act as a confidential human source or informant without first getting the permission of the court.

(12) If the probation officer determines that the defendant poses a risk to another person (including an organization), the probation officer may require the defendant to notify the person about the risk and the defendant shall comply with that instruction. The probation officer may contact the person and confirm that the defendant has notified the person about the risk.

(13) The defendant shall follow the instructions of the probation officer related to the conditions of supervision.

(d) "SPECIAL" CONDITIONS (POLICY STATEMENT)

The following "special" conditions of probation are recommended in the circumstances described and, in addition, may otherwise be appropriate in particular cases:

(1) SUPPORT OF DEPENDENTS

(A) If the defendant has one or more dependents — a condition specifying that the defendant shall support his or her dependents.

(B) If the defendant is ordered by the government to make child support payments or to make payments to support a person caring for a child — a condition specifying that the defendant shall make the payments and comply with the other terms of the order.

(2) DEBT OBLIGATIONS

If an installment schedule of payment of restitution or a fine is imposed — a condition prohibiting the defendant from incurring

new credit charges or opening additional lines of credit
without approval of the probation officer unless the defendant
is in compliance with the payment schedule.

(3) ACCESS TO FINANCIAL INFORMATION

If the court imposes an order of restitution, forfeiture, or notice to victims, or orders the defendant to pay a fine — a condition requiring the defendant to provide the probation officer access to any requested financial information.

(4) SUBSTANCE ABUSE

If the court has reason to believe that the defendant is an abuser of narcotics, other controlled substances or alcohol —

(A) a condition requiring the defendant to participate in a program approved by the United States Probation Office for substance abuse, which program may include testing to determine whether the defendant has reverted to the use of drugs or alcohol; and (B) a condition specifying that the defendant shall not use or possess alcohol.

(5) MENTAL HEALTH PROGRAM PARTICIPATION

If the court has reason to believe that the defendant is in need of psychological or psychiatric treatment — a condition requiring that the defendant participate in a mental health program approved by the United States Probation Office.

(6) DEPORTATION

If (A) the defendant and the United States entered into a stipulation of deportation pursuant to section 238(c)(5) of the Immigration and Nationality Act (8 U.S.C. § 1228(c)(5)*); or (B) in the absence of a stipulation of deportation, if, after notice and hearing pursuant to such section, the Attorney General demonstrates by clear and convincing evidence that the alien is deportable — a condition ordering deportation by a United States district court or a United States magistrate judge.

*So in original. Probably should be 8 U.S.C. § 1228(d)(5).

(7) SEX OFFENSES

If the instant offense of conviction is a sex offense, as defined in Application Note 1 of the Commentary to §5D1.2 (Term of Supervised Release)—

(A) A condition requiring the defendant to participate in a program approved by the United States Probation Office for the treatment and monitoring of sex offenders.

(B) A condition limiting the use of a computer or an interactive computer service in cases in which the defendant used such items.

(C) A condition requiring the defendant to submit to a search, at any time, with or without a warrant, and by any law enforcement or probation officer, of the defendant's person and any property, house, residence, vehicle, papers, computer,

other electronic communication or data storage devices
or media, and effects, upon reasonable suspicion concerning
a violation of a condition of probation or unlawful
conduct by the defendant, or by any probation officer in
the lawful discharge of the officer's supervision functions.

(e) ADDITIONAL CONDITIONS (POLICY STATEMENT)

The following "special conditions" may be appropriate on a case-bycase
basis:

(1) COMMUNITY CONFINEMENT

Residence in a community treatment center, halfway house or
similar facility may be imposed as a condition of probation.
See §5F1.1 (Community Confinement).

(2) HOME DETENTION

Home detention may be imposed as a condition of probation but
only as a substitute for imprisonment. *See* §5F1.2 (Home Detention).

(3) COMMUNITY SERVICE

Community service may be imposed as a condition of probation.
See §5F1.3 (Community Service).

(4) OCCUPATIONAL RESTRICTIONS

Occupational restrictions may be imposed as a condition of probation.
See §5F1.5 (Occupational Restrictions).

(5) CURFEW

A condition imposing a curfew may be imposed if the court concludes
that restricting the defendant to his place of residence
during evening and nighttime hours is necessary to provide
just punishment for the offense, to protect the public from
crimes that the defendant might commit during those hours, or
to assist in the rehabilitation of the defendant. Electronic monitoring
may be used as a means of surveillance to ensure compliance
with a curfew order.

(6) INTERMITTENT CONFINEMENT

Intermittent confinement (custody for intervals of time) may
be ordered as a condition of probation during the first year of
probation. *See* §5F1.8 (Intermittent Confinement).

Commentary

Application Note:

1. **Application of Subsection (c)(4).**—Although the condition in subsection (c)(4) requires
the defendant to "answer truthfully" the questions asked by the probation officer, a defendant's
legitimate invocation of the Fifth Amendment privilege against self-incrimination
in response to a probation officer's question shall not be considered a violation of this
condition.

Historical
Note

Effective November 1, 1987. Amended effective November 1, 1989 (amendments 273, 274, and 302); November
1, 1997 (amendment 569); November 1, 1998 (amendment 584); November 1, 2000 (amendment 605);
November 1, 2001 (amendment 615); November 1, 2002 (amendment 644); November 1, 2004 (amendment
664); November 1, 2007 (amendments 701 and 711); November 1, 2009 (amendment 733); November 1,

2016 (amendment 803).

§5B1.4. [Deleted]

Historical
Note

Effective November 1, 1987. Amended effective November 1, 1989 (amendments 271, 272, and 302), was deleted by consolidation with §§5B1.3 and 5D1.3 effective November 1, 1997 (amendment 569).

PART C — IMPRISONMENT

§5C1.1. Imposition of a Term of Imprisonment

(a) A sentence conforms with the guidelines for imprisonment if it is within the minimum and maximum terms of the applicable guideline range.

(b) If the applicable guideline range is in Zone A of the Sentencing Table, a sentence of imprisonment is not required, unless the applicable guideline in Chapter Two expressly requires such a term.

(c) If the applicable guideline range is in Zone B of the Sentencing Table, the minimum term may be satisfied by—

(1) a sentence of imprisonment; or

(2) a sentence of imprisonment that includes a term of supervised release with a condition that substitutes community confinement or home detention according to the schedule in subsection (e), provided that at least one month is satisfied by imprisonment; or

(3) a sentence of probation that includes a condition or combination of conditions that substitute intermittent confinement, community confinement, or home detention for imprisonment according to the schedule in subsection (e).

(d) If the applicable guideline range is in Zone C of the Sentencing Table, the minimum term may be satisfied by—

(1) a sentence of imprisonment; or

(2) a sentence of imprisonment that includes a term of supervised release with a condition that substitutes community confinement or home detention according to the schedule in subsection (e), provided that at least one-half of the minimum term is satisfied by imprisonment.

(e) Schedule of Substitute Punishments:

(1) One day of intermittent confinement in prison or jail for one day of imprisonment (each 24 hours of confinement is credited as one day of intermittent confinement, provided, however, that one day shall be credited for any calendar day during

which the defendant is employed in the community and confined during all remaining hours);

(2) One day of community confinement (residence in a community treatment center, halfway house, or similar residential facility) for one day of imprisonment;

(3) One day of home detention for one day of imprisonment.

(f) If the applicable guideline range is in Zone D of the Sentencing Table, the minimum term shall be satisfied by a sentence of imprisonment.

Commentary

Application Notes:

1. Subsection (a) provides that a sentence conforms with the guidelines for imprisonment if it is within the minimum and maximum terms of the applicable guideline range specified in the Sentencing Table in Part A of this Chapter. For example, if the defendant has an Offense Level of 20 and a Criminal History Category of I, the applicable guideline range is 33–41 months of imprisonment. Therefore, a sentence of imprisonment of at least thirty-three months, but not more than forty-one months, is within the applicable guideline range.

2. Subsection (b) provides that where the applicable guideline range is in Zone A of the Sentencing Table (*i.e.*, the minimum term of imprisonment specified in the applicable guideline range is zero months), the court is not required to impose a sentence of imprisonment unless a sentence of imprisonment or its equivalent is specifically required by the guideline applicable to the offense. Where imprisonment is not required, the court, for example, may impose a sentence of probation. In some cases, a fine appropriately may be imposed as the sole sanction.

3. Subsection (c) provides that where the applicable guideline range is in Zone B of the Sentencing Table (*i.e.*, the minimum term of imprisonment specified in the applicable guideline range is at least one but not more than nine months), the court has three options:

(A) It may impose a sentence of imprisonment.

(B) It may impose a sentence of probation provided that it includes a condition of probation requiring a period of intermittent confinement, community confinement, or home detention, or combination of intermittent confinement, community confinement, and home detention, sufficient to satisfy the minimum period of imprisonment specified in the guideline range. For example, where the guideline range is 4–10 months, a sentence of probation with a condition requiring at least four months of intermittent confinement, community confinement, or home detention would satisfy the minimum term of imprisonment specified in the guideline range.

(C) Or, it may impose a sentence of imprisonment that includes a term of supervised release with a condition that requires community confinement or home detention. In such case, at least one month must be satisfied by actual imprisonment and the remainder of the minimum term specified in the guideline range must be satisfied

by community confinement or home detention. For example, where the guideline range is 4–10 months, a sentence of imprisonment of one month followed by a term of supervised release with a condition requiring three months of community confinement or home detention would satisfy the minimum term of imprisonment specified in the guideline range.

The preceding examples illustrate sentences that satisfy the minimum term of imprisonment required by the guideline range. The court, of course, may impose a sentence at a higher point within the applicable guideline range. For example, where the guideline range is 4–10 months, both a sentence of probation with a condition requiring six months of community confinement or home detention (under subsection (c)(3)) and a sentence of two months imprisonment followed by a term of supervised release with a condition requiring four months of community confinement or home detention (under subsection (c)(2)) would be within the guideline range.

4. Subsection (d) provides that where the applicable guideline range is in Zone C of the Sentencing Table (*i.e.*, the minimum term specified in the applicable guideline range is ten or twelve months), the court has two options:

(A) It may impose a sentence of imprisonment.

(B) Or, it may impose a sentence of imprisonment that includes a term of supervised release with a condition requiring community confinement or home detention. In such case, at least one-half of the minimum term specified in the guideline range must be satisfied by imprisonment, and the remainder of the minimum term specified in the guideline range must be satisfied by community confinement or home detention. For example, where the guideline range is 10–16 months, a sentence of five months imprisonment followed by a term of supervised release with a condition requiring five months community confinement or home detention would satisfy the minimum term of imprisonment required by the guideline range.

The preceding example illustrates a sentence that satisfies the minimum term of imprisonment required by the guideline range. The court, of course, may impose a sentence at a higher point within the guideline range. For example, where the guideline range is 10–16 months, both a sentence of five months imprisonment followed by a term of supervised release with a condition requiring six months of community confinement or home detention (under subsection (d)), and a sentence of ten months imprisonment followed by a term of supervised release with a condition requiring four months of community confinement or home detention (also under subsection (d)) would be within the guideline range.

5. Subsection (e) sets forth a schedule of imprisonment substitutes.

6. There may be cases in which a departure from the sentencing options authorized for Zone C of the Sentencing Table (under which at least half the minimum term must be satisfied by imprisonment) to the sentencing options authorized for Zone B of the Sentencing Table (under which all or most of the minimum term may be satisfied by intermittent confinement, community confinement, or home detention instead of imprisonment) is appropriate to accomplish a specific treatment purpose. Such a departure should be considered only in cases where the court finds that (A) the defendant is an abuser of narcotics, other controlled substances, or alcohol, or suffers from a significant mental illness, and (B) the defendant's criminality is related to the treatment problem to be addressed.

In determining whether such a departure is appropriate, the court should consider, among other things, (1) the likelihood that completion of the treatment program will successfully address the treatment problem, thereby reducing the risk to the public from further crimes of the defendant, and (2) whether imposition of less imprisonment than required by Zone C will increase the risk to the public from further crimes of the defendant.

Examples: The following examples both assume the applicable guideline range is 12–18 months and the court departs in accordance with this application note. Under Zone C rules, the defendant must be sentenced to at least six months imprisonment. (1) The defendant is a nonviolent drug offender in Criminal History Category I and probation is not prohibited by statute. The court departs downward to impose a sentence of probation, with twelve months of intermittent confinement, community confinement, or home detention and participation in a substance abuse treatment program as conditions of probation.

(2) The defendant is convicted of a Class A or B felony, so probation is prohibited by statute (*see* §5B1.1(b)). The court departs downward to impose a sentence of one month imprisonment, with eleven months in community confinement or home detention and participation in a substance abuse treatment program as conditions of supervised release.

7. The use of substitutes for imprisonment as provided in subsections (c) and (d) is not recommended for most defendants with a criminal history category of III or above.

8. In a case in which community confinement in a residential treatment program is imposed to accomplish a specific treatment purpose, the court should consider the effectiveness of the residential treatment program.

9. Subsection (f) provides that, where the applicable guideline range is in Zone D of the Sentencing Table (*i.e.*, the minimum term of imprisonment specified in the applicable guideline range is 15 months or more), the minimum term must be satisfied by a sentence of imprisonment without the use of any of the imprisonment substitutes in subsection (e).

Historical Note

Effective November 1, 1987. Amended effective January 15, 1988 (amendment 51); November 1, 1989 (amendments 271, 275, and 302); November 1, 1992 (amendment 462); November 1, 2002 (amendment 646); November 1, 2009 (amendment 733); November 1, 2010 (amendment 738).

§5C1.2. Limitation on Applicability of Statutory Minimum Sentences in Certain Cases

(a) Except as provided in subsection (b), in the case of an offense under 21 U.S.C. § 841, § 844, § 846, § 960, or § 963, the court shall impose a sentence in accordance with the applicable guidelines without regard to any statutory minimum sentence, if the court finds that the defendant meets the criteria in 18 U.S.C. § 3553(f)(1)–(5) set forth below:

(1) the defendant does not have more than 1 criminal history point, as determined under the sentencing guidelines before

application of subsection (b) of §4A1.3 (Departures Based on Inadequacy of Criminal History Category);

(2) the defendant did not use violence or credible threats of violence or possess a firearm or other dangerous weapon (or induce another participant to do so) in connection with the offense;

(3) the offense did not result in death or serious bodily injury to any person;

(4) the defendant was not an organizer, leader, manager, or supervisor of others in the offense, as determined under the sentencing guidelines and was not engaged in a continuing criminal enterprise, as defined in 21 U.S.C. § 848; and

(5) not later than the time of the sentencing hearing, the defendant has truthfully provided to the Government all information and evidence the defendant has concerning the offense or offenses that were part of the same course of conduct or of a common scheme or plan, but the fact that the defendant has no relevant or useful other information to provide or that the Government is already aware of the information shall not preclude a determination by the court that the defendant has complied with this requirement.

(b) In the case of a defendant (1) who meets the criteria set forth in subsection (a); and (2) for whom the statutorily required minimum sentence is at least five years, the offense level applicable from Chapters Two (Offense Conduct) and Three (Adjustments) shall be not less than level **17**.

Commentary

Application Notes:

1. "***More than 1 criminal history point, as determined under the sentencing guidelines***," as used in subsection (a)(1), means more than one criminal history point as determined under §4A1.1 (Criminal History Category) before application of subsection (b) of §4A1.3 (Departures Based on Inadequacy of Criminal History Category).

2. "***Dangerous weapon***" and "***firearm***," as used in subsection (a)(2), and "***serious bodily injury***," as used in subsection (a)(3), are defined in the Commentary to §1B1.1 (Application Instructions).

3. "***Offense***," as used in subsection (a)(2)–(4), and "***offense or offenses that were part of the same course of conduct or of a common scheme or plan***," as used in subsection

(a)(5), mean the offense of conviction and all relevant conduct.

4. Consistent with §1B1.3 (Relevant Conduct), the term "***defendant***," as used in subsection (a)(2), limits the accountability of the defendant to his own conduct and conduct that he aided or abetted, counseled, commanded, induced, procured, or willfully caused.

5. "***Organizer, leader, manager, or supervisor of others in the offense, as determined under the sentencing guidelines***," as used in subsection (a)(4), means a defendant who receives an adjustment for an aggravating role under §3B1.1 (Aggravating Role).

6. "***Engaged in a continuing criminal enterprise***," as used in subsection (a)(4), is defined in 21 U.S.C. § 848(c). As a practical matter, it should not be necessary to apply this prong of subsection (a)(4) because (i) this section does not apply to a conviction under 21 U.S.C. § 848, and (ii) any defendant who "engaged in a continuing criminal enterprise" but is convicted of an offense to which this section applies will be an "organizer, leader, manager, or supervisor of others in the offense."

7. Information disclosed by the defendant with respect to subsection (a)(5) may be considered in determining the applicable guideline range, except where the use of such information is restricted under the provisions of §1B1.8 (Use of Certain Information). That is, subsection (a)(5) does not provide an independent basis for restricting the use of information disclosed by the defendant.

8. Under 18 U.S.C. § 3553(f), prior to its determination, the court shall afford the government an opportunity to make a recommendation. *See also* Fed. R. Crim. P. 32(f), (i).

9. A defendant who meets the criteria under this section is exempt from any otherwise applicable statutory minimum sentence of imprisonment and statutory minimum term of supervised release.

Background: This section sets forth the relevant provisions of 18 U.S.C. § 3553(f), as added by section 80001(a) of the Violent Crime Control and Law Enforcement Act of 1994, which limit the applicability of statutory minimum sentences in certain cases. Under the authority of section 80001(b) of that Act, the Commission has promulgated application notes to provide guidance in the application of 18 U.S.C. § 3553(f). *See also* H. Rep. No. 460, 103d Cong., 2d Sess. 3 (1994) (expressing intent to foster greater coordination between mandatory minimum sentencing and the sentencing guideline system).

Historical Note

Effective September 23, 1994 (amendment 509). Amended effective November 1, 1995 (amendment 515); November 1, 1996 (amendment 540); November 1, 1997 (amendment 570); November 1, 2001 (amendment 624); October 27, 2003 (amendment 651); November 1, 2004 (amendment 674); November 1, 2009 (amendment 736).

PART D — SUPERVISED RELEASE

§5D1.1. Imposition of a Term of Supervised Release

(a) The court shall order a term of supervised release to follow imprisonment—

(1) when required by statute (*see* 18 U.S.C. § 3583(a)); or

(2) except as provided in subsection (c), when a sentence of imprisonment of more than one year is imposed.

(b) The court may order a term of supervised release to follow imprisonment in any other case. *See* 18 U.S.C. § 3583(a).

(c) The court ordinarily should not impose a term of supervised release in a case in which supervised release is not required by statute and the defendant is a deportable alien who likely will be deported after imprisonment.

Commentary

Application Notes:

1. **Application of Subsection (a).**—Under subsection (a), the court is required to impose a term of supervised release to follow imprisonment when supervised release is required by statute or, except as provided in subsection (c), when a sentence of imprisonment of more than one year is imposed. The court may depart from this guideline and not impose a term of supervised release if supervised release is not required by statute and the court determines, after considering the factors set forth in Note 3, that supervised release is not necessary.

2. **Application of Subsection (b).**—Under subsection (b), the court may impose a term of supervised release to follow a term of imprisonment in any other case, after considering the factors set forth in Note 3.

3. **Factors to Be Considered.**—

(A) **Statutory Factors.**—In determining whether to impose a term of supervised release, the court is required by statute to consider, among other factors:

(i) the nature and circumstances of the offense and the history and characteristics of the defendant;

(ii) the need to afford adequate deterrence to criminal conduct, to protect the public from further crimes of the defendant, and to provide the defendant with needed educational or vocational training, medical care, or other correctional treatment in the most effective manner;

(iii) the need to avoid unwarranted sentence disparities among defendants with similar records who have been found guilty of similar conduct; and

(iv) the need to provide restitution to any victims of the offense.

See 18 U.S.C. § 3583(c).

(B) **Criminal History.**—The court should give particular consideration to the defendant's criminal history (which is one aspect of the "history and characteristics of the defendant" in subparagraph (A)(i), above). In general, the more serious the defendant's criminal history, the greater the need for supervised release.

(C) **Substance Abuse.**—In a case in which a defendant sentenced to imprisonment is an abuser of controlled substances or alcohol, it is highly recommended that a term of supervised release also be imposed. *See* §5H1.4 (Physical Condition, Including Drug or Alcohol Dependence or Abuse; Gambling Addiction).

(D) **Domestic Violence.**—If the defendant is convicted for the first time of a domestic violence crime as defined in 18 U.S.C. § 3561(b), a term of supervised release is required by statute. *See* 18 U.S.C. § 3583(a). Such a defendant is also required by statute to attend an approved rehabilitation program, if available within a 50-mile radius of the legal residence of the defendant. *See* 18 U.S.C. § 3583(d); §5D1.3(a)(3). In any other case involving domestic violence or stalking in which the defendant is sentenced to imprisonment, it is highly recommended that a term of supervised release also be imposed.

4. **Community Confinement or Home Detention Following Imprisonment.**—A term of supervised release must be imposed if the court wishes to impose a "split sentence" under which the defendant serves a term of imprisonment followed by a period of community confinement or home detention pursuant to subsection (c)(2) or (d)(2) of §5C1.1 (Imposition of a Term of Imprisonment). In such a case, the period of community confinement or home detention is imposed as a condition of supervised release.

5. **Application of Subsection (c).**—In a case in which the defendant is a deportable alien specified in subsection (c) and supervised release is not required by statute, the court ordinarily should not impose a term of supervised release. Unless such a defendant legally returns to the United States, supervised release is unnecessary. If such a defendant illegally returns to the United States, the need to afford adequate deterrence and protect the public ordinarily is adequately served by a new prosecution. The court should, however, consider imposing a term of supervised release on such a defendant if the court

determines it would provide an added measure of deterrence and protection based on the facts and circumstances of a particular case.

Historical Note

Effective November 1, 1987. Amended effective November 1, 1989 (amendment 302); November 1, 1995 (amendment 529); November 1, 2010 (amendment 747); November 1, 2011 (amendment 756); November 1, 2014 (amendment 781).

§5D1.2. Term of Supervised Release

(a) Except as provided in subsections (b) and (c), if a term of supervised release is ordered, the length of the term shall be:

(1) At least two years but not more than five years for a defendant convicted of a Class A or B felony. *See* 18 U.S.C. § 3583(b)(1).

(2) At least one year but not more than three years for a defendant convicted of a Class C or D felony. *See* 18 U.S.C. § 3583(b)(2).

(3) One year for a defendant convicted of a Class E felony or a Class A misdemeanor. *See* 18 U.S.C. § 3583(b)(3).

(b) Notwithstanding subdivisions (a)(1) through (3), the length of the term of supervised release shall be not less than the minimum term of years specified for the offense under subdivisions (a)(1) through (3) and may be up to life, if the offense is—

(1) any offense listed in 18 U.S.C. § 2332b(g)(5)(B), the commission of which resulted in, or created a foreseeable risk of, death or serious bodily injury to another person; or

(2) a sex offense.

(Policy Statement) If the instant offense of conviction is a sex offense, however, the statutory maximum term of supervised release is recommended.

(c) The term of supervised release imposed shall be not less than any statutorily required term of supervised release.

Commentary

Application Notes:

1. **Definitions.**—For purposes of this guideline:

"***Sex offense***" means (A) an offense, perpetrated against a minor, under (i) chapter 109A of title 18, United States Code; (ii) chapter 110 of such title, not including a recordkeeping offense; (iii) chapter 117 of such title, not including transmitting information about a minor or filing a factual statement about an alien individual; (iv) an offense under 18 U.S.C. § 1201; or (v) an offense under 18 U.S.C. § 1591; or (B) an attempt or a conspiracy to commit any offense described in subdivisions (A)(i) through (v) of this note. Such term does not include an offense under 18 U.S.C. § 2250 (Failure to register).

"***Minor***" means (A) an individual who had not attained the age of 18 years; (B) an individual, whether fictitious or not, who a law enforcement officer represented to a participant (i) had not attained the age of 18 years; and (ii) could be provided for the purposes of engaging in sexually explicit conduct; or (C) an undercover law enforcement officer who represented to a participant that the officer had not attained the age of 18 years.

2. **Safety Valve Cases.**—A defendant who qualifies under §5C1.2 (Limitation on Applicability of Statutory Minimum Sentence in Certain Cases) is not subject to any statutory minimum sentence of supervised release. *See* 18 U.S.C. § 3553(f). In such a case, the term of supervised release shall be determined under subsection (a).

3. **Substantial Assistance Cases.**—Upon motion of the Government, a defendant who has provided substantial assistance in the investigation or prosecution of another person who has committed an offense may be sentenced to a term of supervised release that is less

than any minimum required by statute or the guidelines. *See* 18 U.S.C. § 3553(e), §5K1.1 (Substantial Assistance to Authorities).

4. **Factors Considered.**—The factors to be considered in determining the length of a term of supervised release are the same as the factors considered in determining whether to impose such a term. *See* 18 U.S.C. § 3583(c); Application Note 3 to §5D1.1 (Imposition of a Term of Supervised Release). The court should ensure that the term imposed on the defendant is long enough to address the purposes of imposing supervised release on the defendant.

5. **Early Termination and Extension.**—The court has authority to terminate or extend a term of supervised release. *See* 18 U.S.C. § 3583(e)(1), (2). The court is encouraged to exercise this authority in appropriate cases. The prospect of exercising this authority is a factor the court may wish to consider in determining the length of a term of supervised release. For example, the court may wish to consider early termination of supervised release if the defendant is an abuser of narcotics, other controlled substances, or alcohol who, while on supervised release, successfully completes a treatment program, thereby reducing the risk to the public from further crimes of the defendant.

6. **Application of Subsection (c).**—Subsection (c) specifies how a statutorily required minimum term of supervised release may affect the minimum term of supervised release provided by the guidelines.

For example, if subsection (a) provides a range of two years to five years, but the relevant statute requires a minimum term of supervised release of three years and a maximum term of life, the term of supervised release provided by the guidelines is restricted by subsection (c) to three years to five years. Similarly, if subsection (a) provides a range of two years to five years, but the relevant statute requires a minimum term of supervised release of five years and a maximum term of life, the term of supervised release provided by the guidelines is five years.

The following example illustrates the interaction of subsections (a) and (c) when subsection (b) is also involved. In this example, subsection (a) provides a range of two years to five years; the relevant statute requires a minimum term of supervised release of five years and a maximum term of life; and the offense is a sex offense under subsection (b). The effect of subsection (b) is to raise the maximum term of supervised release from five years (as provided by subsection (a)) to life, yielding a range of two years to life. The term of supervised release provided by the guidelines is then restricted by subsection (c) to five years to life. In this example, a term of supervised release of more than five years would be a guideline sentence. In addition, subsection (b) contains a policy statement recommending that the maximum — a life term of supervised release — be imposed.

Background: This section specifies the length of a term of supervised release that is to be imposed. Subsection (c) applies to statutes, such as the Anti-Drug Abuse Act of 1986, that require imposition of a specific minimum term of supervised release.

Historical
Note
Effective November 1, 1987. Amended effective January 15, 1988 (amendment 52); November 1, 1989 (amendment 302); November 1, 1995 (amendment 529); November 1, 1997 (amendment 570); November 1, 2001 (amendment 615); November 1, 2002 (amendments 637 and 646); November 1, 2004 (amendment 664); November 1, 2005 (amendment 679); November 1, 2007 (amendment 701); November 1, 2009 (amendment 736); November 1, 2011 (amendment 756); November 1, 2014 (amendment 786).

§5D1.3. Conditions of Supervised Release

(a) MANDATORY CONDITIONS

(1) The defendant shall not commit another federal, state or local offense (*see* 18 U.S.C. § 3583(d)).

(2) The defendant shall not unlawfully possess a controlled substance (*see* 18 U.S.C. § 3583(d)).

(3) The defendant who is convicted for a domestic violence crime as defined in 18 U.S.C. § 3561(b) for the first time shall attend

a public, private, or private non-profit offender rehabilitation program that has been approved by the court, in consultation with a State Coalition Against Domestic Violence or other appropriate experts, if an approved program is available within a 50-mile radius of the legal residence of the defendant (*see* 18 U.S.C. § 3583(d)).

(4) The defendant shall refrain from any unlawful use of a controlled substance and submit to one drug test within 15 days of release on probation and at least two periodic drug tests thereafter (as determined by the court) for use of a controlled substance, but the condition stated in this paragraph may be ameliorated or suspended by the court for any individual defendant if the defendant's presentence report or other reliable information indicates a low risk of future substance abuse by the defendant (*see* 18 U.S.C. § 3583(d)).

(5) If a fine is imposed and has not been paid upon release to supervised release, the defendant shall adhere to an installment schedule to pay that fine (*see* 18 U.S.C. § 3624(e)).

(6) The defendant shall (A) make restitution in accordance with 18 U.S.C. §§ 2248, 2259, 2264, 2327, 3663, 3663A, and 3664; and (B) pay the assessment imposed in accordance with 18 U.S.C. § 3013. If there is a court-established payment schedule for making restitution or paying the assessment (*see* 18 U.S.C. § 3572(d)), the defendant shall adhere to the schedule.

(7) If the defendant is required to register under the Sex Offender Registration and Notification Act, the defendant shall comply with the requirements of that Act (*see* 18 U.S.C. § 3583(d)).

(8) The defendant shall submit to the collection of a DNA sample from the defendant at the direction of the United States Probation Office if the collection of such a sample is authorized pursuant to section 3 of the DNA Analysis Backlog Elimination Act of 2000 (42 U.S.C. § 14135a).

(b) DISCRETIONARY CONDITIONS

The court may impose other conditions of supervised release to the extent that such conditions (1) are reasonably related to (A) the nature and circumstances of the offense and the history and characteristics of the defendant; (B) the need for the sentence imposed to afford adequate deterrence to criminal conduct; (C) the need to protect the public from further crimes of the defendant; and (D) the need to provide the defendant with needed educational or vocational training, medical care, or other correctional treatment in the most effective manner; and (2) involve no greater deprivation of liberty than is reasonably necessary for the purposes set forth above and are consistent with any pertinent policy statements issued by the Sentencing Commission.

(c) "STANDARD" CONDITIONS (POLICY STATEMENT)

The following "standard" conditions are recommended for supervised release. Several of the conditions are expansions of the conditions required by statute:

(1) The defendant shall report to the probation office in the federal judicial district where he or she is authorized to reside within 72 hours of release from imprisonment, unless the probation officer instructs the defendant to report to a different probation office or within a different time frame.

(2) After initially reporting to the probation office, the defendant will receive instructions from the court or the probation officer about how and when to report to the probation officer, and the defendant shall report to the probation officer as instructed.

(3) The defendant shall not knowingly leave the federal judicial district where he or she is authorized to reside without first getting permission from the court or the probation officer.

(4) The defendant shall answer truthfully the questions asked by the probation officer.

(5) The defendant shall live at a place approved by the probation officer. If the defendant plans to change where he or she lives

or anything about his or her living arrangements (such as the people the defendant lives with), the defendant shall notify the probation officer at least 10 days before the change. If notifying the probation officer at least 10 days in advance is not possible due to unanticipated circumstances, the defendant shall notify the probation officer within 72 hours of becoming aware of a change or expected change.

(6) The defendant shall allow the probation officer to visit the defendant at any time at his or her home or elsewhere, and the defendant shall permit the probation officer to take any items prohibited by the conditions of the defendant's supervision that he or she observes in plain view.

(7) The defendant shall work full time (at least 30 hours per week) at a lawful type of employment, unless the probation officer excuses the defendant from doing so. If the defendant does not have full-time employment he or she shall try to find full-time employment, unless the probation officer excuses the defendant from doing so. If the defendant plans to change where the defendant works or anything about his or her work (such as the position or the job responsibilities), the defendant shall notify the probation officer at least 10 days before the change. If notifying the probation officer in advance is not possible due to unanticipated circumstances, the defendant shall notify the probation officer within 72 hours of becoming aware of a change or expected change.

(8) The defendant shall not communicate or interact with someone

the defendant knows is engaged in criminal activity. If the defendant knows someone has been convicted of a felony, the defendant shall not knowingly communicate or interact with that person without first getting the permission of the probation officer.

(9) If the defendant is arrested or questioned by a law enforcement officer, the defendant shall notify the probation officer within 72 hours.

(10) The defendant shall not own, possess, or have access to a firearm, ammunition, destructive device, or dangerous weapon (*i.e.*, anything that was designed, or was modified for, the specific purpose of causing bodily injury or death to another person, such as nunchakus or tasers).

(11) The defendant shall not act or make any agreement with a law enforcement agency to act as a confidential human source or informant without first getting the permission of the court.

(12) If the probation officer determines that the defendant poses a risk to another person (including an organization), the probation officer may require the defendant to notify the person about the risk and the defendant shall comply with that instruction. The probation officer may contact the person and confirm that the defendant has notified the person about the risk.

(13) The defendant shall follow the instructions of the probation officer related to the conditions of supervision.

(d) "SPECIAL" CONDITIONS (POLICY STATEMENT)

The following "special" conditions of supervised release are recommended in the circumstances described and, in addition, may otherwise be appropriate in particular cases:

(1) SUPPORT OF DEPENDENTS

(A) If the defendant has one or more dependents — a condition specifying that the defendant shall support his or her dependents.

(B) If the defendant is ordered by the government to make child support payments or to make payments to support a person caring for a child — a condition specifying that the defendant shall make the payments and comply with the other terms of the order.

(2) DEBT OBLIGATIONS

If an installment schedule of payment of restitution or a fine is imposed — a condition prohibiting the defendant from incurring new credit charges or opening additional lines of credit without approval of the probation officer unless the defendant is in compliance with the payment schedule.

(3) ACCESS TO FINANCIAL INFORMATION

If the court imposes an order of restitution, forfeiture, or notice to victims, or orders the defendant to pay a fine — a condition requiring the defendant to provide the probation officer access to any requested financial information.

(4) SUBSTANCE ABUSE

If the court has reason to believe that the defendant is an abuser of narcotics, other controlled substances or alcohol — (A) a condition requiring the defendant to participate in a program approved by the United States Probation Office for substance abuse, which program may include testing to determine whether the defendant has reverted to the use of drugs or alcohol; and (B) a condition specifying that the defendant shall not use or possess alcohol.

(5) MENTAL HEALTH PROGRAM PARTICIPATION

If the court has reason to believe that the defendant is in need of psychological or psychiatric treatment — a condition requiring that the defendant participate in a mental health program approved by the United States Probation Office.

(6) DEPORTATION

If (A) the defendant and the United States entered into a stipulation of deportation pursuant to section 238(c)(5) of the Immigration and Nationality Act (8 U.S.C. § 1228(c)(5)*); or (B) in the absence of a stipulation of deportation, if, after notice and hearing pursuant to such section, the Attorney General demonstrates by clear and convincing evidence that the alien is deportable — a condition ordering deportation by a United States district court or a United States magistrate judge.

*So in original. Probably should be 8 U.S.C. § 1228(d)(5).

(7) SEX OFFENSES

If the instant offense of conviction is a sex offense, as defined in Application Note 1 of the Commentary to §5D1.2 (Term of Supervised Release) —

(A) A condition requiring the defendant to participate in a program approved by the United States Probation Office for the treatment and monitoring of sex offenders.

(B) A condition limiting the use of a computer or an interactive computer service in cases in which the defendant used such items.

(C) A condition requiring the defendant to submit to a search, at any time, with or without a warrant, and by any law enforcement or probation officer, of the defendant's person and any property, house, residence, vehicle, papers, computer, other electronic communication or data storage devices or media, and effects upon reasonable suspicion concerning a violation of a condition of supervised release or unlawful conduct by the defendant, or by any probation officer in the lawful discharge of the officer's supervision functions.

(8) UNPAID RESTITUTION, FINES, OR SPECIAL ASSESSMENTS

If the defendant has any unpaid amount of restitution, fines, or special assessments, the defendant shall notify the probation officer of any material change in the defendant's economic circumstances that might affect the defendant's ability to pay.

(e) ADDITIONAL CONDITIONS (POLICY STATEMENT)

The following "special conditions" may be appropriate on a case-bycase basis:

(1) COMMUNITY CONFINEMENT

Residence in a community treatment center, halfway house or similar facility may be imposed as a condition of supervised release. *See* §5F1.1 (Community Confinement).

(2) HOME DETENTION

Home detention may be imposed as a condition of supervised release, but only as a substitute for imprisonment. *See* §5F1.2 (Home Detention).

(3) COMMUNITY SERVICE

Community service may be imposed as a condition of supervised release. *See* §5F1.3 (Community Service).

(4) OCCUPATIONAL RESTRICTIONS

Occupational restrictions may be imposed as a condition of supervised release. *See* §5F1.5 (Occupational Restrictions).

(5) CURFEW

A condition imposing a curfew may be imposed if the court concludes that restricting the defendant to his place of residence during evening and nighttime hours is necessary to protect the public from crimes that the defendant might commit during those hours, or to assist in the rehabilitation of the defendant. Electronic monitoring may be used as a means of surveillance to ensure compliance with a curfew order.

(6) INTERMITTENT CONFINEMENT

Intermittent confinement (custody for intervals of time) may be ordered as a condition of supervised release during the first year of supervised release, but only for a violation of a condition of supervised release in accordance with 18 U.S.C. § 3583(e)(2) and only when facilities are available. *See* §5F1.8 (Intermittent Confinement).

Commentary

Application Note:

1. **Application of Subsection (c)(4).**—Although the condition in subsection (c)(4) requires the defendant to "answer truthfully" the questions asked by the probation officer, a defendant's legitimate invocation of the Fifth Amendment privilege against self-incrimination in response to a probation officer's question shall not be considered a violation of this condition.

Historical
Note

Effective November 1, 1987. Amended effective November 1, 1989 (amendments 276, 277, and 302); November 1, 1997 (amendment 569); November 1, 1998 (amendment 584); November 1, 2000 (amendment 605); November 1, 2001 (amendment 615); November 1, 2002 (amendments 644 and 646); November 1, 2004 (amendment 664); November 1, 2007 (amendments 701 and 711); November 1, 2009 (amendment 733); November 1, 2016 (amendment 803).

PART E — RESTITUTION, FINES, ASSESSMENTS, FORFEITURES

§5E1.1. Restitution

(a) In the case of an identifiable victim, the court shall—

(1) enter a restitution order for the full amount of the victim's loss, if such order is authorized under 18 U.S.C. § 1593, § 2248, § 2259, § 2264, § 2327, § 3663, or § 3663A, or 21 U.S.C. § 853(q); or

(2) impose a term of probation or supervised release with a condition requiring restitution for the full amount of the victim's loss, if the offense is not an offense for which restitution is authorized under 18 U.S.C. § 3663(a)(1) but otherwise meets the criteria for an order of restitution under that section.

(b) *Provided*, that the provisions of subsection (a) do not apply—

(1) when full restitution has been made; or

(2) in the case of a restitution order under 18 U.S.C. § 3663; a restitution order under 18 U.S.C. § 3663A that pertains to an offense against property described in 18 U.S.C. § 3663A(c)(1)(A)(ii); or a condition of restitution imposed pursuant to subsection (a)(2) above, to the extent the court finds, from facts on the record, that (A) the number of identifiable victims is so large as to make restitution impracticable; or (B) determining complex issues of fact related to the cause or amount of the victim's losses would complicate or prolong the sentencing process to a degree that the need to provide restitution to any victim is outweighed by the burden on the sentencing process.

(c) If a defendant is ordered to make restitution to an identifiable victim and to pay a fine, the court shall order that any money paid by the defendant shall first be applied to satisfy the order of restitution.

(d) In a case where there is no identifiable victim and the defendant was convicted under 21 U.S.C. § 841, § 848(a), § 849, § 856, § 861, or § 863, the court, taking into consideration the amount of public harm caused by the offense and other relevant factors, shall order an amount of community restitution not to exceed the fine imposed under §5E1.2.

(e) A restitution order may direct the defendant to make a single, lump sum payment, partial payments at specified intervals, in-kind payments, or a combination of payments at specified intervals and inkind payments. *See* 18 U.S.C. § 3664(f)(3)(A). An in-kind payment may be in the form of (1) return of property; (2) replacement of property;

or (3) if the victim agrees, services rendered to the victim or to a person or organization other than the victim. *See* 18 U.S.C. § 3664(f)(4).

(f) A restitution order may direct the defendant to make nominal periodic payments if the court finds from facts on the record that the economic circumstances of the defendant do not allow the payment of any amount of a restitution order and do not allow for the payment of the full amount of a restitution order in the foreseeable future under any reasonable schedule of payments.

(g) Special Instruction

(1) This guideline applies only to a defendant convicted of an offense committed on or after November 1, 1997. Notwithstanding the provisions of §1B1.11 (Use of Guidelines Manual in Effect on Date of Sentencing), use the former §5E1.1 (set forth in Appendix C, amendment 571) in lieu of this guideline in any other case.

Commentary

Application Note:

1. The court shall not order community restitution under subsection (d) if it appears likely that such an award would interfere with a forfeiture under Chapter 46 or 96 of Title 18, United States Code, or under the Controlled Substances Act (21 U.S.C. § 801 *et seq.*). *See* 18 U.S.C. § 3663(c)(4).

Furthermore, a penalty assessment under 18 U.S.C. § 3013 or a fine under Subchapter C of Chapter 227 of Title 18, United States Code, shall take precedence over an order of community restitution under subsection (d). *See* 18 U.S.C. § 3663(c)(5).

Background: Section 3553(a)(7) of Title 18, United States Code, requires the court, "in determining the particular sentence to be imposed," to consider "the need to provide restitution to any victims of the offense." Orders of restitution are authorized under 18 U.S.C. §§ 1593, 2248, 2259, 2264, 2327, 3663, and 3663A, and 21 U.S.C. § 853(q). For offenses for which an order of restitution is not authorized, restitution may be imposed as a condition of probation or supervised release.

Subsection (d) implements the instruction to the Commission in section 205 of the Antiterrorism and Effective Death Penalty Act of 1996. This provision directs the Commission to develop guidelines for community restitution in connection with certain drug offenses where there is no identifiable victim but the offense causes "public harm."

To the extent that any of the above-noted statutory provisions conflict with the provisions of this guideline, the applicable statutory provision shall control.

Historical Note

Effective November 1, 1987. Amended effective January 15, 1988 (amendment 53); November 1, 1989 (amendments 278, 279, and 302); November 1, 1991 (amendment 383); November 1, 1993 (amendment 501); November 1, 1995 (amendment 530); November 1, 1997 (amendment 571); May 1, 2001 (amendment 612); November 1, 2001 (amendment 627).

§5E1.2. Fines for Individual Defendants

(a) The court shall impose a fine in all cases, except where the defendant establishes that he is unable to pay and is not likely to become able to pay any fine.

(b) The applicable fine guideline range is that specified in subsection (c) below. If, however, the guideline for the offense in Chapter Two provides a specific rule for imposing a fine, that rule takes precedence over subsection (c) of this section.

(c) (1) The minimum of the fine guideline range is the amount shown in column A of the table below.

(2) Except as specified in (4) below, the maximum of the fine guideline range is the amount shown in column B of the table below.

(3) FINE TABLE

OFFENSE A B
LEVEL MINIMUM MAXIMUM
3 and below $200 $9,500
4–5 $500 $9,500
6–7 $1,000 $9,500
8–9 $2,000 $20,000
10–11 $4,000 $40,000
12–13 $5,500 $55,000
14–15 $7,500 $75,000
16–17 $10,000 $95,000
18–19 $10,000 $100,000
20–22 $15,000 $150,000
23–25 $20,000 $200,000
26–28 $25,000 $250,000
29–31 $30,000 $300,000
32–34 $35,000 $350,000
35–37 $40,000 $400,000
38 and above $50,000 $500,000.

(4) Subsection (c)(2), limiting the maximum fine, does not apply if the defendant is convicted under a statute authorizing (A) a maximum fine greater than $500,000, or (B) a fine for each day of violation. In such cases, the court may impose a fine up to the maximum authorized by the statute.

(d) In determining the amount of the fine, the court shall consider:

(1) the need for the combined sentence to reflect the seriousness of the offense (including the harm or loss to the victim and the gain to the defendant), to promote respect for the law, to provide just punishment and to afford adequate deterrence;

(2) any evidence presented as to the defendant's ability to pay the fine (including the ability to pay over a period of time) in light of his earning capacity and financial resources;

(3) the burden that the fine places on the defendant and his dependents relative to alternative punishments;

(4) any restitution or reparation that the defendant has made or is obligated to make;

(5) any collateral consequences of conviction, including civil obligations arising from the defendant's conduct;

(6) whether the defendant previously has been fined for a similar offense;

(7) the expected costs to the government of any term of probation, or term of imprisonment and term of supervised release imposed;

and
(8) any other pertinent equitable considerations.
The amount of the fine should always be sufficient to ensure that the fine, taken together with other sanctions imposed, is punitive.
(e) If the defendant establishes that (1) he is not able and, even with the use of a reasonable installment schedule, is not likely to become able to pay all or part of the fine required by the preceding provisions, or (2) imposition of a fine would unduly burden the defendant's dependents, the court may impose a lesser fine or waive the fine. In these circumstances, the court shall consider alternative sanctions in lieu of all or a portion of the fine, and must still impose a total combined sanction that is punitive. Although any additional

sanction not proscribed by the guidelines is permissible, community service is the generally preferable alternative in such instances.
(f) If the defendant establishes that payment of the fine in a lump sum would have an unduly severe impact on him or his dependents, the court should establish an installment schedule for payment of the fine. The length of the installment schedule generally should not exceed twelve months, and shall not exceed the maximum term of probation authorized for the offense. The defendant should be required to pay a substantial installment at the time of sentencing. If the court authorizes a defendant sentenced to probation or supervised release to pay a fine on an installment schedule, the court shall require as a condition of probation or supervised release that the defendant pay the fine according to the schedule. The court also may impose a condition prohibiting the defendant from incurring new credit charges or opening additional lines of credit unless he is in compliance with the payment schedule.
(g) If the defendant knowingly fails to pay a delinquent fine, the court shall resentence him in accordance with 18 U.S.C. § 3614.
(h) Special Instruction
(1) For offenses committed prior to November 1, 2015, use the applicable fine guideline range that was set forth in the version of §5E1.2(c) that was in effect on November 1, 2014, rather than the applicable fine guideline range set forth in subsection (c) above.

Commentary

Application Notes:

1. A fine may be the sole sanction if the guidelines do not require a term of imprisonment. If, however, the fine is not paid in full at the time of sentencing, it is recommended that the court sentence the defendant to a term of probation, with payment of the fine as a condition of probation. If a fine is imposed in addition to a term of imprisonment, it is recommended that the court impose a term of supervised release following imprisonment as a means of enforcing payment of the fine.
2. In general, the maximum fine permitted by law as to each count of conviction is $250,000 for a felony or for any misdemeanor resulting in death; $100,000 for a Class A misdemeanor; and $5,000 for any other offense. 18 U.S.C. § 3571(b)(3)–(7). However, higher or lower limits may apply when specified by statute. 18 U.S.C. § 3571(b)(1), (e). As an alternative

maximum, the court may fine the defendant up to the greater of twice the gross gain or twice the gross loss. 18 U.S.C. § 3571(b)(2), (d).

3. The determination of the fine guideline range may be dispensed with entirely upon a court determination of present and future inability to pay any fine. The inability of a defendant to post bail bond (having otherwise been determined eligible for release) and

the fact that a defendant is represented by (or was determined eligible for) assigned counsel are significant indicators of present inability to pay any fine. In conjunction with other factors, they may also indicate that the defendant is not likely to become able to pay any fine.

4. The Commission envisions that for most defendants, the maximum of the guideline fine range from subsection (c) will be at least twice the amount of gain or loss resulting from the offense. Where, however, two times either the amount of gain to the defendant or the amount of loss caused by the offense exceeds the maximum of the fine guideline, an upward departure from the fine guideline may be warranted.

Moreover, where a sentence within the applicable fine guideline range would not be sufficient to ensure both the disgorgement of any gain from the offense that otherwise would not be disgorged (*e.g.*, by restitution or forfeiture) and an adequate punitive fine, an upward departure from the fine guideline range may be warranted.

5. Subsection (c)(4) applies to statutes that contain special provisions permitting larger fines; the guidelines do not limit maximum fines in such cases. These statutes include, among others: 21 U.S.C. §§ 841(b) and 960(b), which authorize fines up to $8 million in offenses involving the manufacture, distribution, or importation of certain controlled substances; 21 U.S.C. § 848(a), which authorizes fines up to $4 million in offenses involving the manufacture or distribution of controlled substances by a continuing criminal enterprise; 18 U.S.C. § 1956(a), which authorizes a fine equal to the greater of $500,000 or two times the value of the monetary instruments or funds involved in offenses involving money laundering of financial instruments; 18 U.S.C. § 1957(b)(2), which authorizes a fine equal to two times the amount of any criminally derived property involved in a money laundering transaction; 33 U.S.C. § 1319(c), which authorizes a fine of up to $50,000 per day for violations of the Water Pollution Control Act; 42 U.S.C. § 6928(d), which authorizes a fine of up to $50,000 per day for violations of the Resource Conservation Act; and 52 U.S.C. § 30109(d)(1)(D), which authorizes, for violations of the Federal Election Campaign Act under 52 U.S.C. § 30122, a fine up to the greater of $50,000 or 1,000 percent of the amount of the violation, and which requires, in the case of such a violation, a minimum fine of not less than 300 percent of the amount of the violation.

There may be cases in which the defendant has entered into a conciliation agreement with the Federal Election Commission under section 309 of the Federal Election Campaign Act of 1971 in order to correct or prevent a violation of such Act by the defendant.

The existence of a conciliation agreement between the defendant and Federal Election Commission, and the extent of compliance with that conciliation agreement, may be appropriate factors in determining at what point within the applicable fine guideline range to sentence the defendant, unless the defendant began negotiations toward a conciliation agreement after becoming aware of a criminal investigation.

6. The existence of income or assets that the defendant failed to disclose may justify a larger fine than that which otherwise would be warranted under this section. The court may base its conclusion as to this factor on information revealing significant unexplained expenditures by the defendant or unexplained possession of assets that do not comport with the defendant's reported income. If the court concludes that the defendant willfully misrepresented all or part of his income or assets, it may increase the offense level and resulting sentence in accordance with Chapter Three, Part C (Obstruction and Related Adjustments).

7. In considering subsection (d)(7), the court may be guided by reports published by the

Bureau of Prisons and the Administrative Office of the United States Courts concerning average costs.

Historical Note

Effective November 1, 1987. Amended effective January 15, 1988 (amendment 54); November 1, 1989 (amendments 280, 281, and 302); November 1, 1990 (amendment 356); November 1, 1991 (amendment 384); November 1, 1997 (amendment 572); November 1, 2002 (amendment 646); January 25, 2003 (amendment 648); November 1, 2003 (amendment 656); November 1, 2011 (amendment 758); November 1, 2015 (amendments 791 and 796).

§5E1.3. Special Assessments

A special assessment must be imposed on a convicted defendant in the amount prescribed by statute.

Commentary

Application Notes:

1. This guideline applies only if the defendant is an individual. *See* §8E1.1 for special assessments applicable to organizations.
2. The following special assessments are provided by statute (18 U.S.C. § 3013):

FOR OFFENSES COMMITTED BY INDIVIDUALS ON OR AFTER APRIL 24, 1996:

(A) $100, if convicted of a felony;
(B) $25, if convicted of a Class A misdemeanor;
(C) $10, if convicted of a Class B misdemeanor;
(D) $5, if convicted of a Class C misdemeanor or an infraction.

FOR OFFENSES COMMITTED BY INDIVIDUALS ON OR AFTER NOVEMBER 18, 1988 BUT PRIOR TO APRIL 24, 1996:

(E) $50, if convicted of a felony;
(F) $25, if convicted of a Class A misdemeanor;
(G) $10, if convicted of a Class B misdemeanor;
(H) $5, if convicted of a Class C misdemeanor or an infraction.

FOR OFFENSES COMMITTED BY INDIVIDUALS PRIOR TO NOVEMBER 18, 1988:

(I) $50, if convicted of a felony;
(J) $25, if convicted of a misdemeanor.

3. A special assessment is required by statute for each count of conviction.

Background: Section 3013 of Title 18, United States Code, added by The Victims of Crimes Act of 1984, Pub. L. No. 98–473, Title II, Chap. XIV, requires courts to impose special assessments on convicted defendants for the purpose of funding the Crime Victims Fund established by the same legislation.

Historical Note

Effective November 1, 1987. Amended effective November 1, 1989 (amendments 282 and 302); November 1, 1997 (amendment 573).

§5E1.4. Forfeiture

Forfeiture is to be imposed upon a convicted defendant as provided by statute.

Commentary

Background: Forfeiture provisions exist in various statutes. For example, 18 U.S.C. § 3554 requires the court imposing a sentence under 18 U.S.C. § 1962 (proscribing the use of the proceeds of racketeering activities in the operation of an enterprise engaged in interstate commerce) or Titles II and III of the Comprehensive Drug Abuse Prevention and Control Act of 1970 (proscribing the manufacture and distribution of controlled substances) to order the forfeiture of property in accordance with 18 U.S.C. § 1963 and 21 U.S.C. § 853, respectively. Those provisions require the automatic forfeiture of certain property upon conviction of their respective underlying offenses.

In addition, the provisions of 18 U.S.C. §§ 3681–3682 authorizes the court, in certain circumstances, to order the forfeiture of a violent criminal's proceeds from the depiction of his crime in a book, movie, or other medium. Those sections authorize the deposit of proceeds in an escrow account in the Crime Victims Fund of the United States Treasury. The money is to remain available in the account for five years to satisfy claims brought against the defendant by the victim(s) of his offenses. At the end of the five-year period, the court may require that any proceeds remaining in the account be released from escrow and paid into the Fund. 18 U.S.C. § 3681(c)(2).

Historical
Note
Effective November 1, 1987. Amended effective November 1, 1989 (amendment 302).

§5E1.5. Costs of Prosecution (Policy Statement)

Costs of prosecution shall be imposed on a defendant as required by statute.

Commentary

Background: Various statutes require the court to impose the costs of prosecution: 7 U.S.C. § 13 (larceny or embezzlement in connection with commodity exchanges); 21 U.S.C. § 844 (simple possession of controlled substances) (unless the court finds that the defendant lacks the ability to pay); 26 U.S.C. § 7201 (attempt to defeat or evade income tax); 26 U.S.C. § 7202 (willful failure to collect or pay tax); 26 U.S.C. § 7203 (willful failure to file income tax return, supply information, or pay tax); 26 U.S.C. § 7206 (fraud and false statements); 26 U.S.C. § 7210 (failure to obey summons); 26 U.S.C. § 7213 (unauthorized disclosure of information); 26 U.S.C. § 7215 (offenses with respect to collected taxes); 26 U.S.C. § 7216 (disclosure or use of information by preparers of returns); 26 U.S.C. § 7232 (failure to register or false statement

by gasoline manufacturer or producer); 42 U.S.C. § 1320c-9 (improper FOIA disclosure); 43 U.S.C. § 942-6 (rights of way for Alaskan wagon roads).

Historical
Note
Effective November 1, 1992 (amendment 463). Amended effective November 1, 2010 (amendment 747).

PART F — SENTENCING OPTIONS

§5F1.1. Community Confinement

Community confinement may be imposed as a condition of probation or supervised release.

Commentary

Application Notes:

1. "***Community confinement***" means residence in a community treatment center, halfway house, restitution center, mental health facility, alcohol or drug rehabilitation center, or other community facility; and participation in gainful employment, employment search efforts, community service, vocational training, treatment, educational programs, or similar facility-approved programs during non-residential hours.
2. Community confinement generally should not be imposed for a period in excess of six months. A longer period may be imposed to accomplish the objectives of a specific rehabilitative program, such as drug rehabilitation. The sentencing judge may impose other discretionary conditions of probation or supervised release appropriate to effectuate community confinement.

Historical
Note
Effective November 1, 1987. Amended effective November 1, 1989 (amendment 302); November 1, 2002 (amendment 646); November 1, 2009 (amendment 733).

§5F1.2. Home Detention

Home detention may be imposed as a condition of probation or supervised release, but only as a substitute for imprisonment.

Commentary

Application Notes:

1. "***Home detention***" means a program of confinement and supervision that restricts the

defendant to his place of residence continuously, except for authorized absences, enforced by appropriate means of surveillance by the probation office. When an order of home detention is imposed, the defendant is required to be in his place of residence at all times except for approved absences for gainful employment, community service, religious services, medical care, educational or training programs, and such other times as may be specifically authorized. Electronic monitoring is an appropriate means of surveillance and ordinarily should be used in connection with home detention. However, alternative means of surveillance may be used so long as they are as effective as electronic monitoring.

2. The court may impose other conditions of probation or supervised release appropriate to effectuate home detention. If the court concludes that the amenities available in the residence of a defendant would cause home detention not to be sufficiently punitive, the court may limit the amenities available.

3. The defendant's place of residence, for purposes of home detention, need not be the place where the defendant previously resided. It may be any place of residence, so long as the owner of the residence (and any other person(s) from whom consent is necessary) agrees to any conditions that may be imposed by the court, *e.g.*, conditions that a monitoring system be installed, that there will be no "call forwarding" or "call waiting" services, or that there will be no cordless telephones or answering machines.

Background: The Commission has concluded that the surveillance necessary for effective use of home detention ordinarily requires electronic monitoring. However, in some cases home detention may effectively be enforced without electronic monitoring, *e.g.*, when the defendant is physically incapacitated, or where some other effective means of surveillance is available. Accordingly, the Commission has not required that electronic monitoring be a necessary condition for home detention. Nevertheless, before ordering home detention without electronic monitoring, the court should be confident that an alternative form of surveillance will be equally effective.

In the usual case, the Commission assumes that a condition requiring that the defendant seek and maintain gainful employment will be imposed when home detention is ordered.

Historical Note Effective November 1, 1987. Amended effective November 1, 1989 (amendments 271 and 302).

§5F1.3. Community Service

Community service may be ordered as a condition of probation or supervised release.

Commentary

Application Note:

1. Community service generally should not be imposed in excess of 400 hours. Longer terms of community service impose heavy administrative burdens relating to the selection of suitable placements and the monitoring of attendance.

Historical Note

Effective November 1, 1987. Amended effective November 1, 1989 (amendments 283 and 302); November 1, 1991 (amendment 419).

§5F1.4. Order of Notice to Victims

The court may order the defendant to pay the cost of giving notice to victims pursuant to 18 U.S.C. § 3555. This cost may be set off against any fine imposed if the court determines that the imposition of both sanctions would be excessive.

Commentary

Background: In cases where a defendant has been convicted of an offense involving fraud or "other intentionally deceptive practices," the court may order the defendant to "give reasonable notice and explanation of the conviction, in such form as the court may approve" to the victims of the offense. 18 U.S.C. § 3555. The court may order the notice to be given by mail, by advertising in specific areas or through specific media, or by other appropriate means. In determining whether a notice is appropriate, the court must consider the generally applicable sentencing factors listed in 18 U.S.C. § 3553(a) and the cost involved in giving the notice as it relates to the loss caused by the crime. The court may not require the defendant to pay more than $20,000 to give notice.

If an order of notice to victims is under consideration, the court must notify the government and the defendant. 18 U.S.C. § 3553(d). Upon motion of either party, or on its own motion, the court must: (1) permit the parties to submit affidavits and memoranda relevant to the imposition of such an order; (2) provide counsel for both parties the opportunity to address orally, in open court, the appropriateness of such an order; and (3) if it issues such an order, state its reasons for doing so. The court may also order any additional procedures that will not unduly complicate or prolong the sentencing process.

Historical Note

Effective November 1, 1987. Amended effective November 1, 1989 (amendments 284 and 302).

§5F1.5. Occupational Restrictions

(a) The court may impose a condition of probation or supervised release prohibiting the defendant from engaging in a specified occupation, business, or profession, or limiting the terms on which the defendant may do so, only if it determines that:

(1) a reasonably direct relationship existed between the defendant's occupation, business, or profession and the conduct relevant to the offense of conviction; and

(2) imposition of such a restriction is reasonably necessary to protect the public because there is reason to believe that, absent such restriction, the defendant will continue to engage in unlawful conduct similar to that for which the defendant was convicted.

(b) If the court decides to impose a condition of probation or supervised release restricting a defendant's engagement in a specified occupation, business, or profession, the court shall impose the condition for the minimum time and to the minimum extent necessary to protect the public.

Commentary

Background: The Comprehensive Crime Control Act authorizes the imposition of occupational restrictions as a condition of probation, 18 U.S.C. § 3563(b)(5), or supervised release, 18 U.S.C. § 3583(d). Pursuant to § 3563(b)(5), a court may require a defendant to:

[R]efrain, in the case of an individual, from engaging in a specified occupation, business, or profession bearing a reasonably direct relationship to the conduct constituting the offense, or engage in such a specified occupation, business, or profession only to a stated degree or under stated circumstances.

Section 3583(d) incorporates this section by reference. The Senate Judiciary Committee Report on the Comprehensive Crime Control Act explains that the provision was "intended to be used to preclude the continuation or repetition of illegal activities while avoiding a bar from employment that exceeds that needed to achieve that result." S. Rep. No. 225, 98th Cong., 1st Sess. 96–97. The condition "should only be used as reasonably necessary to protect the public. It should not be used as a means of punishing the convicted person." *Id.* at 96. Section 5F1.5 accordingly limits the use of the condition and, if imposed, limits its scope, to the minimum reasonably necessary to protect the public.

The appellate review provisions permit a defendant to challenge the imposition of a probation condition under 18 U.S.C. § 3563(b)(5) if the sentence includes a more limiting condition of probation or supervised release than the maximum established in the guideline. *See* 18 U.S.C. § 3742(a)(3). The government may appeal if the sentence includes a less limiting condition of probation than the minimum established in the guideline. *See* 18 U.S.C. § 3742(b)(3).

Historical Note

Effective November 1, 1987. Amended effective November 1, 1989 (amendments 285 and 302); November 1, 1991 (amendment 428); November 1, 2002 (amendment 646).

§5F1.6. Denial of Federal Benefits to Drug Traffickers and Possessors

The court, pursuant to 21 U.S.C. § 862, may deny the eligibility for certain Federal benefits of any individual convicted of distribution or possession of a controlled substance.

Commentary

Application Note:

1. "***Federal benefit***" is defined in 21 U.S.C. § 862(d) to mean "any grant, contract, loan, professional license, or commercial license provided by an agency of the United States or by appropriated funds of the United States" but "does not include any retirement, welfare, Social Security, health, disability, veterans benefit, public housing, or other similar benefit, or any other benefit for which payments or services are required for eligibility."

Background: Subsections (a) and (b) of 21 U.S.C. § 862 provide that an individual convicted of a state or federal drug trafficking or possession offense may be denied certain federal benefits. Except for an individual convicted of a third or subsequent drug distribution offense, the period of benefit ineligibility, within the applicable maximum term set forth in 21 U.S.C. § 862(a)(1) (for distribution offenses) and (b)(1)(for possession offenses), is at the discretion of the court. In the case of an individual convicted of a third or subsequent drug distribution

offense, denial of benefits is mandatory and permanent under 21 U.S.C. § 862(a)(1)(C) (unless suspended by the court under 21 U.S.C. § 862(c)).

Subsection (b)(2) of 21 U.S.C. § 862 provides that the period of benefit ineligibility that may be imposed in the case of a drug possession offense "shall be waived in the case of a person who, if there is a reasonable body of evidence to substantiate such declaration, declares himself to be an addict and submits himself to a long-term treatment program for addiction, or is deemed to be rehabilitated pursuant to rules established by the Secretary of Health and Human Services."

Subsection (c) of 21 U.S.C. § 862 provides that the period of benefit ineligibility shall be suspended "if the individual (A) completes a supervised drug rehabilitation program after becoming ineligible under this section; (B) has otherwise been rehabilitated; or (C) has made a good faith effort to gain admission to a supervised drug rehabilitation program, but is unable to do so because of inaccessibility or unavailability of such a program, or the inability of the individual to pay for such a program."

Subsection (e) of 21 U.S.C. § 862 provides that a period of benefit ineligibility "shall not apply to any individual who cooperates or testifies with the Government in the prosecution of a Federal or State offense or who is in a Government witness protection program."

Historical Note

Effective November 1, 1989 (amendment 305); November 1, 1992 (amendment 464).

§5F1.7. Shock Incarceration Program (Policy Statement)

The court, pursuant to 18 U.S.C. §§ 3582(a) and 3621(b)(4), may recommend that a defendant who meets the criteria set forth in 18 U.S.C. § 4046 participate in a shock incarceration program.

Commentary

Background: Section 4046 of title 18, United States Code, provides—

"(a) the Bureau of Prisons may place in a shock incarceration program any person who is sentenced to a term of more than 12, but not more than 30 months, if such person consents to that placement.

(b) For such initial portion of the term of imprisonment as the Bureau of Prisons may

determine, not to exceed six months, an inmate in the shock incarceration program shall be required to—
(1) adhere to a highly regimented schedule that provides the strict discipline, physical training, hard labor, drill, and ceremony characteristic of military basic training; and
(2) participate in appropriate job training and educational programs (including literacy programs) and drug, alcohol, and other counseling programs.

(c) An inmate who in the judgment of the Director of the Bureau of Prisons has successfully completed the required period of shock incarceration shall remain in the custody of the Bureau for such period (not to exceed the remainder of the prison term otherwise required by law to be served by that inmate), and under such conditions, as the Bureau deems appropriate. 18 U.S.C. § 4046."

The Bureau of Prisons has issued an operations memorandum (174-90 (5390), November 20, 1990) that outlines eligibility criteria and procedures for the implementation of this program (which the Bureau of Prisons has titled "intensive confinement program"). Under these procedures, the Bureau will not place a defendant in an intensive confinement program unless the sentencing court has approved, either at the time of sentencing or upon consultation after the Bureau has determined that the defendant is otherwise eligible. In return for the successful completion of the "intensive confinement" portion of the program, the defendant is eligible to serve the remainder of his term of imprisonment in a graduated release program comprised of community corrections center and home confinement phases.

Historical
Note
Effective November 1, 1991 (amendment 424). Amended effective November 1, 2002 (amendment 646).

§5F1.8. Intermittent Confinement

Intermittent confinement may be imposed as a condition of probation during the first year of probation. *See* 18 U.S.C. § 3563(b)(10). It may be imposed as a condition of supervised release during the first year of supervised release, but only for a violation of a condition of supervised release in accordance with 18 U.S.C. § 3583(e)(2) and only when facilities are available. *See* 18 U.S.C. § 3583(d).

Commentary

Application Note:

1. "***Intermittent confinement***" means remaining in the custody of the Bureau of Prisons during nights, weekends, or other intervals of time, totaling no more than the lesser of one year or the term of imprisonment authorized for the offense, during the first year of the term of probation or supervised release. *See* 18 U.S.C. § 3563(b)(10).

Historical
Note
Effective November 1, 2009 (amendment 733).

PART G — IMPLEMENTING THE TOTAL SENTENCE OF IMPRISONMENT

§5G1.1. Sentencing on a Single Count of Conviction

(a) Where the statutorily authorized maximum sentence is less than the minimum of the applicable guideline range, the statutorily authorized maximum sentence shall be the guideline sentence.
(b) Where a statutorily required minimum sentence is greater than the maximum of the applicable guideline range, the statutorily required minimum sentence shall be the guideline sentence.

(c) In any other case, the sentence may be imposed at any point within the applicable guideline range, provided that the sentence—
(1) is not greater than the statutorily authorized maximum sentence, and
(2) is not less than any statutorily required minimum sentence.

Commentary

This section describes how the statutorily authorized maximum sentence, or a statutorily required minimum sentence, may affect the determination of a sentence under the guidelines. For example, if the applicable guideline range is 51–63 months and the maximum sentence authorized by statute for the offense of conviction is 48 months, the sentence required by the guidelines under subsection (a) is 48 months; a sentence of less than 48 months would be a guideline departure. If the applicable guideline range is 41–51 months and there is a statutorily required minimum sentence of 60 months, the sentence required by the guidelines under subsection (b) is 60 months; a sentence of more than 60 months would be a guideline departure. If the applicable guideline range is 51–63 months and the maximum sentence authorized by statute for the offense of conviction is 60 months, the guideline range is restricted to 51–60 months under subsection (c).

Historical Note

Effective November 1, 1987. Amended effective November 1, 1989 (amendment 286).

§5G1.2. Sentencing on Multiple Counts of Conviction

(a) Except as provided in subsection (e), the sentence to be imposed on a count for which the statute (1) specifies a term of imprisonment to be imposed; and (2) requires that such term of imprisonment be imposed to run consecutively to any other term of imprisonment, shall be determined by that statute and imposed independently.

(b) For all counts not covered by subsection (a), the court shall determine the total punishment and shall impose that total punishment on each such count, except to the extent otherwise required by law.
(c) If the sentence imposed on the count carrying the highest statutory maximum is adequate to achieve the total punishment, then the sentences on all counts shall run concurrently, except to the extent otherwise required by law.
(d) If the sentence imposed on the count carrying the highest statutory maximum is less than the total punishment, then the sentence imposed on one or more of the other counts shall run consecutively, but only to the extent necessary to produce a combined sentence equal to the total punishment. In all other respects, sentences on all counts shall run concurrently, except to the extent otherwise required by law.
(e) In a case in which subsection (c) of §4B1.1 (Career Offender) applies, to the extent possible, the total punishment is to be apportioned among the counts of conviction, except that (1) the sentence to be imposed on a count requiring a minimum term of imprisonment shall be at least the minimum required by statute; and (2) the sentence to be imposed on the 18 U.S.C. § 924(c) or § 929(a) count shall be imposed to run consecutively to any other count.

Commentary

Application Notes:

1. **In General.**—This section specifies the procedure for determining the specific sentence to be formally imposed on each count in a multiple-count case. The combined length of the sentences ("total punishment") is determined by the court after determining the adjusted combined offense level and the Criminal History Category and determining the defendant's guideline range on the Sentencing Table in Chapter Five, Part A (Sentencing Table).

Note that the defendant's guideline range on the Sentencing Table may be affected or restricted by a statutorily authorized maximum sentence or a statutorily required minimum sentence not only in a single-count case, *see* §5G1.1 (Sentencing on a Single Count of Conviction), but also in a multiple-count case. *See* Note 3, below.

Except as otherwise required by subsection (e) or any other law, the total punishment is to be imposed on each count and the sentences on all counts are to be imposed to run concurrently to the extent allowed by the statutory maximum sentence of imprisonment for each count of conviction.

This section applies to multiple counts of conviction (A) contained in the same indictment or information, or (B) contained in different indictments or informations for which sentences are to be imposed at the same time or in a consolidated proceeding.

Usually, at least one of the counts will have a statutory maximum adequate to permit imposition of the total punishment as the sentence on that count. The sentence on each of the other counts will then be set at the lesser of the total punishment and the applicable statutory maximum, and be made to run concurrently with all or part of the longest sentence. If no count carries an adequate statutory maximum, consecutive sentences are to be imposed to the extent necessary to achieve the total punishment.

2. **Mandatory Minimum and Mandatory Consecutive Terms of Imprisonment (Not Covered by Subsection (e)).**—

(A) **In General.**—Subsection (a) applies if a statute (i) specifies a term of imprisonment to be imposed; and (ii) requires that such term of imprisonment be imposed to run consecutively to any other term of imprisonment. *See, e.g.*, 18 U.S.C. § 924(c) (requiring mandatory minimum terms of imprisonment, based on the conduct involved, and also requiring the sentence imposed to run consecutively to any other term of imprisonment) and 18 U.S.C. § 1028A (requiring a mandatory term of imprisonment of either two or five years, based on the conduct involved, and also requiring, except in the circumstances described in subdivision (B), the sentence imposed to run consecutively to any other term of imprisonment). Except for certain career offender situations in which subsection (c) of §4B1.1 (Career Offender) applies, the term of years to be imposed consecutively is the minimum required by the statute of conviction and is independent of the guideline sentence on any other count. *See, e.g.*, the Commentary to §§2K2.4 (Use of Firearm, Armor-Piercing Ammunition, or Explosive During or in Relation to Certain Crimes) and 3D1.1 (Procedure for Determining Offense Level on Multiple Counts) regarding the determination of the offense levels for related counts when a conviction under 18 U.S.C. § 924(c) is involved. Subsection (a) also applies in certain other instances in which an independently determined and consecutive sentence is required. *See, e.g.*, Application Note 3 of the Commentary to §2J1.6 (Failure to Appear by Defendant), relating to failure to appear for service of sentence.

(B) **Multiple Convictions Under 18 U.S.C. § 1028A.**—Section 1028A of title 18, United States Code, generally requires that the mandatory term of imprisonment for a violation of such section be imposed consecutively to any other term of imprisonment. However, 18 U.S.C. § 1028A(b)(4) permits the court, in its discretion, to impose the mandatory term of imprisonment on a defendant for a violation of such section "concurrently, in whole or in part, only with another term of imprisonment that is imposed by the court at the same time on that person for an additional violation of this section, provided that such discretion shall be exercised in accordance with any applicable guidelines and policy statements issued by the Sentencing Commission . . .".

In determining whether multiple counts of 18 U.S.C. § 1028A should run concurrently with, or consecutively to, each other, the court should consider the following non-exhaustive list of factors:

(i) The nature and seriousness of the underlying offenses. For example, the court should consider the appropriateness of imposing consecutive, or partially consecutive, terms of imprisonment for multiple counts of 18 U.S.C. § 1028A in a case in which an underlying offense for one of the 18 U.S.C. § 1028A offenses is a crime of violence or an offense enumerated in 18 U.S.C. § 2332b(g)(5)(B).

(ii) Whether the underlying offenses are groupable under §3D1.2 (Groups of Closely Related Counts). Generally, multiple counts of 18 U.S.C. § 1028A

should run concurrently with one another in cases in which the underlying offenses are groupable under §3D1.2.

(iii) Whether the purposes of sentencing set forth in 18 U.S.C. § 3553(a)(2) are better achieved by imposing a concurrent or a consecutive sentence for multiple counts of 18 U.S.C. § 1028A.

(C) **Imposition of Supervised Release.**—In the case of a consecutive term of imprisonment imposed under subsection (a), any term of supervised release imposed is to run concurrently with any other term of supervised release imposed. *See* 18 U.S.C. § 3624(e).

3. **Application of Subsection (b).**—

(A) **In General.**—Subsection (b) provides that, for all counts not covered by subsection (a), the court shall determine the total punishment (*i.e.*, the combined length of the sentences to be imposed) and shall impose that total punishment on each such count, except to the extent otherwise required by law (such as where a statutorily required minimum sentence or a statutorily authorized maximum sentence otherwise requires).

(B) **Effect on Guidelines Range of Mandatory Minimum or Statutory Maximum.**—The defendant's guideline range on the Sentencing Table may be affected or restricted by a statutorily authorized maximum sentence or a statutorily required minimum sentence not only in a single-count case, *see* §5G1.1, but also in a multiple-count case.

In particular, where a statutorily required minimum sentence on any count is greater than the maximum of the applicable guideline range, the statutorily required minimum sentence on that count shall be the guideline sentence on all counts. *See* §5G1.1(b). Similarly, where a statutorily required minimum sentence on any count is greater than the minimum of the applicable guideline range, the guideline range for all counts is restricted by that statutorily required minimum sentence. *See* §5G1.1(c)(2) and accompanying Commentary.

However, where a statutorily authorized maximum sentence on a particular count is less than the minimum of the applicable guideline range, the sentence imposed on that count shall not be greater than the statutorily authorized maximum sentence on that count. *See* §5G1.1(a).

(C) **Examples.**—The following examples illustrate how subsection (b) applies, and how the restrictions in subparagraph (B) operate, when a statutorily required minimum sentence is involved.

Defendant A and Defendant B are each convicted of the same four counts. Counts 1, 3, and 4 have statutory maximums of 10 years, 20 years, and 2 years, respectively. Count 2 has a statutory maximum of 30 years and a mandatory minimum of 10 years.

For Defendant A, the court determines that the final offense level is 19 and the defendant is in Criminal History Category I, which yields a guideline range on the

Sentencing Table of 30 to 37 months. Because of the 10-year mandatory minimum on Count 2, however, Defendant A's guideline sentence is 120 months. *See* subparagraph (B), above. After considering that guideline sentence, the court determines

that the appropriate "total punishment" to be imposed on Defendant A is 120 months. Therefore, subsection (b) requires that the total punishment of 120 months be imposed on each of Counts 1, 2, and 3. The sentence imposed on Count 4 is limited to 24 months, because a statutory maximum of 2 years applies to that particular count.

For Defendant B, in contrast, the court determines that the final offense level is 30 and the defendant is in Criminal History Category II, which yields a guideline range on the Sentencing Table of 108 to 135 months. Because of the 10-year mandatory minimum on Count 2, however, Defendant B's guideline range is restricted to 120 to 135 months. *See* subparagraph (B), above. After considering that restricted guideline range, the court determines that the appropriate "total punishment" to be imposed on Defendant B is 130 months. Therefore, subsection (b) requires that the total punishment of 130 months be imposed on each of Counts 2 and 3. The sentences imposed on Counts 1 and 4 are limited to 120 months (10 years) and 24 months (2 years), respectively, because of the applicable statutory maximums.

(D) **Special Rule on Resentencing.**—In a case in which (i) the defendant's guideline range on the Sentencing Table was affected or restricted by a statutorily required minimum sentence (as described in subparagraph (B)), (ii) the court is resentencing the defendant, and (iii) the statutorily required minimum sentence no longer applies, the defendant's guideline range for purposes of the remaining counts shall be redetermined without regard to the previous effect or restriction of the statutorily required minimum sentence.

4. **Career Offenders Covered under Subsection (e).**—

(A) **Imposing Sentence.**—The sentence imposed for a conviction under 18 U.S.C. § 924(c) or § 929(a) shall, under that statute, consist of a minimum term of imprisonment imposed to run consecutively to the sentence on any other count. Subsection (e) requires that the total punishment determined under §4B1.1(c) be apportioned among all the counts of conviction. In most cases this can be achieved by imposing the statutory minimum term of imprisonment on the 18 U.S.C. § 924(c) or § 929(a) count, subtracting that minimum term of imprisonment from the total punishment determined under §4B1.1(c), and then imposing the balance of the total punishment on the other counts of conviction. In some cases covered by subsection (e), a consecutive term of imprisonment longer than the minimum required by 18 U.S.C. § 924(c) or § 929(a) will be necessary in order both to achieve the total punishment determined by the court and to comply with the applicable statutory requirements.

(B) **Examples.**—The following examples illustrate the application of subsection (e) in a multiple count situation:

(i) The defendant is convicted of one count of violating 18 U.S.C. § 924(c) for possessing a firearm in furtherance of a drug trafficking offense (5 year mandatory minimum), and one count of violating 21 U.S.C. § 841(b)(1)(C) (20 year statutory maximum). Applying §4B1.1(c), the court determines that a sentence of 300 months is appropriate (applicable guideline range of 262–327). The court then imposes a sentence of 60 months on the 18 U.S.C. § 924(c) count, subtracts that 60 months from the total punishment of 300 months and imposes the remainder of 240 months on the 21 U.S.C. § 841 count. As required by statute, the sentence on the 18 U.S.C. § 924(c) count is imposed to run consecutively.

(ii) The defendant is convicted of one count of 18 U.S.C. § 924(c) (5 year mandatory minimum), and one count of violating 21 U.S.C. § 841(b)(1)(C) (20 year statutory maximum). Applying §4B1.1(c), the court determines that a sentence of 327 months is appropriate (applicable guideline range of 262–327). The court then imposes a sentence of 240 months on the 21 U.S.C. § 841 count and a sentence of 87 months on the 18 U.S.C. § 924(c) count to run consecutively to the sentence on the 21 U.S.C. § 841 count.

(iii) The defendant is convicted of two counts of 18 U.S.C. § 924(c) (5 year mandatory minimum on first count, 25 year mandatory minimum on second count) and one count of violating 18 U.S.C. § 113(a)(3) (10 year statutory maximum). Applying §4B1.1(c), the court determines that a sentence of 460 months is appropriate (applicable guideline range of 460–485 months). The court then imposes (I) a sentence of 60 months on the first 18 U.S.C. § 924(c) count; (II) a sentence of 300 months on the second 18 U.S.C. § 924(c) count; and (III) a sentence of 100 months on the 18 U.S.C. § 113(a)(3) count. The sentence on each count is imposed to run consecutively to the other counts.

Historical Note

Effective November 1, 1987. Amended effective November 1, 1989 (amendments 287 and 288); November 1, 1994 (amendment 507); November 1, 1998 (amendment 579); November 1, 2000 (amendment 598); November 1, 2002 (amendment 642); November 1, 2004 (amendment 674); November 1, 2005 (amendments 677 and 680); November 1, 2010 (amendment 747); November 1, 2012 (amendments 767 and 770).

§5G1.3. Imposition of a Sentence on a Defendant Subject to an Undischarged Term of Imprisonment or Anticipated State Term of Imprisonment

(a) If the instant offense was committed while the defendant was serving a term of imprisonment (including work release, furlough, or escape status) or after sentencing for, but before commencing service of, such term of imprisonment, the sentence for the instant offense shall be imposed to run consecutively to the undischarged term of imprisonment.

(b) If subsection (a) does not apply, and a term of imprisonment resulted from another offense that is relevant conduct to the instant offense of conviction under the provisions of subsections (a)(1), (a)(2), or (a)(3) of §1B1.3 (Relevant Conduct), the sentence for the instant offense shall be imposed as follows:

(1) the court shall adjust the sentence for any period of imprisonment already served on the undischarged term of imprisonment if the court determines that such period of imprisonment will not be credited to the federal sentence by the Bureau of Prisons; and

(2) the sentence for the instant offense shall be imposed to run concurrently to the remainder of the undischarged term of imprisonment.

(c) If subsection (a) does not apply, and a state term of imprisonment is anticipated to result from another offense that is relevant conduct to the instant offense of conviction under the provisions of subsections (a)(1), (a)(2), or (a)(3) of §1B1.3 (Relevant Conduct), the sentence for the instant offense shall be imposed to run concurrently to the anticipated term of imprisonment.

(d) (Policy Statement) In any other case involving an undischarged term of imprisonment, the sentence for the instant offense may be imposed to run concurrently, partially concurrently, or consecutively to the prior undischarged term of imprisonment to achieve a reasonable punishment for the instant offense.

Commentary

Application Notes:

1. **Consecutive Sentence — Subsection (a) Cases.** Under subsection (a), the court shall impose a consecutive sentence when the instant offense was committed while the defendant was serving an undischarged term of imprisonment or after sentencing for, but before commencing service of, such term of imprisonment.

2. **Application of Subsection (b).—**

(A) **In General.**—Subsection (b) applies in cases in which all of the prior offense is relevant conduct to the instant offense under the provisions of subsection (a)(1), (a)(2), or (a)(3) of §1B1.3 (Relevant Conduct). Cases in which only part of the prior offense is relevant conduct to the instant offense are covered under subsection (d).

(B) **Inapplicability of Subsection (b).**—Subsection (b) does not apply in cases in which the prior offense was not relevant conduct to the instant offense under §1B1.3(a)(1), (a)(2), or (a)(3) (*e.g.*, the prior offense is a prior conviction for which the defendant received an increase under §2L1.2 (Unlawfully Entering or Remaining in the United States), or the prior offense was a crime of violence for which the defendant received an increased base offense level under §2K2.1 (Unlawful Receipt, Possession, or Transportation of Firearms or Ammunition; Prohibited Transactions Involving Firearms or Ammunition)).

(C) **Imposition of Sentence.**—If subsection (b) applies, and the court adjusts the sentence for a period of time already served, the court should note on the Judgment in a Criminal Case Order (i) the applicable subsection (*e.g.*, §5G1.3(b)); (ii) the amount of time by which the sentence is being adjusted; (iii) the undischarged term of imprisonment for which the adjustment is being given; and (iv) that the sentence imposed is a sentence reduction pursuant to §5G1.3(b) for a period of imprisonment that will not be credited by the Bureau of Prisons.

(D) **Example.**—The following is an example in which subsection (b) applies and an adjustment to the sentence is appropriate:

The defendant is convicted of a federal offense charging the sale of 90 grams of cocaine. Under §1B1.3, the defendant is held accountable for the sale of an additional 25 grams of cocaine, an offense for which the defendant has been convicted

and sentenced in state court. The defendant received a nine-month sentence of imprisonment for the state offense and has served six months on that sentence at the time of sentencing on the instant federal offense. The guideline range applicable to the defendant is 12–18 months (Chapter Two offense level of level 16 for sale of 115 grams of cocaine; 3 level reduction for acceptance of responsibility; final offense level of level 13; Criminal History Category I). The court determines that a sentence of 13 months provides the appropriate total punishment. Because the defendant has already served six months on the related state charge as of the date of sentencing on the instant federal offense, a sentence of seven months, imposed to run concurrently with the three months remaining on the defendant's state sentence, achieves this result.

3. **Application of Subsection (c).**—Subsection (c) applies to cases in which the federal court anticipates that, after the federal sentence is imposed, the defendant will be sentenced in state court and serve a state sentence before being transferred to federal custody for federal imprisonment. In such a case, where the other offense is relevant conduct to the instant offense of conviction under the provisions of subsections (a)(1), (a)(2), or (a)(3) of §1B1.3 (Relevant Conduct), the sentence for the instant offense shall be imposed to run concurrently to the anticipated term of imprisonment.

4. **Application of Subsection (d).—**

(A) **In General.**—Under subsection (d), the court may impose a sentence concurrently,

partially concurrently, or consecutively to the undischarged term of imprisonment. In order to achieve a reasonable incremental punishment for the instant offense and avoid unwarranted disparity, the court should consider the following:
(i) the factors set forth in 18 U.S.C. § 3584 (referencing 18 U.S.C. § 3553(a));
(ii) the type (*e.g.*, determinate, indeterminate/parolable) and length of the prior undischarged sentence;
(iii) the time served on the undischarged sentence and the time likely to be served before release;
(iv) the fact that the prior undischarged sentence may have been imposed in state court rather than federal court, or at a different time before the same or different federal court; and
(v) any other circumstance relevant to the determination of an appropriate sentence for the instant offense.

(B) **Partially Concurrent Sentence.**—In some cases under subsection (d), a partially concurrent sentence may achieve most appropriately the desired result. To impose a partially concurrent sentence, the court may provide in the Judgment in a Criminal Case Order that the sentence for the instant offense shall commence on the earlier of (i) when the defendant is released from the prior undischarged sentence; or (ii) on a specified date. This order provides for a fully consecutive sentence if the defendant is released on the undischarged term of imprisonment on or before the date specified in the order, and a partially concurrent sentence if the defendant is not released on the undischarged term of imprisonment by that date.

(C) **Undischarged Terms of Imprisonment Resulting from Revocations of Probation, Parole or Supervised Release.**—Subsection (d) applies in cases in which the defendant was on federal or state probation, parole, or supervised release at the

time of the instant offense and has had such probation, parole, or supervised release revoked. Consistent with the policy set forth in Application Note 4 and subsection (f) of §7B1.3 (Revocation of Probation or Supervised Release), the Commission recommends that the sentence for the instant offense be imposed consecutively to the sentence imposed for the revocation.

(D) **Complex Situations.**—Occasionally, the court may be faced with a complex case in which a defendant may be subject to multiple undischarged terms of imprisonment that seemingly call for the application of different rules. In such a case, the court may exercise its discretion in accordance with subsection (d) to fashion a sentence of appropriate length and structure it to run in any appropriate manner to achieve a reasonable punishment for the instant offense.

(E) **Downward Departure.**—Unlike subsection (b), subsection (d) does not authorize an adjustment of the sentence for the instant offense for a period of imprisonment already served on the undischarged term of imprisonment. However, in an extraordinary case involving an undischarged term of imprisonment under subsection (d), it may be appropriate for the court to downwardly depart. This may occur, for example, in a case in which the defendant has served a very substantial period of imprisonment on an undischarged term of imprisonment that resulted from conduct only partially within the relevant conduct for the instant offense. In such a case, a downward departure may be warranted to ensure that the combined punishment is not increased unduly by the fortuity and timing of separate prosecutions and sentencings. Nevertheless, it is intended that a departure pursuant to this application note result in a sentence that ensures a reasonable incremental punishment for the instant offense of conviction.

To avoid confusion with the Bureau of Prisons' exclusive authority provided under 18 U.S.C. § 3585(b) to grant credit for time served under certain circumstances, the Commission recommends that any downward departure under this application note be clearly stated on the Judgment in a Criminal Case Order as a downward departure pursuant to §5G1.3(d), rather than as a credit for time served.

5. **Downward Departure Provision.**—In the case of a discharged term of imprisonment, a downward departure is not prohibited if the defendant (A) has completed serving a term of imprisonment; and (B) subsection (b) would have provided an adjustment had that completed term of imprisonment been undischarged at the time of sentencing for the instant offense. *See* §5K2.23 (Discharged Terms of Imprisonment).

Background: Federal courts generally "have discretion to select whether the sentences they impose will run concurrently or consecutively with respect to other sentences that they impose, or that have been imposed in other proceedings, including state proceedings." *See Setser v. United States*, 132 S. Ct. 1463, 1468 (2012); 18 U.S.C. § 3584(a). Federal courts also generally have discretion to order that the sentences they impose will run concurrently with or consecutively to other state sentences that are anticipated but not yet imposed. *See Setser*, 132 S. Ct. at 1468. Exercise of that discretion, however, is predicated on the court's consideration of the factors listed in 18 U.S.C. § 3553(a), including any applicable guidelines or policy statements issued by the Sentencing Commission.

Historical Note

Effective November 1, 1987. Amended effective November 1, 1989 (amendment 289); November 1, 1991 (amendment 385); November 1, 1992 (amendment 465); November 1, 1993 (amendment 494); November 1, 1995 (amendment 535); November 1, 2002 (amendment 645); November 1, 2003 (amendment 660); November 1, 2010 (amendment 747); November 1, 2013 (amendment 776).; November 1, 2014 (amendments 782, 787, and 789); November 1, 2016 (amendment 802).

PART H — SPECIFIC OFFENDER CHARACTERISTICS

Introductory Commentary

This Part addresses the relevance of certain specific offender characteristics in sentencing.

The Sentencing Reform Act (the "Act") contains several provisions regarding specific offender characteristics:

First, the Act directs the Commission to ensure that the guidelines and policy statements "are entirely neutral" as to five characteristics – race, sex, national origin, creed, and socioeconomic status. *See* 28 U.S.C. § 994(d).

Second, the Act directs the Commission to consider whether eleven specific offender characteristics, "among others", have any relevance to the nature, extent, place of service, or other aspects of an appropriate sentence, and to take them into account in the guidelines and policy statements only to the extent that they do have relevance. *See* 28 U.S.C. § 994(d).

Third, the Act directs the Commission to ensure that the guidelines and policy statements, in recommending a term of imprisonment or length of a term of imprisonment, reflect the "general inappropriateness" of considering five of those characteristics – education; vocational skills; employment record; family ties and responsibilities; and community ties. *See* 28 U.S.C. § 994(e).

Fourth, the Act also directs the sentencing court, in determining the particular sentence to be imposed, to consider, among other factors, "the history and characteristics of the defendant". *See* 18 U.S.C. § 3553(a)(1).

Specific offender characteristics are taken into account in the guidelines in several ways.

One important specific offender characteristic is the defendant's criminal history, *see* 28 U.S.C. § 994(d)(10), which is taken into account in the guidelines in Chapter Four (Criminal History and Criminal Livelihood). *See* §5H1.8 (Criminal History). Another specific offender characteristic in the guidelines is the degree of dependence upon criminal history for a livelihood, *see* 28 U.S.C. § 994(d)(11), which is taken into account in Chapter Four, Part B (Career Offenders and Criminal Livelihood). *See* §5H1.9 (Dependence upon Criminal Activity for a Livelihood).

Other specific offender characteristics are accounted for elsewhere in this manual. *See, e.g.*, §§2C1.1(a)(1) and 2C1.2(a)(1) (providing alternative base offense levels if the defendant was a public official); 3B1.3 (Abuse of Position of Trust or Use of Special Skill); and 3E1.1 (Acceptance of Responsibility).

The Supreme Court has emphasized that the advisory guideline system should "continue

to move sentencing in Congress' preferred direction, helping to avoid excessive sentencing disparities while maintaining flexibility sufficient to individualize sentences where necessary."
See United States v. Booker, 543 U.S. 220, 264–65 (2005). Although the court must consider "the history and characteristics of the defendant" among other factors, *see* 18 U.S.C. § 3553(a), in order to avoid unwarranted sentencing disparities the court should not give them excessive weight. Generally, the most appropriate use of specific offender characteristics is to consider them not as a reason for a sentence outside the applicable guideline range but for other reasons, such as in determining the sentence within the applicable guideline range, the type of sentence (*e.g.*, probation or imprisonment) within the sentencing options available for the applicable Zone on the Sentencing Table, and various other aspects of an appropriate sentence.
To avoid unwarranted sentencing disparities among defendants with similar records who have been found guilty of similar conduct, *see* 18 U.S.C. § 3553(a)(6), 28 U.S.C. § 991(b)(1)(B), the

guideline range, which reflects the defendant's criminal conduct and the defendant's criminal history, should continue to be "the starting point and the initial benchmark." *Gall v. United States*, 552 U.S. 38, 49 (2007).
Accordingly, the purpose of this Part is to provide sentencing courts with a framework for addressing specific offender characteristics in a reasonably consistent manner. Using such a framework in a uniform manner will help "secure nationwide consistency," *see Gall v. United States*, 552 U.S. 38, 49 (2007), "avoid unwarranted sentencing disparities," *see* 28 U.S.C. § 991(b)(1)(B), 18 U.S.C. § 3553(a)(6), "provide certainty and fairness," *see* 28 U.S.C. § 991(b)(1)(B), and "promote respect for the law," *see* 18 U.S.C. § 3553(a)(2)(A).
This Part allocates specific offender characteristics into three general categories.
In the first category are specific offender characteristics the consideration of which Congress has prohibited (*e.g.*, §5H1.10 (Race, Sex, National Origin, Creed, Religion, and Socio-Economic Status)) or that the Commission has determined should be prohibited.
In the second category are specific offender characteristics that Congress directed the Commission to take into account in the guidelines only to the extent that they have relevance to sentencing. *See* 28 U.S.C. § 994(d). For some of these, the policy statements indicate that these characteristics may be relevant in determining whether a sentence outside the applicable guideline range is warranted (*e.g.*, age; mental and emotional condition; physical condition). These characteristics may warrant a sentence outside the applicable guideline range if the characteristic, individually or in combination with other such characteristics, is present to an unusual degree and distinguishes the case from the typical cases covered by the guidelines. These specific offender characteristics also may be considered for other reasons, such as in determining the sentence within the applicable guideline range, the type of sentence (*e.g.*, probation or imprisonment) within the sentencing options available for the applicable Zone on the Sentencing Table, and various other aspects of an appropriate sentence.
In the third category are specific offender characteristics that Congress directed the Commission to ensure are reflected in the guidelines and policy statements as generally inappropriate in recommending a term of imprisonment or length of a term of imprisonment.
See 28 U.S.C. § 994(e). The policy statements indicate that these characteristics are not ordinarily relevant to the determination of whether a sentence should be outside the applicable guideline range. Unless expressly stated, this does not mean that the Commission views such circumstances as necessarily inappropriate to the determination of the sentence within the applicable guideline range, the type of sentence (*e.g.*, probation or imprisonment) within the sentencing options available for the applicable Zone on the Sentencing Table, or various other aspects of an appropriate sentence (*e.g.*, the appropriate conditions of probation or supervised release). Furthermore, although these circumstances are not ordinarily relevant to the determination of whether a sentence should be outside the applicable guideline range, they may be relevant to this determination in exceptional cases. They also may be relevant if a combination of such circumstances makes the case an exceptional one, but only if each such circumstance is identified as an affirmative ground for departure and is present in the case to a substantial degree. *See* §5K2.0 (Grounds for Departure).

As with the other provisions in this manual, these policy statements "are evolutionary in nature". *See* Chapter One, Part A, Subpart 2 (Continuing Evolution and Role of the Guidelines); 28 U.S.C. § 994(o). The Commission expects, and the Sentencing Reform Act contemplates, that continuing research, experience, and analysis will result in modifications and revisions. The nature, extent, and significance of specific offender characteristics can involve a range of considerations. The Commission will continue to provide information to the courts on

the relevance of specific offender characteristics in sentencing, as the Sentencing Reform Act contemplates. *See, e.g.*, 28 U.S.C. § 995(a)(12)(A) (the Commission serves as a "clearinghouse and information center" on federal sentencing). Among other things, this may include information on the use of specific offender characteristics, individually and in combination, in determining the sentence to be imposed (including, where available, information on rates of use, criteria for use, and reasons for use); the relationship, if any, between specific offender characteristics and (A) the "forbidden factors" specified in 28 U.S.C. § 994(d) and (B) the "discouraged factors" specified in 28 U.S.C. § 994(e); and the relationship, if any, between specific offender characteristics and the statutory purposes of sentencing.

Historical Note

Effective November 1, 1987. Amended effective November 1, 1990 (amendment 357); November 1, 1991 (amendment 386); November 1, 1994 (amendment 508); October 27, 2003 (amendment 651); November 1, 2010 (amendment 739).

§5H1.1. Age (Policy Statement)

Age (including youth) may be relevant in determining whether a departure is warranted, if considerations based on age, individually or in combination with other offender characteristics, are present to an unusual degree and distinguish the case from the typical cases covered by the guidelines. Age may be a reason to depart downward in a case in which the defendant is elderly and infirm and where a form of punishment such as home confinement might be equally efficient as and less costly than incarceration. Physical condition, which may be related to age, is addressed at §5H1.4 (Physical Condition, Including Drug or Alcohol Dependence or Abuse; Gambling Addiction).

Historical Note

Effective November 1, 1987. Amended effective November 1, 1991 (amendment 386); November 1, 1993 (amendment 475); October 27, 2003 (amendment 651); November 1, 2004 (amendment 674); November 1, 2010 (amendment 739).

§5H1.2. Education and Vocational Skills (Policy Statement)

Education and vocational skills are not ordinarily relevant in determining whether a departure is warranted, but the extent to which a defendant may have misused special training or education to facilitate criminal activity is an express guideline factor. *See* §3B1.3 (Abuse of Position of Trust or Use of Special Skill).

Education and vocational skills may be relevant in determining the conditions of probation or supervised release for rehabilitative purposes, for public protection by restricting activities that allow for the utilization of a certain skill, or in determining the appropriate type of community service.

Historical Note

Effective November 1, 1987. Amended effective November 1, 1991 (amendment 386); November 1, 2004 (amendment 674).

§5H1.3. Mental and Emotional Conditions (Policy Statement)

Mental and emotional conditions may be relevant in determining whether a departure is warranted, if such conditions, individually or in combination with other offender characteristics, are present to an unusual degree and distinguish the case from the typical cases covered by the guidelines. *See also* Chapter Five, Part K, Subpart 2 (Other Grounds for Departure).

In certain cases a downward departure may be appropriate to accomplish a specific treatment purpose. *See* §5C1.1, Application Note 6.

Mental and emotional conditions may be relevant in determining the conditions of probation or supervised release; *e.g.*, participation in a mental health program (*see* §§5B1.3(d)(5) and 5D1.3(d)(5)).

Historical Note

Effective November 1, 1987. Amended effective November 1, 1991 (amendment 386); November 1, 1997 (amendment 569); November 1, 2004 (amendment 674); November 1, 2010 (amendment 739).

§5H1.4. Physical Condition, Including Drug or Alcohol Dependence or Abuse; Gambling Addiction (Policy Statement)

Physical condition or appearance, including physique, may be relevant in determining whether a departure is warranted, if the condition or appearance, individually or in combination with other offender characteristics, is present to an unusual degree and distinguishes the case from the typical cases covered by the guidelines. An extraordinary physical impairment may be a reason to depart downward; *e.g.*, in the case of a seriously infirm defendant, home detention may be as efficient as, and less costly than, imprisonment.

Drug or alcohol dependence or abuse ordinarily is not a reason for a downward departure. Substance abuse is highly correlated to an increased propensity to commit crime. Due to this increased risk, it is highly recommended that a defendant who is incarcerated also be sentenced to supervised release with a requirement that the defendant participate in an appropriate substance abuse program (*see* §5D1.3(d)(4)). If

participation in a substance abuse program is required, the length of supervised release should take into account the length of time necessary for the probation office to judge the success of the program.

In certain cases a downward departure may be appropriate to accomplish a specific treatment purpose. *See* §5C1.1, Application Note 6.

In a case in which a defendant who is a substance abuser is sentenced to probation, it is strongly recommended that the conditions of probation contain a requirement that the defendant participate in an appropriate substance abuse program (*see* §5B1.3(d)(4)).

Addiction to gambling is not a reason for a downward departure.

Historical Note

Effective November 1, 1987. Amended effective November 1, 1991 (amendment 386); November 1, 1997 (amendment 569); October 27, 2003 (amendment 651); November 1, 2010 (amendment 739).

§5H1.5. Employment Record (Policy Statement)

Employment record is not ordinarily relevant in determining whether a departure is warranted.

Employment record may be relevant in determining the conditions of probation or supervised release (*e.g.*, the appropriate hours of home detention).

Historical
Note
Effective November 1, 1987. Amended effective November 1, 1991 (amendment 386); November 1, 2004 (amendment 674).

§5H1.6. Family Ties and Responsibilities (Policy Statement)

In sentencing a defendant convicted of an offense other than an offense described in the following paragraph, family ties and responsibilities are not ordinarily relevant in determining whether a departure may be warranted.

In sentencing a defendant convicted of an offense involving a minor victim under section 1201, an offense under section 1591, or an offense under chapter 71, 109A, 110, or 117, of title 18, United States Code, family ties and responsibilities and community ties are not relevant in determining whether a sentence should be below the applicable guideline range.

Family responsibilities that are complied with may be relevant to the determination of the amount of restitution or fine.

Commentary

Application Note:

1. **Circumstances to Consider.—**

(A) **In General.**—In determining whether a departure is warranted under this policy statement, the court shall consider the following non-exhaustive list of circumstances:

(i) The seriousness of the offense.

(ii) The involvement in the offense, if any, of members of the defendant's family.

(iii) The danger, if any, to members of the defendant's family as a result of the offense.

(B) **Departures Based on Loss of Caretaking or Financial Support.**—A departure under this policy statement based on the loss of caretaking or financial support of the defendant's family requires, in addition to the court's consideration of the non-exhaustive list of circumstances in subdivision (A), the presence of the following circumstances:

(i) The defendant's service of a sentence within the applicable guideline range will cause a substantial, direct, and specific loss of essential caretaking, or essential financial support, to the defendant's family.

(ii) The loss of caretaking or financial support substantially exceeds the harm ordinarily incident to incarceration for a similarly situated defendant. For example, the fact that the defendant's family might incur some degree of financial hardship or suffer to some extent from the absence of a parent through incarceration is not in itself sufficient as a basis for departure because such hardship or suffering is of a sort ordinarily incident to incarceration.

(iii) The loss of caretaking or financial support is one for which no effective remedial or ameliorative programs reasonably are available, making the defendant's caretaking or financial support irreplaceable to the defendant's family.

(iv) The departure effectively will address the loss of caretaking or financial support.

Background: Section 401(b)(4) of Public Law 108–21 directly amended this policy statement to add the second paragraph, effective April 30, 2003.

Historical
Note
Effective November 1, 1987. Amended effective November 1, 1991 (amendment 386); April 30, 2003 (amendment 649); October 27, 2003 (amendment 651); November 1, 2004 (amendment 674).

§5H1.7. Role in the Offense (Policy Statement)

A defendant's role in the offense is relevant in determining the applicable guideline range (*see* Chapter Three, Part B (Role in the Offense)) but is not a basis for departing from that range (*see* subsection (d) of §5K2.0 (Grounds for Departures)).

Historical
Note
Effective November 1, 1987. Amended effective October 27, 2003 (amendment 651).

§5H1.8. Criminal History (Policy Statement)

A defendant's criminal history is relevant in determining the applicable criminal history category. *See* Chapter Four (Criminal History and Criminal Livelihood). For grounds of departure based on the defendant's criminal history, *see* §4A1.3 (Departures Based on Inadequacy of Criminal History Category).

Historical
Note
Effective November 1, 1987. Amended effective October 27, 2003 (amendment 651).

§5H1.9. Dependence upon Criminal Activity for a Livelihood (Policy Statement)

The degree to which a defendant depends upon criminal activity for a livelihood is relevant in determining the appropriate sentence. *See* Chapter Four, Part B (Career Offenders and Criminal Livelihood).

Historical
Note
Effective November 1, 1987.

§5H1.10. Race, Sex, National Origin, Creed, Religion, and Socio-Economic Status (Policy Statement)

These factors are not relevant in the determination of a sentence.

Historical
Note
Effective November 1, 1987.

§5H1.11. Military, Civic, Charitable, or Public Service; Employment-Related Contributions; Record of Prior Good Works (Policy Statement)

Military service may be relevant in determining whether a departure is warranted, if the military service, individually or in combination with other offender characteristics, is present to an unusual degree and distinguishes the case from the typical cases covered by the guidelines.

Civic, charitable, or public service; employment-related contributions; and similar prior good works are not ordinarily relevant in determining whether a departure is warranted.

Historical
Note
Effective November 1, 1991 (amendment 386). Amended effective November 1, 2004 (amendment 674); November 1, 2010 (amendment 739).

§5H1.12. Lack of Guidance as a Youth and Similar Circumstances (Policy Statement)

Lack of guidance as a youth and similar circumstances indicating a disadvantaged upbringing are not relevant grounds in determining whether a departure is warranted.

Historical
Note
Effective November 1, 1992 (amendment 466). Amended effective November 1, 2004 (amendment 674).

PART I — [NOT USED]

PART J — RELIEF FROM DISABILITY
Historical
Note
Effective November 1, 1987. Amended effective June 15, 1988 (amendment 55).
§5J1.1. Relief from Disability Pertaining to Convicted Persons Prohibited from Holding Certain Positions (Policy Statement)
A collateral consequence of conviction of certain crimes described in 29 U.S.C. §§ 504 and 1111 is the prohibition of convicted persons from service and employment with labor unions, employer associations, employee pension and welfare benefit plans, and as labor relations consultants in the private sector. A convicted person's prohibited service or employment in such capacities without having been granted one of the following three statutory procedures of administrative or judicial relief is subject to criminal prosecution. First, a disqualified person whose citizenship rights have been fully restored to him or her in the jurisdiction of conviction, following the revocation of such rights as a result of the disqualifying conviction, is relieved of the disability. Second, a disqualified person convicted after October 12, 1984, may petition the sentencing court to reduce the statutory length of disability (thirteen years after date of sentencing or release from imprisonment, whichever is later) to a lesser period (not less than three years after date of conviction or release from imprisonment, whichever is later). Third, a disqualified person may petition either the United States Parole Commission or a United States District Court judge to exempt his or her service or employment in a particular prohibited capacity pursuant to the procedures set forth in 29 U.S.C. §§ 504(a)(B) and 1111(a)(B). In the case of a person convicted of a disqualifying crime committed before November 1, 1987, the United States Parole Commission will continue to process such exemption applications.
In the case of a person convicted of a disqualifying crime committed on or after November 1, 1987, however, a petition for exemption from disability must be directed to a United States District Court. If the petitioner was convicted of a disqualifying federal offense, the petition is directed to the sentencing judge. If the petitioner was convicted of a disqualifying state or local offense, the petition is directed to the United States District Court for the district in which the offense was committed. In such cases, relief shall not be given to aid rehabilitation, but may be granted only following a clear demonstration by the convicted person that he or she has been rehabilitated since commission of the disqualifying crime and can therefore be trusted not to endanger the organization in the position for which he or she seeks relief from disability.
Historical
Note
Effective November 1, 1987. Amended effective June 15, 1988 (amendment 56).

PART K — DEPARTURES
1. SUBSTANTIAL ASSISTANCE TO AUTHORITIES

§5K1.1. Substantial Assistance to Authorities (Policy Statement)

Upon motion of the government stating that the defendant has provided substantial assistance in the investigation or prosecution of another person who has committed an offense, the court may depart from the guidelines.

(a) The appropriate reduction shall be determined by the court for reasons stated that may include, but are not limited to, consideration of the following:

(1) the court's evaluation of the significance and usefulness of the defendant's assistance, taking into consideration the government's evaluation of the assistance rendered;

(2) the truthfulness, completeness, and reliability of any information or testimony provided by the defendant;

(3) the nature and extent of the defendant's assistance;

(4) any injury suffered, or any danger or risk of injury to the defendant or his family resulting from his assistance;

(5) the timeliness of the defendant's assistance.

Commentary

Application Notes:

1. Under circumstances set forth in 18 U.S.C. § 3553(e) and 28 U.S.C. § 994(n), as amended, substantial assistance in the investigation or prosecution of another person who has committed an offense may justify a sentence below a statutorily required minimum sentence.

2. The sentencing reduction for assistance to authorities shall be considered independently of any reduction for acceptance of responsibility. Substantial assistance is directed to the investigation and prosecution of criminal activities by persons other than the defendant, while acceptance of responsibility is directed to the defendant's affirmative recognition of responsibility for his own conduct.

3. Substantial weight should be given to the government's evaluation of the extent of the defendant's assistance, particularly where the extent and value of the assistance are difficult to ascertain.

Background: A defendant's assistance to authorities in the investigation of criminal activities has been recognized in practice and by statute as a mitigating sentencing factor. The nature, extent, and significance of assistance can involve a broad spectrum of conduct that must be evaluated by the court on an individual basis. Latitude is, therefore, afforded the sentencing judge to reduce a sentence based upon variable relevant factors, including those listed above. The sentencing judge must, however, state the reasons for reducing a sentence under this section. 18 U.S.C. § 3553(c). The court may elect to provide its reasons to the defendant *in camera* and in writing under seal for the safety of the defendant or to avoid disclosure of an ongoing investigation.

Historical
Note
Effective November 1, 1987. Amended effective November 1, 1989 (amendment 290).

§5K1.2. Refusal to Assist (Policy Statement)

A defendant's refusal to assist authorities in the investigation of other persons may not be considered as an aggravating sentencing factor.

Historical
Note
Effective November 1, 1987. Amended effective November 1, 1989 (amendment 291).

* * * * *

2. OTHER GROUNDS FOR DEPARTURE

Historical
Note
Effective November 1, 1987. Amended effective November 1, 1990 (amendment 358).

§5K2.0. Grounds for Departure (Policy Statement)

(a) UPWARD DEPARTURES IN GENERAL AND DOWNWARD DEPARTURES IN CRIMINAL CASES OTHER THAN CHILD CRIMES AND SEXUAL OFFENSES.—

(1) IN GENERAL.—The sentencing court may depart from the applicable guideline range if—

(A) in the case of offenses other than child crimes and sexual offenses, the court finds, pursuant to 18 U.S.C. § 3553(b)(1), that there exists an aggravating or mitigating circumstance; or

(B) in the case of child crimes and sexual offenses, the court finds, pursuant to 18 U.S.C. § 3553(b)(2)(A)(i), that there exists an aggravating circumstance,

of a kind, or to a degree, not adequately taken into consideration by the Sentencing Commission in formulating the guidelines that, in order to advance the objectives set forth in 18 U.S.C. § 3553(a)(2), should result in a sentence different from that described.

(2) DEPARTURES BASED ON CIRCUMSTANCES OF A KIND NOT ADEQUATELY TAKEN INTO CONSIDERATION.—

(A) IDENTIFIED CIRCUMSTANCES.—This subpart (Chapter Five, Part K, Subpart 2 (Other Grounds for Departure)) identifies some of the circumstances that the Commission may have not adequately taken into consideration in determining the applicable guideline range (*e.g.*, as a specific offense characteristic or other adjustment). If any such circumstance is present in the case and has not adequately been taken into consideration in determining the applicable guideline range, a departure consistent with 18 U.S.C. § 3553(b) and the provisions of this subpart may be warranted.

(B) UNIDENTIFIED CIRCUMSTANCES.—A departure may be warranted in the exceptional case in which there is present a circumstance that the Commission has not identified in the guidelines but that nevertheless is relevant to determining the appropriate sentence.

(3) DEPARTURES BASED ON CIRCUMSTANCES PRESENT TO A DEGREE NOT ADEQUATELY TAKEN INTO CONSIDERATION.—A departure may be warranted in an exceptional case, even though the circumstance that forms the basis for the departure is taken into consideration in determining the guideline range, if the court determines that such circumstance is present in the offense to a degree substantially in excess of, or substantially below, that which ordinarily is involved in that kind of offense.

(4) DEPARTURES BASED ON NOT ORDINARILY RELEVANT OFFENDER CHARACTERISTICS AND OTHER CIRCUMSTANCES.—An offender characteristic or other circumstance identified in Chapter Five, Part H (Offender Characteristics) or elsewhere in the guidelines

as not ordinarily relevant in determining whether a departure is warranted may be relevant to this determination

only if such offender characteristic or other circumstance is present to an exceptional degree.

(b) DOWNWARD DEPARTURES IN CHILD CRIMES AND SEXUAL OFFENSES.— Under 18 U.S.C. § 3553(b)(2)(A)(ii), the sentencing court may impose a sentence below the range established by the applicable guidelines only if the court finds that there exists a mitigating circumstance of a kind, or to a degree, that—

(1) has been affirmatively and specifically identified as a permissible ground of downward departure in the sentencing guidelines or policy statements issued under section 994(a) of title 28, United States Code, taking account of any amendments to such sentencing guidelines or policy statements by act of Congress;

(2) has not adequately been taken into consideration by the Sentencing Commission in formulating the guidelines; and

(3) should result in a sentence different from that described.

The grounds enumerated in this Part K of Chapter Five are the sole grounds that have been affirmatively and specifically identified as a permissible ground of downward departure in these sentencing guidelines and policy statements. Thus, notwithstanding any other reference to authority to depart downward elsewhere in this Sentencing Manual, a ground of downward departure has not been affirmatively and specifically identified as a permissible ground of downward departure within the meaning of section 3553(b)(2) unless it is expressly enumerated in this Part K as a ground upon which a downward departure may be granted.

(c) LIMITATION ON DEPARTURES BASED ON MULTIPLE CIRCUMSTANCES.— The court may depart from the applicable guideline range based on a combination of two or more offender characteristics or other circumstances, none of which independently is sufficient to provide a basis for departure, only if—

(1) such offender characteristics or other circumstances, taken together, make the case an exceptional one; and

(2) each such offender characteristic or other circumstance is—

(A) present to a substantial degree; and

(B) identified in the guidelines as a permissible ground for departure, even if such offender characteristic or other circumstance is not ordinarily relevant to a determination of whether a departure is warranted.

(d) PROHIBITED DEPARTURES.—Notwithstanding subsections (a) and (b) of this policy statement, or any other provision in the guidelines, the court may not depart from the applicable guideline range based on

any of the following circumstances:
(1) Any circumstance specifically prohibited as a ground for departure in §§5H1.10 (Race, Sex, National Origin, Creed, Religion, and Socio-Economic Status), 5H1.12 (Lack of Guidance as a Youth and Similar Circumstances), the last sentence of 5H1.4 (Physical Condition, Including Drug or Alcohol Dependence or Abuse; Gambling Addiction), and the last sentence of 5K2.12 (Coercion and Duress).
(2) The defendant's acceptance of responsibility for the offense, which may be taken into account only under §3E1.1 (Acceptance of Responsibility).
(3) The defendant's aggravating or mitigating role in the offense, which may be taken into account only under §3B1.1 (Aggravating Role) or §3B1.2 (Mitigating Role), respectively.
(4) The defendant's decision, in and of itself, to plead guilty to the offense or to enter a plea agreement with respect to the offense (*i.e.*, a departure may not be based merely on the fact that the defendant decided to plead guilty or to enter into a plea agreement, but a departure may be based on justifiable, non-prohibited reasons as part of a sentence that is recommended, or agreed to, in the plea agreement and accepted by the court. *See* §6B1.2 (Standards for Acceptance of Plea Agreement).
(5) The defendant's fulfillment of restitution obligations only to the extent required by law including the guidelines (*i.e.*, a departure may not be based on unexceptional efforts to remedy the harm caused by the offense).
(6) Any other circumstance specifically prohibited as a ground for departure in the guidelines.
(e) REQUIREMENT OF SPECIFIC WRITTEN REASONS FOR DEPARTURE.—If the court departs from the applicable guideline range, it shall state, pursuant to 18 U.S.C. § 3553(c), its specific reasons for departure in open court at the time of sentencing and, with limited exception in

the case of statements received *in camera*, shall state those reasons with specificity in the statement of reasons form.

Commentary

Application Notes:

1. **Definitions.**—For purposes of this policy statement:

"***Circumstance***" includes, as appropriate, an offender characteristic or any other offense factor.

"***Depart***", "***departure***", "***downward departure***", and "***upward departure***" have the meaning given those terms in Application Note 1 of the Commentary to §1B1.1 (Application Instructions).

2. **Scope of this Policy Statement.**—

(A) **Departures Covered by this Policy Statement.**—This policy statement covers departures from the applicable guideline range based on offense characteristics or offender characteristics of a kind, or to a degree, not adequately taken into consideration in determining that range. *See* 18 U.S.C. § 3553(b).

Subsection (a) of this policy statement applies to upward departures in all cases

covered by the guidelines and to downward departures in all such cases except for downward departures in child crimes and sexual offenses.
Subsection (b) of this policy statement applies only to downward departures in child crimes and sexual offenses.
(B) **Departures Covered by Other Guidelines.**—This policy statement does not cover the following departures, which are addressed elsewhere in the guidelines: (i) departures based on the defendant's criminal history (*see* Chapter Four (Criminal History and Criminal Livelihood), particularly §4A1.3 (Departures Based on Inadequacy of Criminal History Category)); (ii) departures based on the defendant's substantial assistance to the authorities (*see* §5K1.1 (Substantial Assistance to Authorities)); and (iii) departures based on early disposition programs (*see* §5K3.1 (Early Disposition Programs)).
3. **Kinds and Expected Frequency of Departures under Subsection (a).**—As set forth in subsection (a), there generally are two kinds of departures from the guidelines based on offense characteristics and/or offender characteristics: (A) departures based on circumstances of a kind not adequately taken into consideration in the guidelines; and (B) departures based on circumstances that are present to a degree not adequately taken into consideration in the guidelines.
(A) **Departures Based on Circumstances of a Kind Not Adequately Taken into Account in Guidelines.**—Subsection (a)(2) authorizes the court to depart if there exists an aggravating or a mitigating circumstance in a case under 18 U.S.C. § 3553(b)(1), or an aggravating circumstance in a case under 18 U.S.C. § 3553(b)(2)(A)(i), of a kind not adequately taken into consideration in the guidelines.
(i) **Identified Circumstances.**—This subpart (Chapter Five, Part K, Subpart 2) identifies several circumstances that the Commission may have not

adequately taken into consideration in setting the offense level for certain cases. Offense guidelines in Chapter Two (Offense Conduct) and adjustments in Chapter Three (Adjustments) sometimes identify circumstances the Commission may have not adequately taken into consideration in setting the offense level for offenses covered by those guidelines. If the offense guideline in Chapter Two or an adjustment in Chapter Three does not adequately take that circumstance into consideration in setting the offense level for the offense, and only to the extent not adequately taken into consideration, a departure based on that circumstance may be warranted.
(ii) **Unidentified Circumstances.**—A case may involve circumstances, in addition to those identified by the guidelines, that have not adequately been taken into consideration by the Commission, and the presence of any such circumstance may warrant departure from the guidelines in that case. However, inasmuch as the Commission has continued to monitor and refine the guidelines since their inception to take into consideration relevant circumstances in sentencing, it is expected that departures based on such unidentified circumstances will occur rarely and only in exceptional cases.
(B) **Departures Based on Circumstances Present to a Degree Not Adequately Taken into Consideration in Guidelines.**—
(i) **In General.**—Subsection (a)(3) authorizes the court to depart if there exists an aggravating or a mitigating circumstance in a case under 18 U.S.C. § 3553(b)(1), or an aggravating circumstance in a case under 18 U.S.C. § 3553(b)(2)(A)(i), to a degree not adequately taken into consideration in the guidelines. However, inasmuch as the Commission has continued to monitor and refine the guidelines since their inception to determine the most appropriate weight to be accorded the mitigating and aggravating circumstances specified in the guidelines, it is expected that departures based on the weight accorded to any such circumstance will occur rarely and only in exceptional

cases.
(ii) **Examples.**—As set forth in subsection (a)(3), if the applicable offense guideline and adjustments take into consideration a circumstance identified in this subpart, departure is warranted only if the circumstance is present to a degree substantially in excess of that which ordinarily is involved in the offense. Accordingly, a departure pursuant to §5K2.7 for the disruption of a governmental function would have to be substantial to warrant departure from the guidelines when the applicable offense guideline is bribery or obstruction of justice. When the guideline covering the mailing of injurious articles is applicable, however, and the offense caused disruption of a governmental function, departure from the applicable guideline range more readily would be appropriate. Similarly, physical injury would not warrant departure from the guidelines when the robbery offense guideline is applicable because the robbery guideline includes a specific adjustment based on the extent of any injury. However, because the robbery guideline does not deal with injury to more than one victim, departure may be warranted if several persons were injured.
(C) **Departures Based on Circumstances Identified as Not Ordinarily Relevant.**—Because certain circumstances are specified in the guidelines as not ordinarily relevant to sentencing (*see, e.g.*, Chapter Five, Part H (Specific Offender Characteristics)), a departure based on any one of such circumstances should occur only in exceptional cases, and only if the circumstance is present in the case to an

exceptional degree. If two or more of such circumstances each is present in the case to a substantial degree, however, and taken together make the case an exceptional one, the court may consider whether a departure would be warranted pursuant to subsection (c). Departures based on a combination of not ordinarily relevant circumstances that are present to a substantial degree should occur extremely rarely and only in exceptional cases.
In addition, as required by subsection (e), each circumstance forming the basis for a departure described in this subdivision shall be stated with specificity in the statement of reasons form.
4. **Downward Departures in Child Crimes and Sexual Offenses.**—
(A) **Definition.**—For purposes of this policy statement, the term "***child crimes and sexual offenses***" means offenses under any of the following: 18 U.S.C. § 1201 (involving a minor victim), 18 U.S.C. § 1591, or chapter 71, 109A, 110, or 117 of title 18, United States Code.
(B) **Standard for Departure.**—
(i) **Requirement of Affirmative and Specific Identification of Departure Ground.**—The standard for a downward departure in child crimes and sexual offenses differs from the standard for other departures under this policy statement in that it includes a requirement, set forth in 18 U.S.C. § 3553(b)(2)(A)(ii)(I) and subsection (b)(1) of this guideline, that any mitigating circumstance that forms the basis for such a downward departure be affirmatively and specifically identified as a ground for downward departure in this part (*i.e.*, Chapter Five, Part K).
(ii) **Application of Subsection (b)(2).**—The commentary in Application Note 3 of this policy statement, except for the commentary in Application Note 3(A)(ii) relating to unidentified circumstances, shall apply to the court's determination of whether a case meets the requirement, set forth in subsection 18 U.S.C. § 3553(b)(2)(A)(ii)(II) and subsection (b)(2) of this policy statement, that the mitigating circumstance forming the basis for a downward departure in child crimes and sexual offenses be of kind, or to a degree, not adequately taken into consideration by the Commission.
5. **Departures Based on Plea Agreements.**—Subsection (d)(4) prohibits a downward departure

based only on the defendant's decision, in and of itself, to plead guilty to the offense or to enter a plea agreement with respect to the offense. Even though a departure may not be based merely on the fact that the defendant agreed to plead guilty or enter a plea agreement, a departure may be based on justifiable, non-prohibited reasons for departure as part of a sentence that is recommended, or agreed to, in the plea agreement and accepted by the court. *See* §6B1.2 (Standards for Acceptance of Plea Agreements). In cases in which the court departs based on such reasons as set forth in the plea agreement, the court must state the reasons for departure with specificity in the statement of reasons form, as required by subsection (e).

Background: This policy statement sets forth the standards for departing from the applicable guideline range based on offense and offender characteristics of a kind, or to a degree, not adequately considered by the Commission. Circumstances the Commission has determined are not ordinarily relevant to determining whether a departure is warranted or are prohibited as bases for departure are addressed in Chapter Five, Part H (Offender Characteristics) and in

this policy statement. Other departures, such as those based on the defendant's criminal history, the defendant's substantial assistance to authorities, and early disposition programs, are addressed elsewhere in the guidelines.

As acknowledged by Congress in the Sentencing Reform Act and by the Commission when the first set of guidelines was promulgated, "it is difficult to prescribe a single set of guidelines that encompasses the vast range of human conduct potentially relevant to a sentencing decision." (*See* Chapter One, Part A). Departures, therefore, perform an integral function in the sentencing guideline system. Departures permit courts to impose an appropriate sentence in the exceptional case in which mechanical application of the guidelines would fail to achieve the statutory purposes and goals of sentencing. Departures also help maintain "sufficient flexibility to permit individualized sentences when warranted by mitigating or aggravating factors not taken into account in the establishment of general sentencing practices." 28 U.S.C. § 991(b)(1)(B). By monitoring when courts depart from the guidelines and by analyzing their stated reasons for doing so, along with appellate cases reviewing these departures, the Commission can further refine the guidelines to specify more precisely when departures should and should not be permitted.

As reaffirmed in the Prosecutorial Remedies and Other Tools to end the Exploitation of Children Today Act of 2003 (the "PROTECT Act", Public Law 108–21), circumstances warranting departure should be rare. Departures were never intended to permit sentencing courts to substitute their policy judgments for those of Congress and the Sentencing Commission. Departure in such circumstances would produce unwarranted sentencing disparity, which the Sentencing Reform Act was designed to avoid.

In order for appellate courts to fulfill their statutory duties under 18 U.S.C. § 3742 and for the Commission to fulfill its ongoing responsibility to refine the guidelines in light of information it receives on departures, it is essential that sentencing courts state with specificity the reasons for departure, as required by the PROTECT Act.

This policy statement, including its commentary, was substantially revised, effective October 27, 2003, in response to directives contained in the PROTECT Act, particularly the directive in section 401(m) of that Act to—

"(1) review the grounds of downward departure that are authorized by the sentencing guidelines, policy statements, and official commentary of the Sentencing Commission; and

(2) promulgate, pursuant to section 994 of title 28, United States Code—

(A) appropriate amendments to the sentencing guidelines, policy statements, and official commentary to ensure that the incidence of downward departures is substantially reduced;

(B) a policy statement authorizing a departure pursuant to an early disposition program; and

(C) any other conforming amendments to the sentencing guidelines, policy statements, and official commentary of the Sentencing Commission necessitated by the Act, including a revision of . . . section 5K2.0".

The substantial revision of this policy statement in response to the PROTECT Act was intended to refine the standards applicable to departures while giving due regard for concepts, such as the "heartland", that have evolved in departure jurisprudence over time.

Section 401(b)(1) of the PROTECT Act directly amended this policy statement to add subsection (b), effective April 30, 2003.

Historical
Note

Effective November 1, 1987. Amended effective June 15, 1988 (amendment 57); November 1, 1990 (amendment 358); November 1, 1994 (amendment 508); November 1, 1997 (amendment 561); November 1, 1998 (amendment 585); April 30, 2003 (amendment 649); October 27, 2003 (amendment 651); November 1, 2008 (amendment 725); November 1, 2010 (amendment 739); November 1, 2011 (amendment 757); November 1, 2012 (amendment 770).

§5K2.1. Death (Policy Statement)

If death resulted, the court may increase the sentence above the authorized guideline range.

Loss of life does not automatically suggest a sentence at or near the statutory maximum. The sentencing judge must give consideration to matters that would normally distinguish among levels of homicide, such as the defendant's state of mind and the degree of planning or preparation. Other appropriate factors are whether multiple deaths resulted, and the means by which life was taken. The extent of the increase should depend on the dangerousness of the defendant's conduct, the extent to which death or serious injury was intended or knowingly risked, and the extent to which the offense level for the offense of conviction, as determined by the other Chapter Two guidelines, already reflects the risk of personal injury. For example, a substantial increase may be appropriate if the death was intended or knowingly risked or if the underlying offense was one for which base offense levels do not reflect an allowance for the risk of personal injury, such as fraud.

Historical
Note

Effective November 1, 1987.

§5K2.2. Physical Injury (Policy Statement)

If significant physical injury resulted, the court may increase the sentence above the authorized guideline range. The extent of the increase ordinarily should depend on the extent of the injury, the degree to which it may prove permanent, and the extent to which the injury was intended or knowingly risked. When the victim suffers a major, permanent disability and when such injury was intentionally inflicted, a substantial departure may be appropriate. If the injury is less serious or if the defendant (though criminally negligent) did not knowingly create the risk of harm, a less substantial departure would be indicated. In general, the same considerations apply as in §5K2.1.

Historical
Note

Effective November 1, 1987.

§5K2.3. Extreme Psychological Injury (Policy Statement)

If a victim or victims suffered psychological injury much more serious than that normally resulting from commission of the offense, the court may increase the sentence above the authorized guideline range. The extent of the increase ordinarily should depend on the severity of the psychological injury and the extent to which the injury was intended or knowingly risked.

Normally, psychological injury would be sufficiently severe to warrant application of this adjustment only when there is a substantial impairment of the intellectual, psychological, emotional, or behavioral functioning of a victim, when the impairment is likely to be of an extended or continuous duration, and when the impairment manifests itself by physical or psychological symptoms or by changes in behavior patterns. The court should consider the extent to which such harm was likely, given the nature of the defendant's conduct.

Historical
Note
Effective November 1, 1987.

§5K2.4. Abduction or Unlawful Restraint (Policy Statement)

If a person was abducted, taken hostage, or unlawfully restrained to facilitate commission of the offense or to facilitate the escape from the scene of the crime, the court may increase the sentence above the authorized guideline range.

Historical
Note
Effective November 1, 1987.

§5K2.5. Property Damage or Loss (Policy Statement)

If the offense caused property damage or loss not taken into account within the guidelines, the court may increase the sentence above the authorized guideline range. The extent of the increase ordinarily should depend on the extent to which the harm was intended or knowingly risked and on the extent to which the harm to property is more serious than other harm caused or risked by the conduct relevant to the offense of conviction.

Historical
Note
Effective November 1, 1987.

§5K2.6. Weapons and Dangerous Instrumentalities (Policy Statement)

If a weapon or dangerous instrumentality was used or possessed in the commission of the offense the court may increase the sentence above the authorized guideline range. The extent of the increase ordinarily should depend on the dangerousness of the weapon, the manner in which it was used, and the extent to which its use endangered others. The discharge of a firearm might warrant a substantial sentence increase.

Historical
Note
Effective November 1, 1987.

§5K2.7. Disruption of Governmental Function (Policy Statement)

If the defendant's conduct resulted in a significant disruption of a governmental function, the court may increase the sentence above the authorized guideline range to reflect the nature and extent of the disruption and the importance of the governmental function affected. Departure from the guidelines ordinarily would not be justified when the offense of conviction is an offense such as bribery or obstruction of justice; in such cases interference with a governmental function is inherent in the offense, and unless the circumstances are unusual the guidelines will reflect the appropriate punishment for such interference.

Historical
Note
Effective November 1, 1987.

§5K2.8. Extreme Conduct (Policy Statement)

If the defendant's conduct was unusually heinous, cruel, brutal, or degrading to the victim, the court may increase the sentence above the guideline range to reflect the nature of the conduct. Examples of extreme conduct include torture of a victim, gratuitous infliction of injury, or prolonging of pain or humiliation.

Historical
Note
Effective November 1, 1987.

§5K2.9. Criminal Purpose (Policy Statement)

If the defendant committed the offense in order to facilitate or conceal the commission of another offense, the court may increase the sentence above the guideline range to reflect the actual seriousness of the defendant's conduct.

Historical
Note
Effective November 1, 1987.

§5K2.10. Victim's Conduct (Policy Statement)

If the victim's wrongful conduct contributed significantly to provoking the offense behavior, the court may reduce the sentence below the guideline range to reflect the nature and circumstances of the offense. In deciding whether a sentence reduction is warranted, and the extent of such reduction, the court should consider the following:

(1) The size and strength of the victim, or other relevant physical characteristics, in comparison with those of the defendant.

(2) The persistence of the victim's conduct and any efforts by the defendant to prevent confrontation.

(3) The danger reasonably perceived by the defendant, including the victim's reputation for violence.

(4) The danger actually presented to the defendant by the victim.

(5) Any other relevant conduct by the victim that substantially contributed to the danger presented.

(6) The proportionality and reasonableness of the defendant's response to the victim's provocation.

Victim misconduct ordinarily would not be sufficient to warrant application of this provision in the context of offenses under Chapter Two, Part A, Subpart 3 (Criminal Sexual Abuse). In addition, this provision usually would not be relevant in the context of non-violent offenses. There may, however, be unusual circumstances in which substantial victim misconduct would warrant a reduced penalty in the case of a non-violent offense.

For example, an extended course of provocation and harassment might lead a defendant to steal or destroy property in retaliation.

Historical Note

Effective November 1, 1987. Amended effective October 27, 2003 (amendment 651).

§5K2.11. Lesser Harms (Policy Statement)

Sometimes, a defendant may commit a crime in order to avoid a perceived greater harm. In such instances, a reduced sentence may be appropriate, provided that the circumstances significantly diminish society's interest in punishing the conduct, for example, in the case of a mercy killing. Where the interest in punishment or deterrence is not reduced, a reduction in sentence is not warranted. For example, providing defense secrets to a hostile power should receive no lesser punishment simply because the defendant believed that the government's policies were misdirected.

In other instances, conduct may not cause or threaten the harm or evil sought to be prevented by the law proscribing the offense at issue. For example, where a war veteran possessed a machine gun or grenade as a trophy, or a school teacher possessed controlled substances for display in a drug education program, a reduced sentence might be warranted.

Historical Note

Effective November 1, 1987.

§5K2.12. Coercion and Duress (Policy Statement)

If the defendant committed the offense because of serious coercion, blackmail or duress, under circumstances not amounting to a complete defense, the court may depart downward. The extent of the decrease ordinarily should depend on the reasonableness of the defendant's actions, on the proportionality of the defendant's actions to the seriousness of coercion, blackmail, or duress involved, and on the extent to which the conduct would have been less harmful under the circumstances as the defendant believed them to be. Ordinarily coercion will be sufficiently serious to warrant departure only when it involves a threat of physical injury, substantial damage to property or similar injury resulting from the unlawful action of a third party or from a natural emergency. Notwithstanding this policy statement, personal financial difficulties and economic pressures upon a trade or business do not warrant a downward departure.

Historical Note

Effective November 1, 1987. Amended effective October 27, 2003 (amendment 651); November 1, 2004 (amendment 674).

§5K2.13. Diminished Capacity (Policy Statement)

A downward departure may be warranted if (1) the defendant committed the offense while suffering from a significantly reduced mental capacity; and (2) the significantly reduced mental capacity contributed substantially to the commission of the offense. Similarly, if a departure is warranted under this policy statement, the extent of the departure should reflect the extent to which the reduced mental capacity contributed to the commission of the offense.

However, the court may not depart below the applicable guideline range if (1) the significantly reduced mental capacity was caused by the voluntary use of drugs or other intoxicants; (2) the facts and circumstances of the defendant's offense indicate a need to protect the public because the offense involved actual violence or a serious threat of violence; (3) the defendant's criminal history indicates a need to incarcerate the defendant to protect the public; or (4) the defendant has been convicted of an offense under chapter 71, 109A, 110, or 117, of title 18, United States Code.

Commentary

Application Note:

1. For purposes of this policy statement—

"***Significantly reduced mental capacity***" means the defendant, although convicted, has a significantly impaired ability to (A) understand the wrongfulness of the behavior comprising the offense or to exercise the power of reason; or (B) control behavior that the defendant knows is wrongful.

Background: Section 401(b)(5) of Public Law 108–21 directly amended this policy statement to add subdivision (4), effective April 30, 2003.

Historical
Note

Effective November 1, 1987. Amended effective November 1, 1998 (amendment 583); April 30, 2003 (amendment 649); October 27, 2003 (amendment 651); November 1, 2004 (amendment 674).

§5K2.14. Public Welfare (Policy Statement)

If national security, public health, or safety was significantly endangered, the court may depart upward to reflect the nature and circumstances of the offense.

Historical
Note

Effective November 1, 1987. Amended effective November 1, 2004 (amendment 674).

§5K2.15. [Deleted]

Historical
Note

Effective November 1, 1989 (amendment 292), was deleted effective November 1, 1995 (amendment 526).

§5K2.16. Voluntary Disclosure of Offense (Policy Statement)

If the defendant voluntarily discloses to authorities the existence of, and accepts responsibility for, the offense prior to the discovery of such offense, and if such offense was unlikely to have been discovered otherwise, a downward departure may be warranted. For example, a downward departure under this section might be considered where a defendant, motivated by remorse, discloses an offense that otherwise would have remained undiscovered. This provision does not apply where the motivating factor is the defendant's knowledge that discovery of the offense is likely or imminent, or where the defendant's disclosure occurs in connection with the investigation or prosecution of the defendant for related conduct.

Historical
Note

Effective November 1, 1991 (amendment 420). Amended effective November 1, 2004 (amendment 674).

§5K2.17. Semiautomatic Firearms Capable of Accepting Large Capacity

Magazine (Policy Statement)

If the defendant possessed a semiautomatic firearm capable of accepting a large capacity magazine in connection with a crime of violence or controlled substance offense, an upward departure may be warranted. A "semiautomatic firearm capable of accepting a large capacity magazine" means a semiautomatic firearm that has the ability to fire many rounds without reloading because at the time of the offense (1) the firearm had attached to it a magazine or similar device that could accept more than 15 rounds of ammunition; or (2) a magazine or similar device that could accept more than 15 rounds of ammunition was in close proximity to the firearm. The extent of any increase should depend upon the degree to which the nature of the weapon increased the likelihood of death or injury in the circumstances of the particular case.

Commentary

Application Note:

1. "***Crime of violence***" and "***controlled substance offense***" are defined in §4B1.2 (Definitions of Terms Used in Section 4B1.1).

Historical Note

Effective November 1, 1995 (amendment 531). Amended effective November 1, 2006 (amendment 691); November 1, 2010 (amendment 746).

§5K2.18. Violent Street Gangs (Policy Statement)

If the defendant is subject to an enhanced sentence under 18 U.S.C. § 521 (pertaining to criminal street gangs), an upward departure may be warranted. The purpose of this departure provision is to enhance the sentences of defendants who participate in groups, clubs, organizations, or associations that use violence to further their ends. It is to be noted that there may be cases in which 18 U.S.C. § 521 applies, but no violence is established. In such cases, it is expected that the guidelines will account adequately for the conduct and, consequently, this departure provision would not apply.

Historical Note

Effective November 1, 1995 (amendment 532).

§5K2.19. [Deleted]

Historical Note

Section 5K2.19 (Post-Sentencing Rehabilitative Efforts) (Policy Statement), effective November 1, 2000 (amendment 602), was deleted effective November 1, 2012 (amendment 768).

§5K2.20. Aberrant Behavior (Policy Statement)

(a) In General.—Except where a defendant is convicted of an offense involving a minor victim under section 1201, an offense under section 1591, or an offense under chapter 71, 109A, 110, or 117, of title 18, United States Code, a downward departure may be warranted in an exceptional case if (1) the defendant's criminal conduct meets the requirements of subsection (b); and (2) the departure is not prohibited under subsection (c).

(b) Requirements.—The court may depart downward under this policy statement only if the defendant committed a single criminal occurrence or single criminal transaction that (1) was committed without significant planning; (2) was of limited duration; and (3) represents a marked deviation by the defendant from an otherwise law-abiding life.

(c) PROHIBITIONS BASED ON THE PRESENCE OF CERTAIN CIRCUMSTANCES.—The court may not depart downward pursuant to this policy statement if any of the following circumstances are present:

(1) The offense involved serious bodily injury or death.

(2) The defendant discharged a firearm or otherwise used a firearm or a dangerous weapon.

(3) The instant offense of conviction is a serious drug trafficking offense.

(4) The defendant has either of the following: (A) more than one criminal history point, as determined under Chapter Four (Criminal History and Criminal Livelihood) before application of subsection (b) of §4A1.3 (Departures Based on Inadequacy of Criminal History Category); or (B) a prior federal or state felony conviction, or any other significant prior criminal behavior, regardless of whether the conviction or significant prior criminal behavior is countable under Chapter Four.

Commentary

Application Notes:

1. **Definitions.**—For purposes of this policy statement:

"***Dangerous weapon***," "***firearm***," "***otherwise used***," and "***serious bodily injury***" have the meaning given those terms in the Commentary to §1B1.1 (Application Instructions).

"***Serious drug trafficking offense***" means any controlled substance offense under title 21, United States Code, other than simple possession under 21 U.S.C. § 844, that provides for a mandatory minimum term of imprisonment of five years or greater, regardless of whether the defendant meets the criteria of §5C1.2 (Limitation on Applicability of Statutory Mandatory Minimum Sentences in Certain Cases).

2. **Repetitious or Significant, Planned Behavior.**—Repetitious or significant, planned behavior does not meet the requirements of subsection (b). For example, a fraud scheme generally would not meet such requirements because such a scheme usually involves repetitive acts, rather than a single occurrence or single criminal transaction, and significant planning.

3. **Other Circumstances to Consider.**—In determining whether the court should depart under this policy statement, the court may consider the defendant's (A) mental and emotional conditions; (B) employment record; (C) record of prior good works; (D) motivation for committing the offense; and (E) efforts to mitigate the effects of the offense.

Background: Section 401(b)(3) of Public Law 108–21 directly amended subsection (a) of this policy statement, effective April 30, 2003.

Historical Note

Effective November 1, 2000 (amendment 603). Amended effective April 30, 2003 (amendment 649); October 27, 2003 (amendment 651).

§5K2.21. Dismissed and Uncharged Conduct (Policy Statement)

The court may depart upward to reflect the actual seriousness of the offense based on conduct (1) underlying a charge dismissed as part of a plea agreement in the case, or underlying a potential charge not pursued in the case as part of a plea agreement or for any other reason; and

(2) that did not enter into the determination of the applicable guideline range.
Historical
Note
Effective November 1, 2000 (amendment 604). Amended effective November 1, 2004 (amendment 674).

§5K2.22. Specific Offender Characteristics as Grounds for Downward Departure in Child Crimes and Sexual Offenses (Policy Statement)

In sentencing a defendant convicted of an offense involving a minor victim under section 1201, an offense under section 1591, or an offense under chapter 71, 109A, 110, or 117, of title 18, United States Code:
(1) Age may be a reason to depart downward only if and to the extent permitted by §5H1.1.
(2) An extraordinary physical impairment may be a reason to depart downward only if and to the extent permitted by §5H1.4.
(3) Drug, alcohol, or gambling dependence or abuse is not a reason to depart downward.

Commentary

Background: Section 401(b)(2) of Public Law 108–21 directly amended Chapter Five, Part K, to add this policy statement, effective April 30, 2003.
Historical
Note
Effective April 30, 2003 (amendment 649). Amended effective November 1, 2004 (amendment 674).

§5K2.23. Discharged Terms of Imprisonment (Policy Statement)

A downward departure may be appropriate if the defendant (1) has completed serving a term of imprisonment; and (2) subsection (b) of §5G1.3 (Imposition of a Sentence on a Defendant Subject to Undischarged Term

of Imprisonment or Anticipated Term of Imprisonment) would have provided an adjustment had that completed term of imprisonment been undischarged at the time of sentencing for the instant offense. Any such departure should be fashioned to achieve a reasonable punishment for the instant offense.
Historical
Note
Effective November 1, 2003 (amendment 660). Amended effective November 1, 2004 (amendment 674); November 1, 2014 (amendment 787).

§5K2.24. Commission of Offense While Wearing or Displaying Unauthorized or Counterfeit Insignia or Uniform (Policy Statement)

If, during the commission of the offense, the defendant wore or displayed an official, or counterfeit official, insignia or uniform received in violation of 18 U.S.C. § 716, an upward departure may be warranted.

Commentary

Application Note:
1. **Definition.**—For purposes of this policy statement, "***official insignia or uniform***" has the meaning given that term in 18 U.S.C. § 716(c)(3).
Historical
Note
Effective November 1, 2007 (amendment 700).
* * * * *

3. EARLY DISPOSITION PROGRAMS

Historical
Note
Effective October 27, 2003 (amendment 651).

§5K3.1. Early Disposition Programs (Policy Statement)

Upon motion of the Government, the court may depart downward not more than **4** levels pursuant to an early disposition program authorized by the Attorney General of the United States and the United States Attorney for the district in which the court resides.

Commentary

Background: This policy statement implements the directive to the Commission in section 401(m)(2)(B) of the Prosecutorial Remedies and Other Tools to end the Exploitation of Children Today Act of 2003 (the "PROTECT Act", Public Law 108–21).

Historical
Note
Effective October 27, 2003 (amendment 651).

CHAPTER SIX
SENTENCING PROCEDURES, PLEA AGREEMENTS, AND CRIME VICTIMS' RIGHTS

Historical
Note
Effective November 1, 1987. Amended effective November 1, 2006 (amendment 694).

PART A — SENTENCING PROCEDURES

Introductory Commentary

This Part addresses sentencing procedures that are applicable in all cases, including those in which guilty or *nolo contendere* pleas are entered with or without a plea agreement between the parties, and convictions based upon judicial findings or verdicts. It sets forth the procedures for establishing the facts upon which the sentence will be based. Reliable fact-finding is essential to procedural due process and to the accuracy and uniformity of sentencing.

Historical
Note
Effective November 1, 1987.

§6A1.1. Presentence Report (Policy Statement)

(a) The probation officer must conduct a presentence investigation and submit a report to the court before it imposes sentence unless—

(1) 18 U.S.C. § 3593(c) or another statute requires otherwise; or

(2) the court finds that the information in the record enables it to meaningfully exercise its sentencing authority under 18 U.S.C. § 3553, and the court explains its finding on the record.

Rule 32(c)(1)(A), Fed. R. Crim. P.

(b) The defendant may not waive preparation of the presentence report.

Commentary

A thorough presentence investigation ordinarily is essential in determining the facts relevant to sentencing. Rule 32(c)(1)(A) permits the judge to dispense with a presentence report in certain limited circumstances, as when a specific statute requires or when the court finds

sufficient information in the record to enable it to exercise its statutory sentencing authority meaningfully and explains its finding on the record.

Historical
Note
Effective November 1, 1987. Amended effective June 15, 1988 (amendment 58); November 1, 1989 (amendment 293); November 1, 1997 (amendment 574); November 1, 2004 (amendment 674).

§6A1.2. Disclosure of Presentence Report; Issues in Dispute (Policy Statement)

(a) The probation officer must give the presentence report to the defendant, the defendant's attorney, and an attorney for the government at least 35 days before sentencing unless the defendant waives this minimum period. Rule 32(e)(2), Fed. R. Crim. P.

(b) Within 14 days after receiving the presentence report, the parties must state in writing any objections, including objections to material information, sentencing guideline ranges, and policy statements contained in or omitted from the report. An objecting party must provide a copy of its objections to the opposing party and to the probation officer. After receiving objections, the probation officer may meet with the parties to discuss the objections. The probation officer may then investigate further and revise the presentence report accordingly. Rule 32(f), Fed. R. Crim. P.

(c) At least 7 days before sentencing, the probation officer must submit to the court and to the parties the presentence report and an addendum containing any unresolved objections, the grounds for those objections, and the probation officer's comments on them. Rule 32(g), Fed. R. Crim. P.

Commentary

Background: In order to focus the issues prior to sentencing, the parties are required to respond in writing to the presentence report and to identify any issues in dispute. *See* Rule 32(f), Fed. R. Crim. P.

Historical Note

Effective November 1, 1987. Amended effective June 15, 1988 (amendment 59); November 1, 1991 (amendment 425); November 1, 1997 (amendment 574); November 1, 2004 (amendment 674).

§6A1.3. Resolution of Disputed Factors (Policy Statement)

(a) When any factor important to the sentencing determination is reasonably in dispute, the parties shall be given an adequate opportunity to present information to the court regarding that factor. In

resolving any dispute concerning a factor important to the sentencing determination, the court may consider relevant information without regard to its admissibility under the rules of evidence applicable at trial, provided that the information has sufficient indicia of reliability to support its probable accuracy.

(b) The court shall resolve disputed sentencing factors at a sentencing hearing in accordance with Rule 32(i), Fed. R. Crim. P.

Commentary

Although lengthy sentencing hearings seldom should be necessary, disputes about sentencing factors must be resolved with care. When a dispute exists about any factor important to the sentencing determination, the court must ensure that the parties have an adequate opportunity to present relevant information. Written statements of counsel or affidavits of witnesses may be adequate under many circumstances. *See, e.g.*, *United States v. Ibanez*, 924 F.2d 427 (2d Cir. 1991). An evidentiary hearing may sometimes be the only reliable way to resolve disputed issues. *See, e.g.*, *United States v. Jimenez Martinez*, 83 F.3d 488, 494–95 (1st Cir. 1996) (finding error in district court's denial of defendant's motion for evidentiary hearing given questionable reliability of affidavit on which the district court relied at sentencing); *United States v. Roberts*, 14 F.3d 502, 521(10th Cir. 1993) (remanding because district court did not hold evidentiary hearing to address defendants' objections to drug quantity determination or make requisite findings of fact regarding drug quantity); *see also*, *United States v. Fatico*, 603 F.2d 1053, 1057 n.9 (2d Cir. 1979), *cert. denied*, 444 U.S. 1073 (1980). The sentencing court must determine the appropriate procedure in light of the nature of the dispute, its relevance to the sentencing determination, and applicable case law.

In determining the relevant facts, sentencing judges are not restricted to information that would be admissible at trial. *See* 18 U.S.C. § 3661; *see also United States v. Watts*, 519 U.S. 148, 154 (1997) (holding that lower evidentiary standard at sentencing permits sentencing court's consideration of acquitted conduct); *Witte v. United States*, 515 U.S. 389, 399–401 (1995) (noting that sentencing courts have traditionally considered wide range of information without the procedural protections of a criminal trial, including information concerning criminal conduct that may be the subject of a subsequent prosecution); *Nichols v. United States*, 511 U.S. 738, 747–48 (1994) (noting that district courts have traditionally considered defendant's prior criminal conduct even when the conduct did not result in a conviction). Any information may be considered, so long as it has sufficient indicia of reliability to support its probable accuracy. *Watts*, 519 U.S. at 157; *Nichols*, 511 U.S. at 748; *United States v. Zuleta-Alvarez*,

922 F.2d 33 (1st Cir. 1990), *cert. denied*, 500 U.S. 927 (1991); *United States v. Beaulieu*, 893 F.2d 1177 (10th Cir.), *cert. denied*, 497 U.S. 1038 (1990). Reliable hearsay evidence may be considered. *United States v. Petty*, 982 F.2d 1365 (9th Cir. 1993), *cert. denied*, 510 U.S. 1040 (1994); *United States v. Sciarrino*, 884 F.2d 95 (3d Cir.), *cert. denied*, 493 U.S. 997 (1989). Outof-court declarations by an unidentified informant may be considered where there is good cause for the non-disclosure of the informant's identity and there is sufficient corroboration by other means. *United States v. Rogers*, 1 F.3d 341 (5th Cir. 1993); *see also United States v. Young*, 981 F.2d 180 (5th Cir.), *cert. denied*, 508 U.S. 980 (1993); *United States v. Fatico*, 579 F.2d 707, 713 (2d Cir. 1978), *cert. denied*, 444 U.S. 1073 (1980). Unreliable allegations shall not be considered. *United States v. Ortiz*, 993 F.2d 204 (10th Cir. 1993).

The Commission believes that use of a preponderance of the evidence standard is appropriate to meet due process requirements and policy concerns in resolving disputes regarding application of the guidelines to the facts of a case.

Historical Note

Effective November 1, 1987. Amended effective November 1, 1989 (amendment 294); November 1, 1991 (amendment 387); November 1, 1997 (amendment 574); November 1, 1998 (amendment 586); November 1, 2004 (amendment 674).

§6A1.4. Notice of Possible Departure (Policy Statement)

Before the court may depart from the applicable sentencing guideline range on a ground not identified for departure either in the presentence report or in a party's prehearing submission, the court must give the parties reasonable notice that it is contemplating such a departure. The notice must specify any ground on which the court is contemplating a departure. Rule 32(h), Fed. R. Crim. P.

Commentary

Background: The Federal Rules of Criminal Procedure were amended, effective December 1, 2002, to incorporate into Rule 32(h) the holding in *Burns v. United States*, 501 U.S. 129, 138–39 (1991). This policy statement parallels Rule 32(h), Fed. R. Crim. P.

Historical Note

Effective November 1, 2004 (amendment 674).

§6A1.5. Crime Victims' Rights (Policy Statement)

In any case involving the sentencing of a defendant for an offense against a crime victim, the court shall ensure that the crime victim is afforded the rights described in 18 U.S.C. § 3771 and in any other provision of Federal law pertaining to the treatment of crime victims.

Commentary

Application Note:

1. **Definition.**—For purposes of this policy statement, "***crime victim***" has the meaning given that term in 18 U.S.C. § 3771(e).

Historical Note

Effective November 1, 2006 (amendment 694).

PART B — PLEA AGREEMENTS

Introductory Commentary

Policy statements governing the acceptance of plea agreements under Rule 11(c), Fed. R. Crim. P., are intended to ensure that plea negotiation practices: (1) promote the statutory purposes of sentencing prescribed in 18 U.S.C. § 3553(a); and (2) do not perpetuate unwarranted sentencing disparity.

These policy statements make clear that sentencing is a judicial function and that the appropriate sentence in a guilty plea case is to be determined by the judge. The policy statements also ensure that the basis for any judicial decision to depart from the guidelines will be explained on the record.

Historical
Note
Effective November 1, 1987. Amended effective November 1, 2004 (amendment 674).

§6B1.1. Plea Agreement Procedure (Policy Statement)

(a) The parties must disclose the plea agreement in open court when the plea is offered, unless the court for good cause allows the parties to disclose the plea agreement in camera. Rule 11(c)(2), Fed. R. Crim. P.

(b) To the extent the plea agreement is of the type specified in Rule 11(c)(1)(B), the court must advise the defendant that the defendant has no right to withdraw the plea if the court does not follow the recommendation or request. Rule 11(c)(3)(B), Fed. R. Crim. P.

(c) To the extent the plea agreement is of the type specified in Rule 11(c)(1)(A) or (C), the court may accept the agreement, reject it, or defer a decision until the court has reviewed the presentence report. Rule 11(c)(3)(A), Fed. R. Crim. P.

Commentary

This provision parallels the procedural requirements of Rule 11(c), Fed. R. Crim. P. Plea agreements must be fully disclosed and a defendant whose plea agreement includes a nonbinding recommendation must be advised that the court's refusal to accept the sentencing recommendation will not entitle the defendant to withdraw the plea.

Section 6B1.1(c) deals with the timing of the court's decision regarding whether to accept or reject the plea agreement. Rule 11(c)(3)(A) gives the court discretion to accept or reject the plea agreement immediately or defer a decision pending consideration of the presentence report. Given that a presentence report normally will be prepared, the Commission recommends that the court defer acceptance of the plea agreement until the court has reviewed the presentence report.

Historical
Note
Effective November 1, 1987. Amended effective November 1, 2004 (amendment 674).

§6B1.2. Standards for Acceptance of Plea Agreements (Policy Statement)

(a) In the case of a plea agreement that includes the dismissal of any charges or an agreement not to pursue potential charges (Rule 11(c)(1)(A)), the court may accept the agreement if the court determines, for reasons stated on the record, that the remaining charges adequately reflect the seriousness of the actual offense behavior and that accepting the agreement will not undermine the statutory purposes of sentencing or the sentencing guidelines.

However, a plea agreement that includes the dismissal of a charge or a plea agreement not to pursue a potential charge shall not preclude the conduct underlying such charge from being considered under the provisions of §1B1.3 (Relevant Conduct) in connection with the count(s) of which the defendant is convicted.

(b) In the case of a plea agreement that includes a nonbinding recommendation (Rule 11(c)(1)(B)), the court may accept the recommendation if the court is satisfied either that:

(1) the recommended sentence is within the applicable guideline

range; or
(2) (A) the recommended sentence is outside the applicable guideline range for justifiable reasons; and (B) those reasons are set forth with specificity in the statement of reasons form.
(c) In the case of a plea agreement that includes a specific sentence (Rule 11(c)(1)(C)), the court may accept the agreement if the court is satisfied either that:
(1) the agreed sentence is within the applicable guideline range; or
(2) (A) the agreed sentence is outside the applicable guideline range for justifiable reasons; and (B) those reasons are set forth with specificity in the statement of reasons form.

Commentary

The court may accept an agreement calling for dismissal of charges or an agreement not to pursue potential charges if the remaining charges reflect the seriousness of the actual offense behavior. This requirement does not authorize judges to intrude upon the charging discretion of the prosecutor. If the government's motion to dismiss charges or statement that potential charges will not be pursued is not contingent on the disposition of the remaining charges, the judge should defer to the government's position except under extraordinary circumstances. Rule 48(a), Fed. R. Crim. P. However, when the dismissal of charges or agreement not to pursue potential charges is contingent on acceptance of a plea agreement, the court's authority to adjudicate guilt and impose sentence is implicated, and the court is to determine whether or not dismissal of charges will undermine the sentencing guidelines.

Similarly, the court should accept a recommended sentence or a plea agreement requiring imposition of a specific sentence only if the court is satisfied either that such sentence is an appropriate sentence within the applicable guideline range or, if not, that the sentence is outside the applicable guideline range for justifiable reasons and those reasons are set forth with specificity in the statement of reasons form. *See* 18 U.S.C. § 3553(c). As set forth in subsection (d) of §5K2.0 (Grounds for Departure), however, the court may not depart below the applicable guideline range merely because of the defendant's decision to plead guilty to the offense or to enter a plea agreement with respect to the offense.

A defendant who enters a plea of guilty in a timely manner will enhance the likelihood of his receiving a reduction in offense level under §3E1.1 (Acceptance of Responsibility). Further reduction in offense level (or sentence) due to a plea agreement will tend to undermine the sentencing guidelines.

The second paragraph of subsection (a) provides that a plea agreement that includes the dismissal of a charge, or a plea agreement not to pursue a potential charge, shall not prevent the conduct underlying that charge from being considered under the provisions of §1B1.3 (Relevant Conduct) in connection with the count(s) of which the defendant is convicted. This paragraph prevents a plea agreement from restricting consideration of conduct that is within the scope of §1B1.3 (Relevant Conduct) in respect to the count(s) of which the defendant is convicted; it does not in any way expand or modify the scope of §1B1.3 (Relevant Conduct). Section 5K2.21 (Dismissed and Uncharged Conduct) addresses the use, as a basis for upward departure, of conduct underlying a charge dismissed as part of a plea agreement in the case, or underlying a potential charge not pursued in the case as part of a plea agreement.

The Commission encourages the prosecuting attorney prior to the entry of a plea of guilty or *nolo contendere* under Rule 11 of the Federal Rules of Criminal Procedure to disclose to the defendant the facts and circumstances of the offense and offender characteristics, then known to the prosecuting attorney, that are relevant to the application of the sentencing guidelines. This recommendation, however, shall not be construed to confer upon the defendant any right not otherwise recognized in law.

Historical

Note
Effective November 1, 1987. Amended effective November 1, 1989 (amendment 295); November 1, 1992 (amendment 467); November 1, 1993 (amendment 495); November 1, 2000 (amendment 604); October 27, 2003 (amendment 651); November 1, 2011 (amendment 757).

§6B1.3. Procedure Upon Rejection of a Plea Agreement (Policy Statement)

If the court rejects a plea agreement containing provisions of the type specified in Rule 11(c)(1)(A) or (C), the court must do the following on the record and in open court (or, for good cause, in camera)—

(a) inform the parties that the court rejects the plea agreement;

(b) advise the defendant personally that the court is not required to follow the plea agreement and give the defendant an opportunity to withdraw the plea; and

(c) advise the defendant personally that if the plea is not withdrawn, the court may dispose of the case less favorably toward the defendant than the plea agreement contemplated.

Rule 11(c)(5), Fed. R. Crim. P.

Commentary

This provision implements the requirements of Rule 11(c)(5). It assures the defendant an opportunity to withdraw his plea when the court has rejected a plea agreement.

Historical
Note
Effective November 1, 1987. Amended effective November 1, 2004 (amendment 674).

§6B1.4. Stipulations (Policy Statement)

(a) A plea agreement may be accompanied by a written stipulation of facts relevant to sentencing. Except to the extent that a party may be privileged not to disclose certain information, stipulations shall:

(1) set forth the relevant facts and circumstances of the actual offense conduct and offender characteristics;

(2) not contain misleading facts; and

(3) set forth with meaningful specificity the reasons why the sentencing range resulting from the proposed agreement is appropriate.

(b) To the extent that the parties disagree about any facts relevant to sentencing, the stipulation shall identify the facts that are in dispute.

(c) A district court may, by local rule, identify categories of cases for which the parties are authorized to make the required stipulation orally, on the record, at the time the plea agreement is offered.

(d) The court is not bound by the stipulation, but may with the aid of the presentence report, determine the facts relevant to sentencing.

Commentary

This provision requires that when a plea agreement includes a stipulation of fact, the stipulation must fully and accurately disclose all factors relevant to the determination of sentence. This provision does not obligate the parties to reach agreement on issues that remain in dispute or to present the court with an appearance of agreement in areas where agreement does not exist. Rather, the overriding principle is full disclosure of the circumstances of the actual offense and the agreement of the parties. The stipulation should identify all areas of agreement, disagreement and uncertainty that may be relevant to the determination of sentence. Similarly, it is not appropriate for the parties to stipulate to misleading or non-existent facts, even when both parties are willing to assume the existence of such "facts" for purposes of the litigation. Rather, the parties should fully disclose the actual facts and then explain to the court the reasons why the disposition of the case should differ from that which such facts ordinarily would require under the guidelines.

Because of the importance of the stipulations and the potential complexity of the factors that can affect the determination of sentences, stipulations ordinarily should be in writing. However, exceptions to this practice may be allowed by local rule. The Commission intends to pay particular attention to this aspect of the plea agreement procedure as experience under the guidelines develops. *See* Commentary to §6A1.2 (Disclosure of Presentence Report; Issues in Dispute).

Section 6B1.4(d) makes clear that the court is not obliged to accept the stipulation of the parties. Even though stipulations are expected to be accurate and complete, the court cannot rely exclusively upon stipulations in ascertaining the factors relevant to the determination of sentence. Rather, in determining the factual basis for the sentence, the court will consider the stipulation, together with the results of the presentence investigation, and any other relevant information.

Historical Note

Effective November 1, 1987.

CHAPTER SEVEN

VIOLATIONS OF PROBATION AND SUPERVISED RELEASE

PART A — INTRODUCTION TO CHAPTER SEVEN

1. Authority

Under 28 U.S.C. § 994(a)(3), the Sentencing Commission is required to issue guidelines or policy statements applicable to the revocation of probation and supervised release. At this time, the Commission has chosen to promulgate policy statements only. These policy statements will provide guidance while allowing for the identification of any substantive or procedural issues that require further review. The Commission views these policy statements as evolutionary and will review relevant data and materials concerning revocation determinations under these policy statements. Revocation guidelines will be issued after federal judges, probation officers, practitioners, and others have the opportunity to evaluate and comment on these policy statements.

2. Background

(a) Probation.

Prior to the implementation of the federal sentencing guidelines, a court could stay the imposition or execution of sentence and place a defendant on probation. When a court found that a defendant violated a condition of probation, the court could continue probation, with or without extending the term or modifying the conditions, or revoke probation and either impose the term of imprisonment previously stayed, or, where no term of imprisonment had originally been imposed, impose any term of imprisonment that was available at the initial sentencing.

The statutory authority to "suspend" the imposition or execution of sentence in order to impose a term of probation was abolished upon implementation of the sentencing guidelines. Instead, the Sentencing Reform Act recognized probation as a sentence in itself. 18 U.S.C. § 3561. Under current law, if the court finds that a defendant violated a condition of probation, the court may continue probation, with or without extending the term or modifying the conditions, or revoke probation and impose any other sentence that initially could have been imposed. 18 U.S.C. § 3565. For certain violations, revocation is required by statute.

(b) Supervised Release.

Supervised release, a new form of post-imprisonment supervision created by the Sentencing Reform Act, accompanied implementation of the guidelines. A term of supervised release may be imposed by the court as a part of the sentence of imprisonment at the time of initial sentencing. 18 U.S.C. § 3583(a). Unlike parole, a term of supervised release does not replace a portion of the sentence of imprisonment, but rather is an order of supervision in addition to any term of imprisonment imposed by the court. Accordingly, supervised release is more analogous to the additional "special parole term" previously authorized for certain drug offenses.

The conditions of supervised release authorized by statute are the same as those for a sentence of probation, except for intermittent confinement. (Intermittent confinement is available for a sentence of probation, but is available as a condition of supervised release only for a violation of a condition of supervised release.) When the court finds that the defendant violated a condition of supervised release, it may continue the defendant on supervised release, with or without extending the term or modifying the conditions, or revoke supervised release and impose a term of imprisonment. The periods of imprisonment authorized by statute for a violation of the conditions of supervised release generally are more limited, however, than those available for a violation of the conditions of probation. 18 U.S.C. § 3583(e)(3).

3. Resolution of Major Issues

(a) Guidelines versus Policy Statements.

At the outset, the Commission faced a choice between promulgating guidelines or issuing advisory policy statements for the revocation of probation and supervised release. After considered debate and input from judges, probation officers, and prosecuting and defense attorneys, the Commission decided, for a variety of reasons, initially to issue policy statements. Not only was the policy statement option expressly authorized by statute, but this approach provided greater flexibility to both the Commission and the courts. Unlike guidelines, policy statements are not subject to the May 1 statutory deadline for submission to Congress, and the Commission believed that it would benefit from the additional time to consider complex issues relating to revocation guidelines provided by the policy statement option.

Moreover, the Commission anticipates that, because of its greater flexibility, the policy statement option will provide better opportunities for evaluation by the courts and the Commission. This flexibility is important, given that supervised release as a method of post-incarceration supervision and transformation of probation from a suspension of sentence to a sentence in itself represent recent changes in federal sentencing practices. After an adequate period of evaluation, the Commission intends to promulgate revocation guidelines.

(b) Choice Between Theories.

The Commission debated two different approaches to sanctioning violations of probation and supervised release.

The first option considered a violation resulting from a defendant's failure to follow the court-imposed conditions of probation or supervised release as a "breach of trust." While the nature of the conduct leading to the revocation would be considered in measuring the extent of the breach of trust, imposition of an appropriate punishment for any new criminal conduct would not be the primary goal of a revocation sentence. Instead, the sentence imposed upon revocation would be intended to sanction the violator for failing to abide by the conditions of the court-ordered supervision, leaving the punishment for any new criminal conduct to the court responsible for imposing the sentence for that offense.

The second option considered by the Commission sought to sanction violators for the particular conduct triggering the revocation as if that conduct were being sentenced as new federal criminal conduct. Under this approach, offense guidelines in Chapters Two and Three of the Guidelines Manual would be applied to any criminal conduct that formed the basis of the violation, after which the criminal history in Chapter Four of the Guidelines Manual would be recalculated to determine the appropriate revocation sentence. This option would also address a violation not constituting a criminal offense.

After lengthy consideration, the Commission adopted an approach that is consistent with the theory of the first option; *i.e.*, at revocation the court should sanction primarily the defendant's breach of trust, while taking into account, to a limited degree, the seriousness of the underlying violation and the criminal history of the violator.

The Commission adopted this approach for a variety of reasons. First, although the Commission found desirable several aspects of the second option that provided for a detailed revocation guideline system similar to that applied at the initial sentencing, extensive testing proved it to be impractical. In particular, with regard to new criminal conduct that constituted a violation of state or local law, working groups expert in the functioning of federal criminal law noted that it would be difficult in many instances for the court or the parties to obtain the information necessary to apply properly the guidelines to this new conduct. The potential unavailability of information and witnesses necessary for a determination of specific offense characteristics or other guideline adjustments could create questions about the accuracy of factual findings concerning the existence of those factors.

In addition, the Commission rejected the second option because that option was inconsistent with its views that the court with jurisdiction over the criminal conduct leading to revocation is the more appropriate body to impose punishment for that new criminal conduct, and that, as a breach of trust inherent in the conditions of supervision, the sanction for the violation of trust should be in addition, or consecutive, to any sentence imposed for the new conduct. In contrast, the second option would have the

revocation court substantially duplicate the sanctioning role of the court with jurisdiction over a defendant's new criminal conduct and would provide for the punishment imposed upon revocation to run concurrently with, and thus generally be subsumed in, any sentence imposed for that new criminal conduct.

Further, the sanctions available to the courts upon revocation are, in many cases, more significantly restrained by statute. Specifically, the term of imprisonment that may be imposed upon revocation of supervised release is limited by statute to not more than five years for persons convicted of Class A felonies, except for certain Title 21 drug offenses; not more than three years for Class B felonies; not more than two years for Class C or D felonies; and not more than one year for Class E felonies. 18 U.S.C. § 3583(e)(3).

Given the relatively narrow ranges of incarceration available in many cases, combined with the potential difficulty in obtaining information necessary to determine specific offense characteristics, the Commission felt that it was undesirable at this time to develop guidelines that attempt to distinguish, in detail, the wide variety of behavior that can lead to revocation. Indeed, with the relatively low ceilings set by statute, revocation policy statements that attempted to delineate with great particularity the gradations of conduct leading to revocation would frequently result in a sentence at the statutory maximum penalty.

Accordingly, the Commission determined that revocation policy statements that provided for three broad grades of violations would permit proportionally longer terms for more serious violations and thereby would address adequately concerns about proportionality, without creating the problems inherent in the second option.

4. The Basic Approach

The revocation policy statements categorize violations of probation and supervised release in three broad classifications ranging from serious new felonious criminal conduct to less serious criminal conduct and technical violations. The grade of the violation, together with the violator's criminal history category calculated at the time of the initial sentencing, fix the applicable sentencing range.

The Commission has elected to develop a single set of policy statements for revocation of both probation and supervised release. In reviewing the relevant literature, the Commission determined that the purpose of supervision for probation and supervised release should focus on the integration of the violator into the community, while providing the supervision designed to limit further criminal conduct. Although there was considerable debate as to whether the sanction imposed upon revocation of probation should be different from that imposed upon revocation of supervised release, the Commission has initially concluded that a single set of policy statements is appropriate.

5. A Concluding Note

The Commission views these policy statements for revocation of probation and supervised release as the first step in an evolutionary process. The Commission expects to issue revocation guidelines after judges, probation officers, and practitioners have had an opportunity to apply and comment on the policy statements.

In developing these policy statements, the Commission assembled two outside working groups of experienced probation officers representing every circuit in the nation, officials from the Probation Division of the Administrative Office of the U.S. Courts, the General Counsel's office at the Administrative Office of the U.S. Courts, and the U.S. Parole Commission. In addition, a number of federal judges, members of the Criminal Law and Probation Administration Committee of the Judicial Conference, and representatives from the Department of Justice and federal and community defenders provided considerable input into this effort.

Historical Note

Effective November 1, 1990 (amendment 362). Amended effective November 1, 2002 (amendment 646); November 1, 2009 (amendment 733).

§§7A1.1 – 7A1.4 [Deleted]

Historical Note

Sections 7A1.1 (Reporting of Violations of Probation and Supervised Release), 7A1.2 (Revocation of Probation), 7A1.3 (Revocation of Supervised Release), and 7A1.4 (No Credit for Time Under Supervision), effective November 1, 1987, were deleted as part of an overall revision of this chapter effective November 1, 1990 (amendment 362).

PART B — PROBATION AND SUPERVISED RELEASE VIOLATIONS

Introductory Commentary

The policy statements in this chapter seek to prescribe penalties only for the violation of the judicial order imposing supervision. Where a defendant is convicted of a criminal charge that also is a basis of the violation, these policy statements do not purport to provide the appropriate sanction for the criminal charge itself. The Commission has concluded that the determination of the appropriate sentence on any new criminal conviction should be a separate determination for the court having jurisdiction over such conviction.

Because these policy statements focus on the violation of the court-ordered supervision, this chapter, to the extent permitted by law, treats violations of the conditions of probation and supervised release as functionally equivalent.

Under 18 U.S.C. § 3584, the court, upon consideration of the factors set forth in 18 U.S.C. § 3553(a), including applicable guidelines and policy statements issued by the Sentencing Commission, may order a term of imprisonment to be served consecutively or concurrently to an undischarged term of imprisonment. It is the policy of the Commission that the sanction imposed upon revocation is to be served consecutively to any other term of imprisonment imposed for any criminal conduct that is the basis of the revocation.

This chapter is applicable in the case of a defendant under supervision for a felony or Class A misdemeanor. Consistent with §1B1.9 (Class B or C Misdemeanors and Infractions), this chapter does not apply in the case of a defendant under supervision for a Class B or C misdemeanor or an infraction.

Historical
Note
Effective November 1, 1990 (amendment 362).

§7B1.1. Classification of Violations (Policy Statement)

(a) There are three grades of probation and supervised release violations:
(1) GRADE A VIOLATIONS — conduct constituting (A) a federal, state, or local offense punishable by a term of imprisonment exceeding one year that (i) is a crime of violence, (ii) is a controlled substance offense, or (iii) involves possession of a firearm or destructive device of a type described in 26 U.S.C. § 5845(a); or (B) any other federal, state, or local offense punishable by a term of imprisonment exceeding twenty years;
(2) GRADE B VIOLATIONS — conduct constituting any other federal, state, or local offense punishable by a term of imprisonment exceeding one year;

(3) GRADE C VIOLATIONS — conduct constituting (A) a federal, state, or local offense punishable by a term of imprisonment of one year or less; or (B) a violation of any other condition of supervision.
(b) Where there is more than one violation of the conditions of supervision, or the violation includes conduct that constitutes more than one offense, the grade of the violation is determined by the violation having the most serious grade.

Commentary

Application Notes:

1. Under 18 U.S.C. §§ 3563(a)(1) and 3583(d), a mandatory condition of probation and supervised release is that the defendant not commit another federal, state, or local crime. A violation of this condition may be charged whether or not the defendant has been the subject of a separate federal, state, or local prosecution for such conduct. The grade of violation does not depend upon the conduct that is the subject of criminal charges or of which the defendant is convicted in a criminal proceeding. Rather, the grade of the violation is to be based on the defendant's actual conduct.
2. "***Crime of violence***" is defined in §4B1.2 (Definitions of Terms Used in Section 4B1.1). *See* §4B1.2(a) and Application Note 1 of the Commentary to §4B1.2.
3. "***Controlled substance offense***" is defined in §4B1.2 (Definitions of Terms Used in Section 4B1.1). *See* §4B1.2(b) and Application Note 1 of the Commentary to §4B1.2.
4. A "***firearm or destructive device of a type described in 26 U.S.C. § 5845(a)***" includes a shotgun, or a weapon made from a shotgun, with a barrel or barrels of less than 18 inches in length; a weapon made from a shotgun or rifle with an overall length of less than 26 inches; a rifle, or a weapon made from a rifle, with a barrel or barrels of less than 16 inches in length; a machine gun; a muffler or silencer for a firearm; a destructive device; and certain large bore weapons.
5. Where the defendant is under supervision in connection with a felony conviction, or has a prior felony conviction, possession of a firearm (other than a firearm of a type described in 26 U.S.C. § 5845(a)) will generally constitute a Grade B violation, because 18 U.S.C. § 922(g) prohibits a convicted felon from possessing a firearm. The term "generally" is used in the preceding sentence, however, because there are certain limited exceptions to the applicability of 18 U.S.C. § 922(g). *See, e.g.*, 18 U.S.C. § 925(c).

Historical
Note
Effective November 1, 1990 (amendment 362). Amended effective November 1, 1992 (amendment 473); November 1, 1997 (amendment 568); November 1, 2002 (amendment 646).

§7B1.2. Reporting of Violations of Probation and Supervised Release (Policy

Statement)

(a) The probation officer shall promptly report to the court any alleged Grade A or B violation.

(b) The probation officer shall promptly report to the court any alleged Grade C violation unless the officer determines: (1) that such violation is minor, and not part of a continuing pattern of violations; and (2) that non-reporting will not present an undue risk to an individual or the public or be inconsistent with any directive of the court relative to the reporting of violations.

Commentary

Application Note:

1. Under subsection (b), a Grade C violation must be promptly reported to the court unless the probation officer makes an affirmative determination that the alleged violation meets the criteria for non-reporting. For example, an isolated failure to file a monthly report or a minor traffic infraction generally would not require reporting.

Historical Note

Effective November 1, 1990 (amendment 362).

§7B1.3. Revocation of Probation or Supervised Release (Policy Statement)

(a) (1) Upon a finding of a Grade A or B violation, the court shall revoke probation or supervised release.

(2) Upon a finding of a Grade C violation, the court may (A) revoke probation or supervised release; or (B) extend the term of probation or supervised release and/or modify the conditions of supervision.

(b) In the case of a revocation of probation or supervised release, the applicable range of imprisonment is that set forth in §7B1.4 (Term of Imprisonment).

(c) In the case of a Grade B or C violation—

(1) Where the minimum term of imprisonment determined under §7B1.4 (Term of Imprisonment) is at least one month but not more than six months, the minimum term may be satisfied by (A) a sentence of imprisonment; or (B) a sentence of imprisonment that includes a term of supervised release with a condition that substitutes community confinement or home detention according to the schedule in §5C1.1(e) for any portion of the minimum term; and

(2) Where the minimum term of imprisonment determined under §7B1.4 (Term of Imprisonment) is more than six months but

not more than ten months, the minimum term may be satisfied by (A) a sentence of imprisonment; or (B) a sentence of imprisonment that includes a term of supervised release with a condition that substitutes community confinement or home detention according to the schedule in §5C1.1(e), provided that at least one-half of the minimum term is satisfied by imprisonment.

(3) In the case of a revocation based, at least in part, on a violation of a condition specifically pertaining to community confinement,

intermittent confinement, or home detention, use of the same or a less restrictive sanction is not recommended.

(d) Any restitution, fine, community confinement, home detention, or intermittent confinement previously imposed in connection with the sentence for which revocation is ordered that remains unpaid or unserved at the time of revocation shall be ordered to be paid or served in addition to the sanction determined under §7B1.4 (Term of Imprisonment), and any such unserved period of community confinement, home detention, or intermittent confinement may be converted to an equivalent period of imprisonment.

(e) Where the court revokes probation or supervised release and imposes a term of imprisonment, it shall increase the term of imprisonment determined under subsections (b), (c), and (d) above by the amount of time in official detention that will be credited toward service of the term of imprisonment under 18 U.S.C. § 3585(b), other than time in official detention resulting from the federal probation or supervised release violation warrant or proceeding.

(f) Any term of imprisonment imposed upon the revocation of probation or supervised release shall be ordered to be served consecutively to any sentence of imprisonment that the defendant is serving, whether or not the sentence of imprisonment being served resulted from the conduct that is the basis of the revocation of probation or supervised release.

(g) (1) If probation is revoked and a term of imprisonment is imposed, the provisions of §§5D1.1–1.3 shall apply to the imposition of a term of supervised release.

(2) If supervised release is revoked, the court may include a requirement that the defendant be placed on a term of supervised release upon release from imprisonment. The length of such a term of supervised release shall not exceed the term of supervised release authorized by statute for the offense that resulted

in the original term of supervised release, less any term of imprisonment that was imposed upon revocation of supervised release.

18 U.S.C. § 3583(h).

Commentary

Application Notes:

1. Revocation of probation or supervised release generally is the appropriate disposition in the case of a Grade C violation by a defendant who, having been continued on supervision after a finding of violation, again violates the conditions of his supervision.
2. The provisions for the revocation, as well as early termination and extension, of a term of supervised release are found in 18 U.S.C. § 3583(e), (g)–(i). Under 18 U.S.C. § 3583(h) (effective September 13, 1994), the court, in the case of revocation of supervised release, may order an additional period of supervised release to follow imprisonment.
3. Subsection (e) is designed to ensure that the revocation penalty is not decreased by credit for time in official detention other than time in official detention resulting from the federal probation or supervised release violation warrant or proceeding. **Example**: A defendant, who was in pre-trial detention for three months, is placed on probation, and subsequently violates that probation. The court finds the violation to be a Grade C violation,

determines that the applicable range of imprisonment is 4–10 months, and determines that revocation of probation and imposition of a term of imprisonment of four months is appropriate. Under subsection (e), a sentence of seven months imprisonment would be required because the Bureau of Prisons, under 18 U.S.C. § 3585(b), will allow the defendant three months' credit toward the term of imprisonment imposed upon revocation.

4. Subsection (f) provides that any term of imprisonment imposed upon the revocation of probation or supervised release shall run consecutively to any sentence of imprisonment being served by the defendant. Similarly, it is the Commission's recommendation that any sentence of imprisonment for a criminal offense that is imposed after revocation of probation or supervised release be run consecutively to any term of imprisonment imposed upon revocation.

5. Intermittent confinement is authorized as a condition of probation during the first year of the term of probation. 18 U.S.C. § 3563(b)(10). Intermittent confinement is authorized as a condition of supervised release during the first year of supervised release, but only for a violation of a condition of supervised release in accordance with 18 U.S.C. § 3583(e)(2) and only when facilities are available. *See* §5F1.8 (Intermittent Confinement).

Historical Note

Effective November 1, 1990 (amendment 362). Amended effective November 1, 1991 (amendment 427); November 1, 1995 (amendment 533); November 1, 2002 (amendment 646); November 1, 2004 (amendment 664); November 1, 2009 (amendment 733).

§7B1.4. Term of Imprisonment (Policy Statement)

(a) The range of imprisonment applicable upon revocation is set forth in the following table:

Revocation Table
(in months of imprisonment)

Grade of Violation	**Criminal History Category***					
	I	**II**	**III**	**IV**	**V**	**VI**
Grade C	3–9	4–10	5–11	6–12	7–13	8–14
Grade B	4–10	6–12	8–14	12–18	18–24	21–27
Grade A (1) Except as provided in subdivision (2) below:	12–18	15–21	18–24	24–30	30–37	33–41
(2) Where the defendant was on probation or supervised release as a result of a sentence for a Class A felony:	24–30	27–33	30–37	37–46	46–57	51–63.

*The criminal history category is the category applicable at the time the defendant originally was sentenced to a term of supervision.

(b) *Provided*, that—

(1) Where the statutorily authorized maximum term of imprisonment that is imposable upon revocation is less than the minimum of the applicable range, the statutorily authorized maximum term shall be substituted for the applicable range; and

(2) Where the minimum term of imprisonment required by statute, if any, is greater than the maximum of the applicable range, the minimum term of imprisonment required by statute shall be substituted for the applicable range.

(3) In any other case, the sentence upon revocation may be imposed at any point within the applicable range, provided that the sentence—

(A) is not greater than the maximum term of imprisonment

authorized by statute; and
(B) is not less than any minimum term of imprisonment required by statute.

Commentary

Application Notes:

1. The criminal history category to be used in determining the applicable range of imprisonment in the Revocation Table is the category determined at the time the defendant originally was sentenced to the term of supervision. The criminal history category is not to be recalculated because the ranges set forth in the Revocation Table have been designed to take into account that the defendant violated supervision. In the rare case in which no criminal history category was determined when the defendant originally was sentenced to the term of supervision being revoked, the court shall determine the criminal history category that would have been applicable at the time the defendant originally was sentenced to the term of supervision. (*See* the criminal history provisions of §§4A1.1–4B1.4.)
2. Departure from the applicable range of imprisonment in the Revocation Table may be warranted when the court departed from the applicable range for reasons set forth in §4A1.3 (Departures Based on Inadequacy of Criminal History Category) in originally imposing the sentence that resulted in supervision. Additionally, an upward departure may be warranted when a defendant, subsequent to the federal sentence resulting in supervision, has been sentenced for an offense that is not the basis of the violation proceeding.
3. In the case of a Grade C violation that is associated with a high risk of new felonious conduct (*e.g.*, a defendant, under supervision for conviction of criminal sexual abuse, violates the condition that the defendant not associate with children by loitering near a schoolyard), an upward departure may be warranted.
4. Where the original sentence was the result of a downward departure (*e.g.*, as a reward for substantial assistance), or a charge reduction that resulted in a sentence below the guideline range applicable to the defendant's underlying conduct, an upward departure may be warranted.
5. Upon a finding that a defendant violated a condition of probation or supervised release by being in possession of a controlled substance or firearm or by refusing to comply with a condition requiring drug testing, the court is required to revoke probation or supervised release and impose a sentence that includes a term of imprisonment. 18 U.S.C. §§ 3565(b), 3583(g).
6. In the case of a defendant who fails a drug test, the court shall consider whether the availability of appropriate substance abuse programs, or a defendant's current or past participation in such programs, warrants an exception from the requirement of mandatory revocation and imprisonment under 18 U.S.C. §§ 3565(b) and 3583(g). 18 U.S.C. §§ 3563(a), 3583(d).

Historical Note

Effective November 1, 1990 (amendment 362); November 1, 1995 (amendment 533); November 1, 2010 (amendment 747).

§7B1.5. No Credit for Time Under Supervision (Policy Statement)

(a) Upon revocation of probation, no credit shall be given (toward any sentence of imprisonment imposed) for any portion of the term of probation served prior to revocation.
(b) Upon revocation of supervised release, no credit shall be given (toward any term of imprisonment ordered) for time previously served on post-release supervision.

(c) *Provided,* that in the case of a person serving a period of supervised release on a foreign sentence under the provisions of 18 U.S.C. § 4106A, credit shall be given for time on supervision prior to revocation, except that no credit shall be given for any time in escape or absconder status.

Commentary

Application Note:

1. Subsection (c) implements 18 U.S.C. § 4106A(b)(1)(C), which provides that the combined periods of imprisonment and supervised release in transfer treaty cases shall not exceed the term of imprisonment imposed by the foreign court.

Background: This section provides that time served on probation or supervised release is not to be credited in the determination of any term of imprisonment imposed upon revocation. Other aspects of the defendant's conduct, such as compliance with supervision conditions and adjustment while under supervision, appropriately may be considered by the court in the determination of the sentence to be imposed within the applicable revocation range.

Historical Note

Effective November 1, 1990 (amendment 362).

CHAPTER EIGHT
SENTENCING OF ORGANIZATIONS

Introductory Commentary

The guidelines and policy statements in this chapter apply when the convicted defendant is an organization. Organizations can act only through agents and, under federal criminal law, generally are vicariously liable for offenses committed by their agents. At the same time, individual agents are responsible for their own criminal conduct. Federal prosecutions of organizations therefore frequently involve individual and organizational co-defendants. Convicted individual agents of organizations are sentenced in accordance with the guidelines and policy statements in the preceding chapters. This chapter is designed so that the sanctions imposed upon organizations and their agents, taken together, will provide just punishment, adequate deterrence, and incentives for organizations to maintain internal mechanisms for preventing, detecting, and reporting criminal conduct.

This chapter reflects the following general principles:

First, the court must, whenever practicable, order the organization to remedy any harm caused by the offense. The resources expended to remedy the harm should not be viewed as punishment, but rather as a means of making victims whole for the harm caused.

Second, if the organization operated primarily for a criminal purpose or primarily by criminal means, the fine should be set sufficiently high to divest the organization of all its assets.

Third, the fine range for any other organization should be based on the seriousness of the offense and the culpability of the organization. The seriousness of the offense generally will be reflected by the greatest of the pecuniary gain, the pecuniary loss, or the amount in a guideline offense level fine table. Culpability generally will be determined by six factors that the sentencing court must consider. The four factors that increase the ultimate punishment of an organization are: (i) the involvement in or tolerance of criminal activity; (ii) the prior history of the organization; (iii) the violation of an order; and (iv) the obstruction of justice. The two factors that mitigate the ultimate punishment of an organization are: (i) the existence of an effective compliance and ethics program; and (ii) self-reporting, cooperation, or acceptance of responsibility.

Fourth, probation is an appropriate sentence for an organizational defendant when needed to ensure that another sanction will be fully implemented, or to ensure that steps will be taken within the organization to reduce the likelihood of future criminal conduct.

These guidelines offer incentives to organizations to reduce and ultimately eliminate criminal conduct by providing a structural foundation from which an organization may selfpolice its own conduct through an effective compliance and ethics program. The prevention and detection of criminal conduct, as facilitated by an effective compliance and ethics program, will assist an organization in encouraging ethical conduct and in complying fully with all applicable laws.

Historical Note

Effective November 1, 1991 (amendment 422). Amended effective November 1, 2004 (amendment 673).

PART A — GENERAL APPLICATION PRINCIPLES

§8A1.1. Applicability of Chapter Eight

This chapter applies to the sentencing of all organizations for felony and Class A misdemeanor offenses.

Commentary

Application Notes:

1. "***Organization***" means "a person other than an individual." 18 U.S.C. § 18. The term includes corporations, partnerships, associations, joint-stock companies, unions, trusts, pension funds, unincorporated organizations, governments and political subdivisions thereof, and non-profit organizations.

2. The fine guidelines in §§8C2.2 through 8C2.9 apply only to specified types of offenses. The other provisions of this chapter apply to the sentencing of all organizations for all felony and Class A misdemeanor offenses. For example, the restitution and probation provisions in Parts B and D of this chapter apply to the sentencing of an organization, even if the fine guidelines in §§8C2.2 through 8C2.9 do not apply.

Historical
Note
Effective November 1, 1991 (amendment 422).

§8A1.2. Application Instructions — Organizations

(a) Determine from Part B, Subpart 1 (Remedying Harm from Criminal Conduct) the sentencing requirements and options relating to restitution, remedial orders, community service, and notice to victims.

(b) Determine from Part C (Fines) the sentencing requirements and options relating to fines:

(1) If the organization operated primarily for a criminal purpose or primarily by criminal means, apply §8C1.1 (Determining the Fine — Criminal Purpose Organizations).

(2) Otherwise, apply §8C2.1 (Applicability of Fine Guidelines) to identify the counts for which the provisions of §§8C2.2 through 8C2.9 apply. For such counts:

(A) Refer to §8C2.2 (Preliminary Determination of Inability to Pay Fine) to determine whether an abbreviated determination of the guideline fine range may be warranted.

(B) Apply §8C2.3 (Offense Level) to determine the offense level from Chapter Two (Offense Conduct) and Chapter Three, Part D (Multiple Counts).

(C) Apply §8C2.4 (Base Fine) to determine the base fine.

(D) Apply §8C2.5 (Culpability Score) to determine the culpability score. To determine whether the organization had an effective compliance and ethics program for purposes of §8C2.5(f), apply §8B2.1 (Effective Compliance and Ethics Program).

(E) Apply §8C2.6 (Minimum and Maximum Multipliers) to determine the minimum and maximum multipliers corresponding to the culpability score.

(F) Apply §8C2.7 (Guideline Fine Range — Organizations) to determine the minimum and maximum of the guideline

fine range.
(G) Refer to §8C2.8 (Determining the Fine Within the Range) to determine the amount of the fine within the applicable guideline range.
(H) Apply §8C2.9 (Disgorgement) to determine whether an increase to the fine is required.
For any count or counts not covered under §8C2.1 (Applicability of Fine Guidelines), apply §8C2.10 (Determining the Fine for Other Counts).
(3) Apply the provisions relating to the implementation of the sentence of a fine in Part C, Subpart 3 (Implementing the Sentence of a Fine).
(4) For grounds for departure from the applicable guideline fine range, refer to Part C, Subpart 4 (Departures from the Guideline Fine Range).
(c) Determine from Part D (Organizational Probation) the sentencing requirements and options relating to probation.
(d) Determine from Part E (Special Assessments, Forfeitures, and Costs) the sentencing requirements relating to special assessments, forfeitures, and costs.

Commentary

Application Notes:

1. Determinations under this chapter are to be based upon the facts and information specified in the applicable guideline. Determinations that reference other chapters are to be made under the standards applicable to determinations under those chapters.
2. The definitions in the Commentary to §1B1.1 (Application Instructions) and the guidelines and commentary in §§1B1.2 through 1B1.8 apply to determinations under this chapter unless otherwise specified. The adjustments in Chapter Three, Parts A (Victim-Related Adjustments), B (Role in the Offense), C (Obstruction and Related Adjustments), and E (Acceptance of Responsibility) do not apply. The provisions of Chapter Six (Sentencing Procedures, Plea Agreements, and Crime Victims' Rights) apply to proceedings in which the defendant is an organization. Guidelines and policy statements not referenced in this chapter, directly or indirectly, do not apply when the defendant is an organization; *e.g.*, the policy statements in Chapter Seven (Violations of Probation and Supervised Release) do not apply to organizations.
3. The following are definitions of terms used frequently in this chapter:
(A) "***Offense***" means the offense of conviction and all relevant conduct under §1B1.3 (Relevant Conduct) unless a different meaning is specified or is otherwise clear from the context. The term "***instant***" is used in connection with "offense," "federal offense," or "offense of conviction," as the case may be, to distinguish the violation for which the defendant is being sentenced from a prior or subsequent offense, or from an offense before another court (*e.g.*, an offense before a state court involving the same underlying conduct).
(B) "***High-level personnel of the organization***" means individuals who have substantial control over the organization or who have a substantial role in the making of policy within the organization. The term includes: a director; an executive officer; an individual in charge of a major business or functional unit of the organization, such as sales, administration, or finance; and an individual with a substantial ownership interest. "***High-level personnel of a unit of the organization***" is defined in the Commentary to §8C2.5 (Culpability Score).

(C) "***Substantial authority personnel***" means individuals who within the scope of their authority exercise a substantial measure of discretion in acting on behalf of an organization. The term includes high-level personnel of the organization, individuals who exercise substantial supervisory authority (*e.g.*, a plant manager, a sales manager), and any other individuals who, although not a part of an organization's management, nevertheless exercise substantial discretion when acting within the scope of their authority (*e.g.*, an individual with authority in an organization to negotiate or set price levels or an individual authorized to negotiate or approve significant contracts). Whether an individual falls within this category must be determined on a case-by-case basis.

(D) "***Agent***" means any individual, including a director, an officer, an employee, or an independent contractor, authorized to act on behalf of the organization.

(E) An individual "***condoned***" an offense if the individual knew of the offense and did not take reasonable steps to prevent or terminate the offense.

(F) "***Similar misconduct***" means prior conduct that is similar in nature to the conduct underlying the instant offense, without regard to whether or not such conduct violated the same statutory provision. For example, prior Medicare fraud would be misconduct similar to an instant offense involving another type of fraud.

(G) "***Prior criminal adjudication***" means conviction by trial, plea of guilty (including an *Alford* plea), or plea of *nolo contendere*.

(H) "***Pecuniary gain***" is derived from 18 U.S.C. § 3571(d) and means the additional before-tax profit to the defendant resulting from the relevant conduct of the offense. Gain can result from either additional revenue or cost savings. For example, an offense involving odometer tampering can produce additional revenue. In such a case, the pecuniary gain is the additional revenue received because the automobiles appeared to have less mileage, *i.e.*, the difference between the price received or expected for the automobiles with the apparent mileage and the fair market value of the automobiles with the actual mileage. An offense involving defense procurement fraud related to defective product testing can produce pecuniary gain resulting from cost savings. In such a case, the pecuniary gain is the amount saved because the product was not tested in the required manner.

(I) "***Pecuniary loss***" is derived from 18 U.S.C. § 3571(d) and is equivalent to the term "loss" as used in Chapter Two (Offense Conduct). *See* Commentary to §2B1.1 (Theft, Property Destruction, and Fraud), and definitions of "tax loss" in Chapter Two, Part T (Offenses Involving Taxation).

(J) An individual was "***willfully ignorant of the offense***" if the individual did not investigate the possible occurrence of unlawful conduct despite knowledge of circumstances that would lead a reasonable person to investigate whether unlawful conduct had occurred.

Historical
Note

Effective November 1, 1991 (amendment 422); November 1, 1997 (amendment 546); November 1, 2001 (amendment 617); November 1, 2004 (amendment 673); November 1, 2010 (amendment 747); November 1, 2011 (amendment 758).

PART B — REMEDYING HARM FROM CRIMINAL CONDUCT, AND EFFECTIVE COMPLIANCE AND ETHICS PROGRAM

Historical
Note

Effective November 1, 1991 (amendment 422). Amended effective November 1, 2004 (amendment 673).

1. REMEDYING HARM FROM CRIMINAL CONDUCT

Historical
Note

Effective November 1, 2004 (amendment 673).

Introductory Commentary

As a general principle, the court should require that the organization take all appropriate steps to provide compensation to victims and otherwise remedy the harm caused or threatened by the offense. A restitution order or an order of probation requiring restitution can be used to compensate identifiable victims of the offense. A remedial order or an order of probation requiring community service can be used to reduce or eliminate the harm threatened, or to repair the harm caused by the offense, when that harm or threatened harm would otherwise not be remedied. An order of notice to victims can be used to notify unidentified victims of the offense.

Historical Note

Effective November 1, 1991 (amendment 422).

§8B1.1. Restitution — Organizations

(a) In the case of an identifiable victim, the court shall—

(1) enter a restitution order for the full amount of the victim's loss, if such order is authorized under 18 U.S.C. § 2248, § 2259, § 2264, § 2327, § 3663, or § 3663A; or

(2) impose a term of probation or supervised release with a condition requiring restitution for the full amount of the victim's loss, if the offense is not an offense for which restitution is authorized under 18 U.S.C. § 3663(a)(1) but otherwise meets the criteria for an order of restitution under that section.

(b) *Provided*, that the provisions of subsection (a) do not apply—

(1) when full restitution has been made; or

(2) in the case of a restitution order under § 3663; a restitution order under 18 U.S.C. § 3663A that pertains to an offense against property described in 18 U.S.C. § 3663A(c)(1)(A)(ii); or

a condition of restitution imposed pursuant to subsection (a)(2) above, to the extent the court finds, from facts on the record, that (A) the number of identifiable victims is so large as to make restitution impracticable; or (B) determining complex issues of fact related to the cause or amount of the victim's losses would complicate or prolong the sentencing process to a degree that the need to provide restitution to any victim is outweighed by the burden on the sentencing process.

(c) If a defendant is ordered to make restitution to an identifiable victim and to pay a fine, the court shall order that any money paid by the defendant shall first be applied to satisfy the order of restitution.

(d) A restitution order may direct the defendant to make a single, lump sum payment, partial payments at specified intervals, in-kind payments, or a combination of payments at specified intervals and inkind payments. *See* 18 U.S.C. § 3664(f)(3)(A). An in-kind payment may be in the form of (1) return of property; (2) replacement of property; or (3) if the victim agrees, services rendered to the victim or to a person or organization other than the victim. *See* 18 U.S.C. § 3664(f)(4).

(e) A restitution order may direct the defendant to make nominal periodic payments if the court finds from facts on the record that the economic circumstances of the defendant do not allow the payment of any amount of a restitution order, and do not allow for the payment of the full amount of a restitution order in the foreseeable future under any reasonable schedule of payments.

(f) Special Instruction

(1) This guideline applies only to a defendant convicted of an offense committed on or after November 1, 1997. Notwithstanding the provisions of §1B1.11 (Use of Guidelines Manual in Effect on Date of Sentencing), use the former §8B1.1 (set forth in Appendix C, amendment 571) in lieu of this guideline in any other case.

Commentary

Background: Section 3553(a)(7) of Title 18, United States Code, requires the court, "in determining the particular sentence to be imposed," to consider "the need to provide restitution to any victims of the offense." Orders of restitution are authorized under 18 U.S.C. §§ 2248, 2259, 2264, 2327, 3663, and 3663A. For offenses for which an order of restitution is not authorized, restitution may be imposed as a condition of probation.

Historical Note

Effective November 1, 1991 (amendment 422); November 1, 1997 (amendment 571).

§8B1.2. Remedial Orders — Organizations (Policy Statement)

(a) To the extent not addressed under §8B1.1 (Restitution — Organizations), a remedial order imposed as a condition of probation may require the organization to remedy the harm caused by the offense and to eliminate or reduce the risk that the instant offense will cause future harm.

(b) If the magnitude of expected future harm can be reasonably estimated, the court may require the organization to create a trust fund sufficient to address that expected harm.

Commentary

Background: The purposes of a remedial order are to remedy harm that has already occurred and to prevent future harm. A remedial order requiring corrective action by the organization may be necessary to prevent future injury from the instant offense, *e.g.*, a product recall for a food and drug violation or a clean-up order for an environmental violation. In some cases in which a remedial order potentially may be appropriate, a governmental regulatory agency, *e.g.*, the Environmental Protection Agency or the Food and Drug Administration, may have authority to order remedial measures. In such cases, a remedial order by the court may not be necessary. If a remedial order is entered, it should be coordinated with any administrative or civil actions taken by the appropriate governmental regulatory agency.

Historical Note

Effective November 1, 1991 (amendment 422).

§8B1.3. Community Service — Organizations (Policy Statement)

Community service may be ordered as a condition of probation where such community service is reasonably designed to repair the harm caused by the offense.

Commentary

Background: An organization can perform community service only by employing its resources or paying its employees or others to do so. Consequently, an order that an organization perform community service is essentially an indirect monetary sanction, and therefore generally less desirable than a direct monetary sanction. However, where the convicted organization possesses knowledge, facilities, or skills that uniquely qualify it to repair damage caused by the offense, community service directed at repairing damage may provide an efficient means of remedying harm caused.

In the past, some forms of community service imposed on organizations have not been related to the purposes of sentencing. Requiring a defendant to endow a chair at a university or to contribute to a local charity would not be consistent with this section unless such community service provided a means for preventive or corrective action directly related to the offense and therefore served one of the purposes of sentencing set forth in 18 U.S.C. § 3553(a).

Historical
Note
Effective November 1, 1991 (amendment 422).

§8B1.4. Order of Notice to Victims — Organizations

Apply §5F1.4 (Order of Notice to Victims).

Historical
Note
Effective November 1, 1991 (amendment 422).

* * * * *

2. EFFECTIVE COMPLIANCE AND ETHICS PROGRAM

Historical
Note
Effective November 1, 2004 (amendment 673).

§8B2.1. Effective Compliance and Ethics Program

(a) To have an effective compliance and ethics program, for purposes of subsection (f) of §8C2.5 (Culpability Score) and subsection (b)(1) of §8D1.4 (Recommended Conditions of Probation — Organizations), an organization shall—

(1) exercise due diligence to prevent and detect criminal conduct; and

(2) otherwise promote an organizational culture that encourages ethical conduct and a commitment to compliance with the law.

Such compliance and ethics program shall be reasonably designed, implemented, and enforced so that the program is generally effective in preventing and detecting criminal conduct. The failure to prevent or detect the instant offense does not necessarily mean that the program is not generally effective in preventing and detecting criminal conduct.

(b) Due diligence and the promotion of an organizational culture that encourages ethical conduct and a commitment to compliance with the law within the meaning of subsection (a) minimally require the following:

(1) The organization shall establish standards and procedures to prevent and detect criminal conduct.

(2) (A) The organization's governing authority shall be knowledgeable about the content and operation of the compliance and ethics program and shall exercise reasonable oversight with respect to the implementation and effectiveness of the compliance and ethics program.

(B) High-level personnel of the organization shall ensure that the organization has an effective compliance and ethics

program, as described in this guideline. Specific individual(s) within high-level personnel shall be assigned overall responsibility for the compliance and ethics program.
(C) Specific individual(s) within the organization shall be delegated day-to-day operational responsibility for the compliance and ethics program. Individual(s) with operational responsibility shall report periodically to high-level personnel and, as appropriate, to the governing authority, or an appropriate subgroup of the governing authority, on the effectiveness of the compliance and ethics program. To carry out such operational responsibility, such individual(s) shall be given adequate resources, appropriate authority, and direct access to the governing authority or an appropriate subgroup of the governing authority.
(3) The organization shall use reasonable efforts not to include within the substantial authority personnel of the organization any individual whom the organization knew, or should have known through the exercise of due diligence, has engaged in illegal activities or other conduct inconsistent with an effective compliance and ethics program.
(4) (A) The organization shall take reasonable steps to communicate periodically and in a practical manner its standards and procedures, and other aspects of the compliance and ethics program, to the individuals referred to in subparagraph (B) by conducting effective training programs and otherwise disseminating information appropriate to such individuals' respective roles and responsibilities.

(B) The individuals referred to in subparagraph (A) are the members of the governing authority, high-level personnel, substantial authority personnel, the organization's employees, and, as appropriate, the organization's agents.
(5) The organization shall take reasonable steps—
(A) to ensure that the organization's compliance and ethics program is followed, including monitoring and auditing to detect criminal conduct;
(B) to evaluate periodically the effectiveness of the organization's compliance and ethics program; and
(C) to have and publicize a system, which may include mechanisms that allow for anonymity or confidentiality, whereby the organization's employees and agents may report or seek guidance regarding potential or actual criminal conduct without fear of retaliation.
(6) The organization's compliance and ethics program shall be promoted and enforced consistently throughout the organization through (A) appropriate incentives to perform in accordance with the compliance and ethics program; and (B) appropriate

disciplinary measures for engaging in criminal conduct and for failing to take reasonable steps to prevent or detect criminal conduct.
(7) After criminal conduct has been detected, the organization shall take reasonable steps to respond appropriately to the criminal conduct and to prevent further similar criminal conduct, including making any necessary modifications to the organization's compliance and ethics program.
(c) In implementing subsection (b), the organization shall periodically assess the risk of criminal conduct and shall take appropriate steps to design, implement, or modify each requirement set forth in subsection (b) to reduce the risk of criminal conduct identified through this process.

Commentary

Application Notes:

1. **Definitions.**—For purposes of this guideline:
"***Compliance and ethics program***" means a program designed to prevent and detect criminal conduct.

"***Governing authority***" means the (A) the Board of Directors; or (B) if the organization does not have a Board of Directors, the highest-level governing body of the organization.
"***High-level personnel of the organization***" and "***substantial authority personnel***" have the meaning given those terms in the Commentary to §8A1.2 (Application Instructions — Organizations).
"***Standards and procedures***" means standards of conduct and internal controls that are reasonably capable of reducing the likelihood of criminal conduct.
2. **Factors to Consider in Meeting Requirements of this Guideline.**—
(A) **In General.**—Each of the requirements set forth in this guideline shall be met by an organization; however, in determining what specific actions are necessary to meet those requirements, factors that shall be considered include: (i) applicable industry practice or the standards called for by any applicable governmental regulation; (ii) the size of the organization; and (iii) similar misconduct.
(B) **Applicable Governmental Regulation and Industry Practice.**—An organization's failure to incorporate and follow applicable industry practice or the standards called for by any applicable governmental regulation weighs against a finding of an effective compliance and ethics program.
(C) **The Size of the Organization.**—
(i) **In General.**—The formality and scope of actions that an organization shall take to meet the requirements of this guideline, including the necessary features of the organization's standards and procedures, depend on the size of the organization.
(ii) **Large Organizations.**—A large organization generally shall devote more formal operations and greater resources in meeting the requirements of this guideline than shall a small organization. As appropriate, a large organization should encourage small organizations (especially those that have, or seek to have, a business relationship with the large organization) to implement effective compliance and ethics programs.
(iii) **Small Organizations.**—In meeting the requirements of this guideline, small organizations shall demonstrate the same degree of commitment to ethical conduct and compliance with the law as large organizations. However, a small organization may meet the requirements of this guideline with less formality and fewer resources than would be expected of large organizations. In appropriate

circumstances, reliance on existing resources and simple systems can demonstrate a degree of commitment that, for a large organization, would only be demonstrated through more formally planned and implemented systems. Examples of the informality and use of fewer resources with which a small organization may meet the requirements of this guideline include the following: (I) the governing authority's discharge of its responsibility for oversight of the compliance and ethics program by directly managing the organization's compliance and ethics efforts; (II) training employees through informal staff meetings, and monitoring through regular "walk-arounds" or continuous observation while managing the organization; (III) using available personnel, rather than employing separate staff, to carry out the compliance and ethics

program; and (IV) modeling its own compliance and ethics program on existing, well-regarded compliance and ethics programs and best practices of other similar organizations.

(D) **Recurrence of Similar Misconduct.**—Recurrence of similar misconduct creates doubt regarding whether the organization took reasonable steps to meet the requirements of this guideline. For purposes of this subparagraph, "***similar misconduct***" has the meaning given that term in the Commentary to §8A1.2 (Application Instructions — Organizations).

3. **Application of Subsection (b)(2).**—High-level personnel and substantial authority personnel of the organization shall be knowledgeable about the content and operation of the compliance and ethics program, shall perform their assigned duties consistent with the exercise of due diligence, and shall promote an organizational culture that encourages ethical conduct and a commitment to compliance with the law.

If the specific individual(s) assigned overall responsibility for the compliance and ethics program does not have day-to-day operational responsibility for the program, then the individual(s) with day-to-day operational responsibility for the program typically should, no less than annually, give the governing authority or an appropriate subgroup thereof information on the implementation and effectiveness of the compliance and ethics program.

4. **Application of Subsection (b)(3).**—

(A) **Consistency with Other Law.**—Nothing in subsection (b)(3) is intended to require conduct inconsistent with any Federal, State, or local law, including any law governing employment or hiring practices.

(B) **Implementation.**—In implementing subsection (b)(3), the organization shall hire and promote individuals so as to ensure that all individuals within the high-level personnel and substantial authority personnel of the organization will perform their assigned duties in a manner consistent with the exercise of due diligence and the promotion of an organizational culture that encourages ethical conduct and a commitment to compliance with the law under subsection (a). With respect to the hiring or promotion of such individuals, an organization shall consider the relatedness of the individual's illegal activities and other misconduct (*i.e.*, other conduct inconsistent with an effective compliance and ethics program) to the specific responsibilities the individual is anticipated to be assigned and other factors such as:

(i) the recency of the individual's illegal activities and other misconduct; and

(ii) whether the individual has engaged in other such illegal activities and other such misconduct.

5. **Application of Subsection (b)(6).**—Adequate discipline of individuals responsible for an offense is a necessary component of enforcement; however, the form of discipline that will be appropriate will be case specific.

6. **Application of Subsection (b)(7).**—Subsection (b)(7) has two aspects.

First, the organization should respond appropriately to the criminal conduct. The organization should take reasonable steps, as warranted under the circumstances, to remedy the harm resulting from the criminal conduct. These steps may include, where appropriate, providing restitution to identifiable victims, as well as other forms of remediation.

Other reasonable steps to respond appropriately to the criminal conduct may include selfreporting and cooperation with authorities.

Second, the organization should act appropriately to prevent further similar criminal conduct, including assessing the compliance and ethics program and making modifications necessary to ensure the program is effective. The steps taken should be consistent with subsections (b)(5) and (c) and may include the use of an outside professional advisor to ensure adequate assessment and implementation of any modifications.

7. **Application of Subsection (c).**—To meet the requirements of subsection (c), an organization shall:

(A) Assess periodically the risk that criminal conduct will occur, including assessing the following:

(i) The nature and seriousness of such criminal conduct.

(ii) The likelihood that certain criminal conduct may occur because of the nature of the organization's business. If, because of the nature of an organization's business, there is a substantial risk that certain types of criminal conduct may occur, the organization shall take reasonable steps to prevent and detect that type of criminal conduct. For example, an organization that, due to the nature of its business, employs sales personnel who have flexibility to set prices shall establish standards and procedures designed to prevent and detect price-fixing. An organization that, due to the nature of its business, employs sales personnel who have flexibility to represent the material characteristics of a product shall establish standards and procedures designed to prevent and detect fraud.

(iii) The prior history of the organization. The prior history of an organization may indicate types of criminal conduct that it shall take actions to prevent and detect.

(B) Prioritize periodically, as appropriate, the actions taken pursuant to any requirement set forth in subsection (b), in order to focus on preventing and detecting the criminal conduct identified under subparagraph (A) of this note as most serious, and most likely, to occur.

(C) Modify, as appropriate, the actions taken pursuant to any requirement set forth in subsection (b) to reduce the risk of criminal conduct identified under subparagraph (A) of this note as most serious, and most likely, to occur.

Background: This section sets forth the requirements for an effective compliance and ethics program. This section responds to section 805(a)(5) of the Sarbanes–Oxley Act of 2002, Public Law 107–204, which directed the Commission to review and amend, as appropriate, the guidelines and related policy statements to ensure that the guidelines that apply to organizations in this chapter "are sufficient to deter and punish organizational criminal misconduct."

The requirements set forth in this guideline are intended to achieve reasonable prevention and detection of criminal conduct for which the organization would be vicariously liable. The prior diligence of an organization in seeking to prevent and detect criminal conduct has a direct bearing on the appropriate penalties and probation terms for the organization if it is convicted and sentenced for a criminal offense.

Historical Note

Effective November 1, 2004 (amendment 673). Amended effective November 1, 2010 (amendment 744); November 1, 2011 (amendment 758); November 1, 2013 (amendment 778).

PART C — FINES

1. DETERMINING THE FINE — CRIMINAL PURPOSE ORGANIZATIONS

§8C1.1. Determining the Fine — Criminal Purpose Organizations

If, upon consideration of the nature and circumstances of the offense and the history and characteristics of the organization, the court determines that the organization operated primarily for a criminal purpose or primarily by criminal means, the fine shall be set at an amount (subject to the statutory maximum) sufficient to divest the organization of all its net assets. When this section applies, Subpart 2 (Determining the Fine — Other Organizations) and §8C3.4 (Fines Paid by Owners of Closely Held Organizations) do not apply.

Commentary

Application Note:

1. "***Net assets***," as used in this section, means the assets remaining after payment of all legitimate claims against assets by known innocent bona fide creditors.

Background: This guideline addresses the case in which the court, based upon an examination of the nature and circumstances of the offense and the history and characteristics of the organization, determines that the organization was operated primarily for a criminal purpose (*e.g.*, a front for a scheme that was designed to commit fraud; an organization established to participate in the illegal manufacture, importation, or distribution of a controlled substance) or operated primarily by criminal means (*e.g.*, a hazardous waste disposal business that had no legitimate means of disposing of hazardous waste). In such a case, the fine shall be set at an amount sufficient to remove all of the organization's net assets. If the extent of the assets of the organization is unknown, the maximum fine authorized by statute should be imposed, absent innocent bona fide creditors.

Historical
Note
Effective November 1, 1991 (amendment 422).

* * * * *

2. DETERMINING THE FINE — OTHER ORGANIZATIONS

§8C2.1. Applicability of Fine Guidelines

The provisions of §§8C2.2 through 8C2.9 apply to each count for which the applicable guideline offense level is determined under:

(a) §§2B1.1, 2B1.4, 2B2.3, 2B4.1, 2B5.3, 2B6.1;
§§2C1.1, 2C1.2, 2C1.6;
§§2D1.7, 2D3.1, 2D3.2;
§§2E3.1, 2E4.1, 2E5.1, 2E5.3;
§2G3.1;
§§2K1.1, 2K2.1;
§2L1.1;
§2N3.1;
§2R1.1;
§§2S1.1, 2S1.3;
§§2T1.1, 2T1.4, 2T1.6, 2T1.7, 2T1.8, 2T1.9, 2T2.1, 2T2.2, 2T3.1; or

(b) §§2E1.1, 2X1.1, 2X2.1, 2X3.1, 2X4.1, with respect to cases in which the offense level for the underlying offense is determined under one of the guideline sections listed in subsection (a) above.

Commentary

Application Notes:

1. If the Chapter Two offense guideline for a count is listed in subsection (a) or (b) above, and the applicable guideline results in the determination of the offense level by use of one of the listed guidelines, apply the provisions of §§8C2.2 through 8C2.9 to that count. For example, §§8C2.2 through 8C2.9 apply to an offense under §2K2.1 (an offense guideline

listed in subsection (a)), unless the cross reference in that guideline requires the offense level to be determined under an offense guideline section not listed in subsection (a).

2. If the Chapter Two offense guideline for a count is not listed in subsection (a) or (b) above, but the applicable guideline results in the determination of the offense level by use of a listed guideline, apply the provisions of §§8C2.2 through 8C2.9 to that count. For example, where the conduct set forth in a count of conviction ordinarily referenced to §2N2.1 (an offense guideline not listed in subsection (a)) establishes §2B1.1 (Theft, Property Destruction, and Fraud) as the applicable offense guideline (an offense guideline listed in subsection (a)), §§8C2.2 through 8C2.9 would apply because the actual offense level is determined under §2B1.1 (Theft, Property Destruction, and Fraud).

Background: The fine guidelines of this subpart apply only to offenses covered by the guideline sections set forth in subsection (a) above. For example, the provisions of §§8C2.2 through 8C2.9 do not apply to counts for which the applicable guideline offense level is determined under Chapter Two, Part Q (Offenses Involving the Environment). For such cases, §8C2.10 (Determining the Fine for Other Counts) is applicable.

Historical Note

Effective November 1, 1991 (amendment 422). Amended effective November 1, 1992 (amendment 453); November 1, 1993 (amendment 496); November 1, 2001 (amendments 617, 619, and 634); November 1, 2005 (amendment 679).

§8C2.2. Preliminary Determination of Inability to Pay Fine

(a) Where it is readily ascertainable that the organization cannot and is not likely to become able (even on an installment schedule) to pay restitution required under §8B1.1 (Restitution — Organizations), a determination of the guideline fine range is unnecessary because, pursuant to §8C3.3(a), no fine would be imposed.

(b) Where it is readily ascertainable through a preliminary determination of the minimum of the guideline fine range (*see* §§8C2.3 through 8C2.7) that the organization cannot and is not likely to become able (even on an installment schedule) to pay such minimum guideline fine, a further determination of the guideline fine range is unnecessary. Instead, the court may use the preliminary determination and impose the fine that would result from the application of §8C3.3 (Reduction of Fine Based on Inability to Pay).

Commentary

Application Notes:

1. In a case of a determination under subsection (a), a statement that "the guideline fine range was not determined because it is readily ascertainable that the defendant cannot and is not likely to become able to pay restitution" is recommended.

2. In a case of a determination under subsection (b), a statement that "no precise determination of the guideline fine range is required because it is readily ascertainable that the defendant cannot and is not likely to become able to pay the minimum of the guideline fine range" is recommended.

Background: Many organizational defendants lack the ability to pay restitution. In addition, many organizational defendants who may be able to pay restitution lack the ability to pay the minimum fine called for by §8C2.7(a). In such cases, a complete determination of the guideline fine range may be a needless exercise. This section provides for an abbreviated determination of the guideline fine range that can be applied where it is readily ascertainable that the fine within the guideline fine range determined under §8C2.7 (Guideline Fine Range — Organizations) would be reduced under §8C3.3 (Reduction of Fine Based on Inability to Pay).

Historical Note

Effective November 1, 1991 (amendment 422).

§8C2.3. Offense Level

(a) For each count covered by §8C2.1 (Applicability of Fine Guidelines), use the applicable Chapter Two guideline to determine the base offense level and apply, in the order listed, any appropriate adjustments contained in that guideline.

(b) Where there is more than one such count, apply Chapter Three, Part D (Multiple Counts) to determine the combined offense level.

Commentary

Application Notes:

1. In determining the offense level under this section, "***defendant***," as used in Chapter Two, includes any agent of the organization for whose conduct the organization is criminally responsible.

2. In determining the offense level under this section, apply the provisions of §§1B1.2 through 1B1.8. Do not apply the adjustments in Chapter Three, Parts A (Victim-Related Adjustments), B (Role in the Offense), C (Obstruction and Related Adjustments), and E (Acceptance of Responsibility).

Historical
Note
Effective November 1, 1991 (amendment 422). Amended effective November 1, 2011 (amendment 758).

§8C2.4. Base Fine

(a) The base fine is the greatest of:

(1) the amount from the table in subsection (d) below corresponding to the offense level determined under §8C2.3 (Offense Level); or

(2) the pecuniary gain to the organization from the offense; or

(3) the pecuniary loss from the offense caused by the organization, to the extent the loss was caused intentionally, knowingly, or recklessly.

(b) *Provided*, that if the applicable offense guideline in Chapter Two includes a special instruction for organizational fines, that special instruction shall be applied, as appropriate.

(c) *Provided, further*, that to the extent the calculation of either pecuniary gain or pecuniary loss would unduly complicate or prolong the sentencing process, that amount, *i.e.*, gain or loss as appropriate, shall not be used for the determination of the base fine.

(d) OFFENSE LEVEL FINE TABLE

Offense Level	Amount
6 or less	$8,500
7	$15,000
8	$15,000
9	$25,000
10	$35,000
11	$50,000
12	$70,000
13	$100,000

14 $150,000
15 $200,000
16 $300,000
17 $450,000
18 $600,000
19 $850,000
20 $1,000,000
21 $1,500,000
22 $2,000,000
23 $3,000,000
24 $3,500,000
25 $5,000,000
26 $6,500,000
27 $8,500,000
28 $10,000,000
29 $15,000,000
30 $20,000,000
31 $25,000,000
32 $30,000,000
33 $40,000,000
34 $50,000,000
35 $65,000,000
36 $80,000,000
37 $100,000,000
38 or more $150,000,000.

(e) Special Instruction

(1) For offenses committed prior to November 1, 2015, use the offense level fine table that was set forth in the version of §8C2.4(d) that was in effect on November 1, 2014, rather than the offense level fine table set forth in subsection (d) above.

Commentary

Application Notes:

1. "***Pecuniary gain***," "***pecuniary loss***," and "***offense***" are defined in the Commentary to §8A1.2 (Application Instructions — Organizations). Note that subsections (a)(2) and (a)(3) contain certain limitations as to the use of pecuniary gain and pecuniary loss in determining the base fine. Under subsection (a)(2), the pecuniary gain used to determine the base fine is the pecuniary gain to the organization from the offense. Under subsection (a)(3), the pecuniary loss used to determine the base fine is the pecuniary loss from the offense caused by the organization, to the extent that such loss was caused intentionally, knowingly, or recklessly.

2. Under 18 U.S.C. § 3571(d), the court is not required to calculate pecuniary loss or pecuniary gain to the extent that determination of loss or gain would unduly complicate or prolong the sentencing process. Nevertheless, the court may need to approximate loss in order to calculate offense levels under Chapter Two. *See* Commentary to §2B1.1 (Theft, Property Destruction, and Fraud). If loss is approximated for purposes of determining the applicable offense level, the court should use that approximation as the starting point for calculating pecuniary loss under this section.

3. In a case of an attempted offense or a conspiracy to commit an offense, pecuniary loss and pecuniary gain are to be determined in accordance with the principles stated in

§2X1.1 (Attempt, Solicitation, or Conspiracy).
4. In a case involving multiple participants (*i.e.*, multiple organizations, or the organization and individual(s) unassociated with the organization), the applicable offense level is to be determined without regard to apportionment of the gain from or loss caused by the offense. *See* §1B1.3 (Relevant Conduct). However, if the base fine is determined under subsections (a)(2) or (a)(3), the court may, as appropriate, apportion gain or loss considering the defendant's relative culpability and other pertinent factors. Note also that under §2R1.1(d)(1), the volume of commerce, which is used in determining a proxy for loss under §8C2.4(a)(3), is limited to the volume of commerce attributable to the defendant.
5. Special instructions regarding the determination of the base fine are contained in §§2B4.1 (Bribery in Procurement of Bank Loan and Other Commercial Bribery); 2C1.1 (Offering, Giving, Soliciting, or Receiving a Bribe; Extortion Under Color of Official Right; Fraud Involving the Deprivation of the Intangible Right to Honest Services of Public Officials; Conspiracy to Defraud by Interference with Governmental Functions); 2C1.2 (Offering, Giving, Soliciting, or Receiving a Gratuity); 2E5.1 (Offering, Accepting, or Soliciting a Bribe or Gratuity Affecting the Operation of an Employee Welfare or Pension Benefit Plan; Prohibited Payments or Lending of Money by Employer or Agent to Employees, Representatives, or Labor Organizations); and 2R1.1 (Bid-Rigging, Price-Fixing or Market-Allocation Agreements Among Competitors).

Background: Under this section, the base fine is determined in one of three ways: (1) by the amount, based on the offense level, from the table in subsection (d); (2) by the pecuniary gain to the organization from the offense; and (3) by the pecuniary loss caused by the organization, to the extent that such loss was caused intentionally, knowingly, or recklessly. In certain cases, special instructions for determining the loss or offense level amount apply. As a general rule, the base fine measures the seriousness of the offense. The determinants of the base fine are selected so that, in conjunction with the multipliers derived from the culpability score in §8C2.5 (Culpability Score), they will result in guideline fine ranges appropriate to deter organizational criminal conduct and to provide incentives for organizations to maintain internal

mechanisms for preventing, detecting, and reporting criminal conduct. In order to deter organizations from seeking to obtain financial reward through criminal conduct, this section provides that, when greatest, pecuniary gain to the organization is used to determine the base fine. In order to ensure that organizations will seek to prevent losses intentionally, knowingly, or recklessly caused by their agents, this section provides that, when greatest, pecuniary loss is used to determine the base fine in such circumstances. Chapter Two provides special instructions for fines that include specific rules for determining the base fine in connection with certain types of offenses in which the calculation of loss or gain is difficult, *e.g.*, price-fixing. For these offenses, the special instructions tailor the base fine to circumstances that occur in connection with such offenses and that generally relate to the magnitude of loss or gain resulting from such offenses.

Historical Note

Effective November 1, 1991 (amendment 422). Amended effective November 1, 1993 (amendment 496); November 1, 1995 (amendment 534); November 1, 2001 (amendment 634); November 1, 2004 (amendments 666 and 673); November 1, 2015 (amendment 791).

§8C2.5. Culpability Score

(a) Start with **5** points and apply subsections (b) through (g) below.

(b) Involvement in or Tolerance of Criminal Activity

If more than one applies, use the greatest:

(1) If—

(A) the organization had 5,000 or more employees and

(i) an individual within high-level personnel of the organization participated in, condoned, or was willfully ignorant of the offense; or

(ii) tolerance of the offense by substantial authority personnel
was pervasive throughout the organization; or
(B) the unit of the organization within which the offense was
committed had 5,000 or more employees and
(i) an individual within high-level personnel of the unit
participated in, condoned, or was willfully ignorant of
the offense; or
(ii) tolerance of the offense by substantial authority personnel
was pervasive throughout such unit,
add **5** points; or

(2) If—
(A) the organization had 1,000 or more employees and
(i) an individual within high-level personnel of the organization
participated in, condoned, or was willfully
ignorant of the offense; or
(ii) tolerance of the offense by substantial authority personnel
was pervasive throughout the organization; or
(B) the unit of the organization within which the offense was
committed had 1,000 or more employees and
(i) an individual within high-level personnel of the unit
participated in, condoned, or was willfully ignorant of
the offense; or
(ii) tolerance of the offense by substantial authority personnel
was pervasive throughout such unit,
add **4** points; or
(3) If—
(A) the organization had 200 or more employees and
(i) an individual within high-level personnel of the organization
participated in, condoned, or was willfully
ignorant of the offense; or
(ii) tolerance of the offense by substantial authority personnel
was pervasive throughout the organization; or
(B) the unit of the organization within which the offense was
committed had 200 or more employees and
(i) an individual within high-level personnel of the unit
participated in, condoned, or was willfully ignorant of
the offense; or
(ii) tolerance of the offense by substantial authority personnel
was pervasive throughout such unit,
add **3** points; or

(4) If the organization had 50 or more employees and an individual
within substantial authority personnel participated in, condoned,
or was willfully ignorant of the offense, add **2** points; or
(5) If the organization had 10 or more employees and an individual

within substantial authority personnel participated in, condoned, or was willfully ignorant of the offense, add **1** point.

(c) PRIOR HISTORY

If more than one applies, use the greater:

(1) If the organization (or separately managed line of business) committed any part of the instant offense less than 10 years after (A) a criminal adjudication based on similar misconduct; or (B) civil or administrative adjudication(s) based on two or more separate instances of similar misconduct, add **1** point; or

(2) If the organization (or separately managed line of business) committed any part of the instant offense less than 5 years after (A) a criminal adjudication based on similar misconduct; or (B) civil or administrative adjudication(s) based on two or more separate instances of similar misconduct, add **2** points.

(d) VIOLATION OF AN ORDER

If more than one applies, use the greater:

(1) (A) If the commission of the instant offense violated a judicial order or injunction, other than a violation of a condition of probation; or (B) if the organization (or separately managed line of business) violated a condition of probation by engaging in similar misconduct, *i.e.*, misconduct similar to that for which it was placed on probation, add **2** points; or

(2) If the commission of the instant offense violated a condition of probation, add **1** point.

(e) OBSTRUCTION OF JUSTICE

If the organization willfully obstructed or impeded, attempted to obstruct or impede, or aided, abetted, or encouraged obstruction of justice during the investigation, prosecution, or sentencing of the instant offense, or, with knowledge thereof, failed to take reasonable steps to prevent such obstruction or impedance or attempted obstruction or impedance, add **3** points.

(f) EFFECTIVE COMPLIANCE AND ETHICS PROGRAM

(1) If the offense occurred even though the organization had in place at the time of the offense an effective compliance and ethics program, as provided in §8B2.1 (Effective Compliance and Ethics Program), subtract **3** points.

(2) Subsection (f)(1) shall not apply if, after becoming aware of an offense, the organization unreasonably delayed reporting the offense to appropriate governmental authorities.

(3) (A) Except as provided in subparagraphs (B) and (C), subsection (f)(1) shall not apply if an individual within high-level personnel of the organization, a person within high-level personnel of the unit of the organization within which the offense was committed where the unit had 200 or more employees, or an individual described in §8B2.1(b)(2)(B) or (C), participated in, condoned, or was willfully ignorant

of the offense.
(B) There is a rebuttable presumption, for purposes of subsection (f)(1), that the organization did not have an effective compliance and ethics program if an individual—
(i) within high-level personnel of a small organization; or
(ii) within substantial authority personnel, but not within high-level personnel, of any organization, participated in, condoned, or was willfully ignorant of, the offense.
(C) Subparagraphs (A) and (B) shall not apply if—
(i) the individual or individuals with operational responsibility for the compliance and ethics program (*see* §8B2.1(b)(2)(C)) have direct reporting obligations to the governing authority or an appropriate subgroup thereof (*e.g.*, an audit committee of the board of directors);
(ii) the compliance and ethics program detected the offense before discovery outside the organization or before such discovery was reasonably likely;

(iii) the organization promptly reported the offense to appropriate governmental authorities; and
(iv) no individual with operational responsibility for the compliance and ethics program participated in, condoned, or was willfully ignorant of the offense.
(g) SELF-REPORTING, COOPERATION, AND ACCEPTANCE OF RESPONSIBILITY
If more than one applies, use the greatest:
(1) If the organization (A) prior to an imminent threat of disclosure or government investigation; and (B) within a reasonably prompt time after becoming aware of the offense, reported the offense to appropriate governmental authorities, fully cooperated in the investigation, and clearly demonstrated recognition and affirmative acceptance of responsibility for its criminal conduct, subtract **5** points; or
(2) If the organization fully cooperated in the investigation and clearly demonstrated recognition and affirmative acceptance of responsibility for its criminal conduct, subtract **2** points; or
(3) If the organization clearly demonstrated recognition and affirmative acceptance of responsibility for its criminal conduct, subtract **1** point.

Commentary

Application Notes:

1. **Definitions.**—For purposes of this guideline, "***condoned***", "***prior criminal adjudication***", "***similar misconduct***", "***substantial authority personnel***", and "***willfully ignorant of the offense***" have the meaning given those terms in Application Note 3 of the Commentary to §8A1.2 (Application Instructions — Organizations).
"***Small Organization***", for purposes of subsection (f)(3), means an organization that, at the time of the instant offense, had fewer than 200 employees.

2. For purposes of subsection (b), "***unit of the organization***" means any reasonably distinct operational component of the organization. For example, a large organization may have several large units such as divisions or subsidiaries, as well as many smaller units such as specialized manufacturing, marketing, or accounting operations within these larger units. For purposes of this definition, all of these types of units are encompassed within the term "unit of the organization."
3. "***High-level personnel of the organization***" is defined in the Commentary to §8A1.2 (Application Instructions — Organizations). With respect to a unit with 200 or more employees, "***high-level personnel of a unit of the organization***" means agents within the unit who set the policy for or control that unit. For example, if the managing agent

of a unit with 200 employees participated in an offense, three points would be added under subsection (b)(3); if that organization had 1,000 employees and the managing agent of the unit with 200 employees were also within high-level personnel of the organization in its entirety, four points (rather than three) would be added under subsection (b)(2).
4. Pervasiveness under subsection (b) will be case specific and depend on the number, and degree of responsibility, of individuals within substantial authority personnel who participated in, condoned, or were willfully ignorant of the offense. Fewer individuals need to be involved for a finding of pervasiveness if those individuals exercised a relatively high degree of authority. Pervasiveness can occur either within an organization as a whole or within a unit of an organization. For example, if an offense were committed in an organization with 1,000 employees but the tolerance of the offense was pervasive only within a unit of the organization with 200 employees (and no high-level personnel of the organization participated in, condoned, or was willfully ignorant of the offense), three points would be added under subsection (b)(3). If, in the same organization, tolerance of the offense was pervasive throughout the organization as a whole, or an individual within high-level personnel of the organization participated in the offense, four points (rather than three) would be added under subsection (b)(2).
5. A "***separately managed line of business***," as used in subsections (c) and (d), is a subpart of a for-profit organization that has its own management, has a high degree of autonomy from higher managerial authority, and maintains its own separate books of account. Corporate subsidiaries and divisions frequently are separately managed lines of business. Under subsection (c), in determining the prior history of an organization with separately managed lines of business, only the prior conduct or criminal record of the separately managed line of business involved in the instant offense is to be used. Under subsection (d), in the context of an organization with separately managed lines of business, in making the determination whether a violation of a condition of probation involved engaging in similar misconduct, only the prior misconduct of the separately managed line of business involved in the instant offense is to be considered.
6. Under subsection (c), in determining the prior history of an organization or separately managed line of business, the conduct of the underlying economic entity shall be considered without regard to its legal structure or ownership. For example, if two companies merged and became separate divisions and separately managed lines of business within the merged company, each division would retain the prior history of its predecessor company. If a company reorganized and became a new legal entity, the new company would retain the prior history of the predecessor company. In contrast, if one company purchased the physical assets but not the ongoing business of another company, the prior history of the company selling the physical assets would not be transferred to the company purchasing the assets. However, if an organization is acquired by another organization in response to solicitations by appropriate federal government officials, the prior history of the acquired organization shall not be attributed to the acquiring organization.
7. Under subsections (c)(1)(B) and (c)(2)(B), the civil or administrative adjudication(s) must have occurred within the specified period (ten or five years) of the instant offense.

8. Adjust the culpability score for the factors listed in subsection (e) whether or not the offense guideline incorporates that factor, or that factor is inherent in the offense.
9. Subsection (e) applies where the obstruction is committed on behalf of the organization; it does not apply where an individual or individuals have attempted to conceal their misconduct from the organization. The Commentary to §3C1.1 (Obstructing or Impeding the

Administration of Justice) provides guidance regarding the types of conduct that constitute obstruction.
10. Subsection (f)(2) contemplates that the organization will be allowed a reasonable period of time to conduct an internal investigation. In addition, no reporting is required by subsection (f)(2) or (f)(3)(C)(iii) if the organization reasonably concluded, based on the information then available, that no offense had been committed.
11. For purposes of subsection (f)(3)(C)(i), an individual has "***direct reporting obligations***" to the governing authority or an appropriate subgroup thereof if the individual has express authority to communicate personally to the governing authority or appropriate subgroup thereof (A) promptly on any matter involving criminal conduct or potential criminal conduct, and (B) no less than annually on the implementation and effectiveness of the compliance and ethics program.
12. "***Appropriate governmental authorities***," as used in subsections (f) and (g)(1), means the federal or state law enforcement, regulatory, or program officials having jurisdiction over such matter. To qualify for a reduction under subsection (g)(1), the report to appropriate governmental authorities must be made under the direction of the organization.
13. To qualify for a reduction under subsection (g)(1) or (g)(2), cooperation must be both timely and thorough. To be timely, the cooperation must begin essentially at the same time as the organization is officially notified of a criminal investigation. To be thorough, the cooperation should include the disclosure of all pertinent information known by the organization. A prime test of whether the organization has disclosed all pertinent information is whether the information is sufficient for law enforcement personnel to identify the nature and extent of the offense and the individual(s) responsible for the criminal conduct. However, the cooperation to be measured is the cooperation of the organization itself, not the cooperation of individuals within the organization. If, because of the lack of cooperation of particular individual(s), neither the organization nor law enforcement personnel are able to identify the culpable individual(s) within the organization despite the organization's efforts to cooperate fully, the organization may still be given credit for full cooperation.
14. Entry of a plea of guilty prior to the commencement of trial combined with truthful admission of involvement in the offense and related conduct ordinarily will constitute significant evidence of affirmative acceptance of responsibility under subsection (g), unless outweighed by conduct of the organization that is inconsistent with such acceptance of responsibility. This adjustment is not intended to apply to an organization that puts the government to its burden of proof at trial by denying the essential factual elements of guilt, is convicted, and only then admits guilt and expresses remorse. Conviction by trial, however, does not automatically preclude an organization from consideration for such a reduction. In rare situations, an organization may clearly demonstrate an acceptance of responsibility for its criminal conduct even though it exercises its constitutional right to a trial. This may occur, for example, where an organization goes to trial to assert and preserve issues that do not relate to factual guilt (*e.g.*, to make a constitutional challenge to a statute or a challenge to the applicability of a statute to its conduct). In each such instance, however, a determination that an organization has accepted responsibility will be based primarily upon pretrial statements and conduct.
15. In making a determination with respect to subsection (g), the court may determine that the chief executive officer or highest ranking employee of an organization should appear at sentencing in order to signify that the organization has clearly demonstrated recognition and affirmative acceptance of responsibility.

Background: The increased culpability scores under subsection (b) are based on three interrelated principles. First, an organization is more culpable when individuals who manage the organization or who have substantial discretion in acting for the organization participate in, condone, or are willfully ignorant of criminal conduct. Second, as organizations become larger and their managements become more professional, participation in, condonation of, or willful ignorance of criminal conduct by such management is increasingly a breach of trust or abuse of position. Third, as organizations increase in size, the risk of criminal conduct beyond that reflected in the instant offense also increases whenever management's tolerance of that offense is pervasive. Because of the continuum of sizes of organizations and professionalization of management, subsection (b) gradually increases the culpability score based upon the size of the organization and the level and extent of the substantial authority personnel involvement.

Historical Note

Effective November 1, 1991 (amendment 422). Amended effective November 1, 2004 (amendment 673); November 1, 2006 (amendment 695); November 1, 2010 (amendment 744).

§8C2.6. Minimum and Maximum Multipliers

Using the culpability score from §8C2.5 (Culpability Score) and applying any applicable special instruction for fines in Chapter Two, determine the applicable minimum and maximum fine multipliers from the table below.

CULPABILITY SCORE	MINIMUM MULTIPLIER	MAXIMUM MULTIPLIER
10 or more	2.00	4.00
9	1.80	3.60
8	1.60	3.20
7	1.40	2.80
6	1.20	2.40
5	1.00	2.00
4	0.80	1.60
3	0.60	1.20
2	0.40	0.80
1	0.20	0.40
0 or less	0.05	0.20.

Commentary

Application Note:

1. A special instruction for fines in §2R1.1 (Bid-Rigging, Price-Fixing or Market-Allocation Agreements Among Competitors) sets a floor for minimum and maximum multipliers in cases covered by that guideline.

Historical Note

Effective November 1, 1991 (amendment 422).

§8C2.7. Guideline Fine Range — Organizations

(a) The minimum of the guideline fine range is determined by multiplying the base fine determined under §8C2.4 (Base Fine) by the applicable minimum multiplier determined under §8C2.6 (Minimum and Maximum Multipliers).

(b) The maximum of the guideline fine range is determined by multiplying the base fine determined under §8C2.4 (Base Fine) by the applicable maximum multiplier determined under §8C2.6 (Minimum and Maximum Multipliers).

Historical Note

Effective November 1, 1991 (amendment 422).

§8C2.8. Determining the Fine Within the Range (Policy Statement)

(a) In determining the amount of the fine within the applicable guideline range, the court should consider:

(1) the need for the sentence to reflect the seriousness of the offense, promote respect for the law, provide just punishment, afford adequate deterrence, and protect the public from further crimes of the organization;

(2) the organization's role in the offense;

(3) any collateral consequences of conviction, including civil obligations arising from the organization's conduct;

(4) any nonpecuniary loss caused or threatened by the offense;

(5) whether the offense involved a vulnerable victim;

(6) any prior criminal record of an individual within high-level personnel of the organization or high-level personnel of a unit of the organization who participated in, condoned, or was willfully ignorant of the criminal conduct;

(7) any prior civil or criminal misconduct by the organization other than that counted under §8C2.5(c);

(8) any culpability score under §8C2.5 (Culpability Score) higher than **10** or lower than **0**;

(9) partial but incomplete satisfaction of the conditions for one or more of the mitigating or aggravating factors set forth in §8C2.5 (Culpability Score);

(10) any factor listed in 18 U.S.C. § 3572(a); and

(11) whether the organization failed to have, at the time of the instant offense, an effective compliance and ethics program within the meaning of §8B2.1 (Effective Compliance and Ethics Program).

(b) In addition, the court may consider the relative importance of any factor used to determine the range, including the pecuniary loss caused by the offense, the pecuniary gain from the offense, any specific offense characteristic used to determine the offense level, and any aggravating or mitigating factor used to determine the culpability score.

Commentary

Application Notes:

1. Subsection (a)(2) provides that the court, in setting the fine within the guideline fine range, should consider the organization's role in the offense. This consideration is particularly appropriate if the guideline fine range does not take the organization's role in the offense into account. For example, the guideline fine range in an antitrust case does not take into consideration whether the organization was an organizer or leader of the conspiracy. A higher fine within the guideline fine range ordinarily will be appropriate for an organization that takes a leading role in such an offense.

2. Subsection (a)(3) provides that the court, in setting the fine within the guideline fine

range, should consider any collateral consequences of conviction, including civil obligations arising from the organization's conduct. As a general rule, collateral consequences that merely make victims whole provide no basis for reducing the fine within the guideline range. If criminal and civil sanctions are unlikely to make victims whole, this may provide a basis for a higher fine within the guideline fine range. If punitive collateral sanctions have been or will be imposed on the organization, this may provide a basis for a lower fine within the guideline fine range.

3. Subsection (a)(4) provides that the court, in setting the fine within the guideline fine range, should consider any nonpecuniary loss caused or threatened by the offense. To the extent that nonpecuniary loss caused or threatened (*e.g.*, loss of or threat to human life; psychological injury; threat to national security) by the offense is not adequately considered in setting the guideline fine range, this factor provides a basis for a higher fine within the range. This factor is more likely to be applicable where the guideline fine range is determined by pecuniary loss or gain, rather than by offense level, because the Chapter Two offense levels frequently take actual or threatened nonpecuniary loss into account.

4. Subsection (a)(6) provides that the court, in setting the fine within the guideline fine range, should consider any prior criminal record of an individual within high-level personnel of the organization or within high-level personnel of a unit of the organization. Since an individual within high-level personnel either exercises substantial control over

the organization or a unit of the organization or has a substantial role in the making of policy within the organization or a unit of the organization, any prior criminal misconduct of such an individual may be relevant to the determination of the appropriate fine for the organization.

5. Subsection (a)(7) provides that the court, in setting the fine within the guideline fine range, should consider any prior civil or criminal misconduct by the organization other than that counted under §8C2.5(c). The civil and criminal misconduct counted under §8C2.5(c) increases the guideline fine range. Civil or criminal misconduct other than that counted under §8C2.5(c) may provide a basis for a higher fine within the range. In a case involving a pattern of illegality, an upward departure may be warranted.

6. Subsection (a)(8) provides that the court, in setting the fine within the guideline fine range, should consider any culpability score higher than ten or lower than zero. As the culpability score increases above ten, this may provide a basis for a higher fine within the range. Similarly, as the culpability score decreases below zero, this may provide a basis for a lower fine within the range.

7. Under subsection (b), the court, in determining the fine within the range, may consider any factor that it considered in determining the range. This allows for courts to differentiate between cases that have the same offense level but differ in seriousness (*e.g.*, two fraud cases at offense level 12, one resulting in a loss of $21,000, the other $40,000). Similarly, this allows for courts to differentiate between two cases that have the same aggravating factors, but in which those factors vary in their intensity (*e.g.*, two cases with upward adjustments to the culpability score under §8C2.5(c)(2) (prior criminal adjudications within 5 years of the commencement of the instant offense, one involving a single conviction, the other involving two or more convictions)).

Background: Subsection (a) includes factors that the court is required to consider under 18 U.S.C. §§ 3553(a) and 3572(a) as well as additional factors that the Commission has determined may be relevant in a particular case. A number of factors required for consideration under 18 U.S.C. § 3572(a) (*e.g.*, pecuniary loss, the size of the organization) are used under the fine guidelines in this subpart to determine the fine range, and therefore are not specifically set out again in subsection (a) of this guideline. In unusual cases, factors listed in this section may provide a basis for departure.

Historical Note

Effective November 1, 1991 (amendment 422). Amended effective November 1, 2004 (amendment 673); November 1, 2015 (amendment 797).

§8C2.9. Disgorgement

The court shall add to the fine determined under §8C2.8 (Determining the Fine Within the Range) any gain to the organization from the offense that has not and will not be paid as restitution or by way of other remedial measures.

Commentary

Application Note:

1. This section is designed to ensure that the amount of any gain that has not and will not be taken from the organization for remedial purposes will be added to the fine. This section typically will apply in cases in which the organization has received gain from an offense but restitution or remedial efforts will not be required because the offense did not result in harm to identifiable victims, *e.g.*, money laundering, obscenity, and regulatory reporting offenses. Money spent or to be spent to remedy the adverse effects of the offense, *e.g.*, the cost to retrofit defective products, should be considered as disgorged gain. If the cost of remedial efforts made or to be made by the organization equals or exceeds the gain from the offense, this section will not apply.

Historical Note

Effective November 1, 1991 (amendment 422).

§8C2.10. Determining the Fine for Other Counts

For any count or counts not covered under §8C2.1 (Applicability of Fine Guidelines), the court should determine an appropriate fine by applying the provisions of 18 U.S.C. §§ 3553 and 3572. The court should determine the appropriate fine amount, if any, to be imposed in addition to any fine determined under §8C2.8 (Determining the Fine Within the Range) and §8C2.9 (Disgorgement).

Commentary

Background: The Commission has not promulgated guidelines governing the setting of fines for counts not covered by §8C2.1 (Applicability of Fine Guidelines). For such counts, the court should determine the appropriate fine based on the general statutory provisions governing sentencing. In cases that have a count or counts not covered by the guidelines in addition to a count or counts covered by the guidelines, the court shall apply the fine guidelines for the count(s) covered by the guidelines, and add any additional amount to the fine, as appropriate, for the count(s) not covered by the guidelines.

Historical Note

Effective November 1, 1991 (amendment 422).

* * * * *

3. IMPLEMENTING THE SENTENCE OF A FINE

§8C3.1. Imposing a Fine

(a) Except to the extent restricted by the maximum fine authorized by statute or any minimum fine required by statute, the fine or fine

range shall be that determined under §8C1.1 (Determining the Fine — Criminal Purpose Organizations); §8C2.7 (Guideline Fine Range — Organizations) and §8C2.9 (Disgorgement); or §8C2.10 (Determining the Fine for Other Counts), as appropriate.

(b) Where the minimum guideline fine is greater than the maximum fine authorized by statute, the maximum fine authorized by statute

shall be the guideline fine.
(c) Where the maximum guideline fine is less than a minimum fine required by statute, the minimum fine required by statute shall be the guideline fine.

Commentary

Background: This section sets forth the interaction of the fines or fine ranges determined under this chapter with the maximum fine authorized by statute and any minimum fine required by statute for the count or counts of conviction. The general statutory provisions governing a sentence of a fine are set forth in 18 U.S.C. § 3571.

When the organization is convicted of multiple counts, the maximum fine authorized by statute may increase. For example, in the case of an organization convicted of three felony counts related to a $200,000 fraud, the maximum fine authorized by statute will be $500,000 on each count, for an aggregate maximum authorized fine of $1,500,000.

Historical Note

Effective November 1, 1991 (amendment 422).

§8C3.2. Payment of the Fine — Organizations

(a) If the defendant operated primarily for a criminal purpose or primarily by criminal means, immediate payment of the fine shall be required.

(b) In any other case, immediate payment of the fine shall be required unless the court finds that the organization is financially unable to make immediate payment or that such payment would pose an undue burden on the organization. If the court permits other than immediate payment, it shall require full payment at the earliest possible date, either by requiring payment on a date certain or by establishing an installment schedule.

Commentary

Application Note:

1. When the court permits other than immediate payment, the period provided for payment shall in no event exceed five years. 18 U.S.C. § 3572(d).

Historical Note

Effective November 1, 1991 (amendment 422).

§8C3.3. Reduction of Fine Based on Inability to Pay

(a) The court shall reduce the fine below that otherwise required by §8C1.1 (Determining the Fine — Criminal Purpose Organizations), or §8C2.7 (Guideline Fine Range — Organizations) and §8C2.9 (Disgorgement), to the extent that imposition of such fine would impair its ability to make restitution to victims.

(b) The court may impose a fine below that otherwise required by §8C2.7 (Guideline Fine Range — Organizations) and §8C2.9 (Disgorgement) if the court finds that the organization is not able and, even with the use of a reasonable installment schedule, is not likely to become able to pay the minimum fine required by §8C2.7 (Guideline Fine Range — Organizations) and §8C2.9 (Disgorgement).

Provided, that the reduction under this subsection shall not be more than necessary to avoid substantially jeopardizing the continued viability of the organization.

Commentary

Application Note:

1. For purposes of this section, an organization is not able to pay the minimum fine if, even with an installment schedule under §8C3.2 (Payment of the Fine — Organizations), the payment of that fine would substantially jeopardize the continued existence of the organization.

Background: Subsection (a) carries out the requirement in 18 U.S.C. § 3572(b) that the court impose a fine or other monetary penalty only to the extent that such fine or penalty will not impair the ability of the organization to make restitution for the offense; however, this section does not authorize a criminal purpose organization to remain in business in order to pay restitution.

Historical
Note
Effective November 1, 1991 (amendment 422).

§8C3.4. Fines Paid by Owners of Closely Held Organizations

The court may offset the fine imposed upon a closely held organization when one or more individuals, each of whom owns at least a 5 percent

interest in the organization, has been fined in a federal criminal proceeding for the same offense conduct for which the organization is being sentenced. The amount of such offset shall not exceed the amount resulting from multiplying the total fines imposed on those individuals by those individuals' total percentage interest in the organization.

Commentary

Application Notes:

1. For purposes of this section, an organization is closely held, regardless of its size, when relatively few individuals own it. In order for an organization to be closely held, ownership and management need not completely overlap.
2. This section does not apply to a fine imposed upon an individual that arises out of offense conduct different from that for which the organization is being sentenced.

Background: For practical purposes, most closely held organizations are the alter egos of their owner-managers. In the case of criminal conduct by a closely held corporation, the organization and the culpable individual(s) both may be convicted. As a general rule in such cases, appropriate punishment may be achieved by offsetting the fine imposed upon the organization by an amount that reflects the percentage ownership interest of the sentenced individuals and the magnitude of the fines imposed upon those individuals. For example, an organization is owned by five individuals, each of whom has a twenty percent interest; three of the individuals are convicted; and the combined fines imposed on those three equals $100,000. In this example, the fine imposed upon the organization may be offset by up to 60 percent of their combined fine amounts, *i.e.*, by $60,000.

Historical
Note
Effective November 1, 1991 (amendment 422).

* * * * *

4. DEPARTURES FROM THE GUIDELINE FINE RANGE

Introductory Commentary

The statutory provisions governing departures are set forth in 18 U.S.C. § 3553(b). Departure may be warranted if the court finds "that there exists an aggravating or mitigating circumstance of a kind, or to a degree, not adequately taken into consideration by the Sentencing Commission in formulating the guidelines that should result in a sentence different from that described." This subpart sets forth certain factors that, in connection with certain offenses, may not have been adequately taken into consideration by the guidelines. In deciding whether departure is warranted, the court should consider the extent to which that factor is adequately taken into consideration by the guidelines and the relative importance or substantiality of that factor in the particular case.

To the extent that any policy statement from Chapter Five, Part K (Departures) is relevant to the organization, a departure from the applicable guideline fine range may be warranted.

Some factors listed in Chapter Five, Part K that are particularly applicable to organi§

zations are listed in this subpart. Other factors listed in Chapter Five, Part K may be applicable in particular cases. While this subpart lists factors that the Commission believes may constitute grounds for departure, the list is not exhaustive.

Historical
Note
Effective November 1, 1991 (amendment 422).

§8C4.1. Substantial Assistance to Authorities — Organizations (Policy Statement)

(a) Upon motion of the government stating that the defendant has provided substantial assistance in the investigation or prosecution of another organization that has committed an offense, or in the investigation or prosecution of an individual not directly affiliated with the defendant who has committed an offense, the court may depart from the guidelines.

(b) The appropriate reduction shall be determined by the court for reasons stated on the record that may include, but are not limited to, consideration of the following:

(1) the court's evaluation of the significance and usefulness of the organization's assistance, taking into consideration the government's evaluation of the assistance rendered;

(2) the nature and extent of the organization's assistance; and

(3) the timeliness of the organization's assistance.

Commentary

Application Note:

1. Departure under this section is intended for cases in which substantial assistance is provided in the investigation or prosecution of crimes committed by individuals not directly affiliated with the organization or by other organizations. It is not intended for assistance in the investigation or prosecution of the agents of the organization responsible for the offense for which the organization is being sentenced.

Historical
Note
Effective November 1, 1991 (amendment 422).

§8C4.2. Risk of Death or Bodily Injury (Policy Statement)

If the offense resulted in death or bodily injury, or involved a foreseeable risk of death or bodily injury, an upward departure may be warranted. The extent of any such departure should depend, among other factors, on the nature of the harm and the extent to which the harm was intended or knowingly risked, and the extent to which such harm or risk is taken into account within the applicable guideline fine range.

Historical
Note
Effective November 1, 1991 (amendment 422).

§8C4.3. Threat to National Security (Policy Statement)

If the offense constituted a threat to national security, an upward departure may be warranted.

Historical
Note
Effective November 1, 1991 (amendment 422).

§8C4.4. Threat to the Environment (Policy Statement)

If the offense presented a threat to the environment, an upward departure may be warranted.

Historical Note

Effective November 1, 1991 (amendment 422).

§8C4.5. Threat to a Market (Policy Statement)

If the offense presented a risk to the integrity or continued existence of a market, an upward departure may be warranted. This section is applicable to both private markets (*e.g.*, a financial market, a commodities market, or a market for consumer goods) and public markets (*e.g.*, government contracting).

Historical Note

Effective November 1, 1991 (amendment 422).

§8C4.6. Official Corruption (Policy Statement)

If the organization, in connection with the offense, bribed or unlawfully gave a gratuity to a public official, or attempted or conspired to bribe or unlawfully give a gratuity to a public official, an upward departure may be warranted.

Historical Note

Effective November 1, 1991 (amendment 422).

§8C4.7. Public Entity (Policy Statement)

If the organization is a public entity, a downward departure may be warranted.

Historical Note

Effective November 1, 1991 (amendment 422).

§8C4.8. Members or Beneficiaries of the Organization as Victims (Policy Statement)

If the members or beneficiaries, other than shareholders, of the organization are direct victims of the offense, a downward departure may be warranted. If the members or beneficiaries of an organization are direct victims of the offense, imposing a fine upon the organization may increase the burden upon the victims of the offense without achieving a deterrent effect. In such cases, a fine may not be appropriate. For example, departure may be appropriate if a labor union is convicted of embezzlement of pension funds.

Historical Note

Effective November 1, 1991 (amendment 422).

§8C4.9. Remedial Costs that Greatly Exceed Gain (Policy Statement)

If the organization has paid or has agreed to pay remedial costs arising from the offense that greatly exceed the gain that the organization received from the offense, a downward departure may be warranted. In such a case, a substantial fine may not be necessary in order to achieve adequate punishment and deterrence. In deciding whether departure is

appropriate, the court should consider the level and extent of substantial authority personnel involvement in the offense and the degree to which the loss exceeds the gain. If an individual within high-level personnel was involved in the offense, a departure would not be appropriate under this section. The lower the level and the more limited the extent of substantial authority personnel involvement in the offense, and the greater the degree to which remedial costs exceeded or will exceed gain, the less will be the need for a substantial fine to achieve adequate punishment and deterrence.

Historical
Note
Effective November 1, 1991 (amendment 422).

§8C4.10. Mandatory Programs to Prevent and Detect Violations of Law (Policy Statement)

If the organization's culpability score is reduced under §8C2.5(f) (Effective Compliance and Ethics Program) and the organization had implemented its program in response to a court order or administrative order specifically directed at the organization, an upward departure may be warranted to offset, in part or in whole, such reduction.

Similarly, if, at the time of the instant offense, the organization was required by law to have an effective compliance and ethics program, but the organization did not have such a program, an upward departure may be warranted.

Historical
Note
Effective November 1, 1991 (amendment 422). Amended effective November 1, 2004 (amendment 673).

§8C4.11. Exceptional Organizational Culpability (Policy Statement)

If the organization's culpability score is greater than **10**, an upward departure may be appropriate.

If no individual within substantial authority personnel participated in, condoned, or was willfully ignorant of the offense; the organization at the time of the offense had an effective program to prevent and detect violations of law; and the base fine is determined under §8C2.4(a)(1), §8C2.4(a)(3), or a special instruction for fines in Chapter Two (Offense Conduct), a downward departure may be warranted. In a case meeting these criteria, the court may find that the organization had exceptionally

low culpability and therefore a fine based on loss, offense level, or a special Chapter Two instruction results in a guideline fine range higher than necessary to achieve the purposes of sentencing. Nevertheless, such fine should not be lower than if determined under §8C2.4(a)(2).

Historical
Note
Effective November 1, 1991 (amendment 422).

PART D — ORGANIZATIONAL PROBATION

Introductory Commentary

Section 8D1.1 sets forth the circumstances under which a sentence to a term of probation is required. Sections 8D1.2 through 8D1.4, and 8F1.1, address the length of the probation term, conditions of probation, and violations of probation conditions.

Historical
Note

Effective November 1, 1991 (amendment 422). Amended effective November 1, 2004 (amendment 673).

§8D1.1. Imposition of Probation — Organizations

(a) The court shall order a term of probation:

(1) if such sentence is necessary to secure payment of restitution (§8B1.1), enforce a remedial order (§8B1.2), or ensure completion of community service (§8B1.3);

(2) if the organization is sentenced to pay a monetary penalty (*e.g.*, restitution, fine, or special assessment), the penalty is not paid in full at the time of sentencing, and restrictions are necessary to safeguard the organization's ability to make payments;

(3) if, at the time of sentencing, (A) the organization (i) has 50 or more employees, or (ii) was otherwise required under law to have an effective compliance and ethics program; and (B) the organization does not have such a program;

(4) if the organization within five years prior to sentencing engaged in similar misconduct, as determined by a prior criminal adjudication, and any part of the misconduct underlying the instant offense occurred after that adjudication;

(5) if an individual within high-level personnel of the organization or the unit of the organization within which the instant offense was committed participated in the misconduct underlying the instant offense and that individual within five years prior to sentencing engaged in similar misconduct, as determined by a prior criminal adjudication, and any part of the misconduct underlying the instant offense occurred after that adjudication;

(6) if such sentence is necessary to ensure that changes are made within the organization to reduce the likelihood of future criminal conduct;

(7) if the sentence imposed upon the organization does not include a fine; or

(8) if necessary to accomplish one or more of the purposes of sentencing set forth in 18 U.S.C. § 3553(a)(2).

Commentary

Background: Under 18 U.S.C. § 3561(a), an organization may be sentenced to a term of probation. Under 18 U.S.C. § 3551(c), imposition of a term of probation is required if the sentence imposed upon the organization does not include a fine.

Historical
Note
Effective November 1, 1991 (amendment 422). Amended effective November 1, 2004 (amendment 673).

§8D1.2. Term of Probation — Organizations

(a) When a sentence of probation is imposed—

(1) In the case of a felony, the term of probation shall be at least one year but not more than five years.

(2) In any other case, the term of probation shall be not more than five years.

Commentary

Application Note:

1. Within the limits set by the guidelines, the term of probation should be sufficient, but not more than necessary, to accomplish the court's specific objectives in imposing the

term of probation. The terms of probation set forth in this section are those provided in 18 U.S.C. § 3561(c).

Historical
Note
Effective November 1, 1991 (amendment 422). Amended effective November 1, 2013 (amendment 778).

§8D1.3. Conditions of Probation — Organizations

(a) Pursuant to 18 U.S.C. § 3563(a)(1), any sentence of probation shall include the condition that the organization not commit another federal, state, or local crime during the term of probation.

(b) Pursuant to 18 U.S.C. § 3563(a)(2), if a sentence of probation is imposed for a felony, the court shall impose as a condition of probation at least one of the following: (1) restitution or (2) community service, unless the court has imposed a fine, or unless the court finds on the record that extraordinary circumstances exist that would make such condition plainly unreasonable, in which event the court shall impose one or more other conditions set forth in 18 U.S.C. § 3563(b).

(c) The court may impose other conditions that (1) are reasonably related to the nature and circumstances of the offense or the history and characteristics of the organization; and (2) involve only such deprivations of liberty or property as are necessary to effect the purposes of sentencing.

Historical
Note
Effective November 1, 1991 (amendment 422). Amended effective November 1, 1997 (amendment 569); November 1, 2009 (amendment 733).

§8D1.4. Recommended Conditions of Probation — Organizations (Policy Statement)

(a) The court may order the organization, at its expense and in the format and media specified by the court, to publicize the nature of the offense committed, the fact of conviction, the nature of the punishment imposed, and the steps that will be taken to prevent the recurrence of similar offenses.

(b) If probation is imposed under §8D1.1, the following conditions may be appropriate:

(1) The organization shall develop and submit to the court an effective compliance and ethics program consistent with §8B2.1 (Effective Compliance and Ethics Program). The organization shall include in its submission a schedule for implementation of the compliance and ethics program.

(2) Upon approval by the court of a program referred to in paragraph (1), the organization shall notify its employees and shareholders of its criminal behavior and its program referred to in paragraph (1). Such notice shall be in a form prescribed by the court.

(3) The organization shall make periodic submissions to the court or probation officer, at intervals specified by the court, (A) reporting on the organization's financial condition and results of

business operations, and accounting for the disposition of all funds received, and (B) reporting on the organization's progress in implementing the program referred to in paragraph (1). Among other things, reports under subparagraph (B) shall disclose any criminal prosecution, civil litigation, or administrative proceeding commenced against the organization, or any investigation or formal inquiry by governmental authorities of which the organization learned since its last report.

(4) The organization shall notify the court or probation officer immediately upon learning of (A) any material adverse change in its business or financial condition or prospects, or (B) the commencement of any bankruptcy proceeding, major civil litigation, criminal prosecution, or administrative proceeding against the organization, or any investigation or formal inquiry by governmental authorities regarding the organization.

(5) The organization shall submit to: (A) a reasonable number of regular or unannounced examinations of its books and records at appropriate business premises by the probation officer or experts engaged by the court; and (B) interrogation of knowledgeable individuals within the organization. Compensation to and costs of any experts engaged by the court shall be paid by the organization.

(6) The organization shall make periodic payments, as specified by the court, in the following priority: (A) restitution; (B) fine; and (C) any other monetary sanction.

Commentary

Application Note:

1. In determining the conditions to be imposed when probation is ordered under §8D1.1, the court should consider the views of any governmental regulatory body that oversees conduct of the organization relating to the instant offense. To assess the efficacy of a compliance and ethics program submitted by the organization, the court may employ appropriate experts who shall be afforded access to all material possessed by the organization that is necessary for a comprehensive assessment of the proposed program. The court should approve any program that appears reasonably calculated to prevent and detect criminal conduct, as long as it is consistent with §8B2.1 (Effective Compliance and Ethics Program), and any applicable statutory and regulatory requirements.

Periodic reports submitted in accordance with subsection (b)(3) should be provided to any governmental regulatory body that oversees conduct of the organization relating to the instant offense.

Historical Note

Effective November 1, 1991 (amendment 422). Amended effective November 1, 2004 (amendment 673); November 1, 2010 (amendment 744).

§8D1.5. [Deleted]

Historical Note

Effective November 1, 1991 (amendment 422); was moved to §8F1.1 effective November 1, 2004 (amendment 673).

PART E — SPECIAL ASSESSMENTS, FORFEITURES, AND COSTS

§8E1.1. Special Assessments — Organizations

A special assessment must be imposed on an organization in the amount prescribed by statute.

Commentary

Application Notes:

1. This guideline applies if the defendant is an organization. It does not apply if the defendant is an individual. *See* §5E1.3 for special assessments applicable to individuals.
2. The following special assessments are provided by statute (*see* 18 U.S.C. § 3013):

FOR OFFENSES COMMITTED BY ORGANIZATIONS ON OR AFTER APRIL 24, 1996:

(A) $400, if convicted of a felony;
(B) $125, if convicted of a Class A misdemeanor;
(C) $50, if convicted of a Class B misdemeanor; or
(D) $25, if convicted of a Class C misdemeanor or an infraction.

FOR OFFENSES COMMITTED BY ORGANIZATIONS ON OR AFTER NOVEMBER 18, 1988 BUT PRIOR TO APRIL 24, 1996:

(E) $200, if convicted of a felony;
(F) $125, if convicted of a Class A misdemeanor;
(G) $50, if convicted of a Class B misdemeanor; or
(H) $25, if convicted of a Class C misdemeanor or an infraction.

FOR OFFENSES COMMITTED BY ORGANIZATIONS PRIOR TO NOVEMBER 18, 1988:

(I) $200, if convicted of a felony;
(J) $100, if convicted of a misdemeanor.

3. A special assessment is required by statute for each count of conviction.

Background: Section 3013 of Title 18, United States Code, added by The Victims of Crimes Act of 1984, Pub. L. No. 98-473, Title II, Chap. XIV, requires courts to impose special assessments on convicted defendants for the purpose of funding the Crime Victims Fund established by the same legislation.

Historical
Note
Effective November 1, 1991 (amendment 422); November 1, 1997 (amendment 573).

§8E1.2. Forfeiture — Organizations

Apply §5E1.4 (Forfeiture).

Historical
Note
Effective November 1, 1991 (amendment 422).

§8E1.3. Assessment of Costs — Organizations

As provided in 28 U.S.C. § 1918, the court may order the organization to pay the costs of prosecution. In addition, specific statutory provisions mandate assessment of costs.

Historical
Note
Effective November 1, 1991 (amendment 422).

PART F — VIOLATIONS OF PROBATION — ORGANIZATIONS

Historical
Note
Effective November 1, 2004 (amendment 673).

§8F1.1. Violations of Conditions of Probation — Organizations (Policy Statement)

Upon a finding of a violation of a condition of probation, the court may extend the term of probation, impose more restrictive conditions of probation, or revoke probation and resentence the organization.

Commentary

Application Notes:

1. **Appointment of Master or Trustee.**—In the event of repeated violations of conditions of probation, the appointment of a master or trustee may be appropriate to ensure compliance with court orders.

2. **Conditions of Probation.**—Mandatory and recommended conditions of probation are specified in §§8D1.3 (Conditions of Probation — Organizations) and 8D1.4 (Recommended Conditions of Probation — Organizations).

Historical
Note
Effective November 1, 2004 (amendment 673).

APPENDIX A

STATUTORY INDEX

INTRODUCTION

This index specifies the offense guideline section(s) in Chapter Two (Offense Conduct) applicable to the statute of conviction. If more than one guideline section is referenced for the particular statute, use the guideline most appropriate for the offense conduct charged in the count of which the defendant was convicted. For the rules governing the determination of the offense guideline section(s) from Chapter Two, and for any exceptions to those rules, *see* §1B1.2 (Applicable Guidelines).

Historical
Note
Effective November 1, 1987. Amended effective November 1, 1989 (amendments 296 and 297); November 1, 1993 (amendment 496); November 1, 2000 (amendment 591); November 1, 2014 (amendment 781).

INDEX

Statute Guideline Statute Guideline

2 U.S.C. § 192 2J1.1, 2J1.5
2 U.S.C. § 390 2J1.1, 2J1.5
7 U.S.C. § 6 2B1.1
7 U.S.C. § 6b(A) 2B1.1
7 U.S.C. § 6b(B) 2B1.1
7 U.S.C. § 6b(C) 2B1.1
7 U.S.C. § 6c 2B1.1
7 U.S.C. § 6h 2B1.1
7 U.S.C. § 6o 2B1.1
7 U.S.C. § 13(a)(1) 2B1.1
7 U.S.C. § 13(a)(2) 2B1.1
7 U.S.C. § 13(a)(3) 2B1.1
7 U.S.C. § 13(a)(4) 2B1.1
7 U.S.C. § 13(c) 2C1.3
7 U.S.C. § 13(d) 2B1.4
7 U.S.C. § 13(e) 2B1.4
7 U.S.C. § 23 2B1.1
7 U.S.C. § 87b 2N2.1
7 U.S.C. § 87f(e) 2J1.1, 2J1.5
7 U.S.C. § 136 2Q1.2
7 U.S.C. § 136j 2Q1.2
7 U.S.C. § 136k 2Q1.2
7 U.S.C. § 136l 2Q1.2
7 U.S.C. § 149 2N2.1
7 U.S.C. § 150bb 2N2.1
7 U.S.C. § 150gg 2N2.1
7 U.S.C. § 154 2N2.1
7 U.S.C. § 156 2N2.1
7 U.S.C. § 157 2N2.1
7 U.S.C. § 158 2N2.1
7 U.S.C. § 161 2N2.1
7 U.S.C. § 163 2N2.1
7 U.S.C. § 195 2N2.1
7 U.S.C. § 270 2B1.1
7 U.S.C. § 281 2N2.1
7 U.S.C. § 472 2N2.1
7 U.S.C. § 473c-1 2N2.1
7 U.S.C. § 491 2N2.1
7 U.S.C. § 499n 2N2.1
7 U.S.C. § 503 2N2.1
7 U.S.C. § 511d 2N2.1
7 U.S.C. § 511i 2N2.1
7 U.S.C. § 516 2N2.1
7 U.S.C. § 610(g) 2C1.3
7 U.S.C. § 2018(c) 2N2.1
7 U.S.C. § 2024(b) 2B1.1
7 U.S.C. § 2024(c) 2B1.1
7 U.S.C. § 2156
(felony provisions only) 2E3.1
7 U.S.C. § 6810 2N2.1
7 U.S.C. § 7734 2N2.1
7 U.S.C. § 8313 2N2.1
8 U.S.C. §
1160(b)(7)(A) 2L2.1, 2L2.2
8 U.S.C. § 1185(a)(1) 2L1.2
8 U.S.C. § 1185(a)(2) 2L1.1
8 U.S.C. § 1185(a)(3) 2L2.1, 2L2.2
8 U.S.C. § 1185(a)(4) 2L2.1
8 U.S.C. § 1185(a)(5) 2L2.2
8 U.S.C. § 1253 2L1.2
8 U.S.C. § 1255a(c)(6) 2L2.1, 2L2.2
8 U.S.C. § 1324(a) 2L1.1
8 U.S.C. § 1325(a) 2L1.2
8 U.S.C. § 1325(c) 2L2.1, 2L2.2
8 U.S.C. § 1325(d) 2L2.1, 2L2.2
8 U.S.C. § 1326 2L1.2
8 U.S.C. § 1327 2L1.1
8 U.S.C. § 1328 2G1.1, 2G1.3
8 U.S.C. §
1375a(d)(5)(B)(i) 2H3.1
8 U.S.C. §
1375a(d)(5)(B)(ii) 2H3.1
8 U.S.C. §
1375a(d)(5)(B)(iii) 2B1.1
10 U.S.C. § 987(f) 2X5.2
12 U.S.C. § 631 2B1.1
12 U.S.C. § 1818(j) 2B1.1
12 U.S.C. § 1844(f) 2J1.1, 2J1.5
12 U.S.C. § 2273 2J1.1, 2J1.5
12 U.S.C. § 3108(b)(6) 2J1.1, 2J1.5
12 U.S.C. § 4636b 2B1.1
12 U.S.C. § 4641 J1.1, 2J1.5

52 U.S.C. § 30120 2C1.8
52 U.S.C. § 30121 2C1.8
52 U.S.C. § 30122 2C1.8
52 U.S.C. § 30123 2C1.8
52 U.S.C. § 30124(a) 2C1.8
52 U.S.C. § 30125 2C1.8
52 U.S.C. § 30126 2C1.8

Historical Note

Effective November 1, 1987. Amended effective January 15, 1988 (amendments 60 and 61); June 15, 1988 (amendments 62 and 63); October 15, 1988 (amendments 64 and 65); November 1, 1989 (amendments 297–301); November 1, 1990 (amendment 359); November 1, 1991 (amendment 421); November 1, 1992 (amendment 468); November 1, 1993 (amendment 496); November 1, 1995 (amendment 534); November 1, 1996 (amendment 540); November 1, 1997 (amendment 575); November 1, 1998 (amendment 589); November 1, 2000 (amendment 592); May 1, 2001 (amendment 612); November 1, 2001 (amendments 617, 622, 626, 627, 628, 633, and 634); November 1, 2002 (amendments 637, 638, 639, and 646); January 25, 2003 (amendments 647 and 648); November 1, 2003 (amendments 653, 654, 655, 656, 658, and 661); November 1, 2004 (amendments 664, 665, 666, 667, 669, and 674); October 24, 2005 (amendments 675 and 676); November 1, 2005 (amendments 677, 679, and 680); November 1, 2006 (amendments 685, 686, 687, 689, and 690); May 1, 2007 (amendment 697); November 1, 2007 (amendments 699, 700, 701, 703, 704, 705, 707, 708, and 711); February 6, 2008 (amendment 714); November 1, 2008 (amendments 718, 720, 721, 724 and 725); November 1, 2009 (amendments 727, 728, 729, 730, 731, 733, 736, and 737); November 1, 2010 (amendments 743, 745, and 746); November 1, 2011 (amendments 749, 753, and 757); November 1, 2012 (amendments 765 and 769); November 1, 2013 (amendments 772, 773, and 777); November 1, 2014 (amendment 781); November 1, 2015 (amendment 796); November 1, 2016 (amendments 800 and 804).

INDEX TO GUIDELINES MANUAL

This index provides an alphabetical list of topics addressed in the Guidelines Manual and refers the reader to provisions that may be relevant to those topics. This index is unofficial and is provided only as a convenience to the reader.

Note that this index generally does not refer the reader to provisions in Chapter Two offense guidelines. This is by design, because this index is not to be used in determining the offense guideline section in Chapter Two (Offense Conduct) that applies in a particular case. Such determinations are made based on the statute of conviction. *See* §1B1.2 (Applicable Guidelines) and Appendix A (Statutory Index).

For example, this index contains an entry for "kidnapping" which refers the reader to the Chapter Three adjustment at §3A1.3 (Restraint of Victim) and the upward departure provision at §5K2.4 (Abduction or Unlawful Restraint), each of which may be relevant to kidnapping. This index does not, however, refer the reader to any of the Chapter Two offense guidelines with provisions that may be relevant to kidnapping. The Chapter Two offense guideline that applies in a case involving a kidnapping is determined by identifying the statute of conviction and consulting §1B1.2 (Applicable Guidelines) and Appendix A (Statutory Index).

INDEX

LIST OF DEPARTURE PROVISIONS

This list identifies provisions in the Guidelines Manual that indicate when a departure based on a specific ground may be warranted.

In the list that follows, the guideline provision is printed in **bold type** if it involves a downward departure and *italic type* if it involves an upward departure. (Where the guideline provision could involve either an upward departure or a downward departure, depending on the circumstances, the guideline provision is printed in normal, roman type.)

For departures generally, including provisions setting forth the standards that apply in determining whether a departure is warranted, provisions indicating certain factors that are not relevant (or not ordinarily relevant) in determining whether a departure is warranted, and provisions indicating certain circumstances that are prohibited as grounds for departure, see Chapter Five, Parts H (Specific Offender Characteristics) and K (Departures). For departures with regard to organizations, *see* Chapter 8, Part C, Subpart 4 (Departures from the Guideline Fine Range).

For the definition of "departure" and related terms, *see* §1B1.1 (Application Instructions), Application Note 1(E).

For the use of departures in determining the sentence, *see* §1B1.1(b). For the information to be used in determining whether a departure is warranted, *see* §§1B1.4 (Information to be Used in Imposing Sentence (Selecting a Point Within the Guideline Range or Departing from the Guideline) and 1B1.8 (Use of Certain Information). Other procedural provisions applicable to departures include §§5K2.0(e) (Requirement of Specific Written Reasons for Departure), 6A1.4 (Notice of Possible Departure), and 6B1.2 (Standards for Acceptance of Plea Agreements).

As an aid to understanding the role of departures in the guidelines, *see* Chapter One, Part A, Subpart 1(4)(b) (Departures).

The list is as follows:

CHAPTER ONE

1B1.3, comment. (n.3(B))
1B1.3, comment. (n.6(B))

CHAPTER TWO

2A1.1, comment. (n.2(B))
2A1.2, comment. (n.1)
2A2.1, comment. (n.2)
2A2.4, comment. (n.3)
2A3.1, comment. (n.6)
2A3.2, comment. (n.6)
2A3.6, comment. (n.4)
2A5.3, comment. (n.2)
2A6.1, comment. (n.4(B))
2A6.2, comment. (n.5)
2B1.1, comment. (n.8(A))
2B1.1, comment. (n.20(A))
2B1.1, comment. (n.20(B))
2B1.1, comment. (n.20(C))
2B1.1, comment. (n.20(D))
2B1.5, comment. (n.9)
2B2.1, comment. (backg'd.)
2B3.1, comment. (n.5)
2B3.2, comment. (n.7)
2B3.2, comment. (n.8)
2B5.3, comment. (n.5)
2C1.1, comment. (n.7)
2C1.1, comment. (n.7)
2C1.8, comment. (n.4)
2D1.1, comment. (n.1)
2D1.1, comment. (n.10)
2D1.1, comment. (n.18(A))
2D1.1, comment. (n.22(B))
2D1.1, comment. (n.27(A))
2D1.1, comment. (n.27(B))
2D1.1, comment. (n.27(C))

2D1.5, comment. (n.2)
2D1.7, comment. (n.1)
2D1.7, comment. (n.1)
2D1.11, comment. (n.1(C))
2D1.11, comment. (n.4)
2D1.12, comment. (n.1)
2D1.12, comment. (n.3)
2D2.1, comment. (n.1)
2D2.3, comment. (backg'd.)
2D2.3, comment. (backg'd.)
2E1.1, comment. (n.4)
2E3.1, comment. (n.2)
2G1.1, comment. (n.2)
2G1.1, comment. (n.6)
2G1.3, comment. (n.7)
2G2.1, comment. (n.8)
2G2.2, comment. (n.6(B)(i))
2G2.2, comment. (n.6(B)(ii))
2G2.2, comment. (n.9)
2G2.2, comment. (n.9)

2H2.1, comment. (n.1)
2H3.1, comment. (n.5)
2H4.1, comment. (n.3)
2H4.1, comment. (n.4)
2J1.2, comment. (n.4)
2J1.2, comment. (n.4)
2J1.3, comment. (n.4)
2J1.6, comment. (n.4)
2K1.3, comment. (n.10)
2K1.3, comment. (n.11)
2K1.4, comment. (n.3)
2K2.1, comment. (n.7)
2K2.1, comment. (n.11)
2K2.1, comment. (n.13(C))
2K2.1, comment. (n.14(D))
2K2.1, comment. (n.15)
2K2.4, comment. (n.2(B))
2K2.4, comment. (n.4)
2K2.5, comment. (n.4)
2L1.1, comment. (n.7)
2L1.2, comment. (n.5)
2L1.2, comment. (n.6)
2L1.2, comment. (n.7)
2L2.1, comment. (n.3)
2L2.1, comment. (n.5)
2L2.2, comment. (n.6)
2M3.1, comment. (n.2)
2M3.1, comment. (n.3)
2M4.1, comment. (n.1)
2M5.1, comment. (n.1)
2M5.1, comment. (n.2)
2M5.2, comment. (n.1)
2M5.2, comment. (n.2)
2M5.3, comment. (n.2(A))
2M5.3, comment. (n.2(B))
2N1.1, comment. (n.1)
2N1.1, comment. (n.1)
2N1.2, comment. (n.1)
2N1.3, comment. (n.1)
2N2.1, comment. (n.1)
2N2.1, comment. (n.3(A))
2N2.1, comment. (n.3(B))
2P1.1, comment. (n.4)
2P1.3, comment. (n.1)
2Q1.1, comment. (n.1)
2Q1.2, comment. (n.4)
2Q1.2, comment. (n.5)
2Q1.2, comment. (n.6)
2Q1.2, comment. (n.7)
2Q1.2, comment. (n.8)
2Q1.2, comment. (n.9(A))
2Q1.2, comment. (n.9(B))
2Q1.2, comment. (n.9(C))
2Q1.3, comment. (n.3)
2Q1.3, comment. (n.4)
2Q1.3, comment. (n.5)
2Q1.3, comment. (n.5)
2Q1.3, comment. (n.6)
2Q1.3, comment. (n.7)
2Q1.3, comment. (n.8)
2Q1.4, comment. (n.3(A))
2Q1.4, comment. (n.3(B))
2Q1.4, comment. (n.3(B))
2Q2.1, comment. (n.5)
2R1.1, comment. (n.7)
2T1.8, comment. (n.1)
2T2.1, comment. (n.2)
Ch. Two, Pt. T, Subpt. 3, intro. comment.
2T3.1, comment. (n.2)
2X5.1, comment. (n.2(B))
2X7.2, comment. (n.1(A))
2X7.2, comment. (n.1(B))

CHAPTER THREE

3A1.1, comment. (n.4)
3A1.2, comment. (n.5)
3A1.3, comment. (n.3)
3A1.4, comment. (n.4)

DEPARTURES

Guidelines Manual (November 1, 2016) ‖ **619**

3B1.1, comment. (n.2)
3B1.4, comment. (n.3)
3C1.2, comment. (n.2)
3C1.2, comment. (n.6)
3D1.3, comment. (n.4)
3D1.4, comment. (backg'd.)
3D1.4, comment. (backg'd.)

CHAPTER FOUR

4A1.2, comment. (n.3(B))
4A1.2, comment. (n.8)
4A1.3(a), p.s.
4A1.3(b), p.s.
4B1.1, comment. (n.4)
4B1.2, comment. (n.4)
4B1.4, comment. (n.2)

CHAPTER FIVE

5C1.1, comment. (n.6)
5D1.1, comment. (n.1)
5E1.2, comment. (n.4)
5E1.2, comment. (n.4)
5G1.3, comment. (n.4(E))
5G1.3, comment. (n.5)
5H1.1, p.s.

Overview of Mandatory Minimum Penalties in the Federal Criminal Justice System

July 2017

United States Sentencing Commission

OVERVIEW OF MANDATORY MINIMUM PENALTIES IN THE FEDERAL CRIMINAL JUSTICE SYSTEM (2017)

Introduction

This publication assesses the impact of mandatory minimum penalties on federal sentencing. It continues the United States Sentencing Commission's work in this area by highlighting recent developments regarding the charging of offenses carrying a mandatory minimum penalty, and providing updated sentencing data regarding the use and impact of mandatory minimum penalties. This publication builds on the Commission's previous reports and publications-particularly, its 2011 Report to the Congress: Mandatory Minimum Penalties in the Federal Criminal Justice Systemand is intended to contribute to the continued examination of federal mandatory minimum penalties. It is the first in a series, with future publications focusing on mandatory minimum penalties for specific offense types.

Congress, released varying data publications, responded to Congressional data requests, and provided Congressional testimony regarding mandatory minimum penalties over the past 30 years. 8 The Commission submitted its first report to Congress about mandatory minimum penalties only a few years after the initial guidelines went into effect.9 At that time, the Commission concluded that "the most efficient and effective way for Congress to exercise its powers to direct sentencing policy is through the established process of the sentencing guidelines, permitting the sophistication of the guidelines structure to work, rather than through mandatory minimums.?'"

Federal statutory mandatory minimum

penalties have existed since the early days of the nation, 1 and they have continually evolved in the centuries since. As policy views have shifted over time, Congress2 and many others3 have continued to examine the role and scope of these mandatory minimum penalties in the federal criminal system.4 For more than thirty years, the United States Sentencing Commission ("the Commission")5 has played a central role in this process, working with the legislative, executive, and judicial branches of government and other interested parties to ensure that sentencing policy promotes the goals of the Sentencing Reform Act of 1984 ("SRA").6

Consistent with its statutory role,' the Commission has continued to inform the ongoing discussion regarding sentencing policy by gathering, analyzing, and disseminating sentencing data, including analyses regarding the use, scope and impact that mandatory minimum penalties have on sentencing in the federal system. The Commission has submitted numerous reports to

Most recently, the Commission issued its comprehensive 2011 Report to the Congress:

Mandatory Minimum Penalties in the Federal Criminal Justice System (2011 Mandatory Minimum Report). That report, which was submitted pursuant to the statutory directive contained in section 4 713 of the Matthew Shepard and James Byrd, Jr. Hate Crimes Prevention Act of 2009, 11 provided detailed historical analyses of the evolution of federal mandatory minimums, 12 scientific and medical literature on the topic, and extensive analysis of the Commission's own data, public comment, and expert testimony.

While expressing a "spectrum of views" regarding mandatory minimum penalties in its 2011 Mandatory Minimum Report, the Commission uniformly concluded that "a strong and effective sentencing guidelines system best serves the purposes of the Sentencing Reform Act."14 The Commission further concluded that where "Congress decides to exercise its power to direct sentencing policy by enacting mandatory minimum penalties, ... such penalties should (1) not be excessively severe, (2) be narrowly tailored to apply only to those offenders who warrant such punishment, and (3) be applied consistently."15

Section One:

INTRODUCTION

Lastly, the Commission encouraged Congress to request prison impact analyses as early as possible in its legislative process whenever it considers enacting or amending criminal penalties to ensure that increasingly strained federal prison resources are focused on offenders who commit the most serious offenses.16 Guided by these general principles, the Commission expressed its belief that the current system of mandatory minimum penalties could be improved, and made several specific recommendations regarding the four major offense types studied in the report.17

In conjunction with its concluding recommendations in the 2011 Mandatory Minimum Report, the Commission explained that it "stands ready to work with Congress on measures that can be taken to enhance the strength and effectiveness of the current guidelines system and address the problems with certain mandatory minimum penalties identified in this report."18 To that end, the Commission has continued to provide timely and objective sentencing data, information, and analysis to assist the efficient and effective exercise of congressional power to direct sentencing policy.

This publication continues the Commission's work in the area of federal mandatory minimums by highlighting recent developments, as well as providing updated sentencing data regarding the use and impact of mandatory minimum penalties. It analyzes the most recently available sentencing data to supplement the data presented in the 2011 Mandatory Minimum Report, providing a detailed empirical research study of the effect of mandatory minimum penalties under federal law, including an updated assessment of the impact of mandatory rmrumum sentencing provisions on the federal prison population.

Like the Commission's recent publications on recidivism of federal offenders, 19 this publication is designed to be the first in a series, with future publications focusing on mandatory minimum penalties for specific offense types.

Key 2011 Recommendations

Report to the Congress: Mandatory Minimum Penalties in the Federal Criminal Justice System (2011}

• A strong and effective sentencing guidelines system best serves the purposes of the Sentencing Reform Act.

• If Congress decides to exercise its power to direct sentencing policy by enacting mandatory minimum penalties, such penalties should (1) not be excessively severe, (2) be narrowly tailored to apply only to those offenders who warrant such punishment, and (3) be applied consistently.

• Congress should request prison impact analyses from the Commission as early as possible in its legislative process whenever it considers enacting or amending criminal penalties.

United States Sentencing Commission

OVERVIEW OF MANDATORY MINIMUM PENALTIES IN THE FEDERAL CRIMINAL JUSTICE SYSTEM (2017)

Key Findings

Building directly on its previous reports and analyses, this publication continues the Commission's examination of mandatory minimum penalties in the federal system.

As part of this overview analysis the Commission makes the following key findings.

Key 2017 Findings

1. Mandatory minimum penalties continue to result in long sentences in the federal system.

• In fiscal year 2016, the average sentence length for offenders who were convicted of an offense carrying a mandatory minimum penalty was 110 months of imprisonment, nearly four times the average sentence (28 months) for offenders not convicted of an offense carrying a mandatory minimum penalty.

• Even when such offenders receive relief from a mandatory minimum penalty, the average sentence (67 months) is still over two times greater than the average sentence for those not convicted of a mandatory minimum.

2. Mandatory minimum penalties continue to have a significant impact on the size and composition of the federal prison population.

• While the percentage decreased slightly between 2010 and 2016, more than half(55.7%) of federal inmates in custody as of September 30, 2016 were convicted of an offense carrying a mandatory minimum penalty.

• Among offenders in federal prison as of September 30, 2016, 42.7 percent were convicted of an offense carrying a mandatory minimum penalty and remained subject to that penalty at sentencing, which compared to 40.4 percent as of September 30, 2010.

3. Offenses carrying a mandatory minimum penalty were used less often, as the number and percentage of offenders convicted of an offense carrying a mandatory minimum penalty has decreased since fiscal year 2010.

• Just over one-fifth of all offenders sentenced in fiscal year 2016 (21.9%) were convicted of an offense carrying a mandatory minimum penalty, a difference of 5.3 percentage points from fiscal year 2010 (27.2%).

Section Two:

SUMMARY OF KEY FINDINGS

Key 2017 Findings

4. While fewer offenders were convicted of an offense carrying a mandatory minimum penalty in recent years, those who were tended to be more serious offenders.

• Offenders convicted of an offense carrying a mandatory minimum penalty were less likely to receive relief from such penalty at sentencing-38.7 percent of such offenders received relief in fiscal year 2016 compared to 46. 7 percent in fiscal year 2010.

• Additionally, convictions for drug trafficking offenses carrying a mandatory minimum penalty were more likely to involve the use of a weapon, violence or credible threats of violence, or death or serious bodily injury (28. 7% of such offenders had a conviction or guideline finding suggesting the existence of these factors compared to 20. 7% in fiscal year 2010).

• Offenders convicted of such offenses were also more likely to have played a leadership role, as evidenced by application of a guideline adjustment for aggravating role (11. 7% in fiscal year 2016 compared to 7.7% in fiscal year 2010), and were more likely to have three criminal history points or more (50.9% in fiscal year 2016 compared to 45.8% in fiscal year 2010).

5. There were significant demographic shifts in the data relating to mandatory minimum penalties.

• As they did in fiscal year 2010 (38.3%), Hispanic offenders continued to represent the largest group of offenders (40.4%) convicted of an offense carrying a mandatory minimum penalty in fiscal year 2016. However, other demographic data has shifted.

• Unlike in fiscal year 2010, White offenders, as opposed to Black offenders, had the highest average sentence among offenders convicted of an offense carrying a mandatory minimum penalty (127 months), offenders relieved of the application of a mandatory minimum penalty at sentencing (73 months), and offenders subject to a mandatory minimum penalty at sentencing (150 months).

• While Black offenders convicted of an offense carrying a mandatory minimum penalty continued to receive relief from the mandatory minimum penalty least often, the gap between Black offenders and White offenders has narrowed. In fiscal year 2016, 73.2 percent of Black offenders convicted of an offense carrying a mandatory minimum penalty remained subject to that penalty, compared to 70.0 percent of White offenders convicted of such an offense. This difference of3 .2 percent in fiscal year 2016, compares to a difference of 11.6 percent in fiscal year 2010 (65.1 % of Black offenders convicted of an offense carrying a mandatory minimum penalty compared to 53.5% of White offenders).

United States Sentencing Commission

: OVERVIEW OF MANDATORY MINIMUM PENALTIES IN THE FEDERAL CRIMINAL JUSTICE SYSTEM (2017)

What are Mandatory Minimum Penalties?

The term "mandatory minimum penalty" refers to a federal criminal statute requiring, upon conviction of a federal criminal offense and the satisfaction of criteria set forth in that statute, the imposition of a specified minimum term of irnprlsonment .v Mandatory minimum penalties vary in length depending on the offense type and specified criteria, from two years for aggravated identity theft, to life in prison for certain drug trafficking offenses.

offender convicted of an offense involving 280 grams is subject to a mandatory minimum penalty of ten years. While drug quantity is the most common triggering factor in these offenses, other triggering characteristics include selling to a person under 21 years of age, selling within 1,000 feet of a school, and employing a person under 18 years of age.21

Statutory Criteria Triggering Mandatory Minimum Penalties

The statutory criteria that trigger mandatory minimum penalties can be classified into at least one of three categories:

- penalties triggered by offense characteristics or elements of the offense of conviction;
- penalties triggered by reference to another underlying offense; or
- penalties triggered by the offender's criminal history.

The first category is best exemplified by the federal mandatory minimum penalties for drug trafficking offenses. As discussed in more detail below, the mandatory minimum penalty applies if the instant offense of conviction involves a specified element of which the offender is found guilty. In the case of drug offenses, these triggering characteristics include manufacturing, trafficking, importing or distributing a particular type of drug at quantities above a specified threshold. For example, under 21 U.S.C. § 84l(a) and (b)(l), an offender convicted of trafficking 28 grams or more of a mixture or substance containing cocaine base (crack cocaine) is subject to a mandatory minimum penalty of not less than five years, whereas an

Under the second category, the mandatory minimum penalty generally does not apply to the underlying offense, but an additional consecutive mandatory minimum penalty applies if criteria specified in a separate statute are met. The most commonly applied mandatory minimum penalty of this type is 18 U.S.C. § 924(c), which requires a mandatory consecutive term of imprisonment for the possession or use of a firearm in connection with certain underlying offenses. Another example is 18 U.S.C. § 1028A, which requires a mandatory consecutive term of imprisonment for identity theft committed in connection with certain underlying offenses. These mandatory minimum penalties are often applied in addition to any sentence imposed for the other underlying offense, although they also can be charged as a sole count in an indictment.

The third category involves mandatory minimum penalties that are triggered when the offender's criminal history includes a conviction for one or more of a specified category of prior offenses. An example of this type of mandatory minimum penalty is found in 18 U.S.C. § 924(e), commonly known as the Armed Career Criminal Act. Section 924(e) provides a mandatory minimum penalty of 15 years of imprisonment if a person commits a firearms offense and has previously been convicted of three or more "violent felonies" or "serious drug offenses." Another example is found in the context of drug trafficking offenses, in which the mandatory minimum penalty increases if the offender has a prior conviction for a felony drug offense.

Section Three:

MANDATORY MINIMUMS IN THE FEDERAL SYSTEM

Common Offenses Involving Mandatory Minimum Penalties

To combat what it perceived as widespread problems resulting from drug trafficking and related crime, Congress made significant changes to mandatory minimum penalties beginning in 19 51. 22 Reversing its prior policy of disfavoring mandatory minimum penalties, Congress lengthened existing mandatory minimum penalties,23 enacted new ones, and expanded its use of them to offenses not previously covered by such penalties.24

The policy shift was short-lived: mandatory minimum penalties-particularly those for drug offenses-became increasingly unpopular by the late 1960s and Congress repealed nearly all of them.25 The pendulum swung back again, however, in the 1980s. Prevailing attitudes toward sentencing shifted away from a rehabilitative model toward controlling crime using "more certain, less disparate, and more appropriately punitive" sentences.26 On the heels of this shift, Congress again enacted many mandatory minimum penalties related to controlled substances and firearms, and significantly increased the length of several existing penalties.27 Today, most convictions under statutes requiring mandatory minimum penalties relate to controlled substances, firearms, identity theft, and child sex offenses.

Mandatory Minimum Penalties for Drug Offenses

Mandatory minimum penalties in the federal system are most commonly associated with controlled substance offenses.28 In recent years, drug trafficking offenses have accounted for approximately two-thirds of the offenses carrying a mandatory minimum penalty, significantly higher than the next largest class of offenses.29

This trend is not surprising given the increase in the number and severity of mandatory minimum penalties for drug trafficking offenses just before the initial guidelines were promulgated. The Anti-Drug Abuse Act of 198630 created mandatory minimum penalties for many drug trafficking offenses committed on or after October 27, 1986. Congress further extended the reach of these mandatory minimum penalties in 1988 to drug trafficking conspiracies, thereby broadening the scope of mandatory minimum penalties to include virtually all offenders in drug trafficking organizations.31

The Anti-Drug Abuse Act also established the tiered penalty structure currently applicable to many federal drug trafficking offenses.32 This tiered structure can be found at 21 U.S.C. §§

84133 and 96034-the most commonly prosecuted drug offenses carrying mandatory minimum penalties.

Under both provisrons, mandatory mmrmum penalties are first tied to the quantity and type of controlled substances in the offense. The first tier establishes a five-year mandatory minimum penalty and a maximum term of 40 years, while higher thresholds increase the mandatory minimum to ten years with a maximum term of life imprisonment.35

Triggering Thresholds for Common Controlled Substances

5-yeor 10-year

21 U.S.C. § 841 Mandatory Minimum

Heroin	100G	1KG
Powder Cocaine	500G	5 KG
Cocaine Bose (crock)	28G	280 G
Marijuana	100 KG	1,000 KG
Methomphetomine (pure)	5G	50G
Methamphetomine (mixture)	50G	500 G

The drug trafficking offense mandatory minimum penalties-including those in sections 841 (b) and 960(b)-may also include enhanced penalties based on the defendant's prior record.36 For example, offenders who otherwise qualify for the five-year mandatory minimum penalty would face an increased statutory range of ten years to life if they had a prior conviction for a felony drug offense.37 Similarly, a qualifying prior conviction increases a ten-year mandatory minimum to a 20- year mandatory minimum (the maximum remains life), while offenders previously convicted of two or more prior drug felonies are subject to a mandatory minimum term of life.38

The penalties for committmg other drug offenses criminalized under title 21, United States Code, are also tied to the above-referenced penalty structure. For example, attempts or conspiracies to commit any drug offense are subject to the same penalty structure as the substantive offense.39 Congress also criminalized distributing drugs to persons who are under the age of 21 or who are pregnant, using persons under the age of 18 in drug operations, and distributing drugs in or near schools and colleges." Higher penalty ranges apply if death or serious bodily injury results from use of the controlled substance.41

2011 RECOMMENDATIONS

In its 2011 Mandatory Minimum Report, the Commission recommended that Congress marginally expand the safety valve at 18 U.S.C. § 3553(f), and reassess the severity and scope of the recidivist enhancements for drug offenses.

Mandatory Minimum Penalties for Firearms

Congress also expanded the scope and severity of mandatory minimum penalties for firearms offenses in the later part of the 20th Century. 42 These firearms mandatory minimum penalties are currently set forth in two subsections of 18 U.S.C. § 924.

18 U.S.C. § 924(c)43

Section 924(c) of title 18, United States Code, prohibits using or carrying a firearm during and in relation to, or possessing a firearm in furtherance of, a crime of violence or a drug trafficking crime.44 The statute prescribes a mandatory minimum penalty of at least five years of imprisonment for committing the offense, with increasingly longer mandatory minimum penalties based on how the firearm was used (seven years if the firearm was brandished and ten years if the firearm was discharged) and the type of firearm involved in the crime (ten years if the firearm was a short-barreled rifle, a short-barreled shotgun, or a semiautomatic assault weapon and 30 years if the firearm was a machinegun, a destructive device, or was equipped with a silencer or muffler).45 Section 924(c) further provides that these mandatory minimum penalties must be imposed in addition to, and must run consecutively to, "any other term of imprisonment imposed on the person, including any term of imprisonment imposed for the [underlying] crime of violence or drug trafficking crime .... "46

Section 924(c) also establishes longer mandatory minimum penalties of 25 years for each "second or subsequent conviction" of a section 924(c) offense.47 The Supreme Court has held that when multiple section 924(c) counts are charged in the same proceeding, this longer mandatory minimum penalty of 25 years applies.48 Thus, the longer recidivist mandatory minimum penalty must be served consecutively to any sentences imposed

Section Three:

MANDATORY MINIMUMS IN THE FEDERAL SYSTEM

for the underlying offenses and other section 924(c) offenses, even when all of the offenses were charged in a single indictment. This practice of charging multiple violations of section 924(c) within the same indictment is commonly known as "stacking" mandatory minimum penalties.

2011 RECOMMENDATIONS

In its 2011 Mandatory Minimum Report, the Commission recommended that Congress consider several changes to the firearms mandatory minimum penalties, including {l) amending 18 U.S.C. § 924(c) so that the enhanced mandatory minimum penalties for a "second or subsequent" offense apply only to prior convictions, and that such penalties be reduced, and (2) eliminating the "stacking" requirement in 18 U.S.C. § 924(c) to give the sentencing court discretion to impose sentences for multiple violations of section 924(c) concurrently.

The Armed Career Criminal Act, 18 U.S.C. § 924(e)49

The Armed Career Criminal Act requires a minimum 15 years of imprisonment if the defendant violates 18 U.S.C. § 922(g) and has at least three prior convictions for a violent felony or a serious drug offense." Section 922(g) makes it unlawful for certain prohibited persons, including convicted felons, fugitives from justice, persons dishonorably discharged from the armed forces, and aliens who are illegally or unlawfully in the United States, to possess a firearm or ammunition that is in or affecting commerce, to ship or transport a firearm or ammunition in interstate or foreign commerce, or to receive any firearm or ammunition which has been shipped or transported in interstate or foreign commerce.51

Mandatory Minimum Penalties for Child Sexual Exploitation and Related Offenses52

Congress has also enacted mandatory minimum penalties to combat child sexual exploitation. These penalties have expanded since Congress first outlawed the production of child pornography in 1978 and included a mandatory minimum penalty of two years of imprisonment for repeat offenders. 53 By 1996, Congress had increased the penalties for production of child pornography to require a mandatory minimum penalty of ten years of imprisonment for first-time offenders, 15 years of imprisonment for offenders with a prior conviction for a child sexual exploitation offense, and at least 30 years of imprisonment for offenders with two such prior convictions.54

The Prosecutorial Remedies and Other Tools to end the Exploitation of Children Today (PROTECT) Act of 200355 established new mandatory minimum penalties and increased existing mandatory minimums for certain child sexual abuse and child pornography crimes. Among other changes, Congress increased the mandatory minimum penalties for producing child pornography and related conduct from ten to 15 years of imprisonment for first-time offenders, from 15 to 25 years of imprisonment for repeat child exploitation offenders, and from 30 to 35 years of imprisonment for offenders with more than two prior child exploitation convictions. 56 The PROTECT Act further increased the mandatory minimum penalty for the buying or selling of children from 20 to 30 years of imprisonment,57 and the mandatory minimum penalty for possession of child pornography by a recidivist offender from two to ten years of imprisonment.58 Finally, Congress established new mandatory minimum penalties for existing offenses, most notably by requiring at least five years of imprisonment for receipt and distribution of child pornography,59 as well as a new mandatory minimum penalty of five years of imprisonment for enticing a minor to travel in interstate commerce for criminal sexual activity.'"

Congress again increased existing mandatory minimum penalties and established new mandatory minimum penalties for certain sex offenses three years later in the Adam Walsh Child Protection and Safety Act of 2006.61 That Act, among other provisions, added a new mandatory minimum penalty of 15 years of imprisonment for sex trafficking,62 increased the mandatory minimum penalty from five to ten years of imprisonment for enticing a minor to engage in criminal activity,63 and established a mandatory minimum penalty of 20 years of imprisonment for engaging in a child exploitation enterprise.64 The Act also created new offenses and mandatory minimum penalties relating to failure to register as a sex offender.65

Thus, as currently in effect, federal law provides numerous mandatory minimum penalties for two types of child exploitation offenses: (1) sexual abuse (also called "contact") offenses, i.e., those offenses involving actual or attempted sexual contact with the victim regardless of the victim's age; and (2) child pornography (other than an offense related to the production of pornography depicting an actual child, which is deemed a "contact" offense). The current penalties for each category are briefly summarized.

Sexual Abuse Offenses

These provisions are primarily found in the following sections of title 18:

• § 159l(b)(l) and (2) (minimum ten- or 15-year term for sex trafficking of a minor depending on the age of the victim);

• § 224l(c) (minimum 30-year term for traveling across state lines with the intent to have sex with a child under 12 years of age or for crossing state lines and having sex with a child between the ages of 12 and 16 under certain aggravating circumstances);

• §§ 225 l(e) and 2260(c)(l) (minimum term of 15 years for production of child pornography and enhanced minimum terms if such a defendant has a prior felony conviction for an enumerated sex offense);

• § 2251A(a) & (b) (minimum term of 30 years for buying or selling, or otherwise transferring, children to participate in the production of child pornography);

• § 2422(b) (minimum term of ten years for using mails or facilities or means of commerce to cause a minor to engage in prostitution or other criminal sexual activity);
• § 2423(a) (minimum term of ten years for transporting a minor in commerce to engage in prostitution or other criminal sexual activity); and
• § 3 5 5 9(e) (mandatory life imprisonment for second conviction for certain sex offenses against minors).

Section Three:
MANDATORY MINIMUMS IN THE FEDERAL SYSTEM
Child Pornography Offenses
The most common child pornography offenses are set forth at 18 U.S.C. §§ 2251, 2252, 2252A, and 2260, which broadly prohibit a variety of acts related to the distribution,66 transportation (including by shipping or mailing),67 importation, receipt, and possession of child pornography, including attempted acts and conspiracies to commit such acts.68 An additional statute, 18 U.S.C. § 1466A, prohibits possession, receipt, distribution, and production of "obscene visual representations of the sexual abuse of children."
The statutory penalty ranges for violations of these provisions vary in severity depending on both the act involved and the defendant's prior criminal record. Simple possession of child pornography is punishable by up to ten years in federal prison, but does not carry a mandatory minimum term of imprisonment. 69 If a defendant has a prior federal or state conviction for one or more enumerated sex offenses," however, the penalty range for simple possession increases to a mandatory minimum term of ten years and a maximum term of 20 years of imprisonment. 71
Child pornography offenses for transportation (including mailing or shipping), receipt, distribution, and possession with the intent to distribute or sell child pornography offenses each carry a mandatory minimum term of five years of imprisonment and a maximum term of 20 years." If a defendant has a prior federal or state conviction for one or more enumerated sex offenses, however, the penalty range increases to a mandatory minimum term of 15 years and a maximum term of 40 years of imprisonment. 73
Violations of section 1466A involving receipt, distribution, or production of "obscene visual representations of the sexual abuse of children"
carry a mandatory minimum penalty of five years and a maximum of 20 years of imprisonment, while violations of section 1466A involving simple possession of such obscene material carry no mandatory minimum penalty and have a statutory maximum of ten years of imprisonment. 74
2011 RECOMMENDATIONS
In its 2011 Mandatory Minimum Report, the Commission recommended that Congress review current mandatory minimum penalties for offenses involving the receipt of child pornography that are virtually indistinguishable from possession offenses. As set forth in the Commission's Report to the Congress: Federal Child Pornography Offenses (2012), available sentencing data suggests that the mandatory minimum penalties for these receipt offenses may be excessively severe and, as a result, are applied inconsistently.
Mandatory Minimum Penalties for Identity Theft75
Section 1028A of title 18 provides enhanced punishment for aggravated identity theft, including a required two-year mandatory minimum penalty. This provision, which was enacted in the

Identity Theft Penalty Enhancement Act of 2004,76 provides, "[w]hoever, during and in relation to any felony violation enumerated in subsection (c), knowingly transfers, possesses, or uses, without lawful authority, a means of identification of another person shall, in addition to the punishment provided for such felony, be sentenced to a term of imprisonment of two years.'?" The enumerated felony offenses include theft offenses, 78 offenses involving false statements and fraud,79 offenses related to nationality and citizenship," offenses related to passports and visas,81 and immigration offenses. Section 1028A requires that the mandatory two year term of imprisonment be imposed consecutively to "any other term of imprisonment imposed on the person under any other provision of law, including any term of imprisonment imposed for the felony during which the means of identification was transferred, possessed, or used. "83 Moreover, the statute directs the sentencing court not to reduce any sentence for the underlying felony, assuming the defendant is convicted separately of the underlying felony, to "compensate for, or otherwise take into account, any separate term of imprisonment" to be imposed for a violation of section 1028A.84

The statute further provides that sentences for multiple violations of section 1028A may be "stacked," but that the court may, in its discretion, run the sentence for any additional section 1028A counts "concurrently, in whole or in part, ... with another term of imprisonment that is imposed by the court at the same time on that person for an additional violation of[section 1028A]."85

How Are Mandatory Minimum Penalties Incorporated Into the Guidelines?

Congress charged the Commission with promulgating guidelines that are "consistent with all pertinent provisions" of federal law86 and with providing sentencing ranges that are "consistent with all pertinent provisions of title 18, United States Code."87 To that end, the Commission has incorporated mandatory minimum penalties into the guidelines since their inception, and has continued to incorporate new mandatory minimum penalties as enacted by Congress. 88

In the initial guidelines, the Commission generally incorporated mandatory mrrumum penalties by establishing guideline ranges slightly above the mandatory minimum penalty for offenders convicted of offenses carrying a mandatory minimum penalty in Criminal History Category I.89 At the time, the Commission determined that incorporating mandatory minimum penalties in this way fulfilled its statutory mandate to "assure that the guidelines reflect the general appropriateness of imposing a lower sentence than would otherwise be imposed, including a sentence that is lower than that established by statute as a minimum sentence, to take into account a defendant's substantial assistance .... "90

While this policy remained in place for much of the guidelines' history, the Commission has varied its methods of incorporating mandatory minimum penalties into the guidelines over time based on its continuing research, experience, and analysis.91 As Congress has enacted new mandatory minimum penalties, the Commission has drawn on its experience with particular offenses and related guidelines to incorporate the new penalties. Furthermore, the Commission has amended its incorporation of certain types of mandatory minimum penalties-most notably, drug offenses-over time to account for other changes in the statutes and the guidelines.

For example, the Commission has changed the way in which mandatory minimum penalties for drug offenses are incorporated in the Drug Quantity Table at USSG §2DI.I in recent years. When Congress passed the Anti-Drug Abuse Act of 1986, the Commission responded by incorporating the statutory mandatory minimum penalties into the guidelines and extrapolating upward and downward to set sentencing guideline ranges for all drug quantities. The quantity thresholds in the Drug Quantity Table were set to provide base offense levels corresponding to guideline ranges that were slightly above the statutory mandatory minimum penalties. Accordingly, offenses involving drug quantities that triggered a five-year statutory minimum were assigned a base offense level (level 26) corresponding to a sentencing guideline range of 63 to 78 months for a defendant in Criminal History Category I (a guideline range that exceeds the five-year statutory minimum penalty for such offenses by at least three months). Similarly, offenses that triggered a ten-year statutory minimum penalty were assigned a base offense level (level 32) corresponding to a sentencing guideline range of 121 to 151 months for a defendant in Criminal History Category I (a guideline range that exceeds the ten-year statutory minimum penalty for such offenses by at least one month)."

The Commission recently reduced the drug guidelines for all drugs by two levels, changing how the applicable statutory mandatory minimum penalties are incorporated into the Drug Quantity Table.93 Specifically, the amendment reduced the offense levels assigned to the quantities that trigger the statutory mandatory minimum penalties by two, resulting in corresponding guideline ranges that include, as opposed to exceed, the mandatory minimum penalties.94 The Commission determined that "changes in the law and recent experience with similar reductions in base offense levels for crack cocaine offenses indicate that setting base offense levels above the mandatory minimum penalties is no longer necessary to provide adequate incentives to plead guilty or otherwise cooperate with authorities."95 Instead, the Commission noted that adequate incentives exist through operation of the statutory "safety valve" provision enacted in 1994, and related guideline reductions." The change also reflected the fact that the guidelines more adequately differentiate among drug trafficking offenders than when the Drug Quantity Table was initially established through numerous enhancements and adjustments.97

As another example, the Commission set a base offense level that produced a guideline range entirely below the mandatory minimum penalty for offenders in Criminal History Category I when Congress established a new mandatory minimum of five years of imprisonment for existing child pornography trafficking and receipt offenses in the PROTECT Act. The Commission modified its general approach at the time because experience and data showed that several existing enhancements (e.g., use of a computer, material involving children under 12 years of age, number of images) in the applicable guideline, USSG §2G2.2, apply in almost every case.98

The Commission also addressed how to incorporate other types of mandatory minimum penalties, including those requiring consecutive terms of imprisonment. To ensure the guidelines' consistency with federal law, the Commission has incorporated consecutive penalties by specifying that the guideline sentence for that count is the minimum term required by the statute. For example, USSG §2K2.4(b) provides that for an offender convicted of violating section 924(c), "the guideline sentence [for that count] is the minimum term of imprisonment required by statute."99

Finally, for those offenses carrying a mandatory minimum penalty not specifically referenced to a particular guideline, 100 or where the mandatory minimum penalty is not specifically incorporated, the guidelines provide a catchall instruction ensuring that any applicable mandatory minimum penalty controls.'?' Similarly, the guidelines ensure that no portion of an offender's guideline range falls below an applicable mandatory minimum penalty by providing that the mandatory minimum penalty becomes the bottom of the guideline range where some,

but not all, of the guideline range falls below the mandatory minimum penalty.!"
United States Sentencing Commission
OVERVIEW OF MANDATORY MINIMUM PENALTIES IN THE FEDERAL CRIMINAL JUSTICE SYSTEM (2017)
Can Offenders Obtain Relief From Mandatory Minimum Penalties?
and policy statements issued by the Sentencing Commission pursuant to section 994 of title 28, United States Code."107
Not all offenders convicted of an offense carrying a mandatory minimum penalty are sentenced to the minimum term of imprisonment specified in the statute of conviction.I'" Under the current system, 104 a sentencing court can impose a sentence below an otherwise applicable statutory mandatory minimum penalty if: (1) the prosecution files a motion based on the defendant's "substantial assistance" to authorities in the investigation or prosecution of another person; or (2) in certain drug trafficking cases, the defendant qualifies for the statutory "safety valve" contained in 18 U.S.C. § 3553(f).
Substantial Assistance
Two related provisions allow a sentencing court to impose a term of imprisonment lower than a mandatory minimum penalty in cases where a defendant provides substantial assistance in the investigation or prosecution of another person: 18 U.S.C. § 3553(e) and Federal Rule of Criminal Procedure 35(b).
18 U.S.C. § 3553(e)
Section 3553(e), which was enacted as part of the Anti-Drug Abuse Act of 1986, ios grants a court limited authority to impose a sentence below a mandatory minimum penalty at the time of sentencing. Specifically, the section provides that "[u]pon motion of the Government, the court shall have the authority to impose a sentence below a level established by statute as a minimum sentence so as to reflect a defendant's substantial assistance in the investigation or prosecution of another person who has committed an offense."!" Section 3553(e) further requires such a sentence to "be imposed in accordance with the guidelines
As directed by Congress, the Commission incorporated this statutory mechanism for relief from mandatory minimum penalties into the guidelines. USSG §5KI.I, consistent with the requirements of the Commission's organic statute, 108 authorizes a departure from the guideline range if the offender has provided substantial assistance to law enforcement. In contrast to section 3553(e), however, §SKI .1 does not explicitly authorize courts to impose a sentence below a mandatory minimum penalty but instead includes a reference to 18 U.S.C. § 3553(e).109 As such, even if the government files a motion under §5KI.I, the sentencing court may not impose a sentence below a statutory mandatory minimum penalty unless the government also files a motion pursuant to 18 U.S.C. § 3553(e).110
Federal Rule of Criminal Procedure 35(b)
Relief under section 3553(e) is, in most respects, identical to the relief provided under Rule 35 of the Federal Rules of Criminal Procedure, as both require substantial assistance and both require a government motion. The most significant difference between the two types of motions is timing: Rule 35(b) motions are made after the original sentencing and so require a resentencing if granted, while section 3553(e) motions are made before sentencing and ruled on at the time of the original sentencing. 111
Rule 35(b) permits a court, upon the government's motion, to impose a new, reduced sentence

that considers post-sentencing substantial assistance. Rule 35(b)(1) provides that, "[u]pon the government's motion made within one year of sentencing, the court may reduce a sentence if the defendant, after sentencing, provided substantial assistance in investigating or prosecuting another person."1l2 Pursuant to Rule 35(b)(2), motions may also be made later than one year after the original sentence if the "defendant's substantial assistance involved": (1) "information not known to the defendant until one year or more after sentencing," (2) information provided within one year that "did not become useful to the government until more than one year after sentencing," or (3) if the defendant could not have "reasonably ... anticipated" that the information in question would be useful until more than a year after sentencing.113 In evaluating whether the substantial assistance is, in fact, sufficient to warrant a reduction under Rule 35(b), "the court may consider the defendant's presentence assistance."114

Rule 35(b) expressly applies to sentences that would otherwise be subject to a mandatory minimum penalty, authorizing the sentencing court to "reduce the sentence to a level below the minimum sentence established by statute."115

Statutory "Safety Valve" Relief

The second relief provision, codified at 18 U.S.C. § 3553(f) (Limitation on Applicability of Mandatory Minimum Penalties in Certain Cases), is commonly referred to as the "safety valve."116 Unlike a substantial assistance departure-which applies to all types of federal offenses carrying a mandatory minimum penalty-the safety valve statute only applies in cases in which a defendant faces a mandatory minimum penalty after being convicted of a drug trafficking offense listed in the statute.117 In addition, the safety valve only applies if the following five criteria are met:

• the defendant does not have more than one criminal history point, as determined under the sentencing guidelines;

• the defendant did not use violence or credible threats of violence or possess a firearm or other dangerous weapon (or induce another participant to do so) in connection with the offense;

• the offense did not result in death or serious bodily injury to any person;

• the defendant was not an organizer, leader, manager, or supervisor of others in the offense, as determined by the sentencing guidelines and was not engaged in a continuing criminal enterprise, as defined in 21 U.S.C. § 848; and

• no later than the time of the sentencing hearing, the defendant has truthfully provided to the Government all information and evidence the defendant has concerning the offense or offenses that were part of the same course of conduct or of a common scheme or plan, but the fact that the defendant has no relevant or useful or other information to provide or that the government is already aware of the information shall not preclude a determination by the court that the defendant has not complied with this requirement.

Where these criteria are met, section 3553(f) provides that judges shall impose a sentence without regard to the statutory mandatory minimum penalty for the covered offenses.

For defendants who qualify for relief from the mandatory minimum penalty pursuant to the statutory safety valve, the guideline at §5Cl.2 directs the court to "impose a sentence in accordance with the applicable guidelines without regard to any statutory minimum sentence."118 The drug trafficking guideline at USSG §2D 1.1 also provides for a 2-level decrease if the defendant meets the safety valve subdivision criteria listed at USSG §5Cl.2.119 This decrease applies regardless of whether the defendant was convicted of an offense carrying a mandatory minimum penalty.

Recent Changes

Since the Commission's 2011 Mandatory Minimum Report was issued in October of 2011, the landscape of federal mandatory minimum penalties has continued to evolve. Congress has continued to explore criminal justice reform, including possible changes to certain mandatory minimum penalties. Additionally, changes to Department of Justice charging policy and recent Supreme Court case law have impacted charging practices relating to mandatory minimum penalties. As these changes likely impacted data trends since the Commission's last report, they are briefly summarized here.

Impact of the Fair Sentencing Act of 2010

The last significant change to mandatory minimum penalties came in the Fair Sentencing Act of 2010 ("FSA"), which amended penalties for crack cocaine offenses.121 The Act, which followed four Commission reports on federal cocaine sentencing policy, 122 altered the mandatory minimum penalties established by Congress in 1986 and 1988 by repealing the mandatory minimum penalty for simple possession of crack cocaine and by increasing the quantities required to trigger the five- and ten-year mandatory minimum penalties for crack cocaine trafficking offenses from five to 28 grams and 50 to 280 grams, respectively.123 The Act also directed the Commission to provide higher guideline sentences for all drug offenders based on the presence of specified aggravating factors, such as bribing a law enforcement official to facilitate the offense, maintaining an establishment for manufacturing or distributing controlled substances, or obstructing justice while holding an aggravating role in the offense. The Act further directed the Commission to provide lower guideline sentences for certain offenders who receive a guideline adjustment for being a minimal participant in the offense. 124

Enactment of the FSA triggered responses from the Commission, the Department of Justice, and the Supreme Court, all of which influenced the impact of the Act's changes. In 2011, the Commission implemented the FSA's new penalties in the guidelines and subsequently made the changes retroactive.125 After initially advising federal prosecutors that the new penalties would apply prospectively only to offense conduct occurring on or after the FSA's enactment date, the Department of Justice issued subsequent guidance that the FSA's new penalties applied to sentencings occurring on or after August 3, 2010, regardless of when the offense took place.126 Finally, the Supreme Court similarly held that the FSA's penalties applied to offenses committed prior to August 3, 2010, but sentenced after that date. 127

As directed by Congress, 128 the Commission studied the impact of the changes made by the FSA and issued a report in August of 2015.129 The Commission's study concluded that the FSA reduced the disparity between crack and powder cocaine sentences, reduced the federal prison population, and appears to have resulted in fewer federal prosecutions for crack cocaine. The report further observed that these impacts occurred while crack cocaine use continued to decline. 130

Criminal Justice Reform

Since passage of the FSA in 2010, Congress has continued to express interest in exploring the scope and severity of current mandatory minimum penalties. Members of Congress have introduced numerous pieces of bipartisan legislation proposing various sentencing changes (many of which reflect recommendations made by the Commission in its 2011 Mandatory Minimum Report), including:

• reducing mandatory minimum penalties for certain drug offenses;

Section Four:
RECENT CHANGES IN THE CHARGING OF MANDATORY MINIMUM OFFENSES
• broadening the existing "safety valve" to include offenders with prior misdemeanor convictions, while excluding offenders with prior felony convictions, or prior violent or drug trafficking convictions;
• creating a second "safety valve" allowing judges to sentence certain low-level offenders below an otherwise applicable ten-year mandatory minimum penalty;
• revising the mandatory minimum penalties for firearms offenses, including changes to section 924(c) and the Armed Career Criminal Act; and
• making the statutory changes in the Fair Sentencing Act of 2010 retroactive.131
While these and other proposals have not proceeded beyond the respective Committees in the U.S. Senate and House of Representatives, Members of Congress have continued to express an intent to explore these issues in the current or future sessions.
Changes in Charging Practices
In addition to legislative changes, there were also significant legal and administrative changes relating to the charging of mandatory minimum penalties that impacted the data presented in this publication.
First, beginning in 2010 and continuing through May of 201 7, the Department of Justice amended its guidance to federal prosecutors regarding which offenses to charge, including more targeted charging of offenses carrying a mandatory minimum penalty. Since 2003, Department of Justice policy had directed prosecutors to charge the most serious, readily provable offenses supported by the facts and that would result in the longest sentence.132 In 2010, however, then-Attorney General Eric Holder issued a memorandum revising this guidance to provide that a prosecutor "should
ordinarily charge" the most serious offense. The memorandum further instructed that this charging decision required an individualized assessment to ensure that the charges fit the specific circumstances of the case, are consistent with the purposes of the federal criminal laws, and maximize the impact of federal resources. The "Holder Memorandum," as it has come to be called, further required the same individualized assessment in plea bargaining and sentencing advocacy.133
Further changes in charging practices came in the wake of the Supreme Court's decision in Alleyne v. United States.134 In Alleyne, the Court revisited a longstanding controversy in criminal law regarding the method of proof the Sixth Amendment requires to impose a mandatory minimum sentence. It has been settled since the Court's 2000 decision in Apprendi v. New Jersey135 that any facts that increase a criminal defendant's maximum possible sentence are considered "elements" of the criminal offense, which must be proved to a jury beyond a reasonable doubt. In the context of mandatory minimums, the Court had previously decided in Harris v. United States136 that Apprendi did not apply to facts that would increase a defendant's mandatory minimum sentence, and therefore that a judge could constitutionally decide to apply a mandatory minimum sentence based on facts not proven to a jury.
Overruling the Harris decision, Alleyne held that facts that increase a mandatory minimum penalty are elements that must be submitted to a jury and found beyond a reasonable doubt.

Relying on the logic of Apprendi, the Court concluded that the definition of "elements" necessarily includes facts that not only increase the maximum penalty, but also those that increase the minimum penalty, because both affect the sentencing range to which a defendant is exposed. As the Court notes, "[i]t is impossible to dissociate the floor of a sentencing range from the penalty affixed to the crime."137 Increasing the legally prescribed floor indisputably aggravates the punishment and "heightens the loss of liberty associated with the crime," because the government can invoke the mandatory minimum to require a harsher punishment than would have resulted otherwise.138 The Court reasoned that "[t]his reality demonstrates that the core crime and the fact triggering the mandatory minimum sentence together constitute a new, aggravated crime, each element of which must be submitted to the jury."139 The Court concluded that, by defining facts that increase the mandatory minimum sentence to be elements of the crime, the defendant can predict the potential penalties from the face of the indictment, and the Court has preserved "the historic role of the jury as an intermediary between the State and criminal defendants."!"

While the issue in Alleyne was a seven year sentence imposed on a defendant for having "brandished" a firearm while "using or carrying [it] during and in relation to a crime of violence," courts have extended its application to other mandatory minimum offenses, including drug offenses. Applying Alleyne, courts have held that a factfinder must determine the type and quantity of controlled substances involved in the offense if the drug type and/or quantity increases the statutorily prescribed minimum sentence.141 These decisions have directly impacted the application of mandatory minimum penalties by altering the way in which mandatory minimum enhancements must be charged and proven by the government.

After Alleyne, the Department of Justice further modified its charging policies as part of then-Attorney General Holder's Smart on Crime Initiative.142 Noting that "the Supreme Court's decision in Alleyne heightens the role a prosecutor plays in determining whether a defendant is subject to a mandatory minimum sentence," the Department of Justice issued a new policy refining

its charging policy regarding mandatory minimums for certain nonviolent, low-level drug offenders.143 Specifically, the memorandum provides that "prosecutors should decline to charge the quantity necessary to trigger a mandatory minimum sentence if the defendant meets each of the following criteria:

• the defendant's relevant conduct does not involve the use of violence, the credible threat of violence, the possession of a weapon, the trafficking of drugs to or with minors, or the death or serious bodily injury of any person;

• the defendant is not an organizer, leader, manager, or supervisor of others within a criminal organization;

• the defendant does not have significant ties to large-scale drug trafficking organizations, gangs, or cartels; and

• the defendant does not have a significant criminal history. A significant criminal history will normally be evidenced by three or more criminal history points but may involve fewer or greater depending on the nature of any prior convictions."144

The memorandum provides that prosecutors should decline to pursue the recidivist enhancements provided for in title 21 (and therefore, not file an information pursuant to 21 U.S.C. § 851) "unless the defendant is involved in conduct that makes the case appropriate for severe sanctions."145

Given their timing, it is likely that many, if not all, of the above changes have in some way impacted the data discussed in this publication, including the current population of the Federal Bureau of Prisons (BOP). The Commission further notes, however, that the impacts from these changes and recent data trends may not be permanent. Different trends may emerge as policies regarding mandatory minimum penalties continue to evolve. This evolving nature is reflected both in the changes between 2010 and 2016 discussed above and in other more recent changes, discussed below, that will also impact charging decisions and sentencing in future years.

First, the Department of Justice recently rescinded the changes made in both the 2010 and 2013 memoranda discussed above. On May 10, 2017, Attorney General Jeff Sessions issued revised guidance emphasizing the Department's "responsibility ... to fulfill [its] role in a way that accords with the law, advances public safety, and promotes respect for our legal system," and "noting that"[i]t is often the most importance to enforce the law fairly and consistently." Relying on these principles, the memorandum instructs that "prosecutors should charge and pursue the most serious, readily provable offense." The memorandum further provides that "the most serious offenses are those that carry the most substantial guidelines sentence, including mandatory minimum sentences." The memorandum provides for "circumstances in which good judgement would lead a prosecutor to conclude that a strict application of the above charging policy is not warranted," thus allowing for exceptions with supervisory approval. 146

Additionally, the Supreme Court recently issued its holding in Dean v. United States, 147 which addressed the issue of sentencing an offender charged with possessing a firearm in furtherance of a crime of violence, in violation of 18 U.S.C. § 924(c). The Court unanimously held that 18U.S.C. § 924(c) does not prevent a sentencing court from considering a mandatory sentence imposed under that provision when determining the sentence for the underlying predicate offense. The Court began by reviewing the factors that sentencing courts are required to consider when setting an appropriate sentence and noted that generally, a court "imposing a sentence on one count of conviction [can] consider sentences imposed on other counts."148 In this case, both the fact that Dean would not be released from prison until after he was 50 years old, and the deterrent effect of the 30-year mandatory minimum sentence (based on the mandatory stacking of consecutive five and 25-year penalties for his two section 924(c) convictions) were factors that the sentencing court could consider. The Court rejected the government's contention that sentencing courts should not consider the effect of other sentences until it is deciding whether sentences should run consecutively or concurrently. Here, the Court noted that this interpretation goes against the practice of the government in "sentencing package cases." In those cases, where some but not all counts of conviction are vacated on appeal, the government "routinely argues" that the entire sentence should be vacated so that the court may increase the sentences for any remaining counts.

The Court also found that there is nothing in the text of section 924(c) that prohibits a court from considering the mandatory sentence when calculating the sentence for the predicate offense. Neither the fact that the mandatory sentence must be imposed "in addition to" the punishment for the predicate offense, nor the fact that the additional sentence must be imposed "consecutively" to the sentence for the predicate offense affects the sentencing court's discretion to consider the mandatory minimum when calculating each individual sentence. The

Court noted that the government was asking for an additional limitation to be read into the text, which is inappropriate, particularly when Congress has shown that it knows how to "make explicit what the Government argues is implicit in § 924(c)." It did this in 18 U.S.C. § 1028A, which deals with identify theft and provides that in determining the sentence for the predicate felony, "a court shall not in any way reduce the term to be imposed for such crime so as to compensate for, or otherwise take into account, any separate term of imprisonment imposed or to be imposed for a violation of this section."149

OVERVIEW OF MANDATORY MINIMUM PENALTIES IN THE FEDERAL CRIMINAL JUSTICE SYSTEM (2017)

The Commission's Updated Study

Since the issuance of its 2011 Mandatory Minimum Report, the Commission has continued its study of the scope, use, and impact of mandatory minimum penalties in the federal system. The Commission has regularly provided updated data on mandatory minimums in various forms throughout the past six years, through the issuance of Quick Facts publications, 150 as well as in testimony on the criminal justice reforms recently under consideration by Congress.151 Nevertheless, given the changes highlighted above, as well as the ongoing interest in this subject, the Commission provides this publication to further update the information and analyses in its 2011 Mandatory Minimum Report regarding the application of mandatory minimum penalties for all offenses. Future publications will provide targeted analyses for specific types of offenses.

It is the Commission's intent that the data in this publication will further inform the ongoing discussion regarding mandatory minimum penalties as Congress, the Department of Justice, and others examine the status of current legislation and policies, and explore the need for additional changes in the future.

Methodology

Records Collection

Pursuant to 28 U.S.C. § 994(w), a district court is directed to submit to the Commission the following sentencing documents in each felony or Class A misdemeanor case: the presentence report (PSR), the judgment and commitment order (J&C), the statement ofreasons form (SOR), the indictment or other charging instrument, and any plea agreement.152 These documents are then analyzed to extract demographic, conviction, sentencing, and guideline application information for each case.

Data Analysis

With the exception of the analysis of the BOP inmate population, the data reported in this publicationisderivedentirelyfromtheCommission's electronic database of information that is routinely collected through the above processes for all federal cases for which the Commission receives full documentation in accordance with 28 U.S.C. § 994(w). In fiscal year 2016,[153] the Commission's individual datafile included 67,742 cases. Of those cases, the Commission received complete guideline application information and sufficient documentation for analysis in this publication in 62,251 cases.[154]

For each of these 62,251 cases, the Commission gathered and analyzed relevant offender and offense characteristics, including demographic data, the types of underlying offenses, and basic criminal history information. This publication provides general comparisons between offenders in the overall federal offender population, offenders convicted of an offense carrying a mandatory minimum penalty,[155] offenders who obtained relief from application of a mandatory minimum penalty, and offenders who remained subject to a mandatory minimum penalty at the time of sentencing. The Commission also provides data about sentencing outcomes involving the application of mandatory minimum penalties. Where appropriate, this publication also highlights key changes between the data set forth in the Commission's 2011 Mandatory Minimum Report and the fiscal year 2016 sentencing data.

Lastly, this publication analyzes and provides updated trends regarding the impact of mandatory minimum sentencing provisions on the federal prison population. Specifically, the Commission provides an overall assessment of the prison impact of statutes carrying mandatory minimum penalties. For this analysis, the Commission obtained prisoner data from the BOP to compare to Commission data.

SENTENCING TABLE

(in months of imprisonment)

	Offense Level	Criminal History Category (Criminal History Points) I (0 or 1)	II (2 or 3)	III (4, 5, 6)	IV (7, 8, 9)	V (10, 11, 12)	VI (13 or more)
	1	0-6	0-6	0-6	0-6	0-6	0-6
	2	0-6	0-6	0-6	0-6	0-6	1-7
	3	0-6	0-6	0-6	0-6	2-8	3-9
	4	0-6	0-6	0-6	2-8	4-10	6-12
Zone A	5	0-6	0-6	1-7	4-10	6-12	9-15
	6	0-6	1-7	2-8	6-12	9-15	12-18
	7	0-6	2-8	4-10	8-14	12-18	15-21
	8	0-6	4-10	6-12	10-16	15-21	18-24
Zone B	9	4-10	6-12	8-14	12-18	18-24	21-27
	10	6-12	8-14	10-16	15-21	21-27	24-30
	11	8-14	10-16	12-18	18-24	24-30	27-33
Zone C	12	10-16	12-18	15-21	21-27	27-33	30-37
	13	12-18	15-21	18-24	24-30	30-37	33-41
	14	15-21	18-24	21-27	27-33	33-41	37-46
	15	18-24	21-27	24-30	30-37	37-46	41-51
	16	21-27	24-30	27-33	33-41	41-51	46-57
	17	24-30	27-33	30-37	37-46	46-57	51-63
	18	27-33	30-37	33-41	41-51	51-63	57-71
	19	30-37	33-41	37-46	46-57	57-71	63-78
	20	33-41	37-46	41-51	51-63	63-78	70-87
	21	37-46	41-51	46-57	57-71	70-87	77-96
	22	41-51	46-57	51-63	63-78	77-96	84-105
	23	46-57	51-63	57-71	70-87	84-105	92-115
	24	51-63	57-71	63-78	77-96	92-115	100-125
	25	57-71	63-78	70-87	84-105	100-125	110-137
	26	63-78	70-87	78-97	92-115	110-137	120-150
Zone D	27	70-87	78-97	87-108	100-125	120-150	130-162
	28	78-97	87-108	97-121	110-137	130-162	140-175
	29	87-108	97-121	108-135	121-151	140-175	151-188
	30	97-121	108-135	121-151	135-168	151-188	168-210
	31	108-135	121-151	135-168	151-188	168-210	188-235
	32	121-151	135-168	151-188	168-210	188-235	210-262
	33	135-168	151-188	168-210	188-235	210-262	235-293
	34	151-188	168-210	188-235	210-262	235-293	262-327
	35	168-210	188-235	210-262	235-293	262-327	292-365
	36	188-235	210-262	235-293	262-327	292-365	324-405
	37	210-262	235-293	262-327	292-365	324-405	360-life
	38	235-293	262-327	292-365	324-405	360-life	360-life
	39	262-327	292-365	324-405	360-life	360-life	360-life
	40	292-365	324-405	360-life	360-life	360-life	360-life
	41	324-405	360-life	360-life	360-life	360-life	360-life
	42	360-life	360-life	360-life	360-life	360-life	360-life
	43	life	life	life	life	life	life

November 1, 2012

Made in United States
North Haven, CT
05 November 2026

21763972R00343